Recent Developments in Smart Healthcare

Special Issue Editors

Wenbing Zhao
Xiong Luo
Tie Qiu

MDPI • Basel • Beijing • Wuhan • Barcelona • Belgrade

MDPI

Special Issue Editors
Wenbing Zhao
Cleveland State University
USA

Xiong Luo
University of Science and Technology Beijing
China

Tie Qiu
Dalian University of Technology
China

Editorial Office
MDPI AG
St. Alban-Anlage 66
Basel, Switzerland

This edition is a reprint of the Special Issue published online in the open access journal *Applied Sciences* (ISSN 2076-3417) from 2016–2017 (available at: http://www.mdpi.com/journal/applsci/special_issues/smart_healthcare).

For citation purposes, cite each article independently as indicated on the article page online and as indicated below:

Author 1, Author 2. Article title. *Journal Name*. **Year**. Article number/page range.

First Edition 2017

ISBN 978-3-03842-644-8 (Pbk)
ISBN 978-3-03842-645-5 (PDF)

Table of Contents

About the Special Issue Editors

Wenbing Zhao, Professor, is a faculty member at the Department of Electrical Engineering and Computer Science, Cleveland State University. He earned his Ph.D. at University of California, Santa Barbara in 2002. Dr. Zhao has been conducting research on smart and connected health since 2010. Dr. Zhao has over 150 peer-reviewed publications, and a US patent (pending) on privacy-aware human activity tracking. He has served on the Organizing and Technical Committees of numerous conferences and on the Editorial Boards of several international journals, including IEEE Access, PeerJ Computer Science, Applied System Innovation, International Journal of Parallel Emergent and Distributed Systems, International Journal of Distributed Systems and Technologies.

Xiong Luo, Professor, received his Ph.D. degree from Central South University, China, in 2004. He currently works as a Professor in the School of Computer and Communication Engineering, University of Science and Technology Beijing, China. His current research interests include machine learning, cloud computing, and computational intelligence. He has published extensively in his areas of interest in journals, such as Future Generation Computer Systems, Computer Networks, IEEE Access, and Personal and Ubiquitous Computing.

Tie Qiu, Associate Professor, received his M.Sc and Ph.D degree in computer science from Dalian University of Technology, in 2005 and 2012, respectively. He is currently Associate Professor at School of Software, Dalian University of Technology. He serves as an Associate Editor of IEEE Access Journal, Computers and Electrical Engineering and Human-centric Computing and Information Sciences; an Editorial Board Member of Ad Hoc Networks and International Journal on AdHoc Networking Systems. He serves as General Chair, PC Chair, Workshop Chair, Publicity Chair, Publication Chair or TPC Member of a number of conferences. He has authored/co-authored eight books, over 100 scientific papers in international journals and conference proceedings. He has contributed to the development of four copyrighted software systems and invented 15 patents. He is a senior member of China Computer Federation and a Senior Member of IEEE and ACM.

Preface to "Recent Developments in Smart Healthcare"

Medicine is undergoing a sector-wide transformation thanks to the advances in computing and networking technologies. Healthcare is changing from reactive and hospital-centered to preventive and personalized, from disease focused to well-being centered. In essence, the healthcare systems, as well as fundamental medicine research, are becoming smarter. We anticipate significant improvements in areas ranging from molecular genomics and proteomics to decision support for healthcare professionals through big data analytics, to support behavior changes through technology-enabled self-management, and social and motivational support. Furthermore, with smart technologies, healthcare delivery could also be made more efficient, of higher quality, and lower cost. In this Special Issue, we received a total of 45 submissions and accepted 19 outstanding papers that span across several interesting topics on smart healthcare, including public health, health information technology (Health IT), and smart medicine.

Wenbing Zhao, Xiong Luo , Tie Qiu
Special Issue Editors

*applied
sciences*

MDPI

Article

Design, Development and Implementation of a Smartphone Overdependence Management System for the Self-Control of Smart Devices

Seo-Joon Lee [1,†], Mi Jung Rho [2,3,†], In Hye Yook [2], Seung-Ho Park [4], Kwang-Soo Jang [4], Bum-Joon Park [4], Ook Lee [4], Dong Kyun Lee [2], Dai-Jin Kim [5,6,*,‡] and In Young Choi [2,3,*,‡]

[1]   BK21 PLUS Program in Embodiment: Health-Society Interaction, Department of Public Health Sciences, Graduate School, Korea University, Seoul 02841, Korea; richardlsj@korea.ac.kr
[2]   Department of Medical Informatics, College of Medicine, The Catholic University of Seoul, 222, Banpo-daero, Seocho-gu, Seoul 06591, Korea; romy1018@naver.com (M.J.R.); whiteeyes89@naver.com (I.H.Y.); alexlee@credoway.com (D.K.L.)
[3]   Catholic Institute for Healthcare Management and Graduate School of Healthcare Management and Policy, The Catholic University of Korea, Seoul 06591, Korea
[4]   Department of Information System, Hanyang University; Seoul 04763, Korea; shpark@tnic.co.kr (S.-H.P.); jks8605@nate.com (K.-S.J.); indev@tnic.co.kr (B.-J.P.); ooklee@hanyang.ac.kr (O.L.)
[5]   Addiction Research Institute, Department of Psychiatry, Seoul St. Mary's Hospital, College of Medicine, The Catholic University of Korea, Seoul 06591, Korea
[6]   Department of Psychiatry, Seoul St. Mary's Hospital, College of Medicine, The Catholic University of Korea, 222, Banpo-daero, Seocho-gu, Seoul 06591, Korea
*   Correspondence: kdj922@catholic.ac.kr (D.-J.K.); iychoi@catholic.ac.kr (I.Y.C.);
    Tel.: +82-2-2258-6086 (D.-J.K.); +82-2-2258-7870 (I.Y.C.); Fax: +82-2-594-3870 (D.-J.K.); +82-2-2258-8257 (I.Y.C.)
†   These authors contributed equally to this work.
‡   These corresponding authors contributed equally to this work.

Academic Editors: Wenbing Zhao, Xiong Luo and Tie Qiu
Received: 27 November 2016; Accepted: 10 December 2016; Published: 16 December 2016

Abstract: Background: Smartphone overdependence is a type of mental disorder that requires continuous treatment for cure and prevention. A smartphone overdependence management system that is based on scientific evidence is required. This study proposes the design, development and implementation of a smartphone overdependence management system for self-control of smart devices. Methods: The system architecture of the Smartphone Overdependence Management System (SOMS) primarily consists of four sessions of mental monitoring: (1) Baseline settlement session; (2) Assessment session; (3) Sensing & monitoring session; and (4) Analysis and feedback session. We developed the smartphone-usage-monitoring application (app) and MindsCare personal computer (PC) app to receive and integrate usage data from smartphone users. We analyzed smartphone usage data using the Chi-square Automatic Interaction Detector (CHAID). Based on the baseline settlement results, we designed a feedback service to intervene. We implemented the system using 96 participants for testing and validation. The participants were classified into two groups: the smartphone usage control group (SUC) and the smartphone usage disorder addiction group (SUD). Results: The background smartphone monitoring app of the proposed system successfully monitored the smartphone usage based on the developed algorithm. The usage minutes of the SUD were higher than the usage minutes of the SUC in 11 of the 16 categories developed in our study. Via the MindsCare PC app, the data were successfully integrated and stored, and managers can successfully analyze and diagnose based on the monitored data. Conclusion: The SOMS is a new system that is based on integrated personalized data for evidence-based smartphone overdependence intervention. The SOMS is useful for managing usage data, diagnosing smartphone overdependence, classifying usage patterns and predicting smartphone overdependence. This system contributes to the diagnosis of an abstract mental status, such as smartphone overdependence, based on specific scientific indicators without reliance on consultation.

Keywords: smartphone; overdependence; telepsychiatry; monitoring system

---

1. Introduction

The use of smartphones has increased convenience in all sectors of everyday lives. However, numerous studies in the previous have stated the following side effects of excessive smartphone usage [1,2]: Due to a lack of self-control [3], smartphone overuse interferes with daily life and sleep [4]; The side effects are severe at times and may cause depressive symptoms and social relationship failure [5]; Negative effects are valid regardless of gender, particularly in the case of hindering academic achievements [6].

The term smartphone overuse includes all addictive activities regarding the problematic use of the Internet [7], playing games, logging on to messengers, or accessing virtual communities to the extent that they neglect positive areas of life [8].

Sufficient evidence supports the fact that the overdependence of smartphones requires continuous mental treatment sessions to cure this disorder and, if possible, prevent the disorder. Both treatment and prevention should be accompanied by a systemized monitoring environment for appropriate intervention. Information technology (IT) has been extensively applied in other healthcare systems, and many variants of medical information systems (MIS), which enable efficient monitoring of health statuses, have been created [9–11]. Although previous studies have addressed telepsychiatry [12], they primarily rely on videoconferencing.

However, the proper management of mental-related issues is difficult compared with the management of physical illness, such as those caused by viruses or bacteria, because these issues do not accompany distinct causal biomarkers. A recent report has stated that studies about reproducible and clinically actionable markers are lacking in the general case of psychiatry, such as overdependence [13].

This is shown in past literature also, with many utilizing smartphone monitoring application on physical indicators that monitors the changes in heart activity [14], screens for hearing loss [15], or assesses mobility of the elderly [16], etc. As mentioned, mental status such as overuse is still a difficult psychological marker to monitor, with conventional treatment relying on "perceived overuse", and not scientific evidence.

Therefore, we propose the Smartphone Overdependence Management System (SOMS), which is a smartphone overdependence management system that delivers mental medical services based on scientific evidence. The goal of the study is to develop a system that scientifically analyzes behavioral patterns that directly cause smartphone overdependence, prevents and monitors smartphone overdependence, and treats patients with integrated information. The system service was developed and implemented for potentially and currently addicted adults and adolescents.

2. Related Research

The majority of studies have focused on social scientific findings regarding the risks and causal pathways of smartphone overuse [17–19]. Few studies consider smartphone overuse as a psychiatric problem and apply telemedicine for intervention. Lee et al. [20] proposed the Smartphone Addiction Management System (SAMS); however, it lacked a proper automated measurement algorithm (as mentioned in their limitations) and appeared to include location information, which exhibits weak importance in the case of smartphone usage monitoring.

Telepsychiatry, which is a variant of telemedicine, has been the center of solutions in medical information systems regarding mental health. Telepsychiatry initially emerged due to the difficulty of providing mental treatment service [21] in rural and geographically isolated regions. Although it is costly and some patients from remote distances are unable to travel to urban medical centers for psychiatric treatment, the expected outcome of this IT-converged service was subjected to skepticism because many experts believed that mental status issues can be solved only with face-to-face consultation. However, previous consecutive studies indicate that telepsychiatry services, such as interactive videoconferencing, are as effective as face-to-face psychiatry treatment [12] in most psychiatry fields. Positive results were similar for adults, adolescents and children. The studies prove that telepsychiatry is a feasible and acceptable approach to providing mental medical services to youths [22] with educational effects [23].

Additional unique possibilities by applying telemedicine facilitates monitoring using up-to-date mobile technology [24]. Focusing on monitoring and preventing the relapse of alcohol addicts using smartphones, Gustafson et al. [25] proved the effectiveness of smartphone monitoring. Specialized and personalized intervention is possible only based on individually monitored specific data and evidence. This study proposes a medical information system that is based on an optimized algorithm that provides monitoring services to patients to diagnose based on objective data.

3. System Overview

3.1. Total System Architecture

The system architecture of the SOMS consists of four main sessions of mental monitoring: (1) Baseline settlement session; (2) Assessment session; (3) Sensing & monitoring session; and (4) Analysis session. Figure 1 shows the total system architecture.

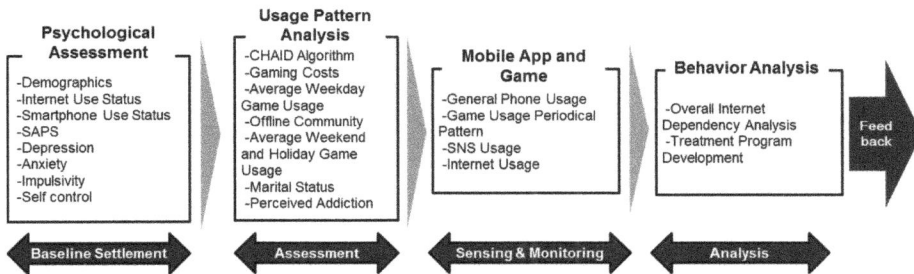

Figure 1. Total System Architecture of the Smartphone Overdependence Management System (SOMS).

In the baseline settlement session, we obtain the psychological information of all patients using surveys and an offline medical test. The psychological information is obtained to assess the socio-demographical status, Internet usage status, smartphone usage status, Smartphone Addiction Proneness Scale (SAPS), depression status, anxiety status, impulsivity status, and self-control status of each patient. In the assessment phase, the patient information is processed using the Chi-square Automatic Interaction Detector (CHAID) algorithm [26]. Six important indicators—gaming costs, average weekday game usage, offline community, average weekend and holiday game usage, marital status, and perceived addiction—are assessed using the CHAID algorithm.

After the assessment phase, the mobile device usage behavior of the patient is sensed and monitored via the mobile application (app), which is developed as a part of the SOMS. The general device usage, game usage periodical pattern, social network service (SNS) and Internet usage are monitored to obtain usage behavior evidence.

The analysis session includes the total Internet dependency analysis of the patient. This session provides a conclusion for the overdependence usage status. Personalized feedback and treatment programs are developed.

Considering the diagnosis based on scientific indicators, the system provides a feedback service for patients when intervention is necessary. The system is implemented to randomly selected adults nationwide and willingly participating middle school and high school adolescents.

3.2. General Specifications

3.2.1. Baseline Settlement Session

We conducted a general survey to assess the psychological status of smartphone overdependence. In the case of adolescents, adolescents who accepted the terms to provide information and had their parents' approval were provided services by the SOMS.

In all surveys, various survey tools, such as the SAPS [27], a behavioral activation system/behavioral inhibition system (BAS/BIS) [28], a short version of the smartphone addiction scale (SAS-SV) [29], depression symptom checklist-90-revision (SCL-90-R) [30], Dickman Functional and Dysfunctional Impulsivity Inventory (DFDII) [31], and belief self-control scale (BSCS) [32], were employed.

The participants were divided into two groups: the smartphone usage control (SUC) group, which included healthy and productive smartphone users, and the smartphone usage disorder (SUD) group, which included negative users with smartphone overdependence.

3.2.2. Assessment Session

The obtained information was input to the developed algorithm based on the CHAID. In our previous study [33], an optimized algorithm to determine the Internet overdependence condition was derived from the CHAID decision tree and applied to the proposed analysis system, as shown in Figure 2.

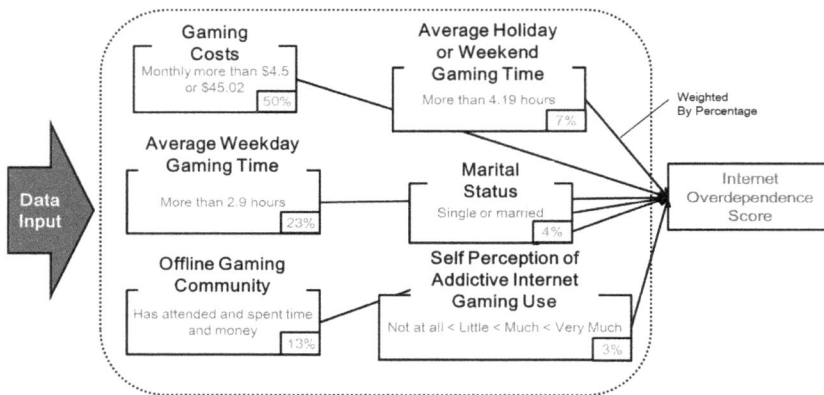

Figure 2. Smartphone overdependence decision algorithm.

When the monitored data are input in the analysis algorithm, the following six indicators are scored and aggregated according to each weight percentage by importance: whether the user has spent more than $4.5–45.02 on gaming (50%); whether the user's average weekday gaming time exceeds 2.9 h (23%); whether the user attends occasional events of the offline gaming community and spends his/her time and money (13%); whether the user's average holiday or weekend gaming time exceeds 4.19 h (7%); the marital status of the user (4%); and the user's self-perception of addictive Internet gaming use (3%). Weight differences were derived from our previous study and were applied in this algorithm. Each of the six indicators' scores is weighted and scored. The aggregated score of the six indicators is the total smartphone over-dependency score of the individual.

3.2.3. Sensing & Monitoring Session

Via the mobile app of the SOMS, the mobile device usage data of the patients are collected and sent to the main server. General phone usage contains all general status information about a phone, even data regarding whether the phone is turned on or off, whether the phone is in an idle state, and whether an Internet connection exists. The most important feature is Internet, SNS, and game usage monitoring. The general application data, exact usage time and period logs are monitored via the background application. The proposed application supports only Android phones. The system architecture is shown in Figure 3.

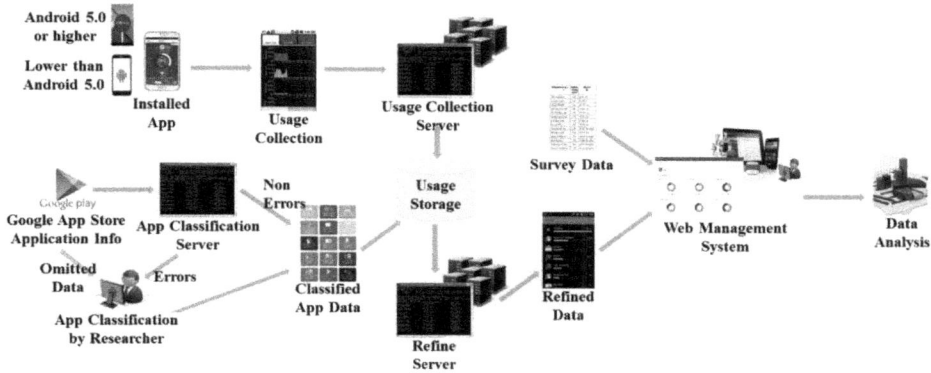

Figure 3. System architecture of sensing and monitoring app.

The installed app collects the application usage information (amount of usage and frequency of usage) and sends it to the usage collection server. The Google app store application information is sent to the app classification server. Only the "application classification" information provided by Google is obtained. However, when the application classification information is omitted, the researcher manually types in the classification information. If data errors occur in the app classification server, the researcher manually corrects the errors. Then, the non-errors and data that are adjusted by the researcher are integrated as classified app data and sent to the usage storage. The application usage and classification information are integrated and sent to the usage storage.

These usage data are useful for analyzing individual application usage information but are not useful for data analysis. In data analysis, the data must be refined. This task is performed by the refine server, which optimizes the refined data for visualization or analysis. The refine server contains a computational algorithm to classify data into meaningful fields, as shown in Table 1. Note that one measurement occurs, for example, when the user begins a game application one time.

In the general measurement information field, classification by day, hour, or ten minutes was conducted to adjust the periods when the smartphone was off or not in use. If the non-usage period is included, the overuse level of the patient is underestimated. The usage data can be analyzed without a smartphone non-usage period bias to manage the data quality. The management fields that are classified and defined based on the binge/chronic status enable researchers to categorize binge overuse and chronic overuse. Binge overuse accounts for people who play games in a certain short period (for example, weekends) but play a lot, whereas chronic overuse accounts for people who play a lot throughout an entire week or period.

With the survey data obtained in the baseline settlement phase, the refined data are sent to a web management system, which is specifically shown in Section 4.5. Using the data from the web management server, researchers can conduct the analysis.

Table 1. Data quality management.

Fields	Definition	Calculation	
General Measurement Information	Measurement Ratio (Standard: Day)	$\frac{Number\ of\ Measurements}{Total\ Measurement\ Period}$	
	Measurement Ratio (Standard: Hour)	$\frac{Number\ of\ Measured\ Hours}{Number\ of\ Measurements \times 24}$	
	Measurement Ratio (Standard: Ten Minutes)	$\frac{Number\ of\ Measured\ 10\ minutes}{Number\ of\ Measured\ Hours \times 6}$	
	Total Number of Measurements Ratio	$\frac{Number\ of\ Measured\ Hours}{Number\ of\ Measurements \times 24 \times 6}$	
	Measurement Period Ratio	$\frac{Number\ of\ Measured\ Hours}{Total\ Measurement\ Period \times 24 \times 6}$	
Measurement Fields Classified by Binge/Chronic Status	-	Binge	Chronic
	Average Usage by Day	$\frac{1\ Day\ Usage\ Amount}{Measured\ Days}$	Not Able
	Average Usage	$\frac{Total\ App\ Usage\ Time}{App\ Usage\ Days}$	$\frac{Total\ App\ Usage\ Time}{Total\ Measured\ Days}$
	Aggregate Average Usage by Category	$\sum\limits_{n=1}^{k} \frac{Total\ App\ Usage\ Time}{App\ Usage\ Days}$ (n indicates the number of all apps in the category)	$\sum\limits_{n=1}^{k} \frac{Total\ App\ Usage\ Time}{Total\ Measured\ Days}$ (n indicates the number of all apps in the category)
	Average Usage by Certain Period (e.g., 2:00 p.m. to 3:00 p.m.)	$\frac{Total\ App\ Usage\ Time\ at\ Certain\ Period}{App\ Usage\ Days\ at\ Certain\ Period}$	$\frac{Total\ App\ Usage\ Time\ at\ Certain\ Period}{Total\ Certain\ Period}$

3.2.4. Analysis Session

The individually targeted diagnosis that considers six indicators of a patient is provided based on an analysis. The total score of smartphone overdependence is provided (as mentioned in the assessment session), and brief specific comments are simultaneously provided. With the total smartphone overdependence score (e.g., 83.3% or 81%), comments such as "Costs for games are pretty high . . . " or "You tend to have many activities related to games . . . " are provided to account for the specific indicator(s) with which the user has a problem.

This simplified recommendation is envisioned to help patients and their physicians understand the nature of their overdependence on the smartphone, monitor the overuse, assess risk and help construct the future mental treatment.

4. Implementation

4.1. Target Population

A baseline settlement survey was conducted with 139 randomly selected participants, who agreed to install the smartphone application of the proposed system. The system was consecutively implemented using these participants. However, 43 participants were excluded due to dropout within seven days or data collection errors. As a result, 96 participants remained (69.06%). The research procedures were performed in accordance with the Declaration of Helsinki. The Institutional Review Board of the Catholic University of South Korea, ST. Mary's Hospital (IRB number: KC15EISI0103).

All 96 participants were classified into two groups: the SUD group and the SUC group. The SUD and SUC groups were distinguished based on the SAPS standards. As a result, the SUD groups had 29 participants, and the SUC groups had 67 participants. The socio-demographic status for the participants in the SUD and SUC groups is listed in Table 2.

Table 2. Socio-demographic status of participants in the smartphone usage disorder (SUD) and smartphone usage control (SUC) groups.

Characteristics		SUD (*n* = 29)		SUC (*n* = 67)		Total (*n* = 96)	
		n	%	*n*	%	*n*	%
Gender	Male	22	75.9	65	97.0	87	90.6
	Female	7	31.8	2	3.4	9	9.4
Age	10–19	15	51.7	57	85.1	72	75.0
	20–29	7	24.1	4	6.0	11	11.5
	30–39	7	24.1	6	9.0	13	13.5
Education	Undergraduate	20	69.0	59	88.1	79	82.3
	Graduate	8	27.6	7	10.4	15	15.6
	Postgraduate	1	3.4	1	1.5	2	2.1
Job	Employed	9	31.0	6	9.0	15	15.6
	Unemployed	20	69.0	61	91.0	81	84.4
Marital Status	Married	5	17.2	5	7.5	10	10.4
	Unmarried	24	82.8	62	92.5	86	89.6
SES	High	3	10.3	15	22.4	18	18.8
	Middle	16	55.2	32	47.8	48	50.0
	Low	8	27.6	18	26.9	26	27.1
	Unknown	2	6.9	2	3.0	4	4.2

Unemployed: Student, Housewife; Abbreviation: SES, Socio-economic Status.

Most participants were male (*n* = 86, 90.6%), and the age of most participants ranged from 10–19 (*n* = 72, 75.0%). Most participants had an undergraduate degree or lower level of education (*n* = 79, 82.3%), were unemployed (*n* = 81, 84.4%), and were not married (*n* = 86, 89.6%), which is also noted by the age demographics. Half of the participants replied that their socio-economic status (SES) was in the middle (*n* = 48, 50%).

4.2. Smartphone Usage Monitoring Implementation

The smartphone application of the SOMS was installed on the mobile phones of the informed participants for additional monitoring. The app monitored the smartphone usage patterns of the participants to obtain objective and specific data to provide evidence of smartphone overdependence.

The SOMS smartphone-usage-monitoring application can be downloaded and installed from app stores. It is not loaded with a user interface (UI); after it is installed and initially executed, it runs as a background app to monitor general usage events. Note that users must approve the app usage access by tapping "on" on the app usage access screen. Then, the data are sent to the personal computer (PC) application of the management servers for the analysis (Section 4.3).

4.3. Management Server: MindsCare PC Application

The aggregated patient data were sent to the server for monitoring. The received data were integrated and mined through the MindsCare PC application and shown as a visual UI, as illustrated in Figures 4 and 5.

On the Dashboard page (Figure 4a), the SUD, SAPS, BAS/BIS, DFDII, and BSCS information is shown in each visual circular chart. The users can view the number of samples when they place the mouse cursor over the circular chart (Figure 4b). The group distribution by age and sex is shown in the bar graphs, and the managers can view the number of samples when they place the mouse cursor over the bar graphs (Figure 4c).

The user smartphone application monitoring information that is obtained via the background-running app Internet Detox is observed on the Smartphone Usage (SMU) page (Figure 5a). The top five smartphone application lists are shown in a circular chart (e.g., Kakao Talk, Chrome, and Google apps). A manager can view the aggregate usage time of each application when they place the mouse cursor over the circular chart (Figure 5b).

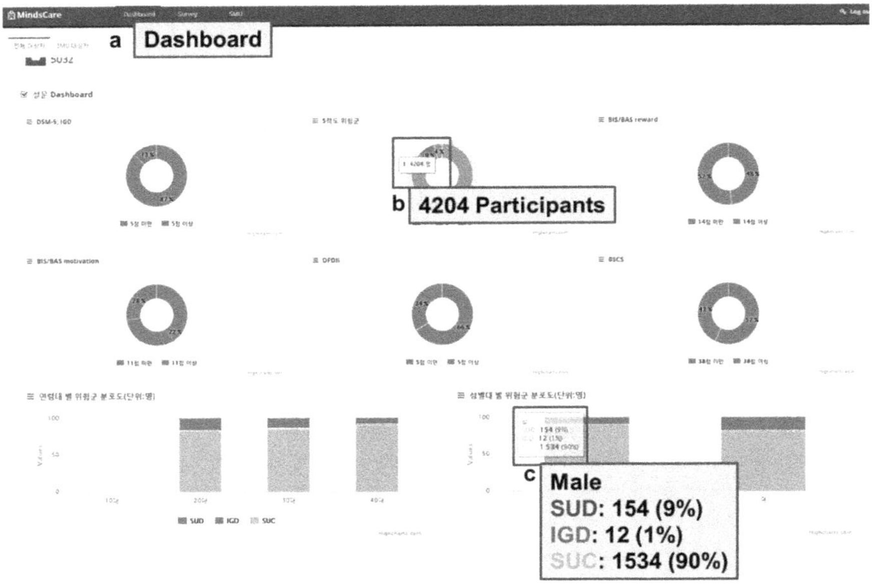

Figure 4. Survey data mining and visualization. SUD: Smartphone Use Disorder; IGD: Internet Gaming Disorder; SUC: Smartphone Use Control.

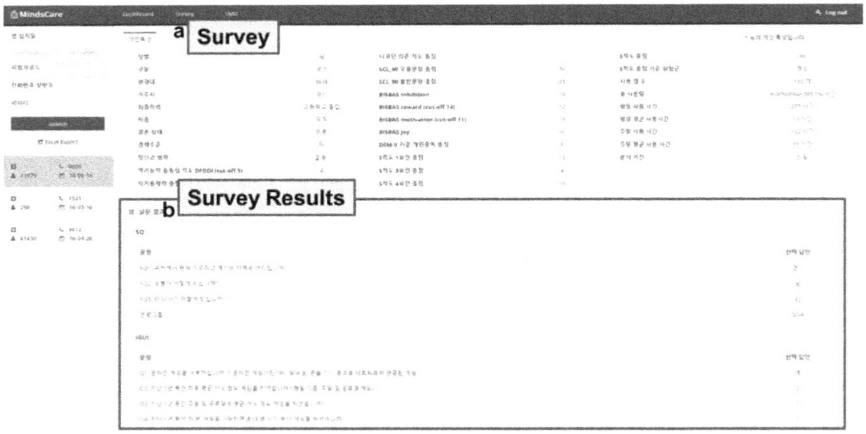

Figure 5. Application usage monitoring.

4.4. Smartphone Usage Results

The smartphone usage monitoring results are listed in Table 3. The results were calculated based on the daily average usage. The Google Play store provides 35 category standards, and registered apps to the store are categorized. However, we identified some categories that can be integrated and reorganized. Thus, the 35 categories were reorganized into the following 16 items: finance, system, web,

SNS, shopping, business, tool/productivity, entertainment, weather, transportation, photo, lifestyle, health/exercise, game, and education, as shown in Table 3.

Table 3. Daily average usage by category.

Category	SUD		SUC		Usage Gap
	User	Usage	User	Usage	
Finance	24	32.5	30	4.5	28.0
System	27	39.7	61	13.8	25.9
Web	27	61.8	57	42.8	19.0
SNS	27	63.7	55	45.0	18.7
Shopping	16	21.5	15	11.6	9.9
Business	21	8.2	28	3.2	5.0
Tool/Productivity	26	14.4	55	10.6	3.8
Entertainment	27	35.0	57	31.2	3.8
Weather	19	4.5	11	1.6	2.9
Transportation	22	5.2	15	3.1	2.1
Photo	23	7.5	38	6.9	0.6
Lifestyle	26	8.8	49	9.3	-0.5
Health/exercise	6	4.1	8	6.4	-2.3
Game	24	20.5	53	23.6	-3.2
Education	14	1.1	14	7.8	-6.7
Decoration	15	92.0	55	102.7	-10.7

Usage: minutes; Usage Gap: SUD − SUC.

"User" refers to the number of users who have used the app of a certain category, and "usage minutes" refers to the time that the user has spent on the app of this category. The usage gap was calculated by subtracting the usage minutes of the SUC from the usage minutes of the SUD. With the exception of five categories (lifestyle, health/exercise, game, education, and decoration), the monitoring results indicate that the SUD usage minutes in all 11 categories were higher than the SUC usage minutes. The most noticeable categories were finance- and system-related apps with usage gaps of 28.0 and 25.9, respectively.

4.5. Discussion

This study attempts to design, develop, and implement a smartphone overdependence management system for self-control of smart devices. Based on the results of this study, we present the discussions below.

In the baseline settlement session, we adapt diverse psychological tools, such as SAPS, BAS/BIS, SAS-SV, SCL-90-R, DFDII, and BSCS, to assess the psychological status of smartphone overdependence. These tools support the system to correctly analyze smartphone usage. Future research may identify other psychological tools to address missing areas.

In the assessment session, we employ the CHAID Algorithm and six indicators to assess the smartphone overdependence. However, the shortcoming is that the six indicators were developed only for Internet dependence. Thus, future research may involve the development of new indicators that are more applicable in other fields.

In the sensing and monitoring session, the background smartphone app monitors specific overuse stats. In the MindsCare PC app, the data are successfully stored and integrated, which enables the monitoring of general application data, exact usage time and period logs. The limitation is that the proposed app only supports Android phones due to security issues at the stage of development, and because more than 85% of smartphone users in South Korea use Android phones. Considering worldwide users, future research should develop the usage collection app for other operating systems (OSs).

In the analysis and feedback session, medical treatment recommendations are provided based on six indicators. If the user has an impediment in two of the six indicators, recommendations are provided based on these two impediments.

Implementation results of the participants of the system indicate that the usage minutes of SUD were higher than the usage minutes of SUC in 11 categories. With the exception of five categories (lifestyle, health/exercise, game, education, and decoration), the daily-average comparison between the SUD group and the SUC group in the 16 categories that were defined from this study indicate that the usage minutes of SUD were higher than the usage minutes of SUC in all 11 categories. In the "game" category, the SUD and SUC groups did not significantly differ (SUD − SUC = −3.2). The smartphone usage time for the SUC group was higher than the smartphone usage for the SUD group. Although games can be easily associated with addiction, and this linkage is sometimes viable [34,35], the proposed results suggest the larger effect of web usage or SNS usage in the case of smartphones. The results also correspond with recent studies that emphasized the importance of considering SNS as a main factor for smartphone overuse [36,37].

A brief comparison with the SAMS is discussed because it is almost the first reference of the smartphone overuse monitoring system. Other related solutions were simple apps that were non-systematic or were not studies. The main difference is that the SAMS simply shows raw smartphone usage, whereas we developed an algorithm to filter raw information and consider the key risks or variables regarding smartphone overuse. The proposed system shows better monitored results based on weekday or weekend usage, which is an important risk factor that was discussed in previous research [38].

Another important point is that we developed 16 new categories to classify the collected app data: finance, system, web, SNS, shopping, business, tool/productivity, entertainment, weather, transportation, photo, lifestyle, health/exercise, game, and education. The previous 35 categories established by Google are overspecified, which render them inappropriate for analysis or research applications. A representative example is that Google separates "Cartoons" and "Entertainment" (based on the most recent Google category in November 2016); however, combining these two terms in the research analysis is more appropriate. It is also a shortcoming of SAMS because they do not address this part. Future related studies are recommended to follow the proposed categories in this study instead of relying on the default category settings of Google.

In the case of "Finance," "System," and "Decoration," the daily average usage minutes were overmeasured because they included usage events such as background security applications and any type of application launchers. These categories may cause bias when monitoring. Thus, future research on monitoring algorithms that filter these events is necessary. A future study should include new categories depending on the app data or research topic.

5. Conclusions

This study developed and implemented the SOMS, which is an original MIS that is based on integrated personalized data for evidence-based smartphone overuse intervention. The SOMS primarily consists of four sessions of mental monitoring: (1) Baseline settlement session; (2) Assessment session; (3) Sensing & monitoring session; and (4) Analysis session. By obtaining integrated data of smartphone overdependent patients, the personalized mental service in the management server can be diagnosed. The uniqueness of the SOMS is that its services are based on specific scientific grounds, which are inferred from specific psychological data. In addition, the proposed system can provide a scientific footwork for personalized smartphone overuse management systems. Additional years of implementation of this study may provide integrated big data in the area of smartphone overdependence, which will cause the abstract mental status, such as smartphone overdependence, to be diagnosed based on specific scientific indicators instead of a dependence on verbal consultation.

Acknowledgments: This study was supported by the Basic Science Research Program through the National Research Foundation of Korea (NRF), which is funded by the Ministry of Science, ICT & Future Planning

(NRF-2014M3C7A1062893). The authors thank the Trend & Innovation Company (TNIC) for their support in system development.

Author Contributions: Seo-Joon Lee and Mi-Jung Rho are both first authors who contributed equally in the article; Seo-Joon Lee wrote the article; Mi-Jung Rho is the assistant executive of the funded research project. Mi-Jung Rho also supported the writing of the article; In Hye Yook analyzed the data and performed the evaluation; Seung-Ho Park, Kwang-Soo Jang and Bum-Joon Park contributed to developing the proposed system; Dong Kyun Lee supported general implementation of the research project; Ook Lee supervised parts of the project and managed researchers; Dai-Jin Kim and In Young Choi are both corresponding authors who contributed equally to this work. SOMS is a large-scale and long-term research project worth $4.5 million, and all 10 authors substantially contributed in each of their expertise.

Conflicts of Interest: The authors declare no conflict of interest.

References

1. Chen, L.; Yan, Z.; Tang, W.J.; Yang, F.Y.; Xie, X.D.; He, J.C. Mobile phone addiction levels and negative emotions among Chinese young adults: The mediating role of interpersonal problems. *Comput. Hum. Behav.* **2016**, *55*, 856–866. [CrossRef]
2. Chóliz, M. Mobile-phone addiction in adolescence: The test of mobile phone dependence (TMD). *Prog. Health Sci.* **2012**, *2*, 33–44.
3. Gokcearslan, S.; Mumcu, F.K.; Haslaman, T.; Çevik, Y.D. Modelling smartphone addiction: The role of smartphone usage, self-regulation, general self-efficacy and cyberloafing in university students. *Comput. Hum. Behav.* **2016**, *63*, 639–649. [CrossRef]
4. Pavia, L.; Cavani, P.; Di Blasi, M.; Giordano, C. Smartphone Addiction Inventory (SPAI): Psychometric properties and confirmatory factor analysis. *Comput. Hum. Behav.* **2016**, *63*, 170–178. [CrossRef]
5. Seo, D.G.; Park, Y.; Kim, M.K.; Park, J. Mobile phone dependency and its impacts on adolescents' social and academic behaviors. *Comput. Hum. Behav.* **2016**, *63*, 282–292. [CrossRef]
6. Hawi, N.S.; Samaha, M. To excel or not to excel: Strong evidence on the adverse effect of smartphone addiction on academic performance. *Comput. Educ.* **2016**, *98*, 81–89. [CrossRef]
7. Yellowlees, P.M.; Marks, S. Problematic Internet use or Internet addiction? *Comput. Hum. Behav.* **2007**, *23*, 1447–1453. [CrossRef]
8. Billieux, J.; Maurage, P.; Lopez-Fernandez, O.; Kuss, D.J.; Griffiths, M.D. Can disordered mobile phone use be considered a behavioral addiction? An update on current evidence and a comprehensive model for future research. *Curr. Addict. Rep.* **2015**, *2*, 156–162. [CrossRef]
9. Alamedine, D.; Khalil, M.; Marque, C. Parameters extraction and monitoring in uterine EMG signals. Detection of preterm deliveries. *IRBM* **2013**, *34*, 322–325. [CrossRef]
10. Konstam, M.A. Home monitoring should be the central element in an effective program of heart failure disease management. *Circulation* **2012**, *125*, 820–827. [CrossRef] [PubMed]
11. Vijayalakshmi, S.R.; Muruganand, S. Real-time monitoring of ubiquitous wireless ECG sensor node for medical care using ZigBee. *Int. J. Electron.* **2012**, *99*, 79–89. [CrossRef]
12. O'Reilly, R.; Bishop, J.; Maddox, K.; Hutchinson, L.; Fisman, M.; Takhar, J. Is telepsychiatry equivalent to face-to-face psychiatry? Results from a randomized controlled equivalence trial. *Psychiatr. Serv.* **2007**, *58*, 836–843. [CrossRef] [PubMed]
13. Insel, T.R. The NIMH Research Domain Criteria (RDoC) Project: Precision Medicine for Psychiatry. *Am. J. Psychiatry* **2014**, *171*, 395–397. [CrossRef] [PubMed]
14. Aliev, T.A.; Rzayeva, N.E.; Sattarova, U.E. Robust correlation technology for online monitoring of changes in the state of the heart by means of laptops and smartphones. *Biomed. Signal Process. Control* **2017**, *31*, 44–51. [CrossRef]
15. Hussein, S.Y.; Swanepoel, D.; de Jager, L.B.; Myburgh, H.C.; Eikelboom, R.H.; Hugo, J. Smartphone hearing screening in mHealth assisted community-based primary care. *J. Telemed. Telecare.* **2016**, *22*, 405–412. [CrossRef] [PubMed]
16. Madhushri, P.; Dzhagary, A.; Jovanov, E.; Milenkovic, A. An mHealth Tool Suite for Mobility Assessment. *Information* **2016**, *7*, 47. [CrossRef]
17. Aljomaa, S.S.; Al Qudah, M.F.; Albursan, I.S.; Bakhiet, S.F.; Abduljabbar, A.S. Smartphone addiction among university students in the light of some variables. *Comput. Hum. Behav.* **2016**, *61*, 155–164. [CrossRef]

18. Kim, D.J.; Kim, J.Y.; Pyeon, A. Altered functional connectivity related smartphone overuse in adolescent. *Int. J. Neuropsychopharmacol.* **2016**, *19*, 158.

19. Inal, E.E.; Demirci, K.; Cetinturk, A.; Akgonul, M.; Savas, S. Effects of smartphone overuse on hand function, pinch strength, and the median nerve. *Muscle Nerve* **2015**, *52*, 183–188. [CrossRef] [PubMed]

20. Lee, H.; Ahn, H.; Choi, S.; Choi, W. The SAMS: Smartphone Addiction Management System and verification. *J. Med. Syst.* **2014**, *38*, 1–10. [CrossRef] [PubMed]

21. El-Guebaly, N.; Kingstone, E.; Rae-Grant, Q.; Fyfe, I. The geographical distribution of psychiatrists in Canada: Unmet needs and remedial strategies. *Can. Psychiatr. Assoc. Rev. Assoc. Psychiatres Can. J.* **1993**, *38*, 212–216.

22. Myers, K.M.; Valentine, J.M.; Melzer, S.M. Feasibility, acceptability, and sustainability of telepsychiatry for children and adolescents. *Psychiatr. Serv.* **2007**, *58*, 1493–1496. [CrossRef] [PubMed]

23. Pesamaa, L.; Ebeling, H.; Kuusimaki, M.L.; Winblad, I.; Isohanni, M.; Moilanen, I. Videoconferencing in child and adolescent telepsychiatry: A systematic review of the literature. *J. Telemed. Telecare* **2004**, *10*, 187–192. [CrossRef] [PubMed]

24. Proudfoot, J. The future is in our hands: The role of mobile phones in the prevention and management of mental disorders. *Aust. N. Z. J. Psychiatry* **2013**, *47*, 111–113. [CrossRef] [PubMed]

25. Ford, J.H.; Alagoz, E.; Dinauer, S.; Johnson, K.A.; Pe-Romashko, K.; Gustafson, D.H. Successful organizational strategies to sustain use of A-CHESS: A mobile intervention for individuals with alcohol use disorders. *JMIR* **2015**, *17*, e201. [CrossRef] [PubMed]

26. Murphy, E.L.; Comiskey, C.M. Using chi-Squared Automatic Interaction Detection (CHAID) modelling to identify groups of methadone treatment clients experiencing significantly poorer treatment outcomes. *J. Subst. Abus. Treat.* **2013**, *45*, 343–349. [CrossRef] [PubMed]

27. Kim, D.; Lee, Y.; Lee, J.; Nam, J.K.; Chung, Y. Development of Korean smartphone addiction proneness scale for youth. *PLoS ONE* **2014**, *9*, e97920. [CrossRef] [PubMed]

28. Kwon, M.; Kim, D.-J.; Cho, H.; Yang, S. The smartphone addiction scale: Development and validation of a short version for adolescents. *PLoS ONE* **2013**, *8*, e83558. [CrossRef] [PubMed]

29. Kwon, M.; Choi, J.-H.; Gu, X.-Y.; Kim, D.-J. Standardization of the smart phone addiction scale (SAS). *Asia Pac. Psychiatry* **2012**, *4*, 160.

30. Engel, K.; Schaefer, M.; Stickel, A.; Binder, H.; Heinz, A.; Richter, C. The role of psychological distress in relapse prevention of alcohol addiction. Can high scores on the SCL-90-R predict alcohol relapse? *Alcohol Alcohol.* **2016**, *51*, 27–31. [CrossRef] [PubMed]

31. Gao, Q.; Zhang, J.; Jia, C. Psychometric properties of the Dickman Impulsivity Instrument in suicide victims and living controls of rural China. *J. Affect. Disord.* **2011**, *132*, 368–374. [CrossRef] [PubMed]

32. Lindner, C.; Nagy, G.; Retelsdorf, J. The dimensionality of the Brief Self-Control Scale-An evaluation of unidimensional and multidimensional applications. *Personal. Individ. Differ.* **2015**, *86*, 465–473. [CrossRef]

33. Rho, M.J.; Jeong, J.E.; Chun, J.W.; Cho, H.; Jung, D.J.; Choi, I.Y.; Kim, D.J. Predictors and patterns of problematic Internet game use using a decision tree model. *J. Behav. Addict.* **2016**, *5*, 500–509. [CrossRef] [PubMed]

34. Chen, C.; Leung, L. Are you addicted to Candy Crush Saga? An exploratory study linking psychological factors to mobile social game addiction. *Telemat. Inform.* **2016**, *33*, 1155–1166. [CrossRef]

35. Munoz-Miralles, R.; Ortega-Gonzalez, R.; Lopez-Moron, M.R.; Batalla-Martinez, C.; Manresa, J.M.; Montella-Jordana, N.; Chamarro, A.; Carbonell, X.; Toran-Monserrat, P. The problematic use of Information and Communication Technologies (ICT) in adolescents by the cross sectional JOITIC study. *BMC Pediatr.* **2016**, *16*, 140. [CrossRef] [PubMed]

36. Jeong, S.-H.; Kim, H.; Yum, J.-Y.; Hwang, Y. What type of content are smartphone users addicted to?: SNS vs. games. *Comput. Hum. Behav.* **2016**, *54*, 10–17. [CrossRef]

37. Kim, H. Exercise rehabilitation for smartphone addiction. *J. Exerc. Rehabil.* **2013**, *9*, 500–505. [CrossRef] [PubMed]

38. Kim, Y.; Jeong, J.E.; Cho, H.; Jung, D.J.; Kwak, M.; Rho, M.J.; Yu, H.; Kim, D.J.; Choi, I.Y. Personality factors predicting smartphone addiction predisposition: Behavioral inhibition and activation systems, impulsivity, and self-control. *PLoS ONE* **2016**, *11*, e0159788. [CrossRef] [PubMed]

Article

A Visual Analytics Approach for Detecting and Understanding Anomalous Resident Behaviors in Smart Healthcare

Zhifang Liao [1], Lingyuan Kong [1], Xiao Wang [2], Ying Zhao [3,*], Fangfang Zhou [3], Zhining Liao [4] and Xiaoping Fan [3,5,*]

[1] School of Software Engineering, Central South University, Changsha 410075, China; zfliao@csu.edu.cn (Z.L.); konglingyuan@outlook.com (L.K.)
[2] Data Center Consolidation (Beijing), Industrial and Commercial Bank of China, Beijing 100000, China; xw14060@my.bristol.ac.uk
[3] School of Information Science and Engineering, Central South University, Changsha 410075, China; zff@csu.edu.cn
[4] Division of Health & Social Care Research, Faculty of Life Sciences &Medicine, King's College London, London WC2R 2LS, UK; liaozn98@yahoo.com
[5] Information Management Department, Hunan University of Finance and Economics, Changsha 410083, China
* Correspondence: zhaoying@csu.edu.cn (Y.Z.); xpfan@csu.edu.cn (X.F.); Tel.: +86-137-8708-4511; +86-135-0731-9135

Academic Editor: Wenbing Zhao
Received: 31 December 2016; Accepted: 27 February 2017; Published: 7 March 2017

Abstract: With the development of science and technology, it is possible to analyze residents' daily behaviors for the purpose of smart healthcare in the smart home environment. Many researchers have begun to detect residents' anomalous behaviors and assess their physical condition, but these approaches used by the researchers are often caught in plight caused by a lack of ground truth, one-sided analysis of behavior, and difficulty of understanding behaviors. In this paper, we put forward a smart home visual analysis system (SHVis) to help analysts detect and comprehend unusual behaviors of residents, and predict the health information intelligently. Firstly, the system classifies daily activities recorded by sensor devices in smart home environment into different categories, and discovers unusual behavior patterns of residents living in this environment by using various characteristics extracted from those activities and appropriate unsupervised anomaly detection algorithm. Secondly, on the basis of figuring out the residents' anomaly degree of every date, we explore the daily behavior patterns and details with the help of several visualization views, and compare and analyze residents' activities of various dates to find the reasons why residents act unusually. In the case study of this paper, we analyze residents' behaviors that happened over two months and find unusual indoor behaviors and give health advice to the residents.

Keywords: smart healthcare; user behaviors; anomaly detection; visual analytics

---

1. Introduction

With the development of Internet of things, various powerful sensors are introduced in household devices frequently, which create a safer, more convenient and comfortable smart home environment [1,2]. At the same time, massive data related to residents' living are continuously captured by the sensors, providing opportunities for researchers to explore residents' behaviors. Through analyzing these behaviors, we can not only recognize indoor activities but also discover residents' living habits, and, more importantly we can detect their unusual behaviors so that we can give them suggestions on how to live a more healthy and environment-friendly life. Furthermore, it can even help conduct health assessment and diagnosis of mobility impaired disease and Alzheimer's disease [3,4].

Recently, detecting anomalous behaviors for smart health in smart home environment has already caught the eyes of some pioneers. Currently, methods of machine learning, frequently used to study these problems [5–7], usually include the following steps: (1) activity recognition; (2) classify these activities and select features; and (3) use the methods of machine learning to figure out the value of residents' health conditions. However, the existing methods have many problems. First, ground truth is generally difficult to obtain, so semi-supervised or supervised machine learning has to rely on a large number of manual annotations. Second, most existing methods are used for a few certain types of activity, which ignores the internal relations between humans and their various activities in smart home. Finally, more human intelligence should be invested, as it is required to comprehend unusual behaviors, analyze causes of anomalous behaviors, recognize, etc.

In this paper, visual analytics technology is introduced to detect and analyze residents' unusual behaviors for health in smart home, which better combines machine intelligence and artificial intelligence. First, we divide more than 30 activities that happen at home into categories, select different characteristics according to activity property, conduct local outlier factor (LOF) based anomaly detection, blend anomaly detection results of events in different categories, and create an overall anomaly appraisal and anomaly indication of separate items. Then, we design a smart home visual analytics system (SHVis) in which original data and anomaly detection results are blended in an interactive visual analysis interface with multiple views. This tool supports interactive exploration of anomaly tendency, analysis of spatial and temporal distribution of daily activities and multi-periods comparative analysis for smart health. It can effectively help analysts analyze, contrast and interpret users' daily activities and anomalous events to predict resident health information. In the case studies, we use several analyses of interesting anomalous events to show the effectiveness of this tool.

The major contribution of this paper includes:

(1) Employing LOF algorithm to anomaly detection of residents' daily activities, which can detect anomalous activities rapidly and effectively.
(2) Designing a series of visual views to analyze, compare and interpret users' various daily activities, which will help researchers locate anomalous events of residents' life rapidly, compare users' behaviors of different dates, and observe detailed information of anomalous events.

2. Related Work

In recent years, there have been number studies focusing on human activity recognition for health in smart home. As the basic steps of analysis of human behavior pattern, the goal of activity recognition is to recognize human daily activities from the data collected from sensors deployed into rooms without disturbing the privacy of the inhabitants [8]. Many machine learning based approaches have been well researched in this area. For example, Kim et al. summarized and compared the performance, features and application scenarios of many machine learning algorithms for activity recognition from the sensor data collecting from smart home [9]. Krishnan et al. proposed a sliding window based SVM (Support Vector Machines) method leading to a real-time performance of activity recognition on streaming sensor data [10]. Some work focus on users' behaviors predication. For example, Liao et al. establishes Markov chain-like models to predict the web resources users need [11].

Based on the study of activity recognition, some researchers have recently carried out many pioneer works on analysis of residents behavior patterns in smart home, especially for the elderly living alone. Some of these works focus on overall evaluation of residents' cognitive ability and life health status according to analysis of data over a period. For example, Prafulla et al. used approximately two years of sensor data in 18 smart homes to train machine learning algorithms for predicting standard clinical assessment scores of residents [5]. Noury et al. evaluated the health status of elderly people living independently at home based on long-term observations on the usage information of electrical devices during months or years [6]. Moreover, other works focus on anomaly detection from daily or weekly perspective based on the monitoring of a single activity or the combination of behaviors. For example, Das et al. proposed a novel one-class classification-based approach to detect errors in daily activities of older adults [12], Jae et al. summarized sensor-based daily behaviors into three aspects, namely activity level, mobility level, and nonresponse interval, and developed a support vector data description method to detect abnormal behavioral patterns of elderly people living alone [13]. Zhao et al. used a novel computer-vision-based system consisting of inexpensive programmable depth sensors, wearable devices, and smart phones to ensure worker safety in the workplace without violating their privacy [14]. Aran et al. proposed an indicator of predictability based on the cross-entropy measure for the detection of anomalies in elderly daily behavior [15]. Alcalá et al. used a novel approach to identify appliance activities from smart meter data and extract the pattern of usage, which is used to monitor the health of the household's occupant [16]. As mentioned above, the machine learning method occupies an absolutely dominant position in the work of residents' behavior assessment and anomaly detection. Our approach aims to solve these problems by combining visual analysis with machine learning.

By now, many studies have introduced visualization and visual analytics into anomaly detection in application domains, such as cyber security and financial crime. There are also some existing works about human abnormal behavior analysis supported by visualization or visual analytics. In terms of human online communication behaviors, Caonan et al. [17,18] designed several novel visualizations to help users understand the analysis results of anomaly recognition algorithm based on machine learning and analyze the behavior patterns of anomalous persons who are potential threats to society. For increased situational awareness and decision making in emergency response, Yuri [19] and Kim [20] visualized people's laws of daily activities in public areas and their movement in emergencies from the data captured by cameras and motion sensors in buildings. On the perspective of human urban life, Liao et al. [21] combined conditional random field model with visual analytics methods to analyze the anomalies in urban taxi Global Positioning System (GPS) traces. Peng et al. [22] performed a visual analysis on heterogeneous trajectories and credit card records of suspects to help investigators obtain their abnormal behaviors and gain evidence. Rohlig et al. [23] presented a novel visual analytics approach for parameter-dependent activity recognition. In general, the analysis and anomaly detection about human behavioral pattern have received extensive attention from visualization and visual analysis communities.

3. Data Description and Task Profile

3.1. Data Description

The Center for Advanced Studies in Adaptive Systems (CASAS) project is a famous smart home research project presented by Washington State University, which treats many houses as intelligent agents where the activities of residents are perceived using multiple sensors [24]. We select two sets of sensor data captured from two houses with two residents living alone in the CASAS project. One dataset has 326,066 rows of data from 18 July 2012 to 17 September 2012 with 28 kinds of daily activities, such as Enter Home, Leave Home, Evening Meds, Morning Meds, Eat Lunch, Eat Dinner, Cook Dinner, Dress, Bathe, Sleep, Toilet, Watch TV, etc. Another dataset has 1,719,553 rows of data from 4 November 2010 to 11 June 2011 with 11 kinds of daily activities, such as Enter Home, Leave Home, Bed to Toilet, Eating, Housekeeping, Relax, Sleeping, Wash Dishes, etc. A sensor event record generally represents four basic fields, namely timestamp, sensorID, sensorStatus, and activityID; an example is shown in Table 1. In these fields, timestamp is accurate to milliseconds, recording the time that the sensor event occurred. Sensor ID represents a certain sensor deployed inside the house. Ssensor status represents the status of the sensor; most sensors only have "ON" and "OFF" statuses, where "ON" means sensor is triggered, and "OFF" means sensor is closed. For a sensor, the time between the nearest "ON" and "OFF" represents the active time of this sensor. Some sensor types, such as temperature sensors and power sensors, are recorded as numbers, and are beyond the scope of this paper. The value of activity ID indicates a specific type of daily activity, which has been pre-processed by activity recognition methods. The field consists of an activity and a status. The words "begin" and "end" of status represent the start and the end of an activity, respectively.

Table 1. Data from sensors.

Timestamp	Sensor ID	Sensor Status	Activity ID
20 July 2012 11:09:18.952332	MA015	ON	Toilet = "begin"
20 July 2012 11:09:20.156992	MA015	OFF	
20 July 2012 11:09:21.252048	MA015	ON	
20 July 2012 11:09:25.563333	MA015	OFF	

3.2. Task Profile

The paper aims at monitoring and exploring users' anomalous behaviors in their smart homes with the help of sensors used to record users' behaviors in a short time. The biggest difficulty in the process of analysis is how to discover and locate anomaly rapidly, how to analyze residents' behavior which has been defined as anomalous from multiple perspectives, and how to discover the false alert from calculation results. Overall, targets of analysis can be divided into the following parts.

3.2.1. Interactive Activity Classification and Summary

In this part, the task is to classify the activities recorded by sensors further so that the features of residents' behaviors can be described more explicitly. For example, "leave home" and "enter home" happen momentarily, while "sleep" and "watch TV" last for a certain period. Thus, we need to classify related activities based on behavior characteristics and offer an interactive manner allowing users to combine these activities freely. Meanwhile, in order to adjust activity categories reasonably, we also need to provide an activity overview to show the information such as the times and the duration of residents' activities.

3.2.2. Combined Anomaly Detection and Summary of Results

In order to get better anomaly detection results, the paper comprehensively takes characteristic parameter of each activity into consideration. We employ a multi-activity and multi-features calculation method to detect and analyze residents' behaviors, and obtain anomaly degrees of residents' activity every day. Researchers carry out characteristics calculation and adjust activities on the basis of analysis results to obtain more precise and accurate value of anomaly degree.

3.2.3. Exploration of Residents' Anomalous Behaviors and Their Spatial and Temporal Distribution

Using the residents' unusual behaviors obtained in T2, T3 is to display and analyze spatial and temporal characters of unusual behaviors by visual analyses methods with multiple dimensions of activity durations, times and start times. With the visual tools, researchers can examine detailed activity information of the date, analyzing activities' information on that very date, such as duration, start time, and times. Furthermore, researchers need to analyze where, when and which resident's behavior is unusual.

3.2.4. Rapid Anomaly Comparison

Researchers not only need to analyze activities in a single date, but compare and contrast behavior patterns of various dates including anomalous and normal dates. In addition, residents' behaviors of some period need to be compared with their general behavior rule. This process offers great help in finding false alert from calculation results.

4. Anomaly Detection

In this section, we detect anomalous behaviors of tested residents through residents' behavior classification, characteristics extraction and anomalous behavior extraction.

4.1. Characteristics Categories

There are many kinds of indoor activities and they are quite different. For example, "sleep" generally happens in bed at nights and lasts for a long time, usually 6 to 9 h. However, although "bath" happens in bathroom regularly, its start time differentiates with each resident's living habits and the duration is generally short. Some other activities happen irregularly in terms of start time and duration, such as "toilet" and "watch TV", without relatively fixed time or duration. Therefore, when we take day as unit to analyze anomaly degree of residents' indoor activities, we need treat different activities in different ways. Table 2 shows part of the data describing activities of an elderly person living alone.

Table 2. Characteristics analysis of various activities.

Activity	Duration	Scene	Start Time	Times	Incidence
Enter Home	short	regular	irregular	irregular	1
Leave home	short	regular	irregular	irregular	1
Dress	short	regular	irregular	irregular	0.98
Phone	short	regular	irregular	irregular	0.33
Cook	short	regular	irregular	irregular	0.22
Eat	short	regular	irregular	irregular	0.216
Bed toilet transition	short	regular	irregular	irregular	0.28
Toilet	short	regular	irregular	irregular	1
Sleep Out of Bed	long	regular	irregular	irregular	1
Relax	long	regular	irregular	irregular	0.58
Watch TV	long	regular	irregular	irregular	1
Entertain guests	long	irregular	regular	irregular	0.066
Groom	short	regular	regular	irregular	0.37
Work at Table	short	regular	regular	irregular	0.05
Read	short	regular	regular	irregular	0.45
Bathe	short	regular	regular	regular	0.93
Sleep	long	regular	regular	regular	0.98

We select three most representative characteristics to calculate anomaly degree of residents' daily behaviors after the analysis of features of indoor activities.

1. Duration: A healthy resident's activity often follows a certain rule, meaning that its value of duration fluctuates around a fixed value. According to the activity's duration, we can calculate anomaly value of residents' activities in each date with LOF algorithm.
2. Times: Similar to Duration, occurrence times of a resident's activity maintain around a fixed value. According to the occurrence times of an activity, we can also calculate anomaly value with LOF algorithm.
3. Start time: Similar to Duration and Times, we can calculate anomaly value of residents' activities in each date with LOF algorithm with the help of standard deviation.

4.2. Characteristics Extraction

Based on the analyses of activity classification, we can select a corresponding activity to calculate residents' anomaly degree according to properties of various characteristics. There are different methods to select activity for each feature. The following are details:

1. Duration: When using Duration to calculate, activities of long duration have greater influence on the calculation of anomaly degree, while activities of short duration such as "leave home" and

"toilet" have few effects on such calculation, which could almost be neglected. Hence, activities of long duration should be chosen when calculating anomaly degree in this category.

2. Times: Activities with short duration are not suitable for calculation of Duration anomaly degree, but they are fit for calculation of Times anomaly degree. For instance, how often a resident goes to bathroom exerts a great influence on reflecting anomaly degree of his behavior on that day, whereas how long a resident takes in toilet totally in a day is insignificant in calculation. Therefore, activities of short duration should be chosen when calculating anomaly degree in the category of Times. In addition, the activity with relatively stable frequency is more valuable when calculating anomaly degree of Times, meaning that it should be given priority in selection.

3. Start time: Start time of some activities can also be regarded as the evidence to judge if anomalous events occurred. For instance, duration of "sleep" may be around a certain number of hours, if they go to bed too early or too late it means they behaved unusually on that day.

On the basis of analyzing various features of activities, we rule out activities without stability on any of the features described above, such as "entertain guests", as this activity only offers no valuable reference for calculating anomaly degree of duration, times and start time, and would affect accuracy of calculation. Table 3 describes activity characteristics which can be used in calculation.

Table 3. Activity characteristics used in calculation.

Features	Duration	Times	Start Time
Activity can be selected from	Sleep, Read, Watch TV, Sleep Out of Bed, Relax	Enter Home, Leave home, Dress, Phone, Cook, Eat, Bed Toilet Transition, Toilet, Groom, Cook Lunch, Eat Lunch, Wash Lunch, Personal Hygiene, Wash Dishs, Bathe, Evening Meds, Morning Meds, Cook Dinner, Cook Breakfast, Eat Breakfast, Eat Dinner, Wash Dinner, Wash Breakfast	Bathe, Evening Meds, Morning Meds, Cook Breakfast, Eat Breakfast, Wash Breakfast, Sleep

4.3. Local Outlier Factor

Abnormity of residents' daily behavior refers to some event deviating from the general rule of events in daily life. For example, a resident with high blood pressure needs to take medicine on time to bring high blood pressure down. If one day he/she does not take medicine on time or take no medicine at all, it will be defined as his unusual behavior. A challenge in detecting residents' anomalous behavior is that residents' behaviors are dynamically changing. Hence, we cannot simply use occurrence of some events to judge if a behavior pattern of the resident some day is abnormal. Besides, anomalous behaviors of a resident are often very few, which cannot represent the distribution of abnormity very well. Since LOF (local outlier factor model) is an unsupervised learning approach and needs no training dataset when detecting outliers, it overcomes the difficulty of annotating anomalous behaviors in residents' behavior dataset and effectively reduces probability of erroneous judgment. Therefore, the paper employs LOF to detect residents' abnormal behavior pattern. Based on the method used to classify residents' behaviors in Section 4.1, this paper uses behavior characteristics, including duration, scene, times and start time, to calculate LOF outliers and show the final results.

Define $X = [x_1, x_2, \ldots, x_t]$, where x_t is an eigenvector used to describe residents' behavior at date $t \in [1, 2, \ldots, T]$. Based on users' every day activity, we find user's anomaly degree on that very day using LOF algorithm. Definition of behavior anomaly degree is shown as Equation (1).

$$LOF_k(x_t) = \frac{\sum_{y \in N_k(x_t)} \frac{lrd_k(y)}{lrd_k(x_t)}}{|N_k(x_t)|} = \frac{\sum_{y \in N_k(x_t)} lrd_k(y)}{|N_k(x_t)| lrd_k(x_t)} \tag{1}$$

In Equation (1), $N_k(x_t)$ is the set of the k-nearest neighbors of x_t in the feature space X. $lrd_k(x_t)$ is local reachability density of the feature vector x which can be calculated by Equation (2).

$$lrd_k(x_t) = 1 / \left(\frac{\sum_{y \in N_k(x_t)} rd_k(x_t, y)}{|N_k(x_t)|} \right) \tag{2}$$

In Equation (2), $rd_k(x, y)$ is the distance used to define what is called reachability distance, which can be calculated by Equation (3). $d(x,y)$ represents the Euclidean distance between feature vector x and y. k distance(x) is the max distance of the feature vector x to its k-nearest neighbors.

$$rd_k(x, y) = \max\{k \; distance(y), d(x, y)\} \tag{3}$$

Since abnormality of behavior is only in comparison to its several neighbors instead of the entire data set, the result is still valid in the case of residents with multiple potential lifestyles. Therefore, we can find resident abnormal behavior by LOF in the data set based on the regularity of resident's life.

5. Analysis Interface and Visualization

In this section, we give the detailed description of the visualization views of SHVis. SHVis is a tool to explore and analyze the residents' daily activities for smart health from multiple views. The overview of SHVis shows in Figure 1, which consists of seven visualization views. Figure 1(1–3) explains three sorts of abnormity distribute on each date by three methods: Tree-map, score and projection view. This part can also provide the information of what kind of activities exert greatest influence on three sorts of abnormity, respectively. Figure 1(4–7) can help researchers analyze concrete conditions of residents' daily activities with Activity Gantt view, Heat Gantt view, Radar view and Space Radar view. These parts help researchers find the specific reasons why unusual behaviors occur. Furthermore, it can help researchers to compare activities of different dates rapidly. SHVis provides an effective way for us to deeper understand the behavioral patterns of residents in smart homes. The detailed description of visual components is as follows.

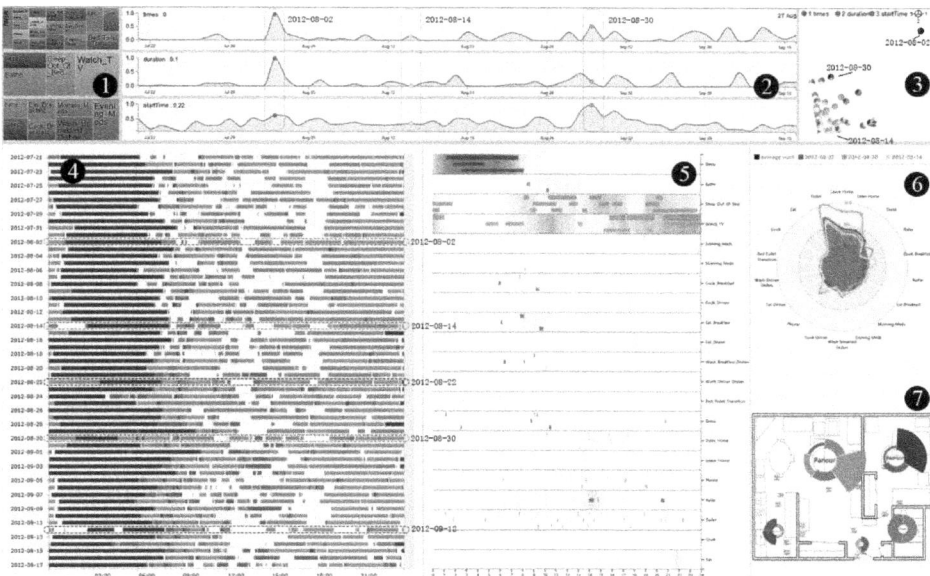

Figure 1. Overview of the visualization views.

5.1. Activity Tree Map View

By using three characteristics, the system works out anomaly degree of everyday's activities. Then, the system uses random forests algorithm to measure weight of the anomaly value of each activity on assessment of abnormal value. Based on activities' weight, we can create a tree map of categories, in which every rectangle represents an activity, different colors stand for different activities, and the size of rectangle shows the weight of the activity on calculations of this category. For example, as Figure 1(1) shows, the second set is the abnormal value figured out based on duration, among which the biggest rectangle is "Watch TV", meaning that "Watch TV" has the greatest effects on residents' activity abnormal value obtained based on duration. The colors here stand for different activities, which are consistent with the codification colors in other views.

5.2. Anomaly Grading View

Anomaly Grading View is divided into three parts corresponding to three sections in Activity Tree Map. The view is designed to display activity anomaly grades, which are calculated by anomaly detection algorithm. Three results of calculation are normalized in interval [0, 1]. This part is a filter for data display in other views. In this view, we can choose different date intervals by dragging to locate the date of abnormal pattern. Besides, we can choose different dates by clicking to look over and compare details of residents' activities. In Figure 1(2), we can see that, according to Times and Duration, the resident behaved abnormally on 2 August; according to Times and Start time, the resident behaved unusually on 30 August; and the 14 August activity abnormal value is relatively small.

5.3. Date Map View

In this map, based on anomaly degree obtained through three features, we project each date on plane using Multidimensional scaling (MDS). Every spot stands for a date, relative position of which shows residents' activity status. Spots further from the cluster of spots, have higher comprehensive anomaly degrees, and vice versa. We divide each spot into three equal sectors and each sector stands for a kind of abnormity. Darker sector colors correspond to higher abnormity values. Clicking the circle options on topside, we can filter abnormal value of three sorts while when the mouse holds on one spot, the date represented by the spot will be shown just beside it. As shown in Figure 2, we can see that, on 2 August, the date with biggest anomaly degree, the resident's abnormal values calculated in terms of Duration and Times are high, and anomaly degree of Start time is in the medium level. Meanwhile, we can see the date 30 August with a relatively high abnormal value is also far from the cluster of spots. The abnormal behavior dates can be looked at in more detail in the following analysis views.

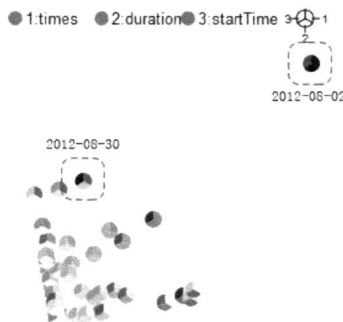

Figure 2. Date map.

5.4. Gantt Chart View

Based on views or maps described above, to look into residents' activity models in a period, researchers need to interactively look through various activity data in a certain period within smart home. First, Gantt chart is used to show the interactive information due to the residents' activities can be ranked and filtered according to dates in the chart which could reduce screen space.

In Gantt Chart, we can choose to display information of specific dates and specific activities. The codification colors are the same as that used in Activity Tree Map View. X-axis in Gantt view is 24 h of a day, and Y-axis is the date, so it is very convenient to compare activities in different dates. For example, as shown in Figure 1(4), we can know that the resident go to bed very late on 22 August and there is a long interruption of sleep on 12 September. Furthermore, the Gantt chart allows users to display activities in layers in an interactive manner and to display accumulative duration of activities. By doing this, we can analyze time regularities and Duration characteristics more clearly and accurately. The details are shown in Figure 3.

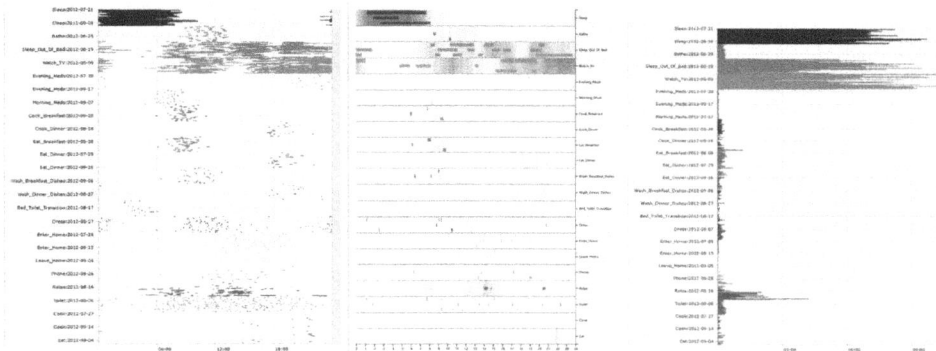

Figure 3. Left Gantt chart display activities in categories corresponding to heat Gantt charts. Right Gantt chart calculates out duration of each activity of each date. Thus, we can check the total duration of a particular activity on a particular date.

Although Gantt Chart is convenient to get the comparison information from different dates, it sacrifices the spatial information of activities, and makes it difficult to discover the general rules of residents' activities and the activity information of short duration. These shortcomings are solved by other views.

5.5. Heat Gantt Chart View

To solve the problem in Gantt Chart for discovering the general rules of residents' activities, we use Heat Gantt Chart to explore these rules. First, we cluster the activities on each date, then we draw out probability of each activity occurred at each time point in 24 h using a grayscale heat Gantt Chart, where white means the activity occurs at that time on no day and deeper colors indicate greater probabilities the event occurred.

When a user selects a date in the view of activity anomaly degree, the system draws activities of the date in Heat Gantt Chart, thus it is convenient to compare the activity of the date to the general rules of the activity. If several dates are selected, the system will compare activities on these days. Generally we can select three dates each time at most and draw different segments representing different dates in the outlines of the activity rectangle. From the information shown in Figure 4, we can guess the resident perhaps has some troubles on 30 August 2012.

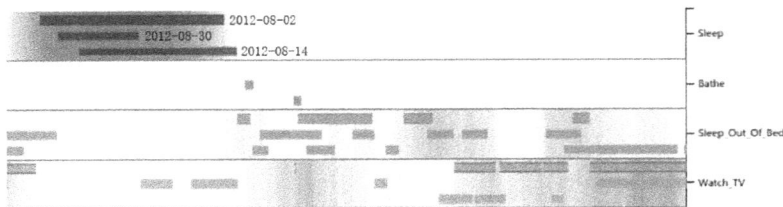

Figure 4. Comparison four activities within three days through Heat Gantt Chart. We can discover the resident sleep activity lasted a short time on 30 August 2012, and the resident slept late on 14 August. We can also find that the residents' Sleep Out Of Bed activities continued until the early hours of 30 August 2012, and on that same day the inhabitant watched TV for a long time during a time that he/she habitually sleeps.

5.6. Radar Map View

To solve the problem in Gantt chart that it is difficult to explain the short duration activity information, we use Radar Map to explore these kinds of activities. The Radar Map uses frequency characteristics of activity to detect short-term behavior anomalies. The initial gray area of Radar Map refers to the average times of each selected activity. As shown in Figure 5, the Radar Map can compare the relationship of different dates, and the relationship between the values of a certain day with the average value, which helps recognize the date when the activity frequency presents anomaly. For example, we can see from Figure 5 that the activity frequency of the resident's "toilet", "leave home" and "enter home" are much higher than the average value on 30 August. The codification colors are in agreement with the counterparts in Heat Gantt Chart.

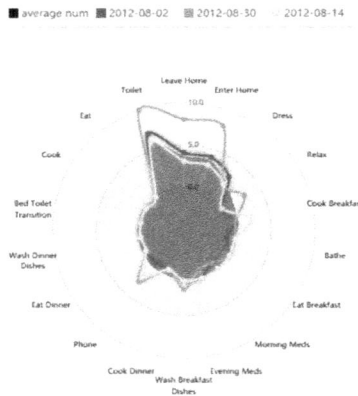

Figure 5. Radar Map: Each axis from the center represents a short-term activity, the grey part refers to the average times of each selected activity, and the different colors refer to different days, where the codification colors are the same as those in Heat Gantt Chart.

5.7. Space Radar Map View

We use Space Radar Map to solve the problem of missing activity space information in Gantt Chart. This view is used to show the spatial distribution of activities, and compare the duration of activities on different days. Figure 6 shows the duration of activities in different places for three days.

The different colors represent different activities. The area is white when no activity occurs on that day. The date corresponds to the selected date of the Radar Map, the fill color is the same as that of the Gantt Chart. It is convenient to examine the spatial distribution of the activity. We should note that the image size of the corresponding date only represents the duration recorded by the sensor at this place triggered by the activity, which is not exactly equal to the duration of the activity on that day. As in Figure 6, the sensor-recorded duration triggered by the resident's sleeping activity is quite long on 30 August, so it could be inferred that the sleeping quality of the inhabitant is rather poor. The fill color of the bathing area in the bathroom is white on 2 August, from which we can tell that the inhabitant did not take a bath that day.

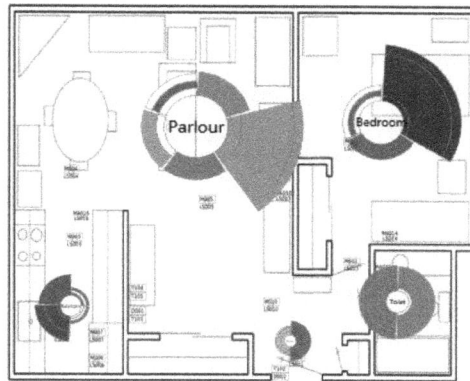

Figure 6. Space Radar Map: One circle refers to one room, and each circle represents the three-day activity selected in the other views, from inside to outside. Sectors with different colors, besides the circle, refer to sensor-recorded duration triggered by different activity.

6. Case Study

The data set consists of the information of an adult living in a smart domestic environment collected by various sensors. Based on the original data, we hope to use this system to analyze the daily behavior of the resident, and find out the date of anomaly behavior pattern and the reason for the anomaly.

The system first analyzes 30 kinds of residents' activities and classifies activities according to the activity classification methods mentioned above, and then determines the strategy of calculating the anomaly for each activity. Furthermore, we can filter activities based on activity features to decide which activities can be used for the calculation of anomaly. Figure 1(1,2) shows the anomaly degree worked out using three methods of activity anomaly measurement and the weight of each activity used for calculations. Consequently, we can see that some daily activities with long duration and activities with strong regularity exert great influence on the measurement of anomaly. This regularity is in accord with the general knowledge of inhabitant's activity. It can be seen in Figure 1(3) that most dates are gathered together, indicating that inhabitant's activities of most dates correspond to their living habits, and only a few dates projected to the edge are judged as anomaly. The anomaly degree on 30 August, 2 August and 1 September arrives at the highest with the projective point at the remotest place from the cluster.

The start time and duration of inhabitants' daily activities can be seen from the Gantt Chart of Figure 1(4). We choose 2 August, 30 August and 14 August for comparison and analysis. In Figure 1(5), we can see that the resident's sleeping activity was quite normal on 2 August. However, the resident lacked the activity of bathing; the time of watching TV was longer than the average value; he/she did not take medicine as usually, and did not take a rest. On 30 August, the resident slept too short, while he/she slept a long time on the sofa, and did not take medicine both in the morning and in the evening. Regarding 14 August, it was a relatively normal day, on which the behavior pattern of the resident had no obvious anomaly. It can be seen in Figure 5 that the resident's activity frequency showed great discrepancy with the average frequency on the radar map at the two days judged as anomaly. Especially, the resident had evident fluctuation in the times of going to toilet, leaving home, taking rest and medicine, and using phone on 30 August. The patient also presented such behavior phenomenon on 2 August, while the normal date of 14 August was nearer to the general activity routines, which accorded with the resident's daily behavioral habits.

Figure 6 shows the duration of sensor at different places triggered by different activities, and the value does not refer to the activity duration of the resident at this place, as the resident would not trigger the sensor at that place after he/she slept in the bedroom. Triggering the sensor for many times will make the duration of triggering sensor longer, indicating the resident may have a poor sleep and get up many times. It can be concluded from the sleeping activity that the resident had a long sleep on 2 and 14 August, but the duration of triggering sensor was quite short, which proved a high quality of sleeping for the resident. The sleeping time on 30 August was quite short, but duration of triggering sensor is relatively long, which explained that the resident slept short and poor.

7. Conclusions

In this paper, we propose a new visual analytics system to analyze the abnormity of resident's behavior pattern in the intelligent environment. Researchers can make analysis through anomaly recognition model without supervision and multi-view visual analysis system to find out the anomaly date of resident's behavior pattern and examine the reason. It will be easy for the rapid check of resident's activities using this system and for the comparison of inhabitant's behavior at different dates, which is significant to find out resident's bad habits and behavior that may influence their health. In the future, we hope that we can further classify the activities and determine the weight of each activity in calculating residents' behavior anomaly to calculate more accurately and discover the anomaly of resident's daily behavior more precisely.

Acknowledgments: This project is supported by the Fundamental Research Funds for the Central Universities of Central South University with No. 2016zzts371, Hunan Provincial 2011 Collaborative Innovation Center for Development and Utilization of the Financial and Economic Big Data Property and the National Natural Science Foundation of China under Grant Nos. 61402540 and 61672538. We would like to thank the Center for Advanced Studies in Adaptive Systems (CASAS) at Washington State University for making available the data set. Ying Zhao and Xiaoping Fan are co-corresponding authors of this work.

Author Contributions: Zhifang Liao and Ying Zhao, Fanngfang Zhou conceived and designed the system; Lingyuan Kong and Xiao Wang performed the experiments and realized the system; Zhining Liao collected the data; Xiaoping Fan offered useful suggestions for the preparation and writing the paper; Zhifang Liao and Lingyuan Kong wrote the paper.

Conflicts of Interest: The authors declare no conflict of interest.

References

1. Acampora, G.; Cook, D.J.; Rashidi, P.; Athanasios, V.V. A Survey on Ambient Intelligence in Healthcare. *Proc. IEEE Inst. Electr. Electron. Eng.* **2013**, *101*, 2470–2494. [CrossRef] [PubMed]
2. Luo, X.; Zhang, D.; Yang, L.T.; Liu, J.; Chang, X.; Ning, H. A Kernel Machine-based Secure Data Sensing and Fusion Scheme in Wireless Sensor Networks for the Cyber-physical Systems. *Future Gen. Comput. Syst.* **2016**, *61*, 85–96. [CrossRef]
3. Dawadi, P.N.; Cook, D.J.; Schmitter-Edgecombe, M. Automated Cognitive Health Assessment Using Smart Home Monitoring of Complex Tasks. *IEEE Trans. Syst. Man Cybern. Syst.* **2013**, *43*, 1302–1313. [CrossRef] [PubMed]
4. Rashidi, P.; Cook, D.J. COM: A Method for Mining and Monitoring Human Activity Patterns in Home-based Health Monitoring Systems. *ACM Trans. Intell. Syst. Technol.* **2013**, *4*, 64. [CrossRef]

5. Dawadi, P.N.; Cook, D.J.; Schmitter-Edgecombe, M. Automated Cognitive Health Assessment from Smart Home-Based Behavior Data. *IEEE J Biomed. Health Inform.* **2015**, *20*, 1188–1194. Available online: http:// ieeexplore.ieee.org/stamp/stamp.jsp?arnumber=7206522 (accessed on 1 March 2017). [CrossRef] [PubMed]

6. Noury, N.; Berenguer, M.; Teyssier, H.; Bouzid, M.J.; Giordani, M. Building an Index of Activity of Inhabitants from Their Activity on the Residential Electrical Power Line. *IEEE Trans. Inform. Technol. Biomed.* **2011**, *15*, 758–766. [CrossRef] [PubMed]

7. Suryadevara, N.K.; Mukhopadhyay, S.C. Wireless Sensor Network Based Home Monitoring System for Wellness Determination of Elderly. *IEEE Sens. J.* **2012**, *12*, 1965–1972. [CrossRef]

8. Cook, D.J. How Smart is Your Home? *Science* **2012**, *335*, 1579–1581. [CrossRef] [PubMed]

9. Kim, E.; Helal, S.; Cook, D. Human Activity Recognition and Pattern Discovery. *IEEE Pervasive Comput.* **2010**, *9*, 48–53. [CrossRef] [PubMed]

10. Krishnan, N.C.; Cook, D.J. Activity Recognition on Streaming Sensor Data. *Pervasive Mob. Comput.* **2014**, *10*, 138–154. [CrossRef] [PubMed]

11. Liao, Z.; Liu, M.; Song, T.; Kuang, L.; Zhang, Y.; Liao, Z. Markov Chain-Like Model for Prediction Service Based on Improved Hierarchical Particle Swarm Optimization Cluster Algorithm. *Int. J. Softw. Eng. Knowl. Eng.* **2016**, *26*, 653–674. [CrossRef]

12. Das, B.; Cook, D.J.; Krishnan, N.C.; Schmitter-Edgecombe, M. One-class Classification-based Real-time Activity Error Detection in Smart Homes. *IEEE J. Sel. Top. Signal Process.* **2016**, *10*, 914–923. [CrossRef] [PubMed]

13. Shin, J.H.; Lee, B.; Park, K.S. Detection of Abnormal Living Patterns for Elderly Living Alone Using Support Vector Data Description. *IEEE Trans. Inf. Technol. Biomed.* **2011**, *15*, 438–448. [CrossRef] [PubMed]

14. Zhao, W.; Lun, R.; Gordon, C.; Fofana, A.B.M.; Espy, D.D.; Reinthal, M.A.; Ekelman, B.; Goodman, G.D.; Niederriter, J.E.; Luo, X. A Human-centered Activity Tracking System: Toward a Healthier Workplace. *IEEE Trans. Hum. Mach. Syst.* **2016**, *PP*, 1–13. [CrossRef]

15. Aran, O.; Sanchez-Cortes, D.; Do, M.T.; Gatica-Perez, D. Anomaly Detection in Elderly Daily Behavior in Ambient Sensing Environments. In Proceedings of the International Workshop on Human Behavior Understanding, Amsterdam, The Netherlands, 16 October 2016; pp. 51–67.

16. Alcalá, J.; Parson, O.; Rogers, A. Detecting Anomalies in Activities of Daily Living of Elderly Residents via Energy Disaggregation and Cox Processes. In Proceedings of the 2nd ACM International Conference on Embedded Systems for Energy-Efficient Built Environments, Seoul, South Korea, 4–5 November 2015; pp. 225–234.

17. Cao, N.; Shi, C.; Lin, S.; Lu, J.; Lin, Y.R.; Lin, C.Y. TargetVue: Visual Analysis of Anomalous User Behaviors in Online Communication Systems. *IEEE Trans. Vis. Comput. Gr.* **2015**, *22*, 280–289. [CrossRef] [PubMed]

18. Zhao, J.; Cao, N.; Wen, Z.; Song, Y. #FluxFlow: Visual Analysis of Anomalous Information Spreading on Social Media. *IEEE Trans. Vis. Comput. Gr.* **2014**, *20*, 1773–1782.

19. Ivanov, Y.; Wren, C.; Sorokin, A.; Kaur, I. Visualizing the History of Living Spaces. *IEEE Trans. Vis. Comput. Gr.* **2007**, *13*, 1153–1160. [CrossRef]

20. Kim, S.Y.; Yun, J.; Mellema, A.; Ebert, D.S.; Collinss, T. Visual Analytics on Mobile Devices for Emergency Response. Available online: http://ieeexplore.ieee.org/stamp/stamp.jsp?arnumber=4388994 (accessed on 1 March 2017).

21. Liao, Z.; Yu, Y.; Chen, B. Anomaly Detection in GPS Data Based on Visual Analytics. Available online: http://ieeexplore.ieee.org/xpls/icp.jsp?arnumber=7206522 (accessed on 1 March 2017).

22. Liao, Z.F.; Li, Y.; Peng, Y.; Zhao, Y.; Zhou, F.F.; Liao, Z.N.; Dudley, S.; Ghavami, M. A Semantic-enhanced Trajectory Visual Analytics for Digital Forensic. *J. Vis.* **2015**, *18*, 173–184. [CrossRef]

23. Röhlig, M.; Luboschik, M.; Krüger, F.; Kirste, T.; Schumann, H.; Bögl, M.; Alsallakh, M.; Miksch, S. Supporting Activity Recognition by Visual Analytics. In Proceedings of the 2015 IEEE Conference on Visual Analytics Science and Technology (VAST), Chicago, IL, USA, 25–30 October 2015; pp. 41–48.

24. Cook, D.; Crandall, A.; Thomas, B.; Krishnan, N. CASAS: A Smart Home in a Box. *IEEE Comput.* **2013**, *46*, 62–69. [CrossRef] [PubMed]

applied sciences

MDPI

Article

An IoT System for Remote Monitoring of Patients at Home

KeeHyun Park *, Joonsuu Park and JongWhi Lee

Computer Engineering Department, Keimyung University, Daegu, 42601, Korea; parkjoonsuu@gmail.com (J.P.); dragon8829@naver.com (J.W.L.)
* Correspondence: khp@kmu.ac.kr; Tel.: +82-10-7705-5266

Academic Editors: Wenbing Zhao, Xiong Luo and Tie Qiu
Received: 18 December 2016; Accepted: 1 March 2017; Published: 8 March 2017

Abstract: Application areas that utilize the concept of IoT can be broadened to healthcare or remote monitoring areas. In this paper, a remote monitoring system for patients at home in IoT environments is proposed, constructed, and evaluated through several experiments. To make it operable in IoT environments, a protocol conversion scheme between ISO/IEEE 11073 protocol and oneM2M protocol, and a Multiclass Q-learning scheduling algorithm based on the urgency of biomedical data delivery to medical staff are proposed. In addition, for the sake of patients' privacy, two security schemes are proposed—the separate storage scheme of data in parts and the Buddy-ACK authorization scheme. The experiment on the constructed system showed that the system worked well and the Multiclass Q-learning scheduling algorithm performs better than the Multiclass Based Dynamic Priority scheduling algorithm. We also found that the throughputs of the Multiclass Q-learning scheduling algorithm increase almost linearly as the measurement time increases, whereas the throughputs of the Multiclass Based Dynamic Priority algorithm increase with decreases in the increasing ratio.

Keywords: IoT; personal healthcare device; protocol conversion; remote monitoring; multiclass Q-learning algorithm; buddy-ACK authentication

1. Introduction

The concept of IoT (Internet of Things) [1,2], which allows smart objects to communicate with each other or with a user, has become increasingly popular. With an IoT, we can obtain much more information more easily than ever before, and control objects much more seamlessly. The IoT concept can be applied in many areas, including metering, traffic control, smart homes, and building management. The objects can be sensors, home equipment, meters, and other similar devices.

The remote monitoring of patients has become a highly active area of research in recent years [3–9]. However, there has not been much research on remote monitoring that employs the IoT concept. Application areas that utilize the concept of IoT can be broadened to healthcare or remote monitoring areas. Personal Healthcare Devices (PHDs) are portable electronic healthcare devices that sense and measure users' biomedical signals. Activity monitors, medication dispensers, pulse oximeters, ECG monitors, blood pressure monitors and falling detectors are representative examples of PHDs [10–15]. PHDs could be objects in an IoT system for health care, and healthcare workers could enjoy most of the advantages of an IoT system by monitoring patients at home via IoT systems.

In this paper, an IoT system for the remote monitoring of patients at home is proposed. With the help of the IoT system for monitoring patients at home, medical staffs can monitor their patients at home much more easily than ever before by receiving diverse biomedical data from PHDs with which the patients are connected. PHDs are considered as objects in the IoT system in this paper, and the system will enable medical staffs to be informed when their patients experience emergency conditions more quickly than ever before. In this study, the IoT monitoring system is proposed and constructed based on the oneM2M (one Machine-to-Machine) communication protocol [16–18], an international communication protocol standard for IoT systems.

To make the patient at home monitoring system more desirable and operable on ordinary IoT networks, we consider the following issues in this paper.

- Multiclass data scheduling/communication: Because many diverse PHDs and their biomedical data are transmitted to medical staffs, each piece of data needs to be classified based on the urgency of its delivery. More urgent of data deliveries are assigned higher classes. For example, falling detector data have to be delivered more urgently than medication dispenser data, and thus falling detector data are assigned to the higher class. Alarm conditions should be assigned to the highest class. For example, abnormal ECG data are assigned to a higher class than normal ECG data, and should be delivered more quickly.
- Communication protocol conversion: To use PHDs as objects in an IoT system based on the oneM2M protocol, a communication protocol conversion process is needed, as PHDs and IoT systems use different standard communication protocols. In other words, the ISO/IEEE 11073 protocol [10,11] is an international standard for PHD communication, while the oneM2M protocol is an international standard for the IoT system considered in this paper.
- Strict authorization: Because the biomedical data obtained by a PHD may involve a patient's privacy, the data need to be handled in a manner that prevents its exposure to unauthorized persons. In this study, two security schemes are proposed. First, a patient's biomedical data obtained by a PHD are not stored as a single unit, but stored in parts in the IoT server. The data are partitioned into several parts (two parts in this study) and stored separately in the IoT server. Furthermore, the separation information is not stored in the IoT server, but in the IoT authentication server. This means that anyone who wants to access the data has to access both the IoT server and the IoT authentication server at the same time. Second, an authentication scheme called the Buddy-ACK (Acknowledgment) authorization scheme is proposed in this study. In the Buddy-ACK authorization scheme, a specific piece of biomedical data can be accessed only after both a patient and the related medical staff are authorized. We call the patient and the related medical staff "buddies". A piece of biomedical data can be accessed only after the acknowledgement (or consent) of the buddy is obtained.

The remainder of this paper is organized as follows. Section 2 describes some related studies, and Section 3 explains the structure of the monitoring IoT system for patients at home proposed in this paper. Section 4 discusses the multiclass Q-learning scheduling algorithm proposed in this study, while Section 5 discusses communication protocol conversion mechanisms between oneM2M and ISO/IEEE 11073. Section 6 identifies some security issues and describes the Buddy-ACK authentication scheme proposed in this study. Section 7 shows the results of some experiments using the system constructed in this study, and engages in a discussion based on the results. Finally, Section 8 draws some conclusions and discusses some possible directions for future research.

2. Related Studies

In [12–15], web-based remote PHD management systems for activity monitors, a medication dispenser, and pulse oximeters were proposed and constructed. In terms of communication protocols, ISO/IEEE 11073 and OMA DM (Open Mobile Alliance Data Management) protocols were used to transmit measured data or remote commands. Gateways located between PHDs and the management server transform the ISO/IEEE 11073 messages into OMA DM messages, and vice versa. Biomedical data measured by PHDs were transmitted in an FCFS (First Come, First Served) manner, and there were neither message classification in data scheduling/transmission, nor data security in data access.

Clinician focused remote monitoring systems for telehealth can be found in [3–9]. In the telehealth system shown in [8], wireless wristwatch-based monitoring devices are attached to elderly patients to continuously collect their temperature and motion data. It was found that the designed health monitoring system can be used for an extended period of time and may help older patients with chronic conditions reside in their own homes for longer. In [3,5], it was found that tortuosity in movement paths by elderly persons was related to cognitive impairment or contributed to an increased fall prediction. Four sensors were installed at each corner of a gathering place in an assisted living facility, to wirelessly sense the location data of tags attached to participants. The location data were used to calculate movement path variability. Even though the data processing and transmission methods used in these studies were not clearly addressed, it seems that the data were transmitted in an FCFS manner, and there was no message classification in data scheduling/transmission. Data security in data access was not mentioned either.

Protocol conversion has been used when there are more than two different communication protocols in a system, or when two systems with different communication protocols need to be connected. In [19], a formal model for protocol conversion was presented. The construction of protocol converters was illustrated also. Protocol conversion between wireless sensors (Lean Transport Protocol) and Web systems (Hyper Text Transfer Protocol) was proposed to extend a Web service oriented architecture to wireless sensors for a Web of Things [20]. In particular, self-description of embedded Web services was proposed through the efficient compression of WSDL documents. Backend IT systems can invoke embedded Web services on sensor nodes and vice versa by providing an open framework for protocol conversion. Protocol conversion between SIP (Session Initiation Protocol) and SOAP (Simple Object Access Protocol) can be found in [21]. This proposes a generic SIP/SOAP gateway that implements message handling and network and storage management while relying on application-specific converters to define session management and message mapping for a specific set of SIP and SOAP communication nodes. Thus far, few studies have proposed protocol conversion between ISO/IEEE 11073 protocol and oneM2M protocol, which we propose in this paper.

Security issues for IoT systems or mobile devices have been addressed in many papers [22–28]. In particular, Mohamed et al. [23] proposed a game-based model for adaptive security in the IoT, with an emphasis on eHealth applications. For the sake of mobile devices, the tradeoff between security-effectiveness and energy-efficiency to evaluate adaptive security strategies was considered also. Authentication is to identify users to enable services for legitimate users only, and is considered one of the key aspects of security issues. Biometric authentication [25–28] has been the most popular method for individual identification. Biometric authentication involves the comparison of an input data with stored biometric data to identify a specific user. Fingerprints, face recognition, hand geometry and iris recognition, and ECG are some examples of this type of biometric authentication. Thus far, few studies have proposed the participation of users and the related medical staff in the process of authentication that we propose in this paper.

Multiclass scheduling can be performed when various data to be scheduled have different characteristics [29,30]. The Multiclass Based Dynamic Priority (MBDP) scheduling algorithm [30] classifies messages used for M2M communication in LTE environments into four types: very small-sized delay-intolerant messages (Type 1), messages requiring a minimum guaranteed bit rate (Type 2), bulk-sized delay-tolerant messages (Type 3), and very small-sized delay-tolerant messages (Type 4). Type 1 messages are classified as class 1 and their delay times are 0. Type 3 and Type 4 messages are classified into class N and their delay times are infinite. Communication resources are assigned to class 1 messages first and subsequently assigned to class 2 messages through class N messages. Thus far, few studies have focused on multiclass scheduling for biometric data with the concept of Q-learning.

3. Structure of the Patient at Home Monitoring IoT System

Figure 1 shows the structure of the IoT system for monitoring patients at home that is proposed in this paper. To prepare for the massive number of Personal Healthcare Devices (PHDs) needed, the system was designed as multilayered. The system consists of Application Dedicated

Nodes—Application Entities (ADN-AEs), Middle Nodes—Common Service Entities (MN-CSEs), the Infrastructure Node—Common Service Entity (IN-CSE), and Infrastructure Nodes—Application Entities (IN-AEs).

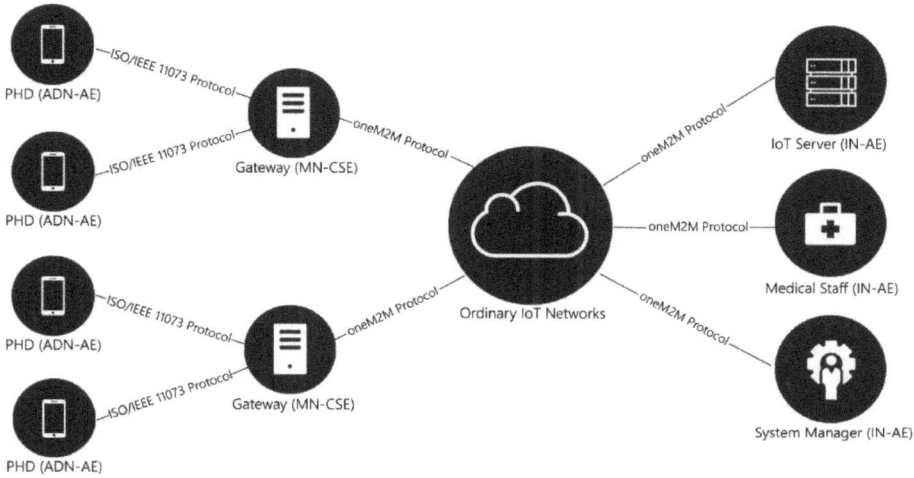

Figure 1. Structure of the IoT (Internet of Things) system for monitoring patients at home.

An ADN-AE is a program installed in a sensor. It senses neighboring signals, processes them to generate data, and finally sends the data to the IN-CSE installed on the patient monitoring IoT server. A (program on a) PHD acts as an ADN-AE in the proposed system. Through an IoT network, MN-CSEs function as gateways for traffic control and/or protocol conversion. In this paper, they transmit patients' biomedical data obtained by a PHD to the IN-CSE (the patient monitoring IoT server). Medical staff or system managers use IN-AEs to access the patients' data stored in the IoT server. An MN-CSE controls or monitors ADN-AEs that belong to the MN-CSE; moreover, it performs processing that is necessary to achieve efficient multiclass communication between ADN-AEs and the IN-CSE. An IN-AE can access patients' data by accessing the patient monitoring IoT server via an IoT network.

In the IoT system, a large amount of diverse biomedical data are transmitted from PHDs to a gateway, and it takes a non-negligible amount of transmission time for the data to be delivered to the patient monitoring IoT server or medical staffs. Therefore, alarm signals that represent abnormal conditions of the patients should be delivered (or "pushed") more quickly than any other data. One of the gateway's responsibilities is to classify and prioritize data received from PHDs, and schedule their data transmissions based on their priorities.

In this study, the oneM2M-based IoT system is constructed in accordance with the oneM2M specifications [16,17]. Then, two modules (Protocol Converter module and MQL Scheduler module) are added, as shown in Figure 2. An ADN-AE consists of a Sensing module and a Network Manager module. The Sensing module senses the biomedical signals of PHD users and processes them to generate biomedical data. The biomedical data are delivered to the Network Manager module, where oneM2M messages are made based on the received biomedical data. A CSE consists of a Network Manager module, a Message Handler module, and a Resource Manager module. The Network Manager module deals with communication with ADN-AEs and controls the entire CSE process. The Resource Manager module manages resource trees in which the information of every object the IoT system manages is stored.

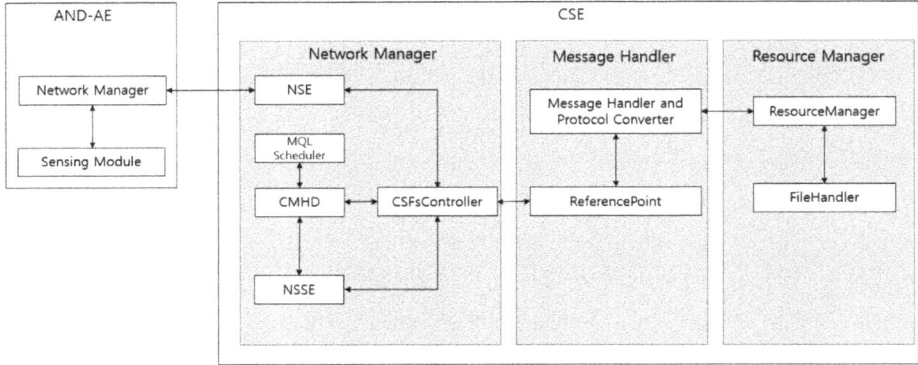

Figure 2. Internal structure of the oneM2M (Machine-to-Machine) IoT system.

The Network Manager module consists of NSE (Network Service Exposure), CMDH (Communication Management and Delivery Handling), NSSE (Network Service Exposure Execution and Triggering) and CSFs (Common Service Functions) Controller. In addition, MQL Scheduler is added for the multiclass Q-learning scheduling proposed in this study. The NSE module transmits oneM2M messages and the CMDH module manages communication (policies) and buffers. The NSSE module performs session management for connection between CSFs and NSE. The MQL Scheduler module makes scheduling decisions for biomedical data transmission on the base of the execution of the MQL scheduling algorithm, which will be discussed in the next section.

The Message Handler module consists of MessageHandler/Protocol Converter and ReferencePoint. The Message Handler module analyzes the incoming messages and performs message conversion between oneM2M primitive messages and HTTP messages. The ReferencePoint module processes XML documents and HTTP headers. The mapping between oneM2M Request/Response primitive messages and HTTP messages is shown in Tables 1 and 2.

Table 1. Mapping between oneM2M primitive Request messages and HTTP messages.

oneM2M Primitive Request Message	HTTP Message
Operation	Method in Header
To	Request-Target in Header
ResourceType	Content-Type in Header
RequestID	X-M2M-RI in Header
Content	Body

Table 2. Mapping between oneM2M primitive Response messages and HTTP messages.

oneM2M Primitive Response Message	HTTP Message
responseCode	Status Code
RequestID	X-M2M-RI in Header
Content	Body

In this study, the Protocol Converter module is added to the MessageHandler module for protocol conversion between ISO/IEEE 11073 messages and oneM2M messages. The proposed protocol conversion mechanism will be discussed in Section 5.

The Resource Manager module consists of ResourceManager and FileHandler. The ResourceManager module performs operations (Create, Retrieve, Update, Delete) on resource trees, based on the received oneM2M primitive Request messages. It also stores the results of the operations in oneM2M primitive Response messages. The FileHandler module manages resource trees stored in physical data stores.

There are two different communication protocols used in the proposed system. The ISO/IEEE 11073 communication protocol is used between PHDs (ADN-AE) and gateways (MN-CSE) for PHD communication, and the oneM2M communication protocol is used between the patient monitoring IoT server (IN-CSE) and gateways for IoT networks. It is natural for the ISO/IEEE 11073 communication protocol to be used for PHD-gateway communication in this paper because the protocol is a standard communication protocol for PHD communication. Similarly, the oneM2M communication protocol is a standard communication protocol for IoT systems, and it is also reasonable that the oneM2M communication protocol is used for the IoT server-gateway communication in this paper. Otherwise, ordinary IoT servers that naturally support the oneM2M standard communication protocol would not understand the message sent from PHDs. As you know, standard communication protocols are used to enable interoperability between different machines or equipment. Therefore, one of the gateway's responsibilities is to convert the ISO/IEEE 11073 protocol into the oneM2M protocol and vice versa to seamlessly transmit a patient's biomedical data from a PHD to the IoT server.

4. Data Classification and Multiclass Q-Learning (MQL) Algorithm

In this study, PHDs such as activity monitors [12], medication dispensers [13], pulse oximeters [14], and ECG monitors, blood pressure monitors and falling detectors are considered as ADN-AEs in the IoT system for monitoring patients at home. For example, Alarm signals of abnormal SpO_2 belong to the highest priority class (Urgent class), and thus are transmitted before any other data. In addition, the alarm signals of the Urgent class are pushed immediately to medical staffs even when the medical staffs do not request the related data from the patient monitoring IoT server.

The multiclass Q-learning scheduling (MQL) algorithm proposed in this study is based on the Q-learning algorithm [31]. As shown in Figure 3, Q-learning is a reinforcement-based learning algorithm that finds an optimal policy by selecting the action with the highest reward in each state.

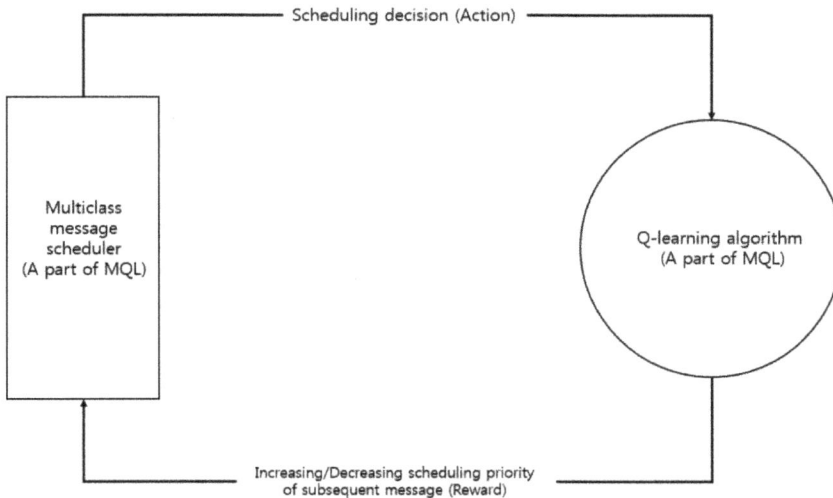

Figure 3. Q-learning algorithm.

The proposed MQL algorithm evaluates the appropriateness of the previous scheduling decision (action); the evaluation result (reward) is then applied to the next scheduling decision. Based on the evaluation result, the scheduling priority of the subsequent message increases or decreases. If a non-urgent message is scheduled for transmission at time T1, and the message is transmitted successfully at T1 without interfering with the transmission of urgent messages, then the scheduling priority of the non-urgent message increases and subsequent non-urgent messages are likely to be scheduled to transmit at T1. Otherwise, the scheduling priority of the non-urgent message decreases and subsequent non-urgent messages are not likely to be scheduled to transmit at time T1. Through successive scheduling decisions, evaluations and applications, the algorithm determines optimal scheduling decisions. The MQL algorithm is designed to transmit urgent messages immediately and transmit non-urgent messages later, when they will not interfere with urgent message transmissions.

When a message arrives for scheduling, the message is inserted into its queue as shown in Algorithm 1 (Insertion of newly arrived message into its queue) discussed below. UrgentQ[*] is a priority queue in which urgent messages wait for scheduling based on their priority basis. NonUrgentQ[t, *] is a priority queue in which non-urgent messages arriving at unit time t wait for scheduling based on their priority basis ($1 \leq t \leq T$; T is the number of unit times). If messages are scheduled every hour (every half hour) for 24 h, T is 24 (48).

Algorithm 1. Insertion of newly arrived message into its queue

---

For a newly arrived urgent message NewM;
Insert NewM at the appropriate position in UrgentQ[*] based on message's
priority basis
For an existing message OldM whose priority is lower than NewM's priority and therefore is pushed back by
one position in UrgentQ[*]:
      Increase OldM's priority by AGE^D
  (AGE: an aging constant, 0.9 in this study,
  D: the distance between the positions of NewM and OldM)
For the newly arrived non-urgent message NewM at unit time At:
Find QTable[At, k] for the maximum reward in QTable[At, *] ($1 \leq k \leq T$)
Insert NewM at the appropriate position in NonUrgentQ[k, *] based on message's priority basis
For an existing message OldM whose priority is lower than NewM's priority and therefore is pushed back by
one position in NonUrgentQ[k, *]:
      Increase OldM's priority by AGE^D

For example, suppose that a new urgent message UM3 (priority 5) arrives at UrgentQ[*] and that two urgent messages UM1 (priority 3) and UM2 (priority 1) are waiting in UrgentQ[*]. Then, UM3, UM1, and UM2 are located at the first, second, and third positions in UrgentQ[*], respectively, based on their priorities. Because UM1 and UM2 are existing messages and are pushed back by one position in UrgentQ[*] owing to the arrival of UM3, their priorities are increased to 3.9 (=3 + 0.9^1) and 1.81 (=1 + 0.9^2), respectively. The priority increase is a type of aging technique that prevents a message with a lower priority from suffering indefinite postponement.

The explanation for a non-urgent message is more complicated. First, by looking at Qtable[*, *], the algorithm finds the QTable[At, k] that obtains the maximum reward in QTable[At, *] to select the transmission time of a non-urgent message whose arrival unit time is At. QTable[At, j] contains the reward obtained when a non-urgent message whose arrival time is unit time At is actually scheduled to transmit at unit time j. The message is then inserted in NonUrgentQ[k, *]. The remainder of the explanation is similar to that of the urgent message case, and has been omitted here.

At unit time t, urgent messages in UrgentQ[*] are scheduled to transmit immediately. However, non-urgent messages in NonUrgentQ[t, *] cannot be scheduled to transmit when UrgentQ[*] is not empty. Therefore, an attempt to transmit a non-urgent message is rewarded negatively and Qtable[*, *] is updated appropriately. Conversely, an attempt to transmit a non-urgent message when UrgentQ[*] is empty is rewarded positively. Algorithm 2 (Transmission scheduling algorithm for non-urgent messages) explains the transmission scheduling algorithm for non-urgent messages.

Algorithm 2. Transmission scheduling algorithm for non-urgent messages

At current unit time Ct:

    If urgent messages are waiting for scheduling in UrgentQ[*],

        Then, transmit the front urgent message in UrgentQ[1]

            QTable[At, Ct] = Qtable[At, Ct] * REC + NR

            (At: arrival unit time of the transmitted urgent message,

            REC: recency constant, 0.9 in this study,

            NR: negative reward, -1 in this study)

    If UrgentQ[*] is empty and non-urgent messages are waiting for

        scheduling in NonUrgentQ[Ct, *],

        Then, transmit the front non-urgent message in NonUrgentQ[Ct, 1]

            QTable[At, Ct] = Qtable[At, Ct] * REC + PR

            (At: arrival time of the transmitted non-urgent message,

            PR: negative reward, +2 in this study)

Let us suppose that Table 3 shows the contents of QTable[*, *] and message queues at unit time 5. When a non-urgent message M18 whose priority is 3.0 arrives at unit time 5, Algorithm 1 determines that QTable[5,9] is the optimum reward (=9.46). The algorithm then inserts M18 into NonUrgentQ[9,1] and the priority of the existing non-urgent message M09 is increased to 2.9. "M18/3.0" in the lower part of Table 3 indicates that a non-urgent message whose ID is 18 and priority is 3.0 is waiting at the front of NonUrgentQ[9, *].

Table 3. Contents of QTable and message queues at unit time 5.

QTable	1	2	3	4	5	6	7	8	9	10
1										
...										
5	5.11	0.23	4.67	9.06	9.26	6.25	2.50	2.32	9.46	6.86
...										
10										

Message Queues	Events	1	2	3	...
UrgentQ	...	M17/5.0	M01/4.9	M02/3.81	...
NonUrgentQ[1]	...	...	...	...	...
...	...	...	...	...	...
NonUrgentQ[9]	Before the arrival of M18	M09/2.0	...	...	
	After the arrival of M18	M18/3.0	M09/2.9	...	

Let us suppose it is unit time 9. At this time, messages in UrgentQ[*] and NonUrgentQ[9, *] are ready to be scheduled. Using Algorithm 2, an urgent message M17 in UrgentQ[1] is scheduled to transmit immediately. However, because NonUrgentQ[9, *] is not empty, the reward of QTable[5,9] is decreased to 7.51 (=Qtable[5,9] $\times$ 0.9 – 1). This means that, owing to the existence of the urgent messages scheduled at unit time 9, a non-urgent message whose arrival unit time is 5 is now less likely to be scheduled to transmit at unit time 9. If three urgent messages are transmitted successfully at unit time 9, the reward of QTable[5,9] will be decreased to 4.18. If there is still sufficient time to schedule a non-urgent message M18 to transmit at unit time 9 after the transmission of M17, M01, and M02, the reward of QTable[5,9] will be increased to 5.76.

5. Protocol Conversion in the IoT System

5.1. Protocol Conversion Modules

As mentioned earlier, in this study protocol conversion is performed between the ISO/IEEE 11073 protocol and the oneM2M protocol. Most PHDs use ISO/IEEE 11073 protocol for their communication because the protocol is a standard communication protocol for PHDs. In addition, most IoT servers and IoT gateways support oneM2M communication protocol for their communication because the protocol is a standard communication protocol for IoT environments. Therefore, protocol conversion between the ISO/IEEE 11073 protocol and the oneM2M protocol is required for interoperability.

Figure 4 shows the program modules for this study that were newly added to the original oneM2M system for the protocol conversion process. Protocol conversion between the ISO/IEEE 11073 protocol and the oneM2M protocol is performed in gateways (MN-CSEs) in the system. The protocol conversion module consists of three classes programmed in C# under a Windows 7 environment.

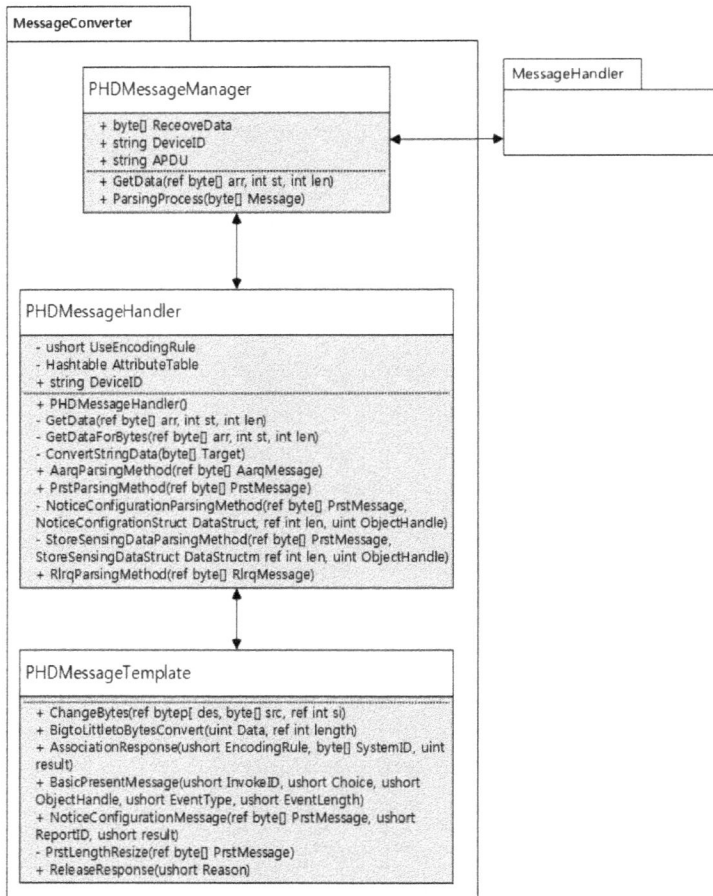

Figure 4. Program modules for the protocol conversion process.

- PHDMessageManager class: Controls the entire flow of the protocol conversion process. It also receives incoming messages to the protocol conversion module and delivers the messages to the PHDMessageHandler.
- PHDMessageHandler class: Performs protocol conversion and sends its results to the ResourceTreeManager, the responsibility of which is to build resource trees for the gateway.

- PHDMessageTemplate class: Handles the templates of various ISO/IEEE 11073 messages. With the templates, the related messages can be built quickly and protocol conversion time can be shortened.

5.2. Protocol Conversion Cases

Table 4 shows the mapping between oneM2M protocol Request messages (right column) and ISO/IEEE 11073 protocol Request messages (left column). The mapping between response messages is similar, and for this reason a description of those is omitted here. In the table, an Association Request (ISO/IEEE 11073) message is converted into a Retrieve Request (oneM2M) message. A Present (Store Sensing Data) Request message is converted into two types of oneM2M messages (i.e., a Retrieve Request message and Update Request messages). Because a Present (Store Sensing Data) Request message can contain multiple biomedical sensing data items, Update Request messages are generated according to the number of sensed data items in the Present (Store Sensing Data) Request message. Before generating the Update Request messages, one Retrieve Request message is generated to access environmental information for the sensed data items. It is not necessary to perform a protocol conversion on the incoming Association Release Request message.

Table 4. Mapping between oneM2M request messages and ISO/IEEE 11073 request messages.

ISO/IEEE 11073 Protocol Request message	oneM2M Protocol Request message
Association Request message	Retrieve primitive Request message
Present (Notice Configuration) Request message	Create primitive Request message(s)
Present (Store Sensing Data) Request message	Retrieve primitive Request message(s) Update primitive Request message(s)
Association Release Request message	-
-	Delete primitive Request message

When a PHD wants to communicate, it initially sends an ISO/IEEE 11073 Association Request message to the other side. Figure 5 shows how to convert an ISO/IEEE 11073 Association Request message into a oneM2M Retrieve primitive Request message in a gateway (MN-CSE). Information related to the thick lines in the figure is involved in the protocol conversion process. In other words, the "System ID" field in the ISO/IEEE 11073 Association Request message is used to make the "<to>" tag field in the oneM2M Retrieve primitive Request message. The "System ID" field is 8 bytes long and contains the identification number of the PHD (ADN-AE). Before building the oneM2M Retrieve primitive Request message, the gateway must check whether the PHD whose ID is in the "System ID" has been registered in the IoT server (IN-CSE) or the gateway. Information in the other fields in the ISO/IEEE 11073 Association Request message is saved for later use (i.e., building the related ISO/IEEE 11073 Association Response message which will be sent in the opposite direction).

Figure 6 shows an example of the process shown in Figure 5. An ISO/IEEE 11073 Association Request message (i.e., a message before conversion) is represented in the upper box, while the resulting oneM2M Retrieve primitive Request message (i.e., a message after conversion) is in the lower box. From the first line of the ISO/IEEE 11073 Association Request message, the gateway knows that "APDU Choice Type" is 0xE2 0x00, which means this message is an ISO/IEEE 11073 Association Request message. "System Type" on the eleventh line is 0x00 0x80 0x00 0x00, which means that the PHD, the source of this message, is an agent. "System ID" of the PHD on the twelfth line is 0x11 0x22 0x33 0x44 0x55 0x66 0x77 0x04, which goes to the "<to>" tag field in the resulting oneM2M Retrieve primitive Request message and it is represented in URL ("//CSEBase/1122334455667704"). Just above the "<to> tag, "<operation>" tag must be defined and "2" is inserted, which means that this message is built for Retrieve operation.

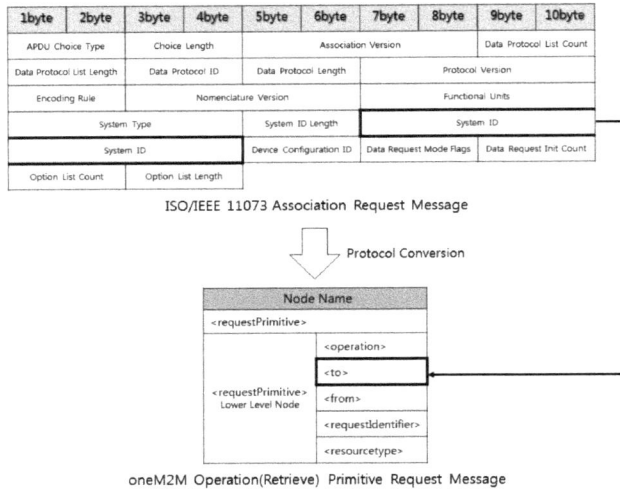

1byte	2byte	3byte	4byte	5byte	6byte	7byte	8byte	9byte	10byte
APDU Choice Type		Choice Length		Association Version				Data Protocol List Count	
Data Protocol List Length		Data Protocol ID		Data Protocol Length		Protocol Version			
Encoding Rule		Nomenclature Version				Functional Units			
System Type				System ID Length		System ID			
System ID				Device Configuration ID		Data Request Mode Flags		Data Request Init Count	
Option List Count		Option List Length							

ISO/IEEE 11073 Association Request Message

Protocol Conversion

Node Name		
<requestPrimitive>		
<requestPrimitive> Lower Level Node		<operation>
		<to>
		<from>
		<requestIdentifier>
		<resourcetype>

oneM2M Operation(Retrieve) Primitive Request Message

Figure 5. Conversion of an ISO/IEEE 11073 Association Request message to a oneM2M Retrieve primitive Request message.

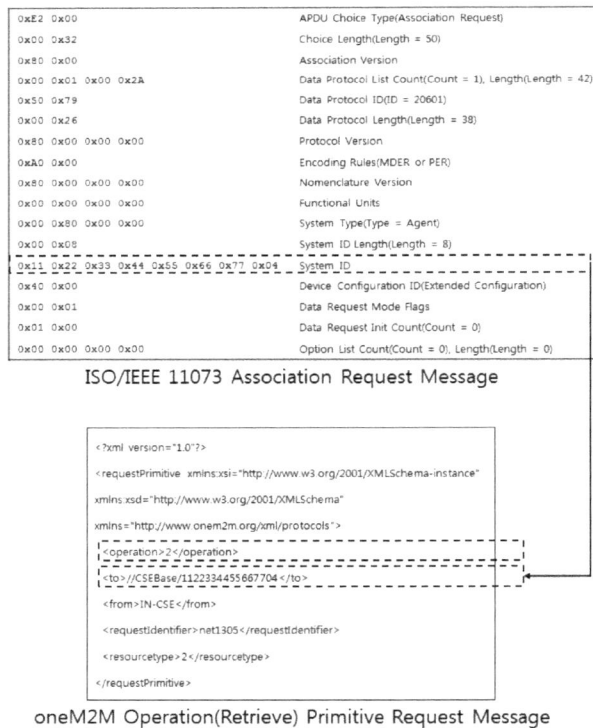

0xE2 0x00	APDU Choice Type(Association Request)
0x00 0x32	Choice Length(Length = 50)
0x80 0x00	Association Version
0x00 0x01 0x00 0x2A	Data Protocol List Count(Count = 1), Length(Length = 42)
0x50 0x79	Data Protocol ID(ID = 20601)
0x00 0x26	Data Protocol Length(Length = 38)
0x80 0x00 0x00 0x00	Protocol Version
0xA0 0x00	Encoding Rules(MDER or PER)
0x80 0x00 0x00 0x00	Nomenclature Version
0x00 0x00 0x00 0x00	Functional Units
0x00 0x80 0x00 0x00	System Type(Type = Agent)
0x00 0x08	System ID Length(Length = 8)
0x11 0x22 0x33 0x44 0x55 0x66 0x77 0x04	System ID
0x40 0x00	Device Configuration ID(Extended Configuration)
0x00 0x01	Data Request Mode Flags
0x01 0x00	Data Request Init Count(Count = 0)
0x00 0x00 0x00 0x00	Option List Count(Count = 0), Length(Length = 0)

ISO/IEEE 11073 Association Request Message

```
<?xml version="1.0"?>
<requestPrimitive xmlns:xsi="http://www.w3.org/2001/XMLSchema-instance"
xmlns:xsd="http://www.w3.org/2001/XMLSchema"
xmlns="http://www.onem2m.org/xml/protocols">
<operation>2</operation>
<to>//CSEBase/1122334455667704</to>
<from>IN-CSE</from>
<requestIdentifier>net1305</requestIdentifier>
<resourcetype>2</resourcetype>
</requestPrimitive>
```

oneM2M Operation(Retrieve) Primitive Request Message

Figure 6. An example of the process described in Figure 5.

When the IoT server decides to communicate with the PHD, the server sends a oneM2M Retrieve primitive Response message. Figure 7 shows how to convert a oneM2M Retrieve primitive Response message into an ISO/IEEE 11073 Association Response message in the gateway. "<responseStatusCode>" tag field in the oneM2M Retrieve primitive Response message is used to make "Result" field in the ISO/IEEE 11073 Association Response message. The "<responseStatusCode>" field contains the results of the registration checking. An example of the process described in Figure 7 is omitted here.

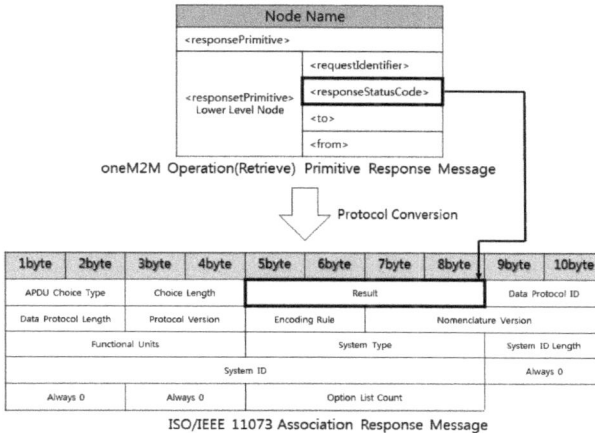

Figure 7. Conversion of a oneM2M Retrieve primitive Response message to an ISO/IEEE 11073 Association Response message.

When the PHD finds that it has not been registered in the IoT server after receiving the ISO/IEEE 11073 Association Response message sent from the gateway, the PHD sends an ISO/IEEE 11073 Present (Notice Configuration) Request message to inform the server of its environmental settings including biomedical data types the PHD will send. Figure 8 shows how to convert an ISO/IEEE 11073 Present (Notice Configuration) Request message into oneM2M Create primitive Request messages. Note that several oneM2M Create primitive Request messages are built from a single ISO/IEEE 11073 Present (Notice Configuration) Request message. This is because a single ISO/IEEE 11073 Present (Notice Configuration) Request message can contain multiple object information ("Object Class", "Object Handle", "Attribute Count", "Attribute Length", "Attribute ID", "Attribute Value Length", "Attribute Value") and a oneM2M Create primitive Request message must be built for every piece of object information in a single ISO/IEEE 11073 Present (Notice Configuration) Request message. In Figure 8, each "Object Handle" field is used to create "<container>" node in the resource tree managed by the gateway or the IoT server. In addition, each ("Attribute ID", "Attribute Value Length", "Attribute Value") is used to create a "<contentInstance>" tag node under the "<container>" tag node in the resource tree. For this paper, an explanation of the conversion of oneM2M Create primitive messages into an ISO/IEEE 11073 Present (Notice Configuration) Request message will be omitted.

Figures 9 and 10 show examples of the process described in Figure 8. In Figure 9, "APDU Choice Type" on the first line is 0xE7 0x00, which means that this message is an ISO/IEEE 11073 Present Request message. "Event Type" on the ninth line indicates that this is a Notice Configuration message. "Configuration Object Count" (0x00 0x03) on the twelfth line indicates that the PHD sends the biomedical data of three objects. The lowest dotted box containing the fourteenth line to the last line represents the information of biomedical data to be delivered. Two more dotted boxes for additional objects are omitted here. In the dotted box, four pulse oximetry information including attributes are contained. Four pulse oximetry information delivered in Figure 9 needs to be stored in the appropriate places in the related resource tree. To store the value information, "<container>" and "<contentInstance>" tag nodes need to be created in the resource tree. In Figure 10, an example of the resulting oneM2M Create primitive Request messages is shown.

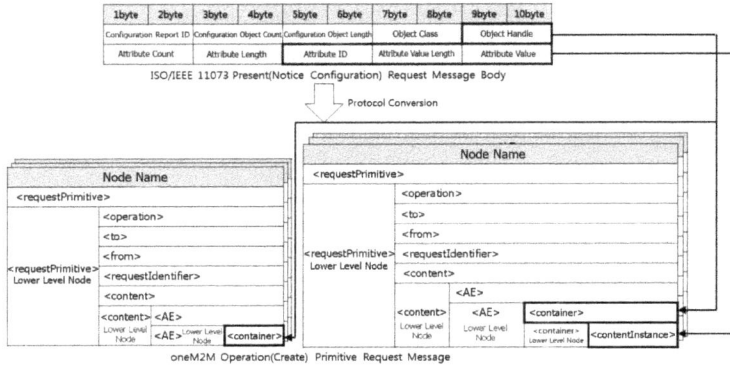

Figure 8. Conversion of an ISO/IEEE 11073 Present (Notice Configuration) Request message to oneM2M Create primitive Request messages.

0xE7 0x00	APDU Choice Type(Present Request)
0x00 0xA8	Choice Length(Length = 168)
0x00 0xA6	OCTET String Length(Length = 166)
0x12 0x36	Invoke ID
0x01 0x01	Choice(Remote Operation Invoke, Confirmed Event Report)
0x00 0xA0	Choice Length(Length = 160)
0x00 0x00	MDS Object(Object Handle = 0)
0xFF 0xFF 0xFF 0xFF	Event Time
0x0D 0x1C	Event Type(MDC_NOTI_CONFIG)
0x00 0x96	Event Information Length(Length = 150)
0x40 0x00	Configuration Report ID
0x00 0x03	Configuration Object Count(Count = 3)
0x00 0x90	Configuration Object Length(Length = 144)
0x00 0x06	Object Class(MDC_MOC_VMO_METRIC_NU)
0x00 0x01	Object Handle(1)
0x00 0x04	Attribute Count(Count = 4)
0x00 0x24	Attribute Length(Length = 36)
0x09 0x2F	Attribute ID(MDC_ATTR_ID_TYPE)
0x00 0x04	Attribute Value Length(Length = 4)
0x00 0x02 0x4B 0xB8	Value(MDC_PART_SCADA, <DC_PULS_OXIM_SAT_02)
0x0A 0x46	Attribute Value ID(MDC_ATTR_METRIC_SPEC_SMALL)
0x00 0x02	Attribute Value Length(Length= 2)
0x40 0xC0	Value(Avail Stored Data, Access Manager Init, Access Agent Init, Measured)
0x09 0x96	Attribute ID(MDC_ATTR_UNIT_CODE)
0x00 0x02	Attribute Value Length(Length = 2)
0x02 0x20	Value(MDC_DIM_PERCENT)
0x0A 0x55	Attribute ID(MDC_ATTR_ATTRIBUTE_VAL_MAP)
0x00 0x0C	Attribute Value Length(Length = 12)
0x00 0x02	Attribute Value Map Count(Count = 2)
0x00 0x08	Attribute Value Map Length(Length = 8)
0x0A 0x4C 0x00 0x02	MDC_ATTR_NU_VAL_OBS_BASIC, Value Length(Length = 2)
0x09 0x90 0x00 0x08	MDC_ATTR_TIME_STAMP_ABS, Value Length(Length = 8)
	⋮

Figure 9. An example of the process described in Figure 8 (ISO/IEEE 11073 Present (Notice Configuration) Request message).

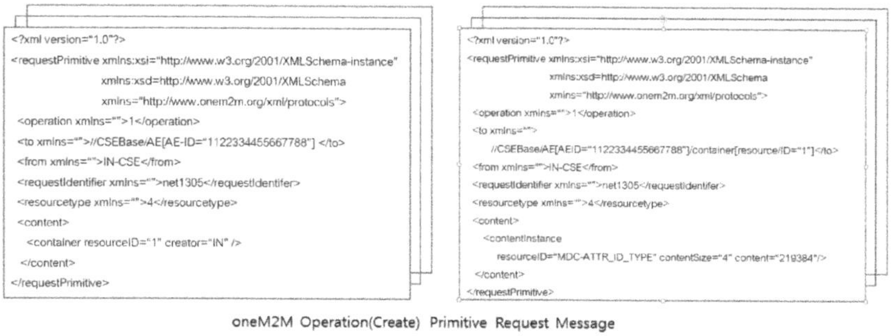

oneM2M Operation(Create) Primitive Request Message

Figure 10. An example of the process described in Figure 8 (oneM2M Create primitive Request message).

Biomedical data measured by a PHD can be delivered in an ISO/IEEE 11073 Present (Store Sensing Data) Request message. Because a single ISO/IEEE 11073 Present (Store Sensing Data) Request message can contain multiple biomedical data, more than oneM2M Update primitive Request messages can be built. Figure 11 shows how to convert an ISO/IEEE 11073 Present (Store Sensing Data) Request message into oneM2M Update primitive Request messages. For an ISO/IEEE 11073 Present (Store Sensing Data) Request message received, the gateway or the IoT server stores the measured biomedical information contained in ("Observed Value", "Absolute Time Stamp") fields into the appropriate places in its resource tree designated by "URL&Value". Figure 12 shows an example of the process described in Figure 11. In the upper image of Figure 12, "APDU Choice Type" on the first line and "Event Type" on the ninth line indicate that this message is an ISO/IEEE 11073 Present Request message and a Store Sensing Data message, respectively. Two measured (observed) values are delivered in the dotted box of the upper figure: 90 is measured at time 6 December 2016, T12:10:0000 and 72 at time 6 December 2016, T12:40:0000. These values and measured times are transmitted in two oneM2M Update primitive Request messages to update the resource tree. Only one oneM2M Update primitive Request message is shown in the dotted box (No. 1) of the lower figure.

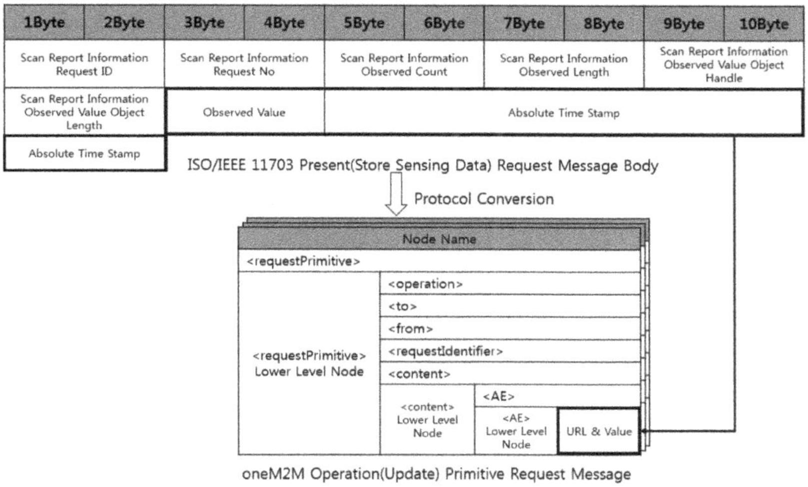

oneM2M Operation(Update) Primitive Request Message

Figure 11. Conversion of an ISO/IEEE 11073 Present (Store Sensing Data) Request message to oneM2M Update primitive Request messages.

0xE7 0x00	APDU Choice Type(Present Request)
0x00 0x36	Choice Length(Length = 54)
0x00 0x34	OCTET String Length(Length = 52)
0x12 0x38	Invoke ID
0x01 0x01	Choice(Remote Operation Invoke, Confirmed Event Report)
0x00 0x2E	Choice Length(Length = 46)
0x00 0x00	MDS Object(Object Handle = 0)
0xFF 0xFF 0xFF 0xFF	Event Time
0x0D 0x1D	Event Type(MDC_NOTI_SCAN_REPORT_FIXED)
0x00 0x24	Event Information Length(Length = 36)
0xF0 0x00	Scan Report Information Request ID
0x00 0x00	Scan Report Information Request No
0x00 0x02	Scan Report Information Observed Count(Count = 2)
0x00 0x1C	Scan Report Information Observed Length(Lerngth = 28)
0x00 0x01	Scan Report Information Observed Value[0] Object Handle(1)
0x00 0x0A	Scan Report Information Observed Value[0] Object Value Length(Length = 10)
0x00 0x62	Basic Numeric Observed Value(Value = 98)
0x20 0x16 0x12 0x06 0x12 0x10 0x00 0x00	Absolute Time Stamp(2016-12-06 T12:10:0000)
0x00 0x0A	Scan Report Information Observed Value[1] Object Handle(10)
0x00 0x0A	Scan Report Information Observed Value[1] Object Length(Length = 10)
0x00 0x48	Simple Numeric Observed Value(Value = 72)
0x20 0x16 0x12 0x06 0x12 0x10 0x00 0x00	Absolute Time Stamp(2016-12-06 T12:40:0000)

ISO/IEEE 11073 Present(Store Sensing Data) Request Message Body

```xml
<?xml version="1.0"?>
<requestPrimitive xmlns:xsi="http://www.w3.org/2001/XMLSchema-instance"
xmlns:xsd="http://www.w3.org/2001/XMLSchema" xmlns="http://www.onem2m.org/xml/protocols">
  <operation xmlns="">3</operation>
  <to xmlns="">//CSEBase/AE[AE-ID="11223344556677 88"]/container[resourceID="1"]/
container[resourceID="MDC_ATTR_ATTRIBUTE_VAL_MAP"]/
contentInstance[resourceID="MDC_ATTR_NU_VAL_OBS_BASIC"]</to>
  <from xmlns="">IN-CSE</from>
  <requestIdentifier xmlns="">net1305</requestIdentifier>
  <resourcetype xmlns="">2</resourcetype>
  <content>
    <contentInstance xmlns:xsi="http://www.w3.org/2001/XMLSchema-instance"
xmlns:xsd="http://www.w3.org/2001/XMLSchema" xmlns="http://www.onem2m.org/xml/protocols">
      <content>98</content>
      <time>2016-12-06 T12:10:0000 <time>
    </contentInstance>
  </content>
</requestPrimitive>
```

oneM2M Operation(Update) Primitive Request Message

Figure 12. An example of the process described in Figure 11.

6. Buddy-ACK Authentication Scheme

Because the biomedical data obtained by a PHD may be very sensitive in terms of a patient's privacy, the data need to be handled in a manner that prevents its exposure to unauthorized persons. In this study, two security schemes are proposed. First, a patient's biomedical data obtained by a PHD are not stored as a single unit, but are stored in parts in the IoT server. The data are partitioned into several parts (two parts in this study) and stored separately in the IoT server. Bytes of the data are stored alternatively into two different locations. Furthermore, the separation information including the locations of the parts is not stored in the IoT server, but in the IoT authentication server. This means that anyone who wants to access the data will need to access both the IoT server and the IoT authentication server simultaneously.

Second, an authentication scheme called the Buddy-ACK authorization scheme is proposed in this study. In a normal authorization scheme, only a user needs to be authorized [32]. However, in the Buddy-ACK authorization scheme, specific biomedical data can be accessed only after both a patient and the related medical staff are authorized. We call the patient and the related medical staff "buddies". Biomedical data can be accessed only after the acknowledgement (or consent) of the related buddy is obtained. In this way, the Buddy-ACK authorization scheme is stricter than normal authorization processes. As far as message authentication is concerned, existing encryption/digital signature schemes can be used [32]; this is not an issue we will discuss further.

The security schemes proposed in this study has the following properties:

- The separation storage of biomedical data: A patient's biomedical data obtained by a PHD are not stored as a single unit, but are stored in parts on the IoT server. The data are partitioned into two parts, each having alternate bytes, and stored separately into the IoT server. The separation information including the locations of the parts is not stored in the IoT server but in the IoT authentication server. Because the IoT authentication server does not have data itself, an attacker would need to successfully breach both servers simultaneously. Even a system administrator of the IoT server cannot obtain the data because the IoT server does not have the separation information that describes where the data parts are located. When data are requested, the IoT server has to request the IoT authentication server for the locations of all the data parts to assemble all of the data parts for complete data.

- The buddy-ACK authentication scheme: For the sake of patient privacy, the buddy-ACK authentication scheme is proposed in this study. A patient and the medical staff responsible for the patient are considered to be "buddies". When a medical staff requests a patient's data, acknowledgement (or consent) of the patient is needed. The IoT authentication server sends the separation information of the data only after the server receives the acknowledgement of the patient. Similarly, even when a patient requests his own data, acknowledgement of the related medical staff must be obtained. The acknowledgement is realized as encrypted IMEI (International Mobile Equipment of Identity) in this study. The encryption key is obtained when a patient (or a medical staff) registers at the IoT authentication server. Thus, the key is shared only by a patient (or a medical staff) and the IoT authentication server. In this way, an attacker may experience significant difficulties in accessing a patient's data because the attacker must know the encryption keys of both the patient and the related medical staff to be successful.

Alarm signals that report the abnormal condition of the patient are exempt from the Buddy-ACK authorization process because the signals should be delivered to the related medical staff immediately. Push operations are used for the signals in the system.

Figure 13 shows the Buddy-ACK authorization scheme process proposed in this study.

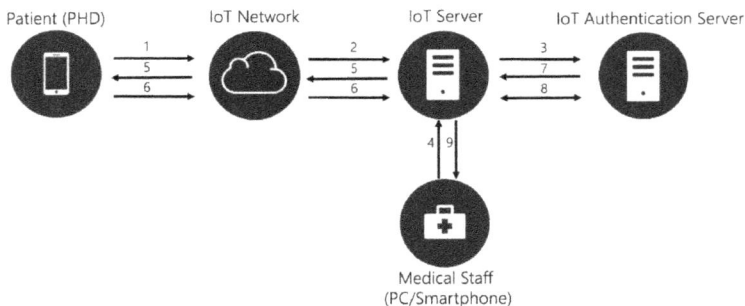

Figure 13. Buddy-ACK authorization scheme process.

The Scheme 1 has the following sequences:

(Storage sequence)

1. PHDa sends measured biomedical data to IoTs through an IoT network.
2. IoTs receives the data, and Splits the data into two parts to store separately
3. IoTs sends the separation information (i.e., the locations of the two parts) to IoTauth and deletes the separation information from IoTs, and IoTauth stores the separation information received from IoTs

(Retrieval sequence performed by Spm)

1. Spm sends Ek(IMEIm) to IoTs to request A's biomedical data
2. IoTs requests ACK of PHDa to initiate the Buddy-ACK authorization process
3. PHDa sends Ek(IMEIa) to IoTs as an ACK
4. IoTs sends (Ek(IMEIm) + Ek(IMEIa)) to IoTauth
5. IoTauth performs Dk(Ek(IDms) + Ek(IDa)) to determine whether it is the legitimate buddy, and IoTauth sends the related separation information to IoTs
6. IoTs locates two parts of A's biomedical data using the received separation information, and Assembles them to send to Ms

(Retrieval sequence performed by PHDa)

PHDa: PHD of patient A
SPm: Smartphone of Medical staff Ms related to A
IMEIa: IMEI of PHDa
IMEIm: IMEI of SPm
IoTs: IoT server
IoTauth: IoT authentication server
Ek(IMEIm): Encryption of IMEIm with the private key k of IoTauth
Dk(IMEIa + IMEIm): Decryption of (IMEIa + IMEIm) with the private key k
 of IoTauth

Scheme 1. Buddy-ACK authorization scheme.

Retrieval sequence performed by PHDa is very similar to Retrieval sequence performed by Spm, except that "Spm" and "Ek(IMEIm)" are replaced by "PHDa" and "Ek(IMEIa)", respectively.

7. Experiments

The proposed IoT system for monitoring patients at home was constructed and evaluated through several experiments. The system was developed in C# under Windows 7 Operating System.

7.1. Experiment on the MQL Scheduling Algorithm

In the experiments to test the MQL scheduling algorithm, four types of PHDs were used to generate pulse oximetry data, ECG data, blood sugar data, and weight data. ECG data, the heaviest data of all, were obtained by gathering 300 data samples per second for 5 ms. Each result in the following graphs was obtained by averaging the results of ten experiments. The characteristics of four types of biomedical data used in these experiments are as follows:

- Pulse oximetry data: Message class (Urgent), Message priority (5.0), Messages size (64 bytes)
- ECG data: Message class (Urgent), Message priority (3.0), Messages size (1024 bytes)
- Blood sugar data: Message class (Non-urgent), Message priority (3.0), Messages size (64 bytes)
- Weight data: Message class (Non-urgent), Message priority (1.0), Messages size (64 bytes)

To compare the proposed MQL scheduling algorithm with other multiclass message scheduling algorithms, the MBDP algorithm was implemented. For the MBDP algorithm, the following maximum delay times were utilized: 0 second for urgent data, 50,000 seconds for blood sugar data, and infinity for weight data. Figure 14 shows the throughputs (the number of messages scheduled for transmission) generated by the MQL and the MBDP algorithms.

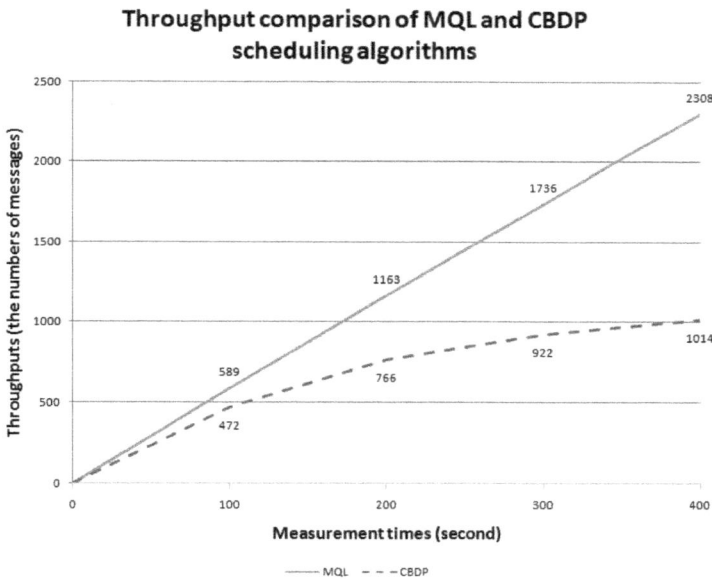

Figure 14. Throughputs of the MQL (Multiclass Q-learning) and the MBDP (Multiclass Based Dynamic Priority) scheduling algorithms.

As seen in Figure 14, the MQL scheduling algorithm proposed in this study performs better than the MBDP scheduling algorithm. In addition, we found that the throughputs of the MQL algorithm increase almost linearly as the measurement time increases, whereas the throughputs of the MBDP algorithm increase with decreases in the increasing ratio. This is partially because the MQL algorithm performs significantly better than the MBDP algorithm, especially when the number of messages waiting to be scheduled becomes quite large. As measurement time increases, the number of messages waiting to be scheduled also increases. Compared to the MQL algorithm, the MBDP algorithm incurs greater overhead when recalculating the RTTS of every message in the waiting queues, and when moving messages between queues upon recalculation.

7.2. Experiment on the Protocol Conversion Process

When a PHD wants to connect to the IoT server, the PHD sends the server an ISO/IEEE 11073 Association Request message for connection. A gateway, located between the PHD and the server, needs to perform the protocol conversion process mentioned in Section 5, because the server does not support the ISO/IEEE 11073 protocol. Figures 15 and 16 show screen captures of the results of the protocol conversion execution for connection establishment. The upper screen in Figure 15 shows the content of the ISO/IEEE 11073 Association Request/Response message, while the lower screen shows that of the oneM2M Operation (Retrieve) primitive Request/Response message. An explanation on the figures is omitted because the same example was explained in detail in Figure 6. The content of the oneM2M message is represented in XML.

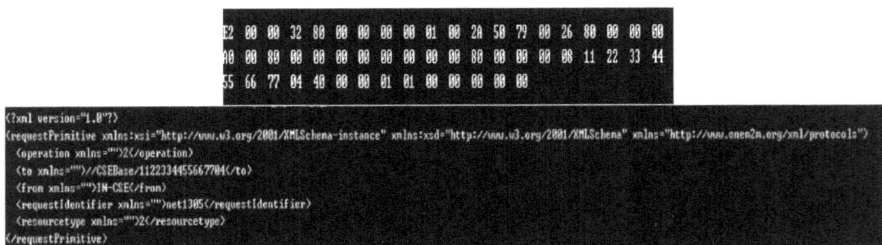

Figure 15. Screen captures of connection establishment (Conversion of an ISO/IEEE 11073 Association Request message into a oneM2M Retrieve primitive Request message).

Figure 16. Screen captures of connection establishment (Conversion of a oneM2M Retrieve primitive Response message into an ISO/IEEE 11073 Association Response message).

In the upper screen of Figure 16, "<responseStatusCode>" is 4004 (on the third line), which means the PHD which requests connection has not been registered in the IoT server. Therefore, the PHD sends the IoT server its configuration in an ISO/IEEE 11073 Present (Notice Configuration) Request message for its registration to the server, as shown in Figure 17.

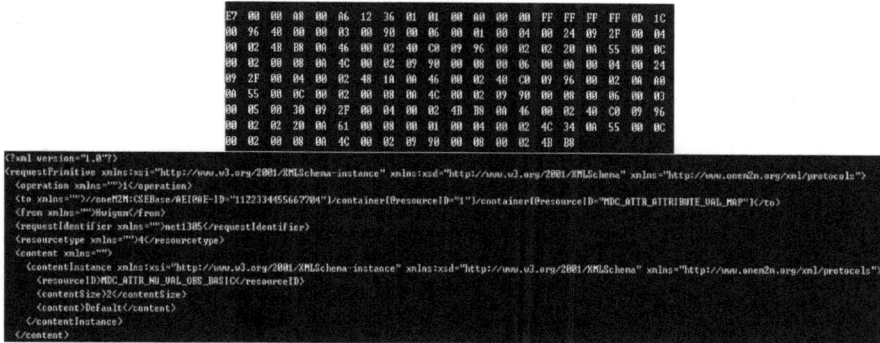

Figure 17. Screen captures of registration (Conversion of an ISO/IEEE 11073 Present (Notice Configuration) Request message into a oneM2M Create primitive Request message).

When the registration process for the PHD finishes, the resource tree shown in Figure 18 is created by the IoT server (IN-CSE). "<AE>" tag node for the PHD is created in the resource tree. Measured biomedical values of three objects by the PHD can be stored in the resource tree later. "content = 'Default'" means that the related measured value will be stored when a oneM2M Operation (Update) primitive Request message arrives later.

```
<AE resourceType="2" xmlns="" creationTime="2015-10-23 오후 7:39:07" AE-ID="1122334455667704" resourceID="resourceID">
  - <container resourceID="1" creator="IN">
      <contentInstance resourceID="MDC_ATTR_ID_TYPE" content="219384" contentSize="4"/>
      <contentInstance resourceID="MDC_ATTR_METRIC_SPEC_SMALL" content="16576" contentSize="2"/>
      <contentInstance resourceID="MDC_ATTR_UNIT_CODE" content="544" contentSize="2"/>
      - <container resourceID="MDC_ATTR_ATTRIBUTE_VAL_MAP" creator="IN">
          <contentInstance resourceID="MDC_ATTR_NU_VAL_OBS_BASIC" content="Default" contentSize="2"/>
          <contentInstance resourceID="MDC_ATTR_TIME_STAMP_ABS" content="Default" contentSize="8"/>
      </container>
  </container>
  - <container resourceID="10" creator="IN">
      <contentInstance resourceID="MDC_ATTR_ID_TYPE" content="218458" contentSize="4"/>
      <contentInstance resourceID="MDC_ATTR_METRIC_SPEC_SMALL" content="16576" contentSize="2"/>
      <contentInstance resourceID="MDC_ATTR_UNIT_CODE" content="2720" contentSize="2"/>
      - <container resourceID="MDC_ATTR_ATTRIBUTE_VAL_MAP" creator="IN">
          <contentInstance resourceID="MDC_ATTR_NU_VAL_OBS_BASIC" content="Default" contentSize="2"/>
          <contentInstance resourceID="MDC_ATTR_TIME_STAMP_ABS" content="Default" contentSize="8"/>
      </container>
  </container>
  - <container resourceID="3" creator="IN">
      <contentInstance resourceID="MDC_ATTR_ID_TYPE" content="219384" contentSize="4"/>
      <contentInstance resourceID="MDC_ATTR_METRIC_SPEC_SMALL" content="16576" contentSize="2"/>
      <contentInstance resourceID="MDC_ATTR_UNIT_CODE" content="544" contentSize="2"/>
      <contentInstance resourceID="MDC_ATTR_SUPPLEMENTAL_TYPES" content="19508" contentSize="2"/>
      - <container resourceID="MDC_ATTR_ATTRIBUTE_VAL_MAP" creator="IN">
          <contentInstance resourceID="MDC_ATTR_NU_VAL_OBS_BASIC" content="Default" contentSize="2"/>
          <contentInstance resourceID="MDC_ATTR_TIME_STAMP_ABS" content="Default" contentSize="8"/>
      </container>
  </container>
</AE>
```

Figure 18. Resource tree created by the IoT server (IN-CSE) after the registration process.

Biomedical values measured by the PHD are delivered in an ISO/IEEE Present (Store Sensing Data) Request message, as shown in the upper screen of Figure 19. The explanation of Figure 19 is similar to what has been previously explained, and will be omitted here.

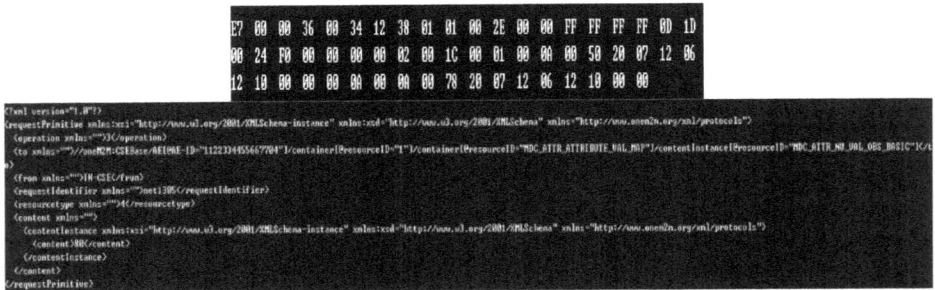

Figure 19. Captured screens of registration (Conversion of an ISO/IEEE 11073 Present (Store Sensing Data) Request message into a oneM2M Update primitive Request message).

8. Conclusions

In this paper, a remote monitoring system for patients at home in IoT environments is proposed, constructed, and evaluated through several experiments. To prepare for the massive number of PHDs needed, the system was designed as multilayered. To use PHDs as objects in an IoT system based on the oneM2M protocol, a protocol conversion process between ISO/IEEE 11073 protocol and oneM2M protocol was proposed and implemented. In addition, a multiclass data communication scheme was proposed and implemented based on the urgency of delivery to medical staff. For the protection of a patient's privacy, two security schemes are proposed in this study. First, a patient's biomedical data obtained by a PHD are not stored as a single unit, but stored in parts in the IoT server. Furthermore, the separated information is stored in the IoT authentication server. In this way, an attacker would need to successfully breach both servers simultaneously to access the data. Second, an authentication scheme called the Buddy-ACK authorization scheme is proposed in this study. In the Buddy-ACK authorization scheme, a specific piece of biomedical data can be accessed only after both a patient and the related medical staff are authorized.

The experiments on the constructed system showed that the system worked well; the protocol conversion process worked efficiently for IoT environments. The experiments also showed the MQL scheduling algorithm proposed in this study transmits urgent messages immediately, and transmits non-urgent messages later, when they will not interfere with urgent message transmissions. In addition, the MQL scheduling algorithm performs better than the MBDP scheduling algorithm. We also found that the throughputs of the MQL algorithm increase almost linearly as the measurement time increases, whereas the throughputs of the MBDP algorithm increase with decreases in the increasing ratio. This is partially because the MQL algorithm performs significantly better than the MBDP algorithm, especially when the number of messages waiting to be scheduled becomes quite large. In addition, despite the heavy traffic, the alarm signals of the highest class were immediately pushed to medical staffs due to the data classification scheme.

Acknowledgments: This research was supported by the Basic Science Research Programs grant through the National Research Foundation of Korea (NRF), funded by the Ministry of Education, Science and Technology (No. NRF-2015R1D1A3A03019278).

Author Contributions: KeeHyun Park conceived the ideas proposed in this paper and designed the Buddy-ACK authentication scheme. Joonsuu Park designed the MQL algorithm and performed the related experiments. JongWhi Lee designed the protocol conversion process and performed the related experiments. Finally, KeeHyun Park wrote the paper.

Conflicts of Interest: The authors declare no conflict of interest.

References

1. Chaouchi, H. *The Internet of Things: Connecting Objects to the Web*; Wiley: Hoboken, NJ, USA, 2013.
2. Hoeller, J.; Tsiatsis, V.; Mulligan, C.; Karnouskos, S.; Avesand, S.; Boyle, D. *From the Machine-to-Machine to the Internet of Things: Introduction to a New Age Intelligence*; Elsevier: Amsterdam, The Netherlands, 2014.
3. Kearns, W.D.; Nams, V.O.; Fozard, J.L. Tortuosity in Movement Paths Is Related to Cognitive Impairment Wireless Fractal Estimation in Assisted Living Facility Residents. *Meth. Inf. Med.* **2010**, *49*, 592–598. [CrossRef] [PubMed]
4. Chen, H.; Kalish, M.C.; Pagán, J.A. Telehealth and Hospitalizations for Medicare Home Healthcare Patients. *Am. J. Manag. Care* **2011**, *17*, 224–230.
5. Kearns, W.D.; Fozard, J.L.; Becker, M.; Jasiewicz, J.M.; Craighead, J.D.; Holtsclaw, L.; Dion, C. Path Tortuosity in Everyday Movements of Elderly Persons Increases Fall Prediction beyond Knowledge of Fall History, Medication Use, and Standardized Gait and Balance Assessments. *J. Am. Med. Dir. Assoc.* **2012**, *13*, 665.e7–665.e13. [CrossRef] [PubMed]
6. Taylor, J.; Coates, E.; Brewster, L.; Mountain, G.; Wessels, B.; Hawley, M.S. Examining the use of telehealth in community nursing: Identifying the factors affecting frontline staff acceptance and telehealth adoption. *J. Adv. Nurs.* **2015**, *71*, 326–337. [CrossRef] [PubMed]
7. Kang, Y.; McHugh, M.D.; Chittams, J.; Bowles, K.H. Utilizing Home Healthcare Electronic Health Records for Telehomecare Patients with Heart Failure: A Decision Tree Approach to Detect Associations with Rehospitalizations. *CIN Comput. Inform. Nurs.* **2016**, *34*, 175–182. [CrossRef] [PubMed]
8. Jarrett, E.; Amy, P.; Tsien, S.S.; Neil, C.; Loretta, S.; Cindy, C.; Michele, M.; Beth, E.C. Remote Health Monitoring for Older Adults and Those with Heart Failure: Adherence and System Usability. *Telemed. e-Health* **2016**, *2*, 480–488.
9. Liu, L.; Stroulia, E.; Nikolaidis, I.; Miguel-Cruz, A.; Rincon, A.R. Smart homes and home health monitoring technologies for older adults: A systematic review. *Int. J. Med. Inform.* **2016**, *91*, 44–59. [CrossRef] [PubMed]
10. Institute of Electrical and Electronics Engineers. Standard for Medical device communication–Part 00000: Framework and overview. *IEEE Std.* **2008**, *1073*. Available online: https://standards.ieee.org/findstds/standard/1073-1996.html (accessed on 7 March 2017).
11. Institute of Electrical and Electronics Engineers. Health informatics-Personal health device communication. *IEEE Std.* **2008**, *11073–20601*. Available online: https://standards.ieee.org/findstds/standard/11073-20601-2008.html (accessed on 3 March 2017).
12. Pak, J.; Park, K. A smart personal activity monitoring system based on wireless device management methods. *Commun. Comput. Inf. Sci.* **2011**, *184*, 335–342.
13. Pak, J.; Park, K. UbiMMS: An ubiquitous medication monitoring system based on remote device management methods. *Healthc. Inf. Manag. J.* **2012**, *41*, 26–30. [CrossRef]
14. Pak, J.; Park, K. Advanced pulse oximetry system for remote monitoring and management. *Biomed. Res. Int.* **2002**. [CrossRef] [PubMed]
15. Park, K.; Lim, S. A multipurpose smart activity monitoring system for personalized health services. *Inf. Sci.* **2015**, *314*, 240–254. [CrossRef]
16. oneM2M. Functional Architecture (TS-0001-V1.6.1). Available online: http://www.onem2m.org (accessed on 10 December 2015).
17. oneM2M. Service Layer Core Protocol Specification (TS-0004-V1.0.1). Available online: http:www.inem2m.org (accessed on 10 December 2015).
18. Grieco, L.A.; Alaya, M.; Montei, T.; Drira, K. Architecting information centric ETSI-M2M systems. In Proceedings of the 2014 IEEE International Conference on Pervasive Computing and Communications Workshops (PERCOM Workshops), Budapest, Hungary, 24–28 March 2014; pp. 211–214.
19. Lam, S. Protocol Conversion. *IEEE Trans. Softw. Eng.* **1988**, *14*, 353–362. [CrossRef]
20. Glombitza, N.; Mietz, R.; Römer, K.; Fischer, S.; Pfisterer, D. Self-Description and Protocol Conversion for a Web of Things. In Proceedings of the 2010 IEEE International Conference on Sensor Networks, Ubiquitous, and Trustworthy Computing (SUTC), Newport Beach, CA, USA, 7–9 June 2010; pp. 229–236.
21. Delac, G.; Budiselic, I.; Zuzak, I.; Skuliber, I.; Stefanec, T. A Methodology for SIP and SOAP Integration Using Application-Specific Protocol Conversion. *ACM Trans. Web* **2012**, *6*, 1–28. [CrossRef]

22. Suo, H.; Wan, J.; Zou, C.; Liu, J. Security in the internet of things: A review. In Proceedings of the 2012 International Conference on Computer Science and Electronics Engineering, ICCSEE 2012, Hangzhou, China, 23–25 March 2012; Volume 3, pp. 648–651.

23. Hamdi, M.; Abie, H. Game-based adaptive security in the Internet of Things for eHealth. In Proceedings of the 2014 IEEE International Conference on Communications, ICC 2014, Sydney, Australia, 10–14 Junuary 2014; pp. 920–925.

24. Arias, O.; Hoang, K. Privacy and Security in Internet of Things and Wearable Devices. *IEEE Trans. Multi-Scale Comput. Syst.* **2015**, *1*, 99–109. [CrossRef]

25. Bhattacharyya, D.; Ranjan, R.; Alisherov, F.; Choi, M. Biometric Authentication: A Review. *Int. J. Serv. Sci. Technol.* **2009**, *2*, 13–28.

26. Schlöglhofer, R.; Sametinger, J. Secure and usable authentication on mobile devices. In Proceedings of the 10th International Conference on Advances in Mobile Computing and Multimedia, New York, NY, USA, 3–5 December 2012; p. 257.

27. Meng, W.; Wong, D.S.; Furnell, S.; Zhou, J. Surveying the development of biometric user authentication on mobile phones. In *IEEE Communications Surveys and Tutorials*; Institute of Electrical and Electronics Engineers Inc.: New York, NY, USA, 2015; Volume 17, Issue 3, pp. 1268–1293.

28. Arteaga-Falconi, J.S.; Al Osman, H.; El Saddik, A. ECG Authentication for Mobile Devices. *IEEE Trans. Instrum. Meas.* **2016**, *65*, 591–600. [CrossRef]

29. Sadiq, B.; Madan, R.; Sampath, A. Downlink scheduling for multiclass traffic in LTE. *EURASIP J. Wired. Commun. Netw.* **2009**, *2009*, 510617. [CrossRef]

30. Giluka, M.K.; Rajoria, N.; Kulkarni, A.C.; Sathya, V.; Tamma, B.R. Class based dynamic priority scheduling for uplink to support M2M communications in LTE. In Proceedings of the 2014 IEEE World Forum on Internet of Things, Seoul, Korea, 6–8 March 2014; pp. 313–317.

31. Watkins, C.; Dayan, P. Q-learning. *Mach. Learn.* **1992**, *8*, 279–292. [CrossRef]

32. Stallings, W. *Crptography and Network Security: Principles and Practices*, 6th ed.; Prentice Hall: Upper Saddle River, NJ, USA, 2014.

applied
sciences

MDPI

Article

Question-Driven Methodology for Analyzing Emergency Room Processes Using Process Mining

Eric Rojas [1,*], Marcos Sepúlveda [1], Jorge Munoz-Gama [1], Daniel Capurro [2,3], Vicente Traver [4,5] and Carlos Fernandez-Llatas [4,5]

[1] Computer Science Department, School of Engineering, Pontificia Universidad Católica de Chile, Santiago 8320000, Chile; marcos@ing.puc.cl (M.S.); jmun@uc.cl (J.M.-G.)
[2] Internal Medicine Department, School of Medicine, Pontificia Universidad Católica de Chile, Santiago 8320000, Chile; dcapurro@med.puc.cl
[3] Department of Biomedical Informatics and Medical Education, School of Medicine, University of Washington, Seattle, WA 98109, USA
[4] Instituto Universitario de las Tecnologías de la Información y de las Comunicaciones (ITACA), Universitat Politécnica de València, Valencia 46022, Spain; vtraver@itaca.upv.es (V.T.); cfllatas@itaca.upv.es (C.F.-L.)
[5] Unidad Mixta de Reingeniería de Procesos Sociosanitarios (eRPSS), Instituto de Investigación Sanitaria del Hospital Universitario y Politecnico La Fe, Bulevar Sur S/N, Valencia 46026, Spain
*   Correspondence: eric.rojas@uc.cl; Tel.: +56(2)-2354-4439

Academic Editors: Wenbing Zhao, Xiong Luo and Tie Qiu
Received: 30 January 2017; Accepted: 15 March 2017; Published: 21 March 2017

Abstract: In order to improve the efficiency and effectiveness of Emergency Rooms (ER), it is important to provide answers to frequently-posed questions regarding all relevant processes executed therein. Process mining provides different techniques and tools that help to obtain insights into the analyzed processes and help to answer these questions. However, ER experts require certain guidelines in order to carry out process mining effectively. This article proposes a number of solutions, including a classification of the frequently-posed questions about ER processes, a data reference model to guide the extraction of data from the information systems that support these processes and a question-driven methodology specific for ER. The applicability of the latter is illustrated by means of a case study of an ER service in Chile, in which ER experts were able to obtain a better understanding of how they were dealing with episodes related to specific pathologies, triage severity and patient discharge destinations.

Keywords: process mining; emergency rooms; frequently-posed questions; methodology

1. Introduction

The Emergency Room (ER) has become one of the most significant first-contact points with the healthcare system [1]. ER must provide the required services to screen, examine and provide care to patients in the most effective way. This has led to increased efforts to improve the service levels, to reduce overcrowding and to provide prompt and efficient care [2]. With these efforts comes a series of questions about what is the best way to make this happen, especially about how to improve ER processes. Based on the knowledge and use of historical information related to process execution within ER, it is possible to provide answers to a number of questions frequently posed by experts in the field. Examples of frequently-posed questions in the ER field include: What exactly generates the bottlenecks that lead to increased waiting times? What do cases in which patients have to endure long waiting times have in common? Are patients being attended to in line with established protocols? Why are there delays in the hospitalization of patients? In the past, multiple techniques have been used in order to provide answers to such questions, as well as to obtain further knowledge about ER processes, such as business process redesign [3], evidence-based medicine [4,5] and lean [6], among others.

Our approach centers on the use of process mining as the main component for responding to the questions posed by the experts. Process mining is a relatively young research discipline that focuses on extracting knowledge from data generated and stored in the databases of (corporate) information systems; in this case, the Hospital Information Systems (HIS). In turn, process execution data are extracted as event logs. An event log can be viewed as a set of traces (also known as cases, or in the emergency room, episodes), each containing all of the activities executed for a particular process instance. Process mining has been applied to Healthcare (HC) in the past, giving rise to a number of significant advantages [7]. For example, it helps to identify and to understand which process is followed in a specific medical procedure (e.g., during surgery [8,9], cardiovascular disease management [10] or during the treatment of cancer patients [11]); it helps to clarify the social relationships between the actors involved in the process (e.g., task delegation or collaboration patterns [12]); and it enables experts to verify levels of compliance with internal or external guidelines [13]. However, since process mining is an emerging discipline, there are still a number of limitations to its application, including the limited implementation of HIS that are process aware and that record event logs, as well as the difficulties involved in data extraction, the limited interpretation of data to respond to questions frequently posed by experts, the lack of methods for responding to the questions and the high dependence of experts on the process mining discipline, among others [7].

Previously, data from ER have been used to conduct three case studies that involve the application of process mining [14–16]. The case studies have provided information regarding the flow of executed activities (e.g., triage and examinations carried out), the relationships between available resources and the identification of opportunities to reduce waiting times for treatment.

In the first case study, undertaken in Portugal [14], a methodology was proposed, through the use of clustering techniques, to help generate simple process models. The models provide insight into the control flow of healthcare processes, their performance and their adherence to institutional guidelines. The methodology provides a series of steps, which should be followed. However, the methodology is not specific for ER, it depends on clustering techniques, and it fails to provide solutions to ER data management. Furthermore, its implementation relates to a suite that is specific to the needs of the particular hospital in which the study was conducted.

The second case was an exploratory study undertaken using data from ER processes from four hospitals in Australia [15]. It identified the process from each respective hospital and subsequently compared the results, highlighting the areas in which processes were executed differently. As part of this comparative study, the steps followed for the creation of the event logs used were described. However, it failed to generate either a detailed method or one specific for ER that might be reused in other medical centers. Both cases illustrate the problems in dealing with complex and interlaced process models, called spaghetti models, and the need to work closely with experts from both the medical and process mining fields.

The third case [16] refers to a study into the process of pediatric patients with asthma attended to in ER, using a visualization tool developed in a hospital in the United States. This case study identified the process model followed for attending to patients. However, it failed to specify a formal method with which to conduct the study, and it does not detail how the method might be replicated in other areas of ER.

As a result of the literature review conducted [7] and previously undertaken case studies, the need to resolve four important requirements has been identified. First, a methodology based on process mining that provides answers to questions frequently posed by ER experts is needed. An ER expert is a professional that works in ER and has knowledge about how ER processes are performed; some roles that are usually included in this group are physicians, nurses, technicians and administrative resources, among others. Previous case studies have merely defined mechanisms for obtaining simple process models, leaving the inclusion of ER experts in the field as work to be conducted in the future.

Second, data reference models that represent the data from ER processes are required in order to ensure that data are stored in a structured manner. Such models need to be process-aware and able to facilitate the creation of event logs. Third, there is a need to reduce the spaghetti effect when discovering ER process models, through the use of a methodology that is driven by specific ER questions. Finally, the fourth is the need to establish methods to apply process mining and data analysis techniques in flexible environments, such as the emergency room.

To fulfill these four requirements a methodology is proposed. This methodology uses both process mining and data analysis techniques, to provide answers to the questions frequently posed by experts, using the data stored in a process-oriented data reference model. The methodology will provide the guide, the data reference model will provide the data structures, and the frequently posed questions will help reduce the spaghetti effect.

ER processes are intrinsically flexible, since they must adapt to the particular characteristics of each patient. This flexible nature is evidenced through the presence of typical and atypical behavior in the ER [17]. However, there have been attempts to establish certain guidelines on how to treat patients, for example by creating guidelines to address specific diagnoses [18]. Our methodology deals with the flexible nature of the ER processes by identifying Frequently-Posed Questions (FPQs) that will guide the different stages of the methodology: which data must be extracted, the data model to be used, the building of the event log and the analysis to be performed. Moreover, episode filtering will help to reduce the event logs to only include the behavior that is desired to be studied for each FPQ.

The structure of the article is as follows: Section 2 defines the questions frequently posed by experts in ER. Section 3 describes the proposed methodology and the proposed data reference models. Section 4 describes a case study in which the methodology has been put into practice. Section 5 provides a discussion of the results obtained, and the article culminates with the conclusions and future work of the authors in Section 6.

2. Frequently-Posed Questions

Prior to explaining the aforementioned methodology and data reference models, it is necessary to identify the type of questions posed by ER experts regarding the relevant processes. Accordingly, two types of frequently-posed questions can be identified (Figure 1): first, general questions that are established in a generic manner for the executed process; and second, episode-oriented questions that are based on specific ER characteristics and the executed activities.

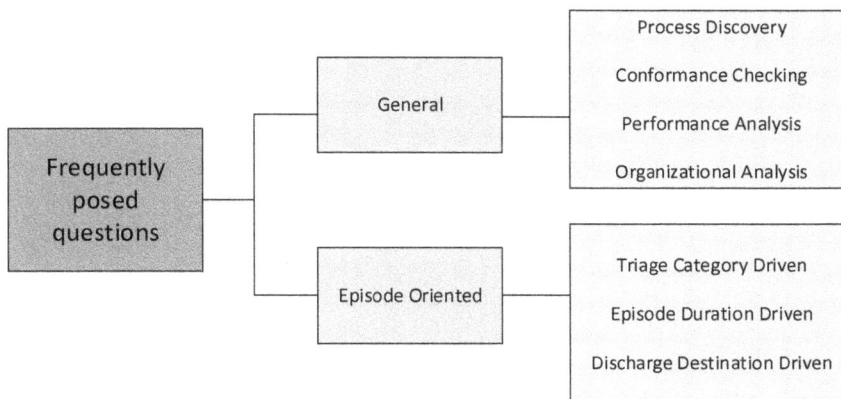

Figure 1. Frequently-posed questions for ER (Emergency Rooms).

We have established the general questions in a previous research work [7], based on the experience of ER experts. The general questions involve understanding how patients are attended to, what activities are executed, how long it takes to attend to patients in accordance with the severity of their particular needs, how resources interact and levels of compliance with associated protocols and standards [19,20]. Many of the questions fit directly with different generic approaches that recommend process mining. The approaches relate to process discovery, conformance checking, performance analysis and organizational analysis, as defined in the process mining literature [19]. Process discovery is directly related to describing the control flow in which process activities are performed by means of a process model. Diverse algorithms, such as heuristic miner or genetic miner, can be used to create a process model from an event log. An example of this type of question is as follows: What is the process (or how are the activities executed) for treating patients with different diagnoses, for example patients with appendicitis or pneumonia? Conformance checking is based on comparing a process model with an event log to verify whether the process is executed in accordance with that model. An example of this type of question is as follows: Are internal protocols being followed in the care provided in the ER? Performance analysis is based on the analysis of the execution times of specific activities, subprocesses or the complete process. An example of this type of question is as follows: What are the activities that increase the episode duration in the ER for patients over 60 years? Finally, organizational analysis is based on discovering the relationships between the resources that execute the tasks included in the event log, by means of social analysis metrics (e.g., "handover of work" or "doing similar tasks"). An example of this type of question is as follows: What is the type of interaction between doctors and nurses during patient care in the emergency room?

The episode-oriented questions are based on certain clinical characteristics or data obtained when executing the process activities that are specific to ER, for example the color of the triage or the discharge destination of a patient. The questions were obtained from gauging the genuine needs of the ER experts regarding their processes, by means of interviews, literature reviews and the personal ER experience of one of the authors of this article. Three different types have been established, which can be extended to include additional data and activities in order to broaden the analysis, as well as the possible combinations thereof: triage-driven questions, stay duration-driven questions and patient discharge-driven questions.

The triage-driven questions are based on the concept of triage, which relates to the process of evaluating patients arriving at ER in order to prioritize attention in accordance with the urgency of their needs and the services required [2]. There are a number of defined systems that establish color-coded classifications according to the needs of the patient, e.g., the Manchester triage system [21]. The Manchester triage system is a five category triage system based on expert knowledge. It helps the classification of patients according to five different colors (red, orange, yellow, green and blue), regarding the severity of the episode and the immediate need of attention; red being the most severe cases and blue being the least [21]. Generally, this task is executed by a nurse. It involves gaining an understanding of the needs of the patient and assigning them a color in line with the severity of their condition, for example red for patients in a critical state. Questions relating to this type are those for which the expert requires information regarding certain types of cases, for example: What process is executed for patients who are triaged green? What are the key activities executed for specific diagnoses in which the majority of patients are triaged orange?

The stay duration-oriented questions are based on the time in which the activities are executed for each case. The stay duration of a patient is the total time in which they are attended in the ER. This value might be denoted in units of time, for example two or four hours, or by means of categories according to a short stay (e.g., episodes of less than six hours) or a long stay (e.g., episodes longer than six hours). The duration values for the questions are established by the expert according to their questions. Examples of the questions include: What are the characteristics of episodes that last less than three hours? What is the process executed for attending to long-stay patients?

The ER patient discharge-driven questions are based on the destination of the patient after leaving ER, e.g., if they are formally admitted to the hospital or discharged home. The options can vary according to the characteristics and circumstances of the medical center, for example the ER may not be located in the patient's preferred hospital, resulting in a request to be moved. In our analysis, the term 'inpatient' will be used to refer to a patient admitted to the hospital following a discharge from ER, whereas 'outpatient' will be used to refer to an ER patient who was sent home. Examples of questions include: What are the clinical characteristics and activities executed during the episodes in which patients are hospitalized? What process is followed for attending to patients that are discharged and sent home?

In addition, compound questions can be detected from several characteristics of the episodes, combining triage, stay duration and patient discharge. For example: What activities are undertaken for patients who are triaged green, have a long stay in ER and whose final destination is to be admitted to the hospital? What characterizes the process followed by short-stay patients, who are triaged yellow or green, and sent home? What process is followed by long-stay patients who are triaged orange? Are there cases in which a patient who is triaged red is sent home? Furthermore, there are additional medical and demographic data that can be used to identify new categories of questions according to the analysis required in ER. For example, other categories may include different types of diagnoses, the resources involved, the physical infrastructure and the age and gender of the patients.

In addition to conducting an analysis led by each of the categories separately, they can be combined to obtain more specific and in-depth results, according to the requirements of the frequently-posed question. For example, those that attempt to describe the process (process discovery) that relate to red or orange category episodes (triage-driven questions) or those that require verification regarding whether they comply with existing regulations or protocols (conformance checking) in long-stay episodes (stay duration oriented questions). As the level of specificity of the question increases, the required level of combination between the categories also increases in order to produce the correct answer. Understanding the frequently-posed questions and their categories can help to produce both a data extraction guide and a methodology for the application of data and process analysis.

3. Methods

This section outlines a proposal for a data reference model for ER and its accompanying methodology. In conjunction, they provide the necessary tools to guide the search for answers to the frequently-posed questions by ER experts. The proposed methodology is evaluated in a case study in Section 4.

3.1. Data Reference Model for ER

This section provides information on how to build a data model, in order to apply process mining techniques to answer FPQs. First the data sources are discussed, followed by the definition of a data model for ER data.

3.1.1. Data Sources

Data from ER processes are stored in Hospital Information Systems (HIS), i.e., information systems designed to manage all aspects of a hospital's operation, including its medical, administrative, financial and legal issues, and the corresponding processing of services. As in general healthcare, the architecture of HIS in ER can be as follows: integrated [14], in which all data are in the same system; distributed [22], in which a specific system provides support for episodes; and the remaining data, such as medication data or medical staff data, are stored on different systems; or any intermediate point between the two extreme cases. Data extraction is challenging because the systems have heterogeneous architectures, including legacy systems developed ad hoc for the needs of each particular hospital. The disadvantage of the systems and repositories is that, despite them being able to store large quantities of data, they are not geared towards recording information regarding processes, which in turn, results in great difficulty when analyzing hospital processes. Accordingly and based on the concept of integrated HIS, we propose a data reference model that allows data to be stored and used for analysis on the process perspective.

3.1.2. Data Reference Model

Data reference models are common across a wide range of areas [23]. For example, in [20,23], the authors propose a general model for HC. However, a model for ER has not yet been proposed. The ER model proposed in this section, as shown in Figure 2, extends the aforementioned HC model, including specific dimensions of ER, such as consultation rooms (boxes) or triage, obtained from the analysis of previous ER case studies and information provided by ER experts. The data model proposed for ER is a model that specifies the data structures and their relationships for representing ER episodes. The data types included in the proposed data reference model were defined or identified from the original HC model and from the HIS studied during the case study. The model does not aim to fit any specific system, but rather to provide a framework that represents, in a generic manner, the data extracted from any ER system.

The proposed data reference model is designed to contain all of the data required to answer any FPQs about ER processes using data mining and process mining techniques. However, not all data are necessary for all questions. In fact, having all data is unusual in real scenarios. Therefore, at the moment of creating the actual data model, we should try to include as much information available as possible, according to the reference data model, but we must be aware that not all data will be available. Then, at the moment of addressing one of the FPQs, we should check whether the available data are sufficient to answer the question.

The data reference model consists of 15 data types used in ER linked by an episode ID. The episode ID is an identification number unique for each episode, in which each episode may be linked to the following: only one patient, one or more payments and zero or more values in the remaining data types. It should be noted that this model can be extended with additional data, which is not included herein, according to the specific characteristics of each ER.

The proposed data reference model retains certain data structures, extends others and adds new ones that are specific to ER. It retains the data structures for payment, patient, referral and radiology, since they already relate to activities generally carried out in all medical centers. It extends the data structures for transportation, internal medication, external medication and facility or building, including additional information, such as the status of a particular transportation, the active ingredient for a medication or information about each consultation room (box) of the ER facility. Finally, the model includes new general structures for all hospital facilities, as well as ones specific to ER. The new structures relate to vital signs, responsibility transfer, detailed professional activity, allergy, diagnosis, triage and ER discharge. Of the included dimensions, those specific to ER are the following: data from the consultation room (box) that form part of the facilities or buildings, triage data and data from the final ER discharge.

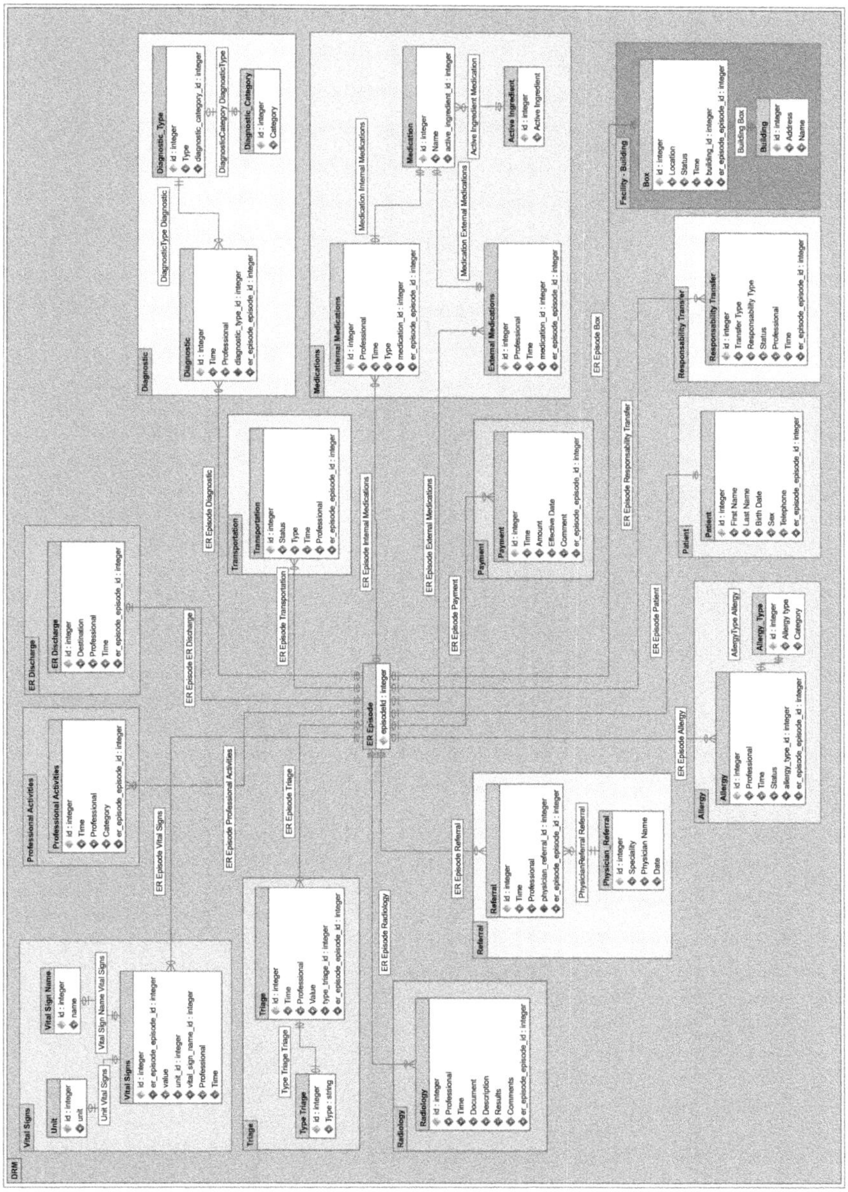

Figure 2. Proposed data reference model for ER.

3.2. New Methodology

This section proposes a methodology based on process mining to analyze ER processes. The methodology is based on the guidelines for process mining projects proposed in [19] and has adapted them to be question driven.

The proposed methodology deals with the flexible nature of ER processes as follows:

- FPQs are established. For each of them, it is possible to identify from the beginning the data in which the analysis should be focused.
- From these data, an event log is extracted that includes only the information required for the analysis of the selected FPQ.
- A list of ad hoc methods is provided to address each FPQ.
- The process can be decomposed into subprocesses, and episodes can be clustered in groups that can be analyzed independently, allowing more comprehensible models to be obtained.
- Moreover, process mining provides a set of tools to deal with unstructured processes: trace clustering gathers episodes into similar groups; identifying more frequent variants of how the process can be performed; and the ability of process mining algorithms, such as fuzzy miner or the one used by Disco, to ignore less frequent behaviors [19].

The proposed methodology is intended to guide a team formed by a domain expert and a process mining expert, so that they have a clear roadmap of how to apply process mining to analysis ER processes. The domain expert contributes with his/her knowledge about and insights about how ER processes are performed. The process mining expert contributes with his/her understanding of how to use the process mining techniques and how to correctly interpret their results.

The methodology consists of six stages (as shown in Figure 3), as follows: (1) extracting data from HIS; (2) creating an event log (main input for process mining techniques) based on the FPQ; (3) filtering the log for any given clinical context; (4) applying data analysis; (5) applying process mining (PM) techniques; and (6) analyzing the results with the experts. Each of the stages is explained below:

Stage 1. Data extraction:

The first stage is to identify the data, extract it from the sources, build a data model, check the presence of timestamps, name the events or activities, create any specific fields and verify the quality of the extracted data. Table 1 sums up the main activities of this stage and provides a series of guidelines to be considered during this stage.

Activity 1.1. Identify available data in HIS and build the data model:

The data may be centralized in a single HIS or distributed across different information systems. A data model should be constructed, based on the reference model proposed in Section 3.1.2, while always identifying each episode with a unique episode ID. Storing data based on a data reference model facilitates data extraction and the use thereof when answering the questions of the experts. It is important at this point to bear in mind a number of challenges when constructing the data reference model, as the quality of the data is not usually optimal, and actions are required as a result.

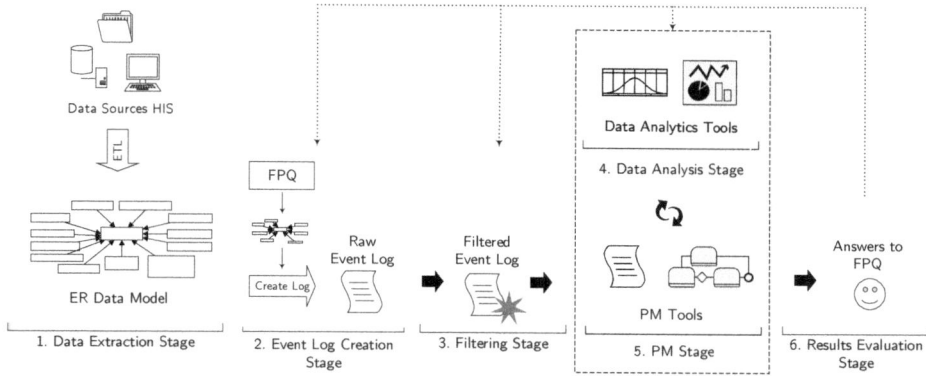

Figure 3. Proposed methodology.

Table 1. Guidelines for the data extraction stage. HIS, Hospital Information System.

Activity	Description	Guidelines
1.1: Identify available data in HIS and build the data model	Have access to the correct data from the direct sources, them being HIS or legacy systems.	- Make sure you have permissions and access granted to them directly or through the data owner. - Identify if data are missing in the data sources, and check if it is feasible to execute the analysis (e.g., timestamps are the minimum required data). - The available data model should contain as many dimensions and attributes of the data reference model as possible. - It should have as much detail granularity as possible.
1.2: Ensure availability of a timestamp for each event	Check that for each event or activity included in the data model, a correct timestamp is included.	- If different levels of accuracy are present, the highest one present in all of the data is recommended, just to have the same level across all of the examined data. - If some data do not have a timestamp, they cannot be used for the analysis.
1.3: Name events	In case any activity or event does not have an appropriate name, one should be assigned to it.	- Use meaningful names for the ER experts, such as "record vital signs".
1.4: Create specific-fields	Create specific-fields based on the required needs.	- It is advisable to group activities into subprocesses (e.g., group the triage activities in one subprocess, when our focus is the rest of the process). - It might also be useful to split activities into sub-activities (e.g., the professional activities could be split according to the role, for example professional activities, such as "physician professional activities" or "nurse professional activities".
1.5: Verify data quality	Further general issues have been identified from the literature review that must be tackled when generating an event log for process mining purposes in healthcare.	- Check lack of data, incorrect data or the inaccuracy and irrelevance of data. - Check in more detail all of the significant challenges previously found in the literature [20,24,25].

Activity 1.2. Ensure the availability of a timestamp for each event:

The first challenge is to ensure that a timestamp is present for each event of an episode. Each timestamp shows the moment in which a relevant event takes place. In addition to verifying the presence of a timestamp, the granularity of the timestamp must also be checked, since some timestamps have a high degree of accuracy (e.g., with a precision up to seconds), whereas others have a low level of accuracy (e.g., with a precision up to hours). As a result, it is necessary to decide the desired level in order to conduct the analysis. Ideally, the timestamp with the highest level of accuracy will be used. If different levels of accuracy are present, the highest one present in all of the data is recommended, just to have the same level across all of the examined data. If some data do not have a timestamp, they cannot be used for the analysis. Check that for each event or activity included in the data model, a correct timestamp is included. This will allow the use of the event or activity in the desired analysis.

Activity 1.3. Name events:

The second challenge is to decide the explicit name used to identify each of the activities included in the event log. In the reference models, data structures are identified for each of the activities undertaken. However, at the precise moment of creating the event log, it is necessary to define a particular name for each of them, in case they do not have one already established. For example, if we decide to include the events outlined in the vital signs data structure, each event must have a particular name, such as "record vital signs" or "taking vital signs". In case any activity or event does not have an appropriate name, one should be assigned to it. The name should be establish according to the knowledge of the domain and taking into consideration the ER expert.

Activity 1.4. Create specific-fields:

Create specific fields based on the required needs. According to the available data and their level of granularity, we can build specific fields to help us through the analysis. This may involve grouping activities into subprocesses or splitting activities into more specific ones, in order to obtain more details of the process. This can be done manually or automatically according to the information provided by the domain expert. Specific fields may be significant for a specific analysis, but not for another, so this task may not apply to all FPQ.

Activity 1.5. Verify data quality:

In addition to the explained challenges, further general issues have been identified from the literature review that must be tackled when generating an event log for process mining purposes in healthcare.

Some of the most significant ones that should be studied and considered are:

1. The definition of 11 patterns that describe the event log quality issues, such as incorrect inputs from UI forms, incorrect time stamps, incorrect format of the data, missing episode IDs related to the characteristics, missing events or activities, repeated events, and others. They should be considered when extracting, building a data reference model and generating an event log. More details can be found in [24].

2. The identification of 27 quality issues regarding the quality of the event log, classified into 4 categories, including process characteristics (amount of data, different types of traces and event granularity) and the quality of the event log (missing, imprecise, incorrect and irrelevant data). The details of the 27 quality issues are described in [20,25].

If the data contain incorrect or inaccurate values, they should be verified and checked with the HIS data owners to see if they are useful or not. If the data can be fixed by the experts to obtain the correct values, they still can be used. In case this is not reliable, the data should not be included in the analysis. It is important to overcome these challenges in the first stage, since it is in this stage that the data model is constructed. This model will facilitate data extraction and filtering processes for the subsequent stage of creating the event log.

Stage 2. Event log creation:

The event log creation stage considers the FPQ, establishes a specific data model and builds an event log to use in the following stages. Table 2 sums up the main activities of this stage and provides a series of guidelines to be considered during this stage.

Table 2. Guidelines for the event log creation stage. FPQ, Frequently-Posed Question.

Activity	Description	Guidelines
2.1: Identify data required to perform the specific analysis	Identify the FPQ to be answered and identify what data from the general data model will be used.	- Have clarity and a good understanding of the FPQs that are desired to be answered. - Not all of the data included in the reference model may be required to answer a specific question.
2.2: Create the event log	Once the data stored in the data model are available, a specific event log must be created each time a question requires a response.	- Establish the format in which the event log will be built. - Tools such as Excel with comma separated values files can be used, but more specific standards (such as XES) should also be considered.
2.3: Include specific characteristics for each event or activity	According to the characteristics of the data and the question that requires an answer, certain data types must be included in the event log.	- After the first version of the event log is built, an inspection should be made to assure that not only the minimum data are included, but also the desired characteristics of the episode with correct values.

Activity 2.1. Identify data required to perform the specific analysis:

Identify the FPQ to be answered and identify what data from the general data model will be used. These data must be extracted to a specific data model for the question, where all of the required data are stored and from where the event log will be built. This specific data model may be built in a database for the specific question or just extracted in a temporary way to build the event log. It is expected that this specific data model may be used for several similar questions, but in the long term will be changing according to questions that are addressed.

Activity 2.2. Create the event log:

Once the data stored in the specific data reference model are available, a specific event log must be created each time a question requires a response. Every event log is guided by the question that requires an answer. Event logs are the input for all process mining techniques and represent the actual execution of a process. An event log is composed of traces (i.e., process instances or episodes in this context), and each trace is represented by the ordered sequence of events that have occurred during the execution of that particular episode. Each event may contain additional information about its execution, such as its performer.

Activity 2.3. Include specific characteristics for each event or activity according to the specific analysis:

According to the characteristics of the data and the question that requires an answer, certain data types must be included in the event log for later use in the discovery or improvement of the process model. For example, in the case of wanting to discover the executed process, it is necessary to have the executed activities and their timestamps for each episode. In the case of wishing to conduct an organizational analysis, information about the health professionals that execute the activities must be included. In the case of wanting greater detail for certain activities, additional information to complement the activity must be included, for example when the requirement is to understand the characteristics of vital signs, including units of measurement and instruments used. Creating the event log is no trivial task, and it is necessary to undertake the process with due caution in order to include all required information. If such caution is lacking, results may be inaccurate and incorrect, meaning that this stage will have to be revisited at a later moment in order to include all missing data.

Stage 3. Filtering stage:

The filtering log stage consists of generating a specific event log for each question based on the filtering capacity of the different tools. It includes doing an analysis of the desired filters and the execution of them.

Once the event log has been created, data can be filtered according to the requirements of the question that requires an answer. This stage enables the event log to be refined in line with detailed characteristics in accordance with the analysis sought, for example establishing ranges of hours or days, clinical characteristics specific to the episodes or patient type. Undertaking this type of filtering is important since it reduces the quantity of episodes in the event log to those that are strictly necessary. This facilitates the application of the techniques and algorithms and the analysis of the data and models obtained. Normally, filters are included in the tools used to apply the process mining methods or techniques. These filter algorithms work by including/excluding episodes from the event log, based on the characteristics or values established in the filtering criteria options [26,27]. Three types of filtering are outlined: basic filtering, clinical domain filtering and question-driven filtering. Table 3 sums up the main activities of this stage and provides a series of guidelines to be considered during this stage.

Table 3. Guidelines for the filtering stage.

Activity	Description	Guidelines
3.1: Basic Filtering	Relates to filters that can be applied to any data characteristic, for example time or location.	- Define which tool is the correct one to execute the filtering. In our case, we propose Disco as a tool with filtering capacities, but additional tools may be considered. - Make sure to have knowledge of the different types of filters that the tools have available. These may include filtering the event log by ranges of dates, filtering by values of the different characteristics or filtering by the execution times of the episodes. - Establish dates, locations and resources or roles to limit the scope of the analysis.
3.2: Clinical Filtering	Relates to filters that can be applied according to the clinical characteristics of the data.	- For each clinical filter that will be done, the values must be known and verified with the ER experts.
3.3: Question-Driven Filtering	Relates to the filtering of data according to the characteristics of the question requiring an answer.	- To make sure that no value is forgotten on the question, split the question regarding the specific characteristics included. For example, if the question is "What is the process for female patients with green category triage and breast cancer as a diagnostic?", a good analysis will identify that filters will be executed regarding the gender, the triage categories and the diagnostic.

Activity 3.1. Basic filtering:

Basic filtering relates to filters that can be applied to any data characteristic, for example filtering by date or time (e.g., data between June and August 2015), filtering by location, clinical facilities or buildings (e.g., only data from the main hospital and not from its branches) and filtering by specific resources (e.g., specialist data or those relating to a specific role), among others.

Activity 3.2. Clinical filtering:

Clinical filtering (based on expert knowledge) relates to filters that can be applied according to the clinical characteristics of the data and which help to specify the data used in an improved manner. Examples of this type of filtering are to filter by diagnostic type (e.g., episodes with a diagnosis of bronchitis or appendicitis) or by medication type (e.g., ibuprofen).

Activity 3.3. Question-driven filtering:

Question-driven filtering relates to the filtering of data according to the characteristics of the question requiring an answer. If a response is required to a question based on triage values, data must be filtered in line with these values. For example, if the question relates to yellow triaged cases, with a diagnosis of bronchitis and with a final discharge to hospital, data must be filtered according to those particular values.

Stage 4. Data analysis stage:

The data analysis stage includes the analysis of data about how the process has been performed, as stored in the different event logs. This stage includes the selection of the data analysis techniques and the corresponding tools and the application of statistical analysis and data mining. Table 4 sums up the main activities of this stage and provides a series of guidelines to be considered during this stage.

Table 4. Guidelines for the data analysis stage.

Activity	Description	Guidelines
4.1: Select Data Analysis Techniques	Select statistical analysis and data mining techniques and tools.	- It is fundamental at this stage to have knowledge about the different types of analysis, to correctly apply them. Applying incorrect analysis to just obtain good visual models will not necessarily help with answering the frequently posed question correctly. - Not only complex models and techniques are required to provide answers to FPQ; exploratory analysis of the data must be executed first.
4.2: Statistical Analysis	Used to characterize an event log, identifying the frequency of activities, the distribution of cases over time and variants of process execution, among others.	- Have an understanding of the statistical and descriptive methods to be applied. - Verify access to the required tools.
4.3: Data Mining Analysis	Discovering different patterns and knowledge on data contained in the event logs.	- Identify the objective to achieve with the data mining techniques. Understanding the objective will provide guidance on which technique and tool to use. - Evaluate previous studies to check their results and see if they are applicable to replicate them. - Make sure to have access, license agreements and the computational resources needed to execute the tools and their included analysis. - Always check for additional libraries with newer techniques added to the tools. This may be an opportunity to apply a new technique to your analysis.

Activity 4.1. Select data analysis techniques:

The data analysis stage includes two possible types of analysis: statistical analysis and data mining analysis. These analyses are executed according to the relevant requirements for answering the specific question posed by the experts. There are types of analysis for specific questions in which only an exploratory statistical analysis is needed using tools, such as Excel (products.office.com/en-us/excel) or Disco (fluxicon.com/disco), and questions that require the use of both statistical analysis and data mining tools.

First, it is required to select the analysis techniques based on the expected outcomes. Outcomes may include a graphical model with data and information about the episodes, or an event log clustered into several sub-event logs. Second, it is required to identify the tools that allow one to perform the chosen techniques.

Activity 4.2. Statistical analysis:

Statistical analysis is used to characterize an event log, identifying the frequency of activities, the distribution of cases over time and variants of process execution, among others. It provides a holistic view of the process from a quantitative perspective and acts as a first step to answering any question. No specific algorithms are associated with this analysis; however, it can be performed using a variety of tools. For example, Disco is more process-oriented, while Excel is more data-oriented. Excel can be useful when the size and amount of data are manageable; but more complex big data solutions may be needed when the size grows, and this is not supported by Excel.

Activity 4.3. Data mining analysis:

Data mining analysis relates to the process of discovering different patterns and knowledge on datasets. There are multiple techniques taken from diverse domains that are applied in data mining in order to obtain the desired results, including, for example, visualization techniques, machine learning, classification algorithms and clustering, among others [28]. Data mining helps to ensure, by means of different techniques and algorithms, diverse types of analysis, including, among others: identifying associations between data; data classification; data clustering; prediction of patterns; and so on. Data mining techniques previously used with process mining include the use of decision mining algorithms in Petri nets and decisions trees to determine the routing of different cases [29], the use of clustering techniques and classification analyses to deconstruct different patient cohorts [30], the use of temporal data mining techniques to analyze clinical time series data and search for patterns in them [31] and the use of association rule mining and sequence mining techniques to discover associations between risk factors and specific outcomes [32]. A wide range of commercial and non-commercial tools are available in data mining that enable the application of the aforementioned analyses, including Rapid Miner (rapidminer.com/products/studio), GNUOctave (www.gnu.org/software/octave), Weka (www.cs.waikato.ac.nz/ml/weka), or R (www.r-project.org).

Stage 5. Process mining stage:

The process mining stage includes all of the steps related to the application of process mining techniques and algorithms, including selecting the appropriate tool and identifying and applying the adequate methods. Table 5 sums up the main activities of this stage and provides a series of guidelines to be considered during this stage.

Table 5. Guidelines for the process mining stage.

Activity	Description	Guidelines
5.1: Identifying the appropriate tool	Select appropriate tools that include the methods and algorithms to execute the desired analysis.	- Identify the available tools, including licensing issues, input and output capacities. - Identify the process mining methods each tool provides. - Each type of analysis may provide different types of data, information, models and results, so it is important to study the desired methods and algorithms to have a clear knowledge of the resulting outputs.
5.2: Process Discovery	Aimed at discovering a process model based on an event log.	- Understand what is the meaning of each event or activity present in each episode. - Have knowledge about the applied algorithm, to understand the correct meaning of its inputs and outputs. - Create process models at different levels of granularity. - Consider analyzing different episode stages (sub-processes) independently.
5.3: Conformance Analysis	Aimed at verifying conformance between a given ideal model and the actual execution as contained in the event log.	- Conformance techniques are complex, so first have a high level of understanding of how the techniques work; this way, the results will be understood and explained accurately when answering the FPQ. - Carefully match the name of events in the ideal model and the event log. - If some events do not appear in the ideal model or the event log, it is better to remove them before applying the conformance techniques.
5.4: Performance Analysis	Aimed at analyzing data regarding activity durations and waiting times between activities.	- It is vital to have the highest level of granularity when executing this analysis. This way, more exact results will be obtained.
5.5: Organizational Analysis	Focuses on the resources' perspective and how people interact during the execution of process activities.	- According to the FPQ, the level of analysis should be defined. It could be at the level of resources, at the level of roles or even at the level of teams or work groups.
5.6: Analysis regarding each type of question	According to the type of FPQ, specific techniques may be applied.	- It is not necessary to executed all of the analysis in the same tool. Different tools may be combined to obtain better models or a deeper analysis.
5.7: Data analysis and process mining cycle	In order to obtain the necessary results to certain questions, a continuous iteration is required for refining the data and the results.	- Several iterations may be done in order to get the exact answer. New iterations may include filtering or modifying the event log, adding new data, applying new filters or incorporating new methods. - Remember that fewer iterations do not guarantee quality results.

Activity 5.1. Identifying the appropriate tool:

The aim of process mining is to discover, monitor and improve real processes by extracting knowledge from event logs obtained from information systems [19]. There is a wide range of process mining algorithms and techniques available, and both commercial and non-commercial tools with which to implement them, including Disco (fluxicon.com/disco), ProM (promtools.org), CoBeFra (processmining.be/cobefra), PALIA (www.sabien.upv.es/proyectos/investigacion/automatizacion-y-mineria-de-procesos), CELONIS (my.celonis.de) and LANA (lana-labs.com). Four types of process mining analyses are required to provide answers to the questions most frequently posed by ER experts: process discovery; conformance analysis; performance analysis; and organizational analysis.

Activity 5.2. Process discovery:

Process discovery is aimed at discovering a process model based on an event log, in which the resulting model includes the activities and paths taken in different cases. Given the flexible nature of ER processes, in which two episodes are never the same, when dealing with questions related to control-flow analysis, we recommend the use of models with more flexible semantics, such as dependency graphs or fuzzy models, as well as the following discovery algorithms, heuristic miner [33] and fuzzy miner [34]. Alternatively, some questions may require models with a more formal semantic (e.g., Petri nets or process trees) and their associated algorithms (e.g., genetic miner [35] or inductive miner [36]) in order to verify conformance. Disco focuses on non-formal semantic models, while ProM includes models and algorithms with more formal semantics.

Activity 5.3. Conformance analysis:

Conformance analysis is aimed at verifying conformance between a given ideal model and the actual execution that is contained in the event log. It is significant because it is able to detect whether the process is being run as expected by the model. It is also possible to check whether or not there is compliance with internal or external guidelines. The authors recommend using algorithms based on conformance alignments in cases where optimal results are desired [37]. If only an exploratory conformance is desired, it is possible to choose conformance based on replay [38]. The algorithms are implemented in tools, such as ProM or CoBeFra.

Activity 5.4. Performance analysis:

Performance analysis is an analysis conducted from the time perspective, which takes into account the data regarding activity durations and waiting times between activities. This type of analysis is able to identify bottlenecks, activities that take longer than expected, excessive waiting times or slow synchronizations. The authors recommend the use of algorithms based on token replay over the model, which are able to obtain performance statistics and annotated Petri net models. The algorithms are implemented in tools, such as ProM.

Activity 5.5. Organizational analysis:

Finally, organizational analysis focuses on the resources perspective and how people behave during the execution of process activities. For example, it identifies who performs each task and how resources interact during a case execution. The authors recommend the use of the organizational metrics implemented in ProM (e.g., working together or handover of work) in order to obtain organizational models.

Activity 5.6. Analysis regarding each type of question:

Section 2 provides a classification of FPQ. For each of them, one or several types of techniques can be applied. For example, some FPQs may need to use discovery techniques to obtain process models, while others may need to use conformance checking techniques to verify conformance. Table 6 provides a general guide of what analysis techniques should be used for each FPQ.

Table 6. Analysis guide for each type of question.

Question	Analysis
General Discovery Questions	Heuristics miner algorithm [33], genetic miner algorithm [35] and inductive miner algorithm [36].
General Conformance Questions	Conformance checking and replay [39].
General Performance Questions	Performance analysis technique [38].
General Organizational Questions	Organizational metrics, such as handover of work, doing similar tasks, working together and subcontracting [40].
Episode Triage Category Questions	Classify and divide the episodes according to the triage categories. Discover a process model for each of the categories and execute the analysis according to the required characteristics of the episode.
Episode Duration Category Questions	Apply clustering techniques to classify the episodes according to their duration characteristics (time attributes), and afterwards, apply discovery or performance analysis techniques.
Episode Discharge Destination Category Questions	Classify and divide the episodes according to the episode discharge destination categories. Discover a process model for each of the categories, and execute the analysis according to the required characteristics of the episode.

Activity 5.7. Data analysis and process mining cycle:

Data analysis and process mining analysis stages are introduced as a cycle, since, in order to obtain the necessary results for responding to certain questions, a continuous iteration is required for refining the data and the results until the desired answers are obtained. For example, process mining discovery techniques are used at the beginning of an analysis to create a process model with a complete event log that includes all activities. These activities have characteristics (e.g., triage color or diagnosis), which help to undertake statistical analyses of the data and filter the event log, as required. The new event log includes only the desired episodes, and during the process mining stage, it helps to create a new model. By means of this series of iterations, it is possible to filter and analyze the dataset and reduce the spaghetti effect [19] in the process models discovered. In addition to analyzing the data in order to reduce or filter the event logs, the data analysis stage also enables the use of more advanced data mining techniques to identify trends, prediction rules and decision trees, among other more complex analyses.

Stage 6. Results evaluation stage:

Regardless of the technique used, it is extremely important to gather feedback from the ER experts, not only about the answers provided, but also about the clinical impact of the data and models obtained. In the results evaluation stage, the results are shown to the ER experts in order to know whether they provide the information, data and models to answer their FPQs. Table 7 sums up the main activities of this stage and provides a series of guidelines to be considered during this stage.

Table 7. Guidelines for the results evaluation stage.

Activity	Description	Guidelines
6.1: Identify ER Experts	Identify the experts responsible for the analysis of the resulting values and models for each question.	- The greater the number of experts available, the more comprehensive the analysis will be.
6.2: Define Feedback Instruments	Establish the instruments that will be used to verify the results with the experts.	- Prepare a presentation with the data, information, models and main conclusions obtained from the analysis. - Consider using questionnaires, interviews or focus groups.
6.3: Obtain feedback	Gather feedback in a systematic way.	- Prepare several questions that were triggered during the analysis and may help clarify the understanding of the data and the FPQ or impact future analysis. - Returning to previous stages is normal and usually allows obtaining more conclusive results. - The more information be provided by the experts, the greater the knowledge of the analyzed process will be, increasing the probability of obtaining better results in future iterations.

Activity 6.1. Identify ER experts:

The first step is to identify who are the relevant ER experts, those that have the knowledge about the complete process and are able to identify and explain each performed task.

Activity 6.2. Define feedback instruments:

Once the results from the analysis stages have been acquired, it is important to establish the instruments that will be used to verify the results in conjunction with the ER experts by analyzing the models and data obtained from each frequently-posed question. Examples of common instruments that might be considered include questionnaires, interviews and focus groups [41]. A questionnaire can be used to ask open or closed questions to identify whether the experts encounter the desired answers in the models and the data shown. This type of questionnaire should be used after the introduction and explanation of the obtained results. General questions may include: Do the data and models help to produce answers to the proposed questions? On the other hand, more specific questions might be used, for example: Is the sequence of activities present in the episodes of patients with appendicitis and a yellow triage as expected based on previous experience? Questionnaires do not have to be completed in person; rather, they can be undertaken digitally.

Feedback on the results of the application of process mining can also be obtained by means of interviews with ER experts. The advantage of interviews is that the answers can be broader than ones stemming from more closed questions in a questionnaire. The disadvantage is that they take longer to conduct. On the other hand, through focus groups, multiple experts from the particular field in question can be included simultaneously. In this instance, not only can the experts be asked specific questions, but also a general discussion can be generated regarding the results of the application of process mining in ER.

Activity 6.3. Obtain feedback:

Finally, the results should be shown to the ER experts in order to gather their feedback. It is not necessarily bad that the experts conclude that the outputs obtained are not enough, are not relevant or are not the expected ones. This is part of the process and will imply going back and checking the previous stages. It is usually required to verify whether the data were correct, the filters were made appropriately, the techniques applied were the proper ones and the results were interpreted correctly. This cycle should be repeated as many times as necessary in order to acquire the desired answers.

4. Results

The following section provides an example of the application of the proposed methodology and the search for answers to one specific question regarding a standard process followed in the ER.

Case Study

The case study relates to ER processes within a university hospital in Santiago, Chile. The data collected correspond to July 2014. Initially, several questions were posed according to the specific needs of an ER expert who works as a member of the ER team. For example: What activities are carried out, and what processes are followed in providing attention to ER patients diagnosed with appendicitis? How long do the activities carried out last in attending to ER patients diagnosed with bronchitis? What process is executed for treating patients who are triaged red? Are there certain diagnoses that are always triaged yellow and last more than ten hours? What are the activities carried out; what are the processes followed; and how long do the activities last in terms of providing attention to ER patients diagnosed with pneumonia? What are the most commonly-requested inter-consultations in cases of a long stay, and what are the main diagnoses?

The aim of the case study was to demonstrate the usefulness and applicability of the data reference model, the methodology and the use of process mining techniques to provide answers specifically to the following question: What activities are carried out, and what process is followed in providing attention to ER patients diagnosed with appendicitis? The decision to answer this question is because the episodes of appendicitis should normally follow a standard process, so we are interested in verifying, through the use of the proposed tools and methodology, whether that is effective in practice. Further research will include additional and more complex questions.

The stages defined in Section 3.2 were applied over a period of three months, during which data cleansing was the most time-consuming activity. The following is a description of the tasks undertaken.

Stage 1. Data extraction:

In order to answer the question, the tasks in the first stage of data extraction were executed. Data were extracted from HIS Alert ADWPhase I, which is the HIS used in the ER of the hospital in question. Subsequently, every data type was extracted by means of specific reports in CSV (comma separated value) format from the database (problems, vital signs, allergies, referrals, transportation, responsibility transfer, diagnosis, professional activities, medications, final discharge and triage). Each report comprehends detailed information about each activity or event considered in the analysis, including: a unique episode ID, the activity name, the resource who performed the activity, a timestamp with a high degree of accuracy and, optionally, a series of attributes about the activity or event. These attributes help to better understand how each episode was performed; for example, the dosage and effects of a drug applied to a patient in an internal medication event for a given episode. Demographic information about patients was not included among these attributes, since it was not required for the analysis.

Standardization tasks were performed on date formats, including: checking and establishing the desired format (e.g., dd/mm/yyyy or mm/dd/yyyy) and the spacer (e.g., - or /). In addition, simple activity columns (e.g., recording vital signs) and compound activity columns (e.g., professional task: medical doctor) may be defined and generated to improve the analysis. It is advisable to perform the data extraction with the help of the HIS owners, to make sure no data are left aside and the correct values are being extracted. Besides, it is important to validate the timestamps to check for any inconsistencies. Details, such as the date format or the spacer, can be seen as insignificant at the beginning, but they are relevant when the event log is created and uploaded into the process mining tools.

Stage 2. Event log creation:

During the second stage of the methodology, an event log was extracted taking into account the specific question we want to answer. In our case, the event log was created including all ER episodes during July 2014. The question specifically relates to the sequence of activities carried out in ER in attending to the patients, for example the activity of taking their vital signs, the medical imaging requested, the medication prescribed and the inter-consultations solicited. The minimum requirements for inclusion of each activity in this event log relate to the episode ID, the activity name and its corresponding timestamp. An example fragment of an event log can be seen in Figure 4.

Episode ID	Activity	Resource	Timestamp
1227078	Vital Signs	R1	25/07/2014 18:50
1227078	Nurse Tasks	R1	25/07/2014 18:54
1227078	Vital Signs	R1	25/07/2014 19:22
1227078	Chief Complaint	R1	25/07/2014 19:35
1227078	Triage	R1	25/07/2014 19:40
1227078	Vital Signs	R2	25/07/2014 20:00
1227078	Nurse Tasks	R2	25/07/2014 20:14
1227078	Nurse Tasks	R3	25/07/2014 20:45
1227078	Nurse Tasks	R4	25/07/2014 21:09
1227078	Physician Tasks	R5	25/07/2014 21:26
1227078	Vital Signs	R2	25/07/2014 21:55
1227078	Nurse Notes	R4	25/07/2014 22:11
1227078	Internal Medication	R5	25/07/2014 22:14
1227078	Physical Exam	R5	25/07/2014 22:25
1227078	Diagnostic Output	R5	25/07/2014 22:35
1227078	Anamnesis	R5	25/07/2014 22:35
1227078	Internal Medication	R4	25/07/2014 22:45
1227078	Clinic Discharge	R5	25/07/2014 22:49
1227078	Final Dicharge	R5	25/07/2014 22:49

Figure 4. Example of an event log fragment.

Stage 3. Filtering:

The goal of the following stage is to filter the previously constructed event log in accordance with the specific characteristics of the question that requires an answer. This was done using Disco, which has techniques to enable filters to be applied to the complete event log. Figure 5 shows an example of a filter generated with the Disco tool, in which episodes triaged red were selected.

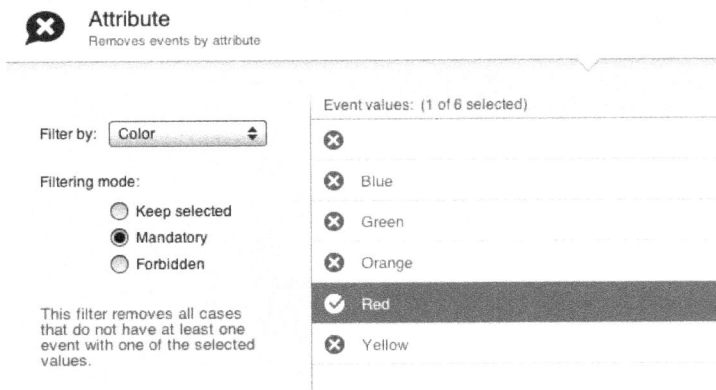

Figure 5. Example of a filter generated using Disco.

In general, the first filter used aims at selecting the completed episodes while excluding the episodes that either do not start or do not end during the desired period. In our case study, complete episodes from July 2014 were kept, excluding those that began prior to July 1 and those that finished after July 31.

Considering the question that needs to be answered, which refers to the analysis of the process followed to treat patients with appendicitis, it is necessary to apply a filter to select all of the episodes in which such a diagnosis has been made.

If additional conditions regarding characteristics relating to the episode or the patient are required, they must be specified by means of filtering during this stage. Once the completed episodes in conjunction with the specific characteristics relating to the relevant question have been obtained, the subsequent step is to analyze the event log with the available tools, exporting the event log itself in the desired event log format (XES, MXML, CSV, among others).

Stages 4 and 5. Data analysis and process mining analysis:

Following the filtering and the generation of event logs with the desired characteristics, data analysis of the included episodes takes place, prior to the subsequent analysis of the process itself, its model and its activities.

The first task undertaken at this stage is descriptive data analysis. At this point, 33 episodes with appendicitis were identified during July 2014. The 33 episodes included one or more of the following activities: nursing tasks, doctor tasks, procedure performance, technical staff tasks, medication prescription, medication administration, undertaking prescription procedures, differential diagnosis, laboratory orders, chief complaints, triage, requested imaging tests, history of present illness, discharge diagnosis, final ER discharge, clinical, biometry and general surgery consultation. The most commonly executed activities related to tasks undertaken by doctors and nurses, followed by activities relating to medication and those performed by the technical staff. The average episode length was 6:48 h, with the shortest lasting 3:24 h and the longest 10:26 h.

To broaden the analysis of the episode data, cases were classified using filters; specifically, according to duration (short and long stay) and triage (blue, green, yellow, orange and red). Table 8 shows the main characteristics of the cases. Of the 33 cases, 14 related to more than 4 h spent in ER (long stay), while 19 related to stays shorter than 4 h (short stay). Overall, 32 patients were hospitalized, and the remaining patient decided to return home. Furthermore, four patients were triaged green, while 28 were triaged yellow, and only one was triaged orange. No cases of either blue or red triage were obtained for this particular diagnosis. In general, and in regard to the data obtained, it is possible to conclude that for episodes in which patients are diagnosed with appendicitis, 100% are hospitalized in cases where the patient chooses not to leave the ER.

Table 8. Characteristics of cases diagnosed with appendicitis.

Color	Short Stay	Long Stay	
Green	3	1	
Yellow	15	13	
Orange	1		
Totals	19	14	33

Following the data analysis, process model discovery took place for the 33 cases included in the event log. Initially, the Disco tool was used to generate a process model, which is shown in Figure 6. As can be seen, neither is sufficiently legible, nor can they be used to clearly identify the activities carried out or the transitions from one to another.

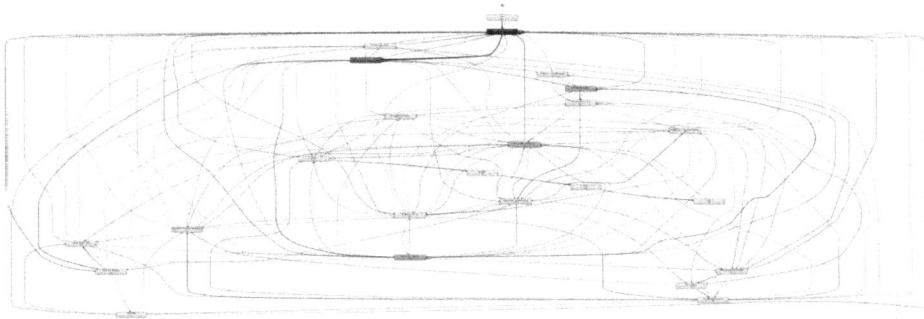

Figure 6. Process model for cases diagnosed with appendicitis (activities: <1%; Paths: <1%).

One way of resolving this problem is to identify the activities and classify them into subprocesses, in conjunction with the ER expert. Accordingly, three important subprocesses were identified. First is the subprocess that contains the triage and diagnosis activities corresponding to the tasks in which the seriousness of the condition of the patient is determined. Second is the subprocess that contains activities relating to treatment, which includes four subtypes grouped into their own subprocesses, as follows: the patient's physical examination subprocess; the procedure execution subprocess; the subprocess of taking exams; and the medication administration subprocess. Third is the subprocess that includes the activities associated with clinical discharge. The subprocesses are shown in Figure 7 in a diagram constructed in BPMN, where it can be seen that the initial subprocess is the triage and diagnostics. Subsequently, the process continues with the physical examination, procedure execution, taking exams and medication, in a loop that can take place more than once, and finally, the discharge subprocess is undertaken. Before executing the discharge subprocess, the condition of the patient must be checked; if the patient is ready to be discharged, the episode continues with this subprocess; otherwise, more procedures and exams should be performed.

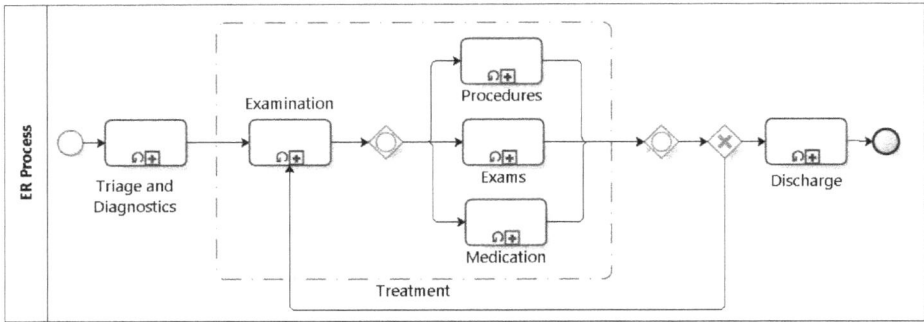

Figure 7. ER process model in Business Process Management Notation.

Owing to medical importance, analysis will only focus on diagnosis and treatment (including the four subprocesses therein). Regarding the activities of the triage and diagnostics subprocess, the activities were filtered and the process model generated in Disco, as shown in Figure 8. Two significant activities were identified in 31 of the cases (90%) and which have a very clear order at the beginning of each episode. First, the chief complaints/entry notes activity was undertaken, followed by the triage.

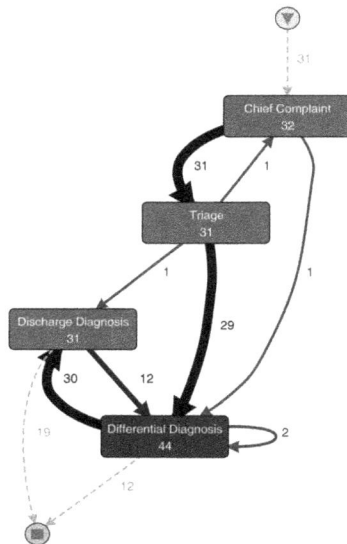

Figure 8. Process model for diagnosis activities activities: <1%; Paths: <1%.

To analyze the subprocesses included in the treatment of the patient, distinct process models were generated in Disco. The first model relates to the activities of the physical examination subprocess (see Figure 9), which includes the activities performed by the doctors, nurses, technical staff and other health professionals, in order to identify the diagnosis of the episode and thereby taking exams, provide medication or execute procedures.

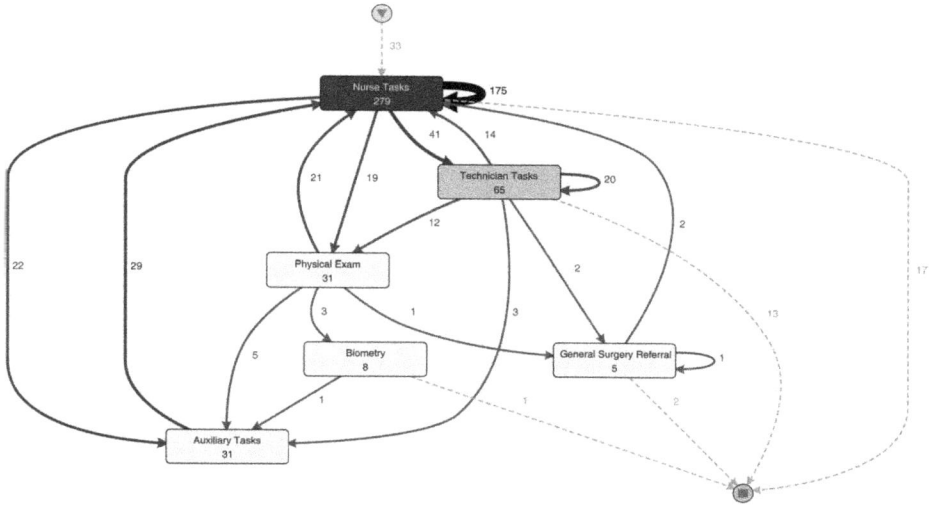

Figure 9. Process model for physical examination activities (activities: <1%; Paths: <1%).

The remaining models relate to the subprocesses of performing medical procedures (see Figure 10a), taking exams (see Figure 10b) and medication (see Figure 10c), which can be undertaken simultaneously, according to the patient diagnosis. The treatment subprocesses (procedures, exams and medication) can be executed one or more times in a continuous manner, alternating between different subprocess activities. The models obtained with the Disco tool help to clarify the details of how activities are performed on each particular subprocess. Based on the obtained models, evaluation by the ER experts can then be performed.

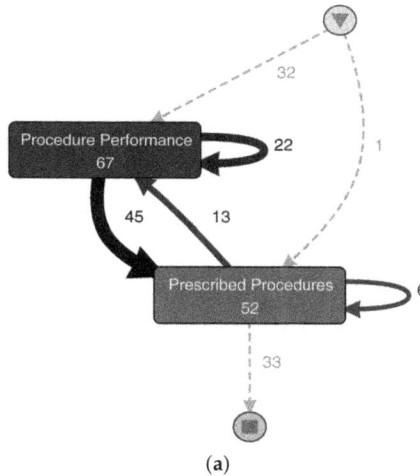

(a)

Figure 10. *Cont.*

(b)

(c)

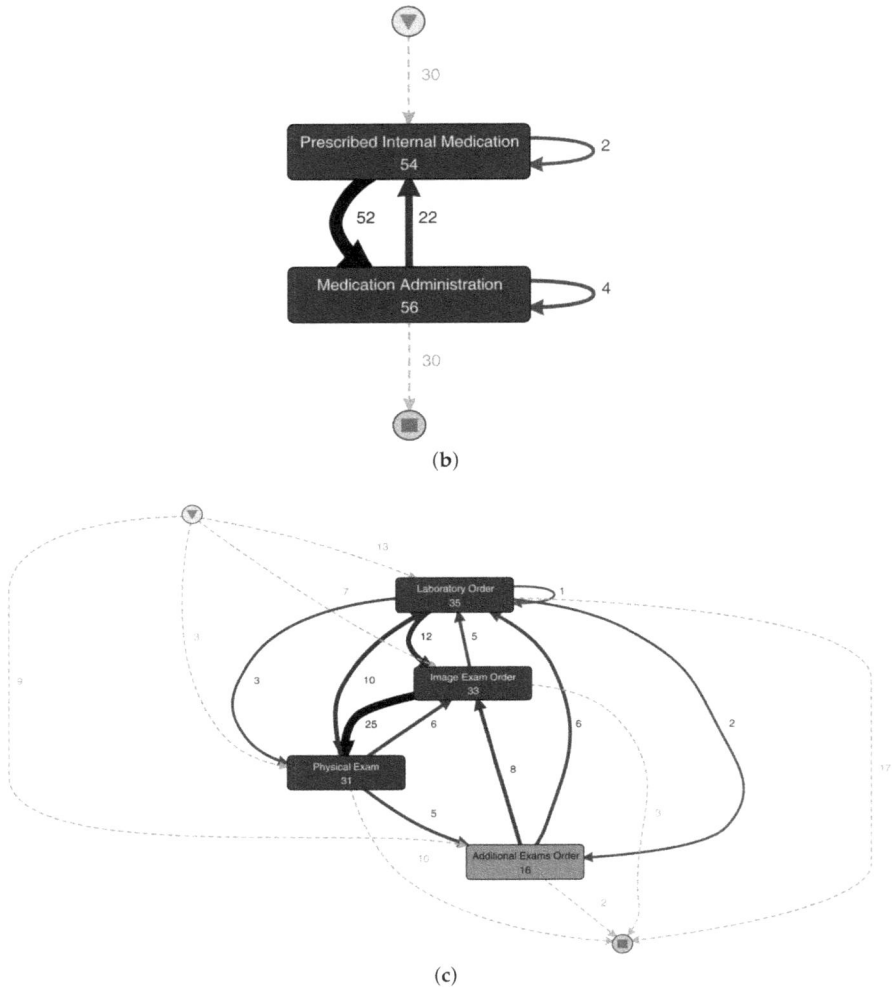

Figure 10. Process models for medical procedures, medication activities and taking exams (activities: <1%; Paths: <1%). (**a**) Process model for activities that relate to the execution of medical procedures; (**b**) process model for medication activities; (**c**) process model for activities that relate to taking exams.

Stage 6. Results evaluation:

Subsequent to obtaining the data, characteristics and models for the analyzed cases, an evaluation was conducted with an ER expert in the emergency room. This evaluation was undertaken by means of an interview with open questions in relation to the results obtained, including the following: Do you consider the model to accurately reflect the reality of the processes followed during the attention of patients with this diagnosis? Do you consider the discovered activities to be correct? In general, do the data and models provide an answer to the frequently-posed questions about this diagnosis? The respondent provided affirmative answers, with the expert confirming that the data and process models can be used to understand the process followed in attending to patients in ER diagnosed with appendicitis. The expert received additional information regarding the cases analyzed and confirmed that the present activities and subprocesses, as well as the behavior identified are correct. The main objective of the interview and the evaluation was to confirm that for a standard, known and understood process (patients diagnosed with appendicitis), process mining and data analysis may provide the details required to answer any questions related with it.

Accordingly, it is possible to confirm that the methodology, in conjunction with the analysis of the data and processes, provides the necessary steps to generate the data and models required in order to answer the questions posed. Additional experts may be required in order to analyze the resulting models and information, and to verify if the process is the best or how it can be improved. For the purpose of this initial phase of the research, the ER expert confirms that the tools and methodology provide the required outputs for further analysis.

5. Discusion

Section 4 outlined a case study in which the proposed methodology was applied. This section discusses the most important results obtained, from two different perspectives: the ER specialist perspective and the process mining specialist perspective.

5.1. The ER Perspective

The use of process mining and data mining techniques allowed answering a question frequently posed by ER experts. The most significant contributions of this research relate to the data model for linking data from ER and the methodology that demonstrates the necessary steps for obtaining data and process models in order to answer the frequently-posed questions.

The data extraction process is the most critical stage of the entire methodology, since in the absence of complete and accurate data in the correct format, the construction of the event logs and the subsequent stages will not produce the desired results. An analysis undertaken by a process mining expert is needed with regard to the minimum data required (timestamp and activity names), in addition to one by an ER expert in order to identify the clinical information relevant to the process analysis (critical activities, such as inter-consultations). The provision of a data model establishes the bases for obtaining the minimum data required to construct an event log for analysis purposes in ER, eliminating the dependency on the experts. It also provides a data structure for storing information stemming from the HIS or other existing data sources in the medical facility.

Furthermore, the methodology acts as a tool to guide an ER expert to use data and process mining analysis techniques in the absence of an expert in those particular fields, after the minimum required data are identified and stored in the data model.

The ER expert fulfills a crucial role in the data extraction process because he/she is able to identify the most important data within the process that, in turn, will help to guide him/her to answer the posed question. For example, if the question relates to a specific neurological diagnosis, the expert can emphasize the importance of the inter-consultation to neurology and the magnetic resonance imaging tests; knowledge that, in most cases, process mining experts lack.

In the stage of verification by the experts, the method includes certain tools for analyzing whether the answer obtained is correct. In case the ER expert is the one leading the analysis, some examples are provided in order to be able to verify the answers with other ER experts.

Regarding the results obtained through the process models and data, it is important to note that such findings do not only provide answers to the frequently posed questions, but they also help to acquire additional knowledge about the process. For example, they can help to do the following: identify the stages undertaken in response to different cases in ER; identify activities undertaken in a sequential or parallel manner or those performed specifically for certain patients; verify whether medical regulations and protocols are being adhered to; identify organizational aspects, such as the work of the team as a whole and individuals' roles therein; and provide performance information relating to each case.

5.2. The PM Perspective

For a process mining specialist, analysis will take place from two distinct perspectives: from the data and from the methodology.

Regarding the data perspective, new and original aspects have been exposed. This article proposes the extraction and storage of data in a data reference model. Usually, with data sources that support ER processes, a challenge arises in terms of data being distributed and stored in multiple systems, making the extraction and use thereof particularly difficult. Accordingly, it is important to establish a unique identification number for each case or episode, which is uniform across all systems. Having a unique identification number means that although the activities or tasks executed for any given episode are not stored in the same place, they can all be identified. In addition to a unique identification number, this article proposes a data model in order to centralize the data within one single repository in a way that facilitates the construction of event logs.

The proposed data model is able to store data from all activities related to an episode. The model identifies the main activities of the ER process, from triage and vital signs to diagnosis and inter-consultations. In addition, a unified source of data enables the moment or timestamp in which an activity is executed, as well as the respective resource, to be stored more easily.

Providing the name of the activity, timestamp and resource and establishing a unique identification number for each episode help the architects to design an HIS that is process-oriented and that facilitates the application of process mining techniques and algorithms. In addition, the data model is used to capture information relating to the clinical context of each episode. This information enables the acquisition of simpler event logs with additional information to generate more detailed process models with increased clinical context. For example, it helps to identify the triaging of patients, considering the standard used and the color assigned and, therefore, adding more meaning to the activity.

Regarding the methodological perspective, the proposal introduces original aspects regarding the steps required for extracting and storing the data, constructing the event logs and complementing the use of process mining and data mining techniques; all in order to obtain answers to questions frequently posed by the experts. Furthermore, tools and examples are mentioned relating to the analysis of the resulting models and data in conjunction with the experts.

The data analysis stage helps to ensure that any analysis does not focus solely on the process. Rather, it enables the use of different techniques, which provide clarity in regard to the patterns, trends and characteristics of the dataset used. It is crucial to indicate that the importance does not revolve around the use of just one or more data mining techniques, but in using them in conjunction with the process mining techniques to ensure a more robust process and, as a consequence, to provide clearer and more accurate answers to the ER expert from the process perspective.

The advantages of data analysis, whether statistical or data mining, is that it provides information that complements the overall process, for example predicting trends or defining case clusters. In addition, it produces information shared between clinical cases and facilitates the identification of patterns to classify cases by trends, which can help to simplify the complexity of the models. There is a wide variety of tools available through which these types of analysis can be undertaken, both free and licensed, and therefore, this should pose no impediment to the application of such techniques.

Regarding the process mining stage, the authors recommend techniques, tools and methods to undertake four types of analysis that will help to generate the models, data and information required to answer the frequently-posed questions that arise. The main limitation of process mining tools is the absence of techniques or algorithms that allow one to handle complex spaghetti-type models, which can be reduced by analyzing event logs for specific questions and not the whole dataset or by identifying subprocesses that can be analyzed independently.

It should be noted that the ER experts must be present throughout the different stages of the process and not simply during the final evaluation. The experts are a key input to data collection, in terms of the definition of the questions that require answering, the establishment of the values for filtering the data and during the analysis stages. In fact, during the stage in which answers are evaluated, the larger the number of experts involved, the greater the levels of trust, accuracy and depth will be, regarding the analysis of the answer obtained.

6. Conclusions and Future Work

This article introduced a methodology that focuses on the application of process mining and data analysis techniques and algorithms in order to provide answers to questions about ER processes that are frequently posed by ER experts. The method used a data model that establishes a structure for the storage of ER data, which facilitates the extraction of data and the construction of event logs.

This methodology was tested in a case study undertaken in the emergency room of a university hospital in Santiago, Chile. It was shown that, with the help of a data reference model for ER, in conjunction with a detailed analysis using data and process mining techniques, answers to the questions frequently posed by ER experts regarding their processes can be given in a simpler and straightforward manner.

As part of our future work, we plan to include additional techniques of data analysis (e.g., prediction rules) to obtain improved results prior to the process mining analysis stage. The proposed methodology brings the basic required steps towards the analysis through data and process mining of ER processes. Further improvements to the methodology may be included to adapt it, more and more, to the flexible nature of these processes. Future work may include new stages, such as visual analytics, artificial intelligence, machine learning and behavioral analysis, among others. Additionally, the case study only was executed in order to validate the methodology, but further interesting and frequently-posed questions exposed by the experts will be analyzed in the future with more statistical and expert validation.

Acknowledgments: This project was partially funded by Fondecyt Grants 1150365 and 11130577 from the Chilean National Commission on Scientific and Technological Research (CONICYT), the Ph.D. Scholarship Program of CONICYT Chile (CONICYT-Doctorado Nacional/2014-63140180), the Ph.D. Scholarship Program of CONICIT Costa Rica and by Universidad de Costa Rica Professor Fellowships.

Author Contributions: All authors undertook writing and review tasks throughout this study. The process was coordinated by Eric Rojas.

Conflicts of Interest: No conflicts of interest are reported by the authors regarding this study.

References

1. Institute of Medicine; Board on Health Care Services; Committee on the Future of Emergency Care in the United States Health System. *Hospital-Based Emergency Care: At the Breaking Point*; National Academy of Sciences: Washington, DC, USA, 2006.
2. Welch, S.J.; Asplin, B.R.; Stone-Griffith, S.; Davidson, S.J.; Augustine, J.; Schuur, J.; Alliance, E.D.B. Emergency department operational metrics, measures and definitions: Results of the second performance measures and benchmarking summit. *Ann. Emerg. Med.* **2011**, *58*, 33–40.
3. Jansen-Vullers, M.; Reijers, H.A. Business Process Redesign in Healthcare: Towards a structured approach. *Inf. Syst. Oper. Res.* **2005**, *43*, 321–339.
4. Grol, R.; Grimshaw, J. Evidence-based implementation of evidence-based medicine. *Jt. Comm. J. Qual. Improv.* **1999**, *25*, 503–513.
5. Fernández-Llatas, C.; Meneu, T.; Traver, V.; Benedi, J.M. Applying evidence-based medicine in telehealth: An interactive pattern recognition approximation. *Int. J. Environ. Res. Public Health* **2013**, *10*, 5671–5682.
6. Radnor, Z.J.; Holweg, M.; Waring, J. Lean in healthcare: The unfilled promise? *Soc. Sci. Med.* **2012**, *74*, 364–371.
7. Rojas, E.; Munoz-Gama, J.; Sepúlveda, M.; Capurro, D. Process mining in healthcare: A literature review. *J. Biomed. Inform.* **2016**, *61*, 224–236.
8. Neumuth, T.; Jannin, P.; Schlomberg, J.; Meixensberger, J.; Wiedemann, P.; Burgert, O. Analysis of surgical intervention populations using generic surgical process models. *Int. J. Comput. Assist. Radiol. Surg.* **2011**, *6*, 59–71.

9. Fernandez-Llatas, C.; Lizondo, A.; Monton, E.; Benedi, J.M.; Traver, V. Process mining methodology for health process tracking using real-time indoor location systems. *Sensors* **2015**, *15*, 29821–29840.

10. Fernandez-Llatas, C.; Bayo, J.L.; Martinez-Romero, A.; Benedí, J.M.; Traver, V. Interactive pattern recognition in cardiovascular disease management: A process mining approach. In Proceedings of the 2016 IEEE-EMBS International Conference on Biomedical and Health Informatics (BHI), Las Vegas, NV, USA, 24–27 February 2016; pp. 348–351.

11. Mans, R.S.; van der Aalst, W.M.; Vanwersch, R.J.; Moleman, A.J. Process mining in healthcare: Data challenges when answering frequently posed questions. In *Process Support and Knowledge Representation in Health Care*; Springer: Berlin/Heidelberg, Germany, 2013; pp. 140–153.

12. Mans, R.; Schonenberg, M.; Song, M.; van der Aalst, W.M.; Bakker, P.J. Application of process mining in healthcare—A case study in a dutch hospital. In Proceedings of the International Joint Conference on Biomedical Engineering Systems and Technologies, Madeira, Portugal, 28–31 January 2008; pp. 425–438.

13. Grando, M.; Schonenberg, M.; van der Aalst, W. Semantic-based conformance checking of computer interpretable medical guidelines. In *Biomedical Engineering Systems and Technologies, Proceedings of the 4th International Joint Conference on Biomedical Engineering Systems and Technologies, Rome, Italy, 26–29 January 2011*; Springer: Berlin, Germany, 2011; pp. 285–300.

14. Rebuge, Á.; Ferreira, D.R. Business process analysis in healthcare environments: A methodology based on process mining. *Inf. Syst.* **2012**, *37*, 99–116.

15. Partington, A.; Wynn, M.; Suriadi, S.; Ouyang, C.; Karnon, J. Process mining for clinical processes: A comparative analysis of four Australian hospitals. *ACM Trans. Manag. Inf. Syst. (TMIS)* **2015**, *5*, 19.

16. Basole, R.C.; Braunstein, M.L.; Kumar, V.; Park, H.; Kahng, M.; Chau, D.H.P.; Tamersoy, A.; Hirsh, D.A.; Serban, N.; Bost, J.; et al. Understanding variations in pediatric asthma care processes in the emergency department using visual analytics. *J. Am. Med. Inform. Assoc.* **2015**, *22*, 318–323.

17. Mejri, A.; Ghannouchi, S.A.; Martinho, R.; Elhadj, F. Enhancing business process flexibility in an emergency care process. In Proceedings of the 2016 IEEE/ACIS 15th International Conference on Computer and Information Science (ICIS), Okayama, Japan, 26–29 June 2016; pp. 1–6.

18. McGregor, C.; Catley, C.; James, A. A process mining driven framework for clinical guideline improvement in critical care. In Proceedings of the Learning from Medical Data Streams Workshop, Bled, Slovenia, 6 July 2011.

19. Van der Aalst, W. *Process Mining: Data Science in Action*; Springer: Cham, Switzerland, 2016.

20. Mans, R.; van der Aalst, W.M.P.; Vanwersch, R.J.B. *Process Mining in Healthcare—Evaluating and Exploiting Operational Healthcare Processes*; Springer Briefs in Business Process Management; Springer: Cham, Switzerland, 2015.

21. Mackway-Jones, K.; Robertson, C. Emergency triage. *BMJ Br. Med. J. Int. Ed.* **1997**, *314*, 1056.

22. Perimal-Lewis, L.; Qin, S.; Thompson, C.; Hakendorf, P. Gaining insight from patient journey data using a process-oriented analysis approach. In Proceedings of the Fifth Australasian Workshop on Health Informatics and Knowledge Management-Volume 129, Melbourne, Australia , 31 January–3 February 2012; Australian Computer Society, Inc.: Darlinghurst, Australia, 2012; pp. 59–66.

23. Silverston, L. *The Data Model Resource Book, Vol. 2: A Library of Data Models for Specific Industries*; Wiley: Hoboken, NJ, USA, 2001.

24. Suriadi, S.; Andrews, R.; ter Hofstede, A.H.; Wynn, M.T. Event log imperfection patterns for process mining: Towards a systematic approach to cleaning event logs. *Inf. Syst.* **2017**, *64*, 132–150.

25. Bose, R.J.C.; Mans, R.S.; van der Aalst, W.M. Wanna improve process mining results? In Proceedings of the 2013 IEEE Symposium on Computational Intelligence and Data Mining (CIDM), Singapore, 16–19 April 2013; pp. 127–134.

26. Günther, C.W.; Rozinat, A. Disco: Discover Your Processes. *Citeseer* **2012**, *940*, 40–44.

27. Claes, J.; Poels, G., Process Mining and the ProM Framework: An Exploratory Survey. In *Business Process Management Workshops: BPM 2012 International Workshops, Tallinn, Estonia, 3 September 2012*; Revised Papers; Springer: Berlin/Heidelberg, Germany, 2013; pp. 187–198.

28. Han, J.; Kamber, M.; Pei, J. *Data Mining: Concepts and Techniques*; Elsevier: Amsterdam, The Netherlands, 2011.

29. Rozinat, A.; van der Aalst, W.M. Decision mining in ProM. In *International Conference on Business Process Management*; Springer: Berlin/Heidelberg, Germany, 2006; pp. 420–425.

30. Suriadi, S.; Mans, R.S.; Wynn, M.T.; Partington, A.; Karnon, J. Measuring patient flow variations: A cross-organisational process mining approach. In Proceedings of the Asia-Pacific Conference on Business Process Management, Brisbane, Australia, 3–4 July 2014; pp. 43–58.

31. Dagliati, A.; Sacchi, L.; Cerra, C.; Leporati, P.; de Cata, P.; Chiovato, L.; Holmes, J.H.; Bellazzi, R. Temporal data mining and process mining techniques to identify cardiovascular risk-associated clinical pathways in Type 2 diabetes patients. In Proceedings of the 2014 IEEE-EMBS International Conference on Biomedical and Health Informatics (BHI), Piscataway, NJ, USA, 1–4 June 2014; pp. 240–243.

32. Kumar, V.; Park, H.; Basole, R.C.; Braunstein, M.; Kahng, M.; Chau, D.H.; Tamersoy, A.; Hirsh, D.A.; Serban, N.; Bost, J.; et al. Exploring clinical care processes using visual and data analytics: Challenges and opportunities. In Proceedings of the 20th ACM SIGKDD Conference on Knowledge Discovery and Data Mining Workshop on Data Science for Social Good, New York, NY, USA, 24–27 August 2014.

33. Weijters, A.; van der Aalst, W.M.; de Medeiros, A.A. Process mining with the heuristics miner-algorithm. *Tech. Univ. Eindh. Tech. Rep. WP* **2006**, *166*, 1–34.

34. Günther, C.W.; van der Aalst, W.M. Fuzzy mining–adaptive process simplification based on multi-perspective metrics. In *Business Process Management*; Springer: Cham, Switzerland, 2007; pp. 328–343.

35. De Medeiros, A.K.A.; Weijters, A.J.; van der Aalst, W.M. Genetic process mining: An experimental evaluation. *Data Min. Knowl. Discov.* **2007**, *14*, 245–304.

36. Leemans, S.J.; Fahland, D.; van der Aalst, W.M. Discovering block-structured process models from event logs containing infrequent behaviour. In *Business Process Management Workshops*; Springer: Cham, Switzerland, 2014; pp. 66–78.

37. Van der Aalst, W.M.P. Business alignment: Using process mining as a tool for Delta analysis and conformance testing. *Requir. Eng.* **2005**, *10*, 198–211.

38. Van der Aalst, W.; Adriansyah, A.; van Dongen, B. Replaying history on process models for conformance checking and performance analysis. *Wiley Interdiscip. Rev. Data Min. Knowl. Discov.* **2012**, *2*, 182–192.

39. Munoz-Gama, J. *Conformance Checking and Diagnosis in Process Mining: Comparing Observed and Modeled Processes*; Springer: Cham, Switzerland, 2017.

40. Song, M.; van der Aalst, W.M. Towards comprehensive support for organizational mining. *Decis. Support Syst.* **2008**, *46*, 300–317.

41. Sampieri, R.H.; Collado, C.F.; Lucio, P.B.; Pérez, M.D.L.L.C. *Metodología de la Investigación*; McGraw-Hill: New York, NY, USA, 1998.

applied
sciences

MDPI

Article

Chinese Medical Question Answer Matching Using End-to-End Character-Level Multi-Scale CNNs

Sheng Zhang *, Xin Zhang, Hui Wang, Jiajun Cheng, Pei Li and Zhaoyun Ding

College of Information Systems and Management, National University of Defense Technology, Changsha 410073, China; ijunzhanggm@gmail.com (X.Z.); huiwang@nudt.edu.cn (H.W.); jiajun.cheng@nudt.edu.cn (J.C.); peili@nudt.edu.cn (P.L.); zyding@nudt.edu.cn (Z.D.)
* Correspondence: zhangsheng@nudt.edu.cn; Tel.: +86-0731-8457-6454

Received: 4 July 2017; Accepted: 26 July 2017; Published: 28 July 2017

Abstract: This paper focuses mainly on the problem of Chinese medical question answer matching, which is arguably more challenging than open-domain question answer matching in English due to the combination of its domain-restricted nature and the language-specific features of Chinese. We present an end-to-end character-level multi-scale convolutional neural framework in which character embeddings instead of word embeddings are used to avoid Chinese word segmentation in text preprocessing, and multi-scale convolutional neural networks (CNNs) are then introduced to extract contextual information from either question or answer sentences over different scales. The proposed framework can be trained with minimal human supervision and does not require any handcrafted features, rule-based patterns, or external resources. To validate our framework, we create a new text corpus, named cMedQA, by harvesting questions and answers from an online Chinese health and wellness community. The experimental results on the cMedQA dataset show that our framework significantly outperforms several strong baselines, and achieves an improvement of top-1 accuracy by up to 19%.

Keywords: question answer matching; medical domain; question answering; answer selection; character embeddings

1. Introduction

Along with the rapid growth of the (mobile) Internet, more and more people in China choose to seek medical help by posting questions on some online health and wellness communities, such as DingXiangYuan (http://dxy.com/) and XunYiWenYao (http://www.xywy.com/). This provides great convenience for users to get medical advice from qualified doctors, as they need not go to the hospital and are able ask questions anywhere and anytime. However, a large number of users—many of whom often ask similar, if not identical, questions—have placed a tremendous burden on the doctor-side, and cause timely reply to be nearly impossible. Thus, to enhance the user experience, it is essential to develop techniques which can efficiently address the problem of medical question answer matching; namely, selecting automatically from some existing medical answer records (e.g., those posted previously by the registered doctors) the one that best matches a user's question.

This paper focuses mainly on the problem of *Chinese medical question answer matching*, in which the languages of questions and answers under consideration are both limited to be Chinese. Compared with open-domain question answer matching in English studied recently by Feng et al. [1] and Tan et al. [2], the problem investigated in this paper is arguably more challenging due to the combination of two main factors: (1) the domain-restricted nature; and (2) some language-specific features of Chinese. The underlying challenges are further discussed as follows.

First of all, due to the lack of delimiters between Chinese words, word segmentation is normally taken as an indispensable preprocessing step for many Chinese natural language processing (NLP) tasks such as part-of-speech (POS) tagging and semantic parsing, and thus considerably impacts the accuracy of those downstream tasks. Though the performance of the off-the-shelf Chinese word segmentation toolkits (e.g., ICTCLAS (http://ictclas.nlpir.org/), Jieba (https://github.com/fxsjy/jieba), THULAC (http://thulac.thunlp.org/), LTP (https://github.com/HIT-SCIR/ltp)) has reached a level satisfactory to many practical applications, they still yield errors [3], which would be inevitably propagated through the framework with a pipelined architecture and hence cause overall performance degradation. Moreover, the great variety of proper terms contained would cause further and sometimes very sharp accuracy decline to those general-purpose word segmentation tools when being directly applied to medical texts. For example, the medical terms "盐酸 西替利嗪 片" (cetirizine hydrochloride tablets) and "葡萄糖酸钙 片" (calcium gluconate tablets) in Table 1 are incorrectly segmented into "盐酸 西替 利嗪 片" and "葡萄糖 酸 钙片" by the Jieba segmentation toolkit (https://github.com/fxsjy/jieba). Although the introduction of domain-specific lexicons can mitigate the negative effect of professional terminology on word segmentation, building such lexicons always seems prohibitive, as it involves a large amount of manual labor and requires a great deal of domain-specific knowledge and expertise. Even worse is that pre-defined lexicons tend to be inappropriate when coping with the user-composed and unedited medical questions and answers posted on online communities, as they are written in an informal style and often contain many short-hand notations, non-standard acronyms, and even typos and ungrammatical sentences. For instance, "坐 (sit)" and "不听使唤 (out of control)" are incorrectly typed as "做 (do)" and "不停使唤 (keep calling)" respectively, in the question given in Table 1.

Table 1. An example of a question with its ground-truth answer and an irrelevant answer from the cMedQA dataset.

我经常做(坐)的太久，站起来，右脚就会不停(听)使唤的像抽筋一样！不知道怎么回事！ **Question**: When I get up after sitting for too long, my right foot is out of control like getting cramps! I don't know what's the matter!
你好：这种情况考虑缺钙引起的症状，最好到医院检查微量元素看看可以结合医生服用 钙片治疗看看，如钙尔奇或葡萄糖酸钙等，注意多吃蔬菜，水果。 **One Good Answer**: Hello: The symptom is caused by calcium deficiency and you'd better get medical tests for trace elements at the hospital. You can also take calcium tablets, such as Caltrate or calcium gluconate tablets, and eat more vegetables and fruits.
你好，根据你的情况，建议口服盐酸西替利嗪片或者葡萄糖酸钙片治疗就可以。 少吃一些辛辣刺激的东西，多吃蔬菜水果等清凉的食物，另外，还要保持皮肤的清洁， 每天洗澡的时候可以用具有杀菌作用的浴液。 **One Irrelevant Answer**: Hello, according to your situation, I suggest that you should take cetirizine hydrochloride tablets or calcium gluconate tablets. You'd better eat less irritating food, and more fruits and vegetables. Moreover, you'd better keep your skin clean, and take a shower every day with sterilized bath liquid.

To address the above issues, we present an end-to-end deep learning framework using character-level multi-scale convolutional neural networks (CNNs). Specifically, the framework adopts a character-level representation, viz. the character embeddings, instead of word embeddings conventionally used, so as to avoid word segmentation during preprocessing as well as its negative impacts on subsequent components. Such representations are pre-trained using the Chinese characters in both questions and answers, and similar to word embeddings, describe each character as a fixed-length vector.

Since characters are less semantically meaningful compared with words in Chinese, the matching task depends more upon the capability of subsequent modules to extract relevant semantic information. This motivates us to introduce CNNs into the proposed framework, which have been proven to be good at capturing the local context of characters and words (i.e., the local interaction and dependency within n-gram). As different Chinese phrases (or words) are often different in length, we employ multi-scale CNNs (multiCNNs) to capture the interaction between them more appropriately, and hence to better encode the semantic association between the questions and answers. The proposed multiCNNs module consists of a stack of feature maps with different scales.

To validate the proposed framework, we develop a dataset by collecting questions and answers from an online Chinese medical questions answering website (http://www.xywy.com), on which questions posted by users mainly contain the description of symptoms, diagnosis and treatment of diseases, use of drugs, psychological counseling, etc., and only certified doctors are permitted to answer questions. The dataset, named cMedQA, consists of 54,000 questions and more than 101,000 answers. We made cMedQA publicly available for academic use only (https://github.com/zhangsheng93/cMedQA). Table 1 gives an example of our data. More details of cMedQA can be found in Section 4.1.

In summary, the contribution of this paper is four-fold:

* To our best knowledge, we are the first to investigate the challenging problem of medical question answer matching in Chinese.
* We propose a character-level multi-scale CNN architecture for representation learning of Chinese medical texts, which employs character embeddings to circumvent the negative influence of Chinese word segmentation, and uses multiple convolutional feature maps to extract semantic information over different scales.
* We create and release the cMedQA dataset, which to the best of our knowledge is the first publicly available Chinese medical questions answer matching corpus.
* The experimental results on the cMedQA dataset demonstrate that the proposed framework significantly outperforms a variety of strong baselines with an improvement of top-1 accuracy by up to 19%.

The rest of the paper is organized as follows: Section 2 briefly overviews the related work; Section 3 presents the end-to-end character-level multi-scale convolutional neural framework; Experimental setting and results are described in Section 4; Finally, we draw conclusions and discuss future work in Section 5.

2. Related Work

Two broad classes of related work pertinent to our work are briefly surveyed in this section. First, we review the previous studies on traditional question answering. Next, we overview the recent work on applying deep learning to open-domain question answer matching.

2.1. Traditional Question Answering

Traditional approaches to medical question answering normally involve rule-based algorithms and statistical methods with handcrafted feature sets.

Jain and Dodiya [4] present rule-based architectures for question-answering systems in the medical domain and also discuss in detail the intricacies of rule-based question processing and answers retrieval. However, as user questions are always presented in a large number of different ways, rule-based methods may not be able to cover all such linguistic variety.

Wang et al. [5] propose an alternative approach, which first splits sentences into words to train the word vector for each sentence and then evaluates the similarity of each question–answer pair by computing the similarity between individual words. Abacha and Zweigenbaum [6] translate questions to machine-readable representations. The approach is thus able to convert a wide range of natural language questions into a standard language form. Later, the authors [7] extend their previous work by applying semantic techniques at both the representation and interrogation levels so as to create a structured query to match the entries in the knowledge base. These methods depend on manually designed patterns and handcrafted features, which often involve tremendous human labor and expertise.

Li [8] employs a multi-label classification method and the BM25 values [9] to retrieve from a pre-built corpus multiple questions, together with their answers, that are similar to the input one. The resulting answers are further ranked to form a single passage using the TextRank algorithm proposed by Mihalcea and Tarau [10]. The proposed approach is essentially an information retrieval (IR)-based one, and the basic ideas are query expansion and retrieval results summarization.

Goodwin and Harabagiu [11] present a novel framework to select and rank scientific articles containing answers for clinical decision support (CDS) [12]. However, this method is likely to suffer from the lack of available external resources and the complexity of parsing differently structured texts.

Some models about Chinese question answering have been proposed recently. Li and Croft [13] constructed a Chinese question answering system named Marsha. The system recognizes known question types and formulates queries, then searches and extracts answers. Li et al. [14] proposed a method to calculate the similarity of two sentences by computing the similarity between words. Li et al. [15] constructed a semantic pattern matching model for musical domain to automatically translate questions to SPARQL queries for building the final answers. However, these methods take word segmentation as an essential step of Chinese text processing, and they do not take the inaccuracy of word segmentation toolkits into consideration, although the accuracy of word segmentation toolkit in general domain is satisfactory. Wang et al. [16] proposed an approach integrating count-based and embedding-based features. They also point out in their work that character-based models outperform word-based models, which gives us a hint that dealing with Chinese characters may avoid the inaccuracy brought by word segmentation.

To summarize, some traditional question answering methods often rely too much on manually developed rules, well-designed patterns, matching of pre-defined labels, and various external resources, which lead them to be human-labor intensive and vulnerable to concept drift frequently occurring when being applied to new datasets. In addition, some previous studies in Chinese question answering do not consider the adverse effect of word segmentation, and the adverse effect may become particularly prominent when we process domain-specific texts. As far as we know, few works have been dedicated to the key task of Chinese medical question answer matching, which is the focus of this paper.

2.2. Deep Learning in Open-Domain Question Answer Matching

As deep learning techniques have the advantage of capturing both low- and high-level semantics, they begin to be applied to open-domain question answer matching in recent years.

Hu et al. [17] proposed two different convolutional models to learn representations of sentences, which is the pioneer work for solving general sentence matching problems using neural networks. Following that, Feng et al. [1] and Zhou et al. [18] employed CNNs to learn the representations of questions and answers, which are further used to compute the similarity between different questions and their candidate answers. Later, in order to extract sequence information from a sentence, Tan et al. [2,19] utilized recurrent neural networks (RNNs) and their variant, long short-term memory networks (LSTMs), to learn the sentence-level representations. It is noteworthy that the authors also exploit attention mechanisms to augment the semantic association between questions and answers.

However, all studies mentioned above are pertinent to English texts. The approaches proposed in them are likely to suffer considerable performance degradation when being applied directly to process Chinese documents, as the latter language differs greatly from English.

3. Methodology

In this Section, we present our novel end-to-end character-level multi-scale convolutional neural framework for Chinese medical questions answering. First, we discuss the correct embedding methods for encoding Chinese medical texts. Next, we describe in detail the basic convolutional neural network architectures and our improved multi-scale convolutional neural network architectures.

Figure 1 illustrates our framework, given a question and its answer which are represented by character embeddings. The embeddings are used as inputs to our architecture. Next, feature maps of convolutional neural networks at different scales are applied to extract different local n-gram information. Max pooling is then applied to simplify the representation and to generate vectors for the question and the answer. Finally, the cosine value of the two vectors is computed to measure the similarity of the question and the answer. It should be noted that layers with the same color share the same parameters and weights [1].

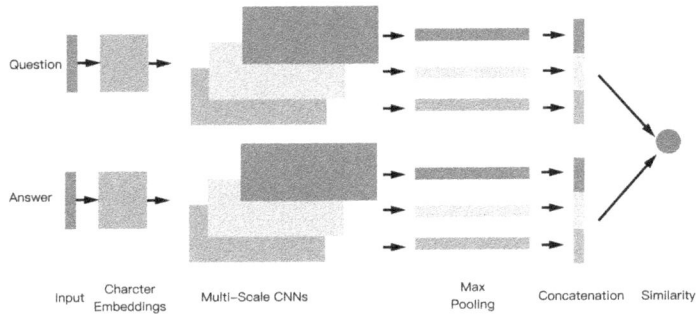

Figure 1. The framework of our model. The question and the answer are first split into characters, and they are represented by character embeddings. The embeddings are then fed into a multi-scale convolutional neural network architecture to extract local information. After that, max pooling layer reduces the representation by choosing the max value along the sequence. Finally, the vectors are concatenated to calculate the similarity of the question and the answer. It should be noted here that layers with the same color share parameters and weights.

3.1. Distributed Representation of Characters

In many natural language processing tasks, one fundamental step is to convert text sequences to machine-readable features, which are always fixed-length vectors. These features determine the upper limit of the effectiveness of the algorithms.

In recent years, embedding-based methods have been used to extract features from text, which shows their utility in semantic representation. A useful and often-mentioned type of embedding method is word embedding, also referred to as the distributed word representation. Bengio et al. [20] proposed a neural network language model (NNLM) which combined a neural network with natural language processing to train word embeddings. After that, Mikolov et al. [21] proposed Word2Vec, a very effective language model inspired from NNLM. Word2Vec has received increasing attention in recent years and has been successfully applied to many tasks, such as document classification [22,23], knowledge graph extraction [24,25], and implicit matrix factorization [26,27].

Shown in Figure 2a is an example of the Word2Vec model. Given a sentence sequence $Sent = [w_1, w_2, \cdots, w_{l_w}]$, where l_w is the length of the sequence and $w_i \in \mathbb{R}^{d_w}$ indicates the word vector of the ith word in the sentence. Let $Context(w_i) = [w_{i-k}, \cdots, w_{i-1}, w_{i+1}, \cdots, w_{i+k}]$ be the context of w_i, where $2k$ is the size of the contextual window. Let $p(w_i|Context(w_i))$ be the probability of the ith word in the sentence being w_i. The target of the model is to optimize the log maximum likelihood estimation (logMLE):

$$\mathcal{L}_w(\text{MLE}) = \sum_{w_i \in s} \log p(w_i|Context(w_i)). \tag{1}$$

However, word-level embedding methods may suffer from the following shortcomings:

1. Word segmentation is an essential preprocessing step for most Chinese NLP tasks. The quality of word segmentation determines the quality of word embeddings, which then influence the

accuracy of the down-stream model. Moreover, word segmentation methods suffer a great reduction in accuracy when directly applied to specific domains (e.g., medical domain).

2. The words that do not or rarely appear in the lexicon or dictionary are called unseen words or rare words. Unseen or rare words may influence the quality of word embeddings.

3. As the number of words is far greater than that of characters, training word embeddings or adopting word embeddings as features may consume a great deal of computing resources and storage resources.

Inspired by Zhang et al. [28], we separate the sentence into individual characters. In order to train distributed representation of characters, we have made minor changes to Word2Vec. As can be seen from Figure 2b, in the context window, each character is used to predict the middle character. After being trained, each character is mapped into a fixed-length vector $c_i \in \mathbb{R}^{d_c}$, where d_c is the dimensionality.

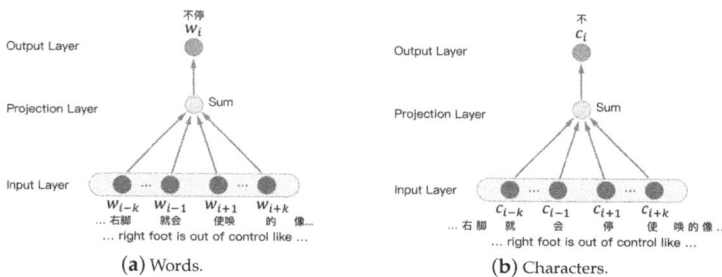

Figure 2. Distributed representation of words and characters.

More specifically, given a sentence sequence $Sent = [c_1, c_2, \cdots, c_{l_c}]$, where l_c is the number of characters in the sequence, the context of c_i is $Context(c_i) = [c_{i-k}, \cdots, c_{i-1}, c_{i+1}, \cdots, c_{i+k}]$. Therefore, Equation (1) can be modified into:

$$\mathcal{L}_c(\text{MLE}) = \sum_{c_i \in s} \log p(c_i | Context(c_i)). \tag{2}$$

Character embeddings reduce the chances of errors brought about by word segmentation algorithms [28]. Furthermore, since the number of characters is much less than the number of words, and the number of unseen or rare characters is also much smaller than that of unseen or rare words, character-level methods reduce the size of the representation of sentences and accelerate the computation. Therefore, character-level embeddings are able to mitigate the adverse effects of word embeddings described above.

Character embeddings have been applied to many tasks, such as neural machine translation [29–32], text classification [33], English factoid question answering [34], and Chinese dependency parsing [28].

Though character embeddings are able to tackle the second and third issues listed above both for English and Chinese, it should be noted that there are still differences between Chinese and English with regard to character embeddings. Character-level methods in Chinese are mainly focused on mitigating the negative impact of word segmentation because there is no natural delimiter in Chinese texts to separate the phrases [28], while various methods in English have been proposed to solve the phenomenon that the words which share the same lexeme have different morphological forms [29]. Besides, the number of Chinese characters is far greater than English characters (only 26) and the characters in Chinese texts also contain more information than those in English.

3.2. A Single Convolutional Neural Network Architecture

As is already known, the meaning of a word (character) is usually affected by its surroundings, especially the context. Currently, the convolutional neural network (CNN) has been proven to be superior in a wide variety of NLP tasks [17,35–37], since the CNN is capable of explicitly capturing local contextual information. The network does not depend on other external information such as part-of-speech tags or a parse tree.

In general, a convolutional neural network architecture consists of two main steps: convolution and pooling. The convolution step extracts local context features using a fixed-size sliding window, while the pooling step selects the maximum or average value of the features extracted from the former layer to reduce the presentation.

More specifically, the question and answer are represented by character embedding sequences having a fixed length: $\{c_1, \cdots, c_{l_c}\}$. We denote the dimensionality of the character vectors by d_c, and each element is a real-valued number, thus $c_i \in \mathbb{R}^{d_c}$. Each sentence is normalized to a fixed length sequence by adding zero paddings if the sentence is short or by truncating the excess otherwise. After embeddings, each question and answer can be presented by matrix $Q_e \in \mathbb{R}^{l_c \times d_c}$ and $A_e \in \mathbb{R}^{l_c \times d_c}$.

Given a sequence $Z = [z_1, z_2, \cdots, z_{l_c-s+1}]$, where the size of feature map is s, and $z_i = [c_i, c_{i+1}, \cdots, c_{i+s-1}] \in \mathbb{R}^{s \times d_c}$ is the concatenation of continuous s character vectors of the sentence, we can define the convolutional operation as follows:

$$O_j = f(W_j \circ [z_1, z_2, \cdots, z_{l_c-s+1}] + b), \tag{3}$$

where $O_j \in \mathbb{R}^{l_c-s+1}$ is the output of convolutional operation, matrix $W_j \in \mathbb{R}^{s \times d}$ and vector b are the parameters to be trained, $f(\cdot)$ is the activation function, and $W \circ Z$ indicates the element-wise multiplication of W with each element in Z. If the number of filter maps is d_o, the output of the layer is $O = [O_1, O_2, \cdots, O_{d_o}] \in \mathbb{R}^{(l_c-s+1) \times d_o}$. Thus, embedding matrices $Q_E \in \mathbb{R}^{l_c \times d_c}$ and $A_E \in \mathbb{R}^{l_c \times d_c}$ are converted into $Q_O \in \mathbb{R}^{(l_c-s+1) \times d_o}$ and $A_O \in \mathbb{R}^{(l_c-s+1) \times d_o}$ through a convolutional neural layer and by sharing the same parameters (W_j and b).

A pooling layer is then applied after the convolutional layer. Max pooling and average pooling are commonly used in the pooling layer, which chooses the max or average value of the features extracted from the former layer to reduce the representation. In this paper, we use 1-max pooling as our method to select the max value of each filter, and max value may be relatively more sensitive to the existence of some pattern in pooled region. The max pooling operation is shown as follows:

$$p = [\max O_1, \max O_2, \cdots, \max O_{d_o}], \tag{4}$$

where $\max O_i$ selects the max value in O_i, and $p \in \mathbb{R}^{d_o}$ is the output vector of the pooling layer.

A vector $q \in \mathbb{R}^{d_o}$ is acquired after max pooling layer, which can be used as a representation of a question. Similarly, a vector $a \in \mathbb{R}^{d_o}$ is also extracted from the answer. The formula that may be used to measure the similarity between the questions and the answers is given as follows:

$$Sim(q, a) = Cos(q, a) = \frac{||q \cdot a||}{||q|| \cdot ||a||}, \tag{5}$$

where $|| \cdot ||$ is the length of the vector.

3.3. A Multi-Scale Convolutional Neural Networks Architecture

As we described above, convolutional neural networks are capable of capturing local contextual information. However, the single CNN architecture usually has single-sized feature maps with a fixed sliding convolutional window. Therefore, the scale of information extracted from the model is limited. Considering the expression structure of Chinese phrases and the variety of expressions available in the language, a single CNN architecture may be insufficient to extract character-level information.

The multi-scale convolutional neural networks (multiCNNs) architecture works in a similar way to the singleCNNs described above, except that they employ feature maps at different scales to extract the information. As shown in Figure 1, the question and the answer are represented using a concatenation of several vectors from the max pooling layer.

More specifically, given a set of filter map sizes $S = \{s_1, s_2, \cdots, s_t\}$, where the ith CNN filter's map size is denoted with s_i, similar to Equation (3), the output of the convolution for the ith CNN is given by:

$$O_j^{s_i} = f(W_j^{s_i} \circ [z_1, z_2, \cdots, z_{l_c - s_i + 1}] + b^{s_i}), \tag{6}$$

where $O_j^{s_i} \in \mathbb{R}^{l_c - s_i + 1}$.

Therefore, the output of the layer becomes $O^{s_i} = [O_1^{s_i}, O_2^{s_i}, \cdots, O_{d_o}^{s_i}]$.

Similarly, after the pooling layer, the output vector from the ith CNN is:

$$p^{s_i} = [\max O_1^{s_i}, \max O_2^{s_i}, \cdots, \max O_{d_o}^{s_i}]. \tag{7}$$

Unlike singleCNN, we concatenate output vectors from different-scale CNNs as the final representation of the question or the answer:

$$p = [p^{s_1}, p^{s_2}, \cdots, p^{s_t}]. \tag{8}$$

After that, the similarity measurement is calculated similarly using Equation (5).

The multiCNNs architecture is fully capable of extracting the relevant language features from Chinese texts. Figure 3 shows an example of the process using which the multiCNNs architecture extracts local information from a region. As we already know, different Chinese phrases usually contain different numbers of characters; therefore, a single convolutional neural network will perform convolutional operation over a fixed-length region, which is similar to combining several adjacent characters into words. Therefore, the multiCNNs architecture performs convolutional operation over different fixed-length regions and extracts a different number of adjacent character embeddings.

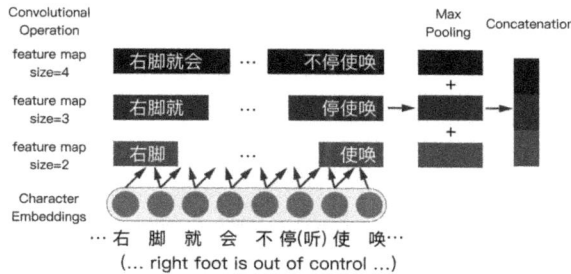

Figure 3. A multi-scale convolutional neural networks architecture. The architecture extracts local features of character embeddings using multi-scale convolutional feature maps. The features are then fed into max pooling layer to reduce the representation. After that, vectors from the pooling layer are concatenated into a single vector.

3.4. Objective Function

Given a question q_i, the ground truth answer is a_i^+, while a_i^- is the incorrect answer randomly sampled from the complete answer pool. A good network would be capable of maximizing $Sim(q_i, a_i^+)$ while minimizing $Sim(q_i, a_i^-)$.

In order to train the neural networks, we follow an approach to [1,17,19], whereby we define the training max-margin loss function as follows:

$$\mathcal{L} = max\{0, M - Sim(q_i, a_i^+) + Sim(q_i, a_i^-)\}, \tag{9}$$

where M is the margin value, which is a constant. If $Sim(q_i, a_i^+) - Sim(q_i, a_i^-) > M$, the cost is zero and no updates are required.

When training the network, we provide each question separately, the ground truth answer and a randomly-sampled negative answer to the network for up to K times. Then, we compute the loss $\mathcal{L}$, and use optimizers such as GradientDescentOptimizer or AdagradOptimizer to update the parameters of networks.

4. Experiments and Results

4.1. Datasets

As there are no public Chinese medical questions and answers datasets available, we have developed and collected a dataset from the Internet. The dataset was acquired from an online Chinese medical question answering forum (http://www.xywy.com/). Questions are proposed by users and are responded to by qualified medical doctors. Each question is often answered by several doctors, and only certified doctors are eligible to answer questions.

To the best of our knowledge, this is the first publicly available dataset based on Chinese medical questions and answers. The dataset is in version 1.0 and is available for non-commercial research (https://github.com/zhangsheng93/cMedQA). We will update and expand the database from time to time. In order to protect privacy, the data is anonymized and no personal information is included.

As shown in Table 2, the data which we refer to as cMedQA is split into three sets—namely, training set, development set, and test set. The second and third columns show the number of questions and answers, respectively. The following two columns illustrate the average number of words per question and answer, while the last two columns indicate the average number of characters.

Table 2. Statistics of the cMedQA dataset.

	#Ques	#Ans	Ave. #Words Per Question	Ave. #Words Per Answer	Ave. #Characters Per Question	Ave. #Characters Per Answer
Train	50,000	94,134	97	169	120	212
Dev	2000	3774	94	172	117	216
Test	2000	3835	96	168	119	211
Total	54,000	101,743	96	169	119	212

While training the framework, for each question q_i in training data, there is a ground truth answer a_i^+ (if a question has multiple ground truth answers, we will choose one randomly each time) and a randomly sampled answer a_i^- from the complete answer pool. Using this mechanism, we generate 30 tuples of (q_i, a_i^+, a_i^-) for each question. Thus, during the training phase, a total of $1,500,000$ tuples are fed into the network at each epoch.

To evaluate the framework, for each question in the development set and test set, we randomly sample 100 candidate answers, including ground truth answers. The development set is used for parameter search and optimization, while the test set is used to evaluate the models. It should be noted that the whole answer space can be regarded as the candidate pool, so each question should be computed for similarities with $101,743$ candidate answers. However, this is impractical because of time-consuming computations [1]. Therefore, we set the pool size to be 100 in our study, which is practical and still a challenging task.

4 2. Metrics

In this study, the top-1 accuracy is used as a metric to evaluate the accuracy of the technique. Top-k accuracy is a commonly used metric in many different information retrieval tasks. The definition of top-k accuracy (*ACC@k*) is given as follows:

$$ACC@k = \frac{1}{N} \sum_{i=1}^{N} 1[a_i \in C_i^k], \tag{10}$$

where a_i is the ground truth answer for question q_i, and C_i^k is the candidate set with top-k highest similar answers. $1[\cdot] \to \{0, 1\}$ denotes the indicator function. When the condition in parentheses is true, the function value is 1, otherwise it is 0.

Unlike traditional information retrieval [38], answering a question requires the provision of the best possible answer rather than a ranked list of answers. Therefore, we have adopted top-1 accuracy (ACC@1) as our metric, which is a highly demanding measurement. Specifically, in terms of a question, if the size of the answers candidate pool is 100, the ACC@1 for random selection methods is only 1%. It should be noted that in our experiment, if a question has multiple ground truth answers, any correctly selected ground truth answer will contribute to the accuracy.

4.3. Baselines

* **Character Matching**: Character matching method counts the number of characters that are the same in the question and the answer.
* **Word Matching**: Similar to the character matching method, the word matching method counts the number of words that are the same. However, this method requires word segmentation; therefore, we use two word segmentation toolkits and present a discussion of the impact of different toolkits.
* **BM25**: BM25 (Best Matching) is a ranking function in Information Retrieval (IR); it has also been used in question answer matching [8,16]. The definition of BM25 is given as follows:

$$BM25(q_i, a_i) = \sum_{w_j \in q_i} IDF(w_j) \cdot \frac{f(w_j, a_i) \cdot (k+1)}{f(w_j, a_i) + k \cdot (1 - b + b \cdot \frac{|a_i|}{|a|_{avg}})}, \tag{11}$$

  where $IDF(w_j)$ is the inverse document frequency (IDF) value of word (character) w_j in question, $|a_i|$ is the length of the answer a_i, $|a|_{avg}$ is the average length of answers, and $f(w_j, a_i)$ is the frequency of w_j in a_i. k and b are free parameters. In our experiment, according to Christopher et al. [39], we set $k = 2.0$ and $b = 0.75$.

* **Average of Embeddings**: Character (Word) embeddings contain semantic and syntactic information, and an average of these can be used to directly represent features. Thus, we compute the average of each question and answer embeddings, and calculate the cosine similarity between the two average embeddings.
* **Embedding Matching**: Inspired by Li et al. [14], we compute the similarity of two sentences by calculating the similarity of words (characters). We modified the algorithm by computing the similarity of every two embeddings, and find the best matching score of each word (character) of the question. The answer with the best matching score will be chosen.
* **biLSTM**: Tan et al. [2] used bi-directional LSTM networks to extract the semantic representations of questions and answers. LSTM networks are a variant of recurrent neural networks (RNN), which are capable of capturing sequence information [2,40,41].

4.4. Experimental Settings

Models presented in our paper were implemented using TensorFlow and TensorLayer from scratch. All questions and answers in the training set are used to train the character embeddings using gensim (https://radimrehurek.com/gensim/). In order to make a comparison between word embeddings and character embeddings, we use two word segmentation toolkits (Jieba and ICTCLAS) for Chinese words segmentation. ICTCLAS is a popular toolkit and reported good F-scores in many segmentation tasks (http://thulac.thunlp.org/). Jieba provides an easy-to-use interface, and we use it as a control. The Python package gensim is used to train both word embeddings and character embeddings. After training, we get dictionaries with $35,933$ (Jieba) words, $20,720$ (ICTCLAS) words, and 3922 characters, respectively. The max sequence length of the question and answer are fixed at 400 for characters and 200 for words. We add paddings to the beginning if the original sequence is short and truncate the excessive parts.

For the CNN, the filter has a size of 3 with 800 feature maps, while the multiCNN architectures have filters of sizes (3,4), respectively, with 800 feature maps each. In this paper, we also use biLSTM [2] to make a comparison. The biLSTM has the output length of 200 in each direction and the hidden states are provided directly for pooling.

AdagradOptimizer is used in this paper, the learning rate is initially set to 0.01, and the margin value is set to 0.05.

4.5. Results

In this section, a detailed examination of the experimental results are presented. Table 3 summarizes the results for different approaches on cMedQA.

Table 3. The top-1 accuracy results of the models. biLSTM: bi-directional long short-term memory network; Multi-CNN: multi-scale CNN.

	Embeddings	Model	Dev (%)	Test (%)
1		Random Selection	01.00	01.00
2		Word Matching (Jieba)	37.05	36.60
3		Word Matching (ICTCLAS)	36.15	37.30
4	None	Character Matching	33.65	34.90
5		BM25 (Jieba)	37.60	40.00
6		BM25 (ICTCLAS)	41.35	41.35
7		BM25 (Character)	44.80	45.40
8	Word (Jieba)		15.60	16.80
9	Word (ICTCLAS)	Average of Embeddings	18.05	18.75
10	Character Embeddings		24.90	24.00
11	Word (Jieba)		24.55	23.65
12	Word (ICTCLAS)	Embedding Matching	27.85	29.10
13	Character Embeddings		30.80	32.30
14		SingleCNN [1]	46.30	47.65
15	Word Embeddings (Jieba)	BiLSTM [2]	51.70	52.70
16		MultiCNNs	48.40	51.15
17		SingleCNN [1]	53.25	53.75
18	Word Embeddings (ICTCLAS)	BiLSTM [2]	56.15	57.65
19		MultiCNNs	54.05	55.40
20		SingleCNN	64.50	64.05
21	Character Embeddings	BiLSTM	61.65	63.20
22		MultiCNNs	**65.35**	**64.75**

Rows 1 to 13 provide a survey of the results of the baseline methods without using neural network architectures. More specifically, as can be seen from Rows 2 to 4, which show the results of matching based methods, the results of the two methods differ by less than 1%. Due to the abundant information contained in words, word-based methods (Rows 2 and Row 3) surpass the character-based method (Row 4). In comparison to word (character) matching methods, BM25 methods (Rows 5 to 7) utilize more statistical information and show up to 11% improvement.

Row 8 to Row 13 show the results of embedding-based shallow methods. Character embedding methods (Row 10,13) take the lead, which indicates that the semantic information of embeddings is better extracted from characters. Word embeddings preprocessed by the ICTCLAS toolkit rank second. However, the average of the embeddings methods is inferior to word matching methods, which may be due to their incomplete semantic information extraction capability.

The following three rows (Rows 14 to 16) illustrate the results of three deep neural models when they are fed with word embeddings preprocessed by the Jieba toolkit. It is observed that the biLSTMs architecture stands out amongst these three models. The potential reason may be that recurrent neural networks include the variant LSTM which is capable of extracting sequence information. They are able to extract the semantic information of the whole sentence, which can effectively reduce the semantic gap between the questions and answers. Our results are consistent with experimental results reported by Tan et al. [19]. Moreover, the multiCNN model shows more than 2 to 3% improvement on the development and test data-sets, respectively.

The next three rows (Rows 17 to 19) show the similarity trends: biLSTM is ranked first, followed by multiCNNs. It is shown that the ICTCLAS method is much more accurate for words segmentation as compared to Jieba in most cases, although it runs slower than Jieba (http://thulac.thunlp.org/). It is also shown in the table that the word embedding methods based on ICTCLAS (Rows 17 to 19) outperform the methods based on Jieba (Rows 14 to 16).

The following three rows (Rows 20 to 22) summarize the results of these models on character embeddings. The multiCNNs architecture achieves the highest performance due to the benefits of multi-scale local information extraction. The singleCNN model ranks second. The performance indicates the effectiveness of the multi-scale convolution operations. Compared to biLSTM models, CNN-based models are shown to be superior to the LSTM-based model with regard to character embeddings. The reason for this is that the CNN models take advantage of local information, which is similar to combining several adjacent characters into words. The biLSTM architecture draws greater attention to sequence information and less attention to local information, as the effectiveness of character-level information extraction is inferior to CNN models.

To summarize, neural network-based methods are superior to word (character) matching methods, which demonstrates that highly diverse and non-formal expressions may confuse the matching methods. Character embedding methods (Rows 20 to 22) significantly outperform the word-level methods (Rows 14 to 19) by up to 19%. The improvements for both CNN-based models and the RNN-based model from character embeddings are remarkable, which demonstrates the effectiveness of our character-level embeddings model for medical-domain questions answer matching.

4.6. Discussion

4.6.1. Random Embeddings vs. Pre-Trained Embeddings

A character embedding matrix is a concatenation of character vectors. The number of rows in the matrix is the total number of characters appearing in texts, while the number of columns is the dimensionality of the character vector.

Normally, there are three approaches to initializing a character (word) embeddings matrix. First, an embedding matrix is randomly initialized with uniformly distributed random real values when constructing a deep neural network. The embeddings matrix is regarded as a parameter and will be updated while training the neural network. This method is used by [35,37,42]. Another initialization method is to use publicly available pre-trained embeddings. These embeddings are pre-trained with some large corpora, such as Wikipedia and Google News. Because of the large number of texts in the corpus, the trained vectors are rich in semantic information and are suitable to be directly used to other models, especially when the dataset is small. This strategy is widely used in general-domain tasks [2,3,43]. Finally, we can also train the embedding matrix with texts according to the specific task. Vectors trained in this way correspond to the dataset. Fundamentally, our proposed architectures belong to the last category.

Since we are focusing on medical care, no pre-trained embedding matrix from a large corpus existed for this application. Hence, we decide to make a comparison between randomly initialized embeddings and pre-trained embeddings from the cMedQA dataset. We also changed the embedding initialization method for the multiCNNs architecture and fixed other parameters.

The multiCNNs architecture with randomly initialized embeddings acquired 62.25% and 63.45% accuracy on development set and test set, respectively. Compared to the results in Table 3, it shows an over 3% decrease on development sets and 1% on test sets, which illustrates that pre-training embeddings from the task-related corpus contributes to the accuracies.

4.6.2. Relationship between SingleCNN and MultiCNNs

From the description in Section 3.3, the multi-scale CNNs architectures can be regarded as an ensemble of different types of CNNs. Therefore, we discuss the relationship between singleCNN and MultiCNNs.

Figure 4 illustrates the top-1 accuracy results for different CNNs with different feature map sizes. As can be seen from the figure, the optimal size of a single feature map is three for both the development set and test set, followed by four and two. It also shows a sharp decrease when the filter size goes up. It is easily understood that words are made up of characters, and two, three, or four are the common number of characters that compose a word.

Table 4 provides a survey of the effect of combining different filter sizes. As can be seen from the table, when we set the filter sizes of multiCNNs to (3,4), it achieves the highest performance, which is in accordance with the results in Table 4. Similarly, when we combine different top sizes (Rows 1 to 4), the performance surpasses that of singleCNN.

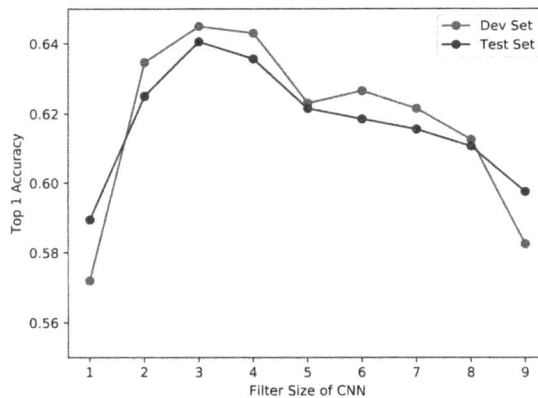

Figure 4. Top-1 Accuracy according to the filter size of CNN.

Table 4. Results of different types of feature maps.

MultiCNNs	Dev (%)	Test (%)
(3,4)	**65.35**	**64.75**
(2,3)	65.00	64.30
(2,4)	64.95	64.15
(2,3,4)	64.90	64.50
(2,4,6)	64.35	64.05
(2,3,5)	64.00	64.25
(3,5,7)	63.40	62.85

4.6.3. Accuracy of Multiple Selection

Traditional information retrieval methods provide several candidates for users to use to select relevant information, while the question answer matching requires the most credible answer rather than a ranked list of answers. However, the lexical gap between questions and answers usually confuses the matching-based methods. Therefore, selecting the correct answer is a crucial step in question answering and requires non-trivial techniques to fully capture the complex and diverse semantic relationship between the questions and answers.

We have proved the effectiveness of our framework in mitigating the lexical gap problem. However, in order to demonstrate that our approaches are superior to existing methods (even when it is allowed to acquire multiple candidate answers for users), we expand top-1 accuracy to top-k accuracy and examine scores for different k values.

Figure 5 shows top-k accuracy results for different k values. Embedding-based methods are applied to multiCNNs architecture. As is shown in the figure, embedding-based multiCNNs architectures outperform matching-based models, regardless of the k value. In addition, these embedding-based methods show rapid growth to 0.95 when k is small. When the accuracy is fixed to 0.90, the k values of green lines are about twice as low as blue lines and four times lower than yellow lines. The same phenomenon occurs when the accuracy is fixed at 0.95, which demonstrates that our character-level embedding-based multiCNNs architecture retrieves relevant information effectively.

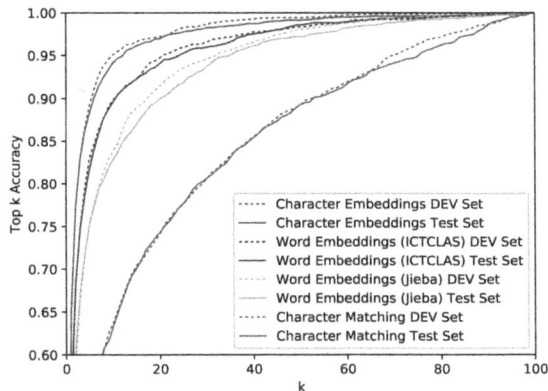

Figure 5. Top-k Accuracy according to k.

5. Conclusions

In this paper, we presented an approach to address the Chinese medical question answer matching task using an end-to-end character-level multi-scale convolutional neural network framework. The framework does not require any extra rule-based patterns, syntactic information, or any other external resources. According to the experimental results, our framework outperforms word-embedding methods, and our multi-scale strategy is capable of capturing character-level information well.

In the future, we would extend our model for disease diagnosis and treatment recommendations according to the description of the symptoms given by users. We aim to construct a hybrid framework that integrates medical domain knowledge into our medical question answering technique. In addition, Chung et al. [41] propose a recurrent neural network model to infer the scale of data by themselves. If the network can discover the latent structure of the sequence, then it can efficiently adjust multi-scale representation of the network to achieve better performance.

Acknowledgments: The work in this paper is financially supported by National Natural Science Foundation of China under grant (No. 71331008) and (No. 61105124).

Author Contributions: Sheng Zhang and Hui Wang conceived and designed the experiments; Sheng Zhang performed the experiments; Sheng Zhang, Jiajun Cheng and Pei Li analyzed the data; Zhaoyun Ding contributed analysis tools; Sheng Zhang, Xin Zhang and Jiajun Cheng wrote the paper.

Conflicts of Interest: The authors declare no conflict of interest. The founding sponsors had no role in the design of the study; in the collection, analyses, or interpretation of data; in the writing of the manuscript, and in the decision to publish the results.

References

1. Feng, M.; Xiang, B.; Glass, M.R.; Wang, L.; Zhou, B. Applying deep learning to answer selection: A study and an open task. In Proceedings of the 2015 IEEE Workshop on Automatic Speech Recognition and Understanding (ASRU), Scottsdale, AZ, USA, 13–17 December 2015; pp. 813–820.
2. Tan, M.; dos Santos, C.; Xiang, B.; Zhou, B. Improved representation learning for question answer matching. In Proceedings of the 54th Annual Meeting of the Association for Computational Linguistics, Berlin, Germany, 7–12 August 2016.
3. Qiu, X.; Huang, X. Convolutional Neural Tensor Network Architecture for Community-Based Question Answering. In Proceedings of the Twenty-Fourth International Joint Conference on Artificial Intelligence (IJCAI), Buenos Aires, Argentina, 25–31 July 2015; pp. 1305–1311.
4. Jain, S.; Dodiya, T. Rule Based Architecture for Medical Question Answering System. In Proceedings of the Second International Conference on Soft Computing for Problem Solving (SocProS 2012), Rajasthan, India, 28–30 December 2012; Springer: New Delhi, India, 2014; pp. 1225–1233.
5. Wang, J.; Man, C.; Zhao, Y.; Wang, F. An answer recommendation algorithm for medical community question answering systems. In Proceedings of the 2016 IEEE International Conference on Service Operations and Logistics, and Informatics (SOLI), Beijing, China, 10–12 July 2016; pp. 139–144.
6. Ben Abacha, A.; Zweigenbaum, P. Medical question answering: Translating medical questions into sparql queries. In Proceedings of the 2nd ACM SIGHIT International Health Informatics Symposium, Miami, FL, USA, 28–30 January 2012; ACM: New York, NY, USA, 2012; pp. 41–50.
7. Abacha, A.B.; Zweigenbaum, P. MEANS: A medical question-answering system combining NLP techniques and semantic Web technologies. *Inf. Process. Manag.* **2015**, *51*, 570–594.
8. Li, C. Research and Application on Intelligent Disease Guidance and Medical Question Answering Method. Master's Thesis, Dalian University of Technology, Dalian, China, 2016.
9. Robertson, S.; Zaragoza, H. The probabilistic relevance framework: BM25 and beyond. *Found. Trends® Inf. Retr.* **2009**, *3*, 333–389.
10. Mihalcea, R.; Tarau, P. *TextRank: Bringing Order into Texts*; Association for Computational Linguistics: Stroudsburg, PA, USA, 2004.
11. Goodwin, T.R.; Harabagiu, S.M. Medical Question Answering for Clinical Decision Support. In Proceedings of the 25th ACM International on Conference on Information and Knowledge Management, Indianapolis, IN, USA, 24–28 October 2016; ACM: New York, NY, USA, 2016; pp. 297–306.
12. Roberts, K.; Simpson, M.; Demner-Fushman, D.; Voorhees, E.; Hersh, W. State-of-the-art in biomedical literature retrieval for clinical cases: A survey of the TREC 2014 CDS track. *Inf. Retr. J.* **2016**, *19*, 113–148.

13. Li, X.; Croft, W.B. Evaluating question-answering techniques in Chinese. In Proceedings of the First International Conference on Human language Technology Research, San Diego, CA, USA, 18–21 March 2001; Association for Computational Linguistics: Stroudsburg, PA, USA, 2001; pp. 1–6.

14. Li, S.; Zhang, J.; Huang, X.; Bai, S.; Liu, Q. Semantic computation in a Chinese question-answering system. *J. Comput. Sci. Technol.* **2002**, *17*, 933–939.

15. Li, T.; Hao, Y.; Zhu, X.; Zhang, X. A Chinese question answering system for specific domain. In *WAIM 2014: Web-Age Information Management, Proceedings of the International Conference on Web-Age Information Management, Macau, China, 3–5 June 2014*; Springer: New York, NY, USA, 2014; pp. 590–601.

16. Wang, B.; Niu, J.; Ma, L.; Zhang, Y.; Zhang, L.; Li, J.; Zhang, P.; Song, D. A Chinese Question Answering Approach Integrating Count-Based and Embedding-Based Features. In *Natural Language Understanding and Intelligent Applications, Proceedings of the International Conference on Computer Processing of Oriental Languages, Kunming, China, 2–6 December 2016*; Springer: New York, NY, USA, 2016; pp. 934–941.

17. Hu, B.; Lu, Z.; Li, H.; Chen, Q. Convolutional neural network architectures for matching natural language sentences. In Proceedings of the Advances in Neural Information Processing Systems, Montreal, QC, Canada, 8–13 December 2014; pp. 2042–2050.

18. Zhou, X.; Hu, B.; Chen, Q.; Tang, B.; Wang, X. Answer sequence learning with neural networks for answer selection in community question answering. *arXiv* **2015**, arXiv:1506.06490.

19. Tan, M.; Xiang, B.; Zhou, B. LSTM-based Deep Learning Models for non-factoid answer selection. *arXiv* **2015**, arXiv:1511.04108.

20. Bengio, Y.; Ducharme, R.; Vincent, P.; Jauvin, C. A neural probabilistic language model. *J. Mach. Learn. Res.* **2003**, *3*, 1137–1155.

21. Mikolov, T.; Sutskever, I.; Chen, K.; Corrado, G.; Dean, J. Distributed Representations of Words and Phrases and their Compositionality. *arXiv* **2013**, arXiv:1310.4546v1.

22. Taddy, M. Document Classification by Inversion of Distributed Language Representations. *arXiv* **2015**, arXiv:1504.07295.

23. Huang, C.; Qiu, X.; Huang, X. Text classification with document embeddings. In *Chinese Computational Linguistics and Natural Language Processing Based on Naturally Annotated Big Data*; Springer, New York, NY, USA, 2014; pp. 131–140.

24. Wang, Z.; Zhang, J.; Feng, J.; Chen, Z. Knowledge Graph Embedding by Translating on Hyperplanes. In Proceedings of the Twenty-Eighth AAAI Conference on Artificial Intelligence, Québec City, QC, Canada, 27–31 July 2014; pp. 1112–1119.

25. Lin, Y.; Liu, Z.; Sun, M.; Liu, Y.; Zhu, X. Learning Entity and Relation Embeddings for Knowledge Graph Completion. In Proceedings of the Twenty-Ninth AAAI Conference on Artificial Intelligence (AAAI), Austin, TX, USA, 25–30 January 2015; pp. 2181–2187.

26. Levy, O.; Goldberg, Y. Neural word embedding as implicit matrix factorization. In Proceedings of the Advances in Neural Information Processing Systems, Montreal, QC, Canada, 8–13 December 2014; pp. 2177–2185.

27. Yang, C.; Liu, Z. Comprehend deepwalk as matrix factorization. *arXiv* **2015**, arXiv:1501.00358.

28. Zhang, M.; Zhang, Y.; Che, W.; Liu, T. Character-level chinese dependency parsing. In Proceedings of the 52nd Annual Meeting of the Association for Computational Linguistics, Baltimore, MD, USA, 23–25 June 2014.

29. Ling, W.; Trancoso, I.; Dyer, C.; Black, A.W. Character-based neural machine translation. *arXiv* **2015**, arXiv:1511.04586.

30. Chung, J.; Cho, K.; Bengio, Y. A character-level decoder without explicit segmentation for neural machine translation. *arXiv* **2016**, arXiv:1603.06147.

31. Luong, M.T.; Manning, C.D. Achieving open vocabulary neural machine translation with hybrid word-character models. *arXiv* **2016**, arXiv:1604.00788

32. Costa-Jussa, M.R.; Fonollosa, J.A. Character-based neural machine translation. *arXiv* **2016**, arXiv:1603.00810.

33. Zhang, X.; Zhao, J.; LeCun, Y. Character-level convolutional networks for text classification. In Proceedings of the Advances in Neural Information Processing Systems, Montreal, QC, Canada, 7–12 December 2015; pp. 649–657.

34. Golub, D.; He, X. Character-level question answering with attention. *arXiv* **2016**, arXiv:1604.00727.

35. Kalchbrenner, N.; Grefenstette, E.; Blunsom, P.; Kartsaklis, D.; Sadrzadeh, M. A Convolutional Neural Network for Modelling Sentences. In Proceedings of the 52nd Annual Meeting of the Association for Computational Linguistics, Baltimore, MD, USA, 22–27 June 2014; pp. 212–217.

36. Kim, Y. Convolutional Neural Networks for Sentence Classification. In Proceedings of the 2014 Conference on Empirical Methods in Natural Language Processing (EMNLP), Doha, Qatar, 25–29 October 2014; pp. 1746–1751.

37. Yin, W.; Schütze, H.; Xiang, B.; Zhou, B. ABCNN: Attention-Based Convolutional Neural Network for Modeling Sentence Pairs. *Trans. Assoc. Comput. Linguist.* **2016**, *4*, 259–272.

38. Goeuriot, L.; Jones, G.J.; Kelly, L.; Müller, H.; Zobel, J. Medical information retrieval: Introduction to the special issue. *Inf. Retr. J.* **2016**, *19*, 1–5.

39. Christopher, D.M.; Prabhakar, R.; Hinrich, S. Introduction to information retrieval. *Introd. Inf. Retr.* **2008**, *151*, 177.

40. Hsu, W.N.; Zhang, Y.; Glass, J. Recurrent Neural Network Encoder with Attention for Community Question Answering. *arXiv* **2016**, arXiv:1603.07044v1.

41. Chung, J.; Ahn, S.; Bengio, Y. Hierarchical multiscale recurrent neural networks. *arXiv* **2016**, arXiv:1609.01704.

42. Cui, Y.; Liu, T.; Chen, Z.; Wang, S.; Hu, G. Consensus attention-based neural networks for chinese reading comprehension. *arXiv* **2016**, arXiv:1607.02250.

43. Yu, L.; Hermann, K.M.; Blunsom, P.; Pulman, S. Deep learning for answer sentence selection. *arXiv* **2014**, arXiv:1412.1632.

applied
sciences

MDPI

Article

Learning Word Embeddings with Chi-Square Weights for Healthcare Tweet Classification

Sicong Kuang * and Brian D. Davison

Department of Computer Science and Engineering, Lehigh University, 19 Memorial Dr. West, Bethlehem, PA 18015, USA; davison@cse.lehigh.edu
* Correspondence: sik211@lehigh.edu

Received: 16 July 2017; Accepted: 11 August 2017; Published: 17 August 2017

Abstract: Twitter is a popular source for the monitoring of healthcare information and public disease. However, there exists much noise in the tweets. Even though appropriate keywords appear in the tweets, they do not guarantee the identification of a truly health-related tweet. Thus, the traditional keyword-based classification task is largely ineffective. Algorithms for word embeddings have proved to be useful in many natural language processing (NLP) tasks. We introduce two algorithms based on an existing word embedding learning algorithm: the continuous bag-of-words model (CBOW). We apply the proposed algorithms to the task of recognizing healthcare-related tweets. In the CBOW model, the vector representation of words is learned from their contexts. To simplify the computation, the context is represented by an average of all words inside the context window. However, not all words in the context window contribute equally to the prediction of the target word. Greedily incorporating all the words in the context window will largely limit the contribution of the useful semantic words and bring noisy or irrelevant words into the learning process, while existing word embedding algorithms also try to learn a weighted CBOW model. Their weights are based on existing pre-defined syntactic rules while ignoring the task of the learned embedding. We propose learning weights based on the words' relative importance in the classification task. Our intuition is that such learned weights place more emphasis on words that have comparatively more to contribute to the later task. We evaluate the embeddings learned from our algorithms on two healthcare-related datasets. The experimental results demonstrate that embeddings learned from the proposed algorithms outperform existing techniques by a relative accuracy improvement of over 9%.

Keywords: word embedding; healthcare; classification

1. Introduction

More and more researchers have realized that Internet data could be a valuable and reliable source for tracking and extracting healthcare-related information. For example, in 2008, Google researchers found that they can "forecast" flu prevalence in real time based on search records [1]. Google later turned this research into one of their projects called Google Flu Trends (GFT) (https://en.wikipedia.org/wiki/Google_Flu_Trends). However, GFT later failed by missing the peak of the 2013 flu season by 140 percent [2]. One reason is the presence of too much noisy data [2]: people who search using the keyword "flu" might know very little about the symptoms of the flu. And some disease, whose symptoms are similar to the symptoms of the flu, is not actually the flu. The failure of GFT does not negate the value of the data but highlights the importance of classification of truly healthcare-related data from irrelevant and noisy data. Healthcare researchers desire to extract more healthcare information from information that people have shared online. Thus, we are more interested in tweets that talk about real disease symptoms as shown in Examples 4–6 which we name healthcare-related tweets, rather than those tweets that simply highlight healthcare information as seen in Examples 1–3 which we name healthcare-noise tweets. The classification task in the healthcare field is a challenging one since both healthcare-related tweets and healthcare-noise tweets might contain some keywords such as "flu" and "health" which makes basic filtering approaches unworkable. Below, we show examples of healthcare-noise tweets (Examples 1–3) versus the truly healthcare-related tweets (Examples 4–6). (The example tweets are all drawn from a published dataset by Lamb et al. [3].) Compared to the healthcare-related tweets, we found that although the healthcare-noise tweets all have keywords such as "swine flu" and "flu shots", they are not really talking about the symptoms of the flu of individuals. With this motivation, the task of this work is to classify truly healthcare-related data from healthcare-noise data that is typically collected through the keyword filtering approach provided by the Twitter API (https://dev.twitter.com/streaming/overview).

1. Worried about swine flu? Here are 10 things you need to know: Since it first emerged in April, the global swine ..
2. Swine Flu - How worried are you? - Take our poll now and check out how others feel!
3. Missed getting a FREE FLU SHOT at Central last night? You've got three more "shots" at it.
4. feels icky. I think I'm getting the flu...not necessarily THE flu, but a flu.
5. Resting 2day ad my mthly blood test last 1 ok got apoint 4 flu jab being lky so far not getting swine flu thats something
6. 38 degrees is possible swine flu watching the thermometer go up. at 36.9 right now im scared :/

Social media, such as Facebook and Twitter, have been widely used by individuals to share real-life data about a person's health. It made the popular social media platforms, such as Twitter, a major source of healthcare-related data. Twitter provides support for accessing tweets via the Twitter API. Healthcare researchers have long been utilizing social media data to conduct their research [3–7]. Because of the popularity of social media platforms such as Twitter, the number of healthcare-related posts is growing fast. To extract further healthcare information, the most basic and crucial task is to discriminate and extract healthcare-related tweets from the massive pool of tweets. Researchers have made efforts to collect healthcare-related tweets [3,8]. Using modern machine learning algorithms and hand-crafted features, such as keyword-based binary features and support vector machines (SVM) with linear kernels [8], researchers are able to collect tweets that are potentially related to healthcare. However, many words are polysemous. For example, "cold" has a potential to talk about the disease but it might refer to the weather; besides the health-related concept, "virus" might also mean computer virus. Thus, tweets that are collected through ambiguous keyword filtering could be irrelevant. Another reason for the limitation of the keywords-based approach is that the set of important words can change over time, e.g., from H1N1, H5N1 to H7N9.

Recent years have seen the success of word embedding algorithms applied to many downstream natural language processing (NLP) tasks such as part-of-speech tagging and sentiment analysis [9–11]. Word embeddings usually learned from neural language models are well-known for representing the fine-granularity of words' semantic meaning. Word2Vec, developed by Mikolov et al. [9], has been shown to establish a new state-of-the-art performance in NLP tasks. Many other researchers have also contributed to the area of neural language model-based word embedding [12–15]. Word embeddings serve as machine-learned features for downstream classification tasks. Compared to the handcrafted keywords approach, the unsupervised word embedding algorithms can be adapted to different tasks and different corpora.

Mikolov et al. presented both the continuous bag of words (CBOW) and skip-gram models in their work. Our work extends the CBOW model. The CBOW model learns to predict the target word from the words in the context window surrounding the target word. The vector representations of the words in the context window are averaged in the process to predict the target word. Thus, the CBOW model treats every word in the context window equally in terms of their contributions to the prediction of the target word.

The CBOW model effectively learns a representation of the semantic meaning of each word as measured by a word-similarity evaluation, as long as the corpus is large enough. Mikolov et al. tested the CBOW model on the 6B-word Google news dataset. News articles are often written by professional reporters. Thus, the sentences are expected to be compact and the sentences should have meaningful semantic words. The intuitive and straightforward idea of equal contribution of every word in the context in the CBOW model is effective enough. However, when the corpus has plenty of slang expressions, abbreviations, emojis and unusual syntactics, such as in a microblog, the default combination that treats every word equally in the CBOW model might not be the optimum solution. We note that not all words in the context window contribute equally to the prediction of the target word. Incorporating all the words in the context window will largely limit the contribution of useful semantic words and bring more noisy or irrelevant words into the learning process.

Some existing word embedding work also learn weighted word embeddings [16–18]. Their weights, however, are based on existing pre-defined syntactic rules while ignoring the ultimate goal of the learned embedding.

Thus, motivated, we propose an alternative, to learn weights based on their relative importance in the classification task. Our intuition is that such learned weights place more emphasis on words that have comparatively more to contribute to the later classification task.

The chi-square (χ^2) statistical test is often used in feature selection for data mining [19]. It calculates the dependency between the individual feature and the class. By utilizing the χ^2 statistics for each word in the corpus as weights, we emphasize words that would later benefit the classification task and de-emphasize words that are usually independent of the class label.

We propose two algorithms based on the CBOW model. Inspired by the max-pooling layer of the convolutional neural network model (CNN), in a small context window setting, the first algorithm selects the word with the maximum χ^2 value to represent the context to predict the target word. The second algorithm keeps every word in the context window but weights them proportionally according to χ^2 values. The main contributions of this work can be summarized as follows:

- We are the first to propose to use the χ^2 statistic to weight the context in the CBOW model to enhance the contribution of the useful semantic words for the classification task and limit the noise brought by comparatively unimportant words.
- We propose two algorithms to train word embeddings using χ^2 on the task of healthcare tweet classification for the purpose of identification of truly health-related tweets from healthcare-noise data collected from a keyword-based approach.
- We evaluate our learned word embeddings for each of the proposed algorithms on two healthcare-related twitter corpora.

2. Related Work

Microblogging sites and online healthcare forums distribute many posts that share aspects of an individual's life and experience each day. The potential for working with great amounts of real healthcare-related clinical records, disease and symptom descriptions and even clinical transcripts attracted many researchers with interesting projects. To further extract and track healthcare information especially from users' social media profiles, the most basic and crucial task is to discriminate the healthcare-related tweets or target users from the massive pool of tweets and users that are irrelevant to the topic. Wang et al. note that prior research on eating disorders only focused on datasets collected from particular forums and communities [4]. Their goal was to identify behavioral patterns and psychometric properties of real users that suffered from eating disorders and not the patterns of people who simply discussed it on Twitter. They proposed a snowball sampling method to collect data based on the labeled eating disorder users' social media connections. Lamb et al. also used tweets to track influenza by distinguishing tweets about truly flu-affected people from the ones that express only concerns and awareness [3]. Because of the subtlety in distinguishing the two types of tweets, a keyword-based approach is insufficient since both sets contain typical keywords. Lamb et al.

proposed handcrafted feature types such as a word lexicon, stylometric features and part-of-speech template features. However, handcrafted features have the problem of scalability. Paul and Dredze [20] build an unsupervised topic model based on latent Dirichlet allocation (LDA) [21] to extract healthcare topics discussed in tweets. Ali et al. designed a platform to detect the trend and breakout of disease at an early stage [8]. They identify healthcare-related tweets from a pre-defined keywords list. Signorini et al. tracked H1N1 activity levels and public concerns on Twitter in real time [5]. They used SVM and handcrafted features such as age, recent clinic visits, etc., to track public sentiment with respect to H1N1, the swine flu. Interestingly, they found hygiene keywords such as "wash hands" positively correlated with the outbreak of the disease.

The popularity of the vector space model lies in its ability to quantify semantic similarities by the distributional structure of the language [22,23]. The assumption here is that words with similar distributional statistics tend to have similar semantic meaning. The distributional structure of the language can be captured by multi-dimensional vectors learned from the words' co-occurrence statistics. The research based on this assumption to quantify words' meaning and similarity is called distributional semantics [24]. There are multiple vector space models implementing distributional semantics, including Latent Semantic Analysis (LSA) [25] and Latent Dirichlet Allocation (LDA) [21]. Landauer and Dumais endowed LSA with a psychological interpretation and used LSA as a computational theory to solve the fundamental problem of knowledge acquisition and knowledge representation [26]. Enlightened by LSA's capability to capture similarity between words and its usage of Singular Value Decomposition (SVD) [27] to smooth the vector and handle the sparseness, Turney proposed capturing the relations between pairs of words and developed a new algorithm called Latent Relational Analysis (LRA) which also used SVD to smooth the data [28]. The context of a target word is defined as a small unordered number of words surrounding the target word in semantic space models. Pado and Lapata incorporated the syntactic information (dependency relations) to represent the context of the target word and formed a general framework for the construction of semantic space models [29]. The development of distributional vector representation of words greatly solves the scalability issue by releasing engineers from tedious handcrafted feature creation work. Neural network language models (NNLM) [30] produce a distributed vector representation of a word, known as a word embedding. The neural language model utilizes the neural network model to predict the word from the words appearing ahead of it [30], thus words with similar context will be mapped to close vector locations. In 2013, Mikolov et al. [9] used a three-layer neural network model to build word embeddings, to capture the semantic and syntactic regularities through the words in the context window of the target word. They proposed two models: the skip-gram and CBOW models. Both learn the vector representation of the word from the context in which the word resides. The skip-gram model trains the weights in the hidden layer and uses a softmax function to produce a probability of appearance in the context for every vocabulary word. Since it is very expensive to compute every word's probability in the corpus for every sample, Mikolov et al. adopt two mechanisms to further reduce the computation: hierarchical softmax and negative sampling. While hierarchical softmax uses a fixed Huffman tree structure with leaves as words in the vocabulary, negative sampling only samples n negative examples instead of the full vocabulary. Tian et al. extended the skip-gram model from Mikolov's work and generated multiple vector representations for each word in a probabilistic manner [31]. Researchers also incorporated syntactic information into neural language models. Levy and Goldberg [16] extended Mikolov et al. [9]'s skip-gram model by replacing the linear context with an NLP dependency-based syntactic context. Their model reported further improvement than the original model in the word similarity task (WordSim353 [32]).

In this work, we focus on an extension of the CBOW model. There are several existing works that also develop this line of research. Trask et al. [33] develop a very simple and effective method, incorporating additional information, the part-of-speech tag attached to each word during training. However, they did not invent a brand new model; instead, they used the CBOW model from Word2Vec. For example, for polysemy disambiguation to train the embedding of (banks, verb) in the sentence

"He banks at the bank", the input of CBOW is ("He", pronoun), ("at", adposition), ("the", determiner), ("bank", noun). For sentiment disambiguation, words are labeled with both the part-of-speech tag and sentiment for adjectives. Similarly, Liu et al. used part-of-speech information to weight the context window in the CBOW model [11]. They argue that in their learning algorithm the part-of-speech tags capture syntactic roles of words and encode inherently the syntactic relationships inside the word vector representation. However, the authors overlook the ultimate goal of the learned embeddings. The usage of the pre-defined syntactic rules to weight the context does not guarantee later success in the classification task in which the trained embeddings will be used.

Statistical measures have long been used in natural language processing. In terminology extraction, a fundamental processing step to extract technical terms from domain-specific textual corpora before complex NLP tasks, statistical measures such as mutual information, log likelihood and *t*-test are used to rank and identify the candidate terms from the texts. Zhang et al. developed a weighted voting algorithm that incorporated five existing term recognition algorithms to recognize both single- and multi-word terms in the text [34]. Most of the five term recognition algorithms adopt both statistical measures and frequency-based measures to rank the terms.

In this work, we propose using χ^2 to weight the context words according to the words' contribution to the classification task. There is existing work which also uses statistical measures in the vector space model. Gamallo introduced a count-based vector space model. Different from most of the co-occurrence context-based word vector space models, the context of the target word in Gamallo's model is the syntactic context (dependencies) of the target word [18]. To store the word–context sparse matrix, Gamallo used a global hash table. One inevitable weakness of count-based model is that the word–context matrix could be huge. Each word can have multiple contexts in the word–context matrix. To reduce dimensionality and only keep the most relevant and informative contexts of the target words, Gamallo used the log likelihood score to select the top R contexts for each word in the corpus. In our proposed algorithms, we also use an informativeness measure, the chi-square statistical test. Different from Gamallo's model, we use the chi-square statistical test to calculate the dependency between each word and the target class. The chi-square value for each word in the context is used as weights based on their relative importance in the later classification task. Another difference is that our work focuses on the neural language model while Gamallo's work extends from the count-based vector space model.

Word embedding algorithms have been applied to the healthcare field. Several studies have shown the performance of word embedding in extracting useful clinical concepts and information from either clinical notes or clinical free text [35,36].

3. Algorithms

In this section, we introduce two algorithms to learn word embeddings for healthcare tweet classification. We first introduce the background knowledge of the Chi-square statistical test and the CBOW model.

3.1. Chi-Square Statistical Test

The Chi-square (χ^2) statistical test has been widely accepted as a statistical hypothesis test to evaluate the dependency among two variables [37]. In natural language processing, the chi-square test is often applied to test the independence between the occurrence of the term and the occurrence of the class. It is often used as a feature selection method in NLP. Formula (1) is used to rank the terms that appear in the corpus [38].

$$\chi^2(\mathbb{D}, t, c) = \sum_{e_t \in \{0,1\}} \sum_{e_c \in \{0,1\}} \frac{(N_{e_t e_c} - E_{e_t e_c})^2}{E_{e_t e_c}} \tag{1}$$

where e_t and e_c are binary variables defined in a contingency table; $e_t = 1$ means the document contains term t and $e_t = 0$ means the document does not contain term t; $e_c = 1$ means the the document is in class c and $e_c = 0$ means the document is not in class c; N is the observed frequency in $\mathbb{D}$ and E is the expected frequency. For example, N_{11} is the observed frequency of documents appearing in class c containing term t; E_{11} is the expected frequency of t and c occurring together in a document assuming the term and class are independent. A higher value of χ^2 indicates that term t and class c are dependent, thus making term t a useful feature since the occurrence of t means the document is more likely to be seen in class c.

Utilizing the property of χ^2 that higher χ^2 values of term t indicate higher likelihood of occurrence in the class c, we use χ^2 to weight the context words in the CBOW model. The key aspect of our discovery is that words with higher χ^2 statistics tend to be keywords for class identification. Thus, we are using the chi-square statistical test to select the lexicon that particularly caters to the specific class identification task of short sentences such as tweets. Our rationale is that in our modified CBOW model, words are weighted according to their χ^2 statistics; words that are likely to be valuable for the classification task are more heavily weighted thus reducing the disturbance of the noise words which are not helpful comparatively to the later task.

3.2. Continuous Bag-of-Words Model (CBOW)

The CBOW model is a neural language model which consists of three layers: an input layer, a projection layer (also known as a hidden layer) and an output layer. In the input layer, the CBOW model uses context words both b before and after the target word to predict it; the vocabulary is represented as an input vocabulary matrix $\mathcal{V} \in \mathbb{R}^{n \times |V|}$; each column in $\mathcal{V}$ is represented as the vector representation of the words in the vocabulary; $\mathcal{V}$ is randomly initialized from the uniform distribution in the range $[-1, 1]$. The matrix $\mathcal{U} \in \mathbb{R}^{|V| \times n}$ is also initialized, which contains parameters learned by the neural language model during training. In the projection layer, the vector representation of the context, $\mathcal{C}$, is calculated as the arithmetic mean of the vector representation of all words w_i in the context window with b words before and after the target word, as shown in Formula (2).

$$\mathcal{C} = \frac{1}{2b} \sum_{i \in [-b,-1] \cup [1,b]} w_i \tag{2}$$

$\mathcal{C}$ is used to calculate the probability of the target word as shown in Formula (3), which is represented as a softmax function over the dot product of the vector representation of the context $\mathcal{C}$ and target word w_t.

$$p(w_t | \mathcal{C}) = \frac{e^{w_t \cdot \mathcal{C}}}{\sum_{w_i \in Vocab} e^{w_i \cdot \mathcal{C}}} \tag{3}$$

Finally, we can depict the loss function of the CBOW model in Formula (4).

$$\mathcal{L} = \sum_{w_t \in \mathbb{C}} \log p(w_t | \mathcal{C}) \tag{4}$$

where over all training tuples in the corpus $\mathbb{C}$, we are maximizing the probability of finding the target word w_t given $\mathcal{C}$, its context. However, to go over all the words in the vocabulary in Formula (3) is expensive. Instead of computing all the words in the vocabulary, distinguishing only the target word from several noise words largely reduces the computation load. This is called negative sampling. In this work, we adopt negative sampling when training the CBOW model. The window size $2b + 1$ and the word embedding dimension n are all hyperparameters.

By averaging the context words, the CBOW model overlooks the fact that the contribution of the words for the prediction should not be equal. We develop two algorithms to re-weight the context words.

3.3. Algorithm I

Inspired by the good performance of the max-pooling layer in the convolutional neural network model (CNN) in which only the maximum value within a window of the feature map is returned, instead of incorporating all the context words, we only select the word with the maximum χ^2 value to represent the context. Thus, Formula (2) of calculating the vector representation of the context is substituted by Formula (5)

$$C = \underset{\chi^2(w_i),\ i\in[-b,-1]\cup[1,b]}{\arg\max}\ w_i \tag{5}$$

where $\chi^2(\cdot)$ represents the chi-square statistical value of w_i for the target class. Although the trained word embedding complies to the property of linear compositionality, in a small context window size, and a corpus containing as much noise such as Twitter, we choose the word from the context window that is likely to contribute the most to the later classification task. The expectation is that this will be more beneficial than the original strategy of averaging all of the context words. We emphasize a small context window size in this algorithm because when the context window is large, there is a greater chance that more than one word with a substantial contribution to the prediction will be included in the context window, thus selecting only the word with the maximum χ^2 statistic might not be beneficial. We test our algorithm in a context window size of $3(b = 1)$, and in Section 4.4 show that our approach can improve performance on data from Twitter.

3.4. Algorithm II

In Algorithm I described above in Section 3.3, we remove all the other words that have smaller χ^2 values and only keep the word with the maximum value to represent the context. In contrast, Algorithm II weights every word in the context window proportionally according to its χ^2 test statistic. Thus, Formula (2) calculating the vector representation of the context is substituted by Formula (6).

$$C = \frac{1}{\sum_{j\in[-b,-1]\cup[1,b]}\chi^2(w_j)} \sum_{i\in[-b,-1]\cup[1,b]} \chi^2(x_i)w_i \tag{6}$$

In the original CBOW model, the words in the context window are treated equally assuming equal contribution to the prediction task. However, the assumption is generally not held based on language characteristics. Previous work also tries to improve this by the pre-defined syntactic rules such as using part-of-speech to weight the words. For example, nouns and verbs are usually more important than prepositions, pronouns and conjunctions; thus they are often weighted heavier comparatively. However, they overlook the purpose and the usage of the learned embedding. The weighting mechanism based on pre-defined rules is not necessarily in line with the classification task. We propose using the χ^2 test statistics as the weighting strategy, which directly links the weights to the term's correlation to the classification task.

4. Experimental Method

In this section, we describe experiments on the two proposed algorithms on two carefully selected datasets.

4.1. Datasets

Our goal is to extract healthcare information from people's profile and Twitter posts. We are more interested in tweets that talk about real disease symptoms as shown in Examples 4–6 which we named healthcare-related tweets, rather than those tweets that popularize the healthcare information as seen in Examples 1–3 in the Introduction which we named healthcare-noise tweets. Our current classification task is a challenging one since both heathcare-related tweets and healthcare-noise tweets might contain keywords such as "flu" and "health" which makes basic filtering approaches unworkable.

We use two datasets in the experiments. The first dataset, called the healthcare dataset, is from Paul and Dredze [20]. It was collected and labeled using Amazon's mechanical turk (AMT) and has two labels: health-related and health-unrelated. All tweets were collected using healthcare keywords filtering as a first step; thus, even health-unrelated tweets contain healthcare keywords. Tweets that were not about a particular person's health (e.g., advertisements of flu shots and news information about the flu) were labeled as unrelated. The statistics of the healthcare dataset are shown in Table 1. The second, called the influenza dataset, is from Lamb et al.'s work [3]. It was also collected from Twitter. It contains tweets posted during the 2009 and 2012 outbreaks of swine and bird influenza. The data is also labeled as influenza-related and influenza-unrelated by AMT workers. The statistics of the influenza dataset are shown in Table 2.

Table 1. Tweet counts for the healthcare dataset (from [20]).

Data	Healthcare-Related	Healthcare-Unrelated	Total
Train	868	1301	2169
Test	217	325	532

Table 2. Tweet counts for the influenza dataset (from [3]).

Data	Influenza-Related	Influenza-Unrelated	Total
Train	2148	1609	3757
Test	537	402	939

4.2. Baselines

We compare the proposed two algorithms with the following baseline methods for healthcare tweet classification.

1. tf-idf + SVM: we calculate the tf-idf scores [39] for the words of each tweet as the features and train a support vector machine (SVM) classifier [40] using the Liblinear library [41].
2. skip-gram + CNN: we train Mikolov et al.'s skip-gram model on the training set for both datasets. We learn the word embedding for each word in the corpus to use as features and train a convolutional neural network model (CNN) for classification [42].
3. CBOW + CNN: we train the original CBOW model and learn the word embeddings for the word in the corpus as a feature and train a convolutional neural network model (CNN) for classification [42].

4.3. Experimental Setup

Preprocessing is necessary when working with the text of tweets. We strip the punctuation, the html tags and hypertext links, and downcase all letters. We use Tensorflow [43] to implement the two proposed algorithms. In both cases, we keep the default model setting as in the Tensorflow skip-gram model codec in Github (https://github.com/tensorflow/models/blob/master/tutorials/embedding/word2vec.py). Word embeddings are learned using a window size of $b = 1$, embedding dimension $n = 128$ and a negative sampling rate of 64. Words with frequency smaller than 3 are eliminated from the vocabulary. We use the stochastic gradient decent optimizer (SGD) to train the two algorithms with a learning rate of 1.0. To perform the χ^2 statistical test, we use sklearn [44] on the training sets of the two corpora. We train CNN models for the two datasets for the classification task. We use filter sizes of 3, 4 and 5 and 128 filters for each filter size in the training process.

4.4. Evaluation and Results

We completed the χ^2 statistical test on the two Twitter datasets. Boxplots for the χ^2 values in both datasets are shown in Figure 1. As we can see, most of the words in the two corpora have a very low χ^2 value. We list the words in Table 3 that ranked highest by χ^2 value. Words with higher χ^2 value are

Appl. Sci. **2017**, *7*, 846

recognizable as plausible keywords for the identification of the health-related tweets. Using the χ^2 statistics in Algorithms I and II, the result of the experiment is shown in Table 4.

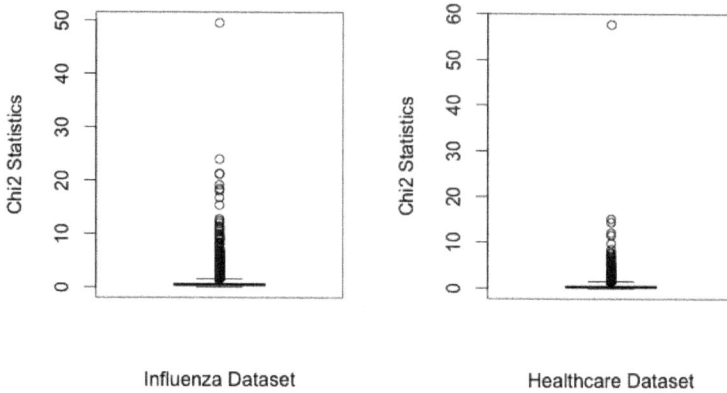

Figure 1. Boxplot of the values of the Chi-square (χ^2) statistical test for the healthcare dataset and the influenza dataset.

Table 3. Words with highest χ^2 value for both datasets.

	Healthcare Dataset	Influenza Dataset
1	headache	sick
2	sick	vaccine
3	allergies	throat
4	feeling	fear
5	flu	news
6	surgery	swineflu
7	cramps	bird
8	throat	shot

Table 4. Comparison of testset classification accuracy across the two datasets using word embeddings from various models. SVM: support vector machine; CNN: convolutional neural network; CBOW: continuous bag of words.

Method	Healthcare Dataset	Influenza Dataset
tf-idf + SVM baseline	59.96	57.18
Skip-gram + CNN baseline	66.61	66.99
CBOW + CNN baseline	69.00	66.67
Algorithm I + CNN	69.19	72.31
Algorithm II + CNN	69.93	72.84

Since we assume equal importance for the identification of both of the two classes, related versus unrelated, we choose accuracy, the commonly used evaluation criteria, as the metric to measure the classification performance as shown in Formula (7).

$$accuracy(y_{lab}, y_{pred}) = \frac{1}{n_{test}} \sum_{i=1}^{n_{test}} 1(y_{pred} = y_{lab}) \tag{7}$$

Since tweets in both classes (related versus unrelated) contain the keywords of the topic, it is not surprising that the keywords-based approach in the tf-idf + SVM baseline behaves poorly for both datasets. For the two Word2Vec baselines, the CBOW model performs better than the skip-gram model for the smaller (healthcare) dataset; they have very similar results in the influenza dataset (which is a larger dataset). Overall, Algorithms I and II improve over the CBOW baseline model by 1.35% and 9.23% respectively. We can see that Algorithm I which chooses the word with the maximum χ^2 value also performs well in terms of accuracy. As we noted earlier, we have a small context window size of $3(b = 1)$. When the context window is larger, more context words are included. It might not be optimal to choose only the word with the maximum statistical measurement score to form the context representation. Our experimental results indicate that the χ^2 weighting scheme of Algorithm II generally outperforms the others.

5. Conclusions

To improve tweet classification accuracy, we use the chi-square (χ^2) statistical test statistic to directly link the weight of each term to its correlation to the tweet classification tasks. We proposed two algorithms: in Algorithm I, assuming a small context window setting, we select the word with the maximum χ^2 value; in Algorithm II, we use the χ^2 statistics to proportionally weight the words in the context window. Our evaluation result shows improvement over the original CBOW Word2Vec model by as much as 9.2%.

Some natural directions for future work include hyperparameter optimization (e.g., selecting the best window size), and testing of other term weighting functions.

Author Contributions: Sicong Kuang and Brian D. Davison conceived the original idea, designed the experiments, and wrote the article; Sicong Kuang performed the experiments and analyzed the data.

Conflicts of Interest: The authors declare no conflict of interest.

References

1. Ginsberg, J.; Mohebbi, M.H.; Patel, R.S.; Brammer, L.; Smolinski, M.S.; Brilliant, L. Detecting influenza epidemics using search engine query data. *Nature* **2009**, *457*, 1012–1014.
2. Butler, D. When Google got flu wrong. *Nature* **2013**, *494*, 155.
3. Lamb, A.; Paul, M.J.; Dredze, M. Separating Fact from Fear: Tracking Flu Infections on Twitter. In Proceedings of the HLT-NAACL, Atlanta, GA, USA, 9–15 June 2013; pp. 789–795.
4. Wang, T.; Brede, M.; Ianni, A.; Mentzakis, E. Detecting and Characterizing Eating-Disorder Communities on Social Media. In Proceedings of the Tenth ACM International Conference on Web Search and Data Mining (WSDM), Cambridge, UK, 6–10 February 2017; pp. 91–100.
5. Signorini, A.; Segre, A.M.; Polgreen, P.M. The use of Twitter to track levels of disease activity and public concern in the US during the influenza A H1N1 pandemic. *PLoS ONE* **2011**, *6*, e19467.
6. Paul, M.J.; Dredze, M. You are what you Tweet: Analyzing Twitter for public health. In Proceedings of the AAAI International Conference on Weblogs and Social Media (ICWSM), Barcelona, Spain, 17–21 July 2011; Volume 20, pp. 265–272.
7. Huang, X.; Smith, M.C.; Paul, M.J.; Ryzhkov, D.; Quinn, S.C.; Broniatowski, D.A.; Dredze, M. Examining Patterns of Influenza Vaccination in Social Media. In Proceedings of the AAAI Joint Workshop on Health Intelligence (W3PHIAI), San Francisco, CA, USA, 4–5 February 2017.
8. Ali, A.; Magdy, W.; Vogel, S. A tool for monitoring and analyzing healthcare tweets. In Proceedings of the ACM SIGIR Workshop on Health Search & Discovery, Dublin, Ireland, 28 July–1 August 2013; p. 23.
9. Mikolov, T.; Sutskever, I.; Chen, K.; Corrado, G.S.; Dean, J. Distributed representations of words and phrases and their compositionality. In Proceedings of the Advances in Neural Information Processing Systems (NIPS), Lake Tahoe, NV, USA, 5–10 December 2013; pp. 3111–3119.
10. Pennington, J.; Socher, R.; Manning, C.D. GloVe: Global Vectors for Word Representation. In Proceedings of the Conference on Empirical Methods in Natural Language Processing (EMNLP), Doha, Qatar, 25–29 October 2014; pp. 1532–1543.
11. Liu, Q.; Ling, Z.H.; Jiang, H.; Hu, Y. Part-of-Speech Relevance Weights for Learning Word Embeddings. *arXiv* **2016**, arXiv:1603.07695.

12. Collobert, R.; Weston, J.; Bottou, L.; Karlen, M.; Kavukcuoglu, K.; Kuksa, P. Natural language processing (almost) from scratch. *J. Mach. Learn. Res.* **2011**, *12*, 2493–2537.

13. Tang, D.; Wei, F.; Yang, N.; Zhou, M.; Liu, T.; Qin, B. Learning Sentiment-Specific Word Embedding for Twitter Sentiment Classification. In Proceedings of the 52nd Annual Meeting of the Association for Computational Linguistics, Baltimore, MD, USA, 23–25 June 2014.

14. Ling, W.; Dyer, C.; Black, A.; Trancoso, I. Two/too simple adaptations of word2vec for syntax problems. In Proceedings of the 2015 Conference of the North American Chapter of the Association for Computational Linguistics: Human Language Technologies, Denver, CO, USA, 31 May–5 June 2015; pp. 1299–1304.

15. Chen, Y.; Perozzi, B.; Al-Rfou, R.; Skiena, S. The Expressive Power of Word Embeddings. In Proceedings of the ICML 2013 Workshop on Deep Learning for Audio, Speech, and Language Processing, Atlanta, GA, USA, 16 June 2013.

16. Levy, O.; Goldberg, Y. Dependency-Based Word Embeddings. In Proceedings of the 52nd Annual Meeting of the Association for Computational Linguistics; Baltimore, MD, USA, 23–25 June 2014; Volume 2, pp. 302–308.

17. Qiu, L.; Cao, Y.; Nie, Z.; Yu, Y.; Rui, Y. Learning Word Representation Considering Proximity and Ambiguity. In Proceedings of the AAAI, Québec City, QC, Canada, 27–31 July 2014; pp. 1572–1578.

18. Gamallo, P. Comparing explicit and predictive distributional semantic models endowed with syntactic contexts. *Lang. Resour. Eval.* **2016**, *51*, 727–743.

19. Howell, D.C. Chi-square test: Analysis of contingency tables. In *International Encyclopedia of Statistical Science*; Springer: Berlin, Germany, 2011; pp. 250–252.

20. Paul, M.J.; Dredze, M. A model for mining public health topics from Twitter. *Health* **2012**, *11*, 16–26.

21. Blei, D.M.; Ng, A.Y.; Jordan, M.I. Latent dirichlet allocation. *J. Mach. Learn. Res.* **2003**, *3*, 993–1022.

22. Harris, Z.S. Distributional structure. *Word* **1954**, *10*, 146–162.

23. Firth, J.R. A synopsis of linguistic theory 1930–1955. In *Studies in Linguistic Analysis (Special Volume of the Philological Society)*; Blackwell: Oxford, UK, 1957; pp. 1–32.

24. Clark, S. Vector space models of lexical meaning. In *Handbook of Contemporary Semantics*; University of Cambridge Computer Laboratory: Cambridge, UK, 2014; pp. 1–43.

25. Deerwester, S.; Dumais, S.T.; Furnas, G.W.; Landauer, T.K.; Harshman, R. Indexing by Latent Semantic Analysis. *J. Am. Soc. Inf. Sci.* **1990**, *41*, 391–407.

26. Landauer, T.K.; Dumais, S.T. A solution to Plato's problem: The latent semantic analysis theory of acquisition, induction, and representation of knowledge. *Psychol. Rev.* **1997**, *104*, 211.

27. Golub, G.H.; Reinsch, C. Singular value decomposition and least squares solutions. *Numer. Math.* **1970**, *14*, 403–420.

28. Turney, P.D. Similarity of semantic relations. *Comput. Linguist.* **2006**, *32*, 379–416.

29. Padó, S.; Lapata, M. Dependency-based construction of semantic space models. *Comput. Linguist.* **2007**, *33*, 161–199.

30. Bengio, Y.; Ducharme, R.; Vincent, P.; Jauvin, C. A neural probabilistic language model. *J. Mach. Learn. Res.* **2003**, *3*, 1137–1155.

31. Tian, F.; Dai, H.; Bian, J.; Gao, B.; Zhang, R.; Chen, E.; Liu, T.Y. A Probabilistic Model for Learning Multi-Prototype Word Embeddings. In Proceedings of the 25th Annual Conference on Computational Linguistics (COLING), Dublin, Ireland, 23–29 August 2014; pp. 151–160.

32. Finkelstein, L.; Gabrilovich, E.; Matias, Y.; Rivlin, E.; Solan, Z.; Wolfman, G.; Ruppin, E. Placing search in context: The concept revisited. In Proceedings of the 10th International Conference on World Wide Web, Hong Kong, China, 1–5 May 2001; ACM: New York, NY, USA, 2011; pp. 406–414.

33. Trask, A.; Michalak, P.; Liu, J. Sense2vec—A Fast and Accurate Method for Word Sense Disambiguation in Neural Word Embeddings. *arXiv* **2015**, arXiv:1511.06388.

34. Zhang, Z.; Brewster, C.; Ciravegna, F. A Comparative Evaluation of Term Recognition Algorithms. In Proceedings of the Sixth International Conference on Language Resources and Evaluation (LREC 2008), Marrakech, Morocco, 28–30 May 2008; pp. 28–31.

35. Kholghi, M.; Vine, L.D.; Sitbon, L.; Zuccon, G.; Nguyen, A.N. The Benefits of Word Embeddings Features for Active Learning in Clinical Information Extraction. In Proceedings of the Australasian Language Technology Association Workshop 2016, Caulfield, Australia, 5–7 December 2016; pp. 25–34.

36. Choi, Y.; Chiu, C.Y.I.; Sontag, D. Learning low-dimensional representations of medical concepts. In Proceedings of the AMIA Summits on Translational Science, San Francisco, CA, USA, 21–24 March 2016; American Medical Informatics Association: Bethesda, MD, USA, 2016; p. 41.

37. Pearson, K. On the Criterion that a given system of deviations from the probable in the case of a correlated system of variables is such that it can be reasonably supposed to have arisen from random sampling. In *Breakthroughs in Statistics: Methodology and Distribution*; Kotz, S., Johnson, N.L., Eds.; Springer: New York, NY, USA, 1992; pp. 11–28.

38. Manning, C.D.; Surdeanu, M.; Bauer, J.; Finkel, J.; Bethard, S.J.; McClosky, D. The Stanford CoreNLP Natural Language Processing Toolkit. In Proceedings of the 52nd Annual Meeting of the Association for Computational Linguistics: System Demonstrations, Baltimore, MD, USA, 22–27 June 2014; pp. 55–60.

39. Robertson, S. Understanding inverse document frequency: On theoretical arguments for IDF. *J. Doc.* **2004**, *60*, 503–520.

40. Cortes, C.; Vapnik, V. Support-vector networks. *Mach. Learn.* **1995**, *20*, 273–297.

41. Fan, R.E.; Chang, K.W.; Hsieh, C.J.; Wang, X.R.; Lin, C.J. LIBLINEAR: A library for large linear classification. *J. Mach. Learn. Res.* **2008**, *9*, 1871–1874.

42. Kim, Y. Convolutional neural networks for sentence classification. In Proceedings of the 2014 Conference on Empirical Methods in Natural Language Processing (EMNLP), Doha, Qatar, 25–29 October 2014; pp. 1746–1751.

43. Abadi, M.; Agarwal, A.; Barham, P.; Brevdo, E.; Chen, Z.; Citro, C.; Corrado, G.S.; Davis, A.; Dean, J.; Devin, M.; et al. TensorFlow: Large-Scale Machine Learning on Heterogeneous Systems. 2015. Available online: tensorflow.org (accessed on 16 June 2017).

44. Buitinck, L.; Louppe, G.; Blondel, M.; Pedregosa, F.; Mueller, A.; Grisel, O.; Niculae, V.; Prettenhofer, P.; Gramfort, A.; Grobler, J.; et al. API design for machine learning software: Experiences from the scikit-learn project. In Proceedings of the ECML/PKDD Workshop: Languages for Data Mining and Machine Learning, Prague, Czech Republic, 23–27 September 2013; pp. 108–122.

![applied sciences logo] *applied sciences*

MDPI

Article

Towards a Predictive Analytics-Based Intelligent Malaria Outbreak Warning System [†]

Babagana Modu [1,*], Nereida Polovina [2], Yang Lan [1], Savas Konur [1], A. Taufiq Asyhari [3] and Yonghong Peng [4]

[1]   School of Electrical Engineering and Computer Science, University of Bradford, Bradford BD7 1DP, UK; y.lan@bradford.ac.uk (Y.L.); s.konur@bradford.ac.uk (S.K.)
[2]   Manchester Metropolitan University Business School, Manchester Metropolitan University, Manchester M15 6BH, UK; n.polovina@mmu.ac.uk
[3]   Centre for Electronic Warfare, Information and Cyber, Cranfield University, Shrivenham SN6 8LA, UK; taufiq-a@ieee.org
[4]   Faculty of Computer Science, University of Sunderland, St Peters Campus, Sunderland SR6 0DD, UK; yonghong.peng@sunderland.ac.uk
*   Correspondence: b.modu@bradford.ac.uk
[†]   This paper is an extended version of our paper published in DIGITALISATION FOR A SUSTAINABLE SOCIETY Embodied, Embedded, Networked, Gothenburg, Sweden, 12–16 June 2017.

Received: 14 July 2017; Accepted: 9 August 2017; Published: 17 August 2017

Abstract: Malaria, as one of the most serious infectious diseases causing public health problems in the world, affects about two-thirds of the world population, with estimated resultant deaths close to a million annually. The effects of this disease are much more profound in third world countries, which have very limited medical resources. When an intense outbreak occurs, most of these countries cannot cope with the high number of patients due to the lack of medicine, equipment and hospital facilities. The prevention or reduction of the risk factor of this disease is very challenging, especially in third world countries, due to poverty and economic insatiability. Technology can offer alternative solutions by providing early detection mechanisms that help to control the spread of the disease and allow the management of treatment facilities in advance to ensure a more timely health service, which can save thousands of lives. In this study, we have deployed an *intelligent malaria outbreak early warning system*, which is a mobile application that predicts malaria outbreak based on climatic factors using machine learning algorithms. The system will help hospitals, healthcare providers, and health organizations take precautions in time and utilize their resources in case of emergency. To our best knowledge, the system developed in this paper is the first publicly available application. Since confounding effects of climatic factors have a greater influence on the incidence of malaria, we have also conducted extensive research on exploring a new ecosystem model for the assessment of hidden ecological factors and identified three confounding factors that significantly influence the malaria incidence. Additionally, we deploy a smart healthcare application; this paper also makes a significant contribution by identifying hidden ecological factors of malaria.

Keywords: malaria; climatic factors; machine learning; prediction; mobile application; structural equation modelling; partial least squares model

1. Introduction

Malaria, as one of the most serious infectious diseases causing public health problems in the world, affects about two-thirds of the world population, with estimated resultant deaths close to a million annually [1]. Its prevalence can be significantly attributed to climate factors, usually worsened by human factors through poor sanitation, overwhelmed sewage and deforestation. These climatic factors were found to contribute to the incidence of malaria [2], which apparently imposes a greater challenge to human life today.

The effects of malaria are much more profound in third world countries due to very limited medical resources. When an intense outbreak occurs, most of these countries cannot cope with the high number of patients due to the lack of medicine, equipment and hospital facilities. The prevention or reduction of the risk factor of this disease is very challenging, especially in these countries, due to poverty, and economic insatiability. Technology can offer alternative solutions by providing early detection mechanisms that help to control the spread of the disease and allow the management of treatment facilities in advance to ensure a more timely health service, which can save thousands of lives. The availability of an early detection system will not only prevent or decrease the large spread of malaria by creating quarantine zones, but also help healthcare providers deliver the necessary medical care on time by managing resources and calling for international aid and support, if needed.

In this study, we aim to design and deploy an *intelligent malaria outbreak early warning system*, which is a mobile application, that predicts malaria outbreak based on climatic factors using machine learning algorithms. The system will help hospitals, healthcare providers, and health organizations take precautions in time and utilize their resources in case of emergency. To our best knowledge, the system developed in this paper is the first publicly available application.

As well as deploying a smart healthcare application, this paper also makes a significant contribution by identifying *hidden ecological factors* of malaria (e.g., temperature, humidity, wind, location, drought, floods, etc.). Since confounding effects of climatic factors have a greater influence on the incidence of malaria, we have also conducted extensive research on exploring a new ecosystem model for the assessment of hidden ecological factors and identified three confounding factors that significantly contribute to the outbreak of malaria.

In this paper, we use an efficient methodology, comprising four stages. In the first stage, we have collected data from some repositories. Unfortunately, most of this data was incomplete in terms of climate factors. We have completed the dataset with the climate variables using satellite-based meteorological data obtained from CFSR (Climate Forecast System Reanalysis).

In the second stage, we have identified hidden ecological factors of malaria. The fundamental concept behind this emanated from the fact that a causal relationship exists among the climatic factors [3]. Some recent studies [4,5] combined meteorological variables together with malaria incidence data and established time series models for predicting malaria incidence. Regression and correlation analysis modelling was applied and using meteorological variables the trend of malaria incidence was determined [6]. Also, one of the most recent studies presented in this direction [7] uses a hybrid approach for time-series modelling and lagged-regression analysis of climate data combined with reported malaria incidence cases. Their result showed that malaria incidence in the area studied has a significant association with relative humidity, whereas temperature and precipitation were found to have negligible effects. This finding might particularly reveal that malaria incidence can be strongly influenced by relative humidity alone. However, this methodology suffers weaknesses due to its inability to capture the pre-determined existing causal relationship among the climate factors.

In this study, we use the partial least squares path modelling (PLS-PM) [8] methodology to analyse the causal relationships among meteorological variables, e.g., minimum average temperature, maximum average temperature, relative humidity, wind speed, precipitation and solar radiation, and explored their impact on the outbreak of malaria. In doing so, we develop an integrated model that provides insight into which lacking pre-determined confounding effects could be identified as hidden ecological factors. In the third stage, we have used machine learning algorithms to identify a pattern/model that will be used to make an accurate prediction of malaria outbreak. We have evaluated the prediction of machine learning algorithms, and obtained a very high accuracy rate. Machine learning has been used for prediction and diagnosis of several diseases, e.g., Parkinson's [9], cancer [10] and heart disease [11]. Among machine learning methods, Support Vector Machines (SVM) [12] have been used in malaria incidence prediction [13]; but this study has several shortcomings:

(i) the dataset used was extremely small (the size is only 33), which makes accuracy of prediction questionable; (ii) the dataset was used without analysing ecological factors, which could result in the inclusion of statistically insignificant variables in the prediction model, and hence could cause overfitting; (iii) there is no systematic methodology to transform this predictor into a smart healthcare system.

In the fourth stage, we have developed a mobile application by embedding the best predictor generated in the previous stage. The application reads climatic information, i.e., temperature, relative humidity, wind speed, solar radiation and precipitation, from free weather and geographical Application Programming Interface (APIs). It then predicts the possibility of malaria outbreak several days in advance (based on available forecasting data).

The subsequent sections of this paper are presented as follows: In Section 2, we present the complete analysis of identification of hidden ecological factors for the incidence of malaria transmission and its health implications to the change in biodiversity. Section 3 presents the intelligent malaria outbreak warning system, comprising data pre-processing, generating a prediction model using a machine learning algorithm and deployment of an intelligent mobile application. Section 4 concludes the paper by providing the summary of our results and our future work.

2. Assessment of Hidden Ecological Factors

Climate factors are the drivers of malaria transmission [14]; however, a study analysing the causal ecological relationship among the climatic factors that affect the incidence of malaria is still lacking, particularly in Sub-Saharan African countries.

The malaria ecosystem comprises four main components: human host, mosquitoes vector, parasites and environmental condition (see Figure 1).

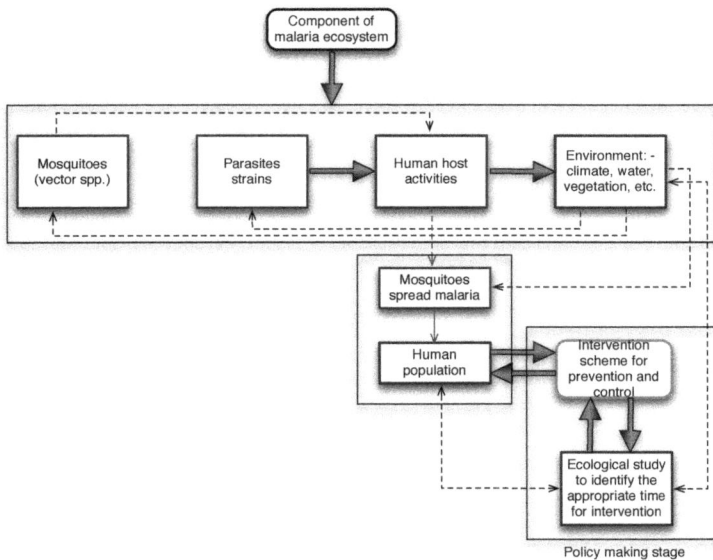

Figure 1. Conceptual framework of the malaria ecosystem describing the dynamic stages of malaria transmission from humans and mosquitoes under the influence of environmental factors. The boxes colored blue indicates the dynamics development of malaria parasite and its interaction between human host with mosquito vector and ecology. While the box colored red is the main scheme for malaria prevention and control indicating the intervention measure taken to mitigate the burden imposed on the human population.

These components are very dynamic in nature due to the inherent characteristics of ecology and the anticipatory change to biodiversity because of global warming. The works by [15–17] reported that ecological changes would adversely affect human health in some ways that are both obvious and obscure. However, the growing evidence also suggests that due to the rise in temperature as a result of the anticipated global warming, some previously unexposed regions of malaria transmission would have a 50% chance of experiencing it due to the link between malaria incidence and ecological factors [18]. The relationship between environmental changes and human health cannot be overemphasized because of the inherent variability and complexity of human nature. In many circumstances, grasslands and forest are converted for agriculture to reduce communicable disease, including wetland drainage for the prevention and control of malaria [17]. These activities can either lead to unintended negative health effects or succeed in the designed purpose. Also, transforming forest to augment food production may, in the long run, lead to the creation of a suitable environment for disease-causing agents such as mosquitoes for malaria transmission [19].

2.1. Study Site and Population

Ejisu-Juaben Municipal has a population of 143,762 [20], lies within latitudes $1°15'$ N and $1°45'$ N also with longitudes $6°15'$ W and $7°00'$ W, occupies a land area of 582.5 km^2 [21]. The vegetation of the municipal is a typical semi-deciduous forest (see Figure 2), with undulating topography and low altitude of about 240 m–300 m above sea level [21]. Also, the rainfall pattern of the area is bi-modal (i.e., two distinct seasons in a year), characterized by major and minor rainfall. The major rainfall begins from March to July with average annual rainfall between 1200 mm–1500 mm, while the minor rainfall begins in September and tapers off in November with annual average rainfall of 900 mm–1120 mm. Usually, December through February is hot, dry and dusty with mean annual temperature 25 °C–32 °C, and the relative humidity is moderately high during the rainy seasons [21]. Figure 2 presents the map of Ejisu-Juaben Municipal, which lies within the red-squared portion labelled Kumasi—the capital city of the Ashanti Region, in southern Ghana.

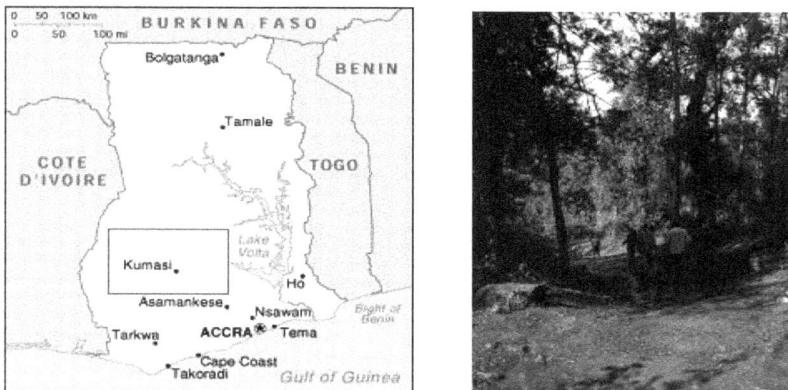

Figure 2. The picture on the left shows the map of Ghana and the portion of Kumasi city, where the study area within which Ejisu-Juaben lies. The picture on the right illustrates the climate vegetational belt characterized by a typical semi-deciduous forest.

2.2. Data Collection and Source

A total of 85,627 confirmed diagnosed cases of malaria incidence for the period of five years from 2009 to 2013, were retrieved in [22]. The distributional pattern of malaria cases reported in the study area shows an indication of high malaria incidence. We sought data on climate factors in the designated weather station of the study area location [20]; unfortunately, very few data are available and also a lot are missing. This is perhaps due to laxity of the weather station staff for not properly keeping up-to-date data. Since the data available is not sufficient for the analysis, we overcome this challenge by using satellite-based meteorological data obtained via [23]. We used the boundary metrics dimensions of [22] at latitude 6.7989° N to 6.6823° S and longitude −1.5656° W to −1.4186° E and demarcate the location of the study area on the satellite globe map. Within the demarcated area, we identify a weather station. We then generate the data of the climate variables of our interest. Moreover, the Ghana malaria incidence data is sufficient for the application of PLS-PM due to its suitability for handling small sample data, non-normality, multi-dimensions and multicollinearity [24,25]. However, the sample set is not sufficient to obtain high precision accuracy when applying machine learning algorithms. A small dataset might also cause the overfitting of data. For that reason, we coupled malaria incidence data used in [26] with [22] and proceed with the analysis.

2.3. Factor Analysis

Exploratory factor analysis (EFA) is one of the techniques for factor analysis (FA). It is primarily used in statistics to describe variance among observed correlated variables in terms of potentially a smaller number of unobserved variables, usually referred to as factors [27]. In this work, EFA was employed to search for confounding ecological factors that are latent [8,27] from the set of observed meteorological variables.

We demonstrate the FA technique using simple mathematical sketches; the observed variables can be expressed as linear combinations of the potential factors plus the residual terms. Consider the following observed variables $Y_1, Y_2, \cdots, Y_M$ of size M, and assume they are linearly related to a small number of unobservable (latent variables) factors $F_1, F_2, \cdots, F_N$, with $N \ll M$ such that:

$$
\begin{aligned}
Y_1 &= \psi_{10} + \psi_{11}F_1 + \cdots + \psi_{1N}F_N + e_1 \\
Y_2 &= \psi_{20} + \psi_{21}F_1 + \cdots + \psi_{1N}F_N + e_2 \\
&\vdots \\
Y_M &= \psi_{M0} + \psi_{M1}F_1 + \cdots + \psi_{MN}F_N + e_M
\end{aligned}
\tag{1}
$$

where $e_1, \cdots, e_M$ are the residual terms, assuming that $E(e_i) = 0$, and $Var(e_i) = \delta_i^2$. While the unobservable factors F_i are independent from each other and $E(F_j) = 0$ and $Var(F_j) = 1$. These two assumptions stand as the robust pre-conditions for the application of structural equation modelling (SEM). The loading scores can be obtained from covariance and variance of any two observed variables using the following formula presented in Equation (2)

$$
\begin{aligned}
Cov(Y_i, Y_j) &= \sum_{\substack{i \neq j}}^{N} \psi_{iN}\psi_{jN} \\
Var(Y_i) &= \sum_{i=1}^{N} \psi_{iK} + \delta_i^2
\end{aligned}
\tag{2}
$$

where the summation sign in Equation (2) denotes communality of the variables, the variance of which is explained by the common factors F_N.

2.4. Structural Equation Modelling

The SEM is a very popular technique that has multidisciplinary applications which combine together both the measurement and structural models [28–30]. In Figure 3a, we present a complex hypothetical SEM showing the causal relationship between malaria incidence and latent ecological factors together with their observed variables. We used ellipse shapes to represent latent factors, while the observed variables are represented by rectangular shapes.

The following system of Equation (3) describes the SEM technique in which the observed variables can be expressed as a linear combination of the potential factors plus residual terms. We therefore present SEM mathematical representations from Figure 3b as follows:

$$\begin{cases} \text{Factor I} = \lambda_{1,1}(\text{minimum temperature}) + \lambda_{1,2}(\text{relative humidity}) + \beta_{1,2}(\text{Factor II}) + \\ \gamma_1(\text{malaria incidence}) + e_1 \\ \text{Factor II} = \lambda_{2,1}(\text{maximum temperature}) + \lambda_{2,2}(\text{solar radiation}) + \beta_{2,3}(\text{Factor III}) + \\ \gamma_2(\text{malaria incidence}) + e_2 \\ \text{Factor III} = \lambda_{3,1}(\text{precipitation}) + \lambda_{3,2}(\text{wind speed}) + \gamma_3(\text{malaria incidence}) + e_3 \end{cases} \quad (3)$$

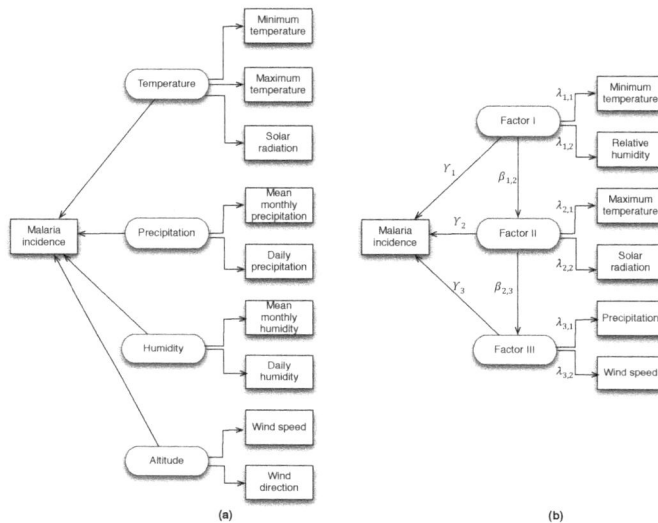

Figure 3. Structural equation model showing the relationship between malaria incidence and climate factors, the black colored rectangle indicating measurement variables while red colored ellipse is latent variables. (**a**) Showing the hypothetical causal relationship between malaria incidence and the climate factors. (**b**) Presenting the reduced causal relationship between malaria incidence and the climate factors after applying factor analysis to identify hidden factors and their dependent measurement variables.

2.5. Estimation of PLS-PM

The technique called PLS-PM or PLS-SEM was developed by [31] and chosen due to its characteristics in terms of small sample size, non-normality, multi-dimensions, and multicollinearity [23,24]. We have identified three hidden factors using EFA, and subsequently applied SEM for construction of the model (see Figure 3b). The PLS-PM is basically divided into three components: estimation of LVs, estimation of inner and outer models and estimation of the structural relations. The PLS algorithm is essentially represented as a sequence of regression in terms of weight vectors [32] and estimates the values of LVs (factor scores) iteratively until convergence is achieved. The fundamental PLS algorithm, as suggested by [30] (see Appendixes A.1–A.3 for detailed procedural descriptions). The PLS-PM is a component-based estimation technique that uses an iteration algorithm, separately analyzes the blocks of the measurement model and estimates the path coefficients in the structural model [33]. We used a package called semPLS in R for the estimation of PLS-SEM parameters including the analysis presented in Section 2.6.

For estimating parameters of SEM, we invoked the PLS technique, and further used 10,000 samples for the bootstrapping analysis instead of the default number of samples set to 500 selections [33]. Also, the PLS-PM latent variable scores were expressed as a linear combination of their observed variables and treated as an error-free substitute for the observed variables [33].

2.5 1. Measurement Model

The model, presented in Figure 3b, shows how observed Measurement Variables (MVs) are related to their Latent Variables (LVs). Hence without any loss of generality, for a good representation of the inner model, the following assumptions must hold:

- Matrix of MVs **Y** are scaled to have zero mean and unit variance.
- Each block of MVs $\mathbf{Y}_g$ is already transformed to be positively correlated for all LVs $x_g, g = 1, \cdots, G$.

The measurement model is broadly classified as either reflective (Mode A) or formative (Mode B) [26], and this depends on the relation between LVs and MVs formation.

2.5.2. Mode A

In this form, each block of MVs reflects its LV and can be represented in multivariate regression form as:

$$\mathbf{Y}_g = \mathbf{x}_g \mathbf{w}_g^\top + \mathbf{F}_g \tag{4}$$

where the $\mathbf{w}_g^\top$ can be estimated using the least squares method.

2.5.3. Mode B

Also, in this form, the LV is considered to be formed by its MVs represented by a multiple regression as:

$$\mathbf{x}_g = \mathbf{Y}_g \mathbf{w}_g + \delta_g \tag{5}$$

using the same method of least squares, the estimate for $\mathbf{w}_g$ can be obtained.

2.6. Presentation of Results

In the application of PLS-SEM, three weighting schemes such as centroid weighting, factorial weighting and path weighting are conceptually used for model specifications and estimations. The conceptual SEM presented in Figure 3a shows the hypothetical causal relationship between latent (hidden) variables and observed meteorological (manifest) variables to the occurrence of malaria incidence. For the identification of confounding hidden variables, we performed factor analysis using exploratory factor analysis (EFA) [34]. From the results, three hidden factors were identified: Factor I (related to the minimum temperature and relative humidity), Factor II (related to the maximum temperature and solar radiation) and Factor III (related to precipitation and wind speed). The identified factors accounted for 64% of the total variance, and at $\alpha = 5\%$ level of significance, $\chi^2 = 13.91$, df = 8, Pvalue = 0.0841. This result provides sufficient evidence to explain malaria incidence in the study area.

We also explored the Guttman–Kaiser Criterion [35] and Cattell scree plots [36], to determine the number of factors to extract, the result of which reconfirmed the existence of three hidden ecological factors to the incidence of malaria. In the Guttman–Kaiser Criterion, we have the eigenvalues 2.71, 1.53, 1.02, 0.82, 0.57, 0.29, 0.05 computed using the correlation matrix (see Table 1); however, the rule for extraction is based on the factors whose eigenvalues are greater than unity. We then discard those factors that have eigenvalues less than unity, and are left with three eigenvalues indicating the number of factors to be considered. Similarly, the Cattell scree plot presented in (Figure 4) facilitates decisions regarding the number of factors to retain.

By analysing Table 1, we obtained the scree plot shown in Figure 4 which represents the relative proportion of variance accounted for by the components. In the scree plot, the eigenvalues of the first three components greater than unity can be seen from the parallel indicator, while the subsequent components below unity also line up beneath the parallel indicator. However, it is important to evaluate the variance accounted for by a few of the eigenvalues regarded as sufficient so that we can focus on them and discard the remaining insufficient factors as noise.

Table 1. Correlation matrix of climate drivers and malaria incidence.

	Mal. Incid.	Max. Temp.	Min. Temp.	Precip.	Rel. Humid	Solar Rad.	Wind Speed
Mal. Incid.	1.00	-	-	-	-	-	-
Max. Temp.	0.28	1.00	-	-	-	-	-
Min. Temp.	0.68	0.04	1.00	-	-	-	-
Precip.	−0.21	−0.36	0.22	1.00	-	-	-
Rel. Humid.	0.51	−0.24	0.90	0.38	1.00	-	-
Solar Rad.	0.19	0.54	−0.33	−0.10	−0.44	1.00	-
Wind Speed	−0.16	0.07	0.45	0.17	0.39	0.01	1.00

Note: (1) Malaria incidence, (2) Maximum temperature, (3) Minimum temperature, (4) Precipitation, (5) Relative humidity, (6) Solar radiation and (7) Wind speed.

In Table 2, we present Pearson's cross-correlation between meteorological variables and occurrence of malaria incidence at various lag effects from 0 to 3 months. The Lag 0, Lag 1 and Lag 2 (e.g., 0 month, 1 month and 2 month) presented in Table 2 which indicates the lagged correlation effects between climate variables and the incidence of malaria in the study area. We observed that at lag effects of 1 month, the minimum temperature, maximum temperature and relative humidity have positive association with malaria incidence as indicated by 0.321, 0.215 and 0.254 respectively. While the precipitation is negatively correlated with malaria incidence at lag effects of 1 month as indicated by −0.292. This explained that the climate drivers at lag of 1 month would be quite enough for the mosquitoes to reproduce and also complete their incubation periods (EIP) to becomes fully active in transmitting malaria infection. We found that the preceding result is consistent with other relevant studies on the influence of meteorological variables on the malaria incidence [37]. The 1 month time lag in the study area is sufficient to capture the pattern of malaria transmission for various strains of plasmodium parasites with definite lengths of EIP. This period usually takes about 10–15 days [38] and temporally varies over location, parasite species and climatic resolution. At Lag 0 and Lag 2, the minimum temperature, precipitation and relative humidity have negative lag effects at 0 month and 2 month except the maximum temperature which has effects of 0.284 and 0.092. These results revealed some clear indications that the malaria transmission in the study area at Lag 0 and Lag 2 suffered a negative effect, which might be attributed to the bi-annual rainfall pattern, low relative humidity—say less than 50%—and inability of mosquitoes completing the EIP cycle. In general, the result showed that maximum temperature, minimum temperature, and relative humidity were related to the malaria incidence at lagged effects of 1 month (i.e., a month in advance) except precipitation which has a negative association in the study area.

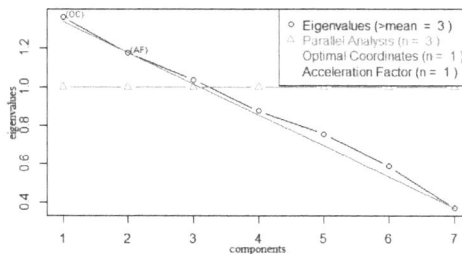

Figure 4. The Cattell scree plot presents the eigenvalues of the components and threshold for identifying the number of hidden ecological factors to be considered using the information in Table 1.

Table 2. Cross-correlation between meteorological variables and malaria incidence; VIF:variance inflated factor.

Variables	Lag 0	Lag 1	Lag 2	VIF	Kurtosis	Standard Error
Maximum temperature	0.284	0.321 [b]	0.092	2.4096	5.48	0.38
Minimum temperature	−0.122	0.215 [b]	−0.237	8.7919	2.07	0.33
Precipitation	−0.214	−0.292 [a]	−0.155	1.4194	20.73	0.27
Relative humidity	−0.134	0.254 [b]	−0.198	9.0065	1.42	0.02
Solar radiation	-	-	-	1.9000	6.73	0.50
Wind speed	-	-	-	1.3452	−0.58	0.04

[a] negative association at lag 1. [b] positive association at lag 1.

Some important summary statistics are presented in Table 2, which describe the distributional pattern of the climate indicators of malaria incidence and variance inflated factor (VIF). In factor analysis, multicollinearity can be used as a diagnostics check prior to application of regression analysis, whereby variables with high-factor loadings are typically multicollinear. We compute VIF of the climate variables to measure the degrees of multicollinearity and identify those factors that are independent of the magnitude of their VIF. In Table 2, the minimum temperature and relative humidity have VIF of 8.7919 and 9.0065 that gives a high degree of multicollinearity. The results revealed a high independent predictor of malaria incidence in the study area, and the degree to which they are independent gives evidence to accurately determine the major factors. However, the values of kurtosis (see Table 2) indicate a high peak of the climate variables with positive values across all the indicators except the wind speed which indicates a flat distribution. Positive values, generally listed in Table 2, indicate that the peakedness of distribution of the climate variables particularly influences the malaria incidence. Also, the standard error estimates provide information on the statistical accuracy of the climate variables; the larger the standard error, the wider the confidence interval of the statistic and vice-versa.

Non-normality of the dataset is one necessity for adopting PLS-SEM, and it is very robust when used on extremely non-normal data [39]. We examined the degree to which the data on malaria incidence are non-normal using the Shapiro–Wilk tests by invoking R software (3.4.1, University of Aukland, New Zealand). The results show that the null hypothesis (Ho) is rejected, indicating that the malaria incidence dataset is non-normal as suggested by the following indices $W = 0.9486$, p-value = 0.0134 and $\alpha = 0.05$, respectively. This method is particularly chosen and useful in smaller samples sizes, less than 2000 [40], and the null hypothesis is that the data are from a normal distribution. Similarly, we used a graphical approach called quantile–quantile (Q–Q) plot [41] and tested for normality of the dataset in similar fashion. The approach creates a plot from the ranked samples of the dataset against a similar number of ranked theoretical samples from a normal distribution. The plot shown in Figure 5, clearly indicates that the data points for malaria incidence are deviating from the straight line. Hence, the malaria incidence dataset is therefore not normally distributed using the Q–Q plot.

In Table 3, we show the results of the factor score estimates for path coefficients of SEM estimated using PLS path modelling, and three different structural model weighting schemes were analysed. We observed that Centroid (A) converges faster after 12 iterations, while factorial (B) and path weighting (C) converge after 15 iterations. The procedure of selecting the best weighting scheme is determined by the maximum number of iterations that will be used for calculating the PLS results and this algorithm did not stop until the maximum number of iterations is reached due to the stop criterion. From Table 3, we can observe that the B and C weighting schemes converge at the same maximum number of iterations in estimating the parameters of SEM. The weighting scheme provides the highest R^2 value for endogenous latent variables in the PLS path model specifications and estimations. This result shows that the C weighting scheme is better than A and B, as suggested by [42] in terms of robustness and also when the path model includes higher-order constructs.

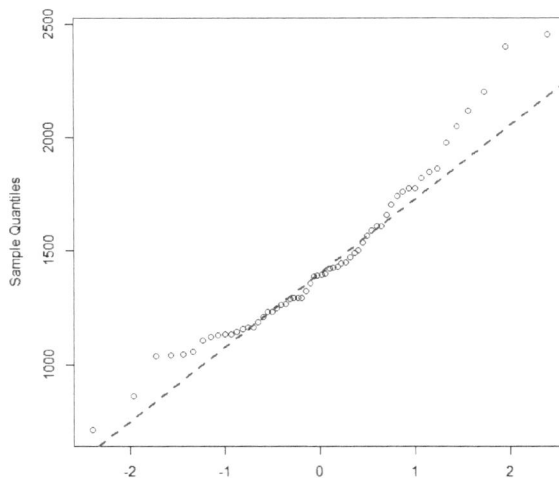

Figure 5. Graphical representation of quantile–quantile (Q–Q) plot normality tests.

Table 3. Factor scores for path coefficients in the PLS-PM using three weighting schemes.

Measurement/Structural Model	Parameter	Estimate	Centroid (A)	Factorial (B)	Path Weighting (C)
Minimum temperature ⟵ FactorI	$\lambda_{1,1}$	0.9479	0.9479	0.9495	0.9495
Relative humidity ⟵ FactorI	$\lambda_{1,2}$	0.9910	0.9910	0.9903	0.9903
Maximum temperature ⟵ FactorII	$\lambda_{2,1}$	0.8816	0.8816	0.8675	0.8675
Solar radiation ⟵ FactorII	$\lambda_{2,2}$	0.8735	0.8735	0.8873	0.8873
Precipitation ⟵ FactorIII	$\lambda_{3,1}$	0.9849	0.9849	0.9852	0.9852
Wind speed ⟵ FactorIII	$\lambda_{3,2}$	0.0017	0.0017	0.0031	0.0031
FactorI ⟶ FactorII	$\beta_{1,2}$	−0.3248	−0.3248	−0.3302	−0.3302
FactorII ⟶ FactorIII	$\beta_{2,3}$	−0.2774	−0.2774	−0.2690	−0.2690
FactorI ⟶ Malaria incidence	γ_1	0.9700	-	-	-
FactorII ⟶ Malaria incidence	γ_2	0.7700	-	-	-
FactorIII ⟶ Malaria incidence	γ_3	0.4900	-	-	-
Maximum number of iterations	-	-	12	15	15

Table 4 presents the results of bootstrapping sampling for outer loadings of the observed variables and path coefficient of the latent variables estimated using PLS-PM. The results also show that all outer loadings and path coefficients are significant at $\alpha = 5\%$, except for the solar radiation with Factor II and wind speed with Factor III that contains zero-point in the bootstrap confidence interval. Furthermore, the interaction effects of the Factors between I and II, II and III were also investigated and the results revealed that none of the Factor combinations is significant in the incidence of malaria in the study area. This result provides sufficient evidence that high malaria incidence in the study area was attributed to the occurrence of minimum temperature and relative humidity which are identified as Factor I.

The decision to select the most influential hidden ecological factor to the incidence of malaria is based on the communality and Dillon–Goldstein's indices. Furthermore, Table 5 summarizes the results, indicating some indices for selecting the hidden ecological factors to the high incidence of malaria in the study area. Among the three factors identified by EFA, we find that Factor I, indicated by minimum temperature and relative humidity, influences malaria transmission with communality index (0.94) and Dillon–Goldstein's ρ (0.97). This result is also consistent with the finding in [37], where a positive association exists between temperature and occurrence of dengue. Factor II and Factor III appear to have less influence on the malaria incidence.

Table 4. Bootstrapping test of the outer loadings and path coefficients in the PLS-PM with a 95% confidence interval.

Measurement/Structural Model	Parameter	Estimate	Bias	Standard Error	Lower	Upper
Minimum ⟵ FactorI	$\lambda_{1,1}$	0.9479	−0.0057	0.0467	0.8240	0.9890
Relative humidity ⟵ FactorI	$\lambda_{1,2}$	0.9910	−0.0055	0.0347	0.9823	1.0000
Maximum temperature ⟵ FactorII	$\lambda_{2,1}$	0.8816	−0.0329	0.1289	0.4769	0.9810
Solar radiation ⟵ FactorII	$\lambda_{2,2}$	0.8735	−0.0343	0.1748	−0.0705	0.9550
Precipitation ⟵ FactorIII	$\lambda_{3,1}$	0.9849	−0.1748	0.4044	0.7666	1.0000
Wind speed ⟵ FactorIII	$\lambda_{3,2}$	0.0017	0.1356	0.4059	−0.6593	0.7300
FactorI ⟶ FactorII	$\beta_{1,2}$	−0.3248	−0.0333	0.1692	−0.4974	0.4260
FactorII ⟶ FactorIII	$\beta_{2,3}$	−0.2774	−0.0264	0.2191	−0.4963	0.3810

Table 5. Indices for selecting the ecological hidden factor of high malaria incidence in the study area.

Factor	Reflective Variables	Communality	Dillon–Goldstein's ρ
I	2	0.94 [c] (94%)	0.97 [c] (97%)
II	2	0.77 (77%)	0.87 (87%)
III	2	0.49 (49%)	0.49 (49%)

[c] the most significant hidden factor.

3. Intelligent Malaria Outbreak Warning System

In the previous section, we identified the hidden ecological factors of malaria using partial least squares path modelling. In this section, we discuss, in detail, the implementation of the malaria outbreak system, based on the identified hidden ecological factors. The deployment comprises of three stages: data processing, generating the predictive model using machine learning and deployment of a mobile application.

3.1. Data Preprocessing

It was a tradition, prior to the application of machine learning algorithms, that datasets need to be pre-processed to enable a faster and more accurate learning process. The heuristic approach involves the discretization techniques most often used in data mining. This involves transforming continuous-valued datasets to discrete datasets by creating a set of contiguous intervals [43]. In this paper, we are making use of a dataset on climate variables as the input while the output variable is malaria incidence data. Our concern is the development of a predictive model using supervised machine learning algorithms that will predict the likelihood of malaria incidence. The output variable appeared to have high-magnitude in-terms of reported number of malaria cases; hence using it directly may cause over-fitting to the predictive model. Therefore, it is pertinent to transform the dataset using some techniques for discretization to enable us to build efficient models.

We have therefore discretized the output variable to form a target variable using the k-means clustering algorithm [44]. This methodology is chosen over equal width (EW) and equal frequency (EF) because it is less sensitive to outliers and also the number of clusters (partitions) can be optimized by analysis rather than pre-determination. In general, the choice of discretization method and choice of k can be guided by the objectives of the discretization task. By invoking R software, we can determine the optimum number of clusters to enable us to partition the output variable.

From the analysis, the optimum number of clusters obtained is k = 4 and the algorithm converges after nine iterations with 89.9% variation. Also, we observed that for k = 5, the number of iterations exceeded the maximum number of tolerable iterations supposed to achieve convergence and in this case it diverges even though the percentage of variation is still good at 93%. For k = 2 and 3, the algorithm converges after three and four iterations with 66.4% and 82% variation, respectively. This gives sufficient evidence to choose the optimum number of clusters as k = 4. Similarly, we have also tried the "NbClust" package in R software for determining the optimal number of clusters. Using the values of k ranging from two to five allows the algorithm to select the optimum number of clusters to be used in order to partition the output variable. The algorithm run and selected k = 4 as the optimum number of clusters to partition the output variables. Hence, both methodologies give the same number of optimum clusters to consider and subsequently prove to be consistent. We then partitioned the output variable into four classes according to the results of k-means algorithm and re-labeled them as: low, medium, high and very high incidence status of malaria. We present, in Table 6, the summary analysis of k-means algorithm clustering.

Table 6. Summary of data discretization using the k-means algorithm. SSB: The sum of squares of errors between the clusters; SST: The total sum of squares of the entire clusters.

Number of Clusters (k)	2	3	4	5
iteration	3	4	9	6
convergence	yes	yes	yes	no
$\frac{SSB}{SST}$	66.4%	82%	89.9%	93%

3.2. Machine Learning

The next stage is to identify a pattern/model from the data processed in Section 3.1 that will be used to make an accurate prediction of malaria incidence. Evolved from traditional pattern recognition approaches, machine learning methods explore the algorithms that can learn from the data and overcome prediction tasks by building a mathematical model with a data sample input. A learning algorithm will mark each given Malaria epidemic data sample as one category, then after being trained using the training dataset, it will build a model to predict which category a forthcoming data sample falls into.

We have applied several machine learning algorithms, including Support Vector Machine (SVM), K-Nearest Neighbours (KNN), Naive Bayes and Decision Trees, to find the best predicting algorithm from the scikit framework [45] in Python.

To evaluate the prediction of machine learning algorithms on the training set, we have used the 10-fold cross-validation technique by selecting a training set and test sets that are mutually independent. Table 7 shows the prediction results in comparison to seven different Machine Learning methods.

Table 7. Comparison of the accuracy of model checking algorithms. LiR: Linear Regression; LoR: Logistic Regression; DT: Decision Tree; SVM: Support Vector Machine; SVM (o): Optimized Support Vector Machine; NB: Naive Bayes; KNN: K-Nearest Neighbours; K-M: K-Means.

Algorithm	LiR	LoR	DT	SVM	SVM (o)	NB	KNN1	KNN5	KNN10	K-M (3)
Accuracy	83.8%	75.0%	63.8%	80.6%	99.0%	63.9%	58.3%	80.6%	80.6%	47.2%

- Linear Regression (LiR) method gives overall good prediction results, but it seems that the method failed to produce any medium predictions.
- Logistic Regression (LoR) method predicts the probability of occurrence of an event by fitting the dataset, as a set of independent variables, into a logic function. In other words, for a correlated data set, LoR may not be able to find the intrinsic-relationships between events.
- Decision Tree (DT) works very well for both categorical and continuous dependent variables; however, this dataset cannot be separated as distinct groups since the edges of the samples are fuzzy. Therefore, DT gave a bad prediction after all.

- Support Vector Machine (SVM) is one of the most efficient supervised machine learning algorithms, which is mainly used for solving classification and regression problems. The best part of this algorithm is that training and testing data can be plotted as a point in a n-dimensional plane, with a feature being the value of a particular coordinate. Without optimisation of the parameters, SVM gave a 80.56% predicting result. After parameter optimisation, especially on the penalty parameter and gamma coefficient adjustment, SVM (o) gave a 99.0% predicting result.
- Naive Bayes (NB) is a well-known classification method, which is based on Bayes' Theorem with an oversimplified assumption of independence between classifiers. Moreover, NB is a conditional probability model, which means that the method needs to be assigned a series of certain events. For this data set, NB did not produce a good prediction overall.
- K-Nearest Neighbours (KNN) method is able to deal with both classification and regression problems. In comparison to KNN5 (where k = 5) and KNN10 (where k = 10), KNN1 (where k = 1) failed to make a good prediction. It means that the data may need to do more pre-process and/or noise removal in a theory; however, most of data from the real world are incomplete; that is why KNN5 and KNN10 make a better prediction.
- K-Means (K-M) is a type of un-supervised method for clustering. In this case, three clusters have been set at the beginning; however, a convergence did not perfectly land; therefore, it cannot give a good overall prediction.

The results, presented in Table 7, show that the best performing algorithm is SVM. We therefore integrate the SVM model into our system.

3.3. Mobile Application

We have developed a mobile application, Malaria Outbreak Warning System, with a built-in SVM model, published at Google Play. The tool can be accessed via [46].

The application is based on the theoretical experiences and practical experiments of the SVM algorithm and model, which has been tested for developing systematic and effective strategies to predict the outbreak of a Malaria epidemic. Meanwhile, the parameters of the model kernel have been optimised and set into this application.

The application consists of three processes: pre-processing the weather forecasting data, processing the data by applying them into the model and implementing the model's interface, and post-processing the prediction data by presenting results on the app's UI front layer. It is a well-suited implementation for location detection.

Figure 6 shows a screen shot of the tool. The application not only supports the automatic gathering of weather forecasting data, but also supports manual data input. The application reads climatic information, i.e., temperature, relative humidity, wind speed, solar radiation and precipitation, from the weather and geographical APIs. When the units of the weather and atmosphere are different from the data set used to construct the predictor, we carry out the required normalisation or feature scaling or similar pre-processing. The tool then predicts the Malaria outbreak a couple of days in advance based on available forecast information acquired from the APIs. The user can slide the screen to see the available outbreak predictions for the current and future days. The additional button on the bottom of the screen is to let the user manually enter a set of weather measurements to make a prediction for customised parameters.

The trained SVM model has been implemented in Java by taking advantage of the LIBSVM (2.88, University of California, Berkeley, CA, USA) [47]. LIBSVM is an integrated software for SVM, regression and distribution estimation. The mobile application has been developed for Android using Android Studio. The weather forecasting data is powered by OpenWeatherMap API (3.0, Riga, Latvia) [48], which is an online service provider for weather data. OpenWeatherMap provides API for searching forecasting data for up to 5 days by coordinates; and the responses served as JavaScript Object Notation (JSON), Extensible Markup Language (XML) and HyperText Markup Language (HTML) endpoints. All of the data provided is under CC BY-SA 4.0 license.

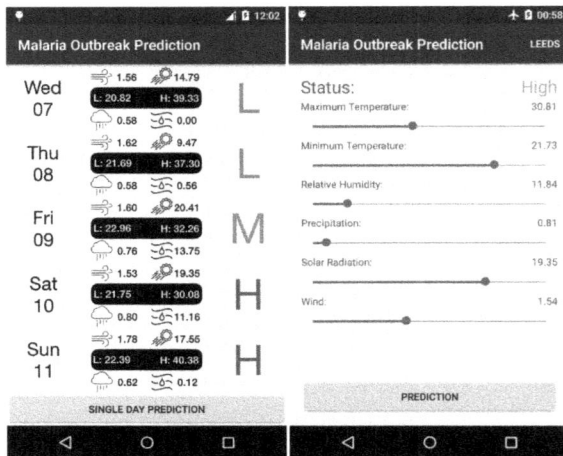

Figure 6. A screen shot of the mobile application.

3.4. Discussion

The current prototype of the intelligent malaria outbreak warning system relies on a batch machine learning process. That is, the learning algorithm is trained and tested offline using the available dataset, and the prediction model is embedded within the tool. Hence, the prediction process relies on the prediction model trained offline at once.

A more effective approach is to make the learning process online. That is, whenever new data is available, the data is automatically updated, and the learning process is run again to encapsulate the new data. This will not only allow an automatic and dynamic learning process, but also increase the accuracy of the prediction by adapting to new patterns in the data.

The online learning approach requires a mechanistic data collection mechanism, which is very challenging to perform as hospitals and health service providers do not make the relevant data available online. Even acquiring permission to have access to the available data is a long and bureaucratic process. On the other hand, as discussed in Section 2.2, most available data cannot be directly used in this system as they are incomplete and/or not processed.

To alleviate these issues and to support the online learning process, the Malaria outbreak warning application can be extended to collect online data from its users. Namely, the users, e.g., hospitals, healthcare providers, individuals etc., report a Malaria case to the system. Using the geographical location of the incident, the application will acquire all the necessary information for the ecological factors. In this way, new data will be collected at run time, and the learning process will be instantiated each time new data is available. We are currently working on the development of this approach.

4. Conclusions

In this study, we have deployed an intelligent malaria outbreak early warning system, predicting malaria outbreaks based on climatic factors using machine learning algorithms. The system will help hospitals, healthcare providers, and health organizations take precautions in time and utilize their resources in case of emergency. To our best knowledge, the system developed in this paper is the first publicly available application.

We have also provided an ecosystem overview for malaria modelling and proposed a new framework for the study of a malaria transmission ecosystem to prevent and control its effects. We have assessed and identified hidden factors that lead to a high malaria outbreak. Our data analysis results have shown that the minimum temperature and relative humidity, which are related to Factor I, have a positive association with the incidence of malaria in the study area. The other observed variables such as maximum temperature, solar radiation, precipitation and wind speed, which are related to hidden Factor II and Factor III, appear to have mildly influenced malaria incidence.

The primary results obtained in this study have demonstrated the power of the proposed predicative analytics-based malaria outbreak warning system. The further development of the system will incorporate automatic data gathering from a variety of sources. We are currently working on further development of our system and methodology to support automatic data collection at run time, and the online learning process. This will not only allow an automatic and dynamic learning process, but also increase the accuracy of the prediction by adapting to new patterns in the data.

Acknowledgments: The authors would like to thank National Centre for Environmental Prediction (NCEP), for their support in providing this work with relevant meteorological data. The author B.M. would like to thank Tertiary Education Trust Fund (tetFund), Nigeria for sponsoring his Ph.D. programme at the University of Bradford, UK. Y.L and S.K. acknowledge Innovate UK KTP010551 grant.

Author Contributions: Savas Konur, Nereida Polovina, Yang Lan, A. Taufiq Asyhari and Yonghong Peng designed the experiments; Babagana Modu performed the experiments; Babagana Modu analysed the data; Babagana Modu, Savas Konur, Nereida Polovina, Yang Lan, A. Taufiq Asyhari and Yonghong Peng contributed reagents/materials/analysis tools; Babagana Modu wrote the paper.

Conflicts of Interest: The authors declare no conflict of interest.

Abbreviations

The following abbreviations are used in this manuscript:

SEM	Structural Equation Modelling
EFA	Exploratory Factor Analysis
PLS-PM	Partial Least Squares Path Modelling
LVs	Latent Variables
MVs	Measurement Variables
FA	Factor Analysis
API	Application Programming Interface
SVM	Support Vector Machine
LiR	Linear Regression
LoR	Logistic Regression
DT	Decision Tree
NB	Naive Bayes
KNN	K-Nearest Neighbours
K-M	K-Means
CFSR	Climate Forecast System Reanalysis
NCEP	National Centre for Environmental Prediction
JSON	JavaScript Object Notation
XML	Extensible Markup Language
HTML	HyperText Markup Language

Appendix A

Appendix A.1. Estimation of Parameters

Step 1   Initialization: Suppose $\mathbf{Y}_1, \cdots, \mathbf{Y}_K$ are the respective MVs, and are scaled such that $\mathbf{E}(\mathbf{Y}_i) = 0$ and $\mathbf{V}(\mathbf{Y}_i) = 1$. We are interested in expressing each LV as a linear combination of MVs, represented in compact form:

$$\hat{\mathbf{X}} = \mathbf{YM}$$
$$\hat{\mathbf{x}}_g = \frac{\hat{x}_g}{\sqrt{VAR(\hat{x}_g)}}, g = 1, \cdots, G \tag{A1}$$

Hence, the LVs are initialized as: $\hat{\mathbf{X}} = \hat{\mathbf{x}}_1, \cdots, \hat{\mathbf{x}}_G$.

Step 2   Inner approximation

Within the inner model domain, the estimation of the path parameter of each LV can be mathematically represented as the weighted sum of its neighbouring LVs.

$$\tilde{\mathbf{X}} = \hat{\mathbf{X}}\mathbf{E}$$
$$\tilde{\mathbf{x}}_g = \frac{\tilde{x}_g}{\sqrt{(VAR(\tilde{\mathbf{x}}_g))}}, g = 1, \cdots, G \tag{A2}$$

The approximate estimation of the inner model path parameter takes: $\tilde{\mathbf{X}} = (\tilde{\mathbf{x}}_1, \cdots, \tilde{\mathbf{x}}_G)$.

Step 3   Outer approximation

The outer approximation is computed based on the weight of the LV loads from the inner approximation. This comes in two forms, Mode A and Mode B. For Mode A, a multivariate regression coefficient with the block of MVs as the response and the LV as the regressor:

$$\hat{\mathbf{w}}_g^\top = (\tilde{\mathbf{x}}_g^\top \tilde{\mathbf{x}}_g)^{-1} \tilde{\mathbf{x}}_g^\top \mathbf{Y}_g \tag{A3}$$

Mode B is a multiple regression coefficient with the block of MVs as the response and its block of MVs as the regressor:

$$\hat{\mathbf{w}}_g = (\mathbf{Y}_g^\top \mathbf{Y}_g)^{-1} \mathbf{Y}_g^t \tilde{\mathbf{x}}_g \tag{A4}$$

Step 4   Outer weight vector

Let $k_g = \{k \in \{1, \cdots, K\} | y_k\, x_g\}$ be a set of indices for MVs related to LV x_g; then, w_g, $g = 1, \cdots, g$, is a column vector of length $|k_g|$. We can write down the matrix of outer weights, W as:

$$W = \begin{pmatrix} w_1 & 0 & \cdots & 0 \\ 0 & w_2 & \cdots & 0 \\ \vdots & \vdots & \ddots & \vdots \\ 0 & 0 & \cdots & w_G \end{pmatrix}$$

The outer weight vectors, $w_1, \cdots, w_G$, in an outer weights matrix W, which we are using now to estimate the factor scores by means of the MVs, are

$$\hat{\mathbf{X}} = \mathbf{YW}$$
$$\hat{\mathbf{X}}_g = \frac{\hat{\mathbf{X}}_g}{\sqrt{VAR(\hat{\mathbf{X}}_g)}}, g = 1, \cdots, G, \tag{A5}$$

Step 5   Iteration

resulting in the outer estimation: $\mathbf{X} = (\hat{\mathbf{x}}_1, \cdots, \hat{\mathbf{x}}_G)$.

If the relative change of all the outer weights from one iteration to the next are smaller than a predefined tolerance,

$$\left| \frac{\hat{w}_{kg}^{old} - \hat{w}_{kg}^{new}}{\hat{w}_{kg}^{new}} \right| < \epsilon, \forall, k = 1, \cdots, K \wedge g = 1, \cdots, G, \tag{A6}$$

the estimation of factor scores done in (A5) is taken to be final. Otherwise, go back to (A2).

Appendix A.2. Weighting Scheme

The weighting schemes are used to estimate the inner weight in (A2) of the PLS algorithm. Generally, there are three weighting schemes, centroid [49], and later [42] introduced the factorial and path weighting schemes.

Appendix A.2.1. Centroid (A)

The centroid weighting scheme takes the form:

$$e_{ij} = \begin{cases} sign(r_{ij}), & \text{for } c_{ij} = 1, i, j = 1, \cdots, G \\ 0, & \text{else} \end{cases} \tag{A7}$$

where $\mathbf{E}$ denotes the matrix of inner weights.

Appendix A.2.2. Factorial (B)

The factorial weighting scheme also takes the form:

$$e_{ij} = \begin{cases} r_{ij}, & \text{for } c_{ij} = 1, i, j = 1, \cdots, G \\ 0, & \text{else} \end{cases} \tag{A8}$$

Appendix A.2.3. Path Weighting (C)

In this weighting scheme, the predecessor and successor of a LV play a different role in the relation. The relation between one specific LV $\mathbf{x}_i$ and its successor is determined by their correlation; for the predecessors it is determined by a multiple regression

$$\begin{aligned} \mathbf{x}_i &= \mathbf{x}_i^{pred} \gamma + \mathbf{z}_i \\ \mathbf{E}[\mathbf{z}_i] &= 0, i = 1, \cdots, G \end{aligned} \tag{A9}$$

where $\mathbf{x}_i^{pred}$ is the predecessor set of the LV $\mathbf{x}_i$. Denoting $\mathbf{x}_i^{succ}$ as the successor set of the LV $\mathbf{x}_i$; the elements of the inner weight matrix are denoted $\mathbf{E}$ as

$$e_{ij} = \begin{cases} \gamma_j, & \text{for } j \in \mathbf{x}_i^{pred}, \\ COR(\mathbf{y}_i, \mathbf{x}_j), & \text{for } j \in \mathbf{x}_i^{succ}, \\ 0, & \text{else} \end{cases} \tag{A10}$$

Appendix A.3. Discriminant Validity Check

In the structural equation model, the factor scores are estimated by the PLS algorithm, while the path coefficients are also estimated using ordinary least squares (OLS). Now, for each LV $\hat{\mathbf{x}}_g$, $g = 1, \cdots, G$, the path coefficient is the regression coefficient in its predecessor set $\hat{\mathbf{x}}_g^{pred}$ defined as:

$$\hat{\beta}_g = (\hat{\mathbf{x}}_g^{pred\top} \hat{\mathbf{x}}_g^{pred})^{-1} \hat{\mathbf{x}}_g^{pred\top} \hat{\mathbf{x}}_g \tag{A11}$$

Using (A11), we can compute the element $\hat{\mathbf{b}}_{ij}, i, j = 1, \cdots, G$, of the estimated matrix of path coefficients $\hat{\beta}$.

Appendix A.3.1. Path Coefficients

$$\hat{\beta}_{ij} = \begin{cases} \hat{\beta}_{gj}, & \text{for } j \in \mathbf{x}_i^{pred}, \\ 0, & \text{else} \end{cases} \tag{A12}$$

Therefore, matrix $\hat{\mathbf{B}}$ denotes a transition matrix for the structural equation model.

Appendix A.3.2. Total Effects

We can calculate the matrix of the total effects $\hat{\mathbf{T}}$ as the sum of the 1 to **G** step transition matrices:

$$\hat{\mathbf{T}} = \sum_{g=1}^{G} \hat{\mathbf{B}}_g \tag{A13}$$

Note that $\hat{\mathbf{B}}^g$ expands to $\overbrace{\hat{\mathbf{B}} \cdot \hat{\mathbf{B}} \cdots \cdot \hat{\mathbf{B}}}^{g-times}$, e.g., $\hat{\mathbf{B}}^2$ contains all the indirect effects mediated by only one LV.

Appendix A.3.3. Outer Loadings

The cross and outer loadings are estimated as:

$$\hat{\wedge}^{cross} = COR(\mathbf{Y}, \hat{\mathbf{X}}) \tag{A14}$$

$$\hat{\lambda}_{kg}^{outer} = \begin{cases} \hat{\lambda}_{kg}^{cross}, & \text{if } m_{kg} = 1 \\ 0, & \text{else} \end{cases} \tag{A15}$$

References

1. World Health Organization. *Malaria Rapid Diagnostic Test Performance: Results of WHO Product Testing of Malaria RDTs: Round 6*; World Health Organization: Geneva, Switzerland, 2015.
2. Haque, U.; Hashizume, M.; Glass, G.E.; Dewan, A.M.; Overgaard, H.J.; Yamamoto, T. The role of climate variability in the spread of malaria in Bangladeshi highlands. *PLoS ONE* **2010**, *5*, e14341.
3. Bonan, G.B.; Shugart, H.H. Environmental factors and ecological processes in boreal forests. *Annu. Rev. Ecol. Syst.* **1989**, *20*, 1–28.
4. Kumar, V.; Mangal, A.; Panesar, S.; Yadav, G.; Talwar, R.; Raut, D.; Singh, S. Forecasting malaria cases using climatic factors in Delhi, India: A time series analysis. *Malar. Res. Treat.* **2014**, doi:10.1155/2014/482851.
5. Ngarakana-Gwasira, E.T.; Bhunu, C.P.; Masocha, M.; Mashonjowa, E. Assessing the Role of Climate Change in Malaria Transmission in Africa. *Malar. Res. Treat.* **2016**, doi:10.1155/2016/7104291.
6. Nath, D.C.; Mwchahary, D.D. Association between Climatic Variables and Malaria Incidence: A Study in Kokrajhar District of Assam, India: Climatic Variables and Malaria Incidence in Kokrajhar District. *Glob. J. Health Sci.* **2013**, *5*, 90.
7. Modu, B.; Asyhari, A.T.; Peng, Y. Data Analytics of climatic factor influence on the impact of malaria incidence. In Proceedings of the 2016 IEEE Symposium Series on Computational Intelligence (SSCI), Athens, Greece, 6–9 December 2016; pp. 1–8.
8. Tenenhaus, M.; Vinzi, V.E.; Chatelin, Y.M.; Lauro, C. PLS path modeling. *Comput. Stat. Data Anal.* **2005**, *48*, 159–205.

9. Sriram, T.; Rao, V.; Narayana, S.; Dowluru, K. Intelligent Parkinson disease prediction using machine learning algorithms. *Int. J. Eng. Innov. Technol.* **2013**, *3*, 212–215.

10. Ganesan, N.; Venkatesh, K.; Rama, M.A. Application of Neural Networks in diagnosing cancer disease using demographic data. *Int. J. Comput. Appl.* **2010**, *1*, 76–85.

11 Aditya, M.; Prince, K.; Himanshu, A.; Pankaj, K. Early heart disease prediction using data mining techniques. *Comput. Sci. Inf. Technol.* **2014**, 53–59, doi:10.5121/csit.2014.4807.

12. Wang, L. (Ed.) *Support Vector Machines: Theory and Applications*; Springer: Berlin, Germany, 2005; Volume 177.

13. Sharma, V.; Kumar, A.; Panat, L.; Karajkhede, G.; Lele, A. Malaria outbreak prediction model using machine learning. *Int. J. Adv. Res. Comput. Eng. Technol.* **2015**, *4*, 4415–4419.

14. Parham, P.E.; Michael, E. Modelling the effects of weather and climate change on malaria transmission. *Environ. Health Perspect.* **2010**, *118*, 620.

15. Myers, S.S.; Patz, J.A. Emerging threats to human health from global environmental change. *Annu. Rev. Environ. Resour.* **2009**, *34*, 223–252.

16. Myers, S.S.; Gaffikin, L.; Golden, C.D.; Ostfeld, R.S.; Redford, K.H.; Ricketts, T.H.; Osofsky, S.A. Human health impacts of ecosystem alteration. *Proc. Natl. Acad. Sci. USA* **2013**, *110*, 18753–18760.

17. Bayles, B.R.; Brauman, K.A.; Adkins, J.N.; Allan, B.F.; Ellis, A.M.; Goldberg, T.L.; Ricketts, T.H. Ecosystem Services Connect Environmental Change to Human Health Outcomes. *EcoHealth* **2016**, *13*, 443–449.

18. The Potsdam Institute for Climate Impact Research and Climate Analytics. *Turn-Down the Heat—Why a 4 Degree Warmer World Must Be Avoided*; International Bank for Reconstruction and Development and World Bank: Washington, DC, USA, 2012.

19. De Castro, M.C.; Monte-Mór, R.L.; Sawyer, D.O.; Singer, B.H. Malaria risk on the Amazon frontier. *Proc. Natl. Acad. Sci. USA* **2006**, *103*, 2452–2457.

20. Nyarko, P. Population and Housing Census, District Analytical Report, Ejisu-Juaben Municipal. Available online: https://www.citypopulation.de/php/ghana-admin.php?adm2id=0117. (accessed on 12 January 2017).

21. Addai, G.; Anyatewon Kwesi, D. *2010 Population and Housing Census: District Analytical Report*, 1st ed.; Ghana Statistical Service: Accra, Ghana, 2014

22. Takyi Appiah, S.; Otoo, H.; Nabubie, I.B. Times Series Analysis Of Malaria Cases In Ejisu-Juaben Municipality. *Int. J. Sci. Technol. Res.* **2015**, *4*, 220–226.

23. Global Weather Data for SWAT. Available online: http://globalweather.tamu.edu (accessed on 24 June 2017).

24. Nitzl, C.; Chin, W.W. The case of partial least squares (PLS) path modeling in managerial accounting research. *J. Manag. Control* **2017**, *28*, 137–156.

25. Bagozzi, R.P.; Yi, Y. Specification, evaluation, and interpretation of structural equation models. *J. Acad. Mark. Sci.* **2012**, *40*, 8–34.

26. Dan, E.D.; Jude, O.; Idochi, O. Modelling and forecasting malaria mortality rate using SARIMA models (a case study of Aboh Mbaise general hospital, Imo State Nigeria). *Sci. J. Appl. Math. Stat.* **2014**, *2*, 31–41.

27. Ruscio, J.; Roche, B. Determining the number of factors to retain in an exploratory factor analysis using comparison data of known factorial structure. *Psychol. Assess.* **2012**, *24*, 282.

28. Kline, R.B. *Principles and Practice of Structural Equation Modelling*; Guilford Publications: New York, NY, USA, 2015.

29. Kelloway, E.K.; Santor, D.A. Using LISREL for Structural Equation Modelling: A Researcher's Guide. *Can. Psychol.* **1999**, *40*, 381.

30. Monecke, A.; Leisch, F. SemPLS: Structural Equation Modeling Using Partial Least Squares. *J. Stat. Softw.* **2012**, *48*, 1–32.

31. Wold, H. Soft Modeling: The Basic Design and Some Extensions. In *Systems under Indirect Observation: Causality– Structure– Prediction*; Part 2; Jöreskog, K.G., Wold, H., Eds.; North-Holland Publishing Company: Amsterdam, The Netherlands, 1982; pp. 1–54.

32. Dijkstra, T.K. Latent variables and indices: Herman Wold's basic design and partial least squares. In *Handbook of Partial Least Squares*; Springer: Berlin, Germany, 2010; pp. 23–46.

33. Byrne, B.M. *Structural Equation Modelling with LISREL, PRELIS, and SIMPLIS: Basic Concepts, Applications, and Programming*; Psychology Press: Hove, UK, 2013.

34. Li, X.X.; Wang, L.X.; Zhang, J.; Liu, Y.X.; Zhang, H.; Jiang, S.W.; Zhou, X.N. Exploration of ecological factors related to the spatial heterogeneity of tuberculosis prevalence in PR China. *Glob. Health Action* **2014**, *7*, doi:10.3402/gha.v7.23620.

35. Yeomans, K.A.; Golder, P.A. The Guttman-Kaiser criterion as a predictor of the number of common factors. *Statistician* **1982**, *31*, 221–229.

36. Ledesma, R.D.; Valero-Mora, P.; Macbeth, G. The scree test and the number of factors: A dynamic graphics approach. *Span. J. Psychol.* **2015**, *18*, doi:10.1017/sjp.2015.13.

37. Xu, L.; Stige, L.C.; Chan, K.S.; Zhou, J.; Yang, J.; Sang, S.; Lu, L. Climate variation drives dengue dynamics. *Proc. Natl. Acad. Sci. USA* **2016**, *114*, 113–118.

38. Srinivasulu, N.; Gujju Gandhi, B.; Naik, R.; Daravath, S. Influence of Climate Change on Malaria Incidence in Mahaboobnagar District of Andhra Pradesh, India. Available online: https://www.ijcmas.com/Archives/vol-2-5/N.%20Srinivasulu,%20et%20al.pdf (accessed on 24 June 2017).

39. Hair, J.F.; Sarstedt, M.; Pieper, T.M.; Ringle, C.M. The use of partial least squares structural equation modelling in strategic management research: A review of past practices and recommendations for future applications. *Long Range Plan.* **2012**, *45*, 320–340.

40. Jarque, C.M.; Bera, A.K. A test for normality of observations and regression residuals. *Int. Stat. Rev./Rev. Int. Stat.* **1987**, *55*, 163–172.

41. Wilk, M.B.; Gnanadesikan, R. Probability plotting methods for the analysis for the analysis of data. *Biometrika* **1968**, *55*, 1–17.

42. Lohmöller, J.B. *Latent Variable Path Analysis with Partial Least Squares*; Physica-Verlag: Heidelberg, Germany, 1989.

43. Lustgarten, J.L.; Gopalakrishnan, V.; Grover, H.; Visweswaran, S. Improving classification performance with discretization on biomedical datasets. In Proceedings of the AMIA Annual Symposium, Hilton Washington and Tower, Washington, DC, USA, 8 November 2008.

44. Maslove, D.M.; Podchiyska, T.; Lowe, H.J. Discretization of continuous features in clinical datasets. *J. Am. Med. Inf. Assoc.* **2013**, *20*, 544–553.

45. Scikit-Learn. Available online: http://www.scikit-learn.org (accessed on 24 June 2017).

46. MLSVM for Research. Available online: https://play.google.com/store/apps/details?id=project.lanydr.mlsvm&hl=en (accessed on 24 June 2017).

47. LIBSVM-A Library for Support Vector Machines. Available online: www.csie.ntu.edu.tw/~cjlin/libsvm/ (accessed on 24 June 2017).

48. Weather API. Available online: http://openweathermap.org/api) (accessed on 24 June 2017).

49. Gang, S. Soft modeling: Intermediate between traditional model building and data analysis. In *Mathematical Statistics*; Polish Scientific Publishers: Warsaw, Poland, 1980; Volume 6, pp. 333–346.

applied sciences

MDPI

Article

A Hospital Recommendation System Based on Patient Satisfaction Survey

Mohammad Reza Khoie [1,*,†], Tannaz Sattari Tabrizi [1,*,†], Elham Sahebkar Khorasani [2], Shahram Rahimi [1] and Nina Marhamati [1]

[1] Department of Computer Science, Southern Illinois University, Carbondale, IL 62901, USA; rahimi@cs.siu.edu (S.R.); nina@siu.edu (N.M.)
[2] Department of Computer Science, University of Illinois at Springfield, Springfield, IL 62703, USA; esahe2@uis.edu
* Correspondence: rezakhoie@siu.edu (M.R.K.); tannaz@siu.edu (T.S.T.); Tel.: +1-618-303-1088 (M.R.K.); +1-618-303-0536 (T.S.T.)
† These authors contributed equally to this work.

Received: 28 July 2017; Accepted: 11 September 2017; Published: 21 September 2017

Abstract: Surveys are used by hospitals to evaluate patient satisfaction and to improve general hospital operations. Collected satisfaction data is usually represented to the hospital administration by using statistical charts and graphs. Although such visualization is helpful, typically no deeper data analysis is performed to identify important factors which contribute to patient satisfaction. This work presents an unsupervised data-driven methodology for analyzing patient satisfaction survey data. The goal of the proposed exploratory data analysis is to identify patient communities with similar satisfaction levels and the major factors, which contribute to their satisfaction. This type of data analysis will help hospitals to pinpoint the prevalence of certain satisfaction factors in specific patient communities or clusters of individuals and to implement more proactive measures to improve patient experience and care. To this end, two layers of data analysis is performed. In the first layer, patients are clustered based on their responses to the survey questions. Each cluster is then labeled according to its salient features. In the second layer, the clusters of first layer are divided into sub-clusters based on patient demographic data. Associations are derived between the salient features of each cluster and its sub-clusters. Such associations are ranked and validated by using standard statistical tests. The associations derived by this methodology are turned into comments and recommendations for healthcare providers and patients. Having applied this method on patient and survey data of a hospital resulted in 19 recommendations where 10 of them were statistically significant with chi-square test's p-value less than 0.5 and an odds ratio z-test's p-value of more than 2 or less than -2. These associations not only are statistically significant but seems rational too.

Keywords: health data analytics; survey analysis; HCAHPS; hospital consumer assessment of healthcare providers and systems; unsupervised learning

---

1. Introduction

Patient satisfaction has been proven to be one of the most valid indicators of the quality of care. Analysis of patient satisfaction data is in demand by many health-care providers. Most health-care providers, from doctor's offices to clinics and hospitals, collect patient satisfaction surveys to evaluate their various services and patient experience. This increasingly growing data is conventionally analyzed by statistical methods, such as analysis of variance (ANOVA) [1], simple regression, Fisher's approach and extensions [2], Neyman's approach to randomization-based inference [2], etc. Such methods typically approach the problem with a specific question in mind and find the relation between one or more independent variables and a dependent variable. For example, they compute the percentage of the patients that have rated each hospital's services similarly or at most provide some correlations between specific groups of patients and their answers to a specific satisfaction question.

For improving patient satisfaction, issues of health care provided at the hospital level and the factors that originate those issues from patients' point of view should be discovered. Therefore, survey data should be either manually analyzed by examining each possible pattern in the data set using conventional methods or an unsupervised methodology is needed to do the analysis with least amount of human interaction. Such methodology should get the satisfaction survey data, find patterns that are repeated among patients' demographics and their satisfaction level in different fields, validate the patterns and compile them into a set of recommendations to help hospitals improve satisfaction within various patient communities.

To this end, a new hybrid methodology is proposed that differs from these conventional approaches in that it is not bound to a single outcome or dependent variable. The focus of this approach is to find patterns in patients' responses to all satisfaction questions and relate them to patients' demographics. The proposed methodology is focused on discovering issues of the health care provided at the hospital level and the factors that originate those issues from the patients' point of view. This methodology is a hybrid unsupervised clustering-labeling method, which finds associations between various levels of patients' satisfaction and demographics. The associations are validated by using standard statistical models and turned into useful recommendations for hospitals in order to improve patients' experience, save cost, and build long-term patient loyalty. The methodology can be generalized to any complex multi-level survey analysis.

The article is organized into eight sections. The next section describes the standard survey instrument used for collecting patient satisfaction data. Section 3 reviews the literature on the analysis of hospital survey data as well as modern survey data analysis methods. The proposed methodology for the analysis of the survey data will be presented in Section 4. Section 5 reports on the experimental results of the analysis using the Hospital Consumer Assessment of Healthcare Providers and Systems (HCAHPS) dataset. The validation of the results of the analysis are discussed in Section 6. Section 7 explains how to convert the associations derived from the analysis into recommendations for healthcare providers. The last section draws a conclusion and future direction of this study.

2. Literature Review

This section describes the HCAHPS dataset and briefly reviews modern survey data analysis methods and their shortcomings in analyzing the HCAHPS dataset.

2.1. HCAHPS Hospital Survey Data

HCAHPS [3] is a standard survey instrument used by many hospitals to evaluate patients' experience. This data is provided by the HCAHPS database, which is funded by U.S. agency for health care research. The centers for Medicaid and Medicare services use the scores from HCAHPS to reimburse hospitals for patient care. Providing a high quality care is directly related to a hospital's revenue and many hospitals are looking for ways to improve patient experience and achieve a higher HCAHPS score.

Table 1 gives a brief description of the satisfaction questions on the HCAHPS survey instrument and the categories that they fall into. As shown in the table, the survey questions are divided into six sections where each section has a number of multiple choice questions. The number of choices for each question is also specified in Table 1. For instance, the section on "care from doctor" measures patient satisfaction with the care provided by doctor(s) using three questions about doctor's respect, listening, and explaining. Each question has four choices (Never, Sometimes, Usually, and Always).

Table 1. Satisfaction Questions Categories.

Section	Number of Question in Each Section	Number of Choices for Each Question
Care from Nurses	5	4
Care from Doctors	3	4
Hospital Environment	2	4
Experience in Hospital	5	4
When You Left	1	2
Overall Rating	1	2
	1	11

Table 2 presents the types of demographic questions in HCAHPS survey instrument. All demographic identifiers (except for "age" and "discharge date") are categorical. The HCAHPS survey questionnaire is brought in the Appendix A.

Table 2. Demographic Data Types.

Questions	Number of Choices
Age	-
Discharge Date	-
State	44
Racial Category	6
Overall Health	5
Education	6
Ethnicity	5
Patient-Filled Race	5
Patient's Language	3
Gender	2
Principal Reason	3
Admission Source	10
Survey Language	2

2.2. Review of Existing Studies on HCAHPS Dataset

There have been several studies on the HCAHPS dataset. Stratford [4] defined a number of objectives to extract useful knowledge from the HCAHPS survey data and studied the effect of such knowledge on hospital care improvement.

Sheetz et al. [5] investigated the relationship between postoperative morbidity and mortality and patients' perspectives of care in surgical patients. In their article, the overall satisfaction score is used along with Michigan Surgical Quality Collaborative clinical registry as a measure of patients' perspective of care.

Quite a few studies have explored specific relationships between a single satisfaction question and one or more of patients' demographic information. Goldstein et al. [6] conducted an analysis of racial/ethnicity in patients' perceptions of inpatient care. Using regression, they concluded that non-Hispanic Whites on average tend to go to hospitals that deliver better patient experiences to all patients as compared to the hospitals that are typically used by African American, Hispanic, Asian/Pacific Islander, or multiracial patients [6].

Elliot et al. analyzed the association of gender with different aspects of satisfaction, [7] and, in a separate study, analyzed hospital ranking variation with patient health status and race/language and slightly with patient's education and age [8].

Klinkenberg [9] explored the relation between the willingness to recommend the hospital and other satisfaction identifiers. This paper discovers that hospitals that focus resources on improving interpersonal aspects of care such as nurses and doctors' courtesy, respect, listening, room cleanliness, etc. will be most likely to see improvements in satisfaction scores. The paper does not consider patients' demographic data.

The existing literature on analysis of the HCAHPS dataset is mostly hypothesis-driven and only considers specific aspects of patient satisfaction or demographics. In contrast, the methodology presented in this paper does not assume any specific hypothesis. Instead, we run a data-driven exploratory analysis which inspects all aspects of patient satisfaction as well as patient demographics and discovers interesting associations in the HCAHPS dataset.

2.3. Shortcomings of Existing Survey Analysis Methods

In addition to the literature on analysis of the HCAHPS dataset; it is also worth reviewing the methods typically used for general survey analysis. Commonly used exploratory data analysis methods such as ANOVA, regression, discriminant analysis, and factor analysis are not applicable to HCAHPS data because of its unique characteristics.

Analysis of variance (ANOVA) is a collection of statistical methods that form an exploratory tool for explaining observations. ANOVA provides a statistical test of whether or not the means of several groups are equal [2]. For finding a specific correlation in the HCAHPS dataset, different levels of ANOVA should be combined. To this end, all possible combinations of satisfaction questions and demographic data should be exhaustively tested, which could be time prohibitive. In addition, ANOVA assumes a normal distribution of the sample observation, continuous dependent variables, and at least one categorical independent variable with two or more levels. The sample data collected for HCAHPS is not guaranteed to be normally distributed. Moreover, the demographic data which form the dependent variables are not always categorical. Given the violation of these assumptions, ANOVA may not produce reliable results for HCAHPS dataset.

Regression analysis is a statistical tool for investigation of relationship between multiple continuous or categorical independent variables and a continuous dependent variable [10]. Regression models can be used for validating correlations, although they are usually used for predicting and forecasting. Variations of this model can be used for the HCAHPS categorical dependent variables and lead to nonlinear models. Using these interpretation, different hypothesis on the data set can be tested by using forward and backward selection of combinations of satisfaction questions and patients' demographic data. However, forward and backward selection is not efficient in the context of HCAHPS data as the search space contains a very large number of combinations of dependent and independent variables. Moreover, fitting a separate model for each satisfaction identifier cannot capture the relationships between different satisfaction questions.

Discriminant analysis is another technique that allows for studying the difference between two or more groups of objects with respect to several variables simultaneously [11]. This model can be fitted to HCAHPS data set in terms of categorical dependent variables as the satisfaction questions and continuous and categorical independent variables such as patient's demographical data. Although this method works better than regression in terms of interpreting categorical variables, it suffers from the same deficiencies when it comes to analyzing the HCAHPS dataset.

Factor analysis is another method that is typically applied to survey data. The main application of this method is to reduce the number of variables and to detect structure in the relationship between variables. In particular, factor analysis can be used to explore the data for patterns, confirm hypotheses, or reduce a large number of variables to a more manageable number [12]. Compared to regression and discriminant analysis, factor analysis is more suitable for an exploratory analysis of the HCAHPS dataset as it does not require a priori hypothesis; however, it has two limitations: (1) the naming of the factors can be problematic and may not accurately reflect the variables within that factor. In particular, it may not be possible to directly compile factors into a set of recommendations for the hospitals. (2) factor analysis is based on the assumption that there is a linear relationship between factors and the variables when computing correlations. The features in the HCAHPS survey data may not necessarily be linearly correlated and factor analysis cannot capture non-linear relations.

3. Analyzing HCAHPS Data

This section describes the proposed methodology for analyzing the HCAHPS data. The analysis is done in three steps: 1—data preparation, 2—two-layer cluster analysis, and 3—salient feature extraction and associations.

3.1. Data Preparation

The first problem that should be handled in data preparation is the nature of some questions, called skip questions. A skip question by itself does not provide any information about a patient but it determines whether some other questions, called dependent questions, are applicable to the patient. For instance, a skip question inquires if the patient has used the bathroom or not. If not, the patient skips all of the dependent questions related to the bathroom cleanliness. Since skip questions, by themselves, do not provide any data about a patient, it would be reasonable to omit them from the dataset and treat their empty dependent questions as missing values. For example, if a patient has not used the bathroom, all of the bathroom-related questions have missing value for that patient.

There are two basic approaches for handling missing values: (1) the complete case analysis which ignores the records with missing data, or (2) the imputation of missing values. The imputation method can be further divided into single imputation where each missing value is replaced by a single value, and multiple imputations where each missing value is replaced by multiple values to reflect the uncertainty. The complete case analysis could introduce a selection bias and may lead to loss of information. The added bias makes the data related to those questions more homogenous. If all of the patients have similar opinion on the related questions the added bias will make those questions insignificant. However, if in fact there are two opposite opinions on this matter that are separated based on the demographic features of patients, the separation will be more statistically significant. Therefore, a single imputation method is applied in this study for handling missing values in HCAHPS dataset. This approach may reduce the variance and add bias to range of the imputed variables but will not result in loss of information. The reduction in the variance of an imputed variable may decrease the chance of that variable being selected as a significant feature when compared to other variables, but there is still a chance of being selected if the data is extensively divided on that variable.

For imputing the missing values, the K-nearest neighbor imputation method (KNNI) [13] is used. This method is chosen because it is applicable to both continuous and categorical variables and it can be applied to the data set automatically and without any supervision. This method imputes the missing value based on the K nearest neighbors of the record with missing value. For categorical features, the missing value is replaced with the category which has the majority in the K nearest neighbors. For continuous features, the missing value is replaced with the weighted average of that feature in the nearest neighbors. To have minimum computational complexity, $K = 3$ has been chosen for KNNI as it is the least number of neighbors that could produce reasonable results for finding majority of classes among categorical variables.

3.2. Two-Layer Cluster Analysis

The goal of this step is to do exploratory data analysis in order to find hidden patterns in the HCAHPS dataset and to identify the main sources of patient dissatisfaction. To this end, two layers of clustering is performed on HCAHP data as illustrated in Figure 1.

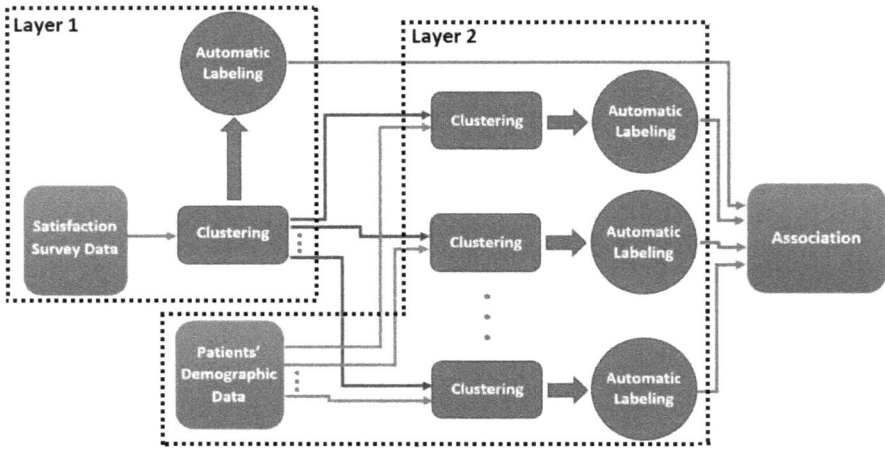

Figure 1. Two-layered analysis method. In the first layer, the clusters and their labels are generated based on the satisfaction questions. In second layer, the clusters of first layer are re-clustered based on patient demographic data.

In the first layer, patient data is clustered based on satisfaction questions (listed in Table 2) to group the patients with similar satisfaction identifiers. We examined various clustering methods such as K-means, DBScan, and Spectral clustering and ultimately decided to choose K-means for its simplicity and efficiency. K-means is the most commonly used clustering method with two main problems. First, it is sensitive to the initialization of the cluster centers and might converge into a local optimum. Second, it requires a pre-specified number of clusters (k). To address the first problem, K-Means++ is typically used to initialize the cluster centroids before proceeding with the standard K-means. With K-means++ initialization, the algorithm is guaranteed to find optimal clusters with $O(\log k)$ competitive with K-means optimal solution [14]. For solving the second problem, there are several techniques offered to extract the optimal number of clusters. The Calinski-Harabasz criterion method is chosen for the estimation of number of clusters for K-means. This method finds the best number of clusters by applying the criterion of minimum within cluster sum of squares. This procedure ensures an effective reduction of the number of possible splits [15], which prevents overfitting in association extraction procedure. This method is implemented in R using the vegan v2.4-2 package by Jari Oksanen based on the Algorithm 1.

Algorithm 1. Optimal number of clusters using Calinski-Harabasz criterion.

Find Number of Clusters (data, minNumClusters = 1, maxNumClusters = 10)
Fit ← cascadeKM (data, inf.gr = minNumClusters, sup.gr = maxNumClusters, iter = 100, criterion = "calinski")
calinski_best ← which.max (fit.results [2,])
Return calinski_best

To apply Kmeans++ algorithm on the HCAHPS data with mixed categorical and continuous variables, the categorical variables are transformed to dummy variables and the continuous variables are normalized using z-score normalization. By this transformation all the variables are in one spatial distance range, which is suitable for applying the Kmeans++ algorithm.

After applying Kmeans++ with selected number of clusters, the salient features of each cluster are derived using automatic cluster labeling to mark the important features that make up a cluster.

The salient features of a cluster are the ones whose values are significantly different (in a statistical sense) in the cluster compared to those in the other clusters.

The clusters of layer one are then fed into the second layer for further analysis. Each satisfaction cluster of the first layer is clustered again; but this time based on the demographic features of each record listed in Table 2 (e.g., patient's age, race, etc.). The salient features of each sub-cluster are then derived to find the important features that make up a sub-cluster.

3.3. Salient Feature Extraction

One can draw associations between the salient features of the outer (satisfaction) cluster and the salient features of its inner (demographic) sub-clusters. For instance, suppose that as a result of the first layer we get an outer cluster whose salient features indicate low values for "satisfaction with Doctor". This cluster is then further clustered into demographic sub-groups. Suppose that the salient features of one of the sub-groups indicates higher values for age and a particular doctor (Doctor X) who visited most patients in this sub-group.

Putting the salient features of a cluster and its sub-clusters together, one can draw an association between older patients who expressed low satisfaction with their doctor and who were visited by Doctor X. Such associations must be further validated through statistical evaluations and can be used to make recommendations to the hospital. For example, the recommendation system might recommend not to assign Doctor X to older patients.

We extract the salient features of each cluster based on the methodology proposed in [16]:

1. The centroid of a cluster k is computed as the average of the points in the cluster:

$$X_k = \frac{\sum_{i=1}^{N} P_i}{N} \tag{1}$$

where X_k is the centroid of cluster k and P_i is a point in cluster k.

2. The Euclidean distance of each point to its cluster centroid is computed:

$$d_i = \sqrt{\sum_j \left(P_{ij} - X_{kj} \right)} \tag{2}$$

3. The points in each cluster are divided into *in-pattern* and *out-pattern* records. The records whose distance lie within the range defined by (3) are called in-pattern records while all other records including the ones in other clusters are called out-pattern records.

$$\mu_k - z\sigma_k < d_i < \mu_k + z\sigma_k \tag{3}$$

where μ_k and σ_k are the mean and standard deviation of the points in cluster k, respectively, and z is a constant factor. Smaller z results in more out-pattern records and larger z result in more in-pattern records.

4. For each feature v and cluster k, the mean of all in-pattern records, $\mu_{in}(k, v)$ and the mean of the out-pattern records, $\mu_{in}(k, v)$, are computed:

$$\mu_{in}(k, v) = \frac{\sum_{P_i \in \varphi_{in}} P_{iv}}{|\varphi_{in}(k)|} \tag{4}$$

$$\mu_{out}(k, v) = \frac{\sum_{P_i \in \varphi_{out}} P_{iv}}{|\varphi_{out}(k)|} \tag{5}$$

where $\varphi_{in}(k)$ and $\varphi_{out}(k)$ are the set of in-pattern and out-pattern points in cluster k, respectively.

5. A difference factor, $df(k, v)$, is calculated for each feature v in cluster k based on Equation (6):

$$df(k, v) = \frac{\mu_{in}(k, v) - \mu_{out}(k, v)}{\mu_{out}(k, v)} \tag{6}$$

6. The mean and standard deviation of the difference factors for all features in cluster k are calculated as follows:

$$\mu_{df}(k) = \frac{\sum_{v-1}^{D} df(k, v)}{D} \tag{7}$$

$$\sigma_{df}(k) = \sqrt{\sum_{v-1}^{D} \left(df(k, v) - \mu_{df}(k) \right)^2 / D} \tag{8}$$

where D is the number of features in the input space.

7. A feature v is a salient feature in cluster k if its corresponding difference factor in k deviates considerably from $\mu_{df}(k)$. More formally, feature v is a salient feature in cluster k if:

$$df(k, v) \leq \mu_{df}(k) - z\sigma_{df}(k) \tag{9}$$

$$df(k, v) \geq \mu_{df}(k) + z\sigma_{df}(k) \tag{10}$$

where z is a constant factor. The smaller the z the more salient features in each cluster. Salient feature extraction method is outlined in Algorithm 2.

Algorithm 2. Salient features extraction.

FindingSalientFeatures (noc, clustered_data, z)
Comment: calculating the center of each clustering by averaging records in the cluster.
    For i ← 0 to noc − 1
        cluster_centers [i] ← average over columns(clustered_data[i])
Comment: calculating distance of records from their assigned cluster center.
    For i ← 0 to noc − 1
        For j ← 0 to length(clustered_data[i]) − 1
            distance_matrix[i][j] ← distance (clustered_data[i][j], cluster_centers [i])
Comment: calculating the average distance of each cluster from its center.
    For i ← 0 to noc − 1
        average_distance[i] ← average over columns(distance_matrix[i])
Comment: calculating standard deviation of distances in each cluster.
    For i ← 0 to noc − 1
        standard_deviation[i]←sqrt (average over j((distance_matrix[i][j] − Average_distance[i]) ˆ2))
Comment: Finding in pattern and out pattern records in each cluster
    counter ← 0
    For i ← 0 to noc − 1
        For j ← to length(clustered_data[i]) − 1
            *If (distance_matrix[i][j] < (average_distance[i] + (z * standard_deviation[i]))*
            *AND distance_matrix[i][j] > (average_distance[i] − (z * standard_deviation[i]))*
                In_patterns[i][counter] ← j
                counter ++
Comment: Calculating the mean of each feature in each cluster for in-pattern neurons.
    For i ← 0 to noc-1
        For j ← 0 to length (clustered_data[i]) − 1
            If (j in In_patterns[i])
                In_pattern_mean[i] ← In_pattern_mean[i] + clustered_data[i]
        else

Algorithm 2. *Cont.*

$$Out\_pattern\_mean[i] \leftarrow Out\_pattern\_mean[i] + clustered\_data[i]$$
$$In\_pattern\_mean[i] \leftarrow In\_pattern\_mean[i]/length(In\_patterns[i])$$
$$Out\_pattern\_mean[i] \leftarrow Out\_pattern\_mean[i]/length(Out\_patterns[i])$$

Comment: *Calculating the difference factor of in and out pattern records.*

For $i \leftarrow 0$ to $noc - 1$

For $j \leftarrow 0$ to $number\_of\_columns(clustered\_data) - 1$

$$difference\_factor\ [i][j] \leftarrow In\_pattern\_mean[i][j] - Out\_pattern\_mean[i][j]$$

Comment: *Calculating the mean difference factor of each dimension.*

$$Mean\_difference\_factor \leftarrow average\ over\ row(difference\_factor)$$

Comment: *Calculating the standard deviation difference factor of each cluster.*

For $i \leftarrow 0$ to $noc - 1$

For $j \leftarrow 1$ to $number\_of\_columns(clustered\_data) - 1$

$$Difference\_factor\_SD[i] \leftarrow Difference\_factor\_SD[i] + difference\_factor\ [i][j] -$$
$$Mean\_difference\_factor\ [i])\hat{}2)$$
$$Difference\_factor\_SD[i] \leftarrow sqrt(Difference\_factor\_SD[i]/$$
$$number\_of\_columns(clustered\_data))$$

Comment: *Calculating a matrix of salient dimentions.*

For $i \leftarrow 0$ to $noc - 1$

For $j \leftarrow \quad number\_of\_columns(clustered\_data) - 1$

If $(difference\_factor\ [i][j] <=$

$(Mean\_difference\_factor[i] - (z * Difference\_factor\_SD[i])))$

$$Salient\_dimension[i][j] = -1$$

else if $(difference\_factor\ [i][j] >=$

$(Mean\_difference\_factor[i] + (z * Difference\_factor\_SD[i])))$

$$Salient\_dimension[i][j] = 1$$

Return *Salient_dimension*

To illustrate the extraction of salient features, suppose, as an example, that we have a dataset with five features as shown in Table 3.

Table 3. Features of Satisfaction Dataset.

Features	Description
D1	Communication with doctor
D2	Communication with Nurse
D3	Pain Management
D4	Cleanliness
D5	Quietness

Suppose that the data points of this feature space are clustered into three groups with the centroids listed in Table 4.

Table 4. Clusters Centroids.

Features	C1	C2	C3
D1	−0.0126243	0.97095961	−0.9913867
D2	0.03791055	−0.07749729	0.02231231
D3	−1.1444478	0.8585494	0.8681821
D4	−1.1509251	0.8681547	0.8681547
D5	−0.00279281	0.009980126	−0.0060900

To find the in-pattern and out-pattern records in the cluster, the distances of each record to all three cluster centroids are computed. In addition, the mean and standard deviation of distances for each cluster centroid are calculated. If a record's distance from a cluster centroid is within one standard deviation from the mean, then it is considered an in-pattern record of that cluster. Otherwise, it is an out-pattern record of the cluster.

Suppose that there are nine records in the dataset. Table 5 shows the distance of each record to all three cluster centroids as well as the mean and standard deviation of each cluster. The in-pattern records of each cluster are shown in bold.

Table 5. Distance of records from centroid. Bold numbers denote in-pattern records which are in range of one standard deviation from the mean.

Records	C1	C2	C3
R1	**1.967133**	0.7958750	**1.3957300**
R2	2.121455	**1.6483554**	0.9116866
R3	**1.675209**	**1.5959835**	**1.7050408**
R4	**1.518996**	**1.6174912**	**1.5210744**
R5	**1.697462**	**1.0558556**	2.1432977
R6	**1.843458**	0.8124378	**1.1173187**
R7	1.191784	2.2571117	**1.3717867**
R8	2.266916	0.7501202	**1.4390353**
R9	**1.706186**	**1.6242395**	**1.7090141**
R10	1.107229	2.0101626	**0.7544890**
μ	1.687192	1.367895	1.367732
σ	0.3833892	0.4231975	0.4307547

After tagging the records in a cluster as in-pattern and out-pattern, the mean of in-pattern records and out-pattern records in each cluster are calculated. Table 6 shows the difference factors of each feature in all three clusters along with the mean and standard deviation of the difference factors of each cluster. The salient features are highlighted in bold. For example, D3 (pain management) and D4 (cleanliness of the hospital) are salient features of cluster 1 while D2 (communication with Nurse) and D5 (quietness) are salient features of cluster 2. The positive values of significant difference factors show high frequency of dichotomous variables and high values for other categorical and continuous variables. Similarly, negative values show a low frequency for dichotomous variables and low values for other categorical and continuous variables. For instance, D3 (pain management) has negative difference factor for cluster one which shows low values of this variable, so the satisfaction with pain management is generally low in this cluster. Similarly, a high satisfaction with pain management can be inferred from cluster three. The salient features of each cluster are presented in Table 7, along with the range of that value or frequency of dichotomous value (High/Low) next to each of them. The salient features with the range of their values are a representation of the cluster, which will be used to create associations.

Table 6. Difference Factor of each Feature in each Cluster. Bold numbers are salient features which are out of range of 1 standard deviation from mean.

Features	C1	C2	C3
D1	−0.03037039	1.18199255	**−1.22503855**
D2	0.04416163	**−0.20817361**	−0.02380192
D3	**−1.537553**	1.033197	**1.041475**
D4	**−1.554513**	1.045382	**1.047448**
D5	−0.06825377	**−0.03673413**	−0.03182003
μ	−0.6293057	0.6031327	0.1616524
Σ	0.7493974	0.5972044	0.8430252

Table 7. Salient features.

Cluster	Salient Features	
C1	Pain Management	Low
	Cleanliness	Low
C2	Communication with Nurse	Low
	Quietness	Low
C3	Communication with doctor	Low
	Pain Management	High
	Cleanliness	High

4. Experiment

The methodology proposed in the previous section is implemented in R and is applied to the HCAHPS dataset of a hospital with 2652 records with the same features explained in Section 2.1. First, K-means++ is used to cluster all records based on the patients' responses to the satisfaction questions. A Self-organizing feature map is used to visualize data distribution in each cluster (Figure 2).

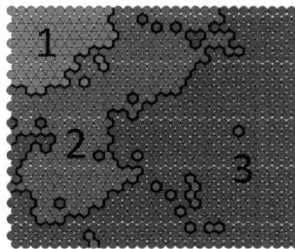

Figure 2. The clusters produced based on patients' responses to satisfaction questions.

The map shows that Kmeans++ divided data according to the Calinski-Harabasz [15] criterion into three clusters based on their responses to the satisfaction questions. These clusters are shown in different colors in Figure 2. In the next step, the salient features of each cluster are extracted to identify the most important features which constitute a cluster. Extracted salient features were interpreted according to nature of each variable whether it is continuing, categorical, or dichotomous. Table 8 asserts the interpretation of the extracted salient features. For example, cluster 1 represent patients who were well-informed about their symptoms after leaving the hospital and expressed high satisfaction with help after discharge and high overall satisfaction.

Table 8. Salient features of clusters in the first layer.

Cluster	Salient Features	
C1	•	High Satisfaction with Help after discharge
	•	High Satisfaction with Symptoms info
	•	High Overall Health
C2	•	High Satisfaction with Help after discharge
	•	High Satisfaction with Symptoms info
C3	•	Low Satisfaction with Help after discharge
	•	Low Satisfaction with Symptoms info
	•	Low Overall Health

Although theoretically salient features are expected be different in different clusters, this expectation could be violated if the clusters are of significantly different sizes. For example, in Table 2, *C1*, and *C2* share some features (i.e., high satisfaction with help after discharge and high satisfaction with symptoms info). This is due to the fact that *C3* is much bigger than *C1* and *C2* (Figure 1). Therefore, it has a significant effect on the value of difference factor, highlighting the shared salient features in *C1* and *C2*. Although it might appear that *C2* is redundant, *C1* and *C2* were divided into two distinct clusters mainly because of their difference in the overall health feature.

The records in each cluster are fed into the second layer of clustering. In this layer, patients are clustered based on their demographic data such as (e.g., age, sex, race, etc.). The first cluster is divided into four demographic sub-clusters and the second and third clusters are both divided into three demographic sub-clusters. The process is outlined in Algorithm 3 and the outcome of this step is visualized in Figure 3.

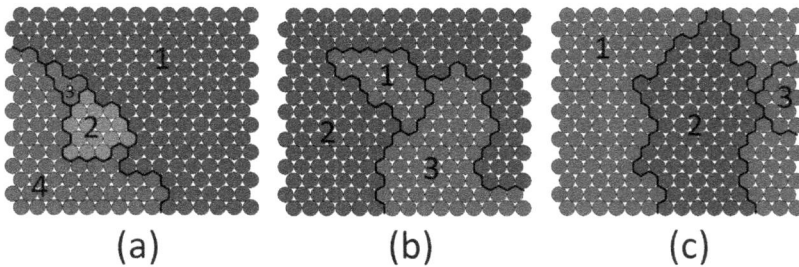

Figure 3. Sub-clusters produced based on patient demographic data (**a**) demographic sub-clusters of the first satisfaction cluster, (**b**)demographic sub-clusters of the second satisfaction cluster, (**c**) demographic subclusters of the third satisfaction cluster.

Algorithm 3. Recommendation extraction.

Find Recommendations (data, split_index)
        Satisfaction_questions_data ← data [:] [0:split_index]
        noc ← FindNumberOfClusters (Satisfaction_questions_data)
        Sq_clustered_data = kmeans (Satisfaction_questions_data)
        Sq_salient_dim ← FindingSalientFeatures (noc, Sq_clustered_data, z)
        For i ← 0 to noc
                For j in Sq_clustered_data[i]
                        Demographic_data ← data[j] [split_index: number_of_columns(data)]
                        D_clustered_data ← kmeans (Demographic_data)
                        D_salient_dim ← FindingSalientFeatures (noc, D_clustered_data, z)
                For sq_salient in Sq_salient_dim[i]:
                    If sq_salient != 0:
                        For d_salient in D_salient_dim:
                            If d_salient != 0:
                              Recommendation
                        [(col_name(sq_salient), sq_salient)].
                            Add ((col_name(d_salient), d_salient))
        Return recommendation

Once again salient feature extraction algorithm is applied on each sub-cluster. The results are asserted in Table 9.

Putting the salient features of a satisfaction cluster and the salient features of its demographic sub-cluster, we derived the associations listed in Table 10. These associations represent a possible source of significant satisfaction questions. For instance, the source of low satisfaction with help after discharge according to *C3* is communication with old people referred from a physician or Spanish speaking patients admitted from the emergency room. Transforming these associations into recommendations can offer hospital policy changes in favor of both patients and hospitals. The proper recommendation in this case can be putting more effort in communication with elderly people and Spanish people, or hiring a Spanish speaking nurse or interpreter.

It is worth noting, that the method explained in this section, works better in terms of performance and accuracy than in methods such as association rule mining, which has its well-known limitations including a brute-force method for extracting association rules and the risk of finding many irrelevant rules.

Table 9. Salient features of all satisfaction clusters and their demographic sub-clusters (Numbers in parenthesis demonstrate the clusters' populations).

Cluster	C1 (1210 Observations)			
Cluster Salient Features	• High Satisfaction with Help after discharge • High Satisfaction with Symptoms info • High Overall Health			
Sub-cluster	SC1 (378 obs.)	SC2 (236 obs.)	SC3 (268 obs.)	SC4 (328)
Sub-cluster Salient Features	• Mostly not Spanish/Hispanic/Latino Ethnicity • Mostly Spanish Language	• Mostly Old • Mostly Emergency Room Admission Source • Mostly Medical Principal Reason of Admission	• Mostly Young • Mostly Female • Mostly Physician Referral Admission Source • Mostly Obstetric Principal Reason of Admission	• Mostly Old • Mostly Physician Referral Admission Source • Mostly Surgical Principal Reason of Admission
Cluster	C2 (602 Observations)			
Cluster Salient Features	• High Satisfaction with Help after discharge • High Satisfaction with Symptoms info			
Sub-cluster	SC1 (141 obs.)	SC2 (224 obs.)	SC3 (237 obs.)	
Sub-cluster Salient Features	• Mostly Old • Mostly Emergency Room Admission Source • Mostly Medical Principal Reason of Admission	• Mostly Physician Referral Admission Source • Rarely Medical Principal Reason of Admission	• Rarely not Spanish/Hispanic/Latino Ethnicity • Mostly Spanish Language	
Cluster	C3 (840 Observations)			
Cluster Salient Features	• Low Satisfaction with Help after discharge • Low Satisfaction with Symptoms info • Low Overall Health			
Sub-cluster	SC1 (278 obs.)	SC2 (296 obs.)	SC3 (266 obs.)	
Sub-cluster Salient Features	• Mostly Old • Mostly Emergency Room Admission Source • Mostly Medical Principal Reason of Admission	• Rarely not Spanish/Hispanic/Latino Ethnicity • Mostly Spanish Language	• Mostly Physician Referral Admission Source • Mostly Obstetric Principal Reason of Admission	

Table 10. Derived Associations.

1	Patients who have high Satisfaction with Help After Discharge, have these qualities: Mostly Physician Referral Admission Source, Mostly not Medical Principal Reason of Admission
2	Patients who have high Satisfaction with Symptoms Info, have these qualities: Mostly Physician Referral Admission Source, Rarely Medical Principal Reason of Admission
3	Patients who have high Satisfaction with Help After Discharge, have these qualities: Rarely White Race
4	Patients who have high Satisfaction with Symptoms Info, have these qualities: Rarely White Race

Table 10. *Cont.*

5	Patients who have high Satisfaction with Help After Discharge, have these qualities: Mostly Old, Mostly Emergency Room Admission Source, Mostly Medical Principal Reason of Admission
6	Patients who have high Satisfaction with Symptoms Info, have these qualities: Mostly Old, Mostly Emergency Room Admission Source, Mostly Medical Principal Reason of Admission
7	Patients who have low Satisfaction with Help After Discharge, have these qualities: Mostly Old, Mostly Physician Referral Admission Source, Mostly Surgical Principal Reason of Admission
8	Patients who have low Satisfaction with Symptoms Info, have these qualities: Mostly Old, Mostly Physician Referral Admission Source, Mostly Surgical Principal Reason of Admission
9	Patients who have low Satisfaction with Help After Discharge, have these qualities: Mostly Young, Mostly Female, Mostly Physician Referral Admission Source, Mostly Obstetric Principal Reason of Admission
10	Patients who have low Satisfaction with Symptoms Info, have these qualities: Mostly Young, Mostly Female, Mostly Physician Referral Admission Source, Mostly Obstetric Principal Reason of Admission
11	Patients who have low Satisfaction with Help After Discharge, have these qualities: Mostly Old, Mostly Emergency Room Admission Source, Mostly Medical Principal Reason of Admission
12	Patients who have low Satisfaction with Symptoms Info, have these qualities: Mostly Old, Mostly Emergency Room Admission Source, Mostly Medical Principal Reason of Admission
13	Patients who have high Satisfaction with Help After Discharge, have these qualities: Mostly Physician Referral Admission Source, Mostly Obstetric Principal Reason of Admission
14	Patients who have high Satisfaction with Symptoms Info, have these qualities: Mostly Physician Referral Admission Source, Mostly Obstetric Principal Reason of Admission
15	Patients who have high Satisfaction with Help After Discharge, have these qualities: Rarely not Spanish/Hispanic/Latino Ethnicity, Rarely English Language
16	Patients who have high Satisfaction with Help After Discharge, have these qualities: Rarely not Spanish/Hispanic/Latino Ethnicity, Rarely English Language
17	Patients who have high Satisfaction with Help After Discharge, have these qualities: Mostly Old, Mostly Emergency Room Admission Source
18	Patients who have high Satisfaction with Symptoms Info, have these qualities: Mostly Old, Mostly Emergency Room Admission Source
19	Patients who have high Overall health, have these qualities: Mostly Old, Mostly Emergency Room Admission Source

5. Validation

The associations derived from the two-layer clustering must be validated through standard statistical tests to ensure that they did not occur by chance. This is a very important step for generating reliable associations. Each of the associations is considered as a hypothesis and it is tested based on the whole data set. As described, almost all of the features in the data set are categorical or even dichotomous, which are of multiple groups of studies with unequal sample sizes. In order to work with such data, chi-square test of independence is used for hypothesis testing.

The Chi-square statistic is a non-parametric tool designed to analyze group differences when the dependent variable is measured at a nominal level [17]. This test is robust to the distribution of data. The null hypothesis is stated as H0: the two classifications are independent, while the alternative hypothesis is H1: the classifications are dependent. The significance of the test is calculated according to the frequency contingency table of the independent classes (Each item in data set belongs only to one class). This value is compared with the critical values in the chi-square table, and if it is larger than this critical value, then the null hypothesis is rejected. Typically, if the chi-square test p-value is lower than 0.05, the independence of the features in the association is rejected.

Before using chi-square test for validating the associations, we have to make sure that the dataset meets the assumptions of the chi-square. The chi-square test requires that no more than 20% of the frequencies of categories are less than five; otherwise the calculated *p*-values may not be accurate. There are many empty or low frequency categories in the patients' contingency table that consists of more than 35% of the frequencies. By combining the columns or rows this issue can be resolved. For example, Table 11 illustrates a 3-way contingency table for testing the 16 association in Table 10. The rows are the satisfaction of symptoms info and the columns are a combination of not Spanish, Hispanic or Latino and the Spanish language. The two-digit binary values in the first row indicate a combination of not Spanish, Hispanic, or Latino Ethnicity (Yes/No) and Spanish Language (Yes/No). For example, 0.0 in the first row indicates that the patients are rarely not Spanish, Hispanic or Latino Ethnicity, and they speak Spanish. In order to get higher frequencies, we can combine the first two rows into a single row to indicate a "low" satisfaction. Similarly, we can merge the last two rows to indicate a "high" satisfaction (Table 12). The rows must be combined in a way to yield an interpretable result. The algorithm proposed for this modification to chi-square test is delineated in Algorithm 4.

Table 11. Contingency Table for Satisfaction with Symptoms Info and rarely not Spanish/Hispanic/ Latino and Spanish Language.

Satisfaction with Symptoms Info	Rarely Not Spanish/Hispanic/Latino Ethnicity Spanish Language			
	0.0	1.0	0.1	1.1
1	3	180	1710	249
2	1	32	521	63
3	0	6	94	7
4	0	5	72	5

Table 12. Contingency Table with Combined Rows.

Satisfaction with Symptoms Info	Rarely Not Spanish/Hispanic/Latino Ethnicity Spanish Language			
	0.0	1.0	0.1	1.1
Low	4	212	2231	256
High	0	11	166	12

Algorithm 4. Modified chi-square test.

Modified_chisquare(interaction_table):
> Comment: Adjusting interaction table not to have values less than five.
> *Col ← 0 to num_col(interaction_table):*
> *If all(table[, col] < 5):*
>> *table1 ← table [, -col]*
>> *table ← table1*
>> *col ← col−1*
>> *numcol ← numcol−1*
> *col ← col + 1*
> *return chisq.test(table)*

The frequencies can further be improved by combining the first two columns as shown in Table 13.

Table 13. Contingency with combined Rows and Columns.

Satisfaction with Symptoms Info	Rarely Not Spanish/Hispanic/Latino Ethnicity Spanish Language		
	X.0	0.1	1.1
Low	216	2231	256
High	11	166	12

The interpretation of the contingency table needs to be done carefully when combining the rows or columns. For example, Table 13 indicates that 216 non-Spanish speaking patients were not satisfied with information provided about their symptoms after discharge. The process of combining the rows and columns continuous until the resulting frequencies satisfy the Chi-square test assumptions.

The chi-square test can be used to prove the validity of an association but it does not give any measure to assess the strength of each valid association. After filtering out the invalid associations using chi-square test, we use odds ratio [18] to measure the strength of each association and to rank them based on their strength. Odds ratio is a measure of association between a condition and an outcome. The odds ratio shows the odds that an outcome will occur in a particular condition, as compared to the odds of the outcome occurring in other conditions. A z-test is used to compare two odds ratios. The significance of the z-test is measured by its p-value. If the p-value is bigger than 2 or smaller than -2, then the association is considered significant both in terms of dependency and strength. Odds ratio is not dependent to the sample size and it can provide a basis to compare the strengths of the associations extracted from the two-layer clustering between patients' satisfaction identifiers and their demographics. Using these two-step validations, recommendations created because of noise in the data are removed, which alleviates the overfitting that could have happened in the process.

Most associations extracted from the patient dataset have more than two features. Before computing the odds ratio, the contingency table should be converted to a two by two table. The converted table is made by calculating the frequencies of instances that meet the demographic conditions in the derived association and the ones that don't meet these conditions. Table 14 converts the contingency table in Table 13 to a two by two table for calculating the odds ratio.

Table 14. Two by Two Table.

Satisfaction with Symptoms Info	Condition: Rarely Not Spanish/Hispanic/Latino Ethnicity High Spanish Language	
	Meet Condition	Do Not Meet Conditions
Low	2447	256
High	177	12

Having converted the contingency table to a two by two table, the odds ratio of each cell in the table is calculated. A z-test is used to compare the odds ratio of the patients meeting the conditions versus the ones who do not having the same satisfaction level. The significance of the z-test is measured by its p-value. If the absolute p-value is greater than 2, then the association is considered significant both in terms of dependency and strength. Unlike chi-square test, the p-value of the z-test can be used both for omitting weak, irrelevant associations and for ranking them. This pseudo code for the validation function used is depicted in Algorithm 5.

Algorithm 5. Validation function.

---

validate_relationships (recommendation)
 Interaction_table ← interact(recommendation)
 Chisqr ← Modifies_chisquare(Interaction_table)
 If Chisqr. P_value < 0.5:
  For row in interaction_table.rows:
   For col in interaction_table.cols:
    Odds_ratio ← Odds_ratio(interaction_table,row,col)
     If odds_ratio.p_value > 2 or odds_ratio.p_value < −2:
      Return True
 Return False

Table 15 lists the *p*-values of the chi-square and the *z*-tests for each association derived in Table 10. Associations with significant values are shown in bold figures. If both *p*-values values are significant, than the association is considered accurate and reliable. Otherwise, the association is omitted as there is not enough evidence to support its significance. The list of cleaned associations is ranked based on the *p*-value of *z*-test and presented in Table 16.

Table 15. Validation results of extracted associations from the HCAHPS data related to one hospital. (Linked to Table 10 by row number). Bold figures are *p*-values in accepted test ranges.

1	*Chi-square*	X-squared = 28.104	*p*-value = **3.455 × 10⁻⁶**
	z-test	*p*-value = **5.00891912614554**	
2	*Chi-square*	X-squared = 7.084	*p*-value = 0.06927
	z-test	*p*-value = 0.0183582852328812	
3	*Chi-square*	X-squared = 1.5969	*p*-value = 0.2063
	z-test	*p*-value = 1.31385601104743	
4	*Chi-square*	X-squared = 0.50012	*p*-value = 0.4794
	z-test	*p*-value = −0.760696016958917	
5	*Chi-square*	X-squared = 30.14	*p*-value = **0.001506**
	z-test	*p*-value = **−2.9118314808416**	
6	*Chi-square*	X-squared = 43.594	*p*-value = **8.558 × 10⁻⁶**
	z-test	*p*-value = **−0.212828628801027**	
7	*Chi-square*	X-squared = 26.86	*p*-value = **0.004825**
	z-test	*p*-value = −1.97247635563556	
8	*Chi-square*	X-squared = 63.926	*p*-value = **1.715 × 10⁻⁹**
	z-test	*p*-value = 3.59338301942709	
9	*Chi-square*	X-squared = 25.48	*p*-value = **0.01271**
	z-test	*p*-value = −3.39514132553282	
10	*Chi-square*	X-squared = 61.28	*p*-value = **1.315 × 10⁻⁸**
	z-test	*p*-value = −5.48685043800752	
11	*Chi-square*	X-squared = 30.14	*p*-value = **0.001506**
	z-test	*p*-value = **2.9118314808416**	
12	*Chi-square*	X-squared = 43.594	*p*-value = **8.558 × 10⁻⁶**
	z-test	*p*-value = 0.212828628801027	
13	*Chi-square*	X-squared = 20.061	*p*-value = **0.0001649**
	z-test	*p*-value = **3.50130627065847**	
14	*Chi-square*	X-squared = 43.489	*p*-value = **1.937 × 10⁻⁹**
	z-test	*p*-value = **5.57545804293131**	
15	*Chi-square*	X-squared = 8.8791	*p*-value = **0.03094**
	z-test	*p*-value = **2.45951143035353**	
16	*Chi-square*	X-squared = 0.9116	*p*-value = 0.8226
	z-test	*p*-value = −0.774093020800148	
17	*Chi-square*	X-squared = 18.715	*p*-value = **0.002172**
	z-test	*p*-value = **−2.85471982135127**	
18	*Chi-square*	X-squared = 27.572	*p*-value = **4.413 × 10⁻⁵**
	z-test	*p*-value = −1.47076729692434	
19	*Chi-square*	X-squared = 24.691	*p*-value = **0.0001599**
	z-test	*p*-value = −0.231962167837976	

Table 16. The list of cleaned associations ranked based on their odds ratio.

1	Patients who have high Satisfaction with Symptoms Info, have these qualities: Mostly Physician Referral Admission Source, Mostly Obstetric Principal Reason of Admission
	z-test — p-value = **5.57545804293131**
2	Patients who have low Satisfaction with Symptoms Info, have these qualities: Mostly Young, Mostly Female, Mostly Physician Referral Admission Source, Mostly Obstetric Principal Reason of Admission
	z-test — p-value = **−5.48685043800752**
3	Patients who have high Satisfaction with Help After Discharge, have these qualities: Mostly Physician Referral Admission Source, Rarely Medical Principal Reason of Admission
	z-test — p-value = **5.00891912614554**
4	Patients who have low Satisfaction with Symptoms Info, have these qualities: Mostly Old, Mostly Physician Referral Admission Source, Mostly Surgical Principal Reason of Admission
	z-test — p-value = **3.59338301942709**
5	Patients who have high Satisfaction with Help After Discharge, have these qualities: Mostly Physician Referral Admission Source, Mostly Obstetric Principal Reason of Admission
	z-test — p-value = **3.50130627065847**
6	Patients who have low Satisfaction with Help After Discharge, have these qualities: Mostly Young, Mostly Female, Mostly Physician Referral Admission Source, Mostly Obstetric Principal Reason of Admission
	z-test — p-value = **−3.39514132553282**
7	Patients who have high Satisfaction with Help After Discharge, have these qualities: Mostly Old, Mostly Emergency Room Admission Source, Mostly Medical Principal Reason of Admission
	z-test — p-value = **−2.9118314808416**
8	Patients who have high Satisfaction with Help After Discharge, have these qualities: Mostly Old, Mostly Emergency Room Admission Source
	z-test — p-value = **−2.85471982135127**
9	Patients who have high Satisfaction with Help After Discharge, have these qualities: Rarely not Spanish/Hispanic/Latino Ethnicity, Rarely English Language
	z-test — p-value = **2.45951143035353**
10	Patients who have high Satisfaction with Symptoms Info, have these qualities: Mostly Old, Mostly Emergency Room Admission Source, Mostly Medical Principal Reason of Admission
	z-test — p-value = **−0.212828628801027**

6. Turning Associations into Recommendations for Hospitals

The associations extracted in the previous section can be used in two ways to improve patient experience for various patient groups:

1. The valid association can be simply transformed into a set of general applicable recommendations. For instance, based on the second association in Table 16, the system can make the recommendation that "Young ladies whose admission source is physician referral and their reason of admission is obstetrical, need more information about their symptoms when they are being discharged". In this approach, one recommendation is generated for each correlation, although, the recommendations which are based on patients' dissatisfaction are probably more useful than ones which are based on patients' satisfaction.

2. The associations can be used to produce target-based recommendations. Assume that a patient is being admitted to a hospital. The reception takes the patient's information and relative recommendations would be popped out. For instance, suppose an old patient with physician referral is being admitted for surgical reason. Based on the 4th correlation in Table 4, a recommendation is shown to the health care provider asserting that this patient needs more information about her/his symptoms. This can be accomplished by a simple rule-based expert system.

7. Conclusions

In this work, an unsupervised exploratory data analysis methodology is introduced to discover associations between patients' demographics and their various satisfaction identifiers. Such associations are extracted using a two-layer cluster analysis together with extracting the salient features of each cluster. The associations are validated using statistical tests and are ranked based on their significance. The goal was to use such associations to create a patient satisfaction based the recommendation system for hospitals. The methodology was applied to HCAHP data obtained from CAHPS Database and the generated recommendations were validated using statistical tests. In the presented case study in this work, the proposed methodology, extracted nineteen associations from the HCAHPS dataset of a hospital with 2652 records. Ten associations out of nineteen were validated through statistical methods of chi-squared independence test, and odds ratio z-test, which shows the reliability of the proposed recommendation system.

The proposed recommendation system provides knowledge that may be hidden to an expert analyzing the surveys and rectifies the need for a subject-matter expert. The analysis approach is designed specifically for the format of the standard HCAHPS survey; however, it can be extended to other domains in which customer survey plays an important role.

The future work of this study will focus on three aspects:

1. **More extensive data collection:** Our long-term goal is to assess how the recommendations produced by our system can improve patients' loyalty and result in saving costs and time in the long run. Using the preliminary results outlined in this paper, our goal is to obtain a more comprehensive data set which includes data on whether the patients have come back to the hospital if medical services were needed, and to examine the relationship between customer loyalty and their satisfaction identifiers.

2. **Handling skip questions:** In this study, a single imputation method based on K-nearest neighbor (KNN) is used to impute missing values. Other popular approaches, such as multiple imputations by chained equations (MICE) [19], should be explored in future for imputing both categorical and continues variables. Also, other approaches for handling skip questions should be examined to better distinguish between non-applicable and missing data.

3. **Alternative distance measures for K-means:** In this study, we used Euclidean distance for clustering. Euclidean distance is typically used for continuous data where data are seen as points in the Euclidean space. Since HCAHPS data consist of mixed numeric and categorical variables, we should examine other types of distance measures such as cosine, Jaccard, Overlap, Occurrence Frequency, etc. [20] and compare the quality of recommendations produced by each measure. In addition, since there are two layers of clustering and the intrinsic characteristics of data points in each layer vary, and a different distance function can be used for each layer.

Acknowledgments: The CAHPS® data used in this analysis were provided by the CAHPS Database. The CAHPS Database is funded by the U.S. Agency for HealthCare Research and Quality (AHRQ) and administered by Westat under Contract No. HHSA290201300003C.

Author Contributions: Shahram Rahimi studied conception and design; Mohammadreza Khoie and Tannaz Sattari Tabrizi and Nina Marhamati acquired data; All authors analysised and interpreted data and evaluated results; Tannaz Sattari Tabrizi and Mohammad Reza Khoie and Elham Sahebkar Khorasani drafted the manuscript; Shahram Rahimi and Elham Sahebkar Khorasani and Nina Marhamati did critical revisions.

Conflicts of Interest: The authors declare no conflict of interest.

Appendix A

The HCAHPS survey has been changed through the time. In this appendix A, we brought the questionnaire of March 2012.

HCAHPS Survey

SURVEY INSTRUCTIONS

♦ You should only fill out this survey if you were the patient during the hospital stay named in the cover letter. Do not fill out this survey if you were not the patient.

♦ Answer <u>all</u> the questions by checking the box to the left of your answer.

♦ You are sometimes told to skip over some questions in this survey. When this happens you will see an arrow with a note that tells you what question to answer next, like this:

    ☐   Yes
    ☑   No   ➜ *If No, Go to Question 1*

> *You may notice a number on the survey. This number is used to let us know if you returned your survey so we don't have to send you reminders.*
> Please note: Questions 1-22 in this survey are part of a national initiative to measure the quality of care in hospitals. OMB #0938-0981

Please answer the questions in this survey about your stay at the hospital named on the cover letter. Do not include any other hospital stays in your answers.

YOUR CARE FROM NURSES

1. **During this hospital stay, how often did nurses treat you with <u>courtesy and respect</u>?**

    ^{1}☐ Never
    ^{2}☐ Sometimes
    ^{3}☐ Usually
    ^{4}☐ Always

2. **During this hospital stay, how often did nurses <u>listen carefully to you</u>?**

    ^{1}☐ Never
    ^{2}☐ Sometimes
    ^{3}☐ Usually
    ^{4}☐ Always

3. **During this hospital stay, how often did nurses <u>explain things</u> in a way you could understand?**

    ^{1}☐ Never
    ^{2}☐ Sometimes
    ^{3}☐ Usually
    ^{4}☐ Always

4. **During this hospital stay, after you pressed the call button, how often did you get help as soon as you wanted it?**

    ^{1}☐ Never
    ^{2}☐ Sometimes
    ^{3}☐ Usually
    ^{4}☐ Always
    ^{9}☐ I never pressed the call button

YOUR CARE FROM DOCTORS

5. **During this hospital stay, how often did doctors treat you with <u>courtesy and respect</u>?**

    [1] Never
    [2] Sometimes
    [3] Usually
    [4] Always

6. **During this hospital stay, how often did doctors <u>listen carefully to you</u>?**

    [1] Never
    [2] Sometimes
    [3] Usually
    [4] Always

7. **During this hospital stay, how often did doctors <u>explain things</u> in a way you could understand?**

    [1] Never
    [2] Sometimes
    [3] Usually
    [4] Always

THE HOSPITAL ENVIRONMENT

8. **During this hospital stay, how often were your room and bathroom kept clean?**

    [1] Never
    [2] Sometimes
    [3] Usually
    [4] Always

9. **During this hospital stay, how often was the area around your room quiet at night?**

    [1] Never
    [2] Sometimes
    [3] Usually
    [4] Always

YOUR EXPERIENCES IN THIS HOSPITAL

10. **During this hospital stay, did you need help from nurses or other hospital staff in getting to the bathroom or in using a bedpan?**

    [1] Yes
    [2] No ➜ **If No, Go to Question 12**

11. **How often did you get help in getting to the bathroom or in using a bedpan as soon as you wanted?**

    [1] Never
    [2] Sometimes
    [3] Usually
    [4] Always

12. **During this hospital stay, did you need medicine for pain?**

    [1] Yes
    [2] No ➜ **If No, Go to Question 15**

13. **During this hospital stay, how often was your pain well controlled?**

    [1] Never
    [2] Sometimes
    [3] Usually
    [4] Always

14. **During this hospital stay, how often did the hospital staff do everything they could to help you with your pain?**

    [1] Never
    [2] Sometimes
    [3] Usually
    [4] Always

15. During this hospital stay, were you given any medicine that you had not taken before?

    ¹☐ Yes

    ²☐ No ➜ If No, Go to Question 18

16. Before giving you any new medicine, how often did hospital staff tell you what the medicine was for?

    ¹☐ Never

    ²☐ Sometimes

    ³☐ Usually

    ⁴☐ Always

17. Before giving you any new medicine, how often did hospital staff describe possible side effects in a way you could understand?

    ¹☐ Never

    ²☐ Sometimes

    ³☐ Usually

    ⁴☐ Always

WHEN YOU LEFT THE HOSPITAL

18. After you left the hospital, did you go directly to your own home, to someone else's home, or to another health facility?

    ¹☐ Own home

    ²☐ Someone else's home

    ³☐ Another health facility ➜ **If Another, Go to Question 21**

19. During this hospital stay, did doctors, nurses or other hospital staff talk with you about whether you would have the help you needed when you left the hospital?

    ¹☐ Yes

    ²☐ No

20. During this hospital stay, did you get information in writing about what symptoms or health problems to look out for after you left the hospital?

    ¹☐ Yes

    ²☐ No

OVERALL RATING OF HOSPITAL

Please answer the following questions about your stay at the hospital named on the cover letter. Do not include any other hospital stays in your answers.

21. Using any number from 0 to 10, where 0 is the worst hospital possible and 10 is the best hospital possible, what number would you use to rate this hospital during your stay?

    ⁰☐ 0   Worst hospital possible

    ¹☐ 1

    ²☐ 2

    ³☐ 3

    ⁴☐ 4

    ⁵☐ 5

    ⁶☐ 6

    ⁷☐ 7

    ⁸☐ 8

    ⁹☐ 9

    ¹⁰☐ 10   Best hospital possible

22. **Would you recommend this hospital to your friends and family?**
    [1] Definitely no
    [2] Probably no
    [3] Probably yes
    [4] Definitely yes

ABOUT YOU

There are only a few remaining items left.

23. **In general, how would you rate your overall health?**
    [1] Excellent
    [2] Very good
    [3] Good
    [4] Fair
    [5] Poor

24. **What is the highest grade or level of school that you have completed?**
    [1] 8th grade or less
    [2] Some high school, but did not graduate
    [3] High school graduate or GED
    [4] Some college or 2-year degree
    [5] 4-year college graduate
    [6] More than 4-year college degree

25. **Are you of Spanish, Hispanic or Latino origin or descent?**
    [1] No, not Spanish/Hispanic/Latino
    [2] Yes, Puerto Rican
    [3] Yes, Mexican, Mexican American, Chicano
    [4] Yes, Cuban
    [5] Yes, other Spanish/Hispanic/Latino

26. **What is your race? Please choose one or more.**
    [1] White
    [2] Black or African American
    [3] Asian
    [4] Native Hawaiian or other Pacific Islander
    [5] American Indian or Alaska Native

27. **What language do you <u>mainly</u> speak at home?**
    [1] English
    [2] Spanish
    [3] Chinese
    [4] Russian
    [5] Vietnamese
    [6] Some other language (please print): _____

THANK YOU
Please return the completed survey in the postage-paid envelope.

References

1. Lehtonen, R.; Pahkinen, E. *Practical Methods for Design and Analysis of Complex Surveys*; John Wiley & Sons: Hoboken, NJ, USA, 2004.
2. Kenett, R.; Salini, S. *Modern Analysis of Customer Surveys: With Applications Using R (Vol. 117)*; John Wiley & Sons: Hoboken, NJ, USA, 2011.
3. Giordano, L.A.; Elliott, M.N.; Goldstein, E.; Lehrman, W.G.; Spencer, P.A. Development, implementation, and public reporting of the HCAHPS survey. *Med. Care Res. Rev.* 2010, *67*, 27–37. [CrossRef] [PubMed]
4. Stratford, N.J. Patient perception of pain care in the United States: A 5-year comparative analysis of hospital consumer assessment of health care providers and systems. *Pain Phys.* 2014, *17*, 369–377.
5. Sheetz, K.H.; Seth, A.W.; Micah, E.G.; Darrell, A.C., Jr.; Michael, J.E. Patients' perspectives of care and surgical outcomes in Michigan: an analysis using the CAHPS hospital survey. *Ann. Surg.* 2014, *260*, 5–9. [CrossRef] [PubMed]
6. Goldstein, E.; Marc, N.E.; William, G.L.; Katrin, H.; Laura, A.G. Racial/ethnic differences in patients' perceptions of inpatient care using the HCAHPS survey. *Med. Care Res. Rev.* 2010, *67*, 74–92. [CrossRef] [PubMed]
7. Elliott, M.N.; William, G.L.; Megan, K.B.; Elizabeth, G.; Katrin, H.; Laura, A.G. Gender differences in patients' perceptions of inpatient care. *Health Serv. Res.* 2012, *47*, 1482–1501. [CrossRef] [PubMed]

8.   Elliott, M.N.; William, G.L.; Elizabeth, G.; Katrin, H.; Megan, K.B.; Laura, A.G. Do hospitals rank differently on HCAHPS for different patient subgroups? *Med. Care Res. Rev.* **2010**, *67*, 56–73. [CrossRef] [PubMed]

9.   Klinkenberg, W.; Dean, S.B.; Brian, M.W.; Koichiro, O.; Joe, M.I.; Jan, C.G.; Wm Claiborne, D. Inpatients' willingness to recommend: A multilevel analysis. *Health Care Manag. Rev.* **2011**, *36*, 349–358. [CrossRef] [PubMed]

10. Kleinbaum, D.; Lawrence, K.; Azhar, N.; Eli, R. *Applied Regression Analysis and Other Multivariable Methods*; Nelson Education: Scarborough, ON, Canada, 2013.

11. Scholkopft, B.; Klaus-Robert, M. Fisher Discriminant Analysis with Kernels. In Proceedings of the Neural Networks for Signal Processing IX, Madison, WI, USA, 25 August 1999.

12. Thurstone, L.L. Multiple factor analysis. *Psychol. Rev.* **1931**, *38*, 406. [CrossRef]

13. Batista, G.E.; Monard, M.C. A Study of K-Nearest Neighbour as an Imputation Method. *HIS* **2002**, *87*, 251–260.

14. Ailon, N.; Ragesh, J.; Claire, M. Streaming *k*-means approximation. In *Advances in Neural Information Processing Systems*; Columbia University: New York, NY, USA, 2009; pp. 10–18.

15. Caliński, T.; Jerzy, H. A dendrite method for cluster analysis. *Commun. Stat.-Theory Methods* **1974**, *3*, 1–27. [CrossRef]

16. Azcarraga, A.P.; Hsieh, M.H.; Pan, S.L.; Setiono, R. Extracting salient dimensions for automatic SOM labeling. *IEEE Trans. Syst. Man Cybern. Part C* **2005**, *35*, 595–600. [CrossRef]

17. McHugh, M.L. The chi-square test of independence. *Biochem. Med.* **2013**, *23*, 143–149. [CrossRef]

18. Bland, J.M.; Douglas, G.A. The odds ratio. *BMJ* **2000**, *320*, 1468. [CrossRef] [PubMed]

19. White, I.R.; Patrick, R.; Angela, M.W. Multiple imputation using chained equations: Issues and guidance for practice. *Stat. Med.* **2011**, *30*, 377–399. [CrossRef] [PubMed]

20. Boriah, S.; Varun, C.; Vipin, K. Similarity measures for categorical data: A comparative evaluation. In Proceedings of the 2008 Society for Industrial and Applied Mathematics (SIAM) International Conference on Data Mining, Atlanta, GA, USA, 24–26 April 2008; pp. 243–254.

applied sciences

Article

Human Emotion Recognition with Electroencephalographic Multidimensional Features by Hybrid Deep Neural Networks

Youjun Li [1], Jiajin Huang [1], Haiyan Zhou [1] and Ning Zhong [1,2,3,*]

[1] Institute of International WIC, Beijing University of Technology, Beijing 100124, China; lyj@ncut.edu.cn (Y.L.); hjj@emails.bjut.edu.cn (J.H.); zhouhaiyan@bjut.edu.cn (H.Z.)

[2] Beijing Advanced Innovation Center for Future Internet Technology, Beijing University of Technology, Beijing 100124, China

[3] Knowledge Information Systems Lab, Department of Life Science and Informatics, Maebashi Institute of Technology, Maebashi 371-0816, Japan

* Correspondence: zhong@maebashi-it.ac.jp; Tel.: +81-27-265-7366

Received: 11 September 2017; Accepted: 11 October 2017; Published: 13 October 2017

Featured Application: The method presented in this study can be applied in many fields, such as mental health care, entertainment consumption behavior, society safety, and so on. For example, in the mental health care field, an automatic emotion analysis system can be constructed with our method to monitor the emotional variation of the subjects. With accurate and objective emotion analysis results from EEG signals, our method can provide useful treatment effect information to the medical staff.

Abstract: The aim of this study is to recognize human emotions by electroencephalographic (EEG) signals. The innovation of our research methods involves two aspects: First, we integrate the spatial characteristics, frequency domain, and temporal characteristics of the EEG signals, and map them to a two-dimensional image. With these images, we build a series of EEG Multidimensional Feature Image (EEG MFI) sequences to represent the emotion variation with EEG signals. Second, we construct a hybrid deep neural network to deal with the EEG MFI sequences to recognize human emotional states where the hybrid deep neural network combined the Convolution Neural Networks (CNN) and Long Short-Term-Memory (LSTM) Recurrent Neural Networks (RNN). Empirical research is carried out with the open-source dataset DEAP (a Dataset for Emotion Analysis using EEG, Physiological, and video signals) using our method, and the results demonstrate the significant improvements over current state-of-the-art approaches in this field. The average emotion classification accuracy of each subject with CLRNN (the hybrid neural networks that we proposed in this study) is 75.21%.

Keywords: emotion recognition; EEG signal; multidimensional features; hybrid neural networks; CNN; LSTM RNN

1. Introduction

Emotion is an important symbol of human intelligence; as such, an important intelligence symbol of artificial intelligence is that the machine can understand human emotions. As early as the 1980s, Minsky, one of the founders of artificial intelligence, proposed that a machine without emotions is not intelligent. Recently, research on human emotion recognition has been applied in many fields such as entertainment [1], safe driving [2,3], health care [4], social security [5], etc. Picard et al. [6] believed that the emotional changes of the human were embodied in speech [7], facial expressions [8], body posture [9], the central nervous system, autonomic nerve physiological activities [10], etc. Thus, the study of human emotions through behavioral, facial, or physiological features has gradually become a focus of much attention. However, voice and facial expressions can be deliberately hidden by people on some social occasions. For this reason, researchers have tended to study human emotion through physiological signals such as electroencephalograms (EEG), electrooculography (EOG), temperature (TEM), blood volume pressure (BVP), electromyograms (EMG), and many other methods. Of all of these physiological signals, the EEG signal is of more interest to researchers as it comes directly from the human brain. Therefore, changes in EEG signals can directly reflect changes in human emotional states.

In this study, we recognize human emotional states with EEG signals. Two important aspects must be ensured during the emotion recognition process: (1) EEG feature extraction and expression and (2) emotion classifiers construction. For the first aspect, most of the previously used methods have only focused on the time and frequency dimension, and rarely combine the spatial dimension. Therefore, how to integrate and present the spatial features of the EEG signal with the time and frequency features is one key problem. For the second aspect, the key problem lies in how to construct a classifier to automatically learn the changes from the EEG multidimensional features over time and classify the changes into different emotion states. Corresponding to these two aspects, we mainly undertook the following work in this study:

- A new method is proposed to integrate the different EEG domain features. With the integration of multidimensional features, a sequence of two-dimensional images is constructed to express the variation in emotion.
- A hybrid deep learning neural network named CLRNN (Convolution al Networks (CNN) and Long-Short-Term-Memory Recurrent Neural Networks (RNN)) is built to undertake the recognitioNeurn of human emotion from the EEG multidimensional feature image sequences.
- Empirical research is conducted with the open-source database DEAP [11] using our method, and the results demonstrate significant improvements over current state-of-the-art approaches in this field.

The rest of the paper is organized as follows: Related work is presented in Section 2. As data preparation, the methods of building EEG MFI and emotion labels are presented in Section 3. Next, we introduce the construction of CLRNN in Section 4. Section 5 describes the procedure of the experiment and reports the results. Finally, the conclusions and their discussion are detailed in Section 6.

2. Related Work

In this section, we review the related work on EEG features extraction and emotion classifying, respectively.

2.1. EEG Feature Extraction

We extend the study in [12] and review a wide range of EEG feature extraction methods proposed in the past 10 years. As seen in Table 1, most previous EEG feature extraction methods only focused on the time and frequency dimensions, and rarely combined them with spatial dimension information.

The time domain features study EEG signal through the variation of signal time series. The features include Hjorth features (Activity, Mobility, and Complexity [13,14]), statistics features (Power, Mean, Standard Deviation, etc. [15]), High Order Crossing features (HOC [16,17]), and so on. Time-domain features are not predominant. However, there are still many studies that have researched human emotion through time domain characteristics.

The frequency domain features study EEG signal by transforming the raw time domain EEG signal into frequency domain EEG signal with Fourier Transform method usually. The most popular features in the frequency domain are power features of different sub-frequency bands known as alpha, beta, theta, and delta. The most widely used algorithm is the Fast Fourier Transform (FFT), which is applied in [18–24], and alternatives include Short-Time Fourier Transform (STFT) [25–28].

Another frequency feature is Power Spectra Density (PSD), which is usually estimated by Welch's method [29].

Table 1. A summary of feature extraction for emotion recognition from EEG [1].

Author and Study	Year	EEG Features	Extraction Method	Dimension
Ansari et al. [13]	2007	Activity, Mobility, and Complexity	Sevcik's method	Time
Chanel et al. [25]	2007	9 sub-bands of the EEG (4–20 Hz)	STFT	Frequency
Horlings [14]	2008	Activity, Mobility, and Complexity	Welch's Method	Time
Khalili and Moradi [18]	2008	Sub-band: θ, α, β, γ	FFT	Frequency
Li and Lu [19]	2009	EEG γ band (30–100 Hz)	FFT	Frequency
Petrantonakis and Hadjileontiadis [16,17]	2010	Higher Order Crossing	DWT	Time
Murugappan et al. [15,30]	2010	Power	DWT	Time
Nie et al. [26]	2011	Sub-band: δ, θ, α (8–13 Hz), β (1–30 Hz), γ (36–40 Hz)	STFT	Frequency
Kroupi et al. [31]	2011	Sub-band: θ, α, β, γ, NLD, NSI	Welch's Method	Frequency
Liu and Sourina [20]	2012	β/α, Sub-band: β	FFT	Frequency
Hadjidimitriou et al. [32]	2012	HHS-based Feature Vectors	HHS	Time and Frequency
Reuderink et al. [33]	2013	The change and asymmetry in Sub-band of α	Welch's Method	Frequency and Spatial
Rozgic et al. [21]	2013	Spectral Power and Spectral Power Differences	FFT	Frequency and Spatial
Lee and Hsieh [22]	2014	Correlation, Coherence, and Phase Synchronization	FFT	Frequency
Zheng et al. [27]	2014	PSD, DE, DASM and RASM	STFT	Frequency
Lahane and Sangaiah [34]	2015	Density Estimate	Kernel Density Estimation	Frequency
Paul et al. [35]	2015	Sub-band: α, β, θ	MFDFA	Frequency
Bashivan et al. [23]	2015	Sum of squared absolute values of the Sub-band: α, β, θ	FFT	Frequency Spatial
Thammasan et al. [29]	2016	Fractal Dimension (FD) and Power Spectral Density (PSD)	Welch's Method	Frequency
Zheng et al. [28]	2016	PSD, DE, DASM, RASM, ASM, and DCAU	STFT	Frequency
Li et al. [36]	2017	Multi-scale entropy	HHT	Time and Frequency
Yin et al. [24]	2017	Frequency Features and Time-Frequency Features	FFT	Time and Frequency

[1] EEG, electroencephalographic; DE, density estimate; DWT, discrete wavelet transform; FFT, Fast Fourier transform; STFT, Short-time Fourier transform; HHS, Hilbert–Huang spectrum; PSD, power spectra density; ASM, asymmetry; DASM, differential asymmetry; RASM, rational asymmetry; DCAU, differential caudality. MFDFA, multifractal detrended fluctuation analysis; NLD, normalized length density; NSI, non-stationarity index.

Since EEG signals are non-stationary, people proposed new methods combining time and frequency domain features to access additional information. The Hilbert–Huang Transform (HHT) is one method of studying EEG signals from both time and frequency domain. It decomposes the signal into Intrinsic Mode Functions (IMF) along with a trend, and obtains instantaneous frequency data. Hadjidimitriou et al. extracted HHS-based energy as the EEG features to study the music liking of the subjects [32]. They found that time–frequency features were more resistant to noise than the STFT-based features, which only extracted frequency features. Li et al. used HHT to improve the extraction of multi-scale entropy as the EEG emotional features [36], and their results demonstrated that the time–frequency combined feature obtained better results than the traditional single-domain features.

EEG signals are obtained by measuring the electrical voltage signals of the multiple electrodes affixed to different positions on the scalp. From the obtaining method of the EEG signal, we can see that the information is highly correlated with the spatial, time, and frequency dimensions. However, seldom have previous studies paid attention to the spatial domain. The spatial information studies were limited to the asymmetry between the electrode pairs. The methods mostly calculate the differences in the power bands of the corresponding electrodes pairs on the left/right hemisphere of the scalp [21,37]. Recently, Bashivan et al. transformed EEG activities into a sequence of topology-preserving multi-spectral images to study human cognitive function [23], but few studies have analyzed human emotions with the spatial information of the EEG signals.

The method to integrate EEG multidimensional features is based on the spatial distribution of EEG electrodes (according to the 10–20 system [38]), and map the frequency domain characteristics to a two-dimensional image. With this method, we obtain a sequence of images from consecutive time windows from the EEG signal. The details of the construction method are presented in Section 3.

2.2. Emotion Classification Methods

In order to provide a comparison to our method, we chose studies that classified human emotions with scales of Valence and Arousal in Table 2. It also lists the classification accuracy and the number of subjects. As seen in Table 2, the most commonly used emotional classification methods include k-Nearest Neighbor (k-NN, used in [15,39]), Support Vector Machine (SVM, used in [14,40–42]), Random Decision Forest (RDF), Bayes Neural Networks (used in [43]) and Neural Networks (used in [44,45]). These methods are all used as baseline methods for comparison with our method, with details given in Section 5.2.

Table 2. Survey of the studies on emotion classification methods with EEG signal [1].

Author and Study	Emotion Classification Basis	Subjects	Accuracy	Classification Method
Horlings [14]	Valence and Arousal (2 classes)	10	81%	SVM
Schaaff [41]	Valence and Arousal (3 classes)	30	66.7%	SVM
Frantzidis [40]	Valence and Arousal (2 classes, respectively)	28	81.3%	SVM
Murugappan [15]	Valence(2 classes)	12	71.3%	k-NN
Brown [39]	Valence (2 classes)	9	82%	SVM, k-NN
Hosseini [42]	Valence and Arousal (2 classes)	15	82%	SVM
Chung [43]	Valence and Arousal (2/3 classes respectively)	32	66.6%, 66.4% (2) 53.4%, 51.0% (3)	Bayes neural network
Li [44]	Valence and Arousal (2 classes, respectively)	32	74.12%	C-RNN
Our Method	Valence and Arousal (4 classes)	32	75.21%	CLRNN

[1] SVM, Support Vector Machine; CNN, Convolution Neural Networks; RNN, Recurrent Neural Networks; C-RNN, CNN+RNN; LSTM, Long Short-Term-Memory; CLRNN, CNN + LSTM RNN.

It is noteworthy that most of the methods listed in Table 2 classify emotions statically, except for the method used in [44] where the LSTM RNN was adopted to learn from the EEG features incrementally and dynamically. Another point worth noting is that only CNN is suitable for automatically extracting features from the image out of these methods. These two points are the reason for selecting CNN and LSTM RNN as parts of our classification method. The second column of Table 2 shows the classification basis and the number of the difference classes in the previous studies. As we can see, previous studies have basically divided emotions into categories two to three. In this study, we divided the emotion state into four classes. All the studies in Table 2 classify the emotion by Valence and Arousal. The third column of Table 2 shows the number of subjects included in the evaluated dataset.

3. Materials and Methods

The data preparation phase mainly included two aspects: the construction of EEG MFI sequences and the building of the emotion classification labels.

3.1. The Construction of EEG MFI Sequences

The International 10–20 System is an internationally recognized method of describing and applying the location of scalp electrodes in the context of an EEG test. The system is based on the relationship between the location of an electrode and the underlying area of the cerebral cortex. The "10" and "20" refer to the fact that the actual distances between the adjacent electrodes are either 10% or 20% of the total front–back or right–left distance of the skull [46].

Figure 1 shows a plan view of the International 10–20 System and a generalized square matrix from it. We can see that the left of Figure 1 is the International 10–20 System, where the EEG electrodes circled in red are the test points used in the DEAP dataset. In this study, we generalized the International 10–20 System with test electrodes used in the DEAP dataset to form a square matrix ($N \times N$), where N is the maximum point number between the horizontal or vertical test points. With the DEAP dataset, N equals 9. The square matrix without filling the EEG frequency features is represented at the right of Figure 1. The gray triangle above the center of the square matrix represents the nasion, while the red points are the electrodes corresponding to the red circles in the International 10–20 System. The gray points are added to form a fully matrix. The value of the red point corresponded to the frequency feature (PSD) of the EEG electrode. The value of the gray point is the interpolation of the red points surrounding it.

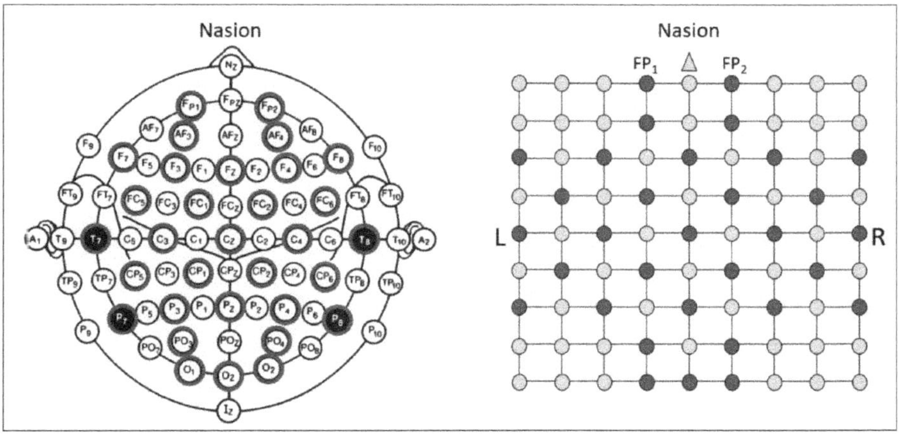

Figure 1. The International 10-20 System and the corresponding square EEG feature matrix (9×9) with tested EEG electrodes (the red points are tested in the trial and the gray points are not tested.

Figure 1 presents the method of mapping the International 10-20 System to a generalized EEG feature matrix. With this method, a single frame EEG MFI can be built from the EEG signal within a time window. With the time window moving forward, an EEG MFI sequence is constructed from the EEG signal. The process is presented in Figure 2. The definition of the red points and gray points is as same as it is defined in Figure 1. The different colors in EEG images represent the value of the EEG feature. The higher the feature is, the closer it is to the dark red. The lower the feature is, the closer it is to the dark blue. And the range of the EEG feature value is from 0 to 1.

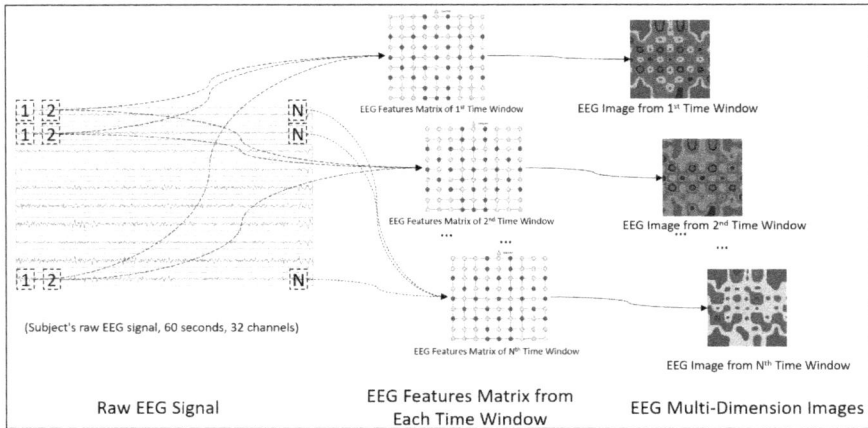

Figure 2. The construction process diagram of the electroencephalographic (EEG) Multidimensional Feature Image (MFI) sequence.

The EEG MFI sequence construction process consists of three steps. First, the raw EEG signals are extracted from DEAP, which included the multi-channel EEG signal of 32 subjects. Each subject has 40 trials where each trial includes the EEG signals of 32 channels, each signal lasting for 60 s. In the leftmost image of Figure 2, we schematically show the raw EEG signal of the first 10 channels. After that, the power spectrum density (PSD, [14,31,33,39,40]) is extracted as a EEG frequency domain feature from the raw signals. The PSD is estimated with Welch's method in MATLAB (R2016a) using a Hamming window and different time window sizes (1, 2, 3, 4, 5, 6, 8, 10, 12, 15, 20, 30 and 60 s) with no overlap as parameters. A number of (32 channels × 60 s/Tl) features are obtained per trial, where Tl is the size of the time window. Using a one-second time window as an example, 1920 (32 × 60) features are obtained from a raw EEG signal. After that, the features of each subject are normalized to reduce inter-participant variability by scaling between 0 and 1, as is shown in Equation (1):

$$F_i' = \frac{F_{\max_i} - F_i}{F_{\max_i} - F_{\min_i}},$$ (1)

where F_i' is the normalized value of the feature; $F_{\max_i}$, $F_{\min_i}$ are the maximum and minimum value of the internal subject features; and F_i is the ith value in the feature sequence. The red points in the feature matrix are directly filled with the normalized feature values. The values of the gray points are calculated with the surrounding point values, and can be expressed as Equation (2):

$$V_{(m,n)} = \frac{V'_{(m+1,n)} + V'_{(m-1,n)} + V'_{(m,n+1)} + V'_{(m,n-1)}}{K}, (0 \le m, n \le 8, m, n \in N),$$ (2)

where V is the value of the gray point (corresponding to $P_{(m,n)}$); and V' is the value of the point surrounding $P_{(m,n)}$. If the index of the surrounding point exceeds the range of 0 and 8, then the value is 0. K is the number of non-zero elements in the numerator, and the default value of K is 1. After the feature matrix is filled, it is used as a base table to generate EEG MFI through the interpolation method.

We generate the EEG MFI in MATLAB (R2016a, MathWorks, Boston, MA, USA, 2016). The code of the interpolation function and MFI generation method is presented in Appendix A. Using this code, the EEG MFI is constructed and saved as .png images with a size of 200×200 pixels. An enlarged EEG MFI is shown in Figure 3. As seen in Figure 3, the frequency domain characteristics are mapped to a two-dimensional plane according to the spatial distribution of the EEG electrodes. This MFI corresponds to a five-second time window. It displays Subject 1's spatial PSD feature of the first-time window. The color legend explains the range of the normalized PSD and the variation. We can see from it that the higher the PSD value is, the closer it is to the dark red end. The lower the PSD value is, the closer it is to the dark blue end. The higher PSD value indicates that the EEG signal contains more energy and the corresponding brain area is more active. With this point, we can find in Figure 3 that the FP1 electrode is with the highest PSD value, and the lowest value appears at the FC_6 (FC_6 is a tested point in 10-20 system, you can find it in left image of Figure 1) electrode.

In this study, in order to find out which time window size is more appropriate for emotion recognition, we build EEG MFI sequence with different length time windows. To illustrate the process of forming a MFI based on different time windows, we formalize the raw feature matrix into a four-dimensional matrix:

$$\mathbf{P}_{(electrode,sequence,trial,subject)}, \tag{3}$$

where the size of the matrix is $(32 \times 60 \times 40 \times 32)$. With the different time windows, it is possible to produce a different number of EEG MFIs. Assuming the number of EEG MFIs is N and the length of the time window is t, N equals sequence/t. The pseudo-code of producing the specific feature matrix is expressed in Appendix B.

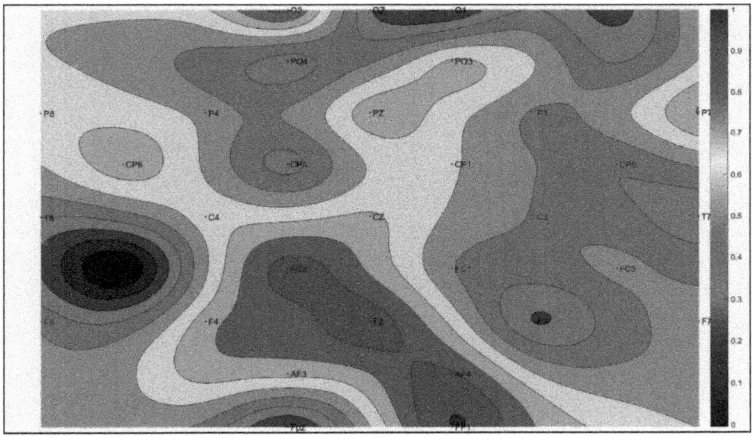

Figure 3. An enlarged EEG MFI with the names of the electrodes and contour lines.

Figure 4 displays the first five MFIs of Subject 1 with different time windows. Each row represents the MFIs with the same time window, and each line represents the MFIs with the same sequence order. Taking the first and the second row in Figure 4 as example, we can see that the first row represents the EEG variation over five seconds with five frames; however, the second row represents the same time variation with two frames. $MFI_{(1,5)}$ and $MFI_{(2,3)}$ are very similar. Accordingly, we can infer that the MFI sequence with a short time window provides more details about the variation than the MFI sequence with a long-time window. The meaning of the color in Figure 4 is the same as it in Figure 3.

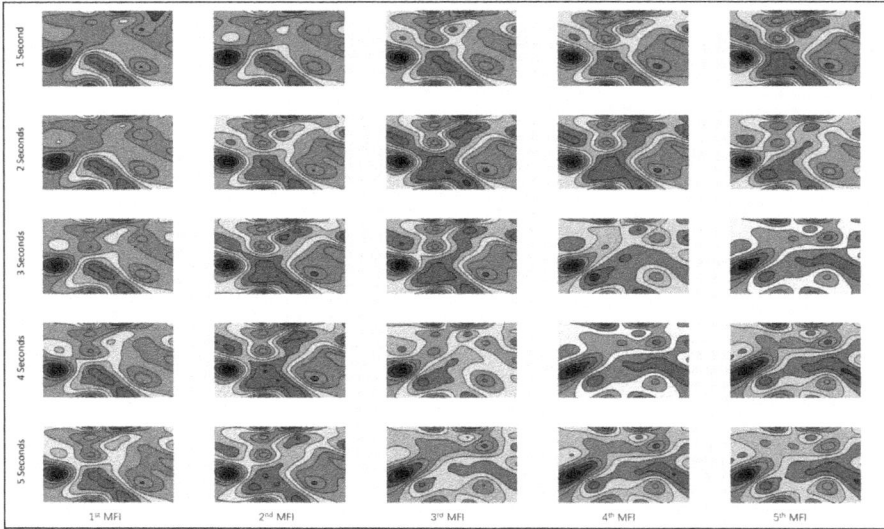

Figure 4. The MFI sequence of Subject 1 with different time windows.

3.2. The Construction of the Emotion Classification Labels

The classification method adopted in this paper is a supervisory machine learning method. Therefore, the corresponding classification labels of the EEG signal also need to be prepared in advance. The DEAP dataset contains the emotional evaluation values (including Valence, Arousal, Dominance, Like, and Familiarity) for the trials. In this paper, Valence and Arousal are extracted as emotional evaluation criteria to generate emotional labels. According to the different levels of Valence and Arousal, we divided the emotional two-dimensional plane into four quadrants. They are High Valence High Arousal (HVHA), High Valence Low Arousal (HVLA), Low Valence Low Arousal (LVLA), and Low Valence High Arousal (LVHA). Each quadrant corresponds to an emotion classification, as shown in Figure 5. According to the positive or negative deviation of the Valence and Arousal, we mapped each trial into the four quadrants to form an emotional classification label.

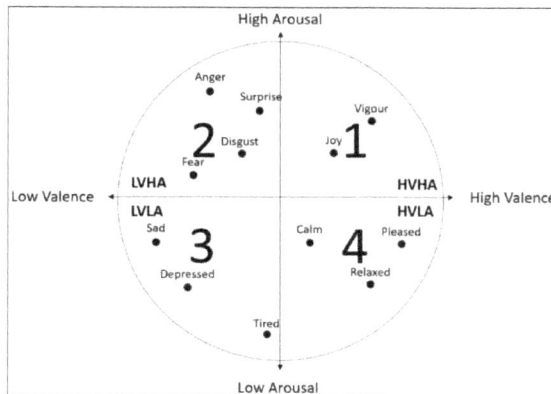

Figure 5. The Valence–Arousal dimension model of human emotion.

Table 3 shows the number of the different emotional samples mapped into the four quadrants. The number of samples contained in different emotional types is basically balanced, which ensured the balance of the neural network classification training.

Table 3. The number of samples in different emotion classifications [1].

Emotion Labels	Number of the Samples
HVHA	348
HVLA	298
LVLA	282
LVHA	352
Total	1280

[1] HVHA, High Valence High Arousal; HVLA, High Valence Low Arousal; LVLA, Low Valence Low Arousal; LVHA, Low Valence High Arousal.

4. The Construction of the Hybrid Deep Neural Networks

We propose a hybrid deep learning model called Convolutional and LSTM Recurrent Neural Networks (CLRNN) to conduct emotion recognition tasks. This model is a composite of two kinds of deep learning structures: CNN and the LSTM recurrent neural network (LSTM RNN). The structure of the model is presented in Figure 6. The CNN is used to extract features from EEG MFI, and the LSTM RNN is used for modeling the context information of the long-term EEG MFI sequences. The features automatically extracted by the CNN reflect the spatial distribution of the EEG signals. In this work, two stacked convolutional layers are adopted as the basic structure of the CNN, which included two convolution layers, two max pooling layers, and a full connection layer. Given the dynamic nature of the EEG data, the LSTM RNN is a reasonable choice for modeling the emotion classification. Before connecting to the LSTM unit, a flattening operation is adopted to transform the final feature maps into a one-dimensional vector.

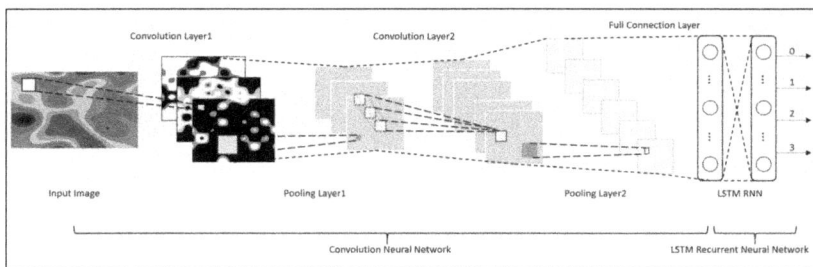

Figure 6. The structure of the hybrid deep neural networks used for emotion classification.

4.1. The Construction of Convolutional Neural Networks

The inputting MFI size of the networks is 200×200 pixels, and it contains three color channels. We set the number of convolutional filters as 30 in the first convolutional layer to extract 30 different kinds of correlation information, namely 30 different features. At the same time, to extract the multiple scale spatial characteristics of MFI, we use different size receptive fields in the first convolutional layer. The field sizes are 2×2 pixels, 5×5 pixels and 10×10 pixels, respectively. Corresponding to the different sizes of the field, the strides are 2, 5 and 10 pixels, respectively, without overlap between the strides. The activation function is ReLU. Following the first convolutional layer is a max pooling layer with pooling size of 2×2, and the strides are 2. The second convolutional layer is set as 10 different filters with a size of 2×2 without overlap between strides. This setting helps to further fuse the information of a specific scale range from the prior features. Like the first convolutional layer, we add a max pooling stage after this convolutional layer for information aggregation. Before connecting to the LSTM unit, a flatten operation is adopted to transform the final features into a one-dimensional feature vector. The configuration of the CNN described above is presented in Table 4. The dense layer in Table 4 is the layer that transforms the final features into a one-dimensional feature vector. In this layer, we set the output at 1/10 of the input to further compress the features and simplify the network. The LSTM RNN layer achieves a full connection to the dense layer. Next, the RNN output layer took 'softmax' as its activation function, and the output size is set to 4, corresponding to the four types of emotion states.

Table 4. The configurations of CNN. The parameters are denoted as <input size/receptive field size/pooling size> × <number of kernels/channels/out size>.

Input Data	Convolutional Layer 1	Max Pooling Layer 1	Convolutional Layer 2	Max Pooling Layer 2	Dense Layer	LSTM RNN	RNN Output
	<2 × 2> × 30	<2 × 2>	<2 × 2> × 10	<2 × 2>	6250:625	625:625	
<200 × 200> × 3	<5 × 5> × 30	<2 × 2>	<2 × 2> × 10	<2 × 2>	4000:400	400:400	4
	<10 × 10> × 30	<2 × 2>	<2 × 2> × 10	<2 × 2>	1000:100	100:100	

4.2. The Construction of LSTM Recurrent Neural Networks

In the DEAP experiment, the stimulus intensity changes over 60 s. The emotion scores by the Subjects are often based on the most exciting part of the entire video. Therefore, we needed to model the context information for long-term sequences. As mentioned before, RNN is good at sequential modeling. However, a simple RNN must face the challenge of 'gradient vanish or explode' in back propagation when its dependencies are too long [47]. LSTM units have been adopted to replace the simple units of a traditional RNN. LSTM units combine gate mechanisms in their structures so that the key features of the timing data are effectively maintained and transmitted during the long-period calculation. The gate is able to forget the used information and the self-loop structure allows the gradient to flow for long durations [48].

A typical structure of a LSTM unit is illustrated in Figure 7. For comparison, Figure 7 shows the structure of two neural network units. The upper left corner of the figure is a simple recurrent neural network unit, and the LSTM unit is below the graph. As seen in Figure 7, the simple RNN unit only contains the feedback from the output to the input. However, the LSTM unit contains three gate structures, i.e., input gate, forget gate, and output gate, which determine what information from the prior step should be forgotten and what information in the current time step should be added into the main data flow. f_i, f_o and f_g are the activation function of the input data, output data, and gate, respectively. In this study, they are all sigmoid functions.

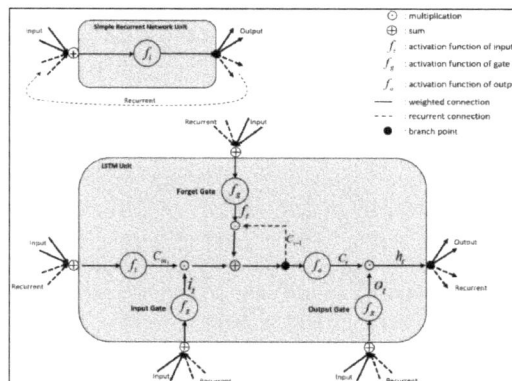

Figure 7. The Long Short-Term-Memory (LSTM) unit and simple recurrent network unit.

Different gates generate decision vectors to decide what candidate information will be selected. Using '*Input Gate*' as an example, this generates vector i_t with the hidden state h_{t-1} from the prior LSTM cell and the current step's input x_t. The process of generating i_t can be formalized as in Equation (4):

$$i_t = f_g(w_i x_t + w_i h_{t-1} + b_i), \tag{4}$$

where w_i is the weighted matrix of the input function; and b_i is the bias. The input candidate information $\widetilde{C}_t$ is also generated with h_{t-1} and x_t. $\widetilde{C}_t$ can be formalized as Equation (5):

$$\widetilde{C}_t = f_i(w_c x_t + w_c h_{t-1} + b_c). \tag{5}$$

The final updating information is the multiplication of the candidate information by the decision vector $\widetilde{C}_t \times i_t$. Another gate is the forget gate, which generates vector f_t to determine if the prior unit's state C_{t-1} should be reserved by multiplication $C_{t-1} \times f_t$. The f_t can be formalized as Equation (6):

$$f_t = f_g(w_{x_f} x_t + w_{h_f} h_{t-1} + b_f), \tag{6}$$

where f_t is scaled between 0 and 1 with the sigmoidal operation. The '0' element causes the corresponding information in C_{t-1} to be wiped out, while the '1' means the corresponding information is allowed to pass. The current unit state C_t is a combination of C_{t-1} and $\widetilde{C}_t$, and can be formalized as Equation (7):

$$C_t = C_{t-1} \times f_t + \widetilde{C}_t \times i_t. \tag{7}$$

The output state of the LSTM unit is determined by the output gate. The output gate also generates a decision vector o_t to decide the hidden state h_t, and they can be formalized as Equations (8) and (9), as follows:

$$o_t = f_g(w_o x_t + w_o h_{t-1} + b_o) \tag{8}$$

$$h_t = f_o(C_t) \times o_t. \tag{9}$$

In this study, the LSTM RNN is adopted to learn contextual information from the spatial features sequence extracted from the MFI.

4.3. The Construction of CLRNN with DL4J

DeepLearning4J is a java based toolkit for building, training and deploying Neural Networks [49]. In this study, DL4J is adopted as the framework to construct the CLRNN. We present the network's configuration in Appendix C. The code in Appendix C is used to construct the network structure of the CLRNN. The size of the kernel in each layer is set according to the configuration given in Table 4. The setting of the learning rate for each layer changed in the tuning process of network training.

5. Results and Discussion

In this section, we present the process of the experiment and compare our method with the baselines to show the effectiveness of our methods.

5.1. Experiment Dataset and Settings

As mentioned earlier, we used the open dataset DEAP to verify the effectiveness of our method, which include EEG signals from 32 channels collected from 32 subjects. Each subject took 40 trials, and each trial lasted 60 s. The sampling frequency of the EEG signal was 512 Hz. With different time windows, we obtained EEG MFI sequences with a different number of EEG MFIs. For example, with a one-second time window, we obtained 2400 MFIs for one EEG MFI sequence. With a two-second time window, we obtained 1200 MFIs for one EEG MFI sequence. However, even with the shortest time window, EEG MFIs are not enough for training a stable emotion recognition model with our method. For this reason, we adoptee data augmentation strategies before training. We added "salt & pepper" noise to the MFIs in MATLAB with the command 'imnoise()'. Image flipping or zooming is not used when augmenting the data. With this method, the original MFI set is expanded 20 times to ensure that we had at least 20,000 MFIs per subject for training. Sufficient training data helps a model with a large number of parameters to converge and generalize well. A five-fold cross-validation method is used to evaluate the performance of our approach, and the average performance of the 5-fold validation processes is taken as the experiment's final results. We trained the model with different time windows to find out if the division of the EEG signal had an impact on the classification's accuracy. The models are trained and tested in the Windows server environment, which included an Intel Xeon® V3 CPU (12 × 2.4 GHz) and 64 Gb RAM. No GPU acceleration is used in the experiment.

5.2. Baseline Methods

To illustrate its effectiveness, we compare our approach with the baseline methods and peer-reviewed studies. The selected baseline classifiers are commonly used in this field, including k-nearest neighbor (k-NN), Random Decision Forest, and Support Vector Machines (SVM). All baseline methods used a 5-fold cross-validation method for comparison with our method. The features trained in the baseline methods included the PSD, the C0 complexity, the power spectrum entropy, the Lyapunov index, and the correlation dimension. We trained the baseline classifiers in two ways: training in segments, and training in trials. The dimensions of each subject's features matrix are (five kinds of features × 32 channels) or (five kinds of features × 60/length of the time window × 32 channels). Principal component analysis is adopted to reduce the features' dimensions. All training processes are tested in the MATLAB (R2016a) environment. Here, we briefly describe the details and parameter settings used in those methods.

k-NN: k-nearest neighbor algorithm (k-NN) is a non-parametric method used for classification. An object is classified by a majority vote of its neighbors. It is useful to assign weight to the contributions of the neighbors, so that nearer neighbors contribute more to the average than more distant ones. Therefore, the main parameters of the k-NN algorithm are the number of neighbors and the weighting scheme of giving each neighbor a weight. In this study, k is selected from the set (k = {5, 10, 15, 20, 25, 30}). Furthermore, the Chebyshev distance is adopted to calculate the distance between the object and the neighbors. The inverse of the distance gives the neighbor a weight, and the weight is used in the vote procedure.

Random Decision Forest: Random Decision Forest (RDF) is an ensemble learning method for classification, which constructs a multitude of decision trees at training time. The training algorithm applies bootstrap aggregating, or bagging, to the tree learners. It selects a random subset of the features during the learning process. The main parameter setting of RDF is the number of the learners. Here, the number of learners is selected from the set (N = {5, 10, 20, 30, 40, 50}).

SVM: SVM hyperparameters consisting of a regularization penalty parameter (C) and inverse of RBF kernel's standard deviation ($\gamma = 1/\sigma$) were selected by grid search through cross-validation on the training set (C = {0.01, 0.1, 1, 10, 100}, γ = {0.1, 0.2, ..., 1, 2, ..., 10}). For the reason of multiple classes, the One-vs.-One strategy is employed during the SVM training.

CNN + RNN (without LSTM units): To show the memory effect of LSTM units in long-period data analysis, we designed a hybrid neural network structure including CNN and RNN without LSTM units. In this network structure, in addition to the RNN network layer not using the LSTM unit, the other network structure is the same as the CLRNN.

For peer-reviewed studies, we chose the studies listed in Table 2 for purposes of comparison.

5.3. Results and Discussion

In this section, we present the results of our experiments. Due to a variation of the parameters in the classification methods, we only present the best results obtained by each method. First, a comparison of the classification accuracies between CLRNN and the baseline methods is presented in Figure 8. We present a boxplot of the mean emotion recognition accuracies with the different time windows for each subject in Figure 8. The comparison shows the effectiveness of our method. The average emotion classification accuracy of each subject with CLRNN is 75.21%, whereas the average accuracies of other classification methods are 69.58% with CNN + RNN, 67.45% with SVM, 45.47% with Random Decision Forest, and 62.84% with k-NN, respectively. The highest accuracy is obtained from Subject 4 with CLRNN, which is 90.54%.

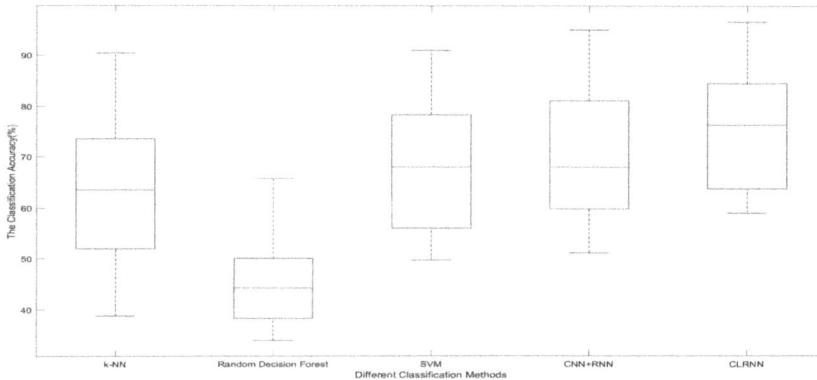

Figure 8. Emotion recognition accuracies with different classification methods.

After a comparison with the baseline methods, we chose relevant studies listed in Table 2 to compare with our method. The selection of the previous studies is based on two aspects: (1) the emotion analysis is based on EEG signals; and (2) the emotion label is produced by the scales of Valence and Arousal. We found that most studies in Table 2 classified emotions into two classes: Pleasant/Unpleasant or Positive/Negative. Some studies [7,43,44] classified emotion into three categories: Pleasant, Neutral, and Unpleasant. In our study, we classify emotion into four types (HVHA, HVLA, LVLA, and LVHA). Two emotion classification problems are relatively simple, and the highest accuracy reached 82%. Multiple (more than two) emotion classification problems are complex, and the accuracy of our method reaches 75.21%, which is higher than the results presented in [43,44]. The studies in [43,44] also employ DEAP as a dataset to recognize human emotions. This shows the effectiveness of our method. In addition, [41,43,44] and this study all employed DEAP as the dataset to undertake the emotion analysis. The performance of our method is better than the others. A similar research method is used in [41], which also built Neural Networks by CNNs and LSTM RNNs, with the difference being that the two-dimensional EEG feature images constructed in [41] ignored the spatial characteristics of EEG signals. In this paper, the spatial features of EEG signals are considered very important for emotion recognition. Through the experiments in this study, we proved the correctness of this point.

To further validate the effectiveness of our method, we investigated the effect of the time window size on the classification analysis. The MFIs with different time windows are trained and tested in CLRNN and CNN + RNN, respectively. For comparison, the features trained in the baseline method are also extracted from the raw EEG signals with the same time window size and are presented in Table 5, which shows the average of the emotional classification accuracy obtained by 32 subjects under different time windows. As seen from the results in Table 5, CLRNN showed sensitivity to the time window size. With an increase in the time window, the classification accuracy showed a decreasing trend. The accuracies of the classification from other methods did not change significantly with the increase of the time window. This further confirmed that the LSTM unit played a role in capturing long-term critical features during the classification process.

Table 5. The classification results with different time window size and methods.

Classification Methods	1 s	2 s	3 s	4 s	5 s	6 s	8 s	10 s	12 s	15 s	20 s	30 s	60 s
k-NN	46.09	52.49	57.29	59.49	61.69	61.39	61.49	61.89	61.79	62.19	62.59	62.19	62.39
Random Decision Forest	39.03	38.17	39.38	40.19	38.53	36.43	44.53	45.38	45.88	46.58	46.68	46.78	46.98
SVM	65.11	65.11	66.11	64.21	63.01	64.31	61.01	63.01	62.61	62.41	63.01	63.41	63.21
CNN + RNN	61.76	59.02	58.07	60.34	61.43	62.13	61.13	59.1	60.1	60.9	61.1	61.5	62.1
CLRNN	74.73	75.21	75.13	74.32	73.25	70.37	67.23	65.01	57.3	60.2	62.1	60.6	61.8

The study in [45] analyzed the emotion classification with DEAP EEG signals from the perspective of time window size and wavelet features and obtained the highest accuracy using the wavelet entropy of three-second signal segments, which is similar to the results we obtained.

Further intuitive investigation is conducted with a graphical representation of the results from CLRNN and 'CNN + RNN', as illustrated in Figure 9. It can be seen from Figure 9 that with the same small time window (before 12 s) CLRNN had higher classification accuracies than CNN + RNN without LSTM units. After 12 s, the difference between the accuracies of the two methods is very small. For this phenomenon, our inference is that the change in the EEG signal presented with the MFIs is overshadowed as the time window becomes larger. Therefore, the MFI sequence corresponding to the large-sized time window does not reflect the change of emotion. To confirm this inference, we select MFI sequences from 32 subjects to seek corresponding evidence. After comparison, Subject 4 is chosen to present the variation, which is shown in Figure 10.

As seen in Figure 10, there are 12 MFI sequences, and each line corresponds to a time widow size. From the first to the fifth line, each line contained the first 10 images of the MFI sequences. Starting from the sixth line, it contains the whole images of the sequence. Studies presented in [50,51] suggested that emotion is related to a group of structures in the center of the brain called the limbic system and other structures such as the prefrontal cortex [52], orbitofrontal cortex, and so on. Out of these areas, the correspondence between the prefrontal cortex and the EEG electrodes FP_1-FP_2 are more direct than others. Therefore, we focused on the area corresponding to FP_1-FP_2. We can see from Figure 10 that the MFI sequences corresponding to time windows 1 s to 3 s reveal more details about the activation in this area. However, starting from the MFI sequence corresponding to the 4 s time window, the activation information for this area is gradually reduced. This also corresponded to the case where emotion recognition accuracy decreased after a 4 s time window by CLRNN in Figure 9.

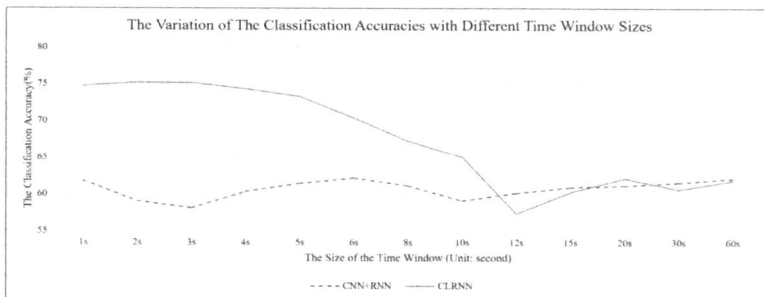

Figure 9. The comparison of the classification accuracies between CLRNN and CNN + RNN with different time window sizes.

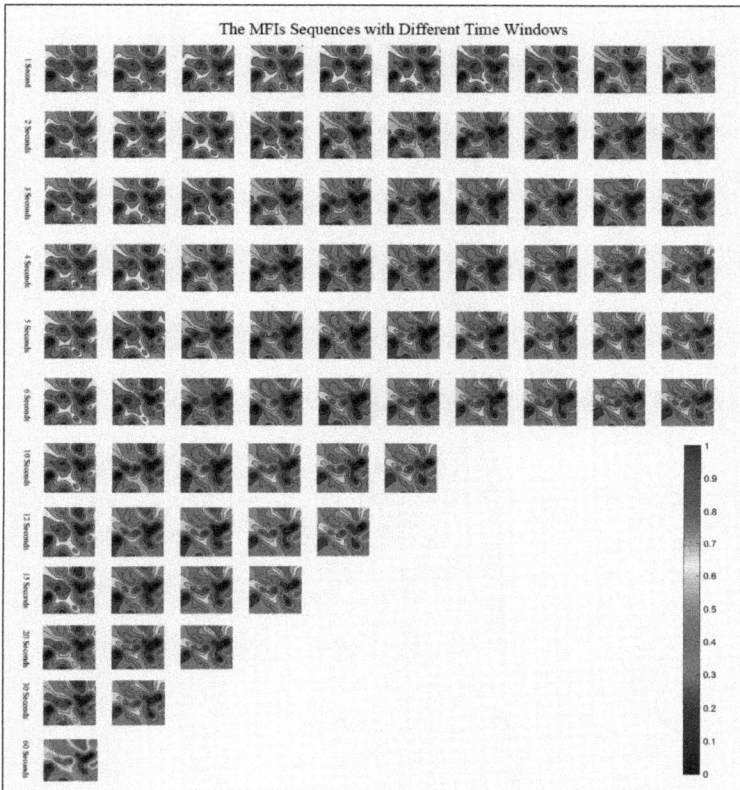

Figure 10. MFI sequences with different time windows corresponding to Subject 4 (corresponding to the emotion HVHA).

6. Conclusions

In this study, we try to improve the accuracy of classifying human emotion by EEG signals. The innovation of our methods involves two aspects. First, we propose a new method for the EEG feature extraction and representation. EEG frequency features (PSD) are extracted from different EEG channels and mapped to a two-dimensional plane to construct the EEG MFI. EEG MFI sequences are built from the raw EEG signal. The EEG MFI sequences fuse together the spatial, frequency domain, and time characteristics of the raw EEG signal. Another aspect is our proposal of a hybrid deep neural network that deals with the EEG MFI sequences and recognizes the emotions. The hybrid deep neural networks combined Convolution Neural Networks and Long-Short-Term-Memory Recurrent Neural Networks. In the hybrid structure, CNN is used to learn temporary image patterns from EEG MFI sequences, and LSTM RNN is used to classify human emotions.

With our method, empirical research is carried out with the DEAP dataset. We compare our results with those from the baseline methods and find that the emotion classification accuracy of our method reached 75.21%, which is higher than the accuracies from the baseline methods. In the baseline methods, we chose a 'CNN + RNN' Neural Network without LSTM unit to compare with our method. We find that the LSTM unit showed the time sensitivity. Furthermore, we reviewed the state of the art of human emotion recognition by EEG signals. Compared with similar studies, our study improves the classification accuracy.

Appl. Sci. **2017**, *7*, 1060

Additionally, we analyzed the effects of different time windows on classification accuracy and found that time windows corresponding to two to three seconds achieved good classification accuracy, and the corresponding classification accuracy decreased from the time window division after four seconds. Given these results, we inferred that MFI sequences from a smaller time window represent more details of the variation of the EEG signal. We select Subject 4 to seek corresponding evidence in the MFI sequence and find that, with smaller size time windows, MFI reveals more details about activation in the FP_1 and FP_2 area.

Acknowledgments: This work is supported by the National Basic Research Program of China (2014CB744600), the National Natural Science Foundation of China (61420106005), and the International Science & Technology Cooperation Program of China (2013DFA32180).

Author Contributions: Youjun Li and Ning Zhong proposed the method of the construction of EEG MFI sequences; Youjun Li and Jiajin Huang proposed the framework of the hybrid neural networks; Haiyan Zhou contributed to the EEG feature extraction and analysis method; Youjun Li and Ning Zhong designed and performed the experiment; Youjun Li wrote the paper.

Conflicts of Interest: The authors declare no conflict of interest.

Appendix A

The code of the interpolation function and MFI generation method (used in MATLAB (R2016a)).

```
function build_EEG_MFI()
    % the feature matrix has been generated and stored in variable basic_matrix (81,3);
            x = basic_matrix (:,1); %Horizontal axis coordinates
            y = basic_matrix (:,2); % Vertical axis coordinates
            z = basic_matrix (:,3); % Feature values of the corresponding electrodes
            nx = linspace(min(x), max(x),1000);
            ny = linspace(min(y), max(y),1000);
            [xx,yy] = meshgrid(nx,ny);
            zz = griddata(x,y,z,xx,yy,'v4');
            contourf(yy,xx,zz,'linestyle','-','LineWidth',0.5);
            colormap('HSV');
            axis off;
            set(gcf,'PaperUnits','inches','PaperPosition',[0 0 2 2]);
            print(1,'-dpng',picWritePath,'-r100');
    end
```

Appendix B

The pseudo-code of producing the specific feature matrix (used in MATLAB (R2016a)).

```
function buildFeatureMatrix(integer theLengthofTheTimeWindow)
    % P is a feature Matrix of four-dimensional: P(electrodeNum,sequenceNum,trialNum,subjectNum)
    %theLengthofTheTimeWindow is set to 1,2,3,4,5, ... , 10;
    the_Num_of_MFIs=sequenceNum/theLengthofTheTimeWindow;
    for subjectNum=1:32
        for trialNum=1:40
         specific_P =P(:,:,subjectNum,trialNum);
         for r1=1:electrodeNum
             for r2=1:the_Num_of_MFIs
                 meanRawData(r1,r2)=mean(specific_P(r1,(r2-1)*theLengthofTheTimeWindow+
                 1:(r2-1)*theLengthofTheTimeWindow+theLengthofTheTimeWindow));
             end
         end
         generate_MFIs(meanRawData);
         end
        end
    end
```

Appendix C

The code to construct the network structure of the CLRNN (built with dl4j).

```
Updater updater = Updater.ADAGRAD; // ADAGRAD function is taken as the updater
   MultiLayerConfiguration conf = new NeuralNetConfiguration.Builder()
      .seed(12345)
      .regularization(true).l2(0.001) //l2 regularization on all layers
      .optimizationAlgo(OptimizationAlgorithm.STOCHASTIC_GRADIENT_DESCENT)
      .iterations(1)
      .learningRate(0.04)
      .list()
      .layer(0, new ConvolutionLayer.Builder(2, 2)
            .nIn(3) //3 channels: RGB
            .nOut(30)
            .stride(2, 2)
            .activation("relu")
            .weightInit(WeightInit.RELU)
            .updater(updater)
            .build())    //Output: (200-2+0)/2+1 = 100 -> 100*100*30
      .layer(1, new SubsamplingLayer.Builder(SubsamplingLayer.PoolingType.MAX)
            .kernelSize(2, 2)
            .stride(2, 2).build())    //Output:(100-2+0)/2+1 = 50
      .layer(2, new ConvolutionLayer.Builder(2, 2)
            .nIn(30)
            .nOut(10)
            .stride(2, 2)
            .activation("relu")
            .weightInit(WeightInit.RELU)
            .updater(updater)
            .build())    //Output: (50-2+0)/2+1 = 25 -> 25*25*10 = 6250
      .layer(3, new DenseLayer.Builder()
            .activation("relu")
            .nIn(6250)
            .nOut(100)
            .weightInit(WeightInit.RELU)
            .updater(updater)
            .gradientNormalization(GradientNormalization.ClipElementWiseAbsoluteValue)
            .gradientNormalizationThreshold(10)
            .learningRate(0.01)
            .build())
      .layer(4, new GravesLSTM.Builder()
            .activation("softsign")
            .nIn(100)
            .nOut(100)
            .weightInit(WeightInit.XAVIER)
            .updater(updater)
            .gradientNormalization(GradientNormalization.ClipElementWiseAbsoluteValue)
            .gradientNormalizationThreshold(10)
            .learningRate(0.001)
            .build())
      .layer(5, new RnnOutputLayer.Builder(LossFunctions.LossFunction.MCXENT)
            .activation("softmax")
            .nIn(100)
            .nOut(4)    //4 possible emotion states
            .updater(updater)
            .weightInit(WeightInit.XAVIER)
            .gradientNormalization(GradientNormalization.ClipElementWiseAbsoluteValue)
            .gradientNormalizationThreshold(10)
            .build())
```

```
.inputPreProcessor(0, new RnnToCnnPreProcessor(200, 200, 2))
.inputPreProcessor(3, new CnnToFeedForwardPreProcessor(50, 50, 10))
.inputPreProcessor(4, new FeedForwardToRnnPreProcessor())
.pretrain(false).backprop(true)
.backpropType(BackpropType.TruncatedBPTT)
.tBPTTForwardLength(60/5)
.tBPTTBackwardLength(60/5)
.build();
```

References

1. Mandryk, R.L.; Inkpen, K.M.; Calvert, T.W. Using psychophysiological techniques to measure user experience with entertainment technologies. *Behav. Inf. Technol.* **2006**, *25*, 141–158. [CrossRef]
2. Healey, J.A.; Picard, R.W. Detecting stress during real-world driving tasks using physiological sensors. *IEEE Trans. Intell. Transp. Syst.* **2005**, *6*, 156–166. [CrossRef]
3. Katsis, C.D.; Katertsidis, N.; Ganiatsas, G.; Fotiadis, D.I. Toward emotion recognition in car-racing drivers: A biosignal processing approach. *IEEE Trans. Syst. Man Cybern.* **2008**, *38*, 502–512. [CrossRef]
4. Katsis, C.D.; Katertsidis, N.S.; Fotiadis, D.I. An integrated system based on physiological signals for the assessment of affective states in patients with anxiety disorders. *Biomed. Signal Process. Control* **2011**, *6*, 261–268. [CrossRef]
5. Verschuere, B.; Ben-Shakhar, G.; Meijer, E. Memory Detection: Theory and Application of the Concealed Information Test. In *Psychopathy and the Detection of Concealed Information*; Verschuere, B., Ben-Shakhar, G.M., Meijer, E., Eds.; Cambridge University Press: Cambridge, UK, 2011; pp. 215–230.
6. Picard, R.W.; Vyzas, E.; Healey, J. Toward machine emotional intelligence: Analysis of affective physiological state. *IEEE Trans. Pattern Anal. Mach. Intell.* **2001**, *23*, 1175–1191. [CrossRef]
7. El Ayadi, M.; Kamel, M.S.; Karray, F. Survey on speech emotion recognition: Features, classification schemes, and databases. *Pattern Recognit.* **2011**, *44*, 572–587. [CrossRef]
8. Venkatesh, Y.V.; Kassim, A.A.; Yuan, J.; Nguyen, T.D. On the simultaneous recognition of identity and expression from BU-3DFE datasets. *Pattern Recognit. Lett.* **2012**, *33*, 1785–1793. [CrossRef]
9. Arnrich, B.; Setz, C.; La Marca, R.; Troster, G.; Ehlert, U. What does your chair know about your stress level? *IEEE Trans. Inf. Technol. Biomed.* **2010**, *14*, 207–214. [CrossRef] [PubMed]
10. Cacioppo, J.T.; Berntson, G.G.; Larsen, J.T.; Poehlmann, K.M. The psychophysiology of emotion. In *Handbook of Emotion*; Lewis, M., Haviland-Jones, J.M., Eds.; Guilford Press: New York, NY, USA, 2000; pp. 173–191.
11. Koelstra, S.; Muhl, C.; Soleymani, M.; Jong-Seok, L.; Yazdani, A.; Ebrahimi, T.; Pun, T.; Nijholt, A.; Patras, I. Deap: A database for emotion analysis ;using physiological signals. *IEEE Trans. Affect. Comput.* **2012**, *3*, 18–31. [CrossRef]
12. Kim, M.-K.; Kim, M.; Oh, E.; Kim, S.-P. A review on the computational methods for emotional state estimation from the human EEG. *Comput. Math. Methods Med.* **2013**, *2013*, 1–13. [CrossRef] [PubMed]
13. Ansari-Asl, K.; Chanel, G.; Pun, T. A channel selection method for EEG classification in emotion assessment based on synchronization likelihood. In Proceedings of the 15th European Signal Processing Conference, Poznan, Poland, 3–7 September 2007; IEEE: Piscataway, NJ, USA, 2007; pp. 1241–1245.
14. Horlings, R.; Datcu, D.; Rothkrantz, L.J.M. Emotion recognition using brain activity. In Proceedings of the 9th international conference on computer systems and technologies and workshop for PhD students in computing, Gabrovo, Bulgaria, 12–13 June 2008; ACM: New York, NY, USA, 2008.
15. Murugappan, M.; Ramachandran, N.; Sazali, Y. Classification of human emotion from EEG using discrete wavelet transform. *J. Biomed. Sci. Eng.* **2010**, *3*, 390–396. [CrossRef]
16. Petrantonakis, P.C.; Hadjileontiadis, L.J. Emotion recognition from EEG using higher order crossings. *IEEE Trans. Inf. Technol. Biomed.* **2010**, *14*, 186–197. [CrossRef] [PubMed]
17. Petrantonakis, P.C.; Hadjileontiadis, L.J. Emotion recognition from brain signals using hybrid adaptive filtering and higher order crossings analysis. *IEEE Trans. Affect. Comput.* **2010**, *1*, 81–97. [CrossRef]
18. Khalili, Z.; Moradi, M.H. Emotion detection using brain and peripheral signals. In Proceedings of the Biomedical Engineering Conference, Cairo, Egypt, 18–20 December 2008; IEEE: Piscataway, NJ, USA, 2009; pp. 1223–1226.

19. Mu, L.; Lu, B.-L. Emotion classification based on gamma-band EEG. In Proceedings of the Annual International Conference of the IEEE, Minneapolis, MN, USA, 3–6 September 2009; IEEE: Piscataway, NJ, USA, 2009; pp. 1223–1226.

20. Liu, Y.; Sourina, O. EEG-based dominance level recognition for emotion-enabled interaction. In Proceedings of the IEEE International Conference on Multimedia and Expo, Melbourne, Australia, 9–13 July 2012; IEEE: Piscataway, NJ, USA, 2012; pp. 1039–1044.

21. Rozgic, V.; Vitaladevuni, S.N.; Prasad, R. Robust EEG emotion classification using segment level decision fusion. In Proceedings of the IEEE International Conference on Acoustics, Speech and Signal Processing, Vancouver, BC, Canada, 26–31 May 2013; IEEE: Piscataway, NJ, USA, 2013; pp. 1286–1290.

22. Daunizeau, J.; Lee, Y.-Y.; Hsieh, S. Classifying different emotional states by means of EEG-based functional connectivity patterns. *PLoS ONE* **2014**, *9*, e95415.

23. Bashivan, P.; Rish, I.; Yeasin, M.; Codella, N. Learning representations from EEG with deep recurrent-convolutional neural networks. In Proceedings of the International Conference on Learning Representations 2016, San Juan, PR, USA, 2–4 May 2016.

24. Yin, Z.; Wang, Y.; Liu, L.; Zhang, W.; Zhang, J. Cross-subject EEG feature selection for emotion recognition using transfer recursive feature elimination. *Front. Neurorobot.* **2017**, *11*, 19. [CrossRef] [PubMed]

25. Chanel, G.; Karim, A.-A.; Thierry, P. Valence-arousal evaluation using physiological signals in an emotion recall paradigm. In Proceedings of the IEEE International Conference on Systems, Man and Cybernetics, Montreal, QC, Canada, 7–10 October 2007; IEEE: Piscataway, NJ, USA, 2008; pp. 2662–2667.

26. Nie, D.; Wang, X.-W.; Shi, L.-C.; Lu, B.-L. EEG-based emotion recognition during watching movies. In Proceedings of the 5th International IEEE/EMBS Conference on Neural Engineering, Cancun, Mexico, 27 April–1 May 2011; IEEE: Piscataway, NJ, USA, 2011; pp. 667–670.

27. Zheng, W.L.; Dong, B.N.; Lu, B.-L. Multimodal emotion recognition using EEG and eye tracking data. In Proceedings of the 36th Annual International Conference of the IEEE Engineering in Medicine and Biology Society, Chicago, IL, USA, 26–30 August 2014; IEEE: Piscataway, NJ, USA, 2014; pp. 5040–5043.

28. Zheng, W.-L.; Zhu, J.-Y.; Lu, B.-L. Identifying stable patterns over time for emotion recognition from EEG. *IEEE Trans. Affect. Comput.* **2017**, *PP*, 1. [CrossRef]

29. Thammasan, N.; Moriyama, K.; Fukui, K.; Numao, M. Continuous music-emotion recognition based on electroencephalogram. *IEICE Trans. Inf. Syst.* **2016**, *99*, 1234–1241. [CrossRef]

30. Murugappan, M.; Rizon, M.; Nagarajan, R.; Yaacob, S. Inferring of human emotional states using multichannel EEG. *Eur. J. Sci. Res.* **2010**, *48*, 281–299.

31. Kroupi, E.; Yazdani, A.; Ebrahimi, T. EEG correlates of different emotional states elicited during watching music videos. In Proceedings of the 4th International Conference on Affective Computing and Intelligent Interaction, Memphis, TN, USA, 9–12 October 2011; Affective Computing and Intelligent Interaction (ACII): Berlin, Germany, 2011; pp. 457–466.

32. Hadjidimitriou, S.K.; Hadjileontiadis, L.J. Toward an EEG-based recognition of music liking using time-frequency analysis. *IEEE Trans. Biomed. Eng.* **2012**, *59*, 3498–3510. [CrossRef] [PubMed]

33. Reuderink, B.; Mühl, C.; Poel, M. Valence, arousal and dominance in the EEG during game play. *Int. J. Auton. Adapt. Commun. Syst.* **2013**, *6*, 45–62. [CrossRef]

34. Lahane, P.; Sangaiah, A.K. An approach to EEG based emotion recognition and classification using kernel density estimation. *Procedia Comput. Sci.* **2015**, *48*, 574–581. [CrossRef]

35. Faul, S.; Mazumder, A.; Ghosh, P.; Tibarewala, D.N.; Vimalarani, G. EEG based emotion recognition system using MFDFA as feature extractor. In Proceedings of the International Conference on Robotics, Automation, Control and Embedded Systems (RACE), Chennai, India, 18–20 February 2015; IEEE: Piscataway, NJ, USA, 2015; pp. 1–5.

36. Li, X.; Qi, X.Y.; Sun, X.Q.; Xie, J.L.; Fan, M.D.; Kang, J.N. An improved multi-scale entropy algorithm in emotion EEG features extraction. *J. Med. Imaging Health Inform.* **2017**, *7*, 436–439.

37. Soleymani, M.; Koelstra, S.; Patras, I.; Pun, T. Continuous emotion detection in response to music videos. In Proceedings of the IEEE International Conference on Automatic Face and Gesture Recognition and Workshops, Santa Barbara, CA, USA, 21–25 March 2011; IEEE: Piscataway, NJ, USA, 2011; pp. 803–808.

38. Klem, G.H.; Luders, H.O.; Jasper, H.H.; Elger, C. The ten-twenty electrode system of the international federation. *Electroencephalogr. Clin. Neurophysiol. Suppl.* **1999**, *52*, 3–6. [PubMed]

39. Brown, L.; Grundlehner, B.; Penders, J. Towards wireless emotional valence detection from EEG. In Proceedings of the Annual International Conference of the IEEE Engineering in Medicine and Biology Society, Boston, MA, USA, 30 August–3 September 2011; IEEE: Piscataway, NJ, USA, 2011; pp. 2188–2191.

40. Frantzidis, C.A.; Bratsas, C.; Papadelis, C.L.; Konstantinidis, E.; Pappas, C.; Bamidis, P.D. Toward emotion aware computing: An integrated approach using multichannel neurophysiological recordings and affective visual stimuli. *IEEE Trans. Inf. Technol. Biomed.* **2010**, *14*, 589–597. [CrossRef] [PubMed]

41. Schaaff, K.; Schultz, T. Towards emotion recognition from electroencephalographic signals. In Proceedings of the 3rd International Conference on Affective Computing and Intelligent Interaction and Workshops, Amsterdam, The Netherlands, 10–12 September 2009; IEEE: Piscataway, NJ, USA, 2009; pp. 1–6.

42. Hosseini, S.A.; Khalilzadeh, M.A.; Naghibi-Sistani, M.B.; Niazmand, V. Higher order spectra analysis of EEG signals in emotional stress states. In Proceedings of the Second International Conference on Information Technology and Computer Science, Kiev, Ukraine, 24–25 July 2010; IEEE: Piscataway, NJ, USA, 2010; pp. 60–63.

43. Chung, S.Y.; Yoon, H.J. Affective classification using Bayesian classifier and supervised learning. In Proceedings of the 12th International Conference on Control, Automation and Systems, JeJu Island, Korea, 17–21 October 2012; IEEE: Piscataway, NJ, USA, 2012; pp. 1768–1771.

44. Li, X.; Song, D.; Zhang, P.; Yu, G.; Hou, Y.; Hu, B. Emotion recognition from multi-channel EEG data through convolutional recurrent neural network. In Proceedings of the IEEE International Conference on Bioinformatics and Biomedicine (BIBM), Shenzhen, China, 15–18 December 2016; IEEE: Piscataway, NJ, USA, 2016; pp. 352–359.

45. Candra, H.; Yuwono, M.; Rifai, C.; Handojoseno, A.; Elamvazuthi, I.; Nguyen, H.T.; Su, S. Investigation of window size in classification of EEG-emotion signal with wavelet entropy and support vector machine. In Proceedings of the 37th Annual International Conference of the IEEE Engineering in Medicine and Biology Society (EMBC), Milan, Italy, 25–29 August 2015; IEEE: Piscataway, NJ, USA, 2015; pp. 7250–7253.

46. 10–20 System (EEG). Available online: https://en.wikipedia.org/wiki/10-20_system_(EEG) (accessed on 10 September 2017).

47. Bengio, Y.; Simard, P.; Frasconi, P. Learning long-term dependencies with gradient descent is difficult. *IEEE Trans. Neural Netw.* **1994**, *5*, 157–166. [CrossRef] [PubMed]

48. Hochreiter, S.; Schmidhuber, J. Long short-term memory. *Neural Comput.* **1997**, *9*, 1735–1780. [CrossRef] [PubMed]

49. DEEPLEARNING4J. Available online: https://deeplearning4j.org/ (accessed on 10 September 2017).

50. Panksepp, J. A role for affective neuroscience in understanding stress: The case of separation distress circuitry. *Psychobiol. Stress* **1990**, *54*, 41–57.

51. Papez, J.W. A proposed mechanism of emotion. *Arch. Neurol. Psychiatry* **1937**, *38*, 725–743. [CrossRef]

52. Davidson, R.J.; Sutton, S.K. Affective neuroscience: The emergence of a discipline. *Curr. Opin. Neurobiol.* **1995**, *5*, 217–224. [CrossRef]

applied
sciences

MDPI

Review

Technology-Facilitated Diagnosis and Treatment of Individuals with Autism Spectrum Disorder: An Engineering Perspective

Xiongyi Liu [1], Qing Wu [2], Wenbing Zhao [2,*] and Xiong Luo [3]

[1] Department of Curriculum and Foundations, Cleveland State University, Cleveland, OH 44115, USA;
    x.liu6@csuohio.edu
[2] Department of Electrical Engineering and Computer Science, Cleveland State University, Cleveland,
    OH 44115, USA; q.wu55@vikes.csuohio.edu
[3] School of Computer and Communication Engineering, University of Science and Technology Beijing,
    Beijing 100083, China; xluo@ustb.edu.cn
*   Correspondence: w.zhao1@csuohio.edu; Tel.: +1-216-523-7480

Received: 8 July 2017; Accepted: 11 October 2017; Published: 13 October 2017

Abstract: The rapid development of computer and robotic technologies in the last decade is giving hope to perform earlier and more accurate diagnoses of the Autism Spectrum Disorder (ASD), and more effective, consistent, and cost-conscious treatment. Besides the reduced cost, the main benefit of using technology to facilitate treatment is that stimuli produced during each session of the treatment can be controlled, which not only guarantees consistency across different sessions, but also makes it possible to focus on a single phenomenon, which is difficult even for a trained professional to perform, and deliver the stimuli according to the treatment plan. In this article, we provide a comprehensive review of research on recent technology-facilitated diagnosis and treat of children and adults with ASD. Different from existing reviews on this topic, which predominantly concern clinical issues, we focus on the engineering perspective of autism studies. All technology facilitated systems used for autism studies can be modeled as human machine interactive systems where one or more participants would constitute as the human component, and a computer-based or a robotic-based system would be the machine component. Based on this model, we organize our review with the following questions: (1) What are presented to the participants in the studies and how are the content and delivery methods enabled by technologies? (2) How are the reactions/inputs collected from the participants in response to the stimuli in the studies? (3) Are the experimental procedure and programs presented to participants dynamically adjustable based on the responses from the participants, and if so, how? and (4) How are the programs assessed?

Keywords: autism spectrum disorder; virtual reality; avatars; social robots; depth sensors; affective computing; emotion recognition; joint attention

1. Introduction

Autism Spectrum Disorder (ASD) is a neurological and developmental disorder. ASD presents with a constellation of physiologic and behavioral symptoms. There are two essential domains of ASD symptoms: (1) restrictive and repetitive behaviors, for example, having a lasting and intense interest in certain topics, including sensory challenges; (2) difficulty in social communication and interaction, such as failing to make proper eye contact during a conversion with another person. Although the exact causes for ASD are not known and there is no cure, research has shown that symptoms can be improved via proper treatment, especially when detected in early childhood.

It was estimated that 1.1% of population in the United States suffer from Autism Spectrum Disorders (ASD), which amounts to more than three million people. The cost of supporting an individual with an ASD ranges from $1.4 million for those without intellectual disability to $2.3 million for those with intellectual disability during his/her lifespan (https://www.autismspeaks. org/about-us/press-releases/annual-cost-of-autism-triples). The largest cost components for children with ASD were special education services and parental productivity loss. Although the final cost is high for people with ASD, the actual damages caused by ASD are far beyond that. Both caregivers and people with ASD can be severely stressed due to the difficulty of proper mutual communication because people with ASD are often overwhelmed and anxious in social interactions. The lack of social skills for people with ASD will also significantly impact their personal lives and hamper their (future) career opportunities, especially for children. Many children with ASD have no friends and even have difficulty interacting with their parents. Not only do they often suffer from strong loneliness, but the frustration may also lead to violent behaviors, which will put both themselves and their loved ones in danger.

The rapid development of computer and robotic technologies in the last decade is giving hope to perform earlier and more accurate diagnosis of ASD, and more effective, consistent, and cost-conscious treatment. Besides the reduced cost, the main benefit of using technology to facilitate treatment is that stimuli produced during each session of the treatment can be controlled, which not only guarantees consistency across different sessions, but also makes it possible to focus on a single phenomenon, which is difficult even for a trained professional to perform, and deliver the stimuli according to the treatment plan. Computer based research typically uses virtual avatars or characters to represent therapists and other related facilitators, while robotic based treatment research typically uses humanoid robots. The computer based approach has the advantage of producing virtual reality scenes and scenarios for a treatment study, while the robotic based approach has the advantage of offering a real-human like physical embodiment.

In this article, we provide a comprehensive review of research on recent technology-facilitated diagnosis and treatment of children and adults with ASD. There are several recent reviews on similar topics. Wieckowski and White [1] provided an excellent review on technology-based interventions for children with social communication impairment. They reviewed work in the most recent seven years. They categorized the research into two major areas: (1) the reception of technology-based communication, and (2) the production of technology-based communication. For each area, the work is further divided into facial communication and non-facial communication. The research is predominately on facial communication. Non-facial communication includes verbal and gestures. The technologies that have been used include computer, mobile, virtual reality, and robotics. The discussions are focused on the clinical impact of these research works.

Aresti-Bartolome and Garcia-Zapirain reviewed the technology facilitated research work on ASD care [2]. They divided the technologies used into four categories: (1) virtual reality; (2) dedicated applications; (3) telehealth applications, and (4) robotic based. For each technology category, three research objectives are considered: (1) communication and interaction; (2) social learning and imitation skills; and (3) other miscellaneous.

There are several reviews on using a particular technology, such as virtual technology, social robotics, and serious games, to treat individuals with ASD. Scassellati et al. [3] reviewed about ten-year's work on using socially assistive robots for autism research up to 2012. The focus was on issues related to robot design, human-robot interaction, and system evaluation. The authors specifically highlighted the need to achieve robot autonomy because the operator-controlled method has severe limitations. Diehl et al. reviewed 15 papers that reported clinical use of social robots for individuals with ASD as of 2012 [4]. This review focused on four aspects of the studies, including the response of individuals with ASD to robots, the various ways of using robots to elicit behaviors, and using robots to teach social skills, and using robots to provide feedback. The authors concluded that most of the work reviewed were exploratory and had severe limitations. Even though it is not our focus, we find the situation has not been improved in our current review. Cabibihan et al. [5] outlined robot design features, complied a list of robotic systems that have been used for ASD therapy up to 2013, and highlighted a set of activities used for ASD therapy, including imitation, eye contact, joint attention, turn-taking, emotion recognition and expression, self-initiated interactions, and triadic interactions. The article also summarized the roles that could be played by a social robot, including as a diagnostic agent, as a friendly playmate, as a behavior eliciting agent, as a social mediator, as a social actor, and as a personal therapist. Pennisi et al. [6] provided a systematic review of research for autism treatment using social robots from a clinical perspective. A major contribution of this review is that it formulated ten questions regarding the essential roles and benefits of robots for ASD treatments, and reported their findings based on the studies that they have collected up to 2015 in light of these questions. Begum et al. [7] reviewed research on using social robots for autism treatment up to 2016. They pointed out that there is little progress in making social robots as clinical useful for ASD treatment.

Parsons provided a review on autism research facilitated by virtual reality technology [8]. This review focuses on the impact of veridicality of the virtual reality technology in autism treatment under two main themes: (1) using virtual environments for learning and intervention for individuals with ASD to better prepare them to handle real world interactions; and (2) using virtual environments to study how individuals with ASD would behave under predefined social scenarios.

Zakari, Ma, and Simmons [9] presented a short review of serious games designed for children with ASD to improve their communication skills and social behavior. These games are designed to be played via touch-enabled mobile devices or via traditional computers using a keyboard and a mouse. Very recently, Grossard et al. provided a more up-to-date review on using serious games to teach individuals with ASD to improve their social interactions and emotion skills [10]. They focused on the target skills of the serious games, and the design principles of the games. They also paid attention to whether or not the games have been validated in a clinical population.

Different from the above reviews, which predominantly concern clinical issues, we focus on the engineering perspective of autism studies. All technology facilitated systems used for autism studies can be considered as a form of human machine interactive systems where one or more participants would constitute as the human component, and a computer-based or a robotic-based system would be the machine component. As shown in Figure 1, the machine can be further divided into two subcomponents: (1) one subcomponent to deliver the output of the machine, typically in terms of visual and possibly audio content; (2) the other subcomponent takes input from the human, which could be directly from the human via a keyboard/mouse or a touch-screen, or indirectly via one or more wearable sensing devices, such as those for heart rate or skin conductance, or one or more remote tracking systems, such as those for eye-tracking or for gesture/body language tracking. Depending on the sophistication level of the human machine system, there may exist a feedback loop where the output of the system is dynamically altered in response to the input to the system. The feedback loop can be pre-programmed into the system, or controlled manually by a trained clinician (typically referred to as the Wizard of Oz scheme [3]). Furthermore, even without a realtime feedback loop, the effectiveness of a program can be evaluated via the data collected by the system objectively via technology, or subjectively from a clinical professional. In some clinical-oriented studies, pre-test and post-test are administered on the social behaviors of participants to assess the effectiveness of the treatment programs using relevant clinically-proven standardized tests.

Based on the model shown in Figure 1, we organize our review with the following questions: (1) What are presented to the participants in the studies and how are the content and delivery methods enabled by technologies? (2) How are the reactions/inputs collected from the participants in response to the stimuli in the studies? (3) Are the experimental procedure and programs presented to participants dynamically adjustable based on the responses from the participants, and if so, how? and (4) How are the programs assessed?

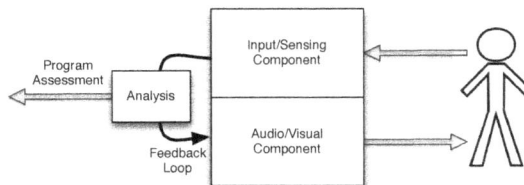

Figure 1. A system model for technology-facilitated systems used for autism research.

Research Contribution

With the rapid development of new technologies, especially information technology and the unprecedented prevalence of autism spectrum disorder among the younger generation, researchers have shown tremendous interest in the field of technology-facilitated diagnosis and treatment of ASD. While it is an emerging field with promising opportunities, it is also one with challenges that are not typically faced by engineers, given that even experts in psychology and medical science are not sure about the causes and best treatment of the many different forms of ASD. Thus timely review of research in this field is crucial for researchers to navigate in this relatively new territory with good understanding of what we have learned from previous research efforts. Compared to previous reviews on similar topics, our review makes unique contribution in several aspects.

First, by utilizing a variety of literature search engines including Web of Science and Google Scholar, it breaks the boundaries among several disciplines that are highly involved in technology-facilitated diagnosis and treatment of ASD (psychology, medical science, education, and engineering) to provide a summary of the collective research efforts by researchers from each discipline.

Second, by focusing on specific technology tools and applications, which serves as the common denominator, it overcomes the barriers caused by the idiosyncratic aspect of different terminology used in each discipline and presents a cross-disciplinary synthesis of the state of art research in the field that researchers can easily relate to regardless of their background. Unlike reviews that focus on specific domains, our review would facilitate more and more efficient sharing and co-construction of knowledge among researchers regarding technology-facilitated diagnosis and treatment of ASD across disciplines.

Third, our review takes into consideration that this is a relatively new and rapidly evolving field and aims at carving out the major areas of scientific exploration, identifying the areas that have been researched heavily as well as areas that demand more attention, evaluating existing evidence supporting the effectiveness of different technologies, and pointing out potentially fruitful directions that researchers can follow in the future.

2. Inclusion of Literature

We aim to provide a semi-systematic review of the studies that employ various technologies in the diagnosis and treatment of individuals with ASD. While it is desirable to have a rigorous systematic review of the topic, where all relevant publications are identified and carefully reviewed, several factors prevented us from doing so: (1) the review of numerous publications takes many months and during this period, new important publications were published and we do not think it is appropriate to ignore these latest publications; (2) there lacks a single search tool that can index all relevant publications and we do not have the manpower to exhaustively search for all databases for relevant publications. Therefore, we decided to rely on the use of Web of Science (all databases) as the main vehicle to find available publications and subjectively identify those that are relevant. We supplemented the search using Google Scholar to find relevant publications that are missing in Web of Science. We decided to focus on literature published since 2012 and only highly cited papers published earlier are included.

We primarily used three search terms, "serious games autism", "virtual reality autism" and "social robots autism". These terms help us obtain publications on autism treatment based on serious games, virtual reality technology, and social robots. The result for each search is manually screened to remove duplicates, misclassified papers (such as a paper on social robots is included in the search result for virtual reality) and out of scope papers (such as those not focused on autism). We selected papers on the diagnosis of individuals with ASD and and those on helping individuals with ASD to improve their social skills and emotion regulation. We intentionally excluded papers that address other aspects of the lives of individuals with ASD, such as helping them to become more literate, to improve their locomotion skills, etc. In addition, we removed papers that do not contain sufficient details on the technology used in their studies. The search results (raw and screened) are summarized in Figure 2. It is interesting to note that the number of publications in each of the three areas are accelerating over the years.

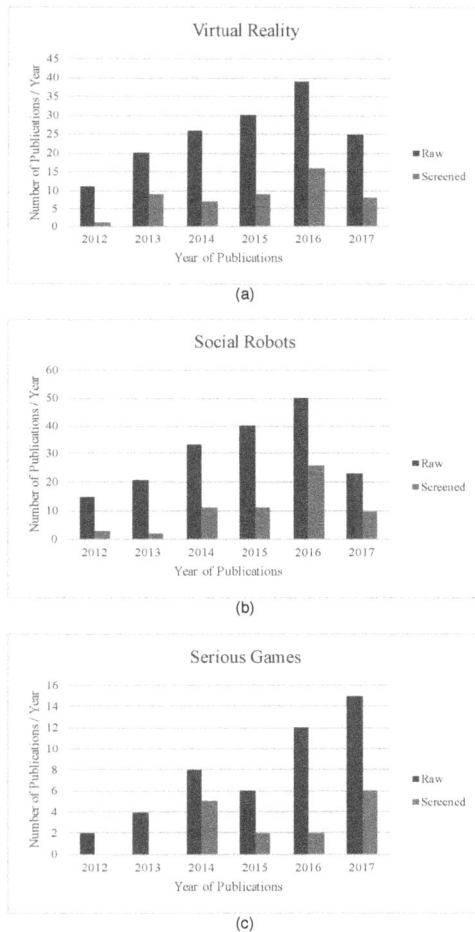

Figure 2. Web of Science search results. (a) The raw and screened number of publications per year using the search term "virtual reality autism"; (b) The raw and screened number of publications per year using the search term "social robots autism"; (c) The raw and screened number of publications per year using the search term "serious games autism".

Based on the publications selected from the filtered Web of Science search results, we further searched Google Scholar to see if the same author(s) have any follow-up studies. If so, these follow-up studies are also included in this review.

The search results include both original research and review articles. We identified ten review papers, two on serious games for children with autism, one on virtual reality based treatment for autism, five for robotic based treatment for autism, and two comprehensive reviews that encompass all technology aspects.

3. Presentation to the Participants

All autism studies use one or more carefully crafted programs to diagnose, treat, or train a participating individual with ASD. The content of such a program is presented to a participant in certain ways, which could be as lightweight as a touch-enabled mobile device, a conventional computer monitor, an immersive virtual reality environment, or via a social robot. Each presentation method has its advantages and shortcomings in terms of cost, convenience, and effectiveness.

The above classification only considers the hardware forms used to deliver the content of a serious game or program to the participants. Except for social robots, the content delivered via all other means of content delivery is virtual in that it is digitally rendered. Even for social robots, some studies used ones that are equipped with a computer monitor for virtual head/face display instead of humanoid physical entity [11]. Furthermore, many studies that employed virtual reality programs used conventional computer monitors/TVs to delivery the content. Hence, the three major categories, i.e., computer and mobile devices, virtual reality systems/devices, and social robots, have certain degree of overlap, as shown in Figure 3.

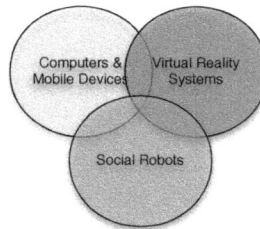

Figure 3. Three major delivery forms of technology-facilitated autism studies.

After introducing the hardware based classification, we further consider user interface design issues in this section, in particular, the primary digital forms used to render the content for the serious games and programs, including images, videos, virtual avatars, non-human objects.

3.1. Computers, Game Consoles and Mobile Devices

Most serious games designed for children with ASD are delivered via conventional computers (such as desktop or laptop computers) or mobile devices [12]. The visual content can be displayed on a laptop screen, a computer monitor, a TV screen, or a touch screen from a mobile device. An advantage of using a mobile device to deliver a game/program to a participant is the convenience [13–17]. A participant could play the game or engage in a program anytime he/she wants and virtually in any posture. Virtually all mobile devices and some newer computers (especially laptop computers) are equipped with touch screens, which enable users to make their choices directly on the screen instead of via a keyboard and mouse [18]. Some of the games designed to run on mobile devices [14] such as iPad, were adapted from traditional assistive tools used for ASD training, such as the cognitive affective training Kit (http://www.cat-kit.com/).

Some serious games involve avatars or a combination of avatars and pictures/videos of real people for various purposes such as the understanding emotions as well as recognition of different emotions via facial expression and body gestures [19]. Another interesting trend in serious games is development of collaborative virtual environment where users can collaborate and communicate during games [15,20,21].

In recent years, motion-based touchless serious games can be played using game consoles (selected from commercial games appropriate for children with ASD) [22–24], or via computer systems [25]. Different from traditional serious games, this type of games engage the full body movements of the participants. In addition to traditional learning targets such as social skills and attention skills, this type of games could enhance motor skills of children with ASD.

On the opposite end is a notion of tangible user interface where a user can directly touch physical objects, such as LEGOs. It is touted that the combination of tangible user interface and the computer-based graphical user interface will lead to more effective education/treatment for children with ASD [26].

Design guidelines for serious games for children with ASD were laid out in [25]. Even though it was introduced in the context of motion-based touchless games, they appear to be applicable for all serious games. In [27], Whyte et al. also provided a set of design principles for serious games. The guidelines include the following key points:

- Strong customizability. The game must be customizable to fit the needs and preferences of each child with autism. Unlike many diseases, autism children may have drastically different strengths and skill deficiencies.
- Increasing levels of complexity of game tasks. As a child acquires more skills, progressively more challenging tasks should be made available. This is the case for virtually all serious games. For example, Chua et al. [14] reported the development of an iPad-based game for children with ASD to learn emotion recognition. At the highest level, there are three worlds. There are six difficulty levels within each world. Each scenario contains one scenario depicted by a video of a human actor. At the end of the video, the headshot of the actor with a facial expression appropriate for the scenario is shown and the participant is asked to identify the emotion expressed by the headshot.
- Clear and easy to understand task goals. For each task, there should be a clear goal that can be easily understand by the participant.
- Multiple means of communicating game instructions, such as text, voice, and visual cues. Some children with low functioning ASD would need visual cues in particular.
- Positive reinforcement with rewards. Game score alone might not be enough to motivate children with ASD. Hence, other forms of rewards such as video or audio effect should be provided to encourage and motivate participants. In [13], a smiley face is shown at the completion of each game regardless of the score. This is referred to as reward-based intervention.
- Repeatability and predictability of game play. Unpredictability may cause anxiety to any children with ASD. The repeatability is needed for participants to learn.
- Smooth transitions. The game must be made easy to repeat and easy to transition to a higher level without noticeable delay so that children with ASD are not discouraged.
- Minimalistic graphics and sound/music. All graphical/sound elements must be included for the game goal because children with ASD maybe subject to sensor overload. Even the use of color may play an important role for improved usability for children with ASD [14].
- Dynamic stimuli. Prolong static scene should be avoided to trigger motor rigidity.

3.2. Virtual Reality Systems/Devices

Three-dimensional immersive virtual reality can be realized via sophisticated immersive virtual reality system with surrounding displays, or head-mounted virtual reality devices. Some studies did use such virtual reality systems/devices [28–36]. However, many studies used conventional computer monitors to display virtual reality scenes with one or more avatars [37–47]. Hence, there is certain degree of overlap between the virtual reality based presentation mode and the conventional computer based presentation mode. We should note that head-mounted display and virtual reality goggles may cause negative experiences such as dizziness and tiredness for some participants, as reported in [48]. Miller et al. provided an excellent review on the impacts of the level of immersion in virtual reality systems on ASD treatment [49].

In [28], a head-mounted display (eMagin Z800 3DVisor from eMagin Corporation at Bellevue, WA, USA) was used to present a virtual classroom containing multiple avatars to a participant. Different from virtual reality scenes provided by a conventional computer monitor, head-mounted display is capable of rendering the scenes in 3-dimension using stereoscopic images [50]. In addition to providing an immersive virtual reality environment, the head-mounted display can be integrated with head position monitor to detect eye gaze in the virtual visual field.

More recently, researchers started to experiment with using consumer-off-the-shelf virtual reality goggles for autism treatment. In [48], the Oculus Rift head-mounted display was used to study the willingness and acceptance of using the device, and the sense of presence and immersion the participants experienced with the device. Oculus Rift was also used in [51] to create immersive 3D scenes.

The term avatar has been used fairly liberally without a universal definition. In [25], Bartoli et al. divided the avatars used in their study into three categories: (1) articulated avatar, where the body parts are represented using lines and simple shapes, which is similar to a stick figure; (2) pointing avatar, where the body can move along a single direction; (3) real avatar, where the avatar is a silhouette of a real person. In other papers, a virtual avatar is typically referred to as a synthetic human character [52]. Carter et al. [52] further divided the avatar into two types: (1) animated avatar, which has an appearance of a 3-dimensional figure, (2) cartoon avatar, which is 2-dimensional like a cartoon character. Yet some literature calls a picture of a human face as an avatar [53]. Note that an avatar does not necessarily have to be human-like. In some programs, animal avatars were used, such as in the virtual pink dolphins project where avatars were dolphins [54–56].

While several different types of avatars, as well as pictures and videos of real persons have been used in many studies, few have compared their impacts to a participant regarding the effectiveness of the social skill learning. Carter et al. reported such a study [52]. In the study, two experiments were conducted. In both experiments, a therapist had a conversation with an individual with ASD. In the first experiment, three presentations of the therapist were used: (1) a realtime video feed of the therapist; (2) an animated avatar that tracks the facial motion of the therapist, and (3) a cartoon avatar that also tracks the facial motion of the therapist limited to 2-dimension. The result shows that there is no apparent variation among participants responses (verbal and nonverbal behaviors) under these three different modes of presentations. The second experiment focused on three different modes of the animated avatar. Exactly because the animated avatar is synthesized based on the therapist's facial expressions and motions, the avatar can be altered to the way the authors' desired. In this experiment, three conditions are tested: (1) direct facial motion tracking without any modification; (2) exaggerated facial motion; (3) dampened facial motion. The result shows that the participants exhibited more positive nonverbal responses for exaggerated facial motion, while there was no difference in verbal responses, which supports the authors' hypothesis that an animated avatar with more exaggerated facial expressions can enhance participant engagement and comprehension.

The virtual avatars used in most studies were produced using 3D animation platforms such as Unity or Vizard. Some studies chose to intentionally use 2D avatars either for comparison or to minimize sensory overload for participants with ASD. Yet some studies chose to use animated photos of real persons as avatars, such as FaceSay [53].

For virtual avatar based serious games and programs, it is essential to produce avatars that can be used to elicit stimuli appropriate for study. Undoubtedly, facial expressions are one of the most important elements in avatar production. In [52], the two-dimensional active appearance models

(AAMs) are used to track a therapist's facial motion. In the first step, AAMs are used to build a set of models based on the appearance and shape of the person's face. The learned models are used to produce an AAM mesh. This mesh is then used to track the facial motion of the person and to retarget to the avatar face.

In [28,37,39–41,57], the Vizard Virtual Reality Toolkit, a commercial product from WorldViz (http://www.worldviz.com/vizard-virtual-reality-software/) was used to produce the avatars in the study. The toolkit contains a PeopleMaker program, which users can use to custom design morphable 3D heads for avatars for different emotion expressions.

In [39], two different experimental paradigms, flashing paradigm and animated paradigm were used. The flashing paradigm involves three scenarios: (1) flashed schematic eyes, where the target event consists of eye balls slightly rotated while the non-target event consists of two eyeballs on the background screen; (2) flashed face with eye position change, where the target event consists of eyes gazing to the face's right and the non-target event consists of a face facing straight front; (3) flashed face with eye and head position change, where the target event consists of the face facing towards the left while the non-target event consists of a face facing direct forward. The animated paradigm involves with two scenarios: (1) animated 3D body with gaze change in one avatar, where the target event consists of the avatar head turning to the right side, and the non-target event consists of the avatar head turning to the left side; (2) animated avatars with gaze change in four avatars, where the scene contains four different avatars and the target event consists of the head of the avatar at the top row turning to the right while the non-target event consists of one of the avatars turning to the right.

In [40], the Vizard Virtual Reality Toolkit is also used. Instead of using the built-in avatars, they chose avatar heads from a database from the Virtual Human Interaction Lab at Stanford University. These avatar heads were converted from 2D photos of teenagers to 3D models using the 3DMeNow software (the company that created the software has ceased to exist). The authors further customized the complexion of the avatar heads using GIMP (GNU Image Manipulation Program), which is a free open source program. The study developed an emotion model that varies the expression from angry (the negative extreme) to happy (the positive extreme). In addition to face expression variations, an avatar can make gestures based on bone-kinematics, and walk around the scene.

In [28], the Vizard Virtual Reality Toolkit is used to develop a virtual 360-degree classroom that is delivered to a participant via a head-mounted display. Due to the 360-degree virtual environment, a participant would have to turn his/her head up to 60 degrees left or right to see all avatars in the scene. Vizard is also used in [44,58] to create virtual reality scenes.

In [59], the Game Studio A6 rendering engine from Conitec, Germany was used to produce the avatars and the corresponding scenes used in their study. In this study, the participants were asked to identify the emotion of the avatar, which could be happy, sad, surprise, anger, disgust, and fear. A participant was allowed to control the virtual distance between the participant and the avatar via joystick so that he/she could position the avatar to the most comfortable distance for emotion identification. For each emotion, there are four levels of emotional intensity (ranging from vague, neutral, to clear and strong) with corresponding facial expression (at 10, 40, 70, and 100%) and body gesture (such as "clasp hands, raise shoulder, shakes head, arms crossed, look down, step back" [59]). Furthermore, the rendering engine also enabled lip-synch animation to increase the fidelity of the verbal interaction.

Another platform used by researchers for virtual avatar-based scene production is the Unity game engine from Unity Technologies. Different from the Vizard Virtual Reality Toolkit and Game Studio A6, other modeling and animation tools are needed for dynamic facial expression design and animation. In [60], the Maya tool from autodesk was used to animate the characters taken from Mixamo (http://www.mixamo.com). In this study, seven universal facial expressions were used, including "joy, surprise, contempt, sadness, fear, disgust, and angle" (page 1644) [60]. For each emotional expression, four emotion intensity levels were animated (low, medium, high, and extreme), which correspond to four different difficulty levels in facial expression recognition where the lower intention level the more difficult to recognize. Unity is also used in [61] for virtual reality production, where both static and animated avatars are used and are capable of making ten different facial motions, including happiness, anger, disgust, fear, sadness, surprise, pain, neutral, and funny face. Unlike other studies, in [61], a game controller (referred to as gamepad in the paper) was used to control the avatars, control the cursors for answering questions, and receive vibration based tactile feedback.

In addition to facial expression, the gait could also reflect the emotion of a person. Hence, some studies have focused using polygonal walking avatars to produce emotional gait stimuli. Similar to facial expressions, gait can also be morphed into different intensity levels. In [62], three levels of intensity are used, ranging from attenuated (50%), prototypical (100%), and exaggerated (150%). The emotion can be expressed via the flexion of the head and arms, as well as the torso positioning [63]. For example, the happy emotion can be expressed by tilting the head backward and leaning back the torso, and the anger emotion can be expressed by tiling the head forward and leaning forward the torso.

In [64], the design of avatar has included the consideration that individuals with ASD tend to suffer from sensory overload, which refers to a phenomenon where an individual with ASD could choose to block all external stimuli when he/she is presented with too many cues concurrently. Hence, the authors of [64] chose to use a 2D cartoon-like avatar with predictable eye blink and head tilt patterns (the avatar links once every 5 s and tilts its head to the side once every 5 s as well).

In some studies, virtual avatars are placed in specific scenes that is consistent with the story told by the avatars. For example, if a story is about an incident in a fast food restaurant, the scene could be McDonald's. In [37,40,41], real 2D pictures of social environments were used for building the scenes. In other works, the scene is often designed using virtual 3D objects, such as [28], where a virtual classroom with multiple avatars is used in the study.

Because typically an avatar would tell a story verbally, the voice becomes an essential component in a virtual reality scene. The voices for avatars were recorded and replayed during a study session [37,41]. In some studies, lip sync, which can be facilitated by the Vizard Virtual Reality Toolkit, is used to make the story telling look more natural [40].

Yet some studies used the Second Life platform to create virtual reality scenes [46,65]. This approach could significantly reduce the development time for virtual reality scenes at the cost of flexibility.

3.3. Social Robots

Many studies have employed humanoid robots for treatment plans for children with ASD [66–79]. However, some research has used non-humanoid robots [11,80–84]. To employ humanoid robots in autism studies, one has to overcome two technical challenges: (1) how to control the movements of the robot, and (2) how to obtain the input from the participant. Unlike virtual avatars, where mature technologies exist to enable high fidelity animation of both facial expressions and body gestures, which are essential to facilitate closed-loop autonomous treatment programs, socially assistive robots used for autism studies so far are scripted in a very limited way (such as raising an arm etc.), presumably due to safety and cost concerns. Furthermore, the use of a social robot is meant to facilitate natural user interaction where the participant would engage in verbal conversations and/or use his/her gestures while doing so. In contrast, a virtual avatar based system can equip the participant with a keyboard and mouse, or a touch screen, which allows the participant to provide his/her input/response to a question by typing, clicking, and touching by hand.

There have been efforts towards an autonomous robotic system. Similar to a virtual reality based system, the eye gaze of the participant with respect to the robot can be detected using eye/head tracking devices, such as a remote desktop eye tracker [85] or a head-mounted eye tracking device [86]. Accurate tracking of eye gaze could enable partial autonomous operation of the treatment program via a social robot. Some studies have also enabled some form of speech recognition functionality. It is limited because for higher recognition accuracy, only scripted simple voice commands can be recognized. There is still a long way to go to support unscripted conversations between a robot and a participant. There is also work on using cameras to track facial expressions [87,88] and gestures made by a participant to understand the emotion of the participant and to allow the participant to give commands to the robots for increased degree of interaction between robots and participants [11].

Despite recent progresses made, such as motion and eye tracking [89–91], in social robotic research, the Wizard of Oz scheme remains the dominant approach to give an illusion that the robot can capture and understand the participant input/response and react/adapt properly while in fact the expression and motion of the robot is controlled, and the user input is captured by a therapist and/or technician.

Many different types of robots have been employed in this line of research, including both humanoid robots and non-humanoid robots. Some robots are stationary in that they do not move around even though they can move their arms, legs and heads in certain ways. Some other robots are mobile in that they can be instructed to move around or even to follow the participant [11]. Most robots are equipped with cameras (for object recognition), microphones (for voice commands or speech recognition), and speakers. Some are equipped with tactile sensors at the head and head to sense touching.

Humanoid robot Nao from Aldebaran Robotics Company is one of the most popular robots used in autism studies [85,92–99]. Nao is a child-sized robot with plastic body (58 cm tall and 4.3 kg weight). It was used in [92] for joint attention and imitation study, in [85] for joint attention study, in [95] for interventions on repetitive behaviors and affective states, in [96] for interventions on verbal communication skills, and in [97,100] for intervention on imitation and interpersonal synchrony of children with ASD. In [95], an additional mobile robot called Rovio from WowWee was used.

Another humanoid robot Zeno R-30 was used in [101] to facilitate imitation training for children with ASD. Zeno R-30 is also a child-like robot produced by Hanson RoboKind. Zeno must be controlled by a separate computer. Zeno R-30 was used for an imitation study where the robot and the participant take turns imitating each other's movement facilitated by a Microsoft Kinect sensor, where the operator's movement was captured and mapped to the robot and similarly the participant's movement was captured for offline analysis.

A newer version of the Zeno robot called Robokind was used in [102,103] to engage children with ASD and emotion recognition training where the participant was asked to identify the emotion expressed by the robot. This robot has a walking body, which is a significant improvement over the Zeno robot. The robot's skin is made of a biomimetic polymer called Frubber, which enables it to make a rich facial expressions. Some research used both Nao and Zeno robots, such as [104].

Lucy is also a humanoid robot used in an autism study [105]. Lucy is about 39 centimeters tall and 6.5 kg in weight. It has a baby-like face and it is capable of talking, recognizing faces and tracking faces. It can make limited types of facial expressions by lighting up some LEDs in the face areas, and limited number of gestures. It is also equipped with motion sensors and touch sensors, and can perform some speech recognition. In [105], Lucy was used to play games (Bingo and quizzes) with children with ASD via a tablet. Lucy was programmed to say encouraging words when the participant provided corrected answers in the quizzes (via a touch panel connected to Lucy instead of speech recognition).

Non-humanoid robots have also been used for autism research. For example, Dehkordi et al. [106] developed a parrot-like robot called RoboParrot for screening autistic children. RoboParrot is placed on a fake wooden base inside a cage mounted with a webcam, with a USB cable coming out of its tail and connecting the embedded hardware with the micro-controller board. The hardware is partially embedded inside the body of RoboParrot and partially embedded in the base. Through this system, input data can be collected via the camera on the cage, and the microphone and various sensors embedded in the robot. Specifically, there are two sensors: an infrared sensor, which is in the chest of RoboParrot and detects if someone tries to touch the chest, and a Hall Effect sensor, which is placed in the beak of RoboParrot and senses the closeness of a person's hand over RoboParrot's head and break.

In [11], a non-traditional robot was designed for autism study. It is equipped with a computer monitor displaying a virtual avatar face and a depth sensor called Asus Xtion PRO for tracking the gesture of the participant and for recognizing the face of the participant. This non-humanoid robot allows the participant to move it around via gestures, and engage in simple pre-scripted conversations via speed recognition and text to speech software. It is important to note that the usability of the robot was not validated via individuals with ASD.

It is interesting to note that social robots are sometimes used in conjunction with conventional computer systems. For example, in [85], two computer monitors are used (one on each side of a robot) in a program designed to improve the joint attention of individuals with ASD where objects were displayed on the monitors when the robot turns it head towards left or right. Furthermore, robotic studies are not just hardware-focused. There was also an effort to develop custom robots with multi-physiological sensing to automatically observe the emotion of a participant [107].

The need for interoperable software architecture for different brands of robots is also getting researchers' attention. In [108], efforts were made to design a platform-agnostic robot control architecture that can be used for various treatment scenarios.

4. Input/Reactions from Participants

In response to stimuli introduced to a participant, various reactions from the participant are collected and often analyzed to different degrees either in realtime or offline. Some of these reactions are directly solicited from the participant where he/she are asked to provide explicitly manual input via a keyboard and mouse, a touch screen, or a specific action such as pointing to a particular object on the screen or touching a designated area in a social robot. Other studies use various sensing technologies, such as computer vision or physiological sensing, to capture more complete reactions produced by the participant, such as eye gaze, physiological characteristics, body language. Yet some studies depend on a trained professional to record reactions of the participant. These common means of getting the input and responses from participants are illustrated in Figure 4.

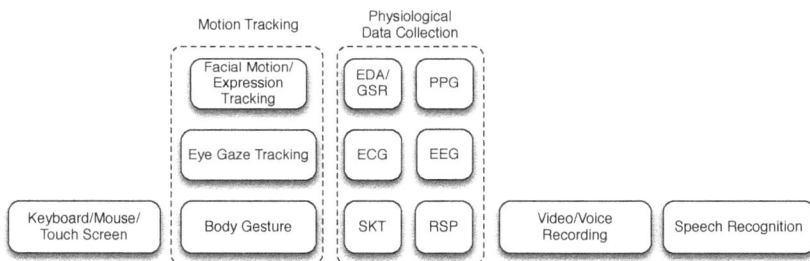

Figure 4. Common means of getting the input and responses from participants.

4.1. Keyboard, Mouse, Touch Screen

To collect direct input from a participant, a conventional approach is to use a menu-driven interface or to display all possible options on the screen where a participant would choose the right answer from several response options using the mouse pointer [40,41,59–61]. It is also common to require a participant to type a key as the answer, for example, "A" for the anger emotion, and "H" for the happy emotion. It is interesting to note that not only the correctness of the selection or input is important, but in some research, the response time, i.e., the time it takes for a participant to make the selection/input since the prompt of the question is also recorded because this delay can be scientifically significant. For example, in [60], the response time was recorded to validate their hypothesis that it takes longer time for a child with ASD to recognize a facial affect than that for a typical developing child.

With the pervasiveness of mobile devices and laptops equipped with touch screen monitors, users could also provide direct input by touching a particular area on the touch screen. This is often the required input method for serious games delivered on devices with touch screens. In [53], participants are required to perform tasks via a touch screen in three different games, including selecting the objects that the avatar is looking at, selecting the right face band aid that would correct the avatar's face, select the correct facial expression, and change the expression of an avatar as suggested.

4.2. Facial Motion/Expression Tracking

There are relatively mature computer vision technology to facilitate facial motion tracking, such as eye gaze, blinks, and mouth motions. For example, two-dimensional active appearance models [109] have been used for facial motion tracking in realtime. In some research [110], head tracking is implemented using a Kinect sensor as an approximation of eye gaze for joint attention study. We have also seen research on using facial expressions recognition to obtain affective feedback [30,111–116]. In some research, head orientation and movement are tracked using inertial sensors embedded in smart glasses instead of cameras [117]. While the tracking itself helps tremendously in producing realistic virtual avatar faces, there is still an open research issue in how to accurately understand the captured motion with respect to nonverbal communicative behaviors of a participant with the exception of eye gaze (and to some extend facial expressions). Hence, the state of the art practice is still to record the video of the participant and then use domain experts to analyze the video regarding the participant's nonverbal communicative behaviors [52,118–120].

4.3. Eye Gaze Tracking

There are two major types of eye tracking technologies. The first one is head-mounted and the other is referred to as desktop based without requiring a participant to wear any device for eye tracking on his/her body. The core technology for eye tracking is identical to head-mounted and desktop eye trackers. An infrared camera is used to detect the rotations of the eyeballs (based on the pupil position and the corneal reflection). The reason why infrared light is used for eye movement tracking is that it renders a better demarcation of the pupil and the iris than visible light. Once the eye movements are determined, the gaze can be computed based on the context.

In [37,41,121], an eye-tracker goggles from Arrington Research Inc. was used to track eye gaze in realtime. The goggles are used in conjunction with a custom designed eye tracking interface platform. The raw eye gaze data were sampled 30 times a second. Then, three features were extracted from the raw data, including the mean pupil diameter, the mean blink rate, and the average fixation duration for each region of interest.

A head-mounted device called WearCam has been used to compute eye gaze offline. This device records the eyes of the participant and the image of the field of view in front of the participant simultaneously [122]. Based on the recorded data, the direction of gaze and focus of attention can be computed. A downside of WearCam is that it requires offline analysis of the recorded video to determine gaze. Hence, this device cannot be used if eye gaze needs to be determined in realtime.

Eye gaze tracking can be made simpler if used in conjunction with head-mounted virtual reality devices, which produces a 360-degree immersive virtual 3D scene. In this case, it is sufficient to track the head movement, which is used in [28]. The head position monitor is integrated with the head-mounted display and it is used to measure the yaw (left/right), pitch (up/down), and tilt movements of the head. From these measurements, the eye gaze direction with respect to the virtual scene can be computed accurately. In [28], the social attention pattern of children with ASD is studied entirely using eye gaze as the sole input from the participants with a head-amounted eye tracker.

Because desktop based eye-trackers are fixated to the monitor, eye tracking alone is not sufficient to accurately determine the gaze direction with respect to the computer monitor. Hence, desktop eye trackers typically integrate with head tracking based on face recognition to compensate for head movement, such as the Eye-Trac 6 desktop eye tracker from Applied Science Laboratories, which is used in [123] in their study.

In [56,60], a similar desktop eye tracking device, called Tobii X120, was used in their study. The device tracks at 120 Hz and allows free head movements within the range of 30 cm by 22 cm by 30 cm (for width, height and depth) and it requires the participant to sit at a distance of 70 cm. The technical specification for Tobii X120 does not state how the head orientation is determined. The authors of [60] designed and implemented an eye tracking application to be used in conjunction with the virtual reality application. The two applications are connected via a high-speed network such that they can determine which and if the participant fixated on one of the regions of interest of the avatar, including forehead, left/right eye, nose, mouth, other face areas, and non-face regions. The same eye tracking device was used in a study with social robots [85]. However, because of the different context where the study wanted to know whether or not the participant was looking at the robot instead of a virtual avatar displayed in a computer monitor, a technician was needed to manually observe the eye gaze and constantly calibrate the system. Automated eye gaze is possible even in this context. However, it would require the participant to wear a head tracker, which was proved to be too uncomfortable for many participants (40% of participants did not want to use it) [124,125].

In [126], another desktop mounted EyeLink 1000 Remote eye tracking system was used in their study. In [127], a remote infrared camera (model D6-HS Remote from Applied Science Laboratories) was used to track the participant's eye gaze.

Zheng et al. reported a system that is capable of automatically detecting head orientation and eye gaze using multiple cameras [128–130]. Based on the detected eye gaze (and engagement level), the system adapts its program content in realtime.

We should note that the trustworthiness of the collected gaze data has rarely been examined carefully with the exception of [131], where the authors studied the raw log files and determined that the quality of recognition is sub-optimal. Future research should pay more attention to the data quality issue, not only for eye gaze data, but all data collected to improve the effectiveness of treatment and to protect the safety of the participants if such data are used in a closed-loop fashion to control the flow of the treatment program.

4.4. Human Motion Tracking via Depth Sensors

Microsoft Kinect and similar depth sensing devices such as Asus Xtion PRO enabled a new way of capturing the gestures as well as facial expressions of the participant [132,133].

In [11], a participant can move the robot to the left or right via the left or right wave gestures. The OpenNI and NITE software packages were used to capture the human motion and to recognize the gestures. In [101], Microsoft Kinect sensor was used to track the participant's movement to determine how closely the participant imitated the pre-scripted and tele-operated movement of the robot. Metrics used include the range of motion of join angles, response delay, and the distance between two time series representing the movement of the robot and that of the participant.

For studies with social robots, depth cameras are often used to track the presence and the activities of the participant for offline analysis regarding the similarity of the imitation and the original actions performed by the robot, as done in [92,101]. In [92], the pose of the participant and the libs were first identified using the depth frames, and subsequently the head region in the corresponding color image frames were cropped. From the cropped face, the pose of the head was determined using a computer vision algorithm. From the head pose data extracted from the logged data during the experiment, the joint attention behaviors of children with ASD and typical developing children are compared. The imitation score was determined by the fraction of postured successfully imitated by the participant.

Enabled by inexpensive depth sensing devices such as Microsoft Kinect, it becomes possible to engage children with ASD with motion-based touchless serious games [22,23,25,134]. Unlike other serious games, a participant engages in the game play by moving his enter body. The participant is being continuously tracked by the depth sensor and an avatar representing the participant becomes part of the game displayed. These types of games not only could be more engaging, but also may enhance the motor skills of the participants too.

Zhang et al. reported their work on using Kinect to track a participant's gesture and assess the quality of the imitation based a set of predefined rules [135]. Feedback is provided in realtime to the participant. Ge et al. [136] used Kinect to track the engagement level of the participant. Yun et al. also used Kinect to track the activity of the participant when he/she is interacting with a social robot [137]. Kinect has also been used to track the movement patterns of the participations [29] and for self-modeling intervention for children with ASD [138].

4.5. Speech Recognition

In some studies, speech recognition is employed to enable a participant to answer questions or engage in a program via predefined voice commands. At this stage, we have yet to see work that has incorporated unscripted conversations.

In [11], a participant can interact with a robot by a number of predefined voice commands, such as move left/right, follow me, stop, and goodbye. The voice commands were captured using the Asus Xtion PRO device, which is equipped with two microphones. The Microsoft Speech Platform Software Development Kit was used to perform speech recognition. In [105], the robot Lucy is said to have speech recognition capability. However, the paper did not provide any technical detail and the use scenarios of the capability in their study.

4.6. Physiological Data Collection

It is well known that physiological characteristics reflect the emotion and attention of a person. Hence, it may be desirable to obtain such information during a session of treatment to gain better insight to the state of an individual with ASD. We have seen more autism research that employs various sensors to collected physiological signals, including Pulse Plethysmogram (PPG), Skin Temperature (ST), Electrodermal Activity (EDA), Electrocardiographic (ECG), and Electroencephalography (EEG) [39,40,51,139,140]. Typically, the classification of such signals was done offline. Hence, the classification accuracy does not impact the flow of the program and cannot cause harm to the participants. Nevertheless, in the long run, obtaining responses through EEG has the potential to develop brain-computer interfaces to improve social skills of individuals with ASD [39]. EEG data were also collected in [141–144]. In [145], Ozcan et al. reported a design for wearable companion toys in which biosensors can be embedded to measure the participant's physiological and emotional state. In [146], physiological data, including PPG, Galvanic Skin Response (GSR), and Respiration (RSP), are collected while a participant with ASD engages in a driving task. Note that in some studies, multimodal data are collected [143]. In addition to physiological data, eye gaze and spoken conversations are also collected [143] to enable adaptive social interaction.

4.7. Video/Voice Recording

Video coding is the standard method for analysis in behavioral research [147,148]. Many autism studies that have been published in clinical journals included video coding, such as [22,38,64,102].

5. Program Customizability and Adaptability

Some programs, especially serious games, may allow users to customize their user interface, including the avatar, if it is used, game scene, as well as difficulty level. In [61], a user is asked to customize the avatar and the virtual environment of his/her choice. The user is also asked to calibrate the tactile feedback of the game controller he/she will be using in the program because the authors anticipated that different users would have different sensitivity preferences. Furthermore, different methods were provided in [61] for a user to indicate the specific emotion they recognized, including a visual non-verbal code where each emotion to be recognized was represented by a particular color/icon (happiness was represented by yellow, angle was represented by red, disgust was represented purple, fear was represented by green, sadness was represented by light blue, surprise was indicated by dark blue, pain was represented by black, neutral was represented by white, and funny face was represented by a trash can), emotional words that told the emotion as it was, and idiomatic expressions, which were short sentences containing a figurative meaning, e.g., an idiomatic expression for fear could be "to get cold feet". In [25], all three motion-based games were designed for customizability. A user could decide on appropriate game speed, object density, and which body parts to enable for game playing.

Different from program customization, it might be desirable for a program to dynamically adjust its flow of control, task difficulty level, or graphic content based on how a user responded to deliver a personalized program for each user [149]. Of course, this does not apply to all programs because some studies were designed to establish patterns of behaviors of individuals with ASD. In these studies, obviously there is no need to adapt the program flow and content based on the input from the participants. Jarrold et al. [28] studied social attention patterns of high functioning children with ASD in a virtual public speaking task based on eye gaze.

Many treatment programs are not adaptive in that the flow of the programs are not changed dynamically based on the input collected while being administered. For mobile games [14], a participant must provide the correct answer to each question before the participant can complete the current level, and only after completing the current level, can the participant continue on to the next level. Such games do not consider how many times a participant has failed a level.

An adaptive program requires the processing of input data from participants in real time. This can be done either automatically using technology and computer algorithms, or by a therapist manually.

5.1. Automatic Adaption of Programs

In [40], the difficulty level is adjusted based on whether or not the participant answered a question correctly via a menu-driven interface. The program has four levels of task difficulty. The difficulty level is reflected from the questions asked for each story. If the answer from the participant is deemed adequate, the next question will be elevated to a higher level unless the current level is already the highest. Mouring and Tang [150] reported an adaptive training for adolescents with ASD using neural network to monitor participant performance and a learning fuzzy inference system to determine deficits to instructional techniques.

Eye tracking is one of the few relatively mature technologies that has been used to retrieve nonverbal communication of a participant in realtime. Some studies used eye gaze information to alter the scene displayed for a participant. In [123], Courgeon et al. studied the joint attention pattern using eye tracking and virtual avatars. The virtual display blurs all the scene except a small rectangular region centered on the point of gaze of the participant. This is done so to provide visual feedback on what the participant is looking at, which enhances self-awareness of gaze.

In [28], the program included a cued condition where an avatar would fade to 70% transparency in six seconds if the participant failed to fixate his/her eyes on the particular avatar when prompted. The entire cued condition is fully automated enabled by the virtual reality program and gaze tracking via a head-mounted display and sensors. The avatar would become opaque again when the participant looked at it again.

An individualized adaptive response module constitutes a core component in the virtual reality system used in [37,41]. The module consists of two adaptive mechanisms, namely, the performance-sensitive system (PS), and the engagement-sensitive system (ES). In PS, the task difficulty is adjusted solely based on the input provided by the participant via the menu-based conversation interface. In ES, the task difficulty is adjusted based on both the input provided by the participant and the engagement level as revealed by the three features obtained from eye gaze tracking data, i.e., the mean pupil diameter, the mean blink rate, and the average fixation duration for each region of interest. For PS, the task difficulty is adjusted based on the performance of the previous task. The performance is determined by the points earned on a task. If the participant earns 70% or more the maximum score possible, then the performance is regarded as adequate. Otherwise, it is regarded as inadequate. If the performance on a task is deemed adequate, then the difficulty level of the next task is elevated to the next higher level. Otherwise, it is switched to a lower difficulty level. For ES, the rule for adjusting difficulty levels is more complicated because it must fuse both the performance from participant direct input (categorized as adequate and inadequate), and the performance from eye gaze analysis, which is categorized into "good enough" and "not good enough".

It is encouraging to see that this line of research is gaining momentum. In addition to eye gaze, we have seen studies that employ various methods to obtain user feedback for adaptive control of a treatment/education program, including facial expression, head orientation, human gesture tracking, and physiological data collection [135,136,141,143,146,151].

5.2. Manual Control

An adaptive program requires realtime analysis of the responses of a participant during a program in one or more aspects and decides on the most appropriate next step autonomously. To a large degree, there is still a gap towards this goal. Hence, a psychologist or a trained clinician is often required to provide their subjectively evaluation based on their observation during the execution of a program. Sometimes, the professional is asked to not only evaluate the response of the participant, but also to control the flow of the program as well, which is true especially for social robotic based studies, where a social robot is controlled manually by the professional based on his/her judgment. This scheme is often referred to as Wizard of Oz scheme [3,152]. The professional evaluation can also be used to assess the effectiveness of the program.

In Carter et al.'s study of interactive avatars [38], the system output was verbal utterances by a human actor that tele-operated the avatar to talk on the screen. The avatar tried to elicit responses (verbal statements and gestures) from the participants and occasionally called on those who raised their hands (and their parents) to engage in one-on-one conversation. In [64], a carton-like avatar was controlled by an actual person. The motivation for doing so is to gain more flexibility during the interactive session because the current state-of-the-art technology is still incapable of handling spontaneous conversations.

In [85], a technician was used to monitor the eye gaze of the participant both for the purpose of calibration of the eye tracking system and for identifying when the participant looked at the robot and the object as directed by the robot. When the participant performed as instructed within 7 s, the technician also triggerred a reward for the participant by pushing a button in the system. Otherwise, a miss event was recorded and the next task was administered.

In Dehkordi et al.'s study [106], the system output consists of simple motions of the robot parrot following the commands of the operator, as well as voice from the speaker uttered by the operator. This involves the use of body motor to control the motions of the wings, the legs, and the neck, and the use of head motor to control the motions of the eyes and the beak. The operator (ideally a therapist) can use the camera on the cage to check the validity of the execution of commands sent to the robot parrot, use the speaker and microphone to verbally communicate with the ASD child, and adjust both the digital commands and verbal output based on what the child says or does.

In [95], the robots were also controlled by a trainer using a laptop running a custom program. The trainer is responsible for deciding when to greet a participant, warming up a game with body stretching activities, playing various games, and deciding when to say goodbye. The same scheme was used in [96].

In motion-based touchless serious games [22,25], a therapist was also tasked to observe the behaviors of participant and to intervene when necessary.

6. Program Evaluation

In addition to program adaptivity, objective evaluation of a program would also need to analyze the input data collected during a study. There are different types of program evaluations.

For a treatment program, the evaluation focuses on its impact on the participants, which typically relies on traditional clinical-proven standard tests, but maybe assessed via technology-based methods as well. For a program aimed to diagnose autism, or a program aimed to establish patterns on social behaviors of individuals with ASD, the purpose of program evaluation is to establish the reliability of the patterns detected or diagnosis [60]. Yet some studies focus on the evaluation of effectiveness of different ways of delivering a treatment plan to individuals with ASD such as [38]. Many pilot studies simply validated a predefined set of hypotheses using their programs [28,38,41,85]. In all studies, the usability of the programs used could also be evaluated [61]. A special case for usability study is testing the acceptability of a new way of delivering content to individuals with ASD, such as [48,153], where a consumer-grade head-mounted virtual reality goggle was experimented.

6.1. Behavioral Pattern Assessment

In [60], the authors studied the patterns of facial emotion recognition and related characteristics for both children with ASD and typical developing children using a virtual avatar based program and eye tracking. They used a number of metrics, including the recognition accuracy of facial emotions, the response time and the confidence level of making the recognition. The authors found that it takes longer for children with ASD to make a recognition with lower confidence level than that of typical developing children. Furthermore, children with ASD have more variation in eye gaze patterns than those of typical developing children. However, the emotion recognition rate is rather similar between the two groups.

6.2. Evaluation of Treatment Effectiveness

In [53], emotion recognition skills of the participants were assessed using six Ekman and Friesen photographs [154] and six drawings of facial expressions, facial recognition skills were evaluated using the Benton Facial Recognition Test [155], social interaction skills in natural environments were rated by the Social Skills Rating System [156] and social skills observation. To validate that a treatment program is effective, these tests are typically administered before and after the treatment sessions and the results are compared.

In a sequence of studies [95–97], Srinivasan et al. presented a systematic evaluation of three different ten-week intervention programs with pretest and posttest using standardized clinical tests. In the first study [95], the repetitive maladaptive behaviors as well as the affective states of participants were coded by clinicians and then compared using statistical analysis. In the second study [96], a standardized test of joint attention was used to determine the verbal communication skills of the participants before and after the ten-week intervention program. In the third study [97], a standardized test of motor performance called BOT-2 was used in the pretest and posttest to access the effectiveness of the intervention program on imitation, interpersonal synchrony, and motor performance of children with ASD. In all these studies, the authors observed that there were no advantages of using social robots compared with rhythm based training.

In [14], a clinician was asked to evaluate the following aspects of the game: (1) how well the game was able to attract the attention of the participant; (2) how well the participant was able to carry out tasks on their own; (3) the degree of effort the participant had made to find the right answer; (4) how well the participant showed signs of anticipation; (5) how well the participant was able to wait patiently to transition from one level to another; and (6) the degree of self-esteem had shown by the participant during the game with respect to the confidence displayed when making successful attempts and despite failures.

In [61], the effectiveness of the treatment program using JeStiMulE was evaluated by comparing the results of the facial emotion recognition accuracy obtained before the four-week long treatment program and after using both the avatars employed in JeStiMulE and the pictures of real-life characters. They observed statistically significant improvement of the treatment plan.

To assess the effectiveness of using motion-based touchless serious games to improve autistic children's learning, two variables, namely selective attention (i.e., how well a participant could focus on an important stimulus in the presence of distractions) and sustained attention (i.e., how well a participant could hold his/her attention to complete a task), were measured and compared using the Bell Test at the beginning, during, and seven days after the end of the treatment [22]. Data for the two variables were extracted from the recorded videos taken during the game plays. The researchers noticed an increase of the two variables for all children. In a follow-up study [25], assessment was made at the beginning and the end of treatment period. In addition to select attention and sustained attention, three additional variables were used, including visual perception (i.e., how well a participant could process visual information), motor coordination (i.e., how well a participant could move body parts coherently), and visuo-motor integration (i.e., how well a participant could control his/her body movement when prompted visually).

In some studies, both parameters collected while a participant was playing a serious game (or a sequence of games) and standardized tests were used to assess the effectiveness of a treatment plan. The data were collected at the beginning and at the end of the six-month treatment plan. In [13], the game-associated parameters used for assessment include the game identifier and level of difficulty, when the game was played, the game score, and the reaction time for a participant to complete a task. The clinical measures include the Autism Diagnosis Observation Schedule, the Vineland Adaptive Behavior Scale II, Weschsler scales, the Child Behavior Checklist, and the Social Communication Questionnaire, and the Parenting Stress Index. The researchers found that computer-based serious games benefited children with ASD. In particular, they found that 4 out of 6 imitation games significantly improved the participants' imitation scores, and 3 out of 4 joint attention games shortened the time it took for participants to complete the task over multiple sessions.

In [19], the Social Responsiveness Scale, 2nd Edition (SRS-2) standardized test was used in pretest and posttest to determine the effectiveness of a serious game called emotiplay.

6.3. Usability Assessment

In [61], the usability of the program called JeStiMulE was evaluated in terms of its adaptability, effectiveness and efficiency with a group of individuals with ASD. For adaptability, the authors observed that all participants managed to use the gamepad to control the avatar, 91% of participants understood the association between facial emotion and the corresponding non-verbal code, and different participants chose their own favorite ways of indicating the facial emotion that they have identified. The effectiveness is determined by the percentage of participants who managed to complete different modules in JeStiMulE. 73% of participants were able to complete all modules. The efficiency is determined by how long the participants were able to complete each module among those who have completed all modules. On average, it takes 49 minutes for a participant to complete each module.

In [48], the acceptability and immersiveness of the consumer-grade head-mounted goggle, Oculus Rift, among individuals with ASD were examined via a two-phase study. The acceptability of the device is determined by the fraction of participants who managed to complete the study. Out of 29 participants, 25 completed the phase I study. 23 participants proceeded on to complete the second phase of the study. For the immsersiveness of the device, the authors chose to use the Independent Television Commission-Sense of Presence Inventory (ITC-SoPI) to evaluate the subjective experiences by participants who have completed the study. ITC-SoPI evaluates user experiences in the following four categories: (1) spatial presence, which is about how a participant feels he/she is really present in the physical environment; (2) user engagement, which is about how involved a participant is in a virtual reality program and how intense it is; (3) ecological validity, which is about how natural a participant feels about the experience; and (4) negative effects, which are about whether or not a participant feels any dizziness, headache, etc. This study also briefly analyzed participant behavior while using the device by first video taping the sessions and then analyzing the recorded video qualitatively manually.

7. Discussion

As we have seen in the reviewed literature, there are two primary means of eliciting proper reactions from individuals with ASD, one using virtual reality technologies, and the other using social robotic technologies. The former typically relies on one or more avatars to serve as an agent to communicate with a participant, while the latter uses a robot. Virtual reality has two advantages over robotics: (1) both the avatar and the virtual scenes can be changed dynamically that fit the treatment scenarios, while a robot cannot easily change its appearance and the treatment environments cannot be changed easily; (2) the virtual reality based systems can be much cheaper than robots. Hence, unless the cost of robots is reduced drastically, virtually reality based systems could be more attractive to home-based uses.

That said, robotic based solutions provide physical embodiment, which is not possible for virtual reality based systems. This advantage may lead to better generalization of skills learned in treatment sessions to the real-world scenarios, although this speculation has yet to be proven in clinical trials.

For virtual reality based systems, even though it is desirable to render 3D views to a participant, which could potentially increase the treatment effectiveness and transferability to real-world skills, the use of head-mounted displays or virtual reality goggles might not be suitable for all individuals with ASD because some are more prone to cyber sickness. This concern is also applicable for wearable devices that take physiological data from a participant.

Another observation is that the current autism studies have predominately focused on treatment programs that target a specific set of social skills. Although temporary improvements in social skills for individuals with ASD have been observed, it is doubtful such improvements can last and can be generalized. More importantly, such training programs do not address the psychological and emotion issues for individuals (especial for children and adolescents) with ASD. What is urgently needed for an individual with ASD is a life coach who he/she trusts, who shares the same interest with him/her with, who knows his/her emotions, and who is never upset no matter how badly he/she behaves. A recently granted patent describes a system that partially fulfill this goal [157]. This system provides an avatar-based mobile interface for an autism child to bound with the avatar character and to learn various lessons on social and emotional regulation skills. The system relies on the use of one or more therapist or parent to interact with an autism child. Essentially, the system presents an illusion that the child with ASD is interacting with an intelligent avatar who he/she feels comfortable interacting with while in reality he/she is communicating with an actual human being who he/she otherwise would be reluctant to communicate with. To help the participating parent or therapist, the system also provides carefully crafted prompts to guide him/her on how to properly interact with the child with ASD. We are currently also working on a system that aims to serve as a virtual life coach for children with ASD [158].

Several publications have reported so called closed-loop autonomous systems based on social robots or virtual avatars [135]. Unfortunately, such systems have achieved autonomy only for very specific scenarios. For example, in [135], the system is capable of assessing a very small set of imitation gestures made by a participant in realtime using predefined rules. This is far from the degree of autonomy needed to train children with ASD towards improved practical social skills. In [159], an ambitious design towards a virtual avatar that can autonomously respond to the participant's emotional reactions and action tendencies was presented. Unfortunately, the authors conceded that it is exceedingly difficult to model the participant accurately based on the limited information collected, including the frequency of touch (on the screen) and eye tracking. In the end, they supplemented their system with a Wizard of Oz control panel for a therapist to intervene when needed.

A much more viable approach is proposed by Esteban et al. where the design goal should be a supervised autonomous system [160]. According to this design, autonomy can be achieved for specific tasks, such as to determine where a social robot (or a virtual avatar) looks at next. With supervised autonomy, a therapist is needed to provide high level guidance and if necessary, to override the decision made autonomously. To accomplish this goal, the system would need to track several primary and secondary variables. The primary variables include the performance of the participant who performs the designated tasks. The secondary variables include: (1) the level of social engagement reflected by eye-contact and verbal utterances; (2) the emotional level (positive or negative); (3) the behavioral level (stereotypical, adaptive, and maladaptive); (4) the cognitive level (rational or irrational). In addition to tracking the participant, the system proposed by Esteban et al. also tracks the behavior of the social robot for maximum safety of the participant [160]. In this system, three regular cameras and three Kinect sensors are used (one of the Kinect sensor is used to self-monitor the social robot).

With the supervised autonomous system design, we believe machine learning and artificial intelligence [161–165], in conjunction with multimodal sensing, will play much more important roles in the next generation autism diagnosis and treatment programs. Considering that good therapists are always in very high demand for the autism population, we envisage that a therapist could operate multiple supervised autonomous systems remotely at different sites, which could benefits more children with ASD while reducing the cost of autism care.

8. Conclusions

In this article, we reviewed the autism research facilitated by various technologies from an engineering perspective. We primarily focused on research results produced in the last five years (2012–2017). As can be seen, while significant progress has been made, there are major challenges to overcome in future research. First, other than manual input via keyboard/mouse/touch-screen, the only mature technology for automatically capturing participant responses is eye gaze. To assess how well a participant responded to an intervention program, current research predominately relied on video tapping and offline analysis of the recorded videos. Even though there have been efforts to use various motion/facial tracking and physiological tracking devices to capture the emotional state of the participant, such efforts are still in preliminary stages. Second, few autism treatment programs are customizable and automatically adaptive. This is obviously a limitation for autism studies because individuals with ASD are known to be highly different in their deficiencies, skill levels and preferences. To overcome this limitation, some studies relied on the use of therapists to operate the virtual avatar or social robot in realtime. However, this approach is not only not conducive for reducing the cost of autism treatment using technology, but also has negative impact on the repeatability of experiments. Furthermore, the quality of the program control also heavily depends on the training and expertise of the therapist. Hence, the solution is not scalable. The resolving of the first issue will open the door for designing and implementing fully autonomous virtual avatars and social robots that help individuals with ASD.

Finally, we provide our observation on how technological limitations might be affecting ASD therapies. First, there lacks a highly reliable and accurate sensing platform that can capture and recognize the affective state of the participant. As pointed in [160], this is the prerequisite to achieving autonomous control of a therapy program that is personalized for each individual and is capable of dynamically adapting the program content based on the affective state of the individual. Many current studies failed to consider the affective state of the participants completely. Even for those that do, the technologies employed are ad-hoc, are often without establishing the ground-truth, and are not processed in realtime.

Second, the therapy program content is typically designed one-size-for-all. It is well known that children with ASD typically have intense interests in certain topics. The therapy programs could be much more effective to an individual if the program content aligns well with the individual's intense interests. Getting to know which participant to have what intense interests would go beyond technology. Ideally, for each child with ASD, an individualized educational placement (IEP) team would be needed to provide intimate knowledge about the child so that the content of the therapy program can be customized for the individual [158].

Third, there lack longitudinal studies on the long-term effectiveness of technology-based therapies. While it is accepted that children with ASD are generally more receptive to technology, for example, they show less anxiety when interacting with virtual avatars or social robots, it is unclear such technologies can truly help children with ASD to gain social skills and emotional regulation skills in practice in the long-run when they have to directly interact with real human beings day-in and day-out.

Acknowledgments: This article was supported in part by the Cleveland State University Graduate Faculty Research Support Program, and by the Cleveland State University Faculty Research and Development—Internet of Things Program. The authors did not receive any fund for covering the costs to publish in open access.

Author Contributions: Xiongyi Liu and Wenbing Zhao conceived and designed the review protocol, Xiongyi Liu, Qing Wu, Wenbing Zhao, and Xiong Luo performed literature search and reviewed the papers collected, and Xiongyi Liu, Qing Wu, Wenbing Zhao and Xiong Luo wrote the paper.

Conflicts of Interest: The authors declare no conflict of interest. The founding sponsors had no role in the design of the study; in the collection, analyses, or interpretation of data; in the writing of the manuscript, and in the decision to publish the results.

Abbreviations

The following abbreviations are used in this manuscript:

ASD	Autism Spectrum Disorder
DOF	Degrees of Freedom
ECG	Electrocardiographic
EDA	Electrodermal Activity
EEG	Electroencephalography
ES	Engagement-Sensitive System
GSR	Galvanic skin response
ITC-SoPI	Independent Television Commission-Sense of Presence Inventory
PPG	Pulse Plethysmogram
RSP	Respiration
SKT	Skin Temperature
PS	Performance-Sensitive System

References

1. Wieckowski, A.T.; White, S.W. Application of technology to social communication impairment in childhood and adolescence. *Neurosci. Biobehav. Rev.* **2017**, doi:10.1016/j.neubiorev.2016.12.030.
2. Aresti-Bartolome, N.; Garcia-Zapirain, B. Technologies as support tools for persons with autistic spectrum disorder: A systematic review. *Int. J. Environ. Res. Public Health* **2014**, *11*, 7767–7802.
3. Scassellati, B.; Admoni, H.; Matarić, M. Robots for use in autism research. *Ann. Rev. Biomed. Eng.* **2012**, *14*, 275–294.
4. Diehl, J.J.; Schmitt, L.M.; Villano, M.; Crowell, C.R. The clinical use of robots for individuals with autism spectrum disorders: A critical review. *Res. Autism Spectr. Disord.* **2012**, *6*, 249–262.
5. Cabibihan, J.J.; Javed, H.; Ang, M.; Aljunied, S.M. Why robots? A survey on the roles and benefits of social robots in the therapy of children with autism. *Int. J. Soc. Robot.* **2013**, *5*, 593–618.
6. Pennisi, P.; Tonacci, A.; Tartarisco, G.; Billeci, L.; Ruta, L.; Gangemi, S.; Pioggia, G. Autism and social robotics: A systematic review. *Autism Res.* **2015**, *9*, 165–183.
7. Begum, M.; Serna, R.W.; Yanco, H.A. Are robots ready to deliver autism interventions? a comprehensive review. *Int. J. Soc. Robot.* **2016**, *8*, 157–181.
8. Parsons, S. Authenticity in Virtual Reality for assessment and intervention in autism: A conceptual review. *Educ. Res. Rev.* **2016**, *19*, 138–157.
9. Zakari, H.M.; Ma, M.; Simmons, D. A review of serious games for children with autism spectrum disorders (ASD). In Proceedings of the International Conference on Serious Games Development and Applications, Berlin, Germany, 9–10 October 2014; Springer: Cham, Switzerland, 2014; pp. 93–106.
10. Grossard, C.; Grynspan, O.; Serret, S.; Jouen, A.L.; Bailly, K.; Cohen, D. Serious games to teach social interactions and emotions to individuals with autism spectrum disorders (ASD). *Comput. Educ.* **2017**, *113*, 195–211.

11. Chuah, M.C.; Coombe, D.; Garman, C.; Guerrero, C.; Spletzer, J. Lehigh instrument for learning interaction (lili): An interactive robot to aid development of social skills for autistic children. In Proceedings of the IEEE 11th International Conference on Mobile Ad Hoc and Sensor Systems, Philadelphia, PA, USA, 28–30 October 2014; pp. 731–736.

12. Marwecki, S.; Rädle, R.; Reiterer, H. Encouraging Collaboration in Hybrid Therapy Games for Autistic Children. In *CHI '13 Extended Abstracts on Human Factors in Computing Systems*; ACM: New York, NY, USA, 2013; pp. 469–474.

13. Jouen, A.L.; Narzisi, A.; Xavier, J.; Tilmont, E.; Bodeau, N.; Bono, V.; Ketem-Premel, N.; Anzalone, S.; Maharatna, K.; Chetouani, M.; et al. GOLIAH (Gaming Open Library for Intervention in Autism at Home): A 6-month single blind matched controlled exploratory study. *Child Adolesc. Psychiatry Ment. Health* **2017**, *11*, 17.

14. Chua, L.; Goh, J.; Nay, Z.T.; Huang, L.; Cai, Y.; Seah, R. ICT-Enabled Emotional Learning for Special Needs Education. In *Simulation and Serious Games for Education*; Springer: Cham, Switzerland, 2017; pp. 29–45.

15. Zhang, L.; Gabriel-King, M.; Armento, Z.; Baer, M.; Fu, Q.; Zhao, H.; Swanson, A.; Sarkar, M.; Warren, Z.; Sarkar, N. Design of a Mobile Collaborative Virtual Environment for Autism Intervention. In Proceedings of the International Conference on Universal Access in Human-Computer Interaction, Toronto, ON, Canada, 17–21 July 2016; Springer: Cham, Switzerland, 2016; pp. 265–275.

16. Vullamparthi, A.J.; Nelaturu, S.C.B.; Mallaya, D.D.; Chandrasekhar, S. Assistive learning for children with autism using augmented reality. In Proceedings of the 2013 IEEE Fifth International Conference on Technology for Education (T4E), Kharagpur, India, 18–20 December 2013; pp. 43–46.

17. Simões, M.; Mouga, S.; Pedrosa, F.; Carvalho, P.; Oliveira, G.; Branco, M.C. Neurohab: a platform for virtual training of daily living skills in autism spectrum disorder. *Procedia Technol.* **2014**, *16*, 1417–1423.

18. Aresti-Bartolome, N.; Garcia-Zapirain, B. Cognitive rehabilitation system for children with autism spectrum disorder using serious games: A pilot study. *Bio-Med. Mater. Eng.* **2015**, *26*, S811–S824.

19. Fridenson-Hayo, S.; Berggren, S.; Lassalle, A.; Tal, S.; Pigat, D.; Meir-Goren, N.; O'Reilly, H.; Ben-Zur, S.; Bölte, S.; Baron-Cohen, S. Emotiplay: A serious game for learning about emotions in children with autism: Results of a cross-cultural evaluation. *Eur. Child Adolesc. Psychiatry* **2017**, *26*, 979–992.

20. Zhao, H.; Swanson, A.; Weitlauf, A.; Warren, Z.; Sarkar, N. A Novel Collaborative Virtual Reality Game for Children with ASD to Foster Social Interaction. In Proceedings of the International Conference on Universal Access in Human-Computer Interaction, Toronto, ON, Canada, 17–21 July 2016; Springer: Cham, Switzerland, 2016; pp. 276–288.

21. Bono, V.; Narzisi, A.; Jouen, A.L.; Tilmont, E.; Hommel, S.; Jamal, W.; Xavier, J.; Billeci, L.; Maharatna, K.; Wald, M.; et al. GOLIAH: A gaming platform for home-based intervention in autism–principles and design. *Front. Psychiatry* **2016**, *7*, 70.

22. Bartoli, L.; Corradi, C.; Garzotto, F.; Valoriani, M. Exploring motion-based touchless games for autistic children's learning. In Proceedings of the 12th International Conference on Interaction Design and Children, New York, NY, USA, 24–27 June 2013; pp. 102–111.

23. Garzotto, F.; Gelsomini, M.; Oliveto, L.; Valoriani, M. Motion-based touchless interaction for ASD children: A case study. In Proceedings of the 2014 International Working Conference on Advanced Visual Interfaces, Como, Italy, 27–29 May 2014; pp. 117–120.

24. Ge, Z.; Fan, L. Social Development for Children with Autism Using Kinect Gesture Games: A Case Study in Suzhou Industrial Park Renai School. In *Simulation and Serious Games for Education*; Springer: Cham, Switzerland, 2017; pp. 113–123.

25. Bartoli, L.; Garzotto, F.; Gelsomini, M.; Oliveto, L.; Valoriani, M. Designing and Evaluating Touchless Playful Interaction for ASD Children. In Proceedings of the 2014 Conference on Interaction Design and Children, Aarhus, Denmark, 17–20 June 2014; ACM: New York, NY, USA, 2014; pp. 17–26.

26. Barajas, A.O.; Al Osman, H.; Shirmohammadi, S. A Serious Game for children with Autism Spectrum Disorder as a tool for play therapy. In Proceedings of the 2017 IEEE 5th International Conference on Serious Games and Applications for Health (SeGAH), Perth, WA, Australia, 2–4 April 2017; pp. 1–7.

27. Whyte, E.M.; Smyth, J.M.; Scherf, K.S. Designing serious game interventions for individuals with autism. *J. Autism Dev. Disord.* **2015**, *45*, 3820–3831.

28. Jarrold, W.; Mundy, P.; Gwaltney, M.; Bailenson, J.; Hatt, N.; McIntyre, N.; Kim, K.; Solomon, M.; Novotny, S.; Swain, L. Social attention in a virtual public speaking task in higher functioning children with autism. *Autism Res.* **2013**, *6*, 393–410.

29. Ip, H.H.; Lai, C.H.Y.; Wong, S.W.; Tsui, J.K.; Li, R.C.; Lau, K.S.Y.; Chan, D.F. Visuospatial attention in children with Autism Spectrum Disorder: A comparison between 2-D and 3-D environments. *Cogent Educ.* **2017**, *4*, 1307709.

30. Lorenzo, G.; Lledó, A.; Pomares, J.; Roig, R. Design and application of an immersive virtual reality system to enhance emotional skills for children with autism spectrum disorders. *Comput. Educ.* **2016**, *98*, 192–205.

31. Bozgeyikli, L.; Bozgeyikli, E.; Raij, A.; Alqasemi, R.; Katkoori, S.; Dubey, R. Vocational training with immersive virtual reality for individuals with autism: Towards better design practices. In Proceedings of the 2016 IEEE 2nd Workshop on Everyday Virtual Reality (WEVR), Greenville, SC, USA, 20 March 2016; pp. 21–25.

32. Bozgeyikli, E.; Raij, A.; Katkoori, S.; Dubey, R. Locomotion in Virtual Reality for Individuals with Autism Spectrum Disorder. In Proceedings of the 2016 Symposium on Spatial User Interaction, Tokyo, Japan, 15–16 October 2016; pp. 33–42.

33. Ip, H.H.; Wong, S.W.; Chan, D.F.; Byrne, J.; Li, C.; Yuan, V.S.; Lau, K.S.; Wong, J.Y. Virtual reality enabled training for social adaptation in inclusive education settings for school-aged children with autism spectrum disorder (ASD). In Proceedings of the International Conference on Blending Learning, Beijing, China, 19–21 July 2016; Springer: Cham, Switzerland, 2016; pp. 94–102.

34. Cheng, Y.; Huang, C.L.; Yang, C.S. Using a 3D immersive virtual environment system to enhance social understanding and social skills for children with autism spectrum disorders. *Focus Autism Other Dev. Disabil.* **2015**, *30*, 222–236.

35. Maskey, M.; Lowry, J.; Rodgers, J.; McConachie, H.; Parr, J.R. Reducing specific phobia/fear in young people with autism spectrum disorders (ASDs) through a virtual reality environment intervention. *PLoS ONE* **2014**, *9*, e100374.

36. Bozgeyikli, L.; Bozgeyikli, E.; Clevenger, M.; Gong, S.; Raij, A.; Alqasemi, R.; Sundarrao, S.; Dubey, R. VR4VR: Towards vocational rehabilitation of individuals with disabilities in immersive virtual reality environments. In Proceedings of the 2014 2nd Workshop on Virtual and Augmented Assistive Technology (VAAT), Minneapolis, MN, USA, 30 March 2014; pp. 29–34.

37. Lahiri, U.; Bekele, E.; Dohrmann, E.; Warren, Z.; Sarkar, N. Design of a virtual reality based adaptive response technology for children with autism. *IEEE Trans. Neural Syst. Rehabil. Eng.* **2013**, *21*, 55–64.

38. Carter, E.J.; Williams, D.L.; Hodgins, J.K.; Lehman, J.F. Are children with autism more responsive to animated characters? A study of interactions with humans and human-controlled avatars. *J. Autism Dev. Disord.* **2014**, *44*, 2475–2485.

39. Amaral, C.P.; Simões, M.A.; Castelo-Branco, M.S. Neural Signals Evoked by Stimuli of Increasing Social Scene Complexity Are Detectable at the Single-Trial Level and Right Lateralized. *PLoS ONE* **2015**, *10*, e0121970.

40. Kuriakose, S.; Lahiri, U. Understanding the psycho-physiological implications of interaction with a virtual reality-based system in adolescents with autism: a feasibility study. *IEEE Trans. Neural Syst. Rehabil. Eng.* **2015**, *23*, 665–675.

41. Lahiri, U.; Bekele, E.; Dohrmann, E.; Warren, Z.; Sarkar, N. A physiologically informed virtual reality based social communication system for individuals with autism. *J. Autism Dev. Disord.* **2015**, *45*, 919–931.

42. Yang, Y.D.; Allen, T.; Abdullahi, S.M.; Pelphrey, K.A.; Volkmar, F.R.; Chapman, S.B. Brain responses to biological motion predict treatment outcome in young adults with autism receiving Virtual Reality Social Cognition Training: Preliminary findings. *Behav. Res. Ther.* **2017**, *93*, 55–66.

43. Wallace, S.; Parsons, S.; Bailey, A. Self-reported sense of presence and responses to social stimuli by adolescents with ASD in a collaborative virtual reality environment. *J. Intellect. Dev. Disabil.* **2017**, *42*, 131–141.

44. Forbes, P.A.; Pan, X.; Hamilton, A.F. Reduced mimicry to virtual reality avatars in Autism Spectrum Disorder. *J. Autism Dev. Disord.* **2016**, *46*, 3788–3797.

45. Didehbani, N.; Allen, T.; Kandalaft, M.; Krawczyk, D.; Chapman, S. Virtual reality social cognition training for children with high functioning autism. *Comput. Hum. Behav.* **2016**, *62*, 703–711.

46. Ke, F.; Im, T. Virtual-reality-based social interaction training for children with high-functioning autism. *J. Educ. Res.* **2013**, *106*, 441–461.

47. Wang, M.; Reid, D. Using the virtual reality-cognitive rehabilitation approach to improve contextual processing in children with autism. *Sci. World J.* **2013**, *2013*, 716890.
48. Newbutt, N.; Sung, C.; Kuo, H.J.; Leahy, M.J.; Lin, C.C.; Tong, B. Brief report: A pilot study of the use of a virtual reality headset in autism populations. *J. Autism Dev. Disord.* **2016**, *46*, 3166–3176.
49. Miller, H.L.; Bugnariu, N.L. Level of immersion in virtual environments impacts the ability to assess and teach social skills in autism spectrum disorder. *Cyberpsychol. Behav. Soc. Netw.* **2016**, *19*, 246–256.
50. Wang, X.; Desalvo, N.; Gao, Z.; Zhao, X.; Lerman, D.C.; Gnawali, O.; Shi, W. Eye Contact Conditioning in Autistic Children Using Virtual Reality Technology. In Proceedings of the International Symposium on Pervasive Computing Paradigms for Mental Health, Tokyo, Japan, 8–9 May 2014; Springer: Cham, Switzerland, 2014; pp. 79–89.
51. Li, Y.; Elmaghraby, A.S.; El-Baz, A.; Sokhadze, E.M. Using physiological signal analysis to design affective VR games. In Proceedings of the 2015 IEEE International Symposium on Signal Processing and Information Technology (ISSPIT), Abu Dhabi, UAE, 7–10 December 2015; pp. 57–62.
52. Carter, E.J.; Hyde, J.; Williams, D.L.; Hodgins, J.K. Investigating the influence of avatar facial characteristics on the social behaviors of children with autism. In Proceedings of the 2016 CHI Conference on Human Factors in Computing Systems, San Jose, CA, USA, 7–12 May 2016; pp. 140–151.
53. Hopkins, I.M.; Gower, M.W.; Perez, T.A.; Smith, D.S.; Amthor, F.R.; Casey Wimsatt, F.; Biasini, F.J. Avatar assistant: improving social skills in students with an ASD through a computer-based intervention. *J. Autism Dev. Disord.* **2011**, *41*, 1543–1555.
54. Cai, Y.; Chiew, R.; Fan, L.; Kwek, M.K.; Goei, S.L. The Virtual Pink Dolphins Project: An International Effort for Children with ASD in Special Needs Education. In *Simulation and Serious Games for Education*; Springer: Cham, Switzerland, 2017; pp. 1–11.
55. Cai, Y.; Chia, N.K.; Thalmann, D.; Kee, N.K.; Zheng, J.; Thalmann, N.M. Design and development of a virtual dolphinarium for children with autism. *IEEE Trans. Neural Syst. Rehabil. Eng.* **2013**, *21*, 208–217.
56. Feng, Y.; Cai, Y. A Gaze Tracking System for Children with Autism Spectrum Disorders. In *Simulation and Serious Games for Education*; Springer: Cham, Switzerland, 2017; pp. 137–145.
57. Kuriakose, S.; Lahiri, U. Design of a Physiology-Sensitive VR-Based Social Communication Platform for Children With Autism. *IEEE Trans. Neural Syst. Rehabil. Eng.* **2017**, *25*, 1180–1191.
58. Halabi, O.; El-Seoud, S.A.; Alja'am, J.M.; Alpona, H.; Al-Hemadi, M.; Al-Hassan, D. Design of Immersive Virtual Reality System to Improve Communication Skills in Individuals with Autism. *Int. J. Emerg. Technol. Learn.* **2017**, *12*, doi:10.3991/ijim.v11i2.6555.
59. Kim, K.; Rosenthal, M.Z.; Gwaltney, M.; Jarrold, W.; Hatt, N.; McIntyre, N.; Swain, L.; Solomon, M.; Mundy, P. A virtual joy-stick study of emotional responses and social motivation in children with autism spectrum disorder. *J. Autism Dev. Disord.* **2015**, *45*, 3891–3899.
60. Bekele, E.; Crittendon, J.; Zheng, Z.; Swanson, A.; Weitlauf, A.; Warren, Z.; Sarkar, N. Assessing the utility of a virtual environment for enhancing facial affect recognition in adolescents with autism. *J. Autism Dev. Disord.* **2014**, *44*, 1641–1650.
61. Serret, S.; Hun, S.; Iakimova, G.; Lozada, J.; Anastassova, M.; Santos, A.; Vesperini, S.; Askenazy, F. Facing the challenge of teaching emotions to individuals with low-and high-functioning autism using a new Serious game: a pilot study. *Mol. Autism* **2014**, *5*, 37.
62. Blain, S.D.; Peterman, J.S.; Park, S. Subtle cues missed: Impaired perception of emotion from gait in relation to schizotypy and autism spectrum traits. *Schizophr. Res.* **2017**, *183*, 157–160.
63. Roether, C.L.; Omlor, L.; Christensen, A.; Giese, M.A. Critical features for the perception of emotion from gait. *J. Vis.* **2009**, *9*, 15.
64. Hsu, C.W.; Teoh, Y.S. Investigating Event Memory in Children with Autism Spectrum Disorder: Effects of a Computer-Mediated Interview. *J. Autism Dev. Disord.* **2017**, *47*, 359–372.
65. Kandalaft, M.R.; Didehbani, N.; Krawczyk, D.C.; Allen, T.T.; Chapman, S.B. Virtual reality social cognition training for young adults with high-functioning autism. *J. Autism Dev. Disord.* **2013**, *43*, 34–44.
66. Li, C.; Jia, Q.; Feng, Y. Human-Robot Interactoin Design for Robot-Assisted Intervention for Children with Autism Based on ES Theory. In Proceedings of the 2016 8th International Conference on Intelligent Human-Machine Systems and Cybernetics (IHMSC), Hangzhou, China, 27–28 August 2016; Volume 2, pp 320–324.

67. Good, J.; Good, J.; Parsons, S.; Parsons, S.; Yuill, N.; Yuill, N.; Brosnan, M.; Brosnan, M. Virtual reality and robots for autism: moving beyond the screen. *J. Assist. Technol.* **2016**, *10*, 211–216.

68. De Haas, M.; Aroyo, A.M.; Barakova, E.; Haselager, W.; Smeekens, I. The effect of a semi-autonomous robot on children. In Proceedings of the 2016 IEEE 8th International Conference on Intelligent Systems (IS), Sofia, Bulgaria, 4–6 September 2016; pp. 376–381.

69. Bernardo, B.; Alves-Oliveira, P.; Santos, M.G.; Melo, F.S.; Paiva, A. An Interactive Tangram Game for Children with Autism. In Proceedings of the International Conference on Intelligent Virtual Agents, Los Angeles, CA, USA, 20–23 September 2016; Springer: Cham, Switzerland, 2016; pp. 500–504.

70. Hong, T.S.; Mohamaddan, S.; Shazali, S.T.S.; Mohtadzar, N.A.A.; Bakar, R.A. A review on assistive tools for autistic patients. In Proceedings of the 2016 IEEE EMBS Conference on Biomedical Engineering and Sciences (IECBES), Kuala Lumpur, Malaysia, 4–8 December 2016; pp. 51–56.

71. Mengoni, S.E.; Irvine, K.; Thakur, D.; Barton, G.; Dautenhahn, K.; Guldberg, K.; Robins, B.; Wellsted, D.; Sharma, S. Feasibility study of a randomised controlled trial to investigate the effectiveness of using a humanoid robot to improve the social skills of children with autism spectrum disorder (Kaspar RCT): A study protocol. *BMJ Open* **2017**, *7*, e017376.

72. Sartorato, F.; Przybylowski, L.; Sarko, D.K. Improving therapeutic outcomes in autism spectrum disorders: Enhancing social communication and sensory processing through the use of interactive robots. *J. Psychiatr. Res.* **2017**, *90*, 1–11.

73. Wong, H.; Zhong, Z. Assessment of robot training for social cognitive learning. In Proceedings of the 2016 16th International Conference on Control, Automation and Systems (ICCAS), Gyeongju, Korea, 16–19 October 2016; pp. 893–898.

74. So, W.C.; Wong, M.Y.; Cabibihan, J.J.; Lam, C.Y.; Chan, R.Y.; Qian, H.H. Using robot animation to promote gestural skills in children with autism spectrum disorders. *J. Comput. Assist. Learn.* **2016**, *32*, 632–646.

75. Bharatharaj, J.; Huang, L.; Al-Jumaily, A.M.; Krageloh, C.; Elara, M.R. Effects of Adapted Model-Rival Method and parrot-inspired robot in improving learning and social interaction among children with autism. In Proceedings of the 2016 International Conference on Robotics and Automation for Humanitarian Applications (RAHA), Kollam, India, 18–20 December 2016; pp. 1–5.

76. Tennyson, M.F.; Kuester, D.A.; Casteel, J.; Nikolopoulos, C. Accessible robots for improving social skills of individuals with autism. *J. Artif. Intell. Soft Comput. Res.* **2016**, *6*, 267–277.

77. Suzuki, R.; Lee, J. Robot-play therapy for improving prosocial behaviours in children with Autism Spectrum Disorders. In Proceedings of the 2016 International Symposium on Micro-NanoMechatronics and Human Science (MHS), Nagoya, Japan, 28–30 November 2016; pp. 1–5.

78. Wainer, J.; Dautenhahn, K.; Robins, B.; Amirabdollahian, F. A pilot study with a novel setup for collaborative play of the humanoid robot KASPAR with children with autism. *Int. J. Soc. Robot.* **2014**, *6*, 45–65.

79. Wainer, J.; Robins, B.; Amirabdollahian, F.; Dautenhahn, K. Using the humanoid robot KASPAR to autonomously play triadic games and facilitate collaborative play among children with autism. *IEEE Trans. Auton. Ment. Dev.* **2014**, *6*, 183–199.

80. Vanderborght, B.; Simut, R.; Saldien, J.; Pop, C.; Rusu, A.S.; Pintea, S.; Lefeber, D.; David, D.O. Using the social robot probo as a social story telling agent for children with ASD. *Interact. Stud.* **2012**, *13*, 348–372.

81. Kajopoulos, J.; Wong, A.H.Y.; Yuen, A.W.C.; Dung, T.A.; Kee, T.Y.; Wykowska, A. Robot-assisted training of joint attention skills in children diagnosed with autism. In Proceedings of the International Conference on Social Robotics, Paris, France, 26–30 October 2015; Springer: Cham, Switzerland, 2015; pp. 296–305.

82. Bharatharaj, J.; Huang, L.; Al-Jumaily, A.M.; Krageloh, C.; Elara, M.R. Experimental evaluation of parrot-inspired robot and adapted model-rival method for teaching children with autism. In Proceedings of the 2016 14th International Conference on Control, Automation, Robotics and Vision (ICARCV), Phuket, Thailand, 13–15 November 2016; pp. 1–6.

83. Bharatharaj, J.; Huang, L.; Mohan, R.E.; Al-Jumaily, A.; Krägeloh, C. Robot-Assisted Therapy for Learning and Social Interaction of Children with Autism Spectrum Disorder. *Robotics* **2017**, *6*, 4.

84. Koch, S.A.; Stevens, C.E.; Clesi, C.D.; Lebersfeld, J.B.; Sellers, A.G.; McNew, M.E.; Biasini, F.J.; Amthor, F.R.; Hopkins, M.I. A Feasibility Study Evaluating the Emotionally Expressive Robot SAM. *Int. J. Soc. Robot.* **2017**, *9*, 601–613.

85. Warren, Z.E.; Zheng, Z.; Swanson, A.R.; Bekele, E.; Zhang, L.; Crittendon, J.A.; Weitlauf, A.F.; Sarkar, N. Can robotic interaction improve joint attention skills? *J. Autism Dev. Disord.* **2015**, *45*, 3726.

86. Wiese, E.; Müller, H.J.; Wykowska, A. Using a gaze-cueing paradigm to examine social cognitive mechanisms of individuals with autism observing robot and human faces. In Proceedings of the International Conference on Social Robotics, Sydney, Australia, 27–29 October 2014; Springer: Cham, Switzerland, 2014; pp. 370–379.

87. Hirokawa, M.; Funahashi, A.; Pan, Y.; Itoh, Y.; Suzuki, K. Design of a robotic agent that measures smile and facing behavior of children with Autism Spectrum Disorder. In Proceedings of the 2016 25th IEEE International Symposium on Robot and Human Interactive Communication (RO-MAN), New York, NY, USA, 26–31 August 2016; pp. 843–848.

88. Yun, S.S.; Choi, J.; Park, S.K. Robotic behavioral intervention to facilitate eye contact and reading emotions of children with autism spectrum disorders. In Proceedings of the 2016 25th IEEE International Symposium on Robot and Human Interactive Communication (RO-MAN), New York, NY, USA, 26–31 August 2016; pp. 694–699.

89. Yun, S.S.; Park, S.K.; Choi, J. A robotic treatment approach to promote social interaction skills for children with autism spectrum disorders. In Proceedings of the 2014 RO-MAN: The 23rd IEEE International Symposium on Robot and Human Interactive Communication, Edinburgh, UK, 25–29 August 2014; pp. 130–134.

90. Hirose, J.; Hirokawa, M.; Suzuki, K. Robotic gaming companion to facilitate social interaction among children. In Proceedings of the 2014 RO-MAN: The 23rd IEEE International Symposium on Robot and Human Interactive Communication, Edinburgh, UK, 25–29 August 2014; pp. 63–68.

91. Mavadati, S.M.; Feng, H.; Gutierrez, A.; Mahoor, M.H. Comparing the gaze responses of children with autism and typically developed individuals in human-robot interaction. In Proceedings of the 2014 14th IEEE-RAS International Conference on Humanoid Robots (Humanoids), Madrid, Spain, 18–20 November 2014; pp. 1128–1133.

92. Anzalone, S.M.; Boucenna, S.; Cohen, D.; Chetouani, M. Autism assessment through a small humanoid robot. In Proceedings of the HRI: A Bridge between Robotics and Neuroscience, Workshop of the 9th ACM/IEEE International Conference on Human-Robot Interaction, Bielefeld, Germany, 3–6 March 2014; pp. 1–2.

93. Anzalone, S.M.; Tilmont, E.; Boucenna, S.; Xavier, J.; Jouen, A.L.; Bodeau, N.; Maharatna, K.; Chetouani, M.; Cohen, D.; Group, M.S.; et al. How children with autism spectrum disorder behave and explore the 4-dimensional (spatial 3D+ time) environment during a joint attention induction task with a robot. *Res. Autism Spectr. Disord.* **2014**, *8*, 814–826.

94. Conti, D.; Di Nuovo, S.; Buono, S.; Trubia, G.; Di Nuovo, A. Use of robotics to stimulate imitation in children with Autism Spectrum Disorder: A pilot study in a clinical setting. In Proceedings of the 2015 24th IEEE International Symposium on Robot and Human Interactive Communication (RO-MAN), Kobe, Japan, 31 August–4 September 2015; pp. 1–6.

95. Srinivasan, S.M.; Park, I.K.; Neely, L.B.; Bhat, A.N. A comparison of the effects of rhythm and robotic interventions on repetitive behaviors and affective states of children with Autism Spectrum Disorder (ASD). *Res. Autism Spectr. Disord.* **2015**, *18*, 51–63.

96. Srinivasan, S.M.; Eigsti, I.M.; Gifford, T.; Bhat, A.N. The effects of embodied rhythm and robotic interventions on the spontaneous and responsive verbal communication skills of children with Autism Spectrum Disorder (ASD): A further outcome of a pilot randomized controlled trial. *Res. Autism Spectr. Disord.* **2016**, *27*, 73–87.

97. Srinivasan, S.M.; Kaur, M.; Park, I.K.; Gifford, T.D.; Marsh, K.L.; Bhat, A.N. The effects of rhythm and robotic interventions on the imitation/praxis, interpersonal synchrony, and motor performance of children with autism spectrum disorder (ASD): A pilot randomized controlled trial. *Autism Res. Treat.* **2015**, *2015*, 736516.

98. Mavadati, S.M.; Feng, H.; Salvador, M.; Silver, S.; Gutierrez, A.; Mahoor, M.H. Robot-based therapeutic protocol for training children with Autism. In Proceedings of the 2016 25th IEEE International Symposium on Robot and Human Interactive Communication (RO-MAN), New York, NY, USA, 26–31 August 2016; pp. 855–860.

99. Chevalier, P.; Martin, J.C.; Isableu, B.; Bazile, C.; Iacob, D.O.; Tapus, A. Joint Attention using Human-Robot Interaction: Impact of sensory preferences of children with autism. In Proceedings of the 2016 25th IEEE International Symposium on Robot and Human Interactive Communication (RO-MAN), New York, NY, USA, 26–31 August 2016; pp. 849–854.

100. Boucenna, S.; Anzalone, S.; Tilmont, E.; Cohen, D.; Chetouani, M. Learning of social signatures through imitation game between a robot and a human partner. *IEEE Trans. Auton. Ment. Dev.* **2014**, *6*, 213–225.

101. Ranatunga, I.; Torres, N.A.; Patterson, R.; Bugnariu, N.; Stevenson, M.; Popa, D.O. RoDiCA: a human-robot interaction system for treatment of childhood autism spectrum disorders. In Proceedings of the 5th International Conference on PErvasive Technologies Related to Assistive Environments, Heraklion, Greece, 6–8 June 2012; p. 50.

102. Costa, S.C.; Soares, F.O.; Pereira, A.P.; Moreira, F. Constraints in the design of activities focusing on emotion recognition for children with ASD using robotic tools. In Proceedings of the 4th IEEE RAS & EMBS International Conference on Biomedical Robotics and Biomechatronics, Rome, Italy, 24–27 June 2012; pp. 1884–1889.

103. Salvador, M.J.; Silver, S.; Mahoor, M.H. An emotion recognition comparative study of autistic and typically-developing children using the zeno robot. In Proceedings of the 2015 IEEE International Conference on Robotics and Automation (ICRA), Seattle, WA, USA, 26–30 May 2015; pp. 6128–6133.

104. Chevalier, P.; Martin, J.C.; Isableu, B.; Bazile, C.; Tapus, A. Impact of sensory preferences of individuals with autism on the recognition of emotions expressed by two robots, an avatar, and a human. *Auton. Robot.* **2017**, *41*, 613–635.

105. Khosla, R.; Nguyen, K.; Chu, M.T. Socially Assistive Robot Enabled Home-Based Care for Supporting People with Autism. In Proceedings of the Pacific Asia Conference on Information Systems, Singapore, 5–9 July 2015; p. 12.

106. Dehkordi, P.S.; Moradi, H.; Mahmoudi, M.; Pouretemad, H.R. The design, development, and deployment of RoboParrot for screening autistic children. *Int. J. Soc. Robot.* **2015**, *7*, 513–522.

107. Mazzei, D.; Greco, A.; Lazzeri, N.; Zaraki, A.; Lanata, A.; Igliozzi, R.; Mancini, A.; Stoppa, F.; Scilingo, E.P.; Muratori, F.; et al. Robotic social therapy on children with autism: preliminary evaluation through multi-parametric analysis. In Proceedings of the International Conference on Social Computing, Amsterdam, The Netherlands, 3–5 September 2012; pp. 766–771.

108. Cao, H.L.; Esteban, P.G.; De Beir, A.; Simut, R.; Van De Perre, G.; Vanderborght, B. A platform-independent robot control architecture for multiple therapeutic scenarios. *arXiv* **2016**, arXiv:1607.04971.

109. Cootes, T.F.; Edwards, G.J.; Taylor, C.J. Active appearance models. *IEEE Trans. Pattern Anal. Mach. Intell.* **2001**, *23*, 681–685.

110. Cazzato, D.; Mazzeo, P.L.; Spagnolo, P.; Distante, C. Automatic joint attention detection during interaction with a humanoid robot. In Proceedings of the International Conference on Social Robotics, Paris, France, 26–30 October 2015; Springer: Cham, Switzerland, 2015; pp. 124–134.

111. Nunez, E.; Matsuda, S.; Hirokawa, M.; Suzuki, K. Humanoid robot assisted training for facial expressions recognition based on affective feedback. In Proceedings of the International Conference on Social Robotics, Paris, France, 26–30 October 2015; Springer: Cham, Switzerland, 2015; pp. 492–501.

112. Leo, M.; Del Coco, M.; Carcagni, P.; Distante, C.; Bernava, M.; Pioggia, G.; Palestra, G. Automatic emotion recognition in robot-children interaction for asd treatment. In Proceedings of the IEEE International Conference on Computer Vision Workshops, Santiago, Chile, 7–13 December 2015; pp. 145–153.

113. Ponce, P.; Molina, A.; Grammatikou, D. Design based on fuzzy signal detection theory for a semi-autonomous assisting robot in children autism therapy. *Comput. Hum. Behav.* **2016**, *55*, 28–42.

114. Yun, S.S.; Kim, H.; Choi, J.; Park, S.K. A robot-assisted behavioral intervention system for children with autism spectrum disorders. *Robot. Auton. Syst.* **2016**, *76*, 58–67.

115. Simut, R.; Van de Perre, G.; Costescu, C.; Saldien, J.; Vanderfaeillie, J.; David, D.; Lebefer, D.; Vanderborght, B. Probogotchi: A novel edutainment device as a bridge for interaction between a child with asd and the typically developed sibling. *J. Evid.-Based Psychother.* **2016**, *16*, 91.

116. Boccanfuso, L.; Scarborough, S.; Abramson, R.K.; Hall, A.V.; Wright, H.H.; O'Kane, J.M. A low-cost socially assistive robot and robot-assisted intervention for children with autism spectrum disorder: Field trials and lessons learned. *Auton. Robot.* **2017**, *41*, 637–655.

117. Liu, R.; Salisbury, J.P.; Vahabzadeh, A.; Sahin, N.T. Feasibility of an autism-focused augmented reality smartglasses system for social communication and behavioral coaching. *Front. Pediatr.* **2017**, *5*, 145.

118. Barakova, E.I.; Bajracharya, P.; Willemsen, M.; Lourens, T.; Huskens, B. Long-term LEGO therapy with humanoid robot for children with ASD. *Expert Syst.* **2015**, *32*, 698–709.

119. Boccanfuso, L.; Barney, E.; Foster, C.; Ahn, Y.A.; Chawarska, K.; Scassellati, B.; Shic, F. Emotional robot to examine different play patterns and affective responses of children with and without ASD. In Proceedings of the 2016 11th ACM/IEEE International Conference on Human-Robot Interaction (HRI), Christchurch, New Zealand, 7–10 March 2016; pp. 19–26.

120. Rudovic, O.; Lee, J.; Mascarell-Maricic, L.; Schuller, B.W.; Picard, R.W. Measuring Engagement in Robot-Assisted Autism Therapy: A Cross-Cultural Study. *Front. Robot. AI* **2017**, *4*, 36.

121. KB, P.R.; Lahiri, U. Design of Eyegaze-sensitive Virtual Reality Based Social Communication Platform for Individuals with Autism. In Proceedings of the 2016 7th International Conference on Intelligent Systems, Modelling and Simulation (ISMS), Bangkok, Thailand, 25–27 January 2016; pp. 301–306.

122. Noris, B.; Nadel, J.; Barker, M.; Hadjikhani, N.; Billard, A. Investigating gaze of children with ASD in naturalistic settings. *PLoS ONE* **2012**, *7*, e44144.

123. Courgeon, M.; Rautureau, G.; Martin, J.C.; Grynszpan, O. Joint attention simulation using eye-tracking and virtual humans. *IEEE Trans. Affect. Comput.* **2014**, *5*, 238–250.

124. Esubalew, T.; Lahiri, U.; Swanson, A.R.; Crittendon, J.A.; Warren, Z.E.; Sarkar, N. A step towards developing adaptive robot-mediated intervention architecture (ARIA) for children with autism. *IEEE Trans. Neural Syst. Rehabil. Eng.* **2013**, *21*, 289–299.

125. Bekele, E.; Crittendon, J.A.; Swanson, A.; Sarkar, N.; Warren, Z.E. Pilot clinical application of an adaptive robotic system for young children with autism. *Autism* **2014**, *18*, 598–608.

126. Caruana, N.; McArthur, G.; Woolgar, A.; Brock, J. Detecting communicative intent in a computerised test of joint attention. *PeerJ* **2017**, *5*, e2899.

127. Grynszpan, O.; Nadel, J.; Martin, J.C.; Simonin, J.; Bailleul, P.; Wang, Y.; Gepner, D.; Le Barillier, F.; Constant, J. Self-monitoring of gaze in high functioning autism. *J. Autism Dev. Disord.* **2012**, *42*, 1642–1650.

128. Zheng, Z.; Fu, Q.; Zhao, H.; Swanson, A.R.; Weitlauf, A.S.; Warren, Z.E.; Sarkar, N. Design of an Autonomous Social Orienting Training System (ASOTS) for Young Children With Autism. *IEEE Trans. Neural Syst. Rehabil. Eng.* **2017**, *25*, 668–678.

129. Zheng, Z.; Nie, G.; Swanson, A.; Weitlauf, A.; Warren, Z.; Sarkar, N. Longitudinal Impact of Autonomous Robot-Mediated Joint Attention Intervention for Young Children with ASD. In Proceedings of the International Conference on Social Robotics, Kansas City, MO, USA, 1–3 November 2016; Springer: Cham, Switzerland, 2016; pp. 581–590.

130. Zhang, L.; Wade, J.; Swanson, A.; Weitlauf, A.; Warren, Z.; Sarkar, N. Cognitive state measurement from eye gaze analysis in an intelligent virtual reality driving system for autism intervention. In Proceedings of the 2015 International Conference on Affective Computing and Intelligent Interaction (ACII), Xi'an, China, 21–24 September 2015; pp. 532–538.

131. Gyori, M.; Borsos, Z.; Stefanik, K.; Csákvári, J. Data Quality as a Bottleneck in Developing a Social-Serious-Game-Based Multi-modal System for Early Screening for High Functioning Cases of Autism Spectrum Condition. In Proceedings of the International Conference on Computers Helping People with Special Needs, Linz, Austria, 13–15 July 2016; Springer: Cham, Switzerland, 2016; pp. 358–366.

132. Lun, R.; Zhao, W. A Survey of Applications and Human Motion Recognition with Microsoft Kinect. *Int. J. Pattern Recognit. Artif. Intell.* **2015**, *29*, 1555008.

133. Zhao, W. A concise tutorial on human motion tracking and recognition with Microsoft Kinect. *Sci. China Inf. Sci.* **2016**, *59*, 93101.

134. Christinaki, E.; Vidakis, N.; Triantafyllidis, G. A novel educational game for teaching emotion identification skills to preschoolers with autism diagnosis. *Comput. Sci. Inf. Syst.* **2014**, *11*, 723–743.

135. Zheng, Z.; Das, S.; Young, E.M.; Swanson, A.; Warren, Z.; Sarkar, N. Autonomous robot-mediated imitation learning for children with autism. In Proceedings of the 2014 IEEE International Conference on Robotics and Automation (ICRA), Hong Kong, China, 31 May–7 June 2014; pp. 2707–2712.

136. Ge, B.; Park, H.W.; Howard, A.M. Identifying Engagement from Joint Kinematics Data for Robot Therapy Prompt Interventions for Children with Autism Spectrum Disorder. In Proceedings of the International Conference on Social Robotics, Kansas City, MO, USA, 1–3 November 2016; Springer: Cham, Switzerland, 2016; pp. 531–540.

137. Yun, S.S.; Choi, J.; Park, S.K.; Bong, G.Y.; Yoo, H. Social skills training for children with autism spectrum disorder using a robotic behavioral intervention system. *Autism Res.* **2017**, *10*, 1306–1323.

138. Uzuegbunam, N.; Wong, W.H.; Cheung, S.c.S.; Ruble, L. MEBook: Kinect-based self-modeling intervention for children with autism. In Proceedings of the 2015 IEEE International Conference on Multimedia and Expo (ICME), Turin, Italy, 29 June–3 July 2015; pp. 1–6.

139. Kuriakose, S.; Kunche, S.; Narendranath, B.; Jain, P.; Sonker, S.; Lahiri, U. A step towards virtual reality based social communication for children with Autism. In Proceedings of the 2013 International Conference on Control, Automation, Robotics and Embedded Systems (CARE), Jabalpur, India, 16–18 December 2013; pp. 1–6.

140. Di Palma, S.; Tonacci, A.; Narzisi, A.; Domenici, C.; Pioggia, G.; Muratori, F.; Billeci, L.; The MICHELANGELO study group. Monitoring of autonomic response to sociocognitive tasks during treatment in children with autism spectrum disorders by wearable technologies: A feasibility study. *Comput. Biol. Med.* **2017**, *85*, 143–152.

141. Zhang, L.; Wade, J.; Bian, D.; Fan, J.; Swanson, A.; Weitlauf, A.; Warren, Z.; Sarkar, N. Cognitive load measurement in a virtual reality-based driving system for autism intervention. *IEEE Trans. Affect. Comput.* **2017**, *8*, 176–189.

142. White, S.W.; Richey, J.A.; Gracanin, D.; Coffman, M.; Elias, R.; LaConte, S.; Ollendick, T.H. Psychosocial and Computer-Assisted Intervention for College Students with Autism Spectrum Disorder: Preliminary Support for Feasibility. *Educ. Train. Autism Dev. Disabil.* **2016**, *51*, 307.

143. Bekele, E.; Wade, J.; Bian, D.; Fan, J.; Swanson, A.; Warren, Z.; Sarkar, N. Multimodal adaptive social interaction in virtual environment (MASI-VR) for children with Autism spectrum disorders (ASD). In Proceedings of the 2016 IEEE Virtual Reality (VR), Greenville, SC, USA, 19–23 March 2016; pp. 121–130.

144. Fan, J.; Wade, J.W.; Bian, D.; Key, A.P.; Warren, Z.E.; Mion, L.C.; Sarkar, N. A Step towards EEG-based brain computer interface for autism intervention. In Proceedings of the 2015 37th Annual International Conference of the IEEE Engineering in Medicine and Biology Society (EMBC), Milan, Italy, 25–29 August 2015; pp. 3767–3770.

145. Özcan, B.; Caligiore, D.; Sperati, V.; Moretta, T.; Baldassarre, G. Transitional wearable companions: A novel concept of soft interactive social robots to improve social skills in children with autism spectrum disorder. *Int. J. Soc. Robot.* **2016**, *8*, 471–481.

146. Bian, D.; Wade, J.; Warren, Z.; Sarkar, N. Online Engagement Detection and Task Adaptation in a Virtual Reality Based Driving Simulator for Autism Intervention. In Proceedings of the International Conference on Universal Access in Human-Computer Interaction, Toronto, ON, Canada, 17–22 July 2016; Springer: Cham, Switzerland, 2016; pp. 538–547.

147. Bakeman, R. Behavioral observation and coding. In *Handbook of Research Methods in Social and Personality Psychology*; Cambridge University Press: New York, NY, USA, 2000; pp. 138–159.

148. Weick, K.E. Systematic observational methods. In *The Handbook of Social Psychology*; John Wiley and Sons: Hoboken, NJ, USA, 1968; Volume 2, pp. 357–451.

149. Khosla, R.; Nguyen, K.; Chu, M.T. Service personalisation of assistive robot for autism care. In Proceedings of the IECON 2015-41st Annual Conference of the IEEE Industrial Electronics Society, Yokohama, Japan, 9–12 November 2015; pp. 002088–002093.

150. Mourning, R.; Tang, Y. Virtual reality social training for adolescents with high-functioning autism. In Proceedings of the 2016 IEEE International Conference on Systems, Man, and Cybernetics (SMC), Budapest, Hungary, 9–12 October 2016; pp. 004848–004853.

151. Bekele, E.; Zheng, Z.; Swanson, A.; Crittendon, J.; Warren, Z.; Sarkar, N. Understanding how adolescents with autism respond to facial expressions in virtual reality environments. *IEEE Trans. Vis. Comput. Graph.* **2013**, *19*, 711–720.

152. Kaboski, J.R.; Diehl, J.J.; Beriont, J.; Crowell, C.R.; Villano, M.; Wier, K.; Tang, K. Brief report: A pilot summer robotics camp to reduce social anxiety and improve social/vocational skills in adolescents with ASD. *J. Autism Dev. Disord.* **2015**, *45*, 3862–3869.

153. Newbutt, N.; Sung, C.; Kuo, H.J.; Leahy, M.J. The potential of virtual reality technologies to support people with an autism condition: A case study of acceptance, presence and negative effects. *Ann. Rev. Cyber Ther. Telemed. (ARCTT)* **2016**, *14*, 149–154.

154. Ekman, P.; Friesen, W.V. *Unmasking the Face: A Guide to Recognizing Emotions from Facial Clues*; ISHK: Los Altos, CA, USA, 2003.

155. Benton, A.L. The neuropsychology of facial recognition. *Am. Psychol.* **1980**, *35*, 176.

156. Gresham, F.M.; Elliott, S.N. *Social Skills Rating System: Manual*; American Guidance Service: Circle Pines, MN, USA, 1990.

157. Suskind, R.; Nguyen, J.; Patterson, S.; Springer, S.; Fanty, M. Guided Personal Companion. U.S. Patent 9,710,613, 18 July 2017.

158. Liu, X.; Zhao, W. Buddy: A Virtual Life Coaching System for Children and Adolescents with High Functioning Autism. In Proceedings of the IEEE Cyber Science and Technology Congress, Orlando, FL, USA, 5–9 November 2017.

159. Bernardini, S.; Porayska-Pomsta, K.; Smith, T.J. ECHOES: An intelligent serious game for fostering social communication in children with autism. *Inf. Sci.* **2014**, *264*, 41–60.

160. Esteban, P.G.; Baxter, P.; Belpaeme, T.; Billing, E.; Cai, H.; Cao, H.L.; Coeckelbergh, M.; Costescu, C.; David, D.; De Beir, A.; et al. How to build a supervised autonomous system for robot-enhanced therapy for children with autism spectrum disorder. *Paladyn J. Behav. Robot.* **2017**, *8*, 18–38.

161. Luo, X.; Deng, J.; Liu, J.; Wang, W.; Ban, X.; Wang, J.H. A quantized kernel least mean square scheme with entropy-guided learning for intelligent data analysis. *China Commun.* **2017**, *14*, 1–10.

162. Luo, X.; Deng, J.; Wang, W.; Wang, J.H.; Zhao, W. A Quantized Kernel Learning Algorithm Using a Minimum Kernel Risk-Sensitive Loss Criterion and Bilateral Gradient Technique. *Entropy* **2017**, *19*, 365.

163. Luo, X.; Lv, Y.; Zhou, M.; Wang, W.; Zhao, W. A laguerre neural network-based ADP learning scheme with its application to tracking control in the Internet of Things. *Pers. Ubiquitous Comput.* **2016**, *20*, 361–372.

164. Luo, X.; Xu, Y.; Wang, W.; Yuan, M.; Ban, X.; Zhu, Y.; Zhao, W. Towards Enhancing Stacked Extreme Learning Machine With Sparse Autoencoder by Correntropy. *J. Frankl. Inst.* **2017**, doi:10.1016/j.jfranklin.2017.08.014.

165. Luo, X.; Zhang, D.; Yang, L.T.; Liu, J.; Chang, X.; Ning, H. A kernel machine-based secure data sensing and fusion scheme in wireless sensor networks for the cyber-physical systems. *Future Gener. Comput. Syst.* **2016**, *61*, 85–96.

applied sciences

MDPI

Article

Efficient Real-Time Lossless EMG Data Transmission to Monitor Pre-Term Delivery in a Medical Information System

Gyoun-Yon Cho [1], Seo-Joon Lee [2] and Tae-Ro Lee [3,*]

[1]   Health Science Institute, Korea University, Seoul 02841, Korea; gycho@korea.ac.kr
[2]   BK21PLUS Program in 'Embodiment: Health-Society Interaction', Department of Public Health Sciences, Graduate School, Korea University, Seoul 02841, Korea; richardlsj@korea.ac.kr
[3]   BK21PLUS Program in 'Embodiment: Health-Society Interaction', School of Health Policy & Management, Korea University, Seoul 02841, Korea
*   Correspondence: trlee@korea.ac.kr; Tel.: +82-10-6697-2391

Academic Editors: Wenbing Zhao, Xiong Luo and Tie Qiu
Received: 17 December 2016; Accepted: 4 April 2017; Published: 6 April 2017

Abstract: An estimated 15 million babies are born prematurely every year worldwide, and suffer from disabilities. Appropriate care of these pre-term babies immediately after birth through telemedicine monitoring is vital. However, problems associated with a limited bandwidth and network overload due to the excessive size of the electromyography (EMG) signal impede the practical application of such medical information systems. Therefore, this research proposes an EMG uterine monitoring transmission solution (EUMTS), a lossless efficient real-time EMG transmission solution that solves such problems through efficient EMG data lossless compression. EMG data samples obtained from the Physionet PhysioBank database were used. Solution performance comparisons were conducted using Lempel-Ziv Welch (LZW) and Huffman methods, in addition to related researches. The LZW and Huffman methods showed *CRs* of 1.87 and 1.90, respectively, compared to 3.61 for the proposed algorithm. This was relatively high compared to related researches, even when considering that those researches were lossy whereas the proposed research was lossless. The results also showed that the proposed algorithm contributes to a reduction in battery consumption by reducing the wake-up time by 1470.6 ms. Therefore, EUMTS will contribute to providing an efficient wireless transmission environment for the prediction of pre-term delivery, enabling immediate interventions by medical professionals. Another novel point of EUMTS is that it is a lossless algorithm, which will prevent any misjudgement by clinicians because the data will not be distorted. Pre-term babies may receive point-of-care immediately after birth, preventing exposure to the development of disabilities.

Keywords: compression; EMG; lossless; medical information system; pre-term birth; telemedicine; wireless

---

1. Introduction

An estimated 15 million babies are born prematurely (pre-term birth) every year worldwide, which is more than one in ten [1]. The World Health Organization (WHO) has indicated that almost one million children die annually, due to complications associated with pre-term birth. Even if the babies survive, they are likely to face a lifetime of disability (learning disabilities, visual disabilities, hearing problems, etc.), which is difficult to resolve using medical treatment.

Globally, prematurity is the leading cause of death in children under the age of five years. The fact that preterm birth rates are increasing in almost all countries is disturbing [2]. There is a growing need for a solution to this problem, as the prevention of pre-term birth is extremely difficult because it is both spontaneous and unpredictable.

One feasible solution, also strongly recommended by WHO, is to provide essential care at the "Golden Time" during the postnatal period. The administration of antibiotics during this time could prevent infections developing in newborns. The appropriate timing for this can be guaranteed using information technology (IT) [3]. By combining health services and IT, uterine parameters can be monitored for signs of pre-term symptoms.

Recent studies of a uterine electromyography (EMG) signal focused on the prediction or detection of pre-term birth [4,5]. These technologies facilitate the remote monitoring of preterm incidents. Furthermore, a hardware feature exists to support such preterm monitoring. A solution [6] issued by Principe proposed a preterm monitoring system and method that monitors the EMG signals of the pregnant mother.

However, the problem of the current features of these platforms is that, due to the massive size of the EMG signal [7], the network bandwidth is constantly overloaded. Hardware and software that support EMG transmission are also overwhelmed, because it is recommended that maternal patients are monitored for 40 weeks (at least 12 weeks) during the gestational period. This results in problems such as rapid battery consumption and overheating. To solve this, compression of the transmitted data is required. This would allow more patients to be supported using a limited bandwidth [8], resulting in a safe EMG signal transmission environment for transmitting maternal patient's signal.

Another problem regarding the transmission of EMG signals is data loss in wireless transmission. There are two cases of data loss; one is natural error, and the other is the loss that occurs from lossy transmission techniques. If data is compressed, it can be transmitted as fast as possible and can be rapidly recovered. However, it is equally important to apply lossless techniques because an EMG signal is a vital sign of the patient's state, and any distortion resulting from data loss may critically affect clinicians' decisions.

Accordingly, this research proposes a real-time wireless lossless EMG data transmission solution termed an EMG uterine monitoring transmission solution (EUMTS), to support the systems for monitoring pregnant women for early symptoms of pre-term labor. Our prior research algorithm regarding an electrocardiography (ECG) was modified and applied to EMG signals, which yielded a high performance result. The significant point of this is that EMG signal compression performance has been lower than expected in other researches thus far, because of its extreme irregularity, and was rarely touched. The proposed research handled this field and produced comparatively high results, even without any data loss. The proposed solution is envisioned to contribute to providing a seamless network platform for preterm telemedicine, facilitating the appropriate care of pre-term babies prior to exposure to infection and contamination. This is a unique contribution.

2. Related Works

2.1. Preterm Prevention Monitoring System

As mentioned earlier, Principe et al. [6] proposed the electrohysterogram (EHG, uterine EMG) monitoring system for sensing the EMG signals of the mother and sending them to the health device through wireless communication. The key specific features are depicted in Figure 1, which is taken from Principe's patent [6].

A surface sensor, which comprises multiple leads, is attached to the uterine surface of the mother (Figures 1a–d and 3a,b). Sensed signals are then sent through the wired network (shown as analog-to-digital convertible shielded cables 4 and 5 in Figure 1) or through a wireless network to the personal health device (shown as 6 in Figure 1), to spatially depict the contraction status (shown as 7 in Figure 1) in real-time. The proposed solution in this study was developed to support the seamless networking of such EMG information monitoring systems, which will be specifically presented in Section 3.

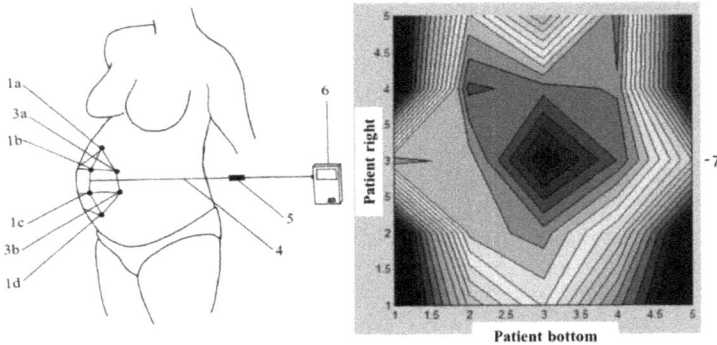

Figure 1. Principe's system and method for analyzing the progress of labor and preterm labor.

2.2. Limited Bandwidth in Practical Real-Time Wireless Communication and Insufficient Battery Life in Pre-Term Monitoring

When using 12 channels, a 32-bit resolution, and a 20 Hz EMG monitoring environment, approximately 7.6 Kbps of bandwidth is required. Considering Bluetooth 4.2. (recent version of Bluetooth), its Low Energy (BLE) specifications are appropriate for monitoring situations, mainly because of its low energy consumption. BLE's throughput specification supports up to 7 Kbps [9]. This is a huge lack of network bandwidth because, realistically, 100% of the 7 Kbps cannot be allocated to EMG channels alone. Headers, security, error correction, and other kinds of data (maybe even other signals than EMG) inevitably take up a considerable portion, even when 100% of the portion alone is not enough for the EMG transmission itself.

Furthermore, in wireless sensor networks, sensors are continuously strained in order to support a seamless network. Engineers are constantly working to increase the run-time of such battery-powered devices [10], because their seamless connection is especially important in smart healthcare networks. However, the need for EMG transmission and a long monitoring length are still large barriers for wireless communications in pre-term monitoring.

It is optimal for a maternal EMG to be monitored for 40 full weeks during the gestation period. At least the 12 weeks (=40 weeks of full period 28 weeks of extremely pre-term period, refer to Section 2.4) before birth should be monitored in real-time, in order to react within the "Golden time". Considering 12 channels, a 32-bit resolution, and a 20 Hz transmission network environment, a minimum of approximately 6.9 Giga Bytes (GB) to a maximum of 23.2 GB of data must be transferred or stored per patient of maternity.

This is affected by the number of maternity patients supported, meaning that an immense amount of data must be transferred and stored for long periods. In reality, this is a great overload to any wireless transmission situation, both to the device and the network.

Therefore, this overloaded environment is practically impossible to support. Heavy battery consumption near wireless networks such as Bluetooth or Wi-Fi suffer from network shortages. Large quantities of EMG data take longer to transmit, and monitoring the pre-term status requires lengthy monitoring periods, resulting in immense battery consumption. If the data size can be reduced, wireless transmission network overload will be lowered and the battery life-span will be increased.

We proposed an algorithm solution to transmit data in a compact size in real-time, thereby contributing to lessening the strains in the wireless communication bandwidth and data transmission strains in battery consumption.

2.3. Prior Research on Term & Pre-Term EMG Signals

Searching the Web of Science (WoS) yielded little research regarding term and pre-term EMG signals. Most researches were concentrated on the monitoring and prediction of preterm birth [11,12], with some focusing on the maternal health system itself. Few other studies were related to the classification of term or pre-term [13] EMG signals for the prediction and detection of preterm birth.

Due to the scarcity of research into the compression of EMG signals of maternal patients, studies of EMG signals, regardless of disease type, were used for comparison (refer to Section 4.2). The studies by Balouchestani [14], Itiki [15], Norris [16], Berger [17], Filho [18], and Trabuco [7] were selected. Specific summary details of the selected researches are shown in Table 1.

Table 1. Selected prior studies.

Study	Notes
Balouchestani [14]	Batch processing algorithm based on analog-compressed sensing (CS) for the receiver side of an ultra-low-power wearable and wireless surface EMG (sEMG) sensor.
Itiki [15]	Compression of high definition (HD) EMG signals recorded by two-dimensional electrode matrices at different muscle-contraction forces. Also includes methodological aspects of compressing HD EMG signals of the non-pinnate (upper trapezius) and pinnate (medial gastrocnemius) muscles using image compression techniques. No real-time supportability.
Norris [16]	Algorithm based on an embedded zero-tree wavelets (EZW) scheme. Does not support real-time.
Berger [17]	Compression algorithm based on wavelet transform, neural network bit allocation procedure and arithmetic entropy coding. Does not support real-time.
Filho [18]	Batch processing algorithm based on a recurrent pattern algorithm.
Trabuco [7]	Algorithm based on discrete wavelet transform for spectral decomposition and de-correlation. Does not support real-time.

The proposed algorithm was not compared to other types of signals, because signals other than EMG have different and unique characteristics. For example, ECG is much regular than that of EMG, so the same optimization technology cannot be applied. In conclusion, in order to objectively evaluate the performance of the proposed algorithm (which is optimized for EMG), comparisons of the same EMG signal-related algorithms should be made. This is also the same case for the prior related researches regarding EMG compression selected above, which also chose to compare similar signal data.

2.4. Term-Preterm Birth

The normal human gestation period is 40 weeks. However, labor prior to the end of the 37th week is known as premature (pre-term) labor, which is abnormal [19]. Pre-term births are classified as shown in Table 2.

Table 2. Classification of Pre-term Birth Based on the Gestational Period.

Sub-Category	Gestational Period
Extremely pre-term	Less than 28 weeks
Very pre-term	28 to 32 weeks
Moderate to late pre-term	32 to less than 37 weeks

Pre-term birth usually leads to unexpected illness, injuries, or disorders that may last a lifetime. Therefore, it is strongly recommended that induction or a caesarean birth is not planned or implemented before 39 weeks [20].

2.5. Digital Signal Compression and EMG

The application of digital signal compression has been practiced in our prior researches [21–23]. An appropriate analysis of digital signal redundancy enables the development of a powerful compression algorithm, and an effective compression ratio.

In this study, compression of the EMG signal of maternal patients was attempted. The EMG signal is generally produced by skeletal muscles and can be used to detect medical abnormalities. Figure 2 shows an example EMG signal of one of the signals used in this study.

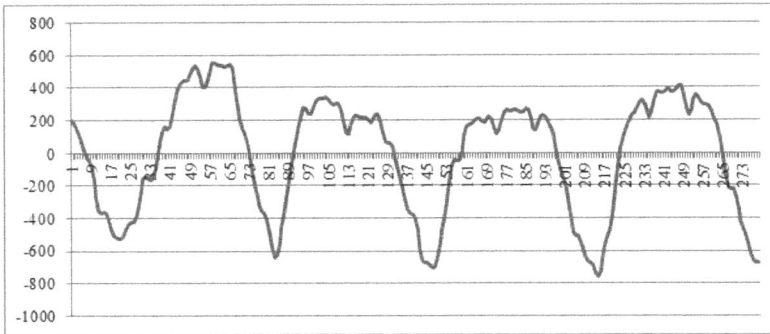

Figure 2. Example EMG signal interval.

There are limitations in efficiently compressing EMG signals because they contain a lower redundancy due to their irregularity (Figure 2). For example, ECG signals contain a very high redundancy due to their distinctive periodical cycles (PQRST interval). Efficient lossless ECG compression in a real-time medical information system environment has been proposed [8], but in this study, a different approach was needed. EMG data had to be analyzed more thoroughly due to its extreme irregularity (low redundancy) compared to ECG (high redundancy). A different compression algorithm was applied, and the main modification was analyzing and developing a different dictionary code word optimized for EMG. The specific features of the algorithm proposed in this research are described in Section 3.2.

3. System Description

3.1. Overall System Architecture

The overall system architecture of a typical term and pre-term monitoring system [24] for mothers is discussed in this Section. The system is depicted in Figure 3.

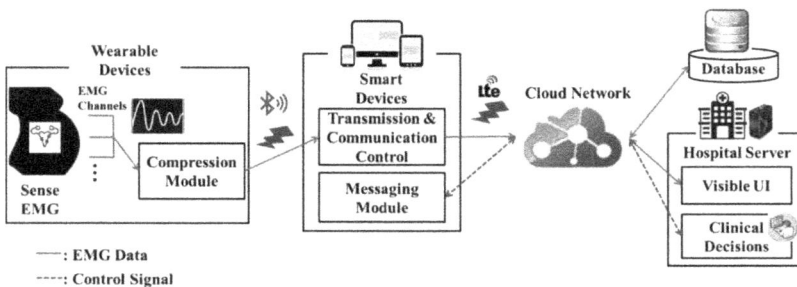

Figure 3. Architecture of a pre-term monitoring system.

Wearable sensors are unobtrusively attached to the patient; these detect the EMG signals, which contain indicators of the term/pre-term condition. Raw EMG data (straight lines) obtained from the sensors in each channel are transmitted to the wearable device (e.g., wearable watch), where they are encoded to be efficiently transmitted through our proposed compression module. The algorithm developed for the compression module is described in Section 3.2.

The compressed EMG signal is sent to the smart device, which contains the transmission direction and communication control module. The network environment used here is usually BLE. The Transmission & Communication module decides where the signals or messages should be sent. If the EMG signal shows no signs of pre-term delivery, it is sent to the database via the cloud network. In this case, the used network may be 4 G (LTE). If the EMG signal shows signs of pre-term delivery, it is sent to the hospital server.

In the hospital server, the visual User Interface (UI) module decodes the compressed EMG data into a user-friendly format, and presents it to the clinician. Clinical decisions or feedbacks are then sent to the smart device (message and control communications are depicted as dotted lines in Figure 3). Finally, the potential patient may receive clinical prevention services through the smart device UI; for example, warning of the risk of pre-term delivery. This facilitates screening for prematurity, allowing precautions to be taken; for example, appropriate interventions after premature birth, preventing the development of complex illness [25] due to a pre-term birth.

An important note that should not be confused is that in the telemonitoring situations for maternal patients shown in Figure 3, real-time interaction is not implemented between the healthcare professional and patient. Physicians are only alerted by the system when abnormality is detected, and vice versa, and they only provide feedback to patients when necessary. Real-time communication is only applied between wearable devices and smart devices (BLE transmission).

3.2. Compression Algorithm

This study developed a compression algorithm for the lossless real-time transmission of the EMG signals of mothers. The mainstream algorithm model of our prior research regarding ECG [8] was used, but its core dictionary code word was modified for the application to EMG signals. The algorithm was designed to be spread throughout the proposed system architecture, contributing to a seamless and lossless transmission network environment. The emphasis on the lossless nature of the system is an important feature, since the network environment proposed in this system handles potentially critical medical information. Any loss in signal may lead to clinical misjudgment or diagnostic errors. A flow chart of the EMG transmission solution is shown in Figure 4.

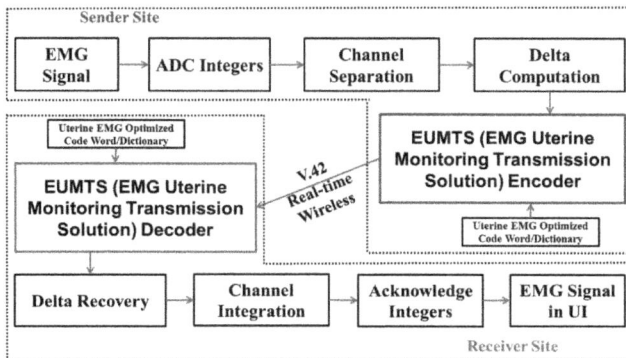

Figure 4. Functional diagram of the proposed system.

The EMG data are first obtained and converted to integers. Channels are then separated according to each EMG lead. Then, delta computation of the samples in each lead is implemented.

Variable bits are dynamically and appropriately allocated for each sample, according to the code word size. Note that the EMG samples originally have 32 bits (EMG machines collect samples in

4 bytes by default). An example histogram regarding the distribution curve of dynamic EMG records after delta computation is shown in Figure 5. An example record was randomly selected from those used in this study.

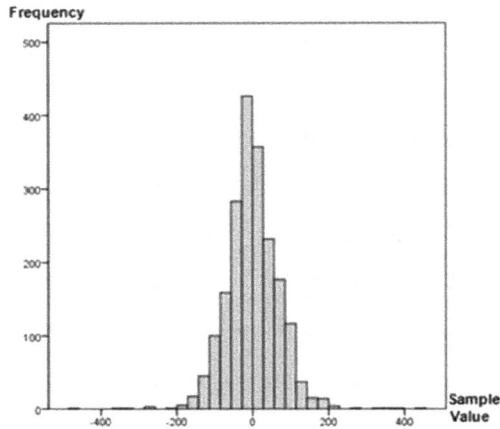

Figure 5. Distribution curve of example records after delta computation.

In Table 3, bit allocation is calculated from the selected example distributions shown in Figure 5. 8 bits (1 byte) were allocated to sample integers from -128 to 127, which were originally 32 bits, and 16 bits (2 bytes) were allocated to sample integers from $-32,768$ to -129 or from 128 to 32,767, which were also originally 32 bits.

Table 3. Frequency of Samples Allocated to 1 and 2 Bytes.

Size	Frequency	Percentage
1 byte	1904	95.2
2 bytes	96	4.8

EUMTS is then applied as the final process of the compression algorithm, creating the final compressed EMG data. Bit allocation and code word modification are the core processes of the EUMTS, and the main difference compared to our prior research [8]. As mentioned in Section 2.3, EMG data have a low redundancy (Table 4). Of the total of 2000 samples, 638 (31.4%) were redundant. Thus, the sample diversity was 1372 (based on Figure 5 and Table 3); therefore, a different code length compared to in cases of high redundancy was needed, not to mention a different dictionary. The proposed algorithm was modified accordingly, and was optimized for the characteristics of EMG signals.

Table 4. Low Redundancy in EMG Signals.

Classification	Frequency	Percentage
Redundant samples	628	31.4
Sample diversity	1372	68.6
Total	2000	100

Efficiently compressed data by EUMTS (lossless) is then transferred by real-time wireless transmission. At the receiver site, the decoding process is the opposite. EUMTS decodes the compressed signal based on a uterine EMG optimized code word/dictionary, delta computed values are recovered, and channels are integrated. Finally, integers are acknowledged and the receiver end users (usually clinicians) check the EMG signal in user interface form.

3.3. Specifications for Real-Time Wireless Transmission

The EUMTS was based on V.42 bis [26]. This is because V.42 bis functions as a wireless transmission environment for real-time compressing and sending data for dictionary-based Lempel-Ziv Welch (LZW) variant methods, enabling the proposed solution to transmit data in real-time packet units. In other words, the proposed algorithm is not a static method that saves, compresses, and transmits EMG signals. The proposed algorithm dynamically compresses and sends real-time EMG signals by data packets. The main specifications of V.42 bis are shown in Figure 6.

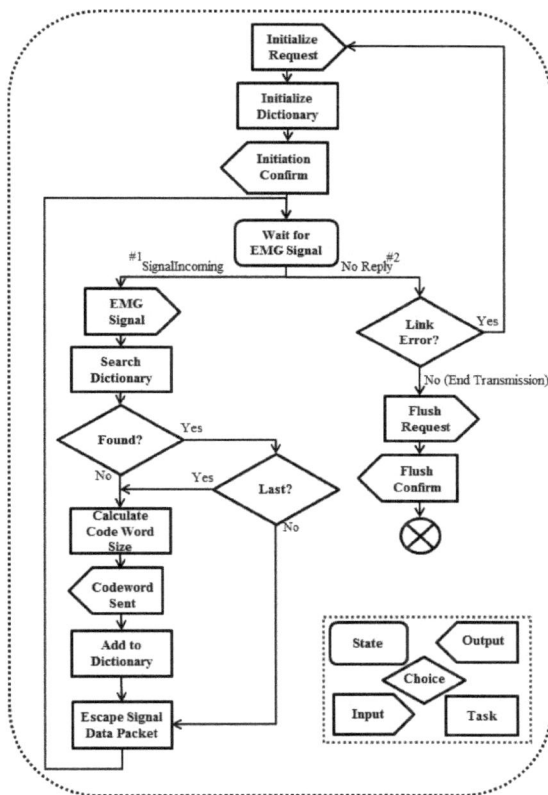

Figure 6. Flow chart specifications of compressing & transmitting real-time data of EUMTS.

After initiating a request and confirming that initiation, the algorithm processes dictionary codes by EMG signal data packets. In scenario #1, the code word and dictionary are calculated, as long as there are incoming signals transmitted in data packets. If the signal sample is not found in the dictionary, it calculates a new code word size, and adds it to the dictionary. The end procedure always matches the newly initialized string signal sequence, so that strings are matched real-time. If the signal sample is found in the dictionary, there is no need for further dictionary addition, so it escapes and waits for another signal sequence. This way, the EMG signal dictionary is trained in real-time through our proposed algorithm. There is no need for delays deriving from statically saving and compressing.

If there is no reply in the incoming character, check first if it's due to a link error. If an error has occurred, re-initiate the request. If it is not an error and it is the end of transmission, request and confirm the flush and end algorithm. The main role of the flush function is to meet the needs of the real-time dynamic bit allocation transmission of LZW. If an error occurs and an empty bit occurs, the flush function fills the empty bit with 0 integer values. Constructed on the real-time specifications of V.42 bis, the proposed algorithm supports dynamic real-time transmission in packet units. In the evaluation Section, the compression performance of the developed algorithm is evaluated.

4. Results

4.1. Materials and Methods

EMG data samples were obtained from the Physionet PhysioBank database [27]. Among the signal databases provided by Physionet, the Term-Preterm EHG Database (TPEHG DB,) was used. According to Physionet, the data were obtained at the Department of Obstetrics and Gynecology of the University Medical Centre, Ljubljana.

The TPEHG DB contains 300 uterine EMG records from 300 pregnant women. Each record consisted of 12 EMG channels, and the sampling frequency was 20 Hz (sampling interval of 0.05 s). In this evaluation, 30 records were randomly chosen for evaluation, each with a length of 2000 samples. As mentioned in Section 3.2, each sample had a resolution of 32 bits.

Solution performance comparisons were conducted for widely used algorithms (LZW, Huffman), and then for related researches. Statistical analysis was conducted using SPSS ver. 23 (IBM, New York, NY, USA). The C programming language was used for algorithm programming, development, and evaluation, with Microsoft Visual Studio 2016 (Microsoft, New York, NY, USA).

4.2. Compression Ratio Results

To evaluate the compression performance of the proposed algorithm, the LZW [28,29] and Huffman [30] algorithms, the most widely used compression algorithms, were first used for comparison. The compression ratio (*CR*) was calculated using the following Equation (1), where *US* is the uncompressed size and *CS* is the compressed size:

$$CR = US/CS \tag{1}$$

A comparison of the *CR* with those of other widely used algorithms is shown in Table 5. LZW and Huffman showed *CR*s of 1.87 and 1.90, respectively, compared to 3.61 for the proposed algorithm, thus exhibiting a significant difference. Therefore, the proposed algorithm yielded a more efficient compression.

Table 5. Comparison of *CR* with those of other algorithms.

CR Values	LZW	Huffman	Proposed Algorithm
Average ± Standard Deviation	1.87 ± 0.03	1.90 ± 0.01	3.61 ± 0.01

For a further subjective evaluation of the performance of the proposed algorithm, a comparison with prior studies was conducted. Few studies of lossless compression of EMG signals of maternal subjects are extant, but recent researches similar to this study were used. Note that the percentage residual difference (*PRD*) is calculated according to Equation (2).

$$PRD = \sqrt{\frac{\sum_{n=0}^{K-1} (x[n] - \hat{x}[n])^2}{\sum_{n=0}^{K-1} x^2[n]}} \times 100\% \tag{2}$$

In Equation (2), x is the uncompressed original signal and $\hat{x}$ is the reconstructed signal after compression. In addition, K is the total sample length of the signal. For instance, the length of K is 2000 in the proposed experiment. A comparison of the *PRD* and *CR* of the proposed algorithm and previous researches is shown in Table 6.

Table 6. Comparison of *CR* with related researches.

Related Researches	PRD	CR	Lossy/Lossless	Real-Time
Balouchestani [14]	0.10	2.00	Lossy	Not Able
Itiki [15]	0.00	1.69	Lossless	Not Able
Norris [16]	3.90	3.33	Lossy	Not Able
Berger [17]	1.79	3.33	Lossy	Not Able
Filho [18]	1.21	3.33	Lossy	Not Able
Trabuco [7]	2.12	3.33	Lossy	Not Able
Proposed algorithm	0.00	3.61	Lossless	Able

For an objective comparison, a *CR* under similar circumstances to *PRD* was compared, because the proposed algorithm was lossy (*PRD* of 0). The lower the *PRD*, the lower the loss rate. Balouchestani reported a *CR* of 2.00, and Itiki a *CR* of 1.69. Norris, Berger, Filho, and Trabuco reported *CRs* of 3.33, but different *PRD* values. The *PRD* values of Norris, Berger, Filho, and Trabuco were 3.90, 1.79, 1.21, and 2.12, respectively.

The proposed algorithm was more efficient (*CR*, 3.61) than those in previous studies. Additionally, Balouchestani, Norris, Berger, Filho, and Trabuco had markedly higher *PRD* values than the proposed algorithm. Although not proposed in their research, their compression performances will be far lower in close-to-zero *PRD* situations.

4.3. Execution Time Difference Results

Basically, microcontrollers are in a 'wake-up' state when processing or transmitting data, and are in a 'sleep' state when not. The duration of time during which the microcontroller is in a 'wake-up' state is when it consumes its battery.

The algorithm contributes to reducing the battery consumption by reducing the packet size of transmitted data, because the transmitting data time is reduced. However, battery consumption not only depends on the transmission time (transmission time needed per packet, *tt*), but also on the processor load (processing time needed per packet, *pt*). The higher the processor load, the higher the consumption, because the processing time (wake-up time) is increased. Since the algorithm increases the processor load, there is some trade-off between transmission time and processing time. Therefore, an assessment of the complex algorithm's contribution to the overall effect in computing time (total computing operations time per packet, *ct*) is needed, and is thus evaluated in this section. The relation between *pt*, *tt*, and *ct* follows Equation (3), and is shown in an example situation in Figure 7.

$$\begin{cases} ct = pt \ (if \ pt > tt) \\ ct = tt \ (if \ pt < tt) \end{cases} \tag{3}$$

Two conditions A and B must be compared for an evaluation of the algorithm's effect on *ct*. A is the time per packet needed to process and transmit data packets using the original system, and B is the time per packet needed to process and transmit data packets using the algorithm that is applied to the original system. The specific steps used to assess A and B are depicted in Figure 8.

To assess the *ct* of A, first set the timer on, input the EMG data, packetize for transmission, transmit the data packets, unpacketize the data, output the EMG data, and set the timer off. On the other hand, to assess the *ct* of B, also set the timer on, input the EMG data, compress the data using EUMTS, packetize for transmission, transmit the data packets, unpacketize the data, uncompress the data using an EUMTS decoder, output the EMG data, and set the timer off. Note that the packet size used in this experiment is 20 samples, because Bluetooth usually sends one packet per second, and because the database used here is 20 Hz. Results of the A and B time comparison in milliseconds are shown in Table 7.

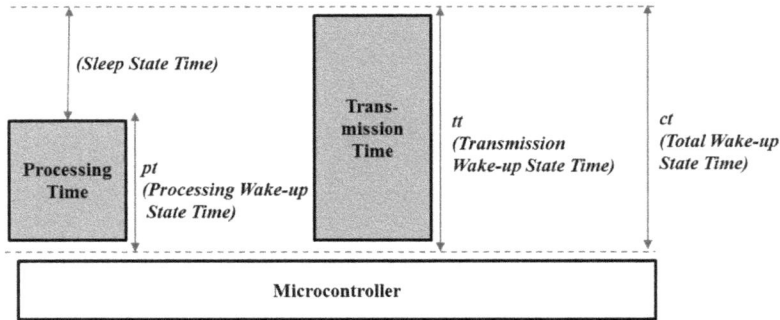

Figure 7. Example relation between *pt*, *tt*, and *ct* when *tt* is longer than *pt*.

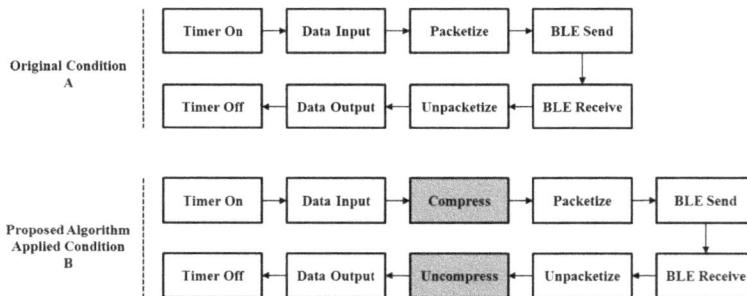

Figure 8. Comparison between original process and proposed algorithm applied process.

Table 7. Operation Second Per Packet Comparison between A and B (Milliseconds, ms).

Conditions	*pt*	*tt*	*ct*
A	2.0 ms	2340.6 ms	2340.6 ms
B	870.0 ms	648.4 ms	870.0 ms

The processor used for evaluation was a recent updated version of microcontroller 8051 that is suitable for wearable operating systems. The network environment was Bluetooth 4.2 Low Energy. Using the database mentioned in Section 4.1, 12 channels of EMG data containing 1000 packets (20,000 samples) in each channel were used in this experiment (size approximately 2 MB).

The results showed that, naturally, the complexity of the proposed algorithm increased the processing time needed per packet from 2.0 ms to 870.0 ms (*pt*). However, EUMTS contributed to the largely decreasing transmission time needed per packet from 2340.6 ms to 648.4 ms, by efficiently compressing the data packet size (*tt*). In conclusion, in spite of a trade-off between the processing time and transmission time, the overall computation time decreased from 2340.6 ms to 870.0 ms (*ct*), thereby contributing to reducing the battery consumption of microcontrollers. In other words, by using the proposed algorithm, the total wake-up state needed in order to process and transmit data decreased for the 8051 microcontroller.

5. Discussion and Conclusions

This research proposed EUMTS, a seamless, lossless real-time transmission solution for the monitoring of preterm birth. A previously published algorithm was modified and applied to uterine EMG signals and optimized for uterine EMG. The developed algorithm had a higher *CR* and lower *PRD* than other widely used algorithms and those proposed by others.

A higher compression digital signal ratio is important, especially for screening for pre-term birth. Without compression, the massive size of the EMG data overloads the network, resulting in network outages and a high battery-power consumption. The results in this proposed research showed that the proposed algorithm contributes to a reduction in battery consumption by reducing the wake-up time by 1470.6 ms. A unique compression technique has additional external affects such as network security and preventing privacy issues [31], blocking any trespassers trying to interrupt the medical system network.

Using the proposed algorithm, maternal EMG signals can be transmitted seamlessly through telemedicine networks. Signals can be compressed with a high efficiency, with more data being transmitted at a higher speed under limited bandwidth situations [32]. Also, the data recovery time is reduced, even if errors occur.

Moreover, digital EMG signals are important indicators of maternal health, and any data loss leads to the possibility of clinical decision errors. The solution proposed in this study is a lossless transmission solution, and is appropriate for EMG signals because EMG signals are precious indicators and information of patients.

The proposed study is also a real-time supporting transmission solution, which is especially fit for telemedicine systems where immediate intervention from medical experts is needed in cases of emergency [33].

In conclusion, EUMTS will contribute to providing a safe, seamless environment for the prediction of pre-term delivery so that immediate interventions by medical professionals can be applied. Pre-term babies may receive appropriate care immediately after birth, before being exposed to infection or contamination, thereby preventing the development of disabilities. Future research should include imbedding the solution algorithm inside a practical EMG acquiring device and performing real tests to measure the power consumption and real-time performance. Moreover, a compatible smartphone app that provides support and advice to the pregnant women should be developed.

Acknowledgments: This research was funded by Korea University, Seoul, South Korea. [Grant number K1605491].

Author Contributions: Gyoun-Yon Cho is the first author and the head developer of this research. Seo-Joon Lee analyzed the data, performed the evaluation, and wrote the article. Tae-Ro Lee is the corresponding author and managed the overall research.

Conflicts of Interest: The authors declare no conflict of interest.

References

1. World Health Organization. Preterm Birth. Available online: http://www.who.int/mediacentre/factsheets/fs363/en/ (accessed on 24 November 2016).
2. World Health Organization. *Born Too Soon the Global Action Report on Preterm Birth*; World Health Organization: Geneva, Switzerland, 2012.
3. Zakane, S.A.; Gustafsson, L.L.; Tomson, G.; Loukanova, S.; Sie, A.; Nasiell, J.; Bastholm-Rahmner, P. Guidelines for maternal and neonatal "point of care": Needs of and attitudes towards a computerized clinical decision support system in rural burkina faso. *Int. J. Med. Inform.* **2014**, *83*, 459–469. [CrossRef] [PubMed]
4. Vinken, M.P.G.C.; Rabotti, C.; Mischi, M.; Oei, S.G. Accuracy of frequency-related parameters of the electrohysterogram for predicting preterm delivery a review of the literature. *Obstet. Gynecol. Surv.* **2009**, *64*, 529–541. [CrossRef] [PubMed]

5. Alamedine, D.; Khalil, M.; Marque, C. Parameters extraction and monitoring in uterine emg signals. Detection of preterm deliveries. *IRBM* **2013**, *34*, 322–325. [CrossRef]

6. Principe, J.C.; Maroserro, D.; Euliano, T.Y.; Neil, R.E.I.I. System and Method for Analyzing Progress of Labor and Preterm Labor. US Patent 8160692 B2, 17 April 2012.

7. Trabuco, M.H.; Costa, M.V.C.; de Oliveira Nascimento, F.A. S-emg signal compression based on domain transformation and spectral shape dynamic bit allocation. *Biomed. Eng. Online* **2014**, *13*, 22. [CrossRef] [PubMed]

8. Cho, G.-Y.; Lee, S.-J.; Lee, T.-R. An optimized compression algorithm for real-time ECG data transmission in wireless network of medical information systems. *J. Med. Syst.* **2015**, *39*, 161. [CrossRef] [PubMed]

9. Microchip Technology Inc. *Bluetooth 4.2 Dual-Mode Module, BM 78*; Microchip Technology Inc.: Chandler, AZ, USA, 2016.

10. Carlo, C. IoT Wireless Sensors and the Problem of Short Battery Life. Available online: http://www.eenewsanalog.com/news/iot-wireless-sensors-and-problem-short-battery-life (accessed on 6 April 2017).

11. Hussain, A.J.; Fergus, P.; Al-Askar, H.; Al-Jumeily, D.; Jager, F. Dynamic neural network architecture inspired by the immune algorithm to predict preterm deliveries in pregnant women. *Neurocomputing* **2015**, *151*, 963–974. [CrossRef]

12. Ren, P.; Yao, S.; Li, J.; Valdes-Sosa, P.A.; Kendrick, K.M. Improved prediction of preterm delivery using empirical mode decomposition analysis of uterine electromyography signals. *PLoS ONE* **2015**, *10*, e0132116. [CrossRef] [PubMed]

13. Smrdel, A.; Jager, F. Separating sets of term and pre-term uterine emg records. *Physiol. Meas.* **2015**, *36*, 341–355. [CrossRef] [PubMed]

14. Balouchestani, M.; Krishnan, S. Robust compressive sensing algorithm for wireless surface electromyography applications. *Biomed. Signal Process. Control* **2015**, *20*, 100–106. [CrossRef]

15. Itiki, C.; Furuie, S.S.; Merletti, R. Compression of high-density emg signals for trapezius and gastrocnemius muscles. *Biomed. Eng. Online* **2014**, *13*, 25. [CrossRef] [PubMed]

16. Norris, J.A.; Englehart, K.; Lovely, D. Steady-State and Dynamic Myoelectric Signal Compression Using Embedded Zero-Tree Wavelets. In Proceedings of the 23rd Annual International Conference of the IEEE Engineering in Medicine and Biology Society, Istanbul, Turkey, 25–28 October 2001; pp. 1879–1882.

17. Berger, P.; Nascimento, F.A.; Rocha, A.F.; Carvalho, J.L. A new wavelet-based algorithm for compression of emg signals. In Proceedings of the 29th Annual International Conference of the IEEE Engineering in Medicine and Biology Society, Lyon, France, 22–26 August 2007; pp. 1554–1557.

18. Filho, E.B.; Silva, E.A.; de Carvalho, M.B. On emg signal compression with recurrent patterns. *IEEE Trans. Biomed. Eng.* **2008**, *55*, 1920–1923. [CrossRef] [PubMed]

19. Steer, P.J. The epidemiology of preterm labour-why have advances not equated to reduced incidence? *BJOG Int. J. Obstet. Gynaecol.* **2008**, *115*, 674–675. [CrossRef] [PubMed]

20. World Health Organization. *Who Recommendations on Interventions to Improve Preterm Birth Outcomes*; World Health Organization: Geneva, Switzerland, 2015.

21. Cho, G.-Y.; Lee, S.-J.; Lee, T.-R. Research on a solution for efficient ecg data transmission in iot environment. *KIPS Trans. Comput. Commun. Syst.* **2014**, *3*, 371–376. [CrossRef]

22. Lee, S.-J.; Cho, G.-Y.; Song, S.-H.; Jang, J.-S.; Lee, K.-I.; Lee, T.-R. Solution for efficient vital data transmission and storing in m-health environment. *J. Dig. Converg.* **2015**, *13*, 227–235. [CrossRef]

23. Yon, C.G.; Lee, S.-J.; Lee, T.R. Research on a solution for efficient ecg data transmission in u-healthcare environment. *J. Dig. Converg.* **2014**, *12*, 397–403.

24. Lee, S.-J.; Sim, H.-J.; Lee, A.-R.; Lee, T.-R. The design of maternity monitoring system using usn in maternity hospital. *J. Dig. Converg.* **2013**, *11*, 347–354.

25. Vinekar, A.; Jayadev, C.; Mangalesh, S.; Shetty, B.; Vidyasagar, D. Role of tele-medicine in retinopathy of prematurity screening in rural outreach centers in india—a report of 20,214 imaging sessions in the kidrop program. *Sem. Fetal Neonat. Med.* **2015**, *20*, 335–345. [CrossRef] [PubMed]

26. International Telecommunication Union. I.T. *Data Compression Procedures for Data Circuit Terminating Equipment (DCE) Using Error Correction Procedures*; International Telecommunication Union: Geneva, Switzerland, 1990.

27. Goldberger, A.L.; Amaral, L.A.N.; Glass, L.; Hausdorff, J.M.; Ivanov, P.C.; Mark, R.G.; Mietus, J.E.; Moody, G.B.; Peng, C.K.; Stanley, H.E. Physiobank, physiotoolkit, and physionet-components of a new research resource for complex physiologic signals. *Circulation* **2000**, *101*, E215–E220. [CrossRef] [PubMed]

28. Ziv, J.; Lempel, A. Universal algorithm for sequential data compression. *IEEE Trans. Inf. Theory* **1977**, *23*, 337–343. [CrossRef]

29. Ziv, J.; Lempel, A. Compression of individual sequences via variable-rate coding. *IEEE Trans. Inf. Theory* **1978**, *24*, 530–536. [CrossRef]

30. Salomon, D. *A Concise Introduction to Data Compression*; Springer: London, UK, 2008.

31. Camara, C.; Pens-Lopez, P.; Tapiador, J.E. Security and privacy issues in implantable medical devices: A comprehensive survey. *J. Biomed. Inf.* **2015**, *55*, 272–289. [CrossRef] [PubMed]

32. Kumar, R.; Kumar, A.; Singh, G.K. Hybrid method based on singular value decomposition and embedded zero tree wavelet technique for ecg signal compression. *Comput. Methods Progr. Biomed.* **2016**, *129*, 135–148. [CrossRef] [PubMed]

33. Lin, B.S. A seamless ubiquitous emergency medical service for crisis situations. *Comput. Methods Progr. Biomed.* **2016**, *126*, 89–97. [CrossRef] [PubMed]

applied
sciences

MDPI

Article

IoT-Based Information System for Healthcare Application: Design Methodology Approach

Damian Dziak [1,*], Bartosz Jachimczyk [2] and Wlodek J. Kulesza [3]

[1] Faculty of Electrical and Control Engineering, Gdansk University of Technology, G. Narutowicza 11/12, 80-233 Gdansk, Poland
[2] BetterSolutions S.A., Al. Grunwaldzka 472, 80-309 Gdansk, Poland; bartosz.jachimczyk@bettersolutions.pl
[3] Department of Applied Signal Processing, Blekinge Institute of Technology, 371 79 Karlskrona, Sweden; wlodek.kulesza@bth.se
* Correspondence: damian.dziak@pg.gda.pl; Tel.: +48-58-347-29-45

Academic Editor: Wenbing Zhao
Received: 28 April 2017; Accepted: 3 June 2017; Published: 8 June 2017

Abstract: Over the last few decades, life expectancy has increased significantly. However, elderly people who live on their own often need assistance due to mobility difficulties, symptoms of dementia or other health problems. In such cases, an autonomous supporting system may be helpful. This paper proposes the Internet of Things (IoT)-based information system for indoor and outdoor use. Since the conducted survey of related works indicated a lack of methodological approaches to the design process, therefore a Design Methodology (DM), which approaches the design target from the perspective of the stakeholders, contracting authorities and potential users, is introduced. The implemented solution applies the three-axial accelerometer and magnetometer, Pedestrian Dead Reckoning (PDR), thresholding and the decision trees algorithm. Such an architecture enables the localization of a monitored person within four room-zones with accuracy; furthermore, it identifies falls and the activities of lying, standing, sitting and walking. Based on the identified activities, the system classifies current activities as normal, suspicious or dangerous, which is used to notify the healthcare staff about possible problems. The real-life scenarios validated the high robustness of the proposed solution. Moreover, the test results satisfied both stakeholders and future users and ensured further cooperation with the project.

Keywords: accelerometers; activity recognition; classification algorithms; design methodology; fall detection; healthcare; dead reckoning; thresholding

1. Introduction

Nowadays, life expectancy significantly differs from that of 25 years ago. Research of the World Health Organization [1] indicates that over the last 25 years, life expectancy in Poland lengthened six years. Moreover, the research of Kontis et al. shows that with high probability, by the year 2030, life expectancy could lengthen for another three years [2]. However, men's and women's life expectancy differs in most cases in favor of women, e.g., in Poland by eight years. Such a situation causes a significant part of the elderly population to live alone. In some cases, such people have mobility difficulties, symptoms of dementia or other health problems, but still would prefer to live in their homes and surroundings. Therefore, there is a need for information systems that could facilitate such a life without compromising people's safety. This can be done by means of an autonomous system, which monitors people's position and their vital signs and is able to distinguish different activities and situations, reacts accordingly to the degree of danger and alarms, e.g., appropriate services or caregivers.

The aim of this paper is to propose an Internet of Things (IoT)-based healthcare information system intended for indoor and outdoor use where a methodological approach to the design process is in focus. A distinguishing feature of this approach is that the contracting authority's and future users' perspectives and needs are included in most stages of the design process. Moreover, in the proposed approach, the designer from the beginning has to think comprehensively to merge human and technical constraints and requirements. The proposed user-driven Design Methodology (DM) is used to solve the problems of the real-life scenario of supporting seniors living alone, especially those with limited abilities to manage their daily lives. The conducted design process results in a system proposal that meets the required assumptions.

The conducted case studies verified that the designed system, consisting of the Inertial Measurement Unit (IMU) with a built-in three-axis accelerometer, gyroscope, magnetometer and altimeter, together with Wi-Fi and heart rate modules and applying thresholding, Pedestrian Dead Reckoning (PDR) and decision trees algorithms, works properly in the tested real environment. The achieved person's localization accuracy within one meter fits the required four room-zone level localization accuracy in an apartment environment. The developed fall detection algorithm proved effectiveness of 98%, and other required activities were recognized with 95% compliance. Moreover, the proposed behavior classification algorithm is able to distinguish normal behaviors from suspicious and dangerous ones, working properly in almost 100% of cases.

2. Survey of Related Work

The Design Methodology (DM) of a product or system has been of interest to many researchers. Already in 1991, A. McKnight proposed a definition of DM as " . . . a sequence of activities required to get from one stage of the design process to another" [3].

K. Prasad and H. Kobayashi, in order to improve hardware description language design productivity, propose the nine-step multi-methodology design process model consisting of system specification, system partitioning, modeling or adaptation, component simulation, system binding, system simulation, pre-synthesis modification, logic synthesis and logic simulation [4]. Their solution enables the diminution of the time required for modeling and simulation-related activities by 31% and 16%, respectively, compared to the classical hardware description language-based design.

The design methodology proposed by S. A. Mengel et al. contains the three stages: requirements, specification and implementation [5]. At the requirements stage, the designers should focus on the key concept of the problem and propose a graph with the structure of the system. At the specification stage, they refine the proposed graph into the content flowchart, which should be easily implementable into the considered system in the last design stage. Moreover, after each DM stage, the validation and verification should be carried out to ensure that the key concepts would have been met.

To improve the productivity of the complex electronics system design, H. Eskelinen proposes to apply two questionnaires to the traditional four-stage electronics system design, which are: system design, electronics design, mechanical design and design for manufacturing [6]. Those questionnaires are used to form requirements lists of electronic system components.

F. Wang and M. J. Hannafin state that the design-based research should be "pragmatic, grounded, interactive, iterative, flexible, integrative, and contextual" [7]. Based on this assumption they form nine principles of the design-based research: support design with research from the outset; set practical goals for theory development and develop an initial plan; conduct the research in representative real-world settings; collaborate closely with participants; implement research methods systematically and purposefully; analyze data immediately, continuously and retrospectively; refine designs continually; document contextual influences with design principles; and validate the generalizability of the design.

A. Saini and P. Yammiyavar chose the user as the focal point of the design of m-health system [8]. They use the object-oriented system design methodology, typical for software development, and then study interactions and relationships between the system requirements and the components of the user's needs and goals. User-driven design becomes especially useful in health applications, where the stakeholders and different kinds of users may express different requirements and constraints.

The suggested DM approach of M. Ahmad considers five design aspects: the target field failure rate, expected use environment, expected environment use conditions, expected enclosure use conditions and expected product internal conditions [9]. The method is applicable to estimate the target's lifetime in the Internet of Things (IoT). It uses the probabilistic approach for estimating hardware reliability with given uncertain use conditions while considering overall system reliability.

Emerging technologies create new opportunities, and the robust monitoring of persons or things, alike, in indoor and outdoor environments, becomes of interest to many scientific and industrial applications, where one of the most important is the healthcare domain. However, the conducted survey reveals that design methodologies, despite their efficacy, have not yet been of great interest to designers in the field of healthcare information systems in IoT. The emerging healthcare applications are possible due to the development in Micro-Electro-Mechanical Systems (MEMS), which enable the integration of various devices like actuators, sensor nodes or mobiles [10,11].

It is preferable that the devices used for monitoring purposes operate wirelessly [12], forming Wireless Sensor Networks (WSNs), which constitute the substantial part of IoT [13]. WSNs are widely used in healthcare applications due to their advantages and diversity. In [14], C. Rotariu and V. Manta propose WSN for monitoring patients' heart rate and oxygen saturation. W. Y. Chung, S. C. Lee and S. H. Toh embed Electrocardiography (ECG) and blood pressure sensors into a cellular phone [15]. The wireless body area network is an example of a suitable approach to the IoT healthcare paradigm. S. -L. Tan, J. Garcia-Guzman and F. Villa-Lopez use Wi-Fi technology to transmit data about the blood pressure, heart rate, body temperature and oxygen saturation to the base station [16]. J. Wannenburg and R. Malekianc apply Bluetooth technology and a smartphone for monitoring the patient's health parameters [17].

In IoT healthcare applications, one of the most frequently-monitored issues is the localization of patient or equipment. For this purpose, depending on the application, various methods and technologies are used. Numerous approaches are based on Received Signal Strength (RSS) [18]. M. Shchekotov uses RSS measurements from several known Wi-Fi access points assuring the localization accuracy at a four room-zone level on a single floor of a building. In order to localize an asset in the healthcare environment, the authors of [19] use the existing infrastructure of the Wireless Local Area Network (WLAN), extended just with six access point beacons. Based on Wi-Fi RSS measurements and small Wi-Fi tags, they are able to localize the assets like wheelchairs, beds, etc., with an accuracy of about 2 m in the hospital clinic environment of 63 m × 46 m size. W. H. Chen et al. use RFID RSS measurements of the reference and monitored tags to estimate the cost function consisting of the disparity and similarity of RSS between monitored and reference tags [20]. In this way, the three optimal reference tags are found, and the position of the monitored tag is determined as the center of mass of the triangle, which they form. The average localization error of a patient or asset in a 5 m × 10 m healthcare environment is about 0.74 m. F. Palumbo et al. propose the stigmergy approach combined with RSS measurements of Bluetooth Low Energy (BLE) [21]. Their approach results in a localization error of less than 1.8 m in 75% cases in a 6 m × 6 m furnished office. J. Wyffels et al. propose a healthcare dedicated indoor localization algorithm based on BLE RSS measurements and least squares-support vector machine, resulting at the four room-zone level localization accuracy [22]. The authors of [23] focus on patients' localization, tracking and monitoring in the nursing institute environment. They use RSS measurements of the ZigBee standard and a particle filter. As a result, they achieved an average localization error of less than 2 m in 80% of cases.

Different algorithms and methods can be used to improve the localization accuracy. In [24], the authors use the Radio Frequency Identification (RFID) fingerprints method and the artificial neural network, which enables a 3D localization accuracy of about 70 cm within a room-sized environment. A different approach to the indoor localization problem is shown in [25] where the authors used fingerprints of Wi-Fi and barometric pressure to localize a target with the floor accuracy of a six-floor building. Their Barometer-aided Wi-Fi (BarFi) floor localization approach detects the target's floor correctly in 96.3% of cases.

An interesting solution of the Pedestrian Dead Reckoning (PDR) algorithm is presented by Kang and Han in [26]. They use data from off-the-shelf three-axis gyroscope, magnetometer and accelerometer smartphone sensors in an in-building environment. The proposed method ensures the mean localization accuracy of 1.35 m with the maximum localization error of 1.62 m. The authors of [27] use data from the accelerometer, magnetometer and gyroscope to recognize a person's posture and to detect the tumbling of the person [28].

Information about the position of a monitored person or equipment is valuable not only for localization, but also it could be used for patient's behavior recognition. This is especially useful while monitoring the elderly living alone or a person at the first stages of dementia. For this purpose, L. Wang et al. apply coin-sized RFID readers on both hands of a patient and one accelerometer on the patient's waist [29]. Using this set, along with a passive RFID tag, they are able to recognize 25 different activities of the supervised person. H. Martin et al. are able to recognize a person's activities and body position by means of Google Nexus S embedded sensors like the magnetometer, gyroscope, accelerometer, light and proximity sensors and a fuzzy classifier [30].

Most of the mentioned monitoring solutions have the common drawback of being dedicated just to indoor environment applications. In the case of an outdoor healthcare monitoring purpose, most of the enable solutions apply the Global Positioning System (GPS) [31], which in the in-city environment provides localization accuracy of about 6 m. Ch. Wu et al. combine GPS data with gyroscope and accelerometer data using the dead reckoning algorithm, which results in an improvement of the in-city localization accuracy up to 4 m [32]. For outdoor behavior recognition, L. Sun et al. apply the mobile embedded accelerometer and Support Vector Machine (SVM)-based classifier, to recognize activities like bicycling, running and walking [33].

The mentioned monitoring solutions are dedicated exclusively to just one, an indoor or outdoor, environment. A multi-environment localization solution was proposed by Millner et al. in [34]. The authors, using the Symeo local positioning radar, are able to localize animals with an accuracy of 0.5 m in 75% of cases in both indoor and outdoor environments; however, the major constraint of the system is its applicability in an environment with low multipath distortions. J. Gonzalez et al. combine Ultra-Wide Band (UWB) and GPS technologies and a particle filter to localize a robot in the indoor and outdoor environments with a localization accuracy of about 2 m [35].

However, these multi-environmental solutions, in turn, are difficult to implement in healthcare applications inter alia due to the size of the devices used. A localization system relatively easily implemented in healthcare, both indoor and outdoor environments, is presented in [36]. It is based on RSS measurements in a ZigBee network [37]. The major drawback of this solution is a significant number of needed reference nodes with known positions and the maximum distance from the reference node of 15 m, which considerably reduces the applicability of the system from the large outdoor environment.

A promising approach to the multi-environmental patient monitoring system is proposed by R. Tabish et al. [38]. They propose a monitoring system of the patient's temperature and ECG based on 3G/Wi-Fi IPv6 over Low Power Wireless Personal Area Networks (6LoWPAN). While the monitored person occurs in an indoor environment, the system uses local Wi-Fi for sensors' data transfer, and in the case of the outdoor environment, the 3G/4G technology is applied. The drawback of this solution is a limited number of monitored vital parameters.

3. Problem Statement and Main Contributions

The number of related publications is enormous, and this review provides only examples of solutions, which in the authors' opinion give a map of the development fields. However, the review of related works indicates that although a variety of solutions is used in the IoT healthcare-monitoring domain for indoor and outdoor environments, a methodological approach to the design process is still missing; where design is understood as "scientific principles, technical information and imagination in the definition of a structure, machine or system to perform pre-specified functions with the maximum economy and efficiency" [39]. Furthermore, using a multi-environmental information system for behavior recognition and classification requires improvement and development.

To fill the gap in the methodological approach to the design of a comprehensive information system for healthcare applications, the objective of this paper is to propose a systematic design procedure, which can enhance the development of healthcare appliances. Apart from technical requirements, the procedure considers multifarious constraints, including the lifetime, energy efficiency, usage comfort and even the price. The case study of the design process is an IoT-based system for monitoring people and things multi-environmentally capable inter alia of behavior recognition and diagnosis. The system is dedicated to support and localize elderly people in their multi-room apartments along with a multi-story building, but even outdoors in the building's surroundings. The system's functionalities consist of monitoring vital signs, posture recognition, suspicious behavior detection and classification.

The development procedure approaches the design target from the perspective of the stakeholders, the authority in charge and the potential users, as the view of the system developers. The proposed design methodology is modelled and then implemented and validated on the case study of the system for multi-environmental monitoring of elderly people living alone. The system has been implemented and validated in real scenarios.

4. Methodology of System Design

The problem of exclusive indoor or outdoor monitoring of patients or elderly people is complex; including both indoor and outdoor cases is even more compounded, especially in the case of IoT. Therefore, to carry out the design of such a system, we propose to systematize the design process. The proposed design methodology illustrated in Figure 1 is composed of two main stages: problem formulation and product development, each consisting of three different steps. Moreover, to avoid the omission of any important aspects of the designed system, the stakeholder's, future user's and designer's perspectives are taken into consideration at each stage of the design process.

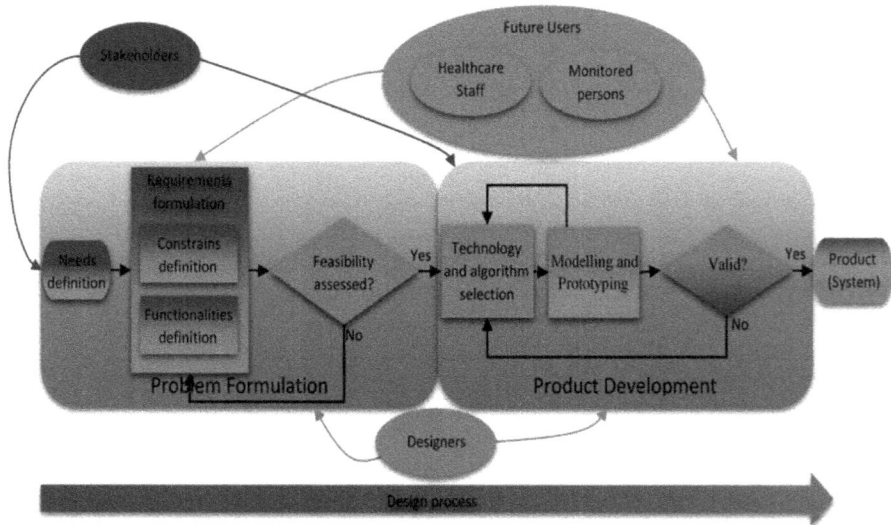

Figure 1. Flowchart of the proposed design methodology.

4.1. Problem Formulation

The problem formulation stage consists of three steps: need definition, requirement formulation and feasibility assessment. Since an essential aspect of the proposed DM is the involvement of all project contributors, i.e., stakeholders, future users and designers, each of them may have a contribution to the problem formulation. However, their goals and expectations of the future system can differ. For example, the user can focus on convenience, safety and confidentiality; the healthcare staff may aim at the system's reliability, ease of operation and maintenance, along with the utility of the obtained information. The stakeholders additionally consider financial and marketing aspects of the product, and then, the designers focus on the design tools and their knowledge and experience.

4.1.1. Needs Definition

This step begins the design process when the stakeholders introduce to the designers the concept and define the general problem. In the proposed DM, this stage should be performed together with the future users in order to include their desires. With such an approach, both stakeholders and future users can express their needs and expectations of the outcome of the working system. In this step, participants should not focus on detailed requirements, but rather general goals of the system, so that the designers would be able to preliminarily assess whether the problem is solvable with their resources.

4.1.2. Requirements Formulation

The requirements formulation is the essential step of the proposed DM. At this stage, the stakeholders and future users firstly formulate the desired system's functionalities such as fall detection or localization of monitored person. Furthermore, the constraints associated with the developed system like costs, size and required lifetime are introduced. In a case of multi-environmental usage, the functionalities and constraints in each of the considered environments have to be defined. These functionalities and constraints constitute the requirements for the designers; moreover, this is how the stakeholders and future users can indirectly affect the structure of the developed healthcare system.

4.1.3. Feasibility Assessment

The designers have to assess the feasibility of the general needs and specified requirements formulated by the stakeholders and future users. Moreover, they have to consider whether the existing possible solutions are able to solve the stated problems and assess whether the needs and requirements are realizable at all. The designers have to take into account also the constraints resulting from the desired working environments. If the designers encounter a problem in accomplishing the requirements, the stakeholders and future users would be asked to modify the requirements in a way that can satisfy them. After assessing that, all requirements can be met, and then, the product development stage can begin.

4.2. Product Development

Usually, due to the challenging trade-offs and diversity of the desired functionalities and constraints, the selection of suitable technologies and algorithms has to be carried out carefully in the following three steps: technologies and algorithms' selection; modeling and prototyping; and then solution validation. Furthermore, at this design phase, the stakeholders and future users are involved; however, it is the designers' responsibility to lead the dialog with all contributors. The main duty of the future users and stakeholders during the product development is to supervise whether all of their needs and requirements are implemented. After verification of the functionalities and constraints, the eventual necessary improvements can be postulated.

4.2.1. Technologies and Algorithms Selection

At this stage, the designers propose technologies and algorithms, which are in line with the desired functionalities and constraints stated by the stakeholders and future users at the problem formulation step. Then, in choosing technologies and algorithms, the constraints arising from the environment, like indoor/outdoor or high humidity, in which the designed system will operate, have to be considered. Furthermore, the suitable technologies and algorithms have to be pondered with respect to the price constraint, and then, after the primary elimination, only a few possible solutions would remain; therefore, the price may indicate the final decision. However, if there are no suitable solutions accomplishing the requirements, or the solutions lack some of the functionalities or constraints, then the designers have to propose and develop new solutions or adapt the existing ones.

4.2.2. Modeling and Prototyping

Modeling and prototyping the system are the main tasks of the designers. These tasks require the most time and may involve experts of different fields. However, in user-oriented design, the models and prototypes have to be endorsed by both designers and future users. This is an iterative process. The designers evaluate the solution's performance, and the future users check if the functionalities and constraints defined by them are accomplished. If something is missing or needs an improvement, the designers have to get rid of bugs and complement any shortcomings. The process continues until all contributors are satisfied. Then, the final outcome has to be validated.

4.2.3. Validation

The stakeholders along with the designers have to validate whether all system's needs and requirements have been accomplished. Now, it is also possible to verify the costs of the product and accept the price. In the case of any discrepancy between the desired needs and requirements and the prototyped multi-environmental healthcare information system, the designers have to examine the proposed technologies and algorithms and come back to the initial stage of product development. Nevertheless, if both stakeholders and designers approve the results, the system is ready to be implemented and launched into a service.

5. Case Study: Problem Formulation

The proposed design methodology is implemented and validated on the case study of a healthcare system for multi-environmental monitoring of elderly people living alone in the Silesia region in Poland. The designed system can be used not only to support and localize the elderly people in their multi-room apartments located in multi-story buildings, but even outdoors in the buildings' neighborhood.

5.1. Needs Definition

The growing number of elderly people is a global problem, and many local authorities, also of the Polish region Silesia, acknowledge its importance and are working on it. The general needs and targets introduced by the stakeholders and future users represented by elderly people and their families have considered possibilities to support elderly people, especially those of limited mobility, living alone or patients with the first symptoms of dementia. The support can be yielded by means of an autonomous system monitoring the target's position, their vital signs and able to recognize different activities and even classify human behavior.

5.2. Requirements Formulation

The functionalities, desired by the stakeholders and future users, consist of the localization of the monitored person in his or her apartment with up to four room-zone level accuracy, but also within a multi-story building, where the apartment is located, with a floor level accuracy. Furthermore, the person's positioning in the building's outdoor neighborhood with an accuracy of at least 10 m is desired. Moreover, the system, in all of these surroundings, should be able to monitor the target's vital signs and even detect the person's fall.

To recognize the required behavioral changes of the monitored person, in addition to the localization and fall detection, there is a need to distinguish the person's postures, like sitting, standing, walking or lying. It is even requested that the system should classify if a current behavior is normal, suspicious or dangerous for the monitored person and, in the case of unusual occurrences, notify the people responsible for care. In the instance of conduct that is classified as suspicious or dangerous, a subsidiary part should provide supplementary information about some vital signs.

According to a division of constraints into the two categories of general and particular, the reliability, size and comfort of device-wearing and even a maximum price of 200 EUR for the complete system are classified as the general constraints of the system. Moreover, the demands that the system should be easy to install, operate and maintain and even assure the subject's privacy are also the general constraints of the system. The operational time of at least one week, necessary for many reasons, can be categorized as particular. The localization accuracy in the considered environments along with the reliabilities of activities and fall recognition are particular constraints. Furthermore, real-time secure non-invasive measurements are crucial particular constraints of the vital signs' monitoring. The high validity of the behavior classification is also considered as a particular constraint. Both general and itemized functionalities, along with the particular requirements, are summarized in Table 1. The table consists of possible technologies and algorithms, and these, which fulfill the stated requirements, are bolded.

Table 1. Technologies and algorithms related to itemized functionalities and particular constraints.

Functionalities		Particular Constraints [1]	Possible Technologies and Algorithms [2]
General	Itemized		
Localization	In apartment	four room-zones level accuracy	Bluetooth, **PDR**, RFID, Wi-Fi fingerprints, UWB
	In building	floor level accuracy	**Atmospheric pressure**, RFID/**Wi-Fi fingerprints**, Bluetooth, UWB
	Outdoor	10 m accuracy	Bluetooth, **GPS**, GSM, **PDR**, Wi-Fi
Activity recognition	Fall Lying Standing Sitting Walking	validity >95% validity >85%	**Accelerometer**, RFID, Wi-Fi, decision trees, genetic algorithms, neural networks, **thresholding**
Vital signs monitoring	Heart rate	non-invasive method	acoustic, electrocardiogram, **infrared**
Behavior classification	Normal Suspicious Danger	high validity	**Decision trees**, genetics algorithms, neural networks, **support vector machines, k-nearest neighborhood**
Control	Easy to handle	fast	**Inter-Integrated Circuit**, Serial Peripheral Interface
Communication	Possible long range up to 40 m	secure	Bluetooth, **Wi-Fi**, RFID

[1] General constraints: wearing comfort, convenience of use, high reliability, assuring privacy, reliable, one-week operation time; [2] selected technologies/algorithms are indicated in bold.

5.3. Feasibility Assessment

The needs, functionalities and constraints presented by both stakeholders and future users need to be scrutinized by the designer. After the comprehensive analysis, the general needs of a system supporting elderly people living alone with limited mobility or with the first signs of dementia are assessed as technically accomplishable and feasible. Furthermore, the performed research proved that the related functionalities and constraints concerning the working environments, activity recognition, vital signs' monitoring and behavior classification are also technically feasible at a moderate level of technical and algorithmic complexity. Nevertheless, the trade-off between the desired low price and the system's reliability and the further constraints has been acknowledged as challenging.

6. Case Study: Product Development

6.1. Technologies and Algorithms' Selection

The selection of appropriate technologies and algorithms from a set of possible solutions was carried out for the preliminary defined functionalities and constraints. Table 1 presents the specified functionalities along with the related constraints and facilitating the possible technologies and algorithms, where the technologies and algorithms recommended by the designer as most suitable are bolded.

For an indoor localization in an apartment at four room-zone level resolution, the PDR algorithm, based on three-axial accelerometer and magnetometer data, is chosen. The reason for this recommendation is the small size of the accelerometers and rotation sensors, which should ensure comfort during use. Another motive of this solution is the use simplicity of the PDR algorithm, which fulfills the convenience of use constraint. Moreover, this solution does not require any extensive infrastructure or any additional sensors, making it easily implementable in any environment. Another advantage of this solution is that the same acceleration and orientation readings can be also used for the recognition of other monitored people's activities.

The BarFi algorithm [25], which applies the Wi-Fi signal and fingerprints of atmospheric pressure measurements, is selected for an indoor localization in a multi-story building with a floor level accuracy. This combination, in addition to meeting the floor level accuracy constraint, maintains the easy operation of the system. Moreover, due to its versatility and simplicity, the Wi-Fi technology can also be useful for communication between the designed device and the PC.

The (GPS) and the PDR-based hybrid method introduced by Ch. Wu et al. [32] are chosen for the outdoor localization with an accuracy of at least 10 meters. This alternative is justified by the GPS's availability and easy feasibility. Moreover, the PDR algorithm is likewise proposed for the indoor localization, which allows increasing the outdoor localization accuracy without any additional equipment.

To detect a subject's fall, we propose to apply the three-axial accelerometer along with the thresholding method. The same set of technologies would either be sufficient for the required identification of the subject's four different postures and activities.

Due to the lack of an accessible suitable behavior classification method, we developed the classification algorithm based on the decision trees algorithm, which should assure the required reliability.

The heart rate can be noninvasively measured by the water-resistant wireless Polar T34 heart rate monitor, which is mounted on the person's chest with an adjustable elastic strap, ensuring comfort while in use. The applied simple noninvasive acoustic-based method does not require any additional electrodes nor gels. Moreover, the adjustable elastic strap can be useful to mount other elements of the designed system.

The general design constraints of the system, including the small size, low energy consumption, easy installation and use along with low price, are supported by applying the Arduino technology and its compatible devices [40]. The system's long-life demand can be assured by using energy-saving adaptive algorithms, which for instance adjust the localization sampling with respect to the actual subject's position.

The selected technologies and algorithms operate in an unobtrusive manner without contravening the integrity of the monitored person. The system collects and processes only insensitive data like the monitored person's position, activity or heart rate. It monitors people without the violation of their privacy. This way of handling personal integrity is appreciated by the future users. Furthermore, the procedures of data treatment assure the restricted access of exclusively trusted people including the healthcare and medical staff, doctors and, if necessary, the liable family members of the monitored person.

6.2. Modeling

6.2.1. Localization Method

The proposed PDR method for the indoor localization applies the measurements from the three-axial accelerometer gathered with a sampling frequency of 90 Hz. In the case study, the accelerometer's normal working position is vertical; Figure 2 shows the orientation of the accelerometer axes. The person's localization is based on the information about the previous position, number of steps, their length and their direction.

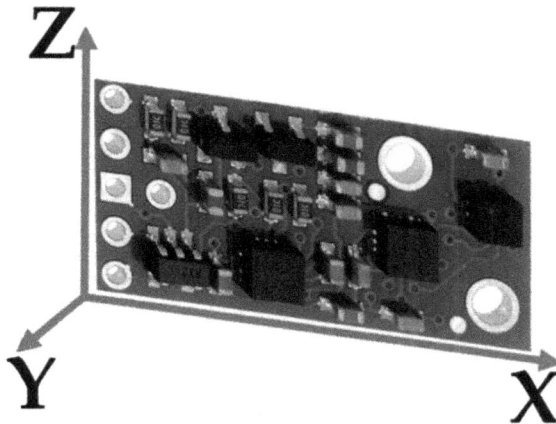

Figure 2. Accelerometer x-, y- and z-axis orientation.

The previously estimated position is stored in the device memory or in the case of the first use of a device, it is set manually at the calibration point. The number of counted steps S_c is estimated using three-axial accelerometer data consisting of acceleration readings in the x, y and z directions, which define the Signal Magnitude Vector (*SMV*) calculated as:

$$SMV = \sqrt{x_i^2 + y_i^2 + z_i^2} \tag{1}$$

where x_i, y_i, z_i are the i-th sample of acceleration in the x-, y- and z-axis, respectively. The step is detected when *SMV* exceeds the empirically chosen threshold. The threshold has to be adjusted to the walking manner of the monitored person.

The step length S_l, approximately unalterable, due to the walking manner of an individual, should be set as fixed and also has to be determined individually. Using such data, the M factor is determined as:

$$M = S_l \times S_c. \tag{2}$$

In the last stage of PDR, the magnetometer along with gyroscope readings are used to estimate the direction θ of the step [26]. Finally, the person's position can be calculated as:

$$\begin{bmatrix} \hat{x}_k \\ \hat{y}_k \end{bmatrix} = \begin{bmatrix} \hat{x}_{k-1} \\ \hat{y}_{k-1} \end{bmatrix} + M \begin{bmatrix} \cos \theta \\ \sin \theta \end{bmatrix} \tag{3}$$

where $\hat{x}_k$ and $\hat{y}_k$ are the coordinates of the estimated position, $\hat{x}_{k-1}$ and $\hat{y}_{k-1}$ are the coordinates of the previously estimated position, θ is the heading direction and M is the factor from (2).

Foremost, occasionally, the system has to be calibrated by activating the device in a known location of the apartment; for instance, while the person is sitting in an armchair or while standing on the clearly marked place in the middle of the antechamber.

6.2.2. Activity Detection

The activity detection means recognition of the subject's posture and/or action. There are five different states that should be distinguished, such as sitting, lying, standing, walking and falling.

As the most dangerous case, reliable fall detection is the most vital. The *SMV* defined by (1) is a suitable measure to detect a fall. The tumble causes changes in the *SMV* with distinctive positive and negative acceleration peaks corresponding to its beginning and the final contact with the floor, as shown in Figure 3. However, in some cases, e.g., a rapid onset of the walk could create similar *SMV* changes. Nevertheless, it is possible to avoid false alarms by monitoring also the accelerometer measures in the *x*-, *y*- and *z*-axes or by an additional localization and posture checking.

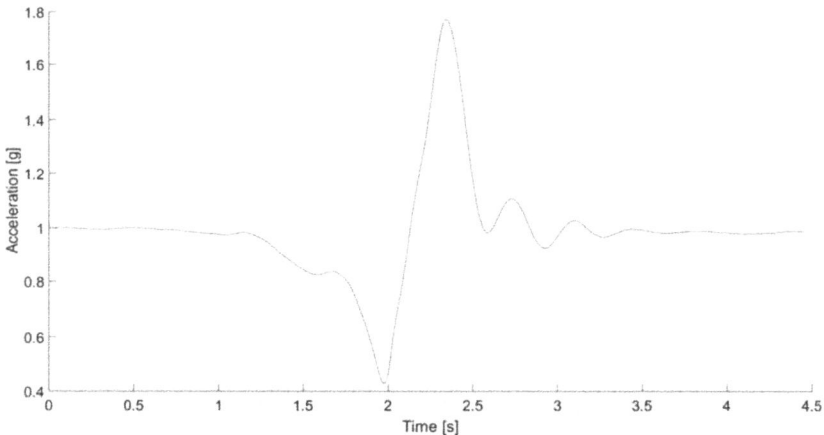

Figure 3. Exemplary *SMV* characteristics for the fall test.

The information about a dynamic posture, such as walking, is determined on the basis of the three-axial accelerometer and magnetometer along with the PDR algorithm, used also for the localization method described in the previous subsection. Whenever the designed system detects a step, the system interprets such activity as walking.

The subject's static postures, such as lying, sitting and standing, can be recognized and distinguished by means of the three-axial accelerometer and magnetometer. The lying position can be easily distinguished from the other postures because in this position, gravity affects mostly the acceleration *z*-component, whereas when standing and sitting, the *y* direction is the dominant acceleration component caused by gravity. Therefore, a suitable discriminator can determine when the *z*-component exceeds the other two components. The most difficult is to distinguish between sitting and standing. These postures cause similar acceleration with just small acceleration deviations resulting from slight movements of the body. Therefore, the system cannot differentiate between characteristic features of sitting and standing; however, it can detect the change of posture. Analyzing the accelerations in the x, y and z directions along with the SMV vector makes it possible to find out the threshold levels to distinguish between sitting down from standing up. Moreover, using appropriate threshold levels makes it possible to distinguish the actions of lying down on a bed from a sitting position and also the action of getting up from the lying down position.

6.2.3. Person's Behavior Recognition

Beside the auxiliary activity recognition, the core function of the designed system is the classification of normal, suspicious and dangerous behaviors of the subject. To make it possible, we propose to create a fingerprint of ordinary behaviors in a given temporal and spatial environment of a subject's life. Following the stakeholder's constraint, Figure 4 illustrates a layout of the possible living environment, which consists of five rooms, including the bathroom, bedroom, corridor, kitchen and living room. Furthermore, each room could be divided into two or three zones dedicated to specific activities. For example, the bedroom could be divided into two zones; one zone around the bed, where sitting and lying activities are considered as normal behaviors, but longer walking or standing should be considered as suspicious and even dangerous when prolonged. The second zone is located near the entrance to the bedroom and around the closet, where standing and walking activities are normal, but sitting and lying should be indicated as suspicious or dangerous.

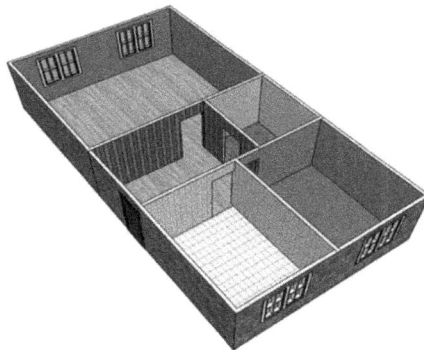

Figure 4. Sketch of an exemplary five-room apartment.

The flowchart of the behavior classification as normal, suspicious or dangerous is presented in Figure 5. Data obtained from the sensors are combined with information about the occurrence, such as the time of day, section of apartment and its zone, then how the current activity is defined and placed in the current activity map. Next, the map is compared with the pattern map of normal behaviors and by means of the machine learning method, and the occurrence is classified.

The behavior classification method can make use of the advantages of different machine learning algorithms like decision trees, Support Vector Machines (SVM), k-Nearest Neighbor (KNN) and the Behavior Vector, (BV). The authors propose to base the behavior classification on the six-component BV consisting of five components based on collected data, such as Time of Day (ToD), Section of Apartment (SoA), Zone of Activity (ZoA), Form of Activity (FoA), Duration of Activity (DoA), and the sixth component is Class of Behavior (CoB), based on the previous observations of the monitored person.

The ToD component is measured using the microcontroller's timer and configurable timeframes, which can be adjusted to personal habits and even changes due to seasons. The SoA and ZoA components are determined from the predefined layout of the apartment and estimates of the PDR indoor localization method. The FoA component results from the proposed activity recognition method, and the DoA component is calculated from timings of recognized activity. The timeframe patterns of normal behaviors of CoB components will be adjusted based on observations of three different elderly persons, two females and one male, during their daily activities.

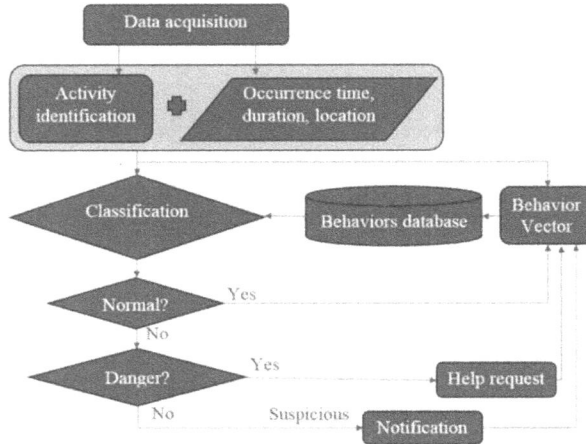

Figure 5. Behavior classification scheme.

The behavior is considered as suspicious if its duration exceeds the timeframe of normal behavior up to the 150%. The dangerous behaviors are those that cannot be recognized either as normal or as suspicious behaviors. Table 2 presents the possible states of each component of BV.

Table 2. Components of the behavior vector.

ToD	SoA	ZoA	FoA	DoA (min)	CoB *
Morning	Bathroom	of lying	Lying	10/15/30/120	Normal
Afternoon	Bedroom	of sitting	Standing	15/23/45/180	Suspicious
Evening	Antechamber	of standing	Sitting	>15/>23/>45/>180	Danger
Night	Kitchen	of walking	Walking	-	-
-	Living room	-	Tumble	-	-

* ToD, Time of Day; SoA, Section of Apartment; ZoA, Zone of Activity; FoA, Form of Activity; DoA, Duration of Activity; CoB, Class of Behavior.

According to the requirements, in the case of suspicious and dangerous behaviors, additional information about the monitored person's heart rate, H_r is required.

6.3. Prototyping

The realized prototype of the system consisting of the designed components is illustrated in Figure 6, where the core of the system is the Arduino-compatible WiDo WiFi WG1300 module equipped with a microcontroller ATmega32u4 and supporting communication with the 2.4-GHz IEEE 802.11 b/g standard. Moreover, the system consists of the Inertial Measurement Unit (IMU), AltIMU-10 v4 with built-in three-axis gyroscope, accelerometer and magnetometer and altimeter. Both devices are mounted on the Polar's T34 Heart Rate Transmitter chest strap and powered with the Li-Pol Redox 1800 mAh 20C 2S 7.4-V battery.

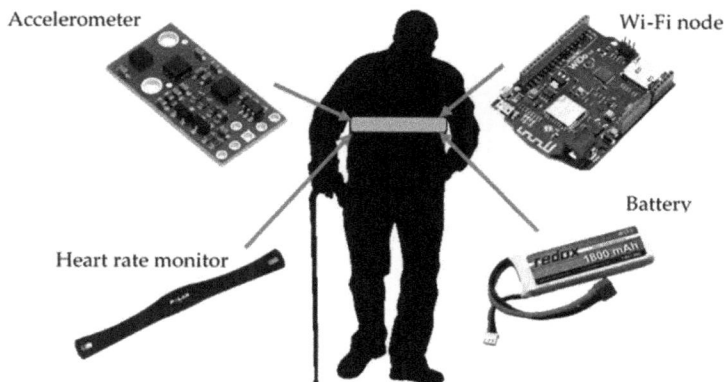

Figure 6. Component setup of the designed system prototype [41].

The behavior identification and its classification are implemented on a Lenovo ThinkPad T440s with i5-4200u 1.6-GHz CPU and 8 GB of RAM with the Windows 7 64-bit operating system and modeling environment MATLAB Version 2015a.

6.4. System Validation

To prove that the proposed solution works properly and fulfills the stated needs and requirements, the validation process is necessary. It begins with an analysis of the accuracy of step detection and direction estimation. Then, the performance analysis of the used localization method is done. Further steps concern the detailed investigation of activity recognition and the developed behavior classification method. The last step of this process is to check if the costs meet the stakeholders' assumptions.

6.4.1. Path Tracking Algorithm

After applying a simple Butterworth low-pass filter of a 2-Hz cutoff frequency to the raw SMV readings of the accelerometer, it was possible to discern single steps with 98% validity for 1500 steps in the test environment. The test of direction estimation, θ, resulted in the mean uncertainty of 1.33°, the standard deviation of 1.15° and the maximal error of 3°. Such high sensitivity causes even the small motions of the body arising from the walking characteristics to be considered as direction changes, imposing an error in the position estimation. The authors' empirical studies indicate that this effect, for a four-meter walk back and forth repeated three times, causes location error in the y-axis of 1 m and 0.5 m in the x-axis. To eliminate the error of walking characteristics, the direction changes smaller than 6° are neglected. This approach allows reducing the localization error from one meter up to 40 cm.

The proposed PDR algorithm with the 6° threshold was investigated in the tested environment. The test path of a walk back and forth each consisted of five sections: I, seven steps ahead, then turn 45° to the left; II, three steps ahead and turn 90° to the left; III, five steps ahead and turn 90° to the left; IV, five steps ahead and 45° turn; and V, five steps ahead; see Figure 7. Then, the volunteer returned to the starting point in the reverse order. The walking pattern was repeated three times.

To comprehend the localization characteristics, Figure 8 shows the localization uncertainty for each step of the test's first round with a division of the path sections for a walk back and forth. The orange dots indicate the localization uncertainty for the first seven steps ahead. The green dots show uncertainty for the three steps after the 45 ° turn to the left.

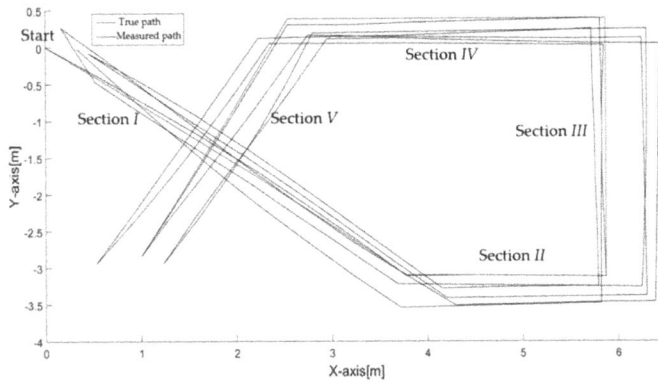

Figure 7. Test path for validation of PDR indoor localization.

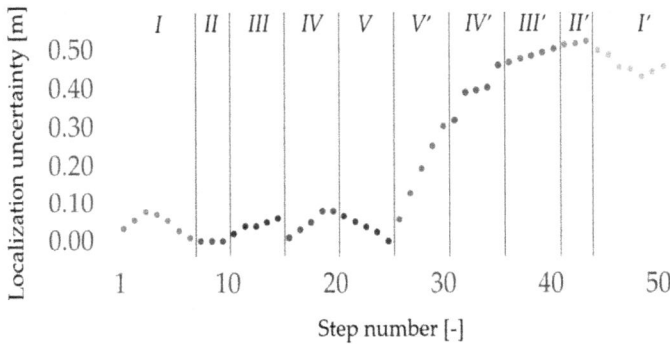

Figure 8. PDR indoor localization uncertainty for each step of the first round of the test path from the start to the end points and in the reverse direction.

The blue dots correspond to the five steps after the 90° turn to the left; the red dots indicate the five steps ahead after another 90° turn to the left; and finally, the purple dots show the last five steps ahead after the 45° turn. For the test path of going one direction, the mean localization uncertainty is 4 cm with a standard deviation of 2 cm. However, the same quantities for the direction of returning to the origin are worse and are 40 cm and 12 cm, respectively. Nevertheless, this difference can be caused by the physiological effect of repeating exactly the same path, especially the *V* section. This effect is further analyzed in the following part of this section.

Figure 9 shows the localization uncertainty for each step of the three rounds of the test five-stage path from the start point to end and in the reverse direction. The mean localization uncertainties for each round are 22 cm, 46 cm and 30 cm, with standard deviations of 20 cm, 12 cm and 11 cm for the first, second and third round, respectively. From these data, one can see that there are clear differences in the two phases of walking back and forth. Probably, this is an effect of a test psychological bias, which cannot necessarily affect the measurements in a real environment. For the whole test path, the mean localization uncertainty is 33 cm, with a standard deviation of 18 cm and a maximal localization error of 66 cm.

Figure 10 shows the averaging of the three rounds of localization uncertainty for each step with distinction for each path section for the two directions. The average of the mean uncertainty for the forward direction is almost the same and equal, about 21 cm. However, the same uncertainty for the back direction is about double and equal, almost 40 cm. The exception is the section *V* when both directions have almost the same average values. It is noticeable that the standard deviations of the measurements are much smaller than the mean uncertainty. It seems that the turns are the cause of the increasing localization uncertainty.

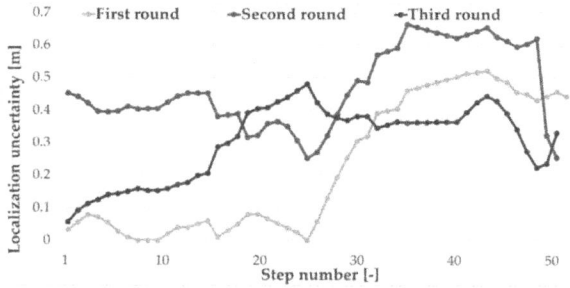

Figure 9. PDR indoor localization uncertainty for each step of three rounds of the test path from the start to end points and in the reverse direction.

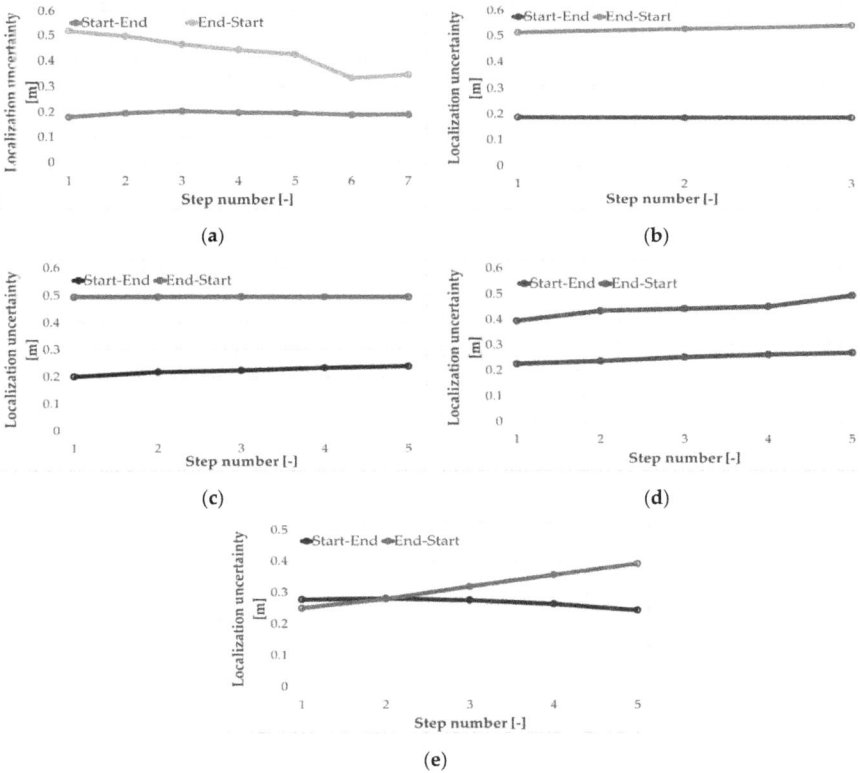

Figure 10. Localization uncertainty for each step for the two directions of the test path sections: (**a**) for *I*; (**b**) for *II*; (**c**) for *III*; (**d**) for *IV*; (**e**) for *V*.

The performed tests prove that the localization accuracy of the proposed algorithm is sufficient for the requirement of the four room-zone level accuracy. However, it also indicates that the longer use of the algorithm causes localization drift, which could lead to losing calibration. Therefore, the load sensors, similar as in car seats, are used as re-calibration points. Those distinguishable sensors, with fixed x and y coordinates, should be mounted at the most frequently-used places, such as the bed, armchair, sofa or kitchen chair. Moreover, those sensors can even be used for the primary calibration of the system. The presented results are consistent with the results reported in [26].

6.4.2. Form of Activity Recognition

One of the requirements, stated by the future users and stakeholders, was to detect a fall of the monitored person in a distinguishable way from the other activities such as standing, sitting, lying down and walking. In order to perform the activity recognition, the SMV and accelerations in the x-, y- and z-axis are measured, and based on the test data, the appropriate identification thresholds for each activity have been justified and set.

To adjust the identification thresholds of a fall, the SMV and accelerations in the x-, y- and z-axis of fall tests of two volunteers were analyzed. Figure 11 presents an example of accelerations in the x-, y- and z-axis along with the SMV measurement of the forward fall test. As one can see, due to the characteristic peaks concerning the beginning of the fall and the contact with the floor, it is possible to justify such thresholds to recognize the fall. Moreover, the decreased levels in the y- and z-axis indicate that the person is lying, which also confirms a fall if at the initial instant, standing positions were recognized.

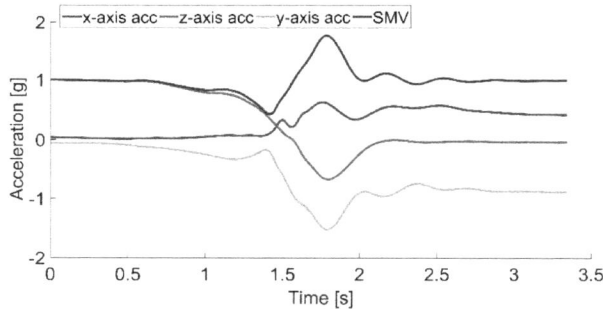

Figure 11. Forward fall test: accelerations in x-, y- and z-axis and SMV characteristic.

The final fall test consisted of 350 different falls including forward, backward, lateral falls to left or right, fainting with rotation to the left or right side and tumbling preceded by flexing the knees, 50 times each case. Up to 342 falls were identified correctly, which gives a satisfying fall detection validity of 98%.

As was predicted, the proposed system cannot directly distinguish between standing and sitting postures, which can be seen in Figure 12a,b, presenting the SMV along with accelerometer readings from the x-, y- and z-axes for standing and sitting activities, respectively. The signals of all four measured variables are not specific for different activities, and the noticeable changes around 0 g of the x- and y-axis in Figure 12a occur due to the natural movement of the body. Therefore, it proves that the observed differences are not sufficient to distinguish between these two activities.

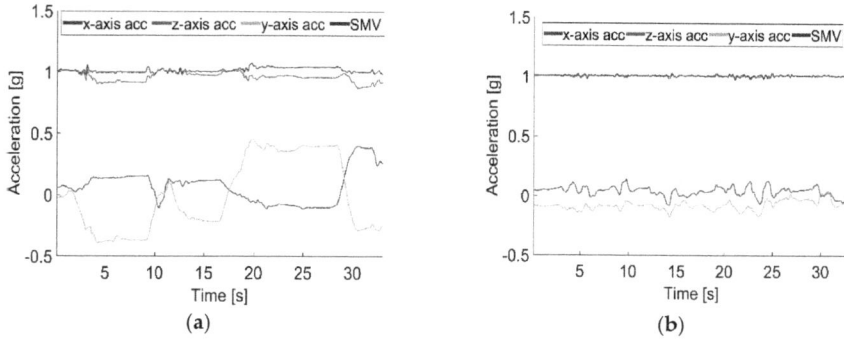

Figure 12. Accelerations in the *x*-, *y*- and *z*-axis and SMV readings during activities: (**a**) standing; (**b**) sitting.

The solution of the problem could be to identify the dynamic activities of sitting down and standing up along with lying down and getting up, instead of static activities of sitting or standing. The volunteers were asked to perform the activities of getting up and sitting down, shown in Figure 13a,b, respectively. As is visible, when the activity of getting up starts, the acceleration in the *y*-axis and hence SMV changes quickly, and when the volunteer straightens, both acceleration in the *y*-axis and SMV gently stabilize. During the sitting down activity, the curves are opposite, while bending, the change is mild, and at the end of sitting down, both acceleration in the *y*-axis and SMV changes quickly. These differences allow for finding the identification thresholds to distinguish between the activities of standing up and sitting down.

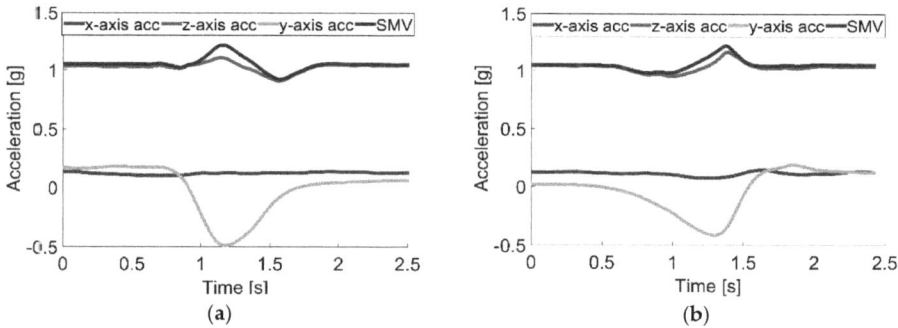

Figure 13. Accelerations in the *x*-, *y*- and *z*-axis and *SMV* readings during activities: (**a**) getting up and (**b**) sitting down.

Figure 14 shows the SMV and accelerometer readings for the activities of lying down on a bed or sofa and getting up from them. During the activity of lying down shown in Figure 14a, the acceleration in the *z*-axis rapidly decreases, and the acceleration of the *y*-axis sharply increases, which is caused by an orientation change of the accelerometer and shifting of an axis, which is most influenced by the gravity force. During the activity of getting up presented in Figure 14b, the acceleration curves of the *z*- and *y*-axes behave conversely; the *z*-axis rapidly increases; and the acceleration of the *y*-axis sharply decreases. These phenomena allow one to distinguish between those two activities.

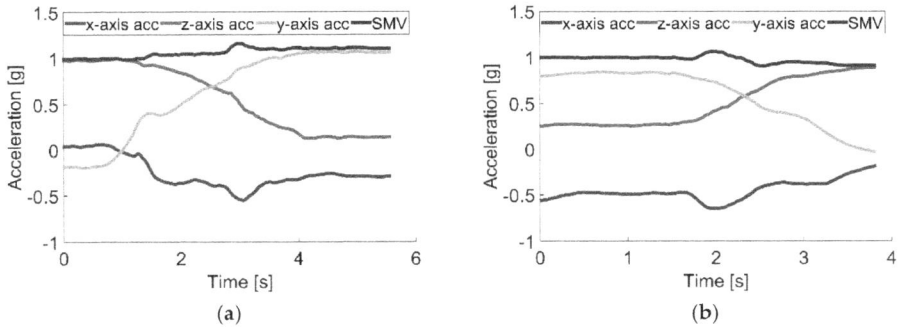

Figure 14. Accelerations in the x-, y- and z-axes and SMV readings during activities: (**a**) lying down; (**b**) getting up.

To validate the proposed solution, volunteers performed different activities: they fell 350 times, laid down almost 200 times, stood over 200 times, sat 400 times down and performed 200 walks. Table 3 summaries the recognition accuracy reached for each activity.

Table 3. Activity recognition accuracy.

Activity	Recognition Accuracy (%)
Falling	98
Standing	94
Lying	96
Sitting	92
Walking	98

The overall system activity detection and identification accuracy was 95.5%, while 2.5% of activities were recognized incorrectly, and 2.0% were not detected at all. The achieved accuracies do not differ from those reported in [27,30].

6.4.3. Behavior Classification

In general, we distinguish three classes of behaviors: normal, suspicious and dangerous. The behaviors identified as dangerous or suspicious require further dedicated actions. The behavior classification procedure starts with the establishing of pattern database of normal, suspicious and dangerous behaviors. Timeframes of the normal behavior are chosen based on the monitoring of three elderly people, two females and one male, during their daily activities for three days. Based on the observation data, the suspicious behavior timeframes are set between 101% and 150% of the timeframes of the normal ones, whereas the timeframes of dangerous behavior exceed the timeframes of normal and suspicious behaviors. However, some activities in an unusual time or place, e.g., standing on a bed, are considered as suspicious or dangerous situations, independently of their timeframes. The behavior classification training-database consists of more than 1200 situations coded as combinations of five variables: ToD, SoA, ZoA, FoA and DoA, similarly as in Table 4, which consists of examples of normal, suspicious and dangerous behaviors from the data gathered during monitoring tests of volunteers. These examples include the morning teeth brushing, sitting on the floor in the middle of the living room and too long standing in one place during the night.

Table 4. Classification of exemplary behaviors.

ToD	SoA	ZoA	FoA	DoA (min)	CoB *
Morning	Bathroom	of standing	Standing	3	Normal
Afternoon	Living room	of standing	Sitting	5	Suspicious
Night	Bedroom	of lying	Standing	17	Danger

* ToD, Time of Day; SoA, Section of Apartment; ZoA, Zone of Activity; FoA, Form of Activity; DoA, Duration of Activity; CoB, Class of Behavior.

The created training database was applied to six different machine learning techniques to establish patterns of normal, suspicious and dangerous behaviors. Using the behavior classification, training-database, the five-fold cross-validation method [42] was applied to evaluate and grade the machine learning techniques. The tested machine learning techniques are: the I and II decision trees, the I and II support vector machines and the I and II k-nearest neighbor classifiers. The I and II decision tree classifiers differ from each other with the maximum possible numbers of splits, which are 20 and 100, respectively. The I and II SVMs differ from each other with the kernel functions, which are linear and cubic, respectively. The difference between I and II KNNs is a distance metric, which is Euclidean and cosine, respectively.

Table 5 shows the percentage of overall classification validity and classification validity including normal, suspicious and dangerous behaviors for the tested machine learning techniques.

Table 5. Classification validity of validated machine learning techniques.

Classifier	Classification Validity (%) of			
	Overall	Normal	Suspicious	Danger
Decision Tree I	82.4	92.8	92.9	74.1
Decision Tree II	94.8	93.7	93.8	96.5
SVM I	54.1	60.0	0.0	50.5
SVM II	85.1	87.2	75.2	86.8
KNN I	96.0	97.9	90.9	96.8
KNN II	95.8	97.6	89.9	97.1
Tuned Decision Tree	99.1	98.8	98.4	99.6

The II decision tree along with I and II KNNs show the highest classification validity; therefore, they were applied for the optimization by tuning their parameters. However, the tuning of I and II KNN classifiers did not lead to improvement of their overall classification validity. Nevertheless, increasing the number of splits up to 140, in the II decision tree classifier, enhances the overall classification validity up to 99.1%. The further increasing of the number of splits did not increase the classification validity.

Table 6 shows the confusion matrix for the optimized decision tree with the maximum possible number of splits, up to 140. The behavior classification validity of normal is at a level of 99.1%, suspicious at a level of 98.4% and dangerous at a level of 99.5%. It is noteworthy that only 0.2% of tested dangerous behaviors were classified as normal, which can be treated as a critical mistake, and 0.3% of them were classified as suspicious, which is less critical since the suspicious behavior should be checked anyway. The classification validity of the proposed method can be justified as up to the mark.

For the final verification of the designed behavior classification method, the tuned decision tree was fed with 50 different behaviors with randomly-chosen timeframes. The test resulted with overall classification accuracy at a level of 100%, and all of the 25 normal, 7 suspicious and 18 dangerous behaviors were classified correctly.

Table 6. Confusion matrix for the optimized decision tree.

True Class \ Predicted Class	Normal	Suspicious	Danger
Normal	99.1%	0.7%	0.2%
Suspicious	1.1%	98.4%	0.5%
Danger	0.2%	0.3%	99.5%

7. Results Discussion

The system design process was conducted using the proposed DM, and based on validation results, the stakeholders and future users approved the solution and continued the project towards implementation and commercialization. The applied DM resulted in the system consisting of hardware and software components, shown in Table 1, suitable to realize required functionalities and fulfilling general constraints.

The presented system validation concerned the crucial requirements of stakeholders and future users such as a four room-zones level localization accuracy, fall detection, activity recognition and classification of normal, suspicious and dangerous situations.

The 1500-step test proved that the proposed step detection method, based on data gathered with the three-axial accelerometer and magnetometer, together with the signal magnitude vector and the pedestrian dead reckoning algorithm, shows a high robustness of 98%. The direction estimation test gave 1.33° of the mean uncertainty of the angular walking direction with a standard deviation of 1.15° and maximal error of 3°. Such high accuracy and sensitivity confirm the usefulness of the method for indoor location monitoring.

However, the further investigation indicated that small natural motions of the body during walking caused up to a 1-m error in the position estimation. Therefore, the 6° threshold filter was applied, which resulted in the reduction of uncertainty in position estimation by up to 40 cm.

For the walk test path consisting of five sections performed back and forth and repeated three times, the mean localization uncertainty was 33 cm with a standard deviation of 18 cm where the maximal localization error was 66 cm. The same test's results indicated that for one round of the walk from the start to end points, the mean localization uncertainty was just 4 cm with a standard deviation of 2 cm. However, for a walk in reverse order, the mean value and standard deviation increased up to 40 cm and 12 cm, respectively. The detailed analysis of the test data resulted in the mean localization uncertainties for each round of 22 cm, 46 cm and 30 cm, with standard deviations of 20 cm, 12 cm and 11 cm for the first, second and third round, respectively. Moreover, average localization uncertainties for the forward direction are almost the same and equal about 21 cm, and the same uncertainty for the back direction is about double and equal to almost 40 cm. This means that the proposed localization algorithm has a small localization uncertainty, and the most distortive movements are turns. It seems that the turns are the cause of the increasing localization uncertainty. The test results verified that the designed method is sufficient for the four room-zone level accuracy requirement.

Analysis of test results of forward fall accelerations in the x-, y- and z-axes and SMV, showing the characteristic peaks concerning the beginning of the fall and the contact with the floor, was applied to define the signal thresholds used to recognize the fall. Moreover, the acceleration change in the z-axis, which the gravity force influences the most, indicating the lying position of the monitored person, is used for the fall confirmation. The performed tests proved that the designed method of fall detection is valid in 98% of cases.

The data gathered during standing and sitting activities indicated that the observed differences in accelerations in the x-, y- and z-axes and SMV are not sufficient to distinguish between these two activities. However, possible identification of getting up and sitting down activities can be used to recognize standing and sitting activities. The beginning of the getting up activity causes the acceleration in the z-axis; hence, SMV changes quickly, and at the end of the activity both acceleration in the z-axis and SMV gently stabilize. In turn, the start of the sitting down activity causes the mild change in acceleration in the z-axis, and at the end of the activity, both acceleration in the z-axis and SMV change quickly. Based on appropriate thresholds, the identification for both of these changes allows one to distinguish between those two activities. Similar analysis can be used to distinguish between lying down and rising activities. When lying down, due to an orientation change of the accelerometer causing a shift of the axis that the gravity force influences the most, the acceleration in the y-axis rapidly decreases, and acceleration of the z-axis sharply increases; while when rising, the acceleration curves of the y- and z-axes behave conversely; the y-axis rapidly increases; and acceleration of the z-axis sharply decreases. These phenomena are used to distinguish these two activities. The proposed activity recognition method was validated based on tests consisting of 350 falls, 200 lying down, 200 standing up, 400 sitting down and 200 walks, and the results are summarized in Table 3. The overall validity of the system activity recognition was 95.5%, where 2.5% of activities were recognized incorrectly and 2.0% not detected at all.

The activity categorization in class of behavior as normal, suspicious or dangerous is based on the analysis of five components: time of day, section of apartment, zone of activity, form of activity and duration of activity. The classification procedure is grounded on the comparison of current measures with the existing behavior database. The behavior database was created from regular three-day observation of three volunteers' activities. From six evaluated machine learning techniques, the decision trees II, KNN I and KNN II showed the highest classification validity of 94.8%, 96.0% and 95.8%, respectively. The conducted optimization of the three best methods indicated that only the tuned decision trees II increased classification accuracy up to 99.1%. The confusion matrix for the tuned decision tree indicates that only 0.2% of the tested dangerous behaviors were classified as normal, which can be treated as a critical mistake, and 0.3% of them were classified as suspicious, which is less critical since the suspicious behavior should be verified anyway. The chosen behavior classification technique of highest validity was verified with a set of 25 normal, 7 suspicious and 18 dangerous behaviors of random timeframes, and as a result, 100% of them were classified correctly.

8. Conclusions and Future Work

Due to the lengthening of life expectancy, society is aging, and more and more people live to an older age. Therefore, it is highly important to assure life quality and safety. Existing and emerging technologies can provide tools that can support elderly people in their everyday life, making it easy and safe. This paper concerns the design methodology of such tools especially for indoor and outdoor localization, health monitoring, fall detection and behavior recognition and classification.

The authors propose the design methodology for the IoT-based home care information system intended for indoor and outdoor environment use. The presented DM approaches the home care problem not only from the designer's perspective, but also considering the contracting authority's and potential users' requirements, which means that apart from the technical requirements, the design procedure considers the multifarious constraints, including the lifetime, energy issue, usage comfort and even the price.

The proposed DM was verified with a case study of real-life scenarios where there is a need for supporting elderly people, especially those of limited mobility living alone. The desire stated by the stakeholders and future users required the system for identifying people's position and their vital signs, but also to be able to recognize basic activities, especially falls, and to classify them as normal, suspicious or dangerous.

The outcome of the conducted design procedure is the system based on IMU, with a built-in three-axis accelerometer, gyroscope, magnetometer and altimeter. It is also equipped with Wi-Fi, GPS and heart rate modules. For an in-apartment localization with four room-zone level resolution, the IMU with PDR algorithm is used. For in-building localization with floor level accuracy, the BarFi algorithm based on pressure and Wi-Fi fingerprints is proposed. For an outdoor localization with an accuracy of at least ten meters, the GPS module and PDR algorithm are applied. In order to detect activities of falling, lying, standing, sitting and walking, the IMU and thresholding algorithms are used. As a method for classifying activities as normal, suspicious or dangerous, the authors developed the six-element behavior vector and used it together with a decision tree algorithm.

The validation procedure performed for the most crucial requirements of the four room-zone level in apartment localization, fall detection, activity recognition and its classification as normal, suspicious and dangerous situations proves that the system works according to the required functionalities and constraints.

The future works concern the verification step, conducted together with the stakeholders and future users, of designed modules and algorithms for a multi-story building environment and nearby outdoor environments. Another future improvement of this system could be further recognition of specific activities like teeth brushing, cooking, watching TV or taking medication. Such information would be informative for caregivers whether the monitored person skipped a meal or forgot to take a medication. Moreover, it could be also included in the behavior vector and inform caregivers about behavior changes within a given period. The other improvement of the system may concern the usefulness of additional sensors for monitoring vital signs. The lifetime extension of the device by means of energy-saving algorithms and methods is another direction for future work.

Acknowledgments: The authors would like to express their thanks to Dariusz Gaszczyk and Robert Dega from the Blekinge Institute of Technology, Sweden, for their support while gathering data used in this research.

Author Contributions: Damian Dziak performed the experimental part, modelled, analyzed data and reported the results. Bartosz Jachimczyk contributed to the experimental part and result analysis. Wlodek J. Kulesza guided the whole research and supported the structure of the paper.

Conflicts of Interest: The authors declare no conflict of interest.

Abbreviations

The following abbreviations are used in this manuscript:

BLE	Bluetooth Low Energy
BV	Behavior Vector
CoB	Class of Behavior
DM	Design Methodology
DoA	Duration of Activity
ECG	Electrocardiography
FoA	Form of Activity
GPS	Global Positioning System
IMU	Inertial Measurement Unit
IoT	Internet of Things
KNN	k-Nearest Neighbor
MEMS	Micro-Electro-Mechanical Systems
PDR	Pedestrian Dead Reckoning
RFID	Radio Frequency Identification
RSS	Received Signal Strength
SMV	Signal Magnitude Vector
SoA	Section of Apartment
SVM	Support Vector Machine
ToD	Time of Day
UWB	Ultra-Wide Band
WSN	Wireless Sensor Networks
ZoA	Zone of Activity

References

1. GHO (By Category). Life Expectancy (Data by Country). Available online: http://apps.who.int/gho/data/node.main.688 (accessed on 20 April 2017).
2. Kontis, V.; Bennett, J.E.; Mathers, C.D.; Li, G.; Foreman, K.; Ezzati, M. Future life expectancy in 35 industrialised countries: Projections with a Bayesian model ensemble. *Lancet* **2017**, *389*, 1323–1335. [CrossRef]
3. McKnight, A. Flexible design methodology management. In Proceedings of the IEE Colloquium on Design Management Environments in CAD, London, UK, 31–31 January 1991; pp. 1/1–1/6.
4. Prasad, R.; Kobayashi, H. Multi-methodology design: An experimental comparison. In Proceedings of the IEEE International Verilog HDL Conference, Santa Clara, CA, USA, 26–28 February 1996; pp. 45–49.
5. Mengel, S.A.; Adams, W.J.; Hagler, M.O. Using a hypertext instructional design methodology in engineering education. In Proceedings of the Frontiers in Education 1997 27th Annual Conference, Teaching and Learning in an Era of Change, Pittsburgh, PA, USA, 5–8 November 1997; pp. 648–652.
6. Eskelinen, H. Improving the productivity of complex electronic systems design by utilizing applied design methodologies. *IEEE Aerosp. Electron. Syst. Mag.* **2001**, *16*, 26–28. [CrossRef]
7. Wang, F.; Hannafin, M.J. Design-based research and technology-enhanced learning environments. *Educ. Technol. Res. Dev.* **2005**, *53*, 5–23. [CrossRef]
8. Saini, A.; Yammiyavar, P. Weak eyesight therapy: A case study in designing an application for m-health systems. In Proceedings of the 2013 International Conference on Human Computer Interactions (ICHCI), Chennai, India, 23–24 August 2013; pp. 1–8.
9. Ahmad, M. Designing for the Internet of Things: A paradigm shift in reliability. In Proceedings of the 2015 IEEE 65th Electronic Components and Technology Conference (ECTC), San Diego, CA, USA, 26–29 May 2015; pp. 1758–1766.
10. Coetzee, L.; Eksteen, J. The Internet of Things—Promise for the future? An introduction. In Proceedings of the 2011 IST-Africa Conference Proceedings, Gaborone, Botswana, 11–13 May 2011; pp. 1–9.
11. Ruffieux, D.; Contaldo, M.; Enz, C. MEMS-based all-digital frequency synthesis for ultralow-power radio for WBAN and WSN applications. In Proceedings of the 2011 IEEE International Symposium on Circuits and Systems (ISCAS), Rio de Janeiro, Brazil, 15–18 May 2011; pp. 157–160.
12. Mainetti, L.; Patrono, L.; Vilei, A. Evolution of wireless sensor networks towards the Internet of Things: A survey. In Proceedings of the SoftCOM 2011, 19th International Conference on Software, Telecommunications and Computer Networks, Split, Croatia, 15–17 September 2011; pp. 1–6.
13. Khalil, N.; Abid, M.R.; Benhaddou, D.; Gerndt, M. Wireless sensors networks for Internet of Things. In Proceedings of the 2014 IEEE Ninth International Conference on Intelligent Sensors, Sensor Networks and Information Processing (ISSNIP), Singapore, 21–24 April 2014; pp. 1–6.
14. Rotariu, C.; Manta, V. Wireless system for remote monitoring of oxygen saturation and heart rate. In Proceedings of the 2012 Federated Conference on Computer Science and Information Systems (FedCSIS), Wroclaw, Poland, 9–12 September 2012; pp. 193–196.
15. Chung, W.-Y.; Lee, S.-C.; Toh, S.-H. WSN based mobile u-healthcare system with ECG, blood pressure measurement function. In Proceedings of the 2008 30th Annual International Conference of the IEEE Engineering in Medicine and Biology Society, Vancouver, BC, Canada, 20–25 August 2008; pp. 1533–1536.
16. Tan, S.-L.; Garcia-Guzman, J.; Villa-Lopez, F. A wireless body area network for pervasive health monitoring within smart environments. In Proceedings of the 2012 IEEE International Conference on Consumer Electronics (ICCE-Berlin), Berlin, Germany, 3–5 September 2012; pp. 47–51.
17. Wannenburg, J.; Malekian, R. Body sensor network for mobile health monitoring, a diagnosis and anticipating system. *IEEE Sens. J.* **2015**, *15*, 6839–6852. [CrossRef]
18. Shchekotov, M. Indoor localization methods based on Wi-Fi lateration and signal strength data collection. In Proceedings of the 2015 17th Conference of Open Innovations Association (FRUCT), Yaroslavl, Russia, 20–24 April 2015; pp. 186–191.
19. Youn, J.H.; Ali, H.; Sharif, H.; Deogun, J.; Uher, J.; Hinrichs, S.H. WLAN-based real-time asset tracking system in healthcare environments. In Proceedings of the Third IEEE International Conference on Wireless and Mobile Computing, Networking and Communications (WiMob 2007), White Plains, NY, USA, 8–10 October 2007; p. 71.

20. Chen, W.H.; Chang, H.H.; Lin, T.H.; Chen, L.K.; Hwang, S.J.; Yen, D.H.J.; Yuan, H.S.; Chu, W.C. Dynamic indoor localization based on active RFID for healthcare applications: A shape constraint approach. In Proceedings of the 2009 2nd International Conference on Biomedical Engineering and Informatics, Tianjin, China, 17–19 October 2009; pp. 1–5.

21. Palumbo, F.; Barsocchi, P.; Chessa, S.; Augusto, J.C. A stigmergic approach to indoor localization using Bluetooth Low Energy beacons. In Proceedings of the 2015 12th IEEE International Conference on Advanced Video and Signal Based Surveillance (AVSS), Karlsruhe, Germany, 25–28 August 2015; pp. 1–6.

22. Wyffels, J.; Brabanter, J.D.; Crombez, P.; Verhoeve, P.; Nauwelaers, B.; Strycker, L.D. Distributed, signal strength-based indoor localization algorithm for use in healthcare environments. *IEEE J. Biomed. Health Inform.* **2014**, *18*, 1887–1893. [CrossRef] [PubMed]

23. Redondi, A.; Tagliasacchi, M.; Cesana, M.; Borsani, L.; Tarrío, P.; Salice, F. LAURA—LocAlization and Ubiquitous monitoRing of pAtients for health care support. In Proceedings of the 2010 IEEE 21st International Symposium on Personal, Indoor and Mobile Radio Communications Workshops (PIMRC Workshops), Istanbul, Turkey, 26–30 September 2010; pp. 218–222.

24. Jachimczyk, B.; Dziak, D.; Kulesza, W.J. RFID-hybrid scene analysis-neural network system for 3D indoor positioning optimal system arrangement approach. In Proceedings of the 2014 IEEE International Instrumentation and Measurement Technology Conference (I2MTC) Proceedings, Montevideo, Uruguay, 12–15 May 2014; pp. 191–196.

25. Shen, X.; Chen, Y.; Zhang, J.; Wang, L.; Dai, G.; He, T. BarFi: Barometer-aided Wi-Fi floor localization using crowdsourcing. In Proceedings of the 2015 IEEE 12th International Conference on Mobile Ad Hoc and Sensor Systems (MASS), Dallas, TX, USA, 19–22 October 2015; pp. 416–424.

26. Kang, W.; Han, Y. SmartPDR: Smartphone-based pedestrian dead reckoning for indoor localization. *IEEE Sens. J.* **2015**, *15*, 2906–2916. [CrossRef]

27. Gjoreski, H.; Lustrek, M.; Gams, M. Accelerometer placement for posture recognition and fall detection. In Proceedings of the 2011 7th International Conference on Intelligent Environments (IE), Dallas, TX, USA, 19–22 October 2011; pp. 47–54.

28. Liu, X.Q.; Cai, W.M. The alarm system of elder tumble at the geracomium based on ZigBee. In Proceedings of the 2011 International Conference on Electronics and Optoelectronics (ICEOE), Dalian, China, 29–31 July 2011; pp. 38–40.

29. Wang, L.; Gu, T.; Chen, H.; Tao, X.; Lu, J. Real-time activity recognition in wireless body sensor networks: From simple gestures to complex activities. In Proceedings of the 2010 IEEE 16th International Conference on Embedded and Real-Time Computing Systems and Applications (RTCSA), Macau, China, 23–25 August 2010; pp. 43–52.

30. Martin, H.; Iglesias, J.; Cano, J.; Bernardos, A.M.; Casar, J.R. Towards a fuzzy-based multi-classifier selection module for activity recognition applications. In Proceedings of the 2012 IEEE International Conference on Pervasive Computing and Communications Workshops (PERCOM Workshops), Lugano, Switzerland, 19–23 March 2012; pp. 871–876.

31. Aranki, D.; Kurillo, G.; Yan, P.; Liebovitz, D.M.; Bajcsy, R. Real-time tele-monitoring of patients with chronic heart-failure using a smartphone: Lessons learned. *IEEE Trans. Affect. Comput.* **2016**, *7*, 206–219. [CrossRef]

32. Wu, C.; Yang, Z.; Xu, Y.; Zhao, Y.; Liu, Y. Human mobility enhances global positioning accuracy for mobile phone localization. *IEEE Trans. Parallel Distrib. Syst.* **2015**, *26*, 131–141. [CrossRef]

33. Sun, L.; Zhang, D.; Li, B.; Guo, B.; Li, S. Activity recognition on an accelerometer embedded mobile phone with varying positions and orientations. In *Ubiquitous Intelligence and Computing*; Springer: Berlin, Germany, 2010; pp. 548–562.

34. Millner, H.; Ebelt, R.; Hoffmann, G.; Vossiek, M. Wireless 3D localization of animals for trait and behavior analysis in indoor and outdoor areas. In Proceedings of the IEEE MTT-S International Microwave Workshop on Wireless Sensing, Local Positioning, and RFID, Cavtat, Croatia, 24–25 September 2009; pp. 1–4.

35. Gonzalez, J.; Blanco, J.L.; Galindo, C.; Ortiz-de-Galisteo, A.; Fernandez-Madrigal, J.A.; Moreno, F.A.; Martinez, J.L. Combination of UWB and GPS for indoor-outdoor vehicle localization. In Proceedings of the 2007 IEEE International Symposium on Intelligent Signal Processing, Alcala de Henares, Spain, 3–5 October 2007; pp. 1–6.

36. Kuo, W.H.; Chen, Y.S.; Jen, G.T.; Lu, T.W. An intelligent positioning approach: RSSI-based indoor and outdoor localization scheme in Zigbee networks. In Proceedings of the 2010 International Conference on Machine Learning and Cybernetics, Qingdao, China, 11–14 July 2010; pp. 2754–2759.

37. The ZigBee Alliance. Control Your World. Available online: http://www.zigbee.org/ (accessed on 5 June 2017).

38. Tabish, R.; Ghaleb, A.M.; Hussein, R.; Touati, F.; Mnaouer, A.B.; Khriji, L.; Rasid, M.F.A. A 3G/WiFi-enabled 6LoWPAN-based U-healthcare system for ubiquitous real-time monitoring and data logging. In Proceedings of the 2nd Middle East Conference on Biomedical Engineering, Doha, Qatar, 17–20 February 2014; pp. 277–280.

39. Fielden, G.D.R. *Engineering Design*; HANSARD: London, UK, 1975.

40. Banzi, M. *Getting Started with Arduino*, 3rd ed.; O'Reilly Media: Sebastopol, CA, USA, 2008.

41. Dziak, D.; Jachimczyk, B.; Kulesza, W.J. Wirelessly interfacing objects and subjects of healthcare system—IoT approach. *Elektronika ir Elektrotechnika* **2016**, *22*, 66–73. [CrossRef]

42. Refaeilzadeh, P.; Tang, L.; Liu, H. Cross-validation. In *Encyclopedia of Database Systems*; Liu, L., Özsu, M.T., Eds.; Springer: New York, NY, USA, 2009; pp. 532–538.

![applied sciences logo] *applied sciences*

MDPI

Article

An Efficient Network Coding-Based Fault-Tolerant Mechanism in WBAN for Smart Healthcare Monitoring Systems

Yuhuai Peng [1,2], Xiaojie Wang [3,*], Lei Guo [1,2], Yichun Wang [3] and Qingxu Deng [1,2,*]

[1] Key Laboratory of Medical Image Computing of Ministry of Education, Northeastern University, Shenyang 110819, China; pengyuhuai@cse.neu.edu.cn (Y.P.); guolei@cse.neu.edu.cn (L.G.)
[2] School of Computer Science and Engineering, Northeastern University, Shenyang 110819, China
[3] School of Software, Dalian University of Technology, Dalian 116620, China; wangych1996@126.com
[*] Correspondence: wangxj1988@mail.dlut.edu.cn (X.W.); dengqx@mail.neu.edu.cn (Q.D.);
Tel.: +86-138-898-62359 (X.W.); +86-138-988-86668 (Q.D.)

Received: 12 July 2017; Accepted: 7 August 2017; Published: 10 August 2017

Abstract: As a key technology in smart healthcare monitoring systems, wireless body area networks (WBANs) can pre-embed sensors and sinks on body surface or inside bodies for collecting different vital signs parameters, such as human Electrocardiograph (ECG), Electroencephalograph (EEG), Electromyogram (EMG), body temperature, blood pressure, blood sugar, blood oxygen, etc. Using real-time online healthcare, patients can be tracked and monitored in normal or emergency conditions at their homes, hospital rooms, and in Intensive Care Units (ICUs). In particular, the reliability and effectiveness of the packets transmission will be directly related to the timely rescue of critically ill patients with life-threatening injuries. However, traditional fault-tolerant schemes either have the deficiency of underutilised resources or react too slowly to failures. In future healthcare systems, the medical Internet of Things (IoT) for real-time monitoring can integrate sensor networks, cloud computing, and big data techniques to address these problems. It can collect and send patient's vital parameter signal and safety monitoring information to intelligent terminals and enhance transmission reliability and efficiency. Therefore, this paper presents a design in healthcare monitoring systems for a proactive reliable data transmission mechanism with resilience requirements in a many-to-one stream model. This Network Coding-based Fault-tolerant Mechanism (NCFM) first proposes a greedy grouping algorithm to divide the topology into small logical units; it then constructs a spanning tree based on random linear network coding to generate linearly independent coding combinations. Numerical results indicate that this transmission scheme works better than traditional methods in reducing the probability of packet loss, the resource redundant rate, and average delay, and can increase the effective throughput rate.

Keywords: wireless body area network (WBAN); real-time monitoring; network coding; fault-tolerant; smart healthcare

1. Introduction

Smart healthcare [1] has attracted more and more worldwide attention due to its advantage of flexibility, mobility, and ease of constant monitoring of the patient. Smart healthcare, an integration of various information technologies including Internet of Things (IoTs) [2], cloud computing, and big data processing, aims at building a remote disease prevention and care platform. As a great driving force of the Fourth Industrial Revolution, the IoT is playing an ever more important role in Intelligent Manufacturing, the Smart Grid, Smart Cities, Vehicular Ad Hoc Networks (VANETs), Smart Healthcare, etc. The notion of the IoT can be regarded as an extension of communication networks and the Internet;

it employs sensing technology and intelligent devices to perceive and recognise the physical world, conducts calculations, processes and mines knowledge through network transmission interconnections. Further, IoT realises information exchanges and seamless connections between things and things and persons and things to effect real-time control, precise management, and scientific decision-making. In future networks, the IoT will be able to integrate sensors, wireless communication, embedded computing, cloud computing, big data, etc., and to apply intelligent terminals, mobile computing and the ubiquitous network to all aspects in people's daily lives. Therefore, IoT is a key to solve growing global demand for satisfactory medical services.

As the core technology of medical IoT, wireless body area network (WBAN) can be used for real-time patients monitoring and home healthcare, has wide application prospects, and has huge market potential. WBAN can automatically collect human Electrocardiograph (ECG), Electroencephalograph (EEG), Electromyogram (EMG), body temperature, blood pressure, blood sugar, blood oxygen, and other life sign parameters from the pre-deployed sensors on the patient's body surface or inside their body. This in in order to achieve real-time, convenient, all-weather healthcare monitoring, thus providing a flexible and effective means for real-time healthcare monitoring of patients inside and outside the hospital room, and in Intensive Care Units (ICUs). In the recent years, the emergence of wireless sensor networks in healthcare systems has significantly increased, mainly in the areas of remote health monitoring, medical data access, and communication with caregivers in emergency situations. Using WSN, we can easily design a simple but efficient system to monitor the conditions of patient continuously. Patients can be tracked and monitored in normal or in emergency conditions at their homes, hospital rooms, and in ICUs.

In most countries, soaring medical expenses and the declining availability of medical services have become the main challenges to be addressed by medical and health services at present. Because of the large global population, overall medical resources are relatively scarce. Furthermore, high-speed economic development will also bring about problems such as population aging, rapid growth of chronic diseases, and high sub-health ratio. Therefore, smart healthcare becomes an effective way to fundamentally solve the problem of inadequate and overly expensive medical services by using information technology to change the existing medical service mode and improve the utilization of medical resources.

Figure 1 depicts the convergence architecture of smart healthcare. Due to the inherent nature of a wireless medium, sensors and link failures often occur because of energy depletion, channel fading, faulty configuration, malicious attacks, etc., in the harsh emergency ward environment. A traditional fault-tolerant scheme with a resource-hungry backup path would require a large amount of redundancy. Additionally, traditional reactive fault-tolerant mechanisms provide protection only after errors occur, resulting in longer delays. Moreover, taking into account the complexity of the smart healthcare environment, previous schemes cannot be applied directly to healthcare monitoring systems. Therefore, this article describes the design and implementation of a proactive, reliable data transmission mechanism with fault-tolerant capacity based on the principle of random linear network coding. This fault-tolerant scheme includes two aspects: the grouping of greedy nodes and the construction of coding trees. As long as the gateway receives a sufficient number of linear independent encoding combinations, original packets can be recovered quickly, even when some errors occur. Numerical results have shown that this resilience transmission mechanism works better than previous methods in increasing the ratio of successful deliveries and the effective throughput rate, and in reducing the degree of resource redundancy and end-to-end delay.

The remainder of this article is organised as follows. Research progress in fault-tolerance is reviewed in Section 2. The network model is then formulated in Section 3. In Section 4, details are presented of how we can generate a spanning tree based on network coding theory. The source-grouping strategy is described in Section 5. Simulation results are discussed in Section 6. Finally, we conclude the paper in Section 7.

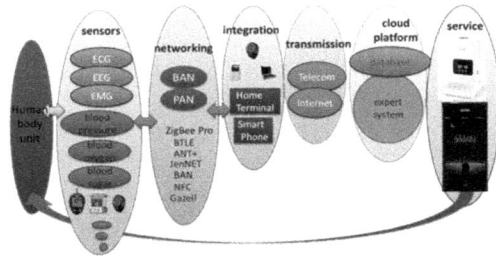

Figure 1. The convergence architecture of smart healthcare.

2. Related Work

During the past few decades, there has been much research on the fault-tolerant problem in network optimization and algorithm design. How to provide a fault-tolerant guarantee is one of the most important challenges. Researchers have drawn attention to this active field and proposed several solutions.

Sterbenz et al. in [3] explored the resilience problem in current communication networks and systematically designed an Internet architecture with survivability as a design consideration. In [4], the authors presented a flow assignment method for computer network design by combining routing and survivability aspects. The authors of [5] investigated the problem of a base station failure in a wireless cellular mobile communication system. In [6], the effects of failures on user mobility and survivability issues in phone/personal communications services networks in a wireless environment were addressed. The authors in [7] took survivability requirements and capacity constraints in wireless access networks into account and designed multi-period optimization. Reddy et al. in [8] designed a novel routing protocol to solve the survivability protection problem against multi-path failures within a minimum packet redundancy restriction. References [9–13] focus on fault-tolerant issues while considering node placement, topology control, and the routing algorithm. Regarding the design of survivability mechanisms in wireless multi-hop networks, researchers have conducted exploratory work with various optimization objectives during the past few years. The authors in [14] studied the maximal network-covering problem in wireless networks. Using binary integer programming methods, the authors solved the maximal-covering problem and offered reliable services provisioning, meeting the network connectivity requirement. This approach was expected to help network planners to deploy Wireless Multi-hop Networks (WMNs) with lower installation costs. The authors in [15] designed a novel scheme to establish a reliable network infrastructure based on the ear decomposition method. The generated topology can guarantee full coverage to all mesh clients and tolerate an error in a single mesh node. The authors of [16] studied the issue of mesh gateway deployment and network topology control, presenting two schemes to address the requirements for delay-tolerance and survivability in backbone wireless mesh networks. The network survival mechanisms in [16] can offer network planners a number of feasible compromise solutions. However, these static proactive network survivability mechanisms lack good flexibility and adaptability. Bisti et al. in [17] presented a new routing protection algorithm to increase network survivability against node or link failures in a wireless multi-hop environment. The method in [17] permits network elements to react to local failures quickly using a proactive backup route. With the joint optimization of scheduling, routing, and channel assignment, the authors of [18] studied the network recovery problem in a multi-interface multi-channel wireless mesh scenario. Their scheme can adjust routing and channel assignments to avoid network congestion. To some degree, these reactive schemes can recover the fault path to ensure packet transmission is uninterrupted. However, longer delays prevent these schemes from being practical.

Al-Kofahi et al. in [19] addressed the survivability problem under a many-to-one traffic pattern and provided sufficient theoretical proof and analysis. They also proposed a network protection mechanism based on network coding to overcome the inadequacies of previous methods. In [20],

Misra et al. studied the fault-tolerance routing problem and developed a learning-automaton-based adaptive fault-tolerant routing scheme in an IOT environment. To improve bandwidth efficiency, Wang et al. in [21] designed a network-coding-based flow allocation and rate-control scheme to tackle the multicast optimization problem for multimedia services in an IOT environment. In [22], Qiu et al. investigated the survivability network topology design problem, and developed a novel model by analysing the roles of different network elements in a heterogeneous wireless sensor network scenario.

Otto et al. in [23] estimate the actual transmission performance of the WBAN prototype system, and analyzes the factors that may cause the network transmission reliability to decline. Latre et al. in [24] evaluated the reliability of the Cascading Information retrieval by Controlling Access with Distributed slot Assignment (CIADIA) protocol, and proposed the improved mechanism based on CIADIA to further improve transmission reliability. Zhou et al. in [25] studied the adaptive resource scheduling mechanism in WBAN to ensure reliable data transmission. Wu et al. in [26] proposed a channel reservation mechanism that can improve the reliability of transmission in a non-ideal WBAN channel environment. However, WBAN system [27] requirements for transmission reliability, energy efficiency, and latency are higher than any previous communication system. If only a single performance index is optimized, it will lead to other performance degradation, which is not conducive to the reliable and efficient transmission of medical services.

3. Network Model

Our network model in Figure 2 consists of three types of nodes: a gateway, sinks, and sensors in a Wireless Body Sensor Network (WBSN) for smart healthcare. We can use a unidirectional connected graph to represent the network topology. Here we use $G = (V, E)$ to indicate backbone network topology of a WBSN, where E refers to the set of wireless links, and V refers to the set of network elements, including a gateway, sinks, and sensor nodes. Network traffic generated from rock-bottom sensors will converge the wireless gateway T. The gateway can be connected to the external wired Internet. In our network model, we mainly investigate a many-to-one traffic model from various sensor nodes to an external gateway. Depending on the number of hops to the gateway node, sink nodes are layered in many levels. It is assumed that nodes in WBSNs are equipped with multi-interface multi-channel functions. In this way, every network element can exchange information with its neighbours at the same time. We assume that every sensor user U_k must be connected to at least two sink nodes L_k for connectivity. We indicate all sensor elements by U_s, in which $U_s = \{S_1, S_2, ..., S_n\}, U_s \subset V, |U_s| = n$. We assume the min-cut between L_s and T to be h. This assumption means that the degree of connection between sink nodes and gateway nodes is very rich. It is assumed that all native or encoding packets are the same size for encoding efficiency. It is assumed that gateways can perform a decoding operation to release original information. According to the well-known Gauss Elimination (GE) method [28], destination nodes have a higher probability of recovering their desired packets by solving groups of linear equations, if the information they receive is sufficient for GE solutions.

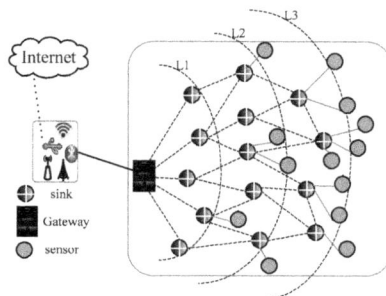

Figure 2. Network model.

4. Design of Network Coding Tree Algorithm

In our model, it is assumed that all sink nodes can encode and decode packets freely, while the rock-bottom sensor nodes cannot. When a particular sink node receives original packets from associated sensor nodes, it attempts to encode the native information into a single message. The sink node will then deliver those encoded messages. An elastic transmission mechanism following the principle of random linear coding [29,30] is presented to ensure that the entire sink node information encoding will be not linearly dependent. This fault-tolerant mechanism consists of two parts: the construction of a network coding tree and the design of a greedy grouping algorithm.

The construction of the spanning tree used for illustration of the coding relationship focuses on generating a tree that can associate all rock-bottom sensor nodes U_s, while all leaf nodes on the tree are located among their associated sink nodes L_s. With this method, destination nodes can construct linearly independent combinations according to the connection relationships of network nodes. The five-step algorithm to establish the spanning tree is given in detail below.

In the first step, a depth-first search (DFS) or breadth-first search (BFS) strategy can be employed to scan the full logical topology established by a WSN. In this way, a spanning tree can be produced with the root node deployed at node L_s.

In the second step, it is assumed that the leaf elements in this spanning tree include some sensor node U_s. If there exist some sensors which are leaf nodes in coding tree, these nodes are denoted as u.

In the third step, the algorithm constantly scans the entire network topology until it finds a neighbour node L_s of u. We indicate this sink node as x. Note that node u cannot be a child node of node x.

In the fourth step, the algorithm pollards this coding spanning tree to ensure its leaf elements do not include any U_s elements. In the fifth step, the algorithm continues to pollard unnecessary L_s nodes if leaf nodes contain any U_s elements.

The fourth step of this algorithm can benefit from a spanning-tree construction proposed in the literature [31,32]. It can be proven that the polynomial time-complexity analysis of establishing this spanning tree will be $O(|V|)$, while the time complexities of both the BFS and DFS algorithms are $O(|E|)$. The pseudo-code of the network coding algorithm is given in Table 1 below.

Table 1. Pseudo-Code of Network Coding Tree Algorithm.

Algorithm for Constructing Coding Tree
1: Use the DFS (depth-first search) or BFS (breadth-first search) algorithm to search the entire network topology to generate a node-rooted tree rooted at L_s.
2: If there exist sensors which are leaf nodes in tree, denote it as u.
3: End if
4: Keep on search until finding one u' neighbor node who is not u' parent node, denote it as x.
5: connect the node u and x to construct a ring, denote it as C.
6: Traverse all the nodes in ring C until finding one sensor v whose L_s neighbor node w in not in ring C.
7: IF node u and v are already connected, then Cut the loop directly in front or behind v.
8: Else
9: Cut the ring on both sides of v, Repeat steps 4–6 until tree trimming ends.
10: End if
11: keep on Pruning trees until There is no leaf node in the tree.
12: The algorithm ends.

In order to better explain the implementation of the coding tree, below is a concrete implementation example. The example network topology is shown in Figure 3. Figure 4a depicts the result of DFS search with C as the root node. Using the steps 2–6, we can get the result in Figure 4b. Figure 4c,d depict cutting off the corresponding edge and trimming off excess leaf nodes.

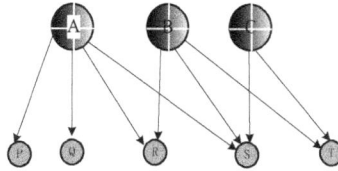

Figure 3. Example network topology for coding tree.

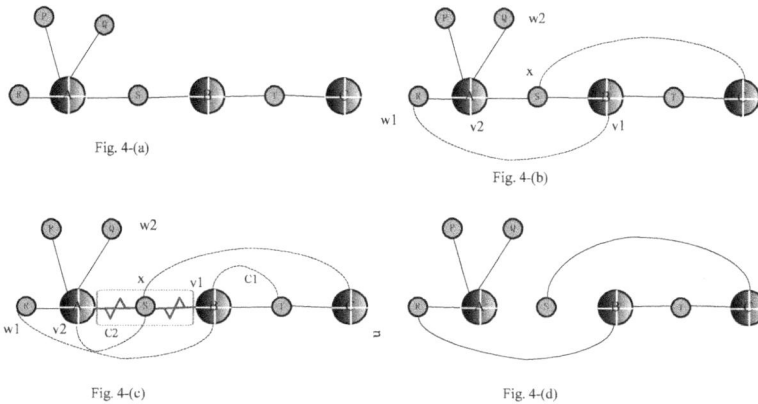

Fig. 4-(a)

Fig. 4-(b)

Fig. 4-(c)

Fig. 4-(d)

Figure 4. Coding tree algorithm implementation process. (**a**) Tree-construction; (**b**) Result of two iterations; (**c**) Result of tree-modification; (**d**) Tree establishment.

Here, it is noted that the condition under which this coding tree algorithm can work well must satisfy $n \prec h$. This condition requires that the full scale of sensor elements in the coding tree must be not more than the scale of their associated sink nodes. However, in actual WSNs, one sink node often associates with multiple sensor elements. If the full scale of source sensors is larger than the full scale of encoded sinks ($n \geq h$), the construction of the network spanning tree following the preset perfect full logical topology would no longer work well. In this situation, the elastic transmission mechanism must follow another grouping strategy to meet the original conditions. This greedy grouping strategy can divide the n sensor nodes, covered by h sink nodes, into groups and ensure that the full network topology constructed by the grouping strategy can continue to employ the coding tree algorithm in Section 4.

The key data structures and their functions are summarised in Table 2.

Table 2. Data Structure and Function of Simulation Program.

Names of Data Structures	Functions
FindTree	Look for DFS_tree
ModTree	Prune DFS_tree and allocate encoding coefficient
Greedy_Group	Logically group the topology that does not meet the coding algorithm condition
GaloisField	Galois field, where encoding is done
nc_node	Define network coding node class
nc_generate_xy	Generate the node coordinates, by which connectivity degree of nodes can be determine
test_connectivity	Measure the connectivity of network topology
nc_independence	Judge whether the received encoding combinations is linearly independent
nc_peform_transmission	Select the node to send packets, and do the encoding operation
nc_update	Judge whether the received encoding combinations is linearly independent, and done the decoding operation

5. Design of Greedy Grouping Algorithm

Without loss of generality, this paper considers the case of a multi-channel multi-interface WSN with a single gateway. The network topology is layered, based on the hops between each sink node and the gateway. Each level of sinks is associated with a group of sensors that continuously monitor mining status and periodically collect data in the smart healthcare environment. It is assumed that L_i and U_i respectively denote the ith level of the sink and sensor sets. Sink nodes normally converse over two orthogonal radio channels. One channel communicates between the sinks to construct the underlying infrastructure, while the other is responsible for communications between the sinks and sensors. This ensures sinks and sensors work simultaneously without mutual interference. The levels of sink nodes occupy the wireless channel using Time Division Multiple Address (TDMA). Each layer of sink nodes is allocated a special time slot for packet transmission. This means that data transmission in each level occurs at the same time. Within each time slot, sensors first deliver data to the relevant level of sinks; the sinks then begin to re-transmit the corresponding data. Typically, each set of sensors and its associated level of sinks is active only during specific time slots assigned to it. The n source nodes represent sensor nodes in the active layer in our network model. If each sensor generates a separate data unit, there will be a total of n data units (from source nodes) that need to be forwarded to the gateway. Here, the binary linear network coding technique is employed to effectively prevent a link failure phenomenon. In our proposal, the minimum number of paths is adopted to provide as much fault-tolerance as possible.

If network latency t is taken into account, the output packet combination can be formulated as in Formula (1):

$$Y_j(t+1) = \sum_{i=1}^{L} g_{ij} X_i(t) + \sum f_j Y(j)(t) \tag{1}$$

In the network model, it is assumed that sensor nodes collect status information periodically. The sink nodes preserve sufficient storage space to accommodate native packets, to encode these original packets and to transmit them. For simplicity, we ignore the delay caused by the encoding operation in our network model. Therefore, here we can calculate the simplified representation of output packets in Formula (2) as follows:

$$Y_j = \sum_{i=1}^{L} g_{ij} X_i \tag{2}$$

For random linear network coding, in Formulas (1) and (2), X_i and Y_j represent the input and output packets, where i and j denote the incoming and output links, respectively. In particular, we use g_{ij} to represent the coding vector generated randomly, L to represent the number of incoming packets, and $Y(j)$ to represent the native packets generated by the sink nodes themselves.

Due to the harsh wireless communication environment in smart healthcare, packet corruption occurs often. Based on the principle of random linear network coding, coded packets are mathematically random linear combinations of the native packets. Based on the GE theory, destination nodes can recover corrupted packets with higher probability. Note that the encoding vector g_{ij} must be recorded in the packet header to assist the destination nodes in the decoding process. Because of the broadcast nature of wireless media, sink nodes can overhear the encoding combinations generated by neighbours. They can then encode them together and forward them. In random linear network coding for our proposal, the coding node encodes the incoming packets with the global encoding vector embedded in the header. The extra fields (or bytes) in messages, as well as storage overhead for coding functions, can also incur a few expenses, compared with traditional methods. Here, note the coding conditions in our proposal target WSNs with omni-directional antenna, in which the sensor and sink nodes are resource-constrained. This means that the memory requirements must be slightly higher than a delay-bandwidth product. In addition, our scheme uses a dynamic cache update scheme, which periodically scans expired packets, so the cache space is not very large. While a sink node can overhear the encoding combinations generated by every sink node in the WBAN, this can create a lot of coding opportunities for sinks. At the expense of this overhead, the proposed fault-tolerant mechanism performs better than traditional schemes in reducing packet loss ratio, end-to-end delay, and resource redundancy degree, and in increasing useful throughput ratio. Therefore, it is worthwhile to pay a small amount of overhead.

A set of sensor nodes that dispatch messages can be considered a group. We can assign a label to a group with a sequence number ID. The decoding process will begin when the destination nodes have received enough native messages with the same sequence number ID. In random linear network coding, the packet information and encoding vectors are mixed at each coding node according to a local coding method. Therefore, the destination node does not need to obtain the knowledge of the whole network topology and global encoding information to recover the native packets. If the rank of matrix made up of global encoding vectors is equal to the number of native packets in each round, the native packets can be released at last. Therefore, as long as the number of linearly independent packets received by destination node is equal to or larger than the number of native packets, all of the native packets can be recovered with high probability through the GE method for solving linear equations over finite fields.

The greedy grouping will first select the candidate sensors with the largest number of neighbour nodes and put them into a grouping labelled as group 1. This selection method can ensure that many connections with L_s nodes can be kept to produce more coding opportunities. The selection method continues putting sensors into this group with the same sequence number until the accumulated degree of this set is not equal to $h - 1$. When group 1 is complete, a subsequent series of groups will be constructed in sequence using this grouping strategy until all sensors are covered, when the greedy grouping algorithm ends. This greedy grouping strategy chooses the source sensors with the most neighbour nodes at every grouping stage. In this way, our greedy algorithm particularly tries to create coding opportunities without regarding other factors that may influence network performance. Therefore, this grouping scheme satisfies the optimal requirement from the local perspective. Globally, however, the optimal grouping combinations are not necessarily achieved [33,34].The pseudo-code of the network coding algorithm is given in Table 3 below.

Table 3. Pseudo-Code of Greedy Grouping Algorithm.

Algorithm for Constructing Greedy Grouping
1: Define the variable
2: Stores the scheduled source node, $SchdSet = \phi$;
3: Initialize the encoding group number, $coding\_lable = 0$;
4: Initialize the cluster number, $cluster\_id = 0$;
5: Start grouping
6: Initialize source node index in group, $index = 0$;
7: Calculate the minimum cut h between L_s and destination node
8: Define a boolean variable Found, If the source node joins the current cluster, it is true, $Found = TRUE$;
9: While$(|SchdSet|<|U_s|)$ do
10: $x = \phi$;
11: if $(index > h - 2 || Found == FALSE)$ then
12: $cluster\_id + +$;
13: $index + +$;
14: **End if**
15: $coding\_lable + +$;
16: x={choose the sensor u with maximum connectivity degree}, $u \notin SchdSet$
17: $if(x == \phi)$ then
18: $Found = FALSE$;
19: **Else**
20: $SchdSet = SchdSet \cup x$;
21: $Schedule[cluster\_id][index] = x$;
22: Complete a node grouping, jump to the next one
23: **End if**
24: **End While**

Finally, the destination nodes will judge if they have received k linearly independent packet combinations. If so, the k original packets can be solved with the GE method. It can be proven that the computational complexity of this greedy grouping algorithm is (k^3). The proof is omitted here because of space. If the wireless channel environment is too unfavourable, the destination nodes will not receive sufficient packets to satisfy the GE condition. In this harsh environment, the source nodes will start there transmission of lost packets. If the destination nodes do not receive enough required information, they will request their neighbour nodes to re-transmit the associated information. The neighbour nodes will also continue to forward lost packets until the GE solution condition is satisfied. For simplicity, it is assumed here that a one-hop retransmission will usually satisfy the GE solution requirement.

In order to better explain the grouping process, Figure 5 gives an example. In Figure 5, there are four source nodes: S1, S2, S3, and S4, and the maximum number of link-disjoint paths between the sinks and the gateway is three. Therefore, the maximum number of source nodes in feasible grouping is 2. Using the greedy grouping algorithm in Table 3, we can derive an output result SET1 = {{S1,S2}, {S3,S4}}. In contrast to the other two grouping results SET2 = {{S1,S2}, {S1,S3}, {S1,S4}} and SET3 = {{S1,S3}, {S2,S4}}, we found that the optimal solution is SET1. Because this scheme obtains a fairness index more than SET2, and consumes less bandwidth resources than SET3. In this greedy strategy, each packet uses only three links to forward data to the minimum cutting edge, while four links in SET3.

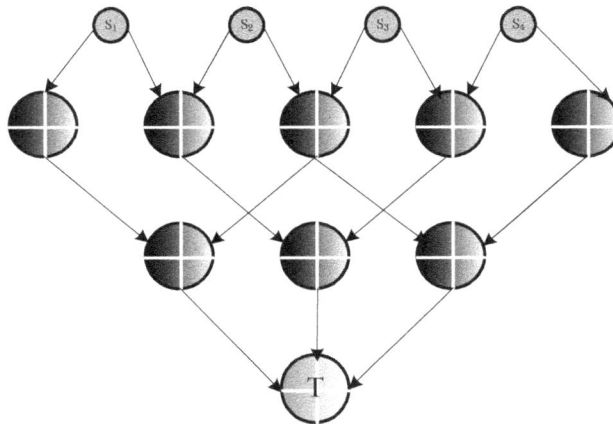

Figure 5. Illustration for grouping algorithm.

6. Numerical Results and Analysis

Extensive simulations have been conducted to compare the transmission reliability and efficiency, resource consumption, and latency performance in the elastic transmission mechanism [35,36] with a resource redundancy protection mechanism and backup path protection mechanism for validation of its effectiveness. We defined four reliability and efficiency performance indicators that we measured by continuing to increase the network traffic and link failure probability. We built a simulation framework in the Windows-environment-based C++language, with the network topology depicted in Figure 6.

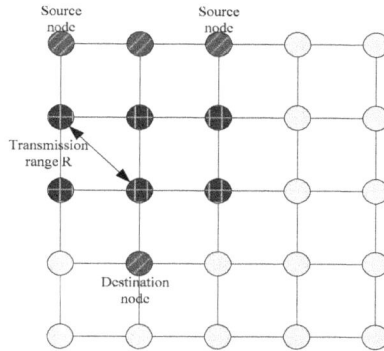

Figure 6. Network topology for simulation experiments.

Figure 7 shows the data transfer arrow signs of three methods, in which the source nodes S1 and S2 need to transmit the packets b1 and b2 to the destination node *T*, respectively.

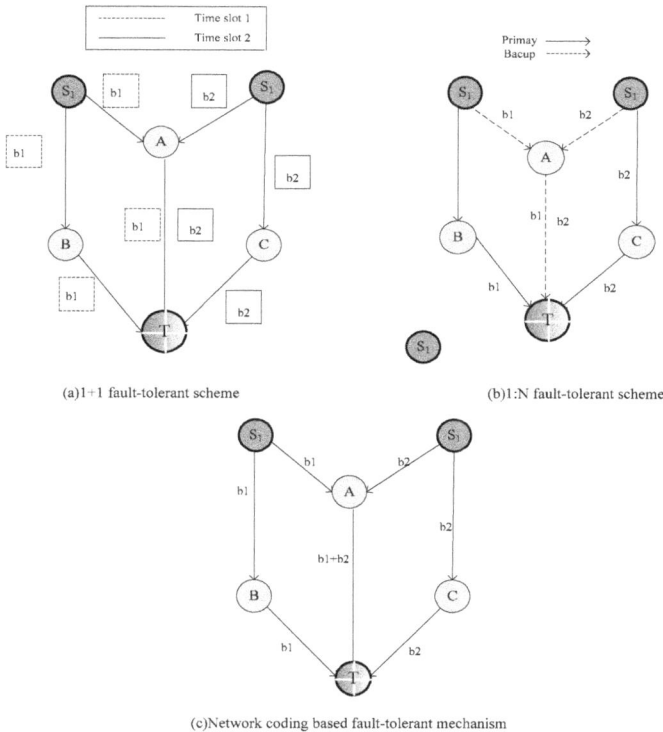

(a)1+1 fault-tolerant scheme

(b)1:N fault-tolerant scheme

(c)Network coding based fault-tolerant mechanism

Figure 7. Packet transmission for three fault-tolerance schemes.

In the process of simulation, it is assumed that the probability of link failure is independent at each hop. The source node sends a steady stream of traffic to the destination node. When each generation of packets is received by destination nodes, they record packet information including packet size, time stamp, encoding operation, decoding operation, and other statistics. The sensor and sink nodes also calculate the transmitting times of packets.

In our simulation configuration, we adopt the following method: the traffic flow is established between each pair of source and destination nodes. This traffic flow would generate new packets according to the assumed statistical distribution (e.g., Poisson distribution), meanwhile, it would specify the size of packet and the average rate of generating packets. In this way, we can configure the dynamic packets. The main simulation parameter values are listed in Table 4 below.

Table 4. Simulation Parameters Settings.

Parameters Value
Attenuation model two ray
Channel capacity 2 Mbit/s
Signal transmission range 250 m
Signal interference range 550 m
Packet size 512 Byte
Output queue type FIFO (First-In First-Out)
Cache capacity 50 packets
energy model generic radio energy model
Simulation area 1000 m × 1000 m

A. Performance Indicators

In our simulation experiments, we adopted four performance indicators:

● Successful delivery ratio

We define the Successful Delivery Ratio (*SDR*) as the percentage of network traffic received at destination nodes relative to the network traffic generated at sources. We use this *SDR* indicator to weigh the probability of successful packet transmission. A larger *SDR* means a higher probability of successful delivery. The *SDR* is computed using Formula (3):

$$SDR = \frac{\sum_{d_k \in (S,D)} P_r}{\sum_{s_k \in (S,D)} P_s} \tag{3}$$

● Resource redundancy degree

We define the Resource Redundancy Degree (*RRD*) as the percentage of redundant network traffic relative to the network traffic generated at sources. These copied packets consist of two parts: duplicates and linearly dependent packets. This *RRD* indicator can be used to measure the cost of the fault-tolerant mechanism. The *RRD* can be computed using Formula (4):

$$RRD = \frac{\sum_{i=1}^{n} R^i_{packet\_useless}}{\sum_{j=1}^{n} R^j_{packet\_emitted}} \tag{4}$$

● End-to-end delay

We define End-to-end delay (*ED*) as the sum of the latencies for every message received by the destination nodes. This *ED* indicator can be used to weigh the timeliness of the fault-tolerant mechanism. Because the network coding operation incurs some latency, the *ED* indicator consists of four parts: encoding latency $d_{encoding}$, decoding latency $d_{decoding}$, transmission latency $d_{transmission}$, and waiting latency d_{wait}. The ED can be calculated using Formulas (5) and (6):

$$ED = \frac{1}{n}\sum_{j=1}^{n} D_j \tag{5}$$

$$D = d_{wait} + d_{transmission} + d_{encoding} + d_{decoding} \tag{6}$$

● Useful throughput ratio

We define the Useful Throughput Ratio (UTR) as the percentage of the scale of effective network information relative to the scale of full network information received by destination nodes. We use this UTR indicator to weigh the transmission efficiency of the fault-tolerant mechanism. Therefore, a larger UTR value means more effective delivery. This UTR indicator can be computed using Formula (7):

$$UTR = \frac{\sum_{d_i \in (S,D)} P_{useful}}{\sum_{d_j \in (S,D)} P_{received}} \tag{7}$$

B. Simulation Results and Analysis

To compare the advantages and disadvantages of the DFS and BFS schemes, some simulation experiments were conducted employing these two search algorithms in the network coding tree algorithm. The range of sink nodes in WSNs could be changed between $|U_s| + 1$ and $2 |U_s|$. Additionally, we continued to increase the number of sensor nodes, keeping the number of sink nodes at twice as many. The experiments were executed 100 times to obtain average values. Figure 8 depicts the number of sink nodes needed while increasing the number of sensor nodes. We observe that the number of leaves generated using the BFS method is larger than that generated by the DFS method. Although global optimization was not achieved, the introduction of the BFS search algorithm was more beneficial than DFS in generating more leaf combinations in the network coding tree.

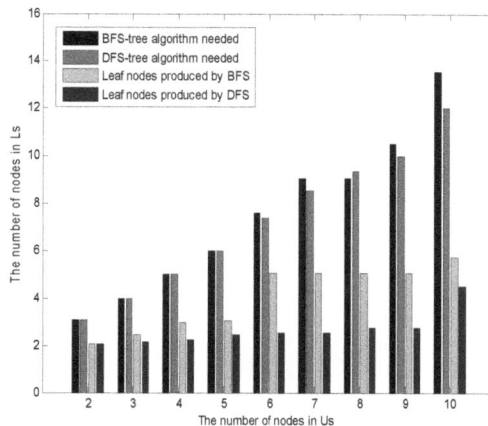

Figure 8. Comparison of the total number of generated leaves nodes between breadth-first search (BFS) and depth-first search (DFS) algorithms.

Figure 9 presents the probability of successful transmission as link failure probability changes. It can be observed that the SDR values of these three fault-tolerant mechanisms shrink as the link failure probability increases. In particular, the SDR values drop abruptly to zero when the link failure probability exceeds 0.3. This is because the NCFM, 1:N and 1 + 1 fault-tolerant mechanisms cannot receive correct packets in harsh channel conditions when the maximum number of retransmissions is reached. In addition, we observe that the *SDR* of the 1 + 1 scheme is more or less the same as that of the 1:N scheme. This is because we reserve just one backup path to retransmit the lost packet in the 1:N scheme; the difference between the 1 + 1 and 1:N schemes can be shown from the analysis of *RRD* and *ED*. Therefore, we conclude that the fault-tolerant capacity of the NCFM algorithm is stronger than those of the 1 + 1 and 1:N schemes. Additionally, the NCFM algorithm has an evident advantage over 1:N and 1 + 1 when the link failure probability is lower than 0.3.

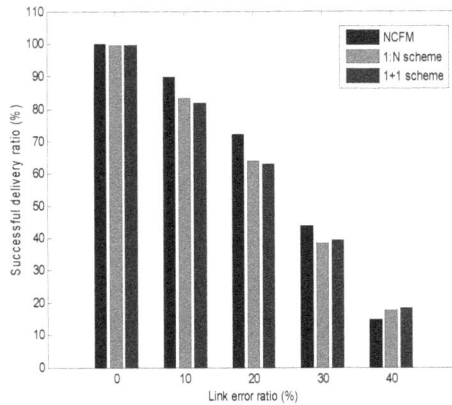

Figure 9. Comparison of successful delivery ratios.

Figure 10 presents the average latency performance analysis for the three fault-tolerant mechanisms as the link failure probability increases. The end-to-end delay curve of the elastic transmission mechanism varies with those of the 1:N and 1 + 1 protection mechanisms if the link failure probability is zero in perfect channel conditions. When the link failure probability rises, the average latency curve of the elastic transmission mechanism will become better than those of the 1:N and 1 + 1 protection mechanisms. This is because the random linear network coding operation can reduce the number of packet transmissions or retransmission times as much as possible when the maximum transmissions bottleneck is reached. Here it is assumed that a node can finish only one packet delivery each time. The 1:N fault-tolerant mechanism must continue to switch the backup path for the retransmission of lost packets, which results in longer *ED*. For the 1 + 1 scheme, packet delivery will be postponed when transmissions fail on both the working and backup paths. In particular, the average latency curves of all schemes will rise rapidly if the wireless link quality degrades. In this situation, it is likely that the destination node cannot receive sufficient packets for decoding with the NCFM algorithm. Therefore, the *ED* performance will fail when the link failure probability is greater than 40%.

Figure 11 shows the average end-to-end delay analysis for the three fault-tolerant mechanisms as the network traffic continues to increase. The simulation experiments were conducted assuming that the link failure probability was 8%. As increased network traffic is injected into the WSN, the average end-to-end delay of the three fault-tolerant mechanisms shows an upward trend. As the number of source packets continues to increase, the *ED* benefit achieved by NCFM becomes gradually evident. The reason is that NCFM exploits the encoding function to cut down the wireless resource redundancy with more information. Under some *SDR* levels, the destination can still receive sufficient packets to restore the original packets. Therefore, this proactive NCFM algorithm outperforms the 1:N and 1 + 1 protection mechanisms. The 1:N method in lossy networks can guarantee the reliability of data transmission to some degree, but the latency caused by path switching and packet retransmission is longer than those of the other two fault-tolerant mechanisms. Therefore, the conclusion can be drawn that the 1:N fault-tolerant mechanism is not suitable if network users have strict real-time demands. The proactive NCFM method can make full use of limited bandwidth resources to supply fast recovery for delay-sensitive traffic.

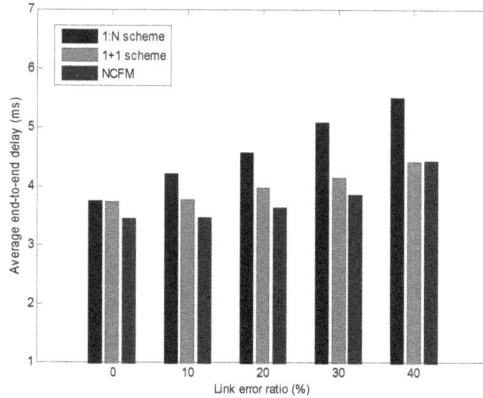

Figure 10. Comparison of average end-to-end delay.

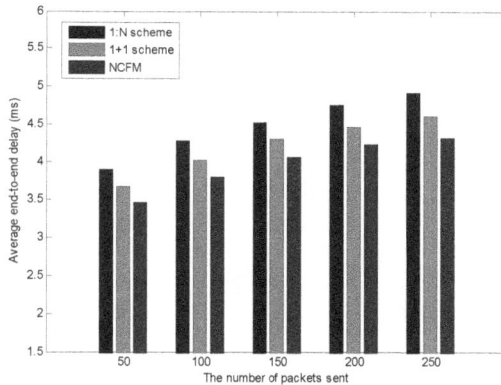

Figure 11. Comparison of ED with the number of packets sent forNetwork Coding-based Fault-tolerant Mechanism (NCFM), 1 + 1 and 1:N.

Figure 12 displays the analysis of the degrees of resource redundancy for the three fault-tolerant mechanisms when the link failure probability is increased. As the link failure probability increases, the degrees of resource redundancy continue to rise, as shown in Figure 12. With the deterioration of channel conditions, packet loss frequently occurs in certain nodes. Partial nodes need to resend the missing packets to ensure that all destination nodes can receive their packets error-free. A large number of retransmissions can cause many redundant packets in WSNs. As depicted in Figure 12, the cost of an elastic transmission mechanism and resource redundancy protection mechanism in terms of the degree of resource redundancy seems to be less than that of a backup path protection mechanism. This is because many different packets are encouraged to mix together into one packet before transmission. This operation can decrease the number of packet transmissions or retransmissions as much as possible, and improve wireless resource utilization. Although some packets are lost, the destination can still exploit the received encoded packets to recover the original packets without retransmission. In particular, the *RRD* of the 1:N method rises sharply after the link error rate reaches 0.1. This is because poor channel quality causes much retransmission, resulting in network congestion, which incurs many more redundant packets. To a certain extent, *RRD* is similar to the energy consumption efficiency. We can conclude that the elastic transmission mechanism is more economical than the 1 + 1 and 1:N mechanisms. Although NCFM increases the data processing burden of nodes, energy consumption in the computer hardware is much smaller than that needed to process packet transmission, so this part of energy consumption can be ignored.

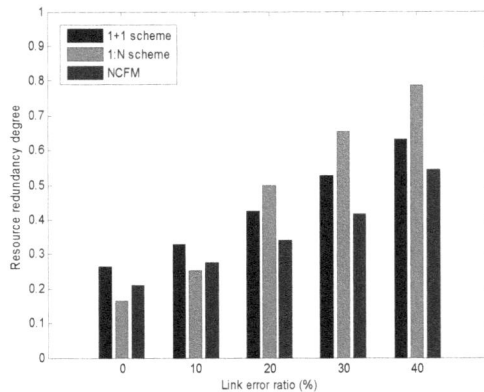

Figure 12. Comparison of resource redundancy degrees.

Figure 13 presents an analysis of the degree of resource redundancy for the three fault-tolerant mechanisms as the network traffic continues to increase. The simulation experiments ran with a link failure probability of 10%. As the injected network traffic grows, the *RRD*s of the three fault-tolerant mechanisms trend steadily upward. When the link failure probability is relatively low, it can be observed that the expense of NCFM in the degree of resource redundancy is smaller than that of the 1:N and 1 + 1 protection mechanisms. The reason for this is similar to the analysis for Figure 12. Therefore, we can conclude that for identical link error rates, the NCFM is the most economical fault-tolerant scheme for network resources.

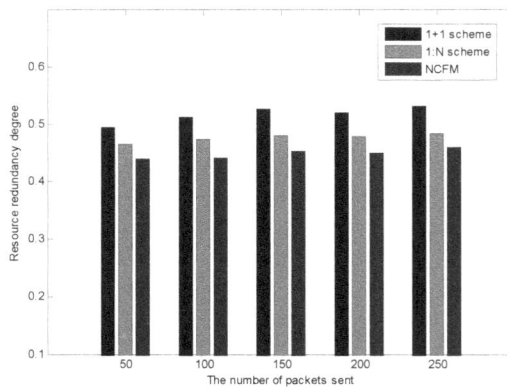

Figure 13. Comparison of RRD with the number of packets sent for NCFM, 1 + 1 and 1:N.

Figure 14 shows the analysis of the useful throughput ratio for the three fault-tolerant mechanisms. The simulations were conducted with a link failure probability of 8%. It can be observed that the useful throughput ratio performance of NCFM is much better than that of the 1:N and 1 + 1 protection mechanisms. From the comparison results in Figure 14, it can be concluded that NCFM can proactively offer fault-tolerant functions for native packets only if the network coding condition is satisfied. Compared with the traditional 1:N and 1 + 1 fault-tolerant mechanisms, we observe that NCFM has higher transmission efficiency, lower network expenses, and a more reliable fault-tolerant capacity.

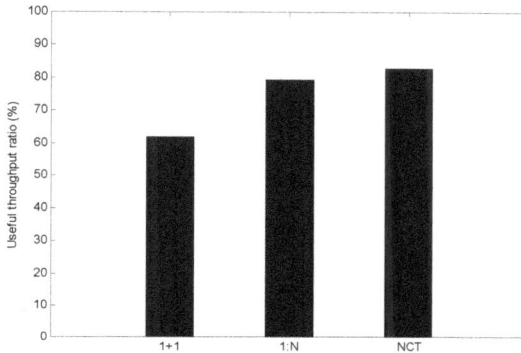

Figure 14. Comparison of useful throughput ratio.

7. Conclusions

To tackle the fault-tolerant problem in a many-to-one stream model in a smart healthcare monitoring scenario, we have designed a proactive resilient data transmission mechanism with the principle of random linear network coding. This fault-tolerant scheme includes two aspects: the greedy grouping of nodes and coding tree construction. As long as the gateway receives a sufficient number of linearly independent encoding combinations, original packets can be recovered quickly even when some errors occur. Additionally, a scalable simulation framework with encoding and decoding functions has been devised to verify the performance of three different fault-tolerant mechanisms. Based on this platform, a number of experiments have been conducted comparing transmission reliability, costs of resource consumption, latency performance, and transmission efficiency. Numerical statistics have shown that this elastic transmission mechanism outperforms traditional network protection mechanisms in improving the successful delivery ratio and the useful throughput ratio, and reduces the degree of resource redundancy and average end-to-end delay. The performance analysis offers some guidelines for effectively and efficiently designing survivability protection methods under different traffic patterns. In the future, this proactive network-coding-based elastic-transmission mechanism will be implemented in a real-time healthcare monitoring systems.

Acknowledgments: The preliminary work of this paper was presented at the International Conference on Computer Science and Software Engineering (ICCSSE) 2013. The work was supported by the National Natural Science Foundation of China (61501105, 61471109, 61471110), the National Key Research and Development Program of China (Grant No. 2016YFC0801607), the China Postdoctoral Science Foundation (2013M541243), the Fundamental Research Funds for the Central Universities (N150404018, N130304001, 150404015, N150401002, N161608001), and the Postdoctoral Science Foundation of Northeast University (20140319).

Author Contributions: Y.P. performed the experimental part, modelled, analyzed data and reported the results. X.W. and Y.W. contributed to the experimental part and result analysis. Q.D. and L.G. guided the whole research and supported the structure of the paper.

Conflicts of Interest: The authors declare no conflict of interest.

References

1. Zhang, C.; Lai, C.; Lai, Y.; Wu, Z.; Chao, H. An inferential real-time falling posture reconstruction for Internet of healthcare things. *J. Netw. Comput. Appl.* **2017**, *89*, 86–95. [CrossRef]
2. Ning, Z.; Xia, F.; Hu, X.; Chen, Z.; Obaidat, M. Social-oriented Adaptive Transmission in Opportunistic Internet of Smartphones. *IEEE Trans. Ind. Inform.* **2017**, *13*, 810–820. [CrossRef]
3. Ning, Z.; Xia, F.; Ullah, N.; Kong, X.; Hu, X. Vehicular Social Networks: Enabling Smart Mobility. *IEEE Commun. Mag.* **2017**, *55*, 49–55. [CrossRef]
4. Pierre, S.; Beaubrun, R. Integrating routing and survivability in fault-tolerant computer network design. *Comput. Commun.* **2000**, *23*, 317–327. [CrossRef]
5. Chu, K.-C.; Lin, F.Y.-S. Survivability and performance optimization of mobile wireless communication networks in the event of base station failure. *Comput. Electr. Eng.* **2006**, *32*, 50–64. [CrossRef]
6. Tipper, D.; Dahlberg, T.; Shin, H.; Charnsripinyo, C. Providing fault tolerance in wireless access networks. *IEEE Commun. Mag.* **2002**, *40*, 58–64. [CrossRef]
7. Bose, I.; Eryarsoy, E.; He, L. Multi-period design of survivable wireless access networks under capacity constraints. *Decis. Support Syst.* **2005**, *38*, 529–538. [CrossRef]
8. Reddy, T.; Sriram, S.; Manoj, B.S.; Murthy, C. MuSeQoR: Multi-path failure-tolerant security-aware QoS routing in ad hoc wireless networks. *Comput. Netw.* **2006**, *50*, 1349–1383. [CrossRef]
9. Qiu, T.; Zhao, A.; Xia, F.; Si, W.; Wu, D. ROSE: Robustness Strategy for Scale-Free Wireless Sensor Networks. *IEEE/ACM Trans. Netw.* **2017**, *1–16*. [CrossRef]
10. Chen, X.; Kim, Y.-A.; Wang, B.; Wei, W.; Shi, Z.; Song, Y. Fault-tolerant monitor placement for out-of-band wireless sensor network monitoring. *Ad Hoc Netw.* **2012**, *10*, 62–74. [CrossRef]
11. Boukerche, A.; NelemPazzi, R.W.; Araujo, R.B. Fault-tolerant wireless sensor network routing protocols for the supervision of context-aware physical environments. *J. Parallel Distrib. Comput.* **2006**, *66*, 586–599. [CrossRef]
12. Ning, Z.; Liu, L.; Xia, F.; Jedari, B.; Lee, I.; Zhang, W. CAIS: A Copy Adjustable Incentive Scheme in Community-based Socially-Aware Networking. *IEEE Trans. Veh. Technol.* **2017**, *66*, 3406–3419. [CrossRef]
13. Qiu, T.; Chen, N.; Li, K.; Qiao, D.; Fu, Z. Heterogeneous ad hoc networks: Architectures, advances and challenges. *Ad Hoc Netw.* **2017**, *55*, 143–152. [CrossRef]
14. Lee, G.; Murray, A.T. Maximal covering with network survivability requirements in wireless mesh networks, Computers. *Environ. Urban Syst.* **2010**, *34*, 49–57. [CrossRef]
15. Benyamina, D.; Hafid, A.; Gendreau, M.; Maureira, J.C. On the design of reliable wireless mesh network infrastructure with QoS constraints. *Comput. Netw.* **2011**, *55*, 1631–1647. [CrossRef]
16. Hsu, C.-Y.; Wu, J.-L.C.; Wang, S.-T.; Hong, C.-Y. Survivable and delay-guaranteed backbone wireless mesh network design. *J. Parallel Distrib. Comput.* **2008**, *68*, 306–320. [CrossRef]
17. Bisti, L.; Lenzini, L.; Mingozzi, E.; Vallati, C.; Erta, A.; Malesci, U. Improved network resilience of wireless mesh networks using MPLS and Fast Re-Routing techniques. *Ad Hoc Netw.* **2011**, *9*, 1448–1460. [CrossRef]
18. Jiang, S.; Xue, Y. Providing survivability against jamming attack for multi-radio multi-channel wireless mesh networks. *J. Netw. Comput. Appl.* **2011**, *34*, 443–454. [CrossRef]
19. Al-Kofahi, O.; Kamal, A. Network coding-based protection of many-to-one wireless flows. *IEEE J. Sel. Areas Commun.* **2009**, *27*, 797–813. [CrossRef]
20. Misra, S.; Gupta, A.; Krishna, P.V.; Agarwal, H.; Obaidat, M.S. An adaptive learning approach for fault-tolerant routing in Internet of Things. In Proceedings of the IEEE Wireless Communications and Networking Conference (WCNC 2012), Paris, France, 1–4 April 2012; pp. 815–819.
21. Wang, J.; Liu, Z.; Shen, Y.; Chen, H.; Zheng, L.; Qiu, H.; Shu, S. A distributed algorithm for inter-layer network coding-based multimedia multicast in Internet of Things. *Comput. Electr. Eng.* **2015**. [CrossRef]
22. Qiu, T.; Liu, X.; Feng, L.; Zhou, Y.; Zheng, K. An efficient tree-based self-organizing protocol for internet of things. *IEEE Access* **2016**, *4*, 3535–3546. [CrossRef]
23. Otto, C.; Milenkovic, A.; Sanders, C.; Jovanov, E. System architecture of a wireless body area sensor network for ubiquitous health monitoring. *J. Mob. Multimedia* **2006**, *1*, 307–326.
24. Latre, B.; Braem, B.; Moerman, I.; Blondia, C.; Reusens, E.; Joseph, W.; Demeester, P. A low-delay protocol for multi-hop wireless body area networks. In Proceedings of the Fourth Annual International Conference on Mobile and Ubiquitous Systems: Networking & Services, Philadelphia, PA, USA, 6–10 August 2007; pp. 1–8.

25. Zhou, G.; Lu, J.; Wan, C.-Y.; Yarvis, M.D.; Stankovic, J.A. Body QoS: Adaptive and radio-agnostic QoS for body sensor networks. In Proceedings of the IEEE 27th Conference on Computer Communications (INFOCOM 2008), Phoenix, AZ, USA, 13–18 April 2008; pp. 565–573.

26. Wu, G.; Ren, J.; Xia, F.; Xu, Z. An adaptive fault-tolerant communication scheme for body sensor networks. *Sensors* **2010**, *10*, 9590–9608. [CrossRef] [PubMed]

27. Qiu, T.; Qiao, R.; Wu, D. EABS: An Event-Aware Backpressure Scheduling Scheme for Emergency Internet of Things. *IEEE Trans. Mob. Comput.* **2017**. [CrossRef]

28. Lipschutz, S.; Lipson, M. *Schaum's Outlines of Linear Algebra*, Tata McGraw-hill edition; The McGraw-Hill Companies, Inc.: Delhi, India, 2001; pp. 69–80.

29. Li, S.Y.; Yeung, R.W.; Cai, N. Linear network coding. *IEEE Trans. Inf. Theory* **2003**, *49*, 371–381. [CrossRef]

30. Ahlswede, R.; Cai, N.; Li, S.; Yeung, R. Network information flow. *IEEE Trans. Inf. Theory* **2000**, *46*, 1204–1216. [CrossRef]

31. Hou, W.; Ning, Z.; Guo, L. Temporal, Functional and Spatial Big Data Computing Framework for Large-Scale Smart Grid. *IEEE Trans. Emerg. Top. Comput.* **2017**. [CrossRef]

32. Guo, L.; Ning, Z.; Song, Q.; Huang, F.; Jamalipour, A. Joint Encoding and Grouping Multiple Node Pairs for Physical-Layer Network Coding with Low-Complexity Algorithm. *IEEE Trans. Veh. Technol.* **2017**. [CrossRef]

33. Qiu, T.; Liu, X.; Han, M.; Li, M.; Zhang, Y. SRTS: A Self-Recoverable Time Synchronization for Sensor Networks of Healthcare IoT. *Comput. Netw.* **2017**. [CrossRef]

34. Park, K.; Park, J.; Lee, J. An IoT System for Remote Monitoring of Patients at Home. *Appl. Sci.* **2017**, *7*. [CrossRef]

35. Aly, S.A.; Kamal, A.E.; Al-Kofahi, O.M. Network protection codes: Providing self-healing in autonomic networks using network coding. *Comput. Netw.* **2012**, *56*, 99–111. [CrossRef]

36. Rouayheb, S.; Sprintson, A.; Georghiades, C. Robust Network codes for unicast connections: A case study. *IEEE/ACM Trans. Netw.* **2011**, *19*, 644–656. [CrossRef]

applied
sciences

Article

Reformulation-Linearization Technique Approach for Kidney Exchange Program IT Healthcare Platforms

Junsang Yuh [1,2], Seokhyun Chung [2] and Taesu Cheong [2,*]

[1]   R&D Center, Begas, Seoul 06179, Korea; yuhjunsang@gmail.com
[2]   School of Industrial Management Engineering, Korea University, Seoul 02841, Korea; csh98016@gmail.com
*   Correspondence: tcheong@korea.ac.kr; Tel.: +82-2-3290-3382

Received: 8 July 2017; Accepted: 11 August 2017; Published: 17 August 2017

Abstract: Kidney exchange allows a potential living donor whose kidney is incompatible with his intended recipient to donate a kidney to another patient so that the donor's intended recipient can receive a compatible kidney from another donor. These exchanges can include cycles of longer than two donor–patient pairs and chains produced by altruistic donors. Kidney exchange programs (KEPs) can be modeled as a maximum-weight cycle-packing problem in a directed graph. This paper develops a new integer programming model for KEPs by applying the reformulation-linearization technique (RLT) to enhance a lower bound obtained by its linear programming (LP) relaxation. Given the results obtained from the proposed model, the model is expected to be utilized in the integrated KEP IT (Information Technology) healthcare platform to obtain plans for optimized kidney exchanges.

Keywords: kidney exchange program; integer programming; reformulation-linearization technique; IT healthcare platform

---

1. Introduction

Kidney transplants are essential for many end-stage renal disease sufferers. However, finding compatible kidneys may be difficult because of blood or tissue incompatibilities between donors and their intended recipients. The issue of incompatibility can be overcome by establishing a kidney exchange program (KEP). The first of these was performed in South Korea [1–3] in 1991 and they have since been widely performed in many countries, including the United States of America [4–9], the United Kingdom [10–12] and Australia [13]. A KEP helps a potential living donor to donate his or her kidney, which is incompatible with the intended recipient, to another recipient so that the donor's intended recipient can also receive a compatible kidney from another donor. The Korea Centers for Disease Control & Prevention (KCDC), the government ministry that maintains a unified administration to avoid disease and to improve public health welfare in South Korea, has recently paid attention to the contribution of the KEP, which increases the number of renal disease sufferers able to receive kidney transplants. The KCDC has pushed ahead with a plan for the development of an integrated IT healthcare platform for the KEP. On the platform, hospitals can register the essential information for verifying the compatibility of their renal disease sufferers. Then, the proposed KEP platform would provide matching plans to maximize the number of possible kidney exchanges in the program. Hence, it is important to establish an efficient optimization model for KEPs that can provide optimized kidney exchange plans within a reasonable time, and, in this paper, we intend to provide a high-performance mathematical programming model easily solvable by commercial optimization solvers (e.g., Cplex, Gurobi) to support the integrated KEP IT healthcare platform of South Korea. We remark that, as in our case, operations research (OR) techniques have been applied and utilized to tackle many important and challenging optimization issues in healthcare (e.g., [14] for an overview of recent research on several OR applications in healthcare, and [15,16] for medical resident scheduling problems and sensor-based patient monitoring problems, respectively).

Figure 1 illustrates two-way and three-way KEPs. Figure 1a illustrates a case consisting of only two pairs. Within each pair, the patient and donor are incompatible. However, the patient in pair 1 is compatible with the donor in pair 2 and the patient in pair 2 is compatible with the donor in pair 1. We note that in precedent times, when exchanges between pairs were not allowed, there was no way to perform the transplants. However, with the KEP, exchanges between the pairs become possible, and the two transplants can be performed. As we will explain in detail below, the KEP can be expressed as a digraph for which a node corresponds to an incompatible donor–recipient pair and a directed arc is introduced if a donor in an initial node is compatible with a recipient in the terminal node of the arc (see the graph in Figure 1a). In practice, three-way exchanges are the most complicated exchanges performed because one of all the operations on an exchange cycle must be performed simultaneously to avoid the risk of one of the donors reneging, and it is technically difficult to simultaneously reserve operation rooms for more than six patients in a hospital. Figure 1b illustrates three-way kidney exchanges.

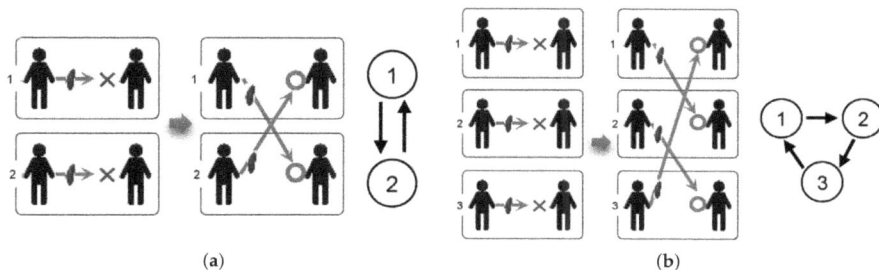

Figure 1. Illustration of (**a**) two-way and (**b**) three-way kidney exchange program (KEP).

As we briefly mentioned before, the KEP model can be expressed by a digraph $G(V, A)$, called a *KEP graph* in this paper, where V and A indicate the set of vertices and arcs of the graph G, respectively. Figure 2 presents an example of G and a solution to the model (i.e., possible kidney exchanges on a KEP graph). In Figure 2a, a vertex $i \in V$ corresponds to a current incompatible pair consisting of a patient i and a donor i, and an arc $(i, j) \in A$ indicates the compatibility between donor i and patient j, which means that donor i can provide his or her kidney to patient j. Figure 2b demonstrates an example of a feasible solution. The thick arrows represent an exchange cycle among pairs 1, 2, and 4.

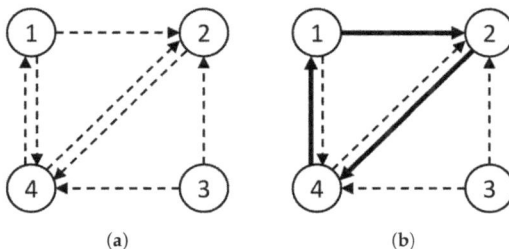

Figure 2. Kidney exchange program (KEP) graph (**a**) and its feasible solution (**b**).

We now discuss the optimization problem for a KEP, given a KEP graph G. The objective of the optimization of a KEP is generally to maximize the number of possible kidney exchanges in a given pool of candidates, and the KEP can be mathematically modeled as an integer programming problem, which is the main focus of this paper. Roth et al. [17] proposed an edge formulation and a cycle formulation for KEPs, and Abraham et al. [7] developed a solution algorithm for those formulations. Furthermore, Constantino et al. [18] proposed two compact formulations—that is, an edge-assignment (EA) formulation and an extended edge (EE) formulation. Manlove and O'Malley [19] presented how the cycle formulation by Roth et al. [17] can be extended to find optimal solutions for the KEP in the United Kingdom, which are compatible with U.K. National Living Donor Kidney Sharing Schemes (NLDKSS).

The reformulation-linearization technique (RLT), which we intend to utilize in this paper, is a procedure that can be used to generate a tight linear programming (LP) relaxation for a discrete optimization problem. Various strong formulations on several classes of structured problems are generated by the RLT. Sherali et al. [20] developed a new integer programming model for the traveling salesman problem (TSP) by applying the RLT to the Miller–Tucker–Zemlin (MTZ) formulation. Moreover, they showed that the resulting formulation dominates the lifted-MTZ formulation of Desrochers and Laporte [21]. Sherali et al. [22] applied the RLT to the path-based TSP model using logical restrictions. They proposed a variety of new formulations for the TSP, and exploited several dominance relationships between them. Park et al. [23] dealt with a two-level facility location–allocation problem arising from the access network design of a telecommunication network. They developed a mixed-integer program for the problem and applied the RLT to improve computational effectiveness.

In this paper, we focus on the best-known compact formulations for the KEP in the literature, which are the EA and EE formulations proposed by Constantino et al. [18]. We first induce the EE formulation by applying the partial level 1 RLT to the EA formulation. After that, we further strengthen the formulation via the level 1 RLT and propose a new integer programming model that dominates existing formulations. Computational results are provided to demonstrate the effectiveness of our formulation compared to that of those previous. Therefore, the contribution of our study can be summarized as below.

- We propose a new integer programming model, which is proved to be more compact and effective than previous optimization models through computational experiments. Although our new formulation gives a solution that allows only one more patient to have a kidney transplant than the matching solutions made by existing formulations, this is a meaningful result because a kidney transplant is immediately related to the precious life of a patient. Furthermore, our proposed model would be directly related to the performance of the KEP IT healthcare platform.

- We derive the EE formulation from the EA formulation by applying a systematic approach, the RLT. As presented by Constantino et al. [18], establishing a more compact integer programming formulation requires the exploitation of the special structures inherent to the problem of interest. On the other hand, by using our approach, such a formulation can be derived by a simple and systematic application of the RLT independent of the problem-specific structures. This difference suggests the possibility that our approach can be applied to other real-world optimization problems to obtain more significant formulations.

This paper is organized as follows: Section 2 briefly provides the overview of the RLT for the reference. Section 3 reviews the two representative integer programming models (i.e., the EE and EA formulations) for the KEP in literature. Section 4 presents how the EE formulation can be derived from the EA formulation by applying the RLT and how we could further strengthen the EE formulation. Section 5 presents the computational results. Finally, we conclude the discussion in Section 6.

2. Reformulation-Linearization Technique

In this section, we briefly describe the concept of the RLT process in the context of zero-one integer problems. Let us define the feasible region of a zero-one integer problem as

$$X = \{x : \mathbf{A}x \leq b, \ x \in \mathbb{B}^r\}$$

where $\mathbf{A}$ is a $q \times r$ matrix, b is a q vector, and $N = \{1, 2, \ldots, r\}$ is the index set of all variables. Without loss of generality, we assume that every component of $\mathbf{A}$ and b is an integer. Additionally, the inequalities accommodate the upper bounds of $x_j \leq 1$ for $j \in N$. As usual, $\mathbb{B}$ and $\mathbb{R}$ denote the sets of binary and real numbers, respectively.

The RLT process by Sherali and Adams [24] to construct relaxation X_d at any level $d \in \{1, \ldots, r\}$ in higher dimensional space consists of two steps, as follows:

Step 1. (Reformulation) Multiply each constraint defining the feasible region with every product factor of the form $\prod_{i \in J_1} x_i \prod_{i \in J_2}(1 - x_i)$, where $J_1, J_2 \subseteq N$, $J_1 \cap J_2 = \varnothing$, and $|J_1 \cup J_2| = d$, and then apply the identity $x_i^2 = x_i$ for all $i \in N$.

Step 2. (Linearization) Linearize the resulting polynomial system by substituting a variable λ_J for every distinct product term $\prod_{i \in J} x_i$, where $J \subseteq N$.

The results of Sherali and Adams [24] show that, by denoting the projection of X_d onto the space of the original variables x by $X_{P_d} = \{x : (x, \lambda) \in X_d\}$, we obtain the hierarchy of relaxations

$$X_{P_0} \equiv X_0 \supseteq X_{P_1} \supseteq X_{P_2} \supseteq \cdots \supseteq X_{P_r} \equiv conv(X)$$

where $X_{P_0} \equiv X_0$ denotes the linear programming relaxation of X. The results above imply that we can theoretically obtain the convex hull of the feasible solution set X via the level r RLT and can hence obtain the optimal solution by solving the linear programming problem over X_{P_r}.

For a better understanding, we illustrate the RLT process through the following example [25].

Example 1. *Consider the following polytope:*

$$X = \{x \in \mathbb{R}^2 : 2x_1 + 3x_2 \leq 4, \ x_j \in \{0, 1\}, \ j = 1, 2\}.$$

The linear programming of this polytope is given as $X_0 = \{x \in R^2 : 2x_1 + 3x_2 \leq 4, \ 0 \leq x_1 \leq 1, \ 0 \leq x_2 \leq 1\}$, and the convex hull of X is given as $conv(X) = \{x \in R^2 : x_1 + x_2 \leq 1, \ x_1 \geq 0, \ x_2 \geq 0\}$ (see Figure 3).

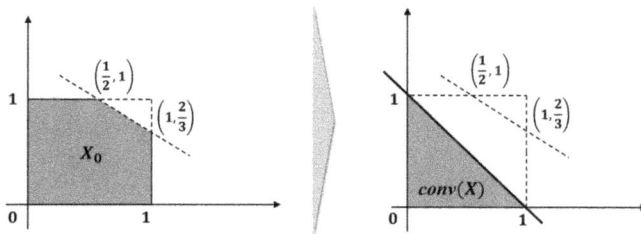

Figure 3. Illustration of polytope X_0 (**left**) and its convex hull $conv(X)$ (**right**).

Now, we apply the level 2 RLT to X_0 to illustrate how $conv(X)$ can be obtained by the RLT process.

Step 1. *(Reformulation) Multiply each constraint of X_0 by each of the factors $x_1 x_2$, $x_1(1 - x_2)$, $(1 - x_1)x_2$, and $(1 - x_1)(1 - x_2)$. This process generates various duplicated or redundant inequalities; thus, we summarize the valid inequalities only, as follows:*

$$
\begin{aligned}
(2x_1 + 3x_2 \le 4) \times x_1 x_2 &\quad\rightarrow\quad 2x_1 x_2 + 3x_1 x_2 \le 4 x_1 x_2 \\
&\quad\hookrightarrow\quad x_1 x_2 \le 0 \\
(2x_1 + 3x_2 \le 4) \times (1 - x_1)(1 - x_2) &\quad\rightarrow\quad 0 \le 4(1 - x_1)(1 - x_2) \\
&\quad\hookrightarrow\quad x_1 + x_2 \le 1 + x_1 x_2 \\
(x_1 \ge 0) \times x_1 x_2 &\quad\rightarrow\quad x_1 x_2 \ge 0 \\
(x_1 \ge 0) \times x_1(1 - x_2) &\quad\rightarrow\quad x_1 - x_1 x_2 \ge 0 \\
(x_2 \ge 0) \times (1 - x_1)x_2 &\quad\rightarrow\quad x_2 - x_1 x_2 \ge 0
\end{aligned}
$$

Step 2. *(Linearization) After linearizing the resulting polynomial system by substituting a variable z_{12} for the product term $x_1 x_2$, we have*

$$
\begin{aligned}
z_{12} &\le 0 \\
x_1 + x_2 &\le 1 + z_{12} \\
z_{12} &\ge 0 \\
x_1 - z_{12} &\ge 0 \\
x_2 - z_{12} &\ge 0
\end{aligned}
$$

By $z_{12} \le 0$ and $z_{12} \ge 0$, we have $z_{12} = 0$. Therefore, the last set of inequalities produces

$$
\{x \in R^2 : x_1 + x_2 \le 1, \ x_1 \ge 0, \ x_2 \ge 0\}
$$

which is $conv(X)$.

3. Two Representative Models for the KEP: EA and EE Formulations

In this section, we present two compact formulations, the EA and EE formulations, which were proposed by Constantino et al. [18] as reference models. In these formulations, the possible cycles in G and L are considered to be defined as a set composed of indices $\{1, ..., l_u\}$, where l_u indicates the upper bound on the possible number of cycles in G. The additional parameters and decision variables used in the formulation are given as follows:

Parameters
w_{ij}: Weight of edge $(i, j) \in A$, representing the level of compatibility between donor i and recipient j.
k: Maximum cycle length.

Decision Variables
x_{ij}: 1 if a kidney is transplanted from donor i to patient j, and 0 otherwise.
y_i^l: 1 if node i is included in cycle l, and 0 otherwise.

Appl. Sci. **2017**, *7*, 847

Then, the EA formulation is given as follows:

$$\text{EA}: \text{Maximize} \sum_{(i,j) \in A} w_{ij} x_{ij} \tag{1a}$$

$$\text{subject to} \sum_{j:\,(j,i) \in A} x_{ji} = \sum_{j:\,(i,j) \in A} x_{ij}, \quad \forall i \in V \tag{1b}$$

$$\sum_{j:\,(i,j) \in A} x_{ij} \leq 1, \quad \forall i \in V \tag{1c}$$

$$\sum_{i \in V} y_i^l \leq k, \quad \forall l \in L \tag{1d}$$

$$\sum_{l \in L} y_i^l = \sum_{j:\,(i,j) \in A} x_{ij}, \quad \forall i \in V \tag{1e}$$

$$y_i^l + x_{ij} \leq 1 + y_j^l, \quad \forall (i,j) \in A, \forall l \in L \tag{1f}$$

$$x_{ij} \in \{0, 1\}, \quad \forall (i,j) \in A \tag{1g}$$

$$y_i^l \in \{0, 1\}, \quad \forall i \in V, l \in L \tag{1h}$$

The objective function of Equation (1a) is to maximize the sum of weights of the transplantations. Because the weight of each edge indicates the appropriateness of the corresponding transplantation, the KEP maximizing the total appropriateness of all transplantations is planned. We note that setting w_{ij} to the same value for all $(i,j) \in A$ allows the maximum number of possible kidney exchanges in a given pool of candidates to be obtained. Constraint (1b) indicates that if a donor in pair i donates his or her kidney to a patient in another pair, then the patient in pair i must receive a kidney. This constraint further implies that if a donor does not participate in transplantation, the paired patient would not receive a kidney. Constraint (1c) implies that a donor cannot donate more than one kidney. Constraint (1d) ensures that the length of each cycle cannot be greater than k. Constraint (1e) assigns a pair to a cycle if it takes part in kidney exchanges. We note that because $\sum_{j:(i,j) \in A} x_{ij} \leq 1$, a pair has to be assigned to one of the cycles. Constraint (1f) implies that if a donor in pair i gives his or her kidney to a patient in pair j and if the pair i is assigned to a cycle l, then pair j also has to be included in cycle l. Constraints (1g) and (1h) indicate that all the decision variables in the model are binary variables.

We now present the EE formulation. We suppose that there are copies of graph G and we let the index of each copy be $l \in L$, where L is a set of the copies of G. Then, the EE formulation requires the additional decision variables x_{ij}^l, as follows:

Decision Variable

x_{ij}^l: 1 if a kidney is transplanted from donor i to patient j in copy l, and 0 otherwise.

Then, the EE formulation is given as follows:

$$\text{EE}: \text{Maximize} \sum_{l \in L} \sum_{(i,j) \in A} w_{ij} x_{ij}^l \tag{2a}$$

$$\text{Subject to} \sum_{j:\,(j,i) \in A} x_{ji}^l = \sum_{j:\,(i,j) \in A} x_{ij}^l, \quad \forall i \in V, \forall l \in L \tag{2b}$$

$$\sum_{l \in L} \sum_{j:\,(i,j) \in A} x_{ij}^l \leq 1, \quad \forall i \in V \tag{2c}$$

$$\sum_{(i,j) \in A} x_{ij}^l \leq k, \quad \forall l \in L \tag{2d}$$

$$x_{ij} \in \{0, 1\}, \quad \forall (i,j) \in A \tag{2e}$$

The objective function of Equation (2a) indicates that the model maximizes the total weight of arcs among all copies of G. Constraint (2b) ensures that the number of kidneys given by donor i and received by patient i should be same at each pair i for each copy l. Constraint (2c) indicates that a pair can donate or receive at most one kidney. We note that the constraint holds for all copies $l \in L$ and that an arc cannot be selected for more than two copies of G. Constraint (2d) restricts the length of exchange cycles to less than or equal to k.

In addition, in order to have further simplified formulations, symmetry elimination constraints were applied, as discussed by Constantino et al. [18]:

$$y_i^l \leq y_l^l, \qquad \forall i \in V, \, l \in L, \, i > l \tag{3}$$

for the EA formulation, and

$$\sum_{j: \, (i, \, j) \in A} x_{ij}^l \leq \sum_{j: \, (l, \, j) \in A} x_{lj}^l, \qquad \forall i > l$$

for the EE formulation. These inequalities enforce node l to be in cycle l and enforce all other nodes in the cycle to have indices larger than l. For further details, we refer the readers to Constantino et al. [18].

4. RLT Applications

In this section, we will present the application of the RLT to two existing compact formulations (i.e., the EA and EE formulations). We first show that the EE formulation can be derived by applying the RLT to the EA formulation systemically without relying on any problem-specific structures or insights. After that, we derive a new compact formulation that dominates the EE formulation by further applying the RLT to it.

4.1. Derivation of the EE Formulation from the EA Formulation

We now apply a specialized version of the RLT to the EA formulation by following the discussion by Sherali and Adams [24,26]. To contain the size of the resulting relaxation, we apply only a partial first-level version of this approach. Our approach is to first reformulate the EA formulation by generating the additional (nonlinear) implied constraints. By applying a linearization, which substitutes variables in place of each distinct nonlinear term, we can expose the useful relationships between the new and original variables that intend to enforce the nonlinear relationships. Specifically, we perform the following operations:

- **Reformulation Phase.** Construct additional sets of constraints via (R1)–(R5) stated below.

    (R1) Similarly to Constraint (1f), construct the following valid inequalities:

    $$y_j^l + x_{ij} \leq 1 + y_i^l, \qquad \forall (i, \, j) \in A, \, \forall l \in L \tag{4}$$

    Using Constraints (1f) and (4), construct the valid inequalities

    $$x_{ij}(y_i^l + x_{ij} - 1 - y_j^l) \leq 0 \quad \text{for} \quad (i, \, j) \in A, \, l \in L$$

    and

    $$x_{ij}(y_j^l + x_{ij} - 1 - y_i^l) \leq 0 \quad \text{for} \quad (i, \, j) \in A, \, l \in L.$$

    (R2) For each $i \in V$, multiply the equation $\sum_{j: \, (j, \, i) \in A} x_{ji} = \sum_{j: \, (i, \, j) \in A} x_{ij}$ of Constraint (1b) by $y_i^l \geq 0$ for each $i \in V$, $l \in L$.

    (R3) For each $i \in V$, multiply the inequality $\sum_{j: \, (i, \, j) \in A} x_{ij} \leq 1$ of Constraint (1c) by $y_i^l \geq 0$ for each $i \in V$, $l \in L$.

    (R4) From Constraints (1c) and (1e), we can derive $\sum_{l \in L} y_i^l \leq 1$ for $i \in V$. For each $i \in V$, multiply $\sum_{l \in L} y_i^l \leq 1$ and $\sum_{l \in L} y_i^l = \sum_{j: \, (i, \, j) \in A} x_{ij}$ by $y_i^{l'}$ for each $i \in V$, $l' \in L$.

(R5) For each $i \in V$, multiply the inequality $\sum_{j:\,(i,\,j) \in A} x_{ij} \leq 1$ of Constraint (1c) by $x_{ij'}$ for each $(i, j') \in A$, and for each $i \in V$, multiply the equation $\sum_{l \in L} y_i^l = \sum_{j:\,(i,\,j) \in A} x_{ij}$ by $x_{ij'}$ for each $(i, j') \in A$.

- **Linearization Phase.** Linearize the new classes of constraints generated by (R1)–(R5) above by using the substitutions

$$u_{ij}^l = y_i^l x_{ij} \quad \text{and} \quad v_{ij}^l = y_j^l x_{ij} \quad \forall (i, j) \in A, \, \forall l \in L.$$

Reformulation step (R1) produces $u_{ij}^l \leq v_{ij}^l$ for $(i, j) \in A$, $l \in L$ and $v_{ij}^l \leq u_{ij}^l$ for $(i, j) \in A$, $l \in L$. Therefore, we have $u_{ij}^l = v_{ij}^l$ for $(i, j) \in A$, $l \in L$ and we only use u variables for the linearization. Step (R2) produces $\sum_{j:\,(j,\,i) \in A} u_{ji}^l = \sum_{j:\,(i,\,j) \in A} u_{ij}^l$ for $i \in V$, $l \in L$. Step (R3) gives $\sum_{j:\,(i,\,j) \in A} u_{ij}^l \leq y_i^l$ for $i \in V$, $l \in L$, and surrogates them for each $l \in L$, which results in $\sum_{l \in L} \sum_{j:\,(i,\,j) \in A} u_{ij}^l \leq \sum_{l \in L} y_i^l$ for $i \in V$. By Constraints (1c) and (1e), we have $\sum_{l \in L} \sum_{j:\,(i,\,j) \in A} u_{ij}^l \leq 1$ for $i \in V$. Reformulation step (R4) generates $y_i^{l'} + \sum_{l(\neq l') \in L} y_i^l y_i^{l'} \leq y_i^{l'}$ for $i \in V$, which leads to $\sum_{l(\neq l') \in L} y_i^l y_i^{l'} = 0$. Therefore, $\sum_{l \in L} y_i^l = \sum_{j:\,(i,\,j) \in A} x_{ij}$ multiplied by $y_i^{l'}$ for each $i \in V$, $l' \in L$ yields $y_i^l = \sum_{j:\,(i,\,j) \in A} u_{ij}^l$ for $i \in V$, $l \in L$ (l' is substituted by l for convenience). Next, surrogating $y_i^l = \sum_{j:\,(i,\,j) \in A} u_{ij}^l$ for each $i \in V$ gives $\sum_{i \in V} y_i^l = \sum_{(i,\,j) \in A} u_{ij}^l$ for $l \in L$. Hence, by Constraint (1d), we have $\sum_{(i,\,j) \in A} u_{ij}^l \leq k$ for $l \in L$. According to the first statement of step (R5) along with $x_{ij} \geq 0$ for $(i, j) \in A$, we can obtain $\sum_{j \neq j':\,(i,\,j) \in A} x_{ij} x_{ij'} = 0$ for $i \in V$. The next statement along with the first result produces $x_{ij} = \sum_{l \in L} u_{ij}^l$ for $i \in V$. Therefore, we can replace the objective function of Equation (1a) with $\sum_{l \in L} \sum_{(i,\,j) \in A} w_{ij} u_{ij}^l$. Consequently, after substituting x_{ij}^l for u_{ij}^l, the RLT application constructs the EE formulation. We again emphasize that the aforementioned procedures do not rely on any problem-specific structures or insights, but they derive the same compact formulation, the EE formulation, from the EA formulation.

4.2. Extended Formulation Derived from the EE Formulation

In this subsection, we further strengthen the EE formulation by applying the RLT while maintaining the y variables. The specific RLT procedure we perform is explained in detail below.

- **Reformulation Phase.** Construct the additional set of constraints via (R6)–(R9) stated below.

  (R6) For each $i \in V$, multiply the inequality $\sum_{j:\,(i,\,j) \in A} x_{ij} \leq 1$ of Constraint (1c) by $y_i^l \geq 0$ for each $i \in V$, $l \in L$.

  (R7) For each $(i, j) \in A$ and $l \in L$, multiply the inequality $y_i^l + x_{ij} \leq 1 + y_j^l$ of Constraint (1f) by $y_i^l \geq 0$ and y_j^l. Similarly, for each $(i, j) \in A$ and $l \in L$, multiply the inequality $y_j^l + x_{ij} \leq 1 + y_i^l$ by $y_i^l \geq 0$.

  (R8) For each $l \in L$, multiply the inequality $\sum_{i \in V} y_i^l \leq k$ of Constraint (1d) by $y_j^l \geq 0$ for each $j \in V$.

  (R9) For each $i \in V$, $l \in L$, $i > l$, multiply the inequality $y_i^l \leq y_l^l$ of the symmetry elimination constraints (3) by $y_i^l \geq 0$, $y_l^l \geq 0$, and $y_j^l \geq 0$ for each $j \in V$.

- **Linearization Phase.** Linearize the new classes of constraints generated by (R6)–(R9) above by using the substitutions

$$x_{ij}^l = y_i^l x_{ij} = y_j^l x_{ij} \quad \forall (i, j) \in A, \, \forall l \in L \quad \text{and} \quad z_{(ij)}^l = y_i^l y_j^l \quad \forall i, j \in V, \, \forall l \in L.$$

Reformulation step (R6) produces $\sum_{j:\,(i,\,j) \in A} x_{ij}^l \leq y_i^l$ for $i \in V$, $l \in L$. Step (R7) gives three classes of valid inequalities $x_{ij}^l \leq z_{(ij)}^l$, $z_{(ij)}^l + x_{ij}^l \leq 2y_j^l$, and $z_{(ij)}^l + x_{ij}^l \leq 2y_i^l$ for $(i, j) \in A$, $l \in L$. Step (R8) generates $\sum_{j(\neq i) \in V} z^l_{(ij)} \leq (k-1)y^l_i$ for $i \in V$, $l \in L$. The last step (R9) produces $y^l_i \leq z^l_{il} \leq y^l_i$ for $i \in V$, $l \in L$, and $z^l_{(ij)} \leq z^l_{jl}$ for $i, j \in V$, $l \in L$.

We summarize the overall RLT process above to derive a new compact formulation from the EE formulation in Figure 4. By augmenting the valid inequalities generated above to some set of constraints from the EE and EA formulations, we derive a new integer programming model for the KEP, which is more compact and tighter than the EE formulation, as follows:

$$\text{RLT}: \text{Maximize} \sum_{l \in L} \sum_{(i,j) \in A} w_{ij} x^l_{ij} \tag{5a}$$

Subject to Constraints (2b), (2c), (2d), (2e), (1h)

$$\sum_{j:(i,j) \in A} x^l_{ij} \leq y^l_i, \qquad \forall i \in V, l \in L \tag{5b}$$

$$x^l_{ij} \leq z^l_{(ij)}, \qquad \forall (i,j) \in A, l \in L \tag{5c}$$

$$z^l_{(ij)} + x^l_{ij} \leq 2y^l_j, \qquad \forall (i,j) \in A, l \in L \tag{5d}$$

$$z^l_{(ij)} + x^l_{ij} \leq 2y^l_i, \qquad \forall (i,j) \in A, l \in L \tag{5e}$$

$$\sum_{j(\neq i) \in V} z^l_{(ij)} \leq (k-1)y^l_i, \qquad \forall i \in V, l \in L \tag{5f}$$

$$y^l_i \leq z^l_{il} \leq y^l_i, \qquad \forall i \in V, l \in L \tag{5g}$$

$$z^l_{(ij)} \leq z^l_{jl}, \qquad \forall i, j \in V, l \in L \tag{5h}$$

$$z^l_{(ij)} \in \{0, 1\}, \qquad \forall i, j \in V, l \in L. \tag{5i}$$

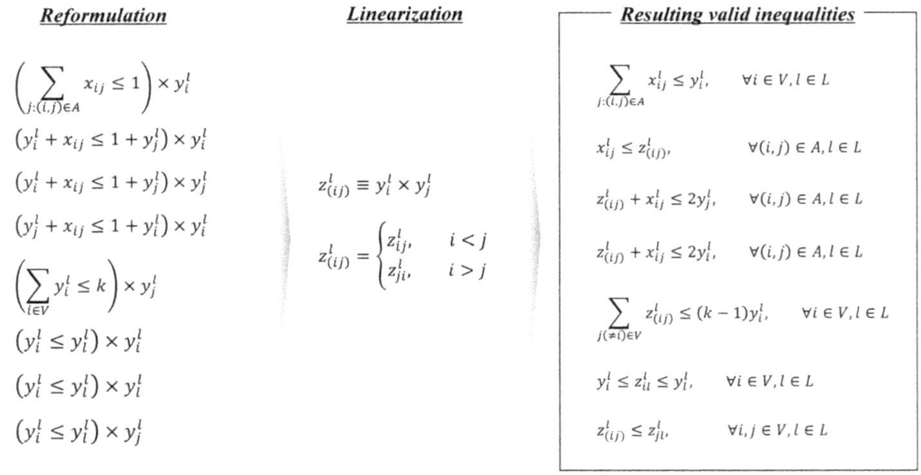

Reformulation	**Linearization**	**Resulting valid inequalities**
$\left(\sum_{j:(i,j)\in A} x_{ij} \leq 1\right) \times y^l_i$		$\sum_{j:(i,j)\in A} x^l_{ij} \leq y^l_i, \quad \forall i \in V, l \in L$
$(y^l_i + x_{ij} \leq 1 + y^l_j) \times y^l_i$		$x^l_{ij} \leq z^l_{(ij)}, \quad \forall (i,j) \in A, l \in L$
$(y^l_i + x_{ij} \leq 1 + y^l_j) \times y^l_j$	$z^l_{(ij)} \equiv y^l_i \times y^l_j$	$z^l_{(ij)} + x^l_{ij} \leq 2y^l_j, \quad \forall (i,j) \in A, l \in L$
$(y^l_j + x_{ij} \leq 1 + y^l_i) \times y^l_i$		$z^l_{(ij)} + x^l_{ij} \leq 2y^l_i, \quad \forall (i,j) \in A, l \in L$
$\left(\sum_{i\in V} y^l_i \leq k\right) \times y^l_j$	$z^l_{(ij)} = \begin{cases} z^l_{ij}, & i < j \\ z^l_{ji}, & i > j \end{cases}$	$\sum_{j(\neq i)\in V} z^l_{(ij)} \leq (k-1)y^l_i, \quad \forall i \in V, l \in L$
$(y^l_i \leq y^l_l) \times y^l_i$		$y^l_i \leq z^l_{il} \leq y^l_i, \quad \forall i \in V, l \in L$
$(y^l_i \leq y^l_l) \times y^l_j$		$z^l_{(ij)} \leq z^l_{jl}, \quad \forall i,j \in V, l \in L$

Figure 4. Illustration of the reformulation-linearization technique (RLT) for deriving new valid inequalities.

5. Computational Results

In this section, we present the results of the computational experiments for the KEP. The experiments were performed using an Intel(R) Core(TM) i7-4770 CPU @ 3.40 GHz, and CPLEX 12.4 as a LP/MIP (mixed integer programming) optimization solver. The experiments were designed to compare the EA, EE, and RLT formulations in terms of performance. Problem instances were constructed as by Constantino et al. [18]. A random generator that created random KEP graphs of chosen certain arc densities was used. To be specific, on each position of the node adjacency matrix of a graph, a probability p is used to determine whether the element equals 1 or 0. Constantino et al. [18] used values of 0.2, 0.5, and 0.7 for the probability p. However, it was found that with probabilities of 0.5 and 0.7, almost every instance had an optimal objective n equal to the number of nodes. Because n is the trivial upper bound of these KEP problems, no formulation can improve the linear relaxation bound of such problem instances. Thus, because an important goal of this paper is to compare the tightness of KEP formulations, p was set to 0.1, 0.2, and 0.5 for low-, medium-, and high-density instances, respectively. For each density, we generated the problem instances with the input parameter $k = 3, 4, 5, 6$. In addition, n, the number of pairs, was further set to 10, 20, and 30 for each k. For each n and k, 10 instances were generated and tested. All the cases were executed within a time limit of 3600 s. The formulations were compared in terms of the optimality gap (GAP) and the execution time. The GAP is calculated by $(Z_{LP} - Z_{IP})/Z_{IP}$, where Z_{IP} is the best objective function value of the integer programming model and Z_{LP} is the optimal objective function value of the corresponding linear programming relaxation. Hence, the lower the GAP obtained, the better the solution (i.e., closer to the optimal solution). On the other hand, T_{IP} and T_{LP} are the average elapsed time of the integer programming model and its linear programming relaxation, respectively.

Table 1. Computational results for low-density instances. EA: edge-assignment; EE: extended edge; RLT: reformulation-linearization technique; GAP: optimality gap.

Problem Instances		EA			EE			RLT		
		T_{LP}	T_{IP}	GAP	T_{LP}	T_{IP}	GAP	T_{LP}	T_{IP}	GAP
$k = 3$	$n = 10$	0.00	0.00	10.7%	0.00	0.00	8.7%	0.00	0.01	6.7%
	$n = 20$	0.00	0.01	87.5%	0.00	0.00	68.2%	0.02	0.03	67.8%
	$n = 30$	0.02	0.53	98.1%	0.01	0.01	84.2%	0.29	0.11	83.9%
$k = 4$	$n = 10$	0.00	0.00	4.3%	0.00	0.00	3.3%	0.00	0.00	3.0%
	$n = 20$	0.00	0.01	45.1%	0.00	0.00	39.0%	0.00	0.00	38.1%
	$n = 30$	0.02	1.68	37.3%	0.01	0.02	33.2%	0.22	0.05	33.1%
$k = 5$	$n = 10$	0.00	0.00	4.7%	0.00	0.00	4.2%	0.00	0.00	3.8%
	$n = 20$	0.00	0.01	17.9%	0.00	0.01	14.8%	0.02	0.03	14.1%
	$n = 30$	0.02	0.76	18.0%	0.01	0.07	15.9%	0.34	0.10	14.9%
$k = 6$	$n = 10$	0.00	0.00	0.0%	0.00	0.00	0.0%	0.00	0.00	0.0%
	$n = 20$	0.00	0.01	10.5%	0.00	0.01	9.6%	0.02	0.04	9.5%
	$n = 30$	0.01	0.59	10.9%	0.01	0.12	9.6%	0.59	0.27	9.6%

Table 1 summarizes the computational results for low-density instances. The EE formulation found the optimal upper bound for 43 out of 120 low-density instances. Of the remaining 77 instances for which the EE formulation could not find the optimal solution, the upper bounds of 36 instances were improved by our RLT model. Subsequently, the average value of the GAP was improved by our RLT formulation. On the other hand, the improvement in the GAP obtained by the RLT formulation tended to be smaller as k grew.

Figure 5 presents box plots of the GAPs (%) produced by each formulation from problem instances for each combination of (n, k). From the figure, we can observe that our RLT formulation yielded the lowest average GAPs, and that furthermore, the variability of the GAPs produced by our RLT formulation was also lower than that of the best-known compact formulations. Specifically, both the maximum and minimum GAPs, as well as the difference between the lower and upper quartiles, significantly dropped from the EA formulation to the EE formulation, and then further again to the RLT formulation. Moreover, such observations were consistent for every combination of (n, k). The results imply that the EA formulation is highly dominated by the EE and RLT formulations, and moreover, that our proposed RLT formulation is more reliable than the EE formulation in terms of solution quality—that is, our approach produces more reliable and higher quality solutions than the best-known compact formulations, without compromising computational time.

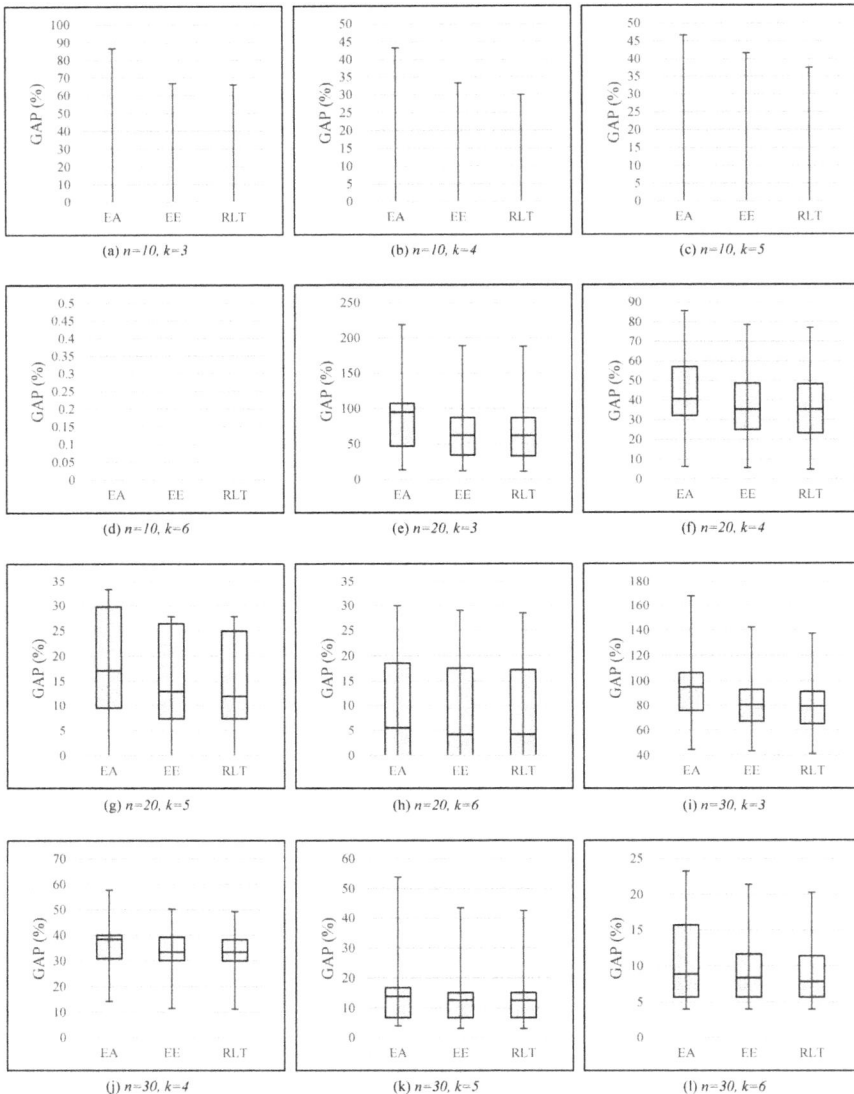

Figure 5. Box plots of optimality gaps (GAPs) for low-density instances.

Similarly, Table 2 demonstrates the computational results for medium-density instances. According to the results, the average GAP was smaller than for the low-density instances for all the formulations. Having such a result is intuitive because the medium-density graph had more arcs representing compatibility; thus, feasible solutions could be more easily found than in the low-density cases. In the experiments, the EE formulation found the optimal upper bounds for 83 out of 120 instances. Our RLT formulation improved the upper bounds of 17 out of the remaining

37 instances whose optimal solutions were not obtained by the EE formulation. When it comes to the box plots of the GAPs for the medium-density problem instances, we are able to make similar observations to those for the low-density instances as presented in Figure 6. As mentioned previously, compared to the low-density case, there were more combinations of (n, k) for which the GAPs of all the problem instances were equal to zero (i.e., (j), (k) and (l) in Figure 6).

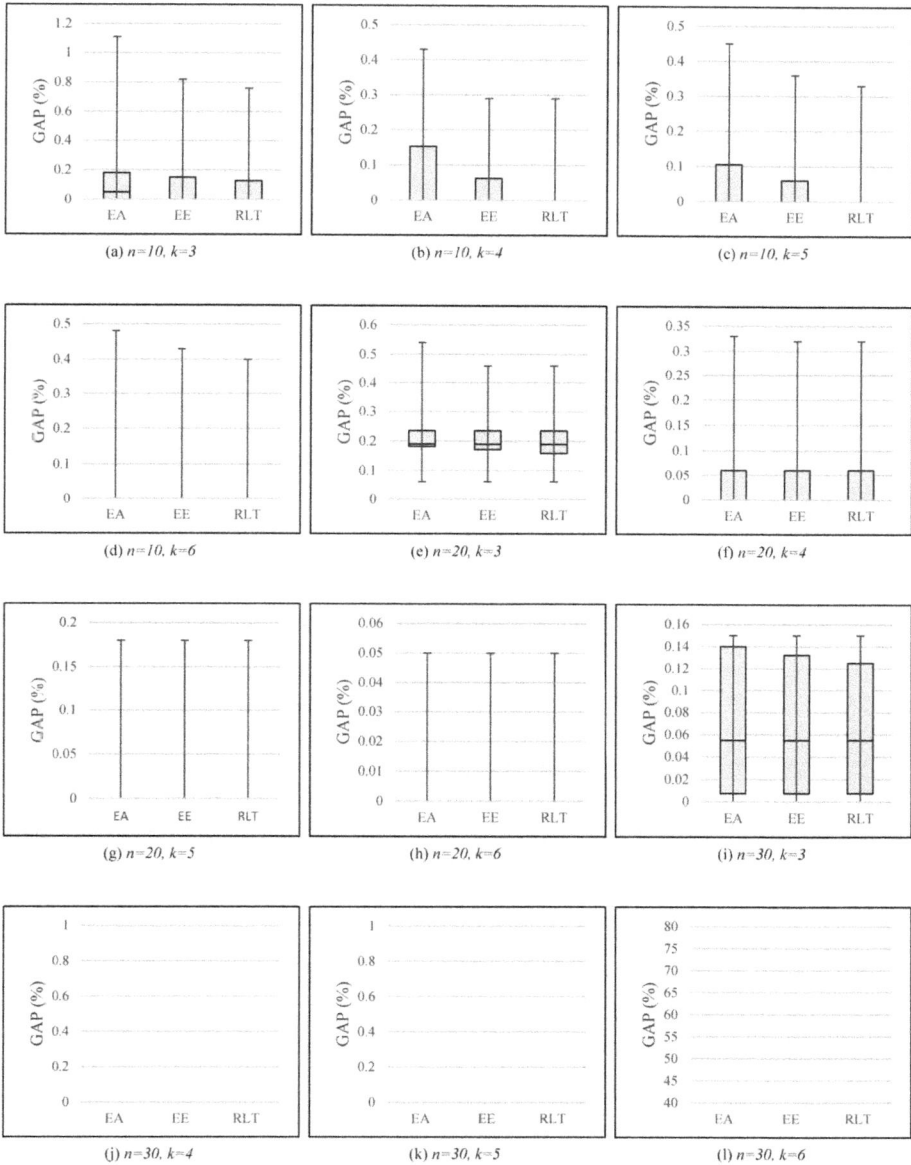

Figure 6. Box plots of optimality gaps (GAPs) for medium-density instances.

Table 2. Computational results for medium-density instances.

Problem Instances		EA			EE			RLT		
		T_{LP}	T_{IP}	GAP	T_{LP}	T_{IP}	GAP	T_{LP}	T_{IP}	GAP
	$n = 10$	0.00	0.00	22.0%	0.00	0.00	16.2%	0.00	0.00	16.0%
$k = 3$	$n = 20$	0.01	0.95	22.2%	0.00	0.01	20.8%	0.05	0.07	20.5%
	$n = 30$	0.03	238.11	7.1%	0.03	0.09	7.0%	0.05	0.12	6.9%
	$n = 10$	0.00	0.00	9.7%	0.00	0.02	6.3%	0.00	0.01	5.1%
$k = 4$	$n = 20$	0.01	0.41	6.2%	0.00	0.06	6.0%	0.53	0.41	6.0%
	$n = 30$	0.02	100.95	0.0%	0.03	0.93	0.0%	0.68	1.55	0.0%
	$n = 10$	0.00	0.00	7.8%	0.00	0.00	5.7%	0.00	0.00	3.8%
$k = 5$	$n = 20$	0.01	0.22	2.9%	0.00	0.07	2.9%	0.40	0.58	2.9%
	$n = 30$	0.02	12.55	0.0%	0.02	0.38	0.0%	0.29	0.67	0.0%
	$n = 10$	0.00	0.00	6.3%	0.00	0.00	5.5%	0.00	0.01	4.8%
$k = 6$	$n = 20$	0.01	0.11	1.1%	0.00	0.07	1.1%	0.27	0.76	1.1%
	$n = 30$	0.02	3.91	0.0%	0.03	0.25	0.0%	0.19	0.42	0.0%

Finally, the computational results for the high-density instances are presented in Table 3. We observe that the GAPs of all the formulations were equal to 0 for all the instances; hence, we here compare them in terms of the computational time only. As presented in Table 3, in terms of computational time, the RLT formulation outperformed the EA formulation, but the EE formulation performed slightly better than the RLT formulation. However, both cases were reasonably acceptable for practical-size problems. We remark that high-density instances rarely appear in real-world situations, as a donor is unlikely to find as many compatible patients as in high-density cases in a given pool of candidates.

Table 3. Computational results for high-density instances.

Problem Instances		EA			EE			RLT		
		T_{LP}	T_{IP}	GAP	T_{LP}	T_{IP}	GAP	T_{LP}	T_{IP}	GAP
	$n = 10$	0.00	0.02	0.0%	0.00	0.01	0.0%	0.02	0.03	0.0%
$k = 3$	$n = 20$	0.01	1.20	0.0%	0.01	0.14	0.0%	0.96	0.31	0.0%
	$n = 30$	0.03	57.15	0.0%	0.03	0.71	0.0%	0.86	1.87	0.0%
	$n = 10$	0.00	0.03	0.0%	0.00	0.01	0.0%	0.01	0.03	0.0%
$k = 4$	$n = 20$	0.01	0.32	0.0%	0.01	0.09	0.0%	0.68	0.49	0.0%
	$n = 30$	0.03	35.29	0.0%	0.04	0.43	0.0%	0.82	0.99	0.0%
	$n = 10$	0.00	0.01	0.0%	0.00	0.01	0.0%	0.01	0.02	0.0%
$k = 5$	$n = 20$	0.01	0.23	0.0%	0.01	0.08	0.0%	0.65	0.48	0.0%
	$n = 30$	0.03	10.02	0.0%	0.04	0.29	0.0%	0.57	0.88	0.0%
	$n = 10$	0.00	0.01	0.0%	0.00	0.01	0.0%	0.01	0.02	0.0%
$k = 6$	$n = 20$	0.01	0.17	0.0%	0.01	0.07	0.0%	0.51	0.46	0.0%
	$n = 30$	0.02	2.53	0.0%	0.04	0.26	0.0%	1.04	0.82	0.0%

6. Conclusions

In this paper, we first show that the EE formulation, until now considered to be the most compact formulation, can be systematically derived from the EA formulation through the RLT process. A previous study developed the EE formulation by exploiting special structures inherent to the problem. However, we show that we can readily apply the RLT procedure to the EA formulation to obtain the same EE formulation. Furthermore, we apply the RLT to the EA and EE formulations and thereby derive a tighter and more compact formulation. Computational results show that the proposed RLT model outperforms the existing EA and EE formulations in terms of solution quality as well as computational time. Specifically, the RLT model provides improved GAPs in several instances for which the EE formulation could not find the optimal solutions within the time limit—especially for low- and medium-density graphs. For high-density instances, although the RLT model does not significantly reduce the execution time, it can produce the same high-quality solutions as the existing formulations. We believe that, given the results obtained by the proposed model, it could be utilized in the integrated KEP IT healthcare platform to obtain optimized KEP exchange plans.

As extended research, several models derived from that proposed in this paper can be considered. For example, firstly, a problem dealing with fair allocations, such as in terms of donor and patient age and health, among the pairs in the candidate pool may be interesting. Indeed, some problems of fairness in kidney transplantation or kidney exchange are discussed by Bertsimas et al. [27] and by Anderson [15] respectively in literature. Secondly, some limitations of this study include that all data (e.g., w_{ij}) were considered to be certain. When a KEP solution is actually implemented, it may be possible to have several unexpected events, including last-minute incompatibility and unavailability of either donors or recipients [28,29]. To handle the data or event uncertainty in KEPs, Alvelos et al. [29], for example, examined an optimization problem whose objective was to maximize the expected number of transplants in a KEP given that all the arcs and vertices in a KEP graph have equal probabilities of failure, and there are some attempts to apply robust optimization theory [30,31] to a KEP [28]. Thus, we can extend our model to incorporate the aforementioned uncertainties and take the solution approaches, such as stochastic optimization or robust optimization techniques, into account. Finally, proposing an efficient heuristic-based approach for solving highly large-scale problems more generally would be the topic for future research.

Acknowledgments: This work was supported by the National Research Foundation of Korea(NRF) grant funded by the Korea government(Ministry of Science, ICT & Future Planning) (No. NRF-2015R1C1A1A02036682).

Author Contributions: Junsang Yuh developed the mathematical programming models and performed the experiments. Seokhyun Chung contributed to the literature review, experimental part and result analysis. Taesu Cheong guided the whole research, supported the structure of the paper and prepared the manuscript. All authors read and approved the final manuscript.

Conflicts of Interest: The authors declare no conflict of interest.

References

1. Kwak, J.Y.; Kwon, O.J.; Lee, K.S.; Kang, C.M.; Park, H.Y.; Kim, J.H. Exchange-donor program in renal transplantation: A single-center experience. *Transplant. Proc.* **1999**, *31*, 344–345.
2. Park, K.; Lee, J.H.; Huh, K.H.; Kim, S.I.; Kim, Y.S. Exchange living-donor kidney transplantation: Diminution of donor organ shortage. *Transplant. Proc.* **2004**, *36*, 2949–2951.
3. Huh, K.H.; Kim, M.S.; Ju, M.K.; Chang, H.K.; Ahn, H.J.; Lee, S.H.; Park, K. Exchange living-donor kidney transplantation: Merits and limitations. *Transplantation* **2008**, *86*, 430–435.
4. Ellison, M.D.; McBride, M.A.; Taranto, S.E.; Delmonico, F.L.; Kauffman, H.M. Living kidney donors in need of kidney transplants: A report from the organ procurement and transplantation network. *Transplantation* **2002**, *74*, 1349–1351.
5. Segev, D.L.; Gentry, S.E.; Warren, D.S.; Reeb, B.; Montgomery, R.A. Kidney paired donation and optimizing the use of live donor organs. *JAMA* **2005**, *293*, 1883–1890.
6. Saidman, S.L.; Roth, A.E.; Sönmez, T.; Ünver, M.U.; Delmonico, F.L. Increasing the opportunity of live kidney donation by matching for two- and three-way exchanges. *Transplantation* **2006**, *81*, 773–782.
7. Abraham, D.J.; Blum, A.; Sandholm, T. Clearing algorithms for barter exchange markets: Enabling nationwide kidney exchanges. In Proceedings of the 8th ACM Conference on Electronic Commerce, San Diego, CA, USA, 11–15 June 2007; pp. 295–304.
8. Veale, J.; Hil, G. National Kidney Registry: 213 transplants in three years. *Clin. Transpl.* **2010**, 333–344. Available online: http://www.kidneyregistry.org/docs/nkr_transplants_2010_chain_chapter.pdf (accessed on 10 April 2017).
9. Wallis, C.; Samy, K.; Roth, A.; Rees, M. Kidney paired donation. *Nephrol. Dial. Transplant.* **2011**, *26*, 2091–2099, doi:10.1093/ndt/gfr155.

10. Johnson, R.; Collett, D.; Birch, R.; Fuggle, S.; Rudge, C. Kidney donation and transplantation in the UK from 1998 to 2007. *Clin. Transpl.* **2008**, 75–88, doi:10.1201/9781420086423.ch10.

11. Johnson, R.J.; Allen, J.E.; Fuggle, S.V.; Bradley, J.A.; Rudge, C. Early experience of paired living kidney donation in the United Kingdom. *Transplantation* **2008**, *86*, 1672–1677.

12. Biro, P.; Manlove, D.F.; Rizzi, R. Maximum weight cycle packing in directed graphs, with application to kidney exchange programs. *Discret. Math. Algorithms Appl.* **2009**, *1*, 499–517.

13. Ferrari, P.; Woodroffe, C.; Christiansen, F.T. Paired kidney donations to expand the living donor pool: The Western Australian experience. *Med. J. Australia* **2009**, *190*, 700.

14. Rais, A.; Viana, A. Operations Research in Healthcare: A Survey. *Int. Trans. Oper. Res.* **2011**, *18*, 1–31.

15. Anderson, R.M. Stochastic Models and Data Driven Simulations for Healthcare Operations. Ph.D. Thesis, Massachusetts Institute of Technology, Cambridge, MA, USA, 2014.

16. D'Andreagiovanni, F.; Nardin, A. Towards the Fast and Robust Optimal Design of Wireless Body Area Networks. *Appl. Soft Comput.* **2015**, *37*, 971–982.

17. Roth, A.E.; Sönmez, T.; Ünver, M.U. Efficient Kidney Exchange: Coincidence of Wants in Markets with Compatibility-Based Preferences. *Am. Econ. Rev.* **2007**, *97*, 828–851.

18. Constantino, M.; Klimentova, X.; Viana, A.; Rais, A. New insights on integer-programming models for the kidney exchange problem. *Eur. J. Oper. Res.* **2013**, *231*, 57–68.

19. Manlove, D.F.; O'Malley, G. Paired and Altruistic Kidney Donation in the UK: Algorithms and Experimentation. *ACM J. Exp. Algorithmics* **2015**, *19*, doi:10.1145/2670129.

20. Sherali, H.D.; Driscoll, P.J. On Tightening the Relaxations of Miller-Tucker-Zemlin Formulations for Asymmetric Traveling Salesman Problems. *Oper. Res.* **2002**, *50*, 656–669.

21. Desrochers, M.; Laporte, G. Improvements and Extensions to the Miller-Tucker-Zemlin Subtour Elimination Constraints. *Oper. Res. Lett.* **1991**, *10*, 27–36.

22. Sherali, H.D.; Sarin, S.C.; Tsai, P. A Class of Lifted Path and Flow-Based Formulations for the Asymmetric Traveling Salesman Problem with and without Precedence Constraints. *Discret. Optim.* **2006**, *3*, 20–32.

23. Park, G.; Lee, Y.; Han, J. A Two-Level Location-Allocation Problem in Designing Local Access Fiber Optic Networks. *Comput. Oper. Res.* **2014**, *51*, 52–63.

24. Sherali, H.D.; Adams, W.P. A hierarchy of relaxations and convex hull characterizations for mixed-integer zero-one programming problems. *Discret. Appl. Math.* **1994**, *52*, 83–106.

25. Sherali, H.D.; Lee, Y.; Kim, Y. Partial convexification cuts for 0–1 mixed-integer programs. *Eur. J. Oper. Res.* **2005**, *165*, 625–648.

26. Sherali, H.D.; Adams, W.P. A hierarchy of relaxations between the continuous and convex hull representations for zero-one programming problems. *SIAM J. Discret. Math.* **1990**, *3*, 411–430.

27. Bertsimas, D.; Farias, V.F.; Trichakis, N. Fairness, Efficiency, and Flexibility in Organ Allocation for Kidney Transplantation. *Oper. Res.* **2013**, *61*, 73–87.

28. Dickerson, J.P. Robust Dynamic Optimization with Application to Kidney Exchange. In Proceedings of the 13th International Conference on Autonomous Agents and Multiagent Systems, Paris, France, 5–9 May 2014; pp. 1701–1702.

29. Alvelos, F.; Klimentova, X.; Rais, A. A Compact Formulation for Maximizing the Expected Number of Transplants in Kidney Exchange Programs. *J. Phys. Conf. Ser.* **2015**, *616*, 012011.

30. Bertsimas, D.; Sim, M. The Price of Robustness. *Oper. Res.* **2004**, *52*, 35–53.

31. Büsing, C.; D'Andreagiovanni, F. New Results about Multi-Band Uncertainty in Robust Optimization. In *Experimental Algorithms—SEA 2012, Lecture Notes in Computer Science*; Klasing, R., Ed.; Springer: Berlin/Heidelberg, Germany, 2012; Volume 7276, 63–74.

applied
sciences

MDPI

Article

Secure Authentication and Prescription Safety Protocol for Telecare Health Services Using Ubiquitous IoT

Zahid Mahmood [1], Huansheng Ning [1,*], Ata Ullah [2] and Xuanxia Yao [1]

[1] School of Computer and Communication Engineering University of Science and Technology Beijing (USTB), Beijing 10008, China; b20140561@xs.ustb.edu.cn (Z.M.); kathy.yao@163.com (X.Y.)
[2] Department of Computer Science, National University of Modern Languages, Islamabad 44000, Pakistan; aullah@numl.edu.pk
* Correspondence: ninghuansheng@ustb.edu.cn; Tel.: +86-10-6233-3015

Received: 16 September 2017; Accepted: 12 October 2017; Published: 16 October 2017

Abstract: Internet-of-Things (IoT) include a large number of devices that can communicate across different networks. Cyber-Physical Systems (CPS) also includes a number of devices connected to the internet where wearable devices are also included. Both systems enable researchers to develop healthcare systems with additional intelligence as well as prediction capabilities both for lifestyle and in hospitals. It offers as much persistence as a platform to ubiquitous healthcare by using wearable sensors to transfer the information over servers, smartphones, and other smart devices in the Telecare Medical Information System (TMIS). Security is a challenging issue in TMIS, and resourceful access to health care services requires user verification and confidentiality. Existing schemes lack in ensuring reliable prescription safety along with authentication. This research presents a Secure Authentication and Prescription Safety (SAPS) protocol to ensure secure communication between the patient, doctor/nurse, and the trusted server. The proposed procedure relies upon the efficient elliptic curve cryptosystem which can generate a symmetric secure key to ensure secure data exchange between patients and physicians after successful authentication of participants individually. A trusted server is involved for mutual authentication between parties and then generates a common key after completing the validation process. Moreover, the scheme is verified by doing formal modeling using Rubin Logic and validated using simulations in NS-2.35. We have analyzed the SAPS against security attacks, and then performance analysis is elucidated. Results prove the dominance of SAPS over preliminaries regarding mutual authentication, message integrity, freshness, and session key management and attack prevention.

Keywords: authentication; key agreement; telecare medical information system; anonymity; un-traceability

1. Introduction

With the development of computing technologies and the expansion of smart-devices and inter-network protocols, hospitals and healthcare organizations are adopting the Telecare Medical Information System (TMIS). The medical identification process has become more resourceful, trustworthy, and efficient by using TMIS. Some Telecare services have been projected in the modern age to ease the workload on the professionals, for example, by methods such as automated healthcare devices, distant health nursing, and patient's health monitoring for remote areas. It is considered as a time-saving, economical, and easy way to access health care facilities remotely. TMIS can lower societal and medical operating cost with improved quality and efficiency [1]. Patient authentication is mandatory to guard against data forgery, misuse, and falsifying the original information by unauthorized active or passive parties. In TMIS, a trusted medical server is responsible for registering all participants, including doctors, nursing staff, and patients, as illustrated in Figure 1. The remote healthcare server keeps the advanced clinical information of the register patients and gives different administrations like healthcare education, doctors, doctor's facilities, remote medical aid, general healthcare, private care benefit, and the most important is medical prescription. Registered TMIS users for medical services can utilize smart cards to access medical devices and transmit collected statistics to the medical server using a public channel. An intruder may likewise find access over the public open channel. The adversary can eavesdrop, block service, modify, delete records, and can also reply to a message broadcasted over an open channel. Therefore, authentication is mandatory for providing information security, records honesty, and confidentiality of data. It is necessary to overcome all existing threats that are major hurdles and make TMIS trustworthy. A session key must be established for a short-time secure communication between two parties where a new key is established for every new session. We have considered various advanced cryptographic calculations like non-revertible one-way hash function, Rivest-Shamir-Adelman (RSA), Elliptic Curve Cryptography (ECC), and chaotic maps cryptosystem. Despite the fact that both ECC and RSA cryptosystems offer an equal level of security, ECC is additionally advantageous as compared to RSA with respect to computational efficiency [2].

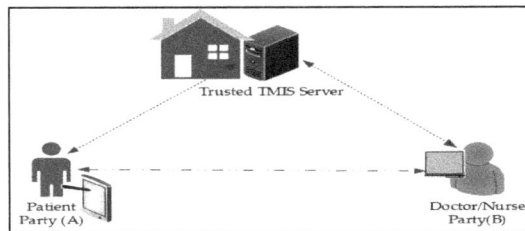

Figure 1. Telecare Medical Information System (TMIS) architecture.

An Internet of Things (IoT) is composed of a vast number of small and large devices that are using the internet for sharing data across the nodes of different networks. In an IoT environment, TMIS can serve patients to save time by remotely accessing consultants and doctors by using the new generation of internet. IoT supports a collection of objects, devices, and networks in surroundings to develop a large number of smart applications. It can undeniably improve the identification and dissemination of information regarding emergency situations where appropriate medical aid is mandatory to save precious lives. IoT can also support integration mechanisms for all physical objects with embedded systems or cyber physical systems for monitoring patients at distant locations. It improves diagnosis at the patient's home for better usefulness and effectiveness regarding medical services [3]. IoT promises an attractive future networking prototype.

Secure authentication and session key establishment schemes enable secure communication for health care services. A three-party password authentication key exchange (3-PAKE) scheme provides mutual authentication between doctor-patient-TS at the same time and hides identities from the adversary [4]. It helps in maintaining a secure link by using a common session key for specific communication. Schemes [5–7] discuss secure session key establishment between participants but later [8–10] identified that these plans are vulnerable to man-in-the-middle attack and undetectable online and offline dictionary attacks for guessing passwords. ECC-based schemes are also explored to evaluate the applicability of efficient solutions with desired security strengths using small key sizes as compared to preliminaries.

The main problem and common deficiency in these schemes are that user anonymity is not provided because the user's identity is sent without encryption on an open channel. The participants' credentials are insecure, causing a lack of anonymity and un-tractability [11]. The scheme is also vulnerable to identification-guessing attacks and tracking attacks. Specifically, a participant's identification might get exposed by an intruder when it gets disconnected from the internet. Furthermore, an adversary can tune into a selected user with the information the user provided within the login request message.

This paper presents a Secure Participant Authentication and Prescription Safety (SAPS) scheme for TMIS to accomplish participant's anonymity and un-traceability. The process begins when the patient registers with the trusted server that validates the communicating parties and then establishes the session key. We have used ECC in this study; results showed that an anonymous ECC-based presented technique has secure and well-organized authentication protocols with foolproof security along with user confidentiality protection which is practical for TMIS. Formal protocol secure analysis using Rubin Logic was used to evaluate their safety performance and reliability. Using the proposed protocol patient can get a medical prescription from physician securely and interacts with health service provider anonymously using TMIS keeping identities secret.

The rest of paper is organized as follows; Section 2 includes the previous work which has some related information regarding the present study and an overview of existing practices. The system model and problem statement are presented in Section 3. Section 4 explores the proposing anonymous SAPS scheme in details with formal steps. Formal analysis using Rubin Logic is presented along with security analysis in Section 5. The performance measures and results have been included in Section 6. Section 7 presents the conclusions of the work and a future roadmap.

2. Literature Review

This section explores some well-known existing schemes related to the security of TMIS and health care services. In this regard, different 3-PAKE and ECC-based schemes are reviewed to analyze the effectiveness, usefulness, and security strengths for providing reliable security solutions. Xie et al. have proposed an ECC-based efficient 3-PAKE scheme [12] that overcomes the flaws mentioned above but suffers from offline password guessing attacks. Che et al. have proposed modular exponentiation on an ECC-based 3-PAKE scheme [13] to make it more complicated for the attacker, but these operations require huge computational cost as compared to existing counterparts. Wu et al. have presented the concept of the secret password and smart card-based verification protocol [14] for TMIS by utilizing the discrete hard logarithm problem (DHLP). It pre-registers to stay away from the exponential mathematical computations during authentication stage. In three-party key exchanges (TPKE) [15], He et al. has found some flaws in [14] and presented an improved scheme that handles impersonation and insider attacks which made the existing scheme vulnerable. Later on, in scheme [16], Wei et al. explored both [14,15] schemes and identified the vulnerability of these schemes for offline password guessing attacks, dictionary attacks, and inability to maintain user un-traceability. To overcome these drawbacks, Wei et al. have improved protocols and presented a user authentication scheme for TMIS that can uphold different attacks. Moreover, Zhu et al. [17] also identified the offline password guessing attacks in these schemes. To overcome issues in [17], Pu et al. [18] has devised a new user authentication scheme applying smart care which is a user password-based identification that provides user anonymity. This scheme is based on an elliptic curve cryptosystem that provides the same security level as RSA with less key size.

Chen et al. [11] highlighted the client anonymity of Khan et al.'s technique [19] but it might be defenseless against insider attacks because all the lawful clients share the secret key. It presented an efficient and secret identity-based validation and secure protocol for TMIS that generates random identities for every exchange in a session to sustain a strategic distance bwetween individual data about the client and the danger of identity theft attack and ensured that their protocol accomplished client privacy. The scheme is a successor and much preferable to the previous responses for use on mobile devices. The scheme does not provide anonymity of the user and is vulnerable for identity guessing and tracking attacks.

In [20] Kumar et al. has presented a smart device authentication scheme in a WSN environment and found that these schemes are suitable for TMIS and fulfill all prerequisites for medical device networks. Later on, He et al. [21] found that some special insider attacks in medical device networks such as offline password guessing attacks occurred and the system was unable to handle anonymity in [20]. A user anonymous authentication scheme has been presented to handle remote medical services applying in WSN to resolve this issues. Nam et al. [22] pointed out some flaws in [21] for user anonymity and smart card theft. By exploiting symmetric encryption and secure key management for message integrity, Xue et al. [23] presented a temporary credential-based secure key using a one-way hash function and XOR operations. It enhances security fundamets without considerably expanding the memory requirements. In [24], Li et al. pointed out that scheme [23] is unable to protect against stolen-verifier attacks, denial of service attacks, smart card theft, and participant's signing attacks. Turkanovic et al. presented a secure hash function-based user prediction and secure key management protocol [25] that ensures security with low energy consumption. Amin et al. [26] identified that the scheme [25] is vulnerable to offline dictionary attacks, password guessing attacks, smart card theft, and has an inefficient authentication process.

IoT can be an appropriate approach to support health care systems by the technological advancements that enable the outlining of new advanced strategies for the treatment of many diseases, e.g., by the surveillance of chronic diseases to assist doctors to work out the best treatments, as projected by [27]. Due to the ubiquitous computational nature of IoT, all the TMIS entities may be monitored and managed continually. Mobile healthcare (m-Healthcare) is an associate economic model to give patients with the right of entry to resources, about past and present health records, blood pressure, and heart rate measurements. Additionally, hospitals and healthcare associations offer on-demand services hosted in the cloud, reducing the equipped costs and overcoming the constraints of standard medical treatment. On the contrary, the privacy of private healthcare information continues to be a challenge to be faced [28].

Rahimi et al. [29,30] introduced a more secure and powerful user authentication and key agreement technique for fitness-IoT structures which requires considerable processing power. It exploits the property of a sensible gateway in fog computing for critical and security services-associated organization. IoT technologies for healthcare achieve standardized medical care [31] that is frequently improved by further automating the tasks that can be performed without human interaction. In this experience, IoT-based healthcare permits remote monitoring and management of large amounts of medical data using cloud services. Yeh et al. [32] highlighted the idea of an ECC-based unique participant's verification protocol to get higher performance and security in a smart medical information system. ECC was first presented in [33,34] by utilizing a logarithm problem that can do a much better job with a smaller key length as compared to well-known existing schemes with larger key sizes [35]. By these assumptions, it is stated that ECC authentication schemes are very appropriate for resource-constrained and remotely accessible devices.

3. System Model and Problem Identification

TMIS requires strong security to provide a dependable user validation and secret key management system for an IoT-based medical environment as depicted in Figure 2. In TMIS, patients remotely present their healthcare services information to a trusted server using a medicinal gadget. Subsequently, accepting the medical records of patients in the network, the servers diagnose the issue and suggest medicines to the online patients. Such systems are rapidly growing in our society and hence require privacy of patient's data. Nonetheless, the private data transmitted over the internet using the public network are not ensured in many TMIS conditions. The system can be subject to a variety of attacks from external parties. Social insurance solutions linked with TMIS should fulfill critical security and protection necessities to ensure patient's medical records and prescriptions are secure, and that they are constantly provided validation, privacy, trustworthiness, and anonymity. Authentication restricts the medical data from being accessed by malicious and dangerous attackers. The secret key is used to encrypt the data packet to guarantee the confidentiality of medical information during data exchange.

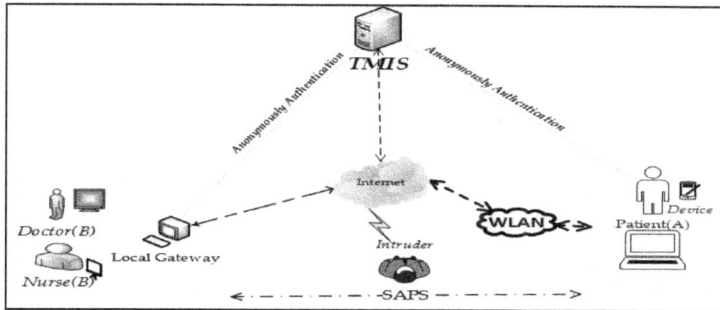

Figure 2. TMIS System Model.

In TMIS, when a patient wishes to become a new legitimate user, denoted as U_i, then the following steps are accomplished; validity of server-assigned timestamp and IDs. The user authenticated process is done after verifying smart card holding parameters to grant or reject authentication. Anonymity and un-traceability are two fundamental and attracting concerns during basic user privacy, where the former ensures secure user identity in transit, and no one else knows the exact IDs except the communication agents. The stronger property of privacy is un-traceability of the user, such that no one can find the sources of secret data during mutual authentication of the two parties by the trusted third party. Due to un-traceability, the outflow of client personal information in one session would be unusable for the adversary to recognize the user characteristics in another session [36].

Security Model

In this section, the identification of the possible threat scenarios that can be launched by exploiting user identity is discussed. An adversary can expose the user ID through exhaustive offline guessing because it is usually shorter and has a certain format which can be easily guessed [37]. To secure participants' medicinal prescription, the identity must not be disclosed at intermediate nodes when the information is being exchanged over the uncertain channel. An intruder can attempt to get the private information of the participant from the system, causing a potential risk for confidential data. There is no check of the rightness of a client's old secret key amid the secret password change stage, implying that an individual [38] who has other individual's smart card can change secret code and bio-metric without giving the original password. Other conceivable assaults are participant impersonation attacks, brute-force attacks, or dictionary assaults. Furthermore, an illegal participant may misuse the other participant's personal information to conduct various login sessions and follow participant's exercises by phishing techniques [30]. Also, the breaching of user privacy and their routine activities may likewise encourage an unapproved user to follow the participant's login history and even their current location. After obtaining the password by off-line password guessing, the user can easily guess or deduce common shared secret keys between end users like A and B after intercepting the transmitted messages R_A and R_B.

An intruder can attempt to retrieve the identity of the legitimate user from their login message. As the user's identity is short, the adversary (A) finds AId_i with polynomial time by executing exhaustive guessing. During multiple valid user sessions using the same unique password, forgery is possible [37]. The well-known threats that can be launched to breech the security of legitimate users are as follows.

(i)   Applying reverse engineering by monitoring user activities, the adversary extracts the privately stored data in the participant's device [38].

(ii)   During private information transmission over an open channel, there are possibilities of eavesdropping, intercepting, content modification, and reply attacking to influence overall communication.

(iii) A user registers with a true identity but acts as a malicious user in the TMIS.

(iv)   To overcome low entropy issues, the password must be robust enough to defend against password guessing attacks.

Using two parameters, such as a secret password and unique identity, is more feasible and is cannot be guessed by an attacker in polynomial time. Considering this assumption, a malicious user can obtain private data from the location of data storage of the user and re-transmit all messages using the public channel. In case a security protocol is unable to handle these issues, then it cannot protect users from password guessing attacks (which is possible offline), replay attacks (by altering the original message), denial of services, man-in-the-middle attacks, and cannot provide seamless forward privacy.

By the above analysis, Chen's scheme [11] cannot survive tracking attacks and it has failed to uphold user un-traceability. It is defenseless against guessing attacks and tracking attacks. A smart card holds a secret number (r) and this can be determined from the fix value of $W = h(r||pw_i)$. An adversary (A) can eavesdrop on a legal user's login request message $R_m = h(Id_i, W)$ and get the value of W to subvert the privacy of the participant unless a new authentication session is established [37]. Moreover, tracking attacks are possible by monitoring different session of same user using W.

4. Secure Authentication and Prescription Safety Protocol

A novel protocol for TMIS is presented to protect patient's privacy and satisfy the security requirements. Mutual authentication enables the communicating parties to verify each other's identities. The proposed Secure Authentication and Prescription Safety (SAPS) protocol demonstrates that it is dynamic and overcomes the above-highlighted flaws in the existing schemes. In SAPS, user authentication and verification are performed by the trusted server (TS). The patient and doctor/nurse are the sender and receiver nodes, respectively, in the proposed scenario to establish the secret keys using SAPS. In this section, all the protocol steps are elaborated on, along with a description of the message contents of a SAPS scenario. It includes a trusted server (TS), patient (A), and a doctor/nurse (B). ASAP provides a secure link for the Patient (A) to communicate securely with a physician to obtain a medical opinion. We highlight that ECC-based mutual authentication is secure against numerous significant attacks and improves the communication and memory requirements of authentication. Considering the positive characteristics of ECC, such as the shorter secret key size and computational efficiency, it is attractive to establish an ECC-based anonymous 3-PAKE protocol to protect TMIS users. By exploring existing literature and studies, there is no such system based on ECC that gives anonymous 3-PAKE protocol to authenticate users without knowing their private information publicly. It achieves its security benefits due to the hardness property of the EC Discrete Logarithm Problem (ECDLP). A list of useful notation for SAPS is listed in Table 1.

In the SAPS protocol, we have assumed that during the registration phase, the TS provides masked identities for both the patient and doctors at the point of registration. Participants provide some secret credentials, such as biometrics, to verify their original identities and record the time of service request. The TS uses the parties' secret credentials for future verification, keeping their original identities and private information secret. Besides this, the authentication protocol satisfies the following functions and security requirements to achieve credible and secure authentication and data sharing in TMIS.

Table 1. Abbreviations and acronyms for Secure Authentication and Prescription Safety (SAPS).

Notations	Descriptions
$TMIS$	Telecare medical information system
E	A large-order finite field on elliptic curve
P	EC generator of a large order n
$H(.)$	Digestive Hash Function.
A	Patient that is participant A in TMIS
B	Doctor/nurse that is user B in TMIS
MAC	Message Authentication Code
$E_{K_{A-TS}}$	Pre-Shared key between TS and User A
$E_{K_{B-TS}}$	Pre-Shared key between TS and User B
TS	Trusted Server as a trusted third party in TMIS
Pw_P	TS shared password for Patient
$Pw_{D,N}$	Doctor/Nurse password shared with TS
ID_A, ID_B, ID_{TS}	Masked Identities of A, B and TS respectively
$E_{K_{TS-A/B}}$	Temporary Encryption key between TS & Ends
d	Private/Public key of TS
$E_k(.), D_k(.)$	Using key (k) perform Encryption/Decryption
T_1, T_2, T_3	User (A, B, TS) Time Stamp
N_1, N_2, N_3	User (A, B, TS) Nonce No
M_A, M_B	Message at User A (Patient) & B (Doctor/Nurse)
C_A, C_B	Cipher Text at A and B

1. Person anonymity: In an authentication mechanism, despite the fact that an attacker extracts some and can eavesdrop on the shared message within the communication network, the legal participant's identity is kept anonymous from the intruder.
2. Identity proof: the process in which both the user and authentication server prove their identities before accessing each other. Numerous steps are performed to achieve mutual authentication to check the integrity of all transmitted messages.
3. Session key management: When the verification method is consummated, the consumer and server must present the consultation key to each other.
4. Password verification manner: If a person has entered an incorrect password within the authentication section, the password has to be detected earlier than the check phase.
5. Person cordiality: An authentication mechanism system provides a password change method through which an individual may facilely change their password without communicating with the server.
6. Robustness: An authenticated key acquisition mechanism has been engendered, and has to be resistant to extraordinary types of assaults, insider attacks, off-line password conjecturing attacks, replay assaults, and consumer impersonation assaults. Besides this, in the proposed protocol, the TS partially establishes a session key between each party. Using the secret credentials generated by the TS, the ends parties establish a session key for the particular session which helps to protect participant identities and ensure un-traceability.

During authentication, a new patient (A) and doctor (B) submit their original identity to the TS using a secure channel. After receiving their network joining request, the TS generates shadow-IDs for each participant and stores them in its database. The shadow-IDs of each participant is to establish anonymous joining of the patient and doctor and to keep prescriptions and private data secret. SAPS is explored in a stepwise manner as follows.

A. Step-I: Initialization by Patient (A)

At the beginning, Patient (A) chooses a random number R_p from a finite field and computes secret parameters. After that, X_A is calculated by multiplying random number R_p by an ECC-based generator P of large order n. Similarly, Y_A is the resultant of R_p and the TS's public key F that is equal to dP, where d is random number a from finite field selected by TS. For level 1 encryption of security credentials, a hash of Y_A is taken to prepare key H_{Y_A}. Patient (A) prepares a message M_A that contains hash of IDs and PW_p as the patient's password and Message Authentication Code (MAC) is used for providing message integrity on the server side. Patient (A) calculates $H(PW_p||ID_A||ID_B)$ and includes PWp to keep it more secure. In our proposed scheme, an intruder is not able to get the IDs of A and B but if in any case these values are exposed, then the exact hash value cannot be calculated because of the missing PWp that is held by the Patient (A) and TS only. For transmission to the server, the patient computes cipher text P_A which is encrypted by the patient's generated secret key H_{Y_A} as shown in step (iv). After that, a cipher text C_A is generated using a pre-established key K_{A-TS}. In step (vi), a temporary ID as ID_{A_T} of the patient is obtained by taking the hash of the $H(X_A, P_A, N_1)$ and is used for the current session only. The new $ID_{A\sim T}$ is never transmitted and can be calculated at the TS using $H(X_A, P_A, N_1)$ where N_1 can be extracted after decryption. It encrypts the parameters $\{X_A, P_A, T_1\}$ using K_{A-TS} where, T_1 is timestamp. Patient (A) transmits $\{ID_{A\sim T}, C_A\}$ to trusted server $\{TS\}$ for authentication.

(i) $X_A = R_p P$

(ii) $Y_A = R_p F$

(iii) $M_A = H(PW_p||ID_A||ID_B)$

(iv) $P_A = E_{H_{Y_A}}(ID_A||M_A||N_1||\text{MAC}(M_A)||ID_B)$

(v) $C_A = E_{K_{A-TS}}(X_A||P_A||T_1)$

(vi) $ID_{A\sim T} = \{H(X_A, P_A, N_1)\}$

B.   Step-II: Verification at Trusted Server

Upon receiving $\{ID_{A\sim T}, C_A\}$ form Patient (A), the TS decrypts the cipher text C_A to get $(X_A||P_A||T_1)$. It also checks the message freshness by taking the difference from T_1 to guard against replay attacks. After that, the TS computes the temporary key of the patient by multiplying the received X_A with d which was pre-generated by the TS as $Y'_A = dX_A$. To verify whether the message is original, the TS computes the Patient's (A) masked identity as $R_p F = R_p dP = dX_A$. It also decrypts P_A to obtain security credentials, including ID_A, M_A, N1, MAC (M_A), and ID_B. The hash of these values is calculated as $M'_A = H(PW_p||ID_A||ID_B)$ and is then compared to verify the equality of M_A and M'_A to ensure message integrity. Otherwise, the message is discarded. The (MAC(M_A)) provides data integrity for M_A. The trusted server computes the following steps.

(i)   Decrypt C_A using K_{A-TS} to get $\{(X_A||P_A||T_1)\}$

(ii)   Computer $Y'_A = dX_A$

(iii)   Decrypts P_A using $K_{H(YA)}$ to get $\{ID_A, M_A, N_1, \text{MAC}(M_A), ID_B\}$

(iv)   Compute: $M'_A = H(PW_p||ID_A||ID_B)$

(v)   If Verify $(MAC'(M_A)\ != \text{MAC}(M_A))$ then discard

(vi)   If M_A NOT equals M'_A then discard message

C.   Step-III: TS-based Mutual Authentication of B&A

After verification, the TS picks a random number R_{Ts} and then computes $Z_{TS} = H(ID_{TS}||ID_B||R_{Ts})$ using identities of B and TS. It also generates a nonce number N_2 to get its hash with identities of communicating parties A and B. After that, TS calculates the XOR of hash value with Z_{TS} to get a new temporary ID for B. The value of C_{TS} is obtained by encrypting $(ID_A||Z_{TS}||T_2||N_2)$ using the pre-established key K_{TS-B}. The TS transmits the temporary identity ID_{B_T} and cipher text C_{TS} to B.

(i) $Z_{TS} = H(ID_{TS}||ID_B||R_{Ts})$

(ii) $ID_{B\sim T} = Z_{TS}\ XOR\ \{H(ID_B||ID_A||N_2)\}$

(iii) $C_{TS} = E_{K_{TS-B}}(ID_A||Z_{TS}||\ T_2||N_2||ID_{B\sim T})$

$TS \rightarrow B : \{ID_{TS}, C_{TS}\}$

Doctor/Nurse (B) receives the message $\{ID_{TS}, C_{TS}\}$ and decrypts it to get the other party's prescription details and TS validity by computing the set time stamp threshold value, nonce number, received masked-ID values, and decrypted message using the pre-share key from the TS. At each end, entity $E_{K_{TS}}$ is used as a key to encrypt secure credentials in addition to MAC and the hash function application to make them more secure.

(i)   Decrypt using K_{TS-B} to get $\{(ID_A||Z_{TS}||\ T_2||\ N_2)\}$
(ii)   If $\{Z_{TS}\ XOR\ \{H(ID_B||ID_A||N_2)\}\}$ NOT Equals $ID_{B\sim T}$ then discard
(iii) $X_B = R_B P, Y_B = R_B F$
(iv) $M_B = H(PW_B||ID_{TS}||ID_B)$
(v) $P_B = E_{H_{Y_B}}(ID_B||M_B||N_3||\ \text{MAC}(M_B)||ID_{TS})$
(vi) $C_B = E_{K_{B-TS}}(X_B||\ P_B||\ T_3)$

$B \rightarrow TS : \{ID_{B\sim T}, C_B\}$

TS receives the message $\{ID_{B\sim T}, C_B\}$ and decrypts it to get $(X_B||\ P_B||\ T_3)$. After that, the TS computes $Y'_B = dX_B$ which is equal to $dR_B P = R_B dP = R_B F = Y_B$ calculated at Doctor/Nurse (B). It further decrypts the P_B to get $ID_B, M_B, N_3, \text{MAC}(M_B)$ and ID_{TS}, as illustrated in steps below. After that, the TS verifies the message's integrity by computing and comparing the hash of the message. Finally, it computes the common parameters CP_A and CP_B for both parties and forwards them to the Patient (A) and doctor/nurse (B) for session key computation.

(i)   Decrypt C_B to get $[(X_B||\ P_B||\ T_3)]$
(ii)   Computes $Y'_B = dX_B$
(iii) Decrypt P_B to get $[(ID_B||M_B||N_3||\ \text{MAC}(M_B)||ID_{TS})]$
(iv)   Calculate $M'_B = H(PW_B||ID_{TS}||ID_B)$
(v)   If M'_B *NOT equals* M_B then drop message
(vi) $CP_A = \{\ E_{H_{Y'_A}}(X_B||ID_A||ID_B||\ Y'_A||N_1\ )\}$
(vii) $CP_B = \{\ E_{H_{Y'_B}}(X_A||ID_A||ID_B||\ Y'_B||N_2\ )\}$

$TS \rightarrow A : \{ID_{A\sim T}, CP_A\}$
$TS \rightarrow B : \{ID_{B\sim T}, CP_B\}$

D.   Step-IV: Participant Validation and Common Session Key Generation

Patient (A) decrypts CP_A, verified by its own nonce and MAC which provide integrity and validity of the TS and the message. The common parameters generated by the trusted server are transmitted securely on each end. Upon receiving the secret credentials, the participating parties first verify message integrity and authority by verifying Y'_A and Y'_B, respectively. After that, MAC, nonce, TS-ID, and the time stamp are also used for double-checking the source's integrity before processing secret credentials. After successful validation of both parties' identities and that of the TS, participants start to compute the common key. The proposed protocol along with stepwise execution is elaborated in Figure 3.

a.   Party (A) gets: $\{X_B, ID_A,\ ID_B,\ Y'_A\}$
b.   Patient (A): $S_{kA} = H(dX_B, ID_B,\ ID_A)$
a.   Party (B) gets: $\{X_A, ID_A,\ ID_B,\ Y'_B\}$
b.   Doctor/Nurse (B): $S_{kB} = H(dX_A, ID_B,\ ID_A)$

Patient

$X_A = R_p P$

$Y_A = R_p F = R_p dP = dX_A$

$M_A = \{H(PW_p \| ID_A \| ID_B)\}$

$P_A = E_{H_{(YA)}} \{(ID_A \| M_A \| N_1 \| MAC(M_A) \| ID_B)\}$

$C_A = E_{K_{(A-T)}} [(X_A \| P_A \| T_1)]$

$ID_{A-T} = \{H(X_A, P_A, N_1)\}$

$\{H(X_A, P_A, N_1)\}$

Trusted Server(TS)

Decrypt C_A using $K_{(A-TS)}$ to get $\{(X_A \| P_A \| T_1)\}$

Compute $Y'_A = dX_A$

Decrypt P_A using $K_{H(YA)}$ to get $\{ID_A, M_A, N_1, MAC(M_A), ID_B\}$

Compute $M'_A = H(PW_p \| ID_A \| ID_B)$

if verify (MAC (M'_A) not equal to MAC(M_A) discard

if M'_A not equals M_A then discard message

Computation at TS

$Z_{TS} = H(ID_B \| ID_B \| R_{TS})$

$ID_{B-T} = Z_{TS} \otimes \{H(ID_B \| ID_A \| N_2)\}$

$C_{TS} = E_{K_{(B-t)}} (ID_A \| Z_{TS} \| T_2 \| N_2 \| ID_{B-T})$

$\{ID_{TT}, C_{TT}\}$

Decrypt C_A to get $[(X_A \| P_A \| T_1)]$

Computes $Y'_b = dX_b$

Decrypt P_b to get $\{(ID_B \| M_3 \| N_3 \| MAC(M_3)\}$

Calculate $M'_b = H(PW_b \| ID_{TS} \| ID_B)$

If M'_b Not equals M_b then drop message

$CP_A = \{E_{k(Y_A)} (X_B \| ID_A \| ID_B \| Y_A \| N_1\}$

$CP_B = \{E_{k(Y_A)} (X_A \| ID_A \| ID_B \| Y_A \| N_3\}$

$\{ID_{A-T}, CP_A\}$ $\{ID_{A-T}, CP_B\}$

Doctor/Nurse

Decrypt using K_{TS-B} to get $\{(ID_A \| Z_{TS} \| T_2 \| N_2)\}$

If $\{Z_{TS} \otimes (H(ID_B \| ID_A \| N_2)\}! = ID_{BT}$ then discard

$X_B = R_p P$, $Y_B = R_p F$

$M_B = H(PW_B \| ID_A \| ID_B)$

$P_B = E_{H(ID)} [(ID_B \| M_B \| N_3 \| MAC(M_B) \| ID_{TS})]$

$C_B = E_{K_{(b-TS)}} (X_B \| P_B \| T_3)$

$\{ID_{TT}, C_B\}$

Party A-Gets
$\{X_B, ID_A, ID_B, Y_A\}$

Party B-Gets
$\{X_A, ID_A, ID_B, Y_B\}$

$S_{EA} = H(dX_B, ID_B, ID_A)$

$S_{EB} = H(dX_B, ID_B, ID_A)$

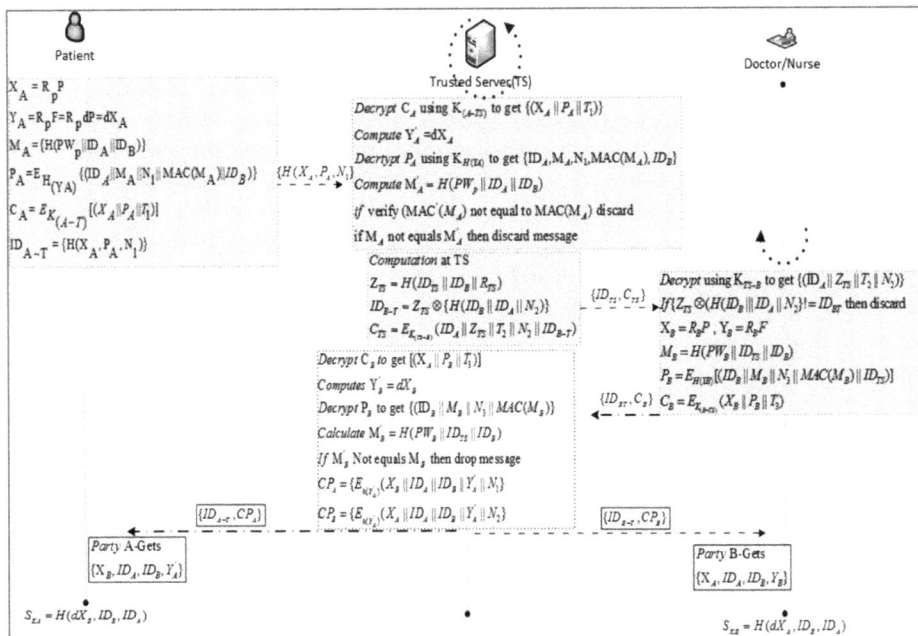

Figure 3. Secure authentication and prescription safety protocol steps.

The novelty of our study is relying upon the creation of secret credentials of the session key for multiparty computing using ECC and symmetric parameters which have less computation cost and are hard to compromise. Upon successful authentication of end parties and common session key generation, both ends share private data securely and efficiently. SAPS attains shared verification, better forward privacy, un-traceability, and participant anonymity. It can launch a secure data sharing connection between the end user and a trusted authority. It also ensures that various attacks, such as offline password guessing, untraceable online secret parameters guessing, confidential insider attacks, card theft attacks, and replay attacks. Intruders cannot enter the system, and the user remains protected at all times.

5. Formal Modeling and Analysis of SAPS

We have performed formal modeling using a method known as Nonmonotonic Cryptographic Protocol (NCP), also called Rubin Logic [39]. The analysis verification of the SAPS protocol is as per its previous terms and specification of NCP. NCP authenticates the proposed scheme as per the regular necessities of cryptographic procedures, considering parameters such as authenticity, data integrity, the freshness of received data, message encryption, and decryption, etc. This will also help identify the lack of certain properties in the presented scheme and for potential data compromising scenarios. This analysis is similar to the actual operation functionalities in a programming scenario. When we talk about Rubin Logic, the units are assigned specific roles, and a universal set of information is maintained. It also maintains current state of the parameters of users after each update operation. Global sets are accessible to all the member nodes and can be categorized into four types which are secret, observer, rule, and first sets. A detailed discussion of the formal specification for WSAN protocols is provided in [26,29], along with appropriate case studies. Entity or node contains a local set that can be categorized into ownership, represented as POSS (), a set of beliefs known as belief BEL (), and to represent the behavior, set BL (). Detailed specification of these sets can be explored in [14,30]. Table 2 represents the local set for the application scenario of Rubin logic on SAPS-AN. The details of SAPS, its verification, and analysis provide a detailed overview of all sets maintained under the category of the local set. All the participating entities, including sender, receiver, and Trusted Server are separately maintained locally. An ownership set, POSS (entity), contains all the parameters involved in encryption, decryption, and other processes accomplished in a local memory of each entity, as described in the section below. For the operations and input arguments that are performed in implementation steps, a Behavior List BL () is maintained. Local sets for the entities of the Trusted Server (TS), patient (A) as first party, and Doctor (B) as the second party are presented in Tables 2–4, respectively.

Table 2. Local set at (Patient) (A).

$POSS(A) = \{ID_A, P, R_p, K_{A\text{-}TS}, F, PW_p\}$
$BEL(A) = \{\#(ID_A), \#(P), \#(R_p), \#(K_{(A\text{-}TS)}), \#(F), \#(PW_p)\}$
$BL(A) =$
$Mul\ (R_p, P) \rightarrow X_A, Mul\ (R_p, F) \rightarrow Y_A$
$Hash(h(.); Concat(PW_p, ID_A, ID_B)) \rightarrow M_A$
$Concat(ID_A, M_A, N_1, MAC(M_A), ID_B) \rightarrow Q_A$
$Hash(h(.); Y_A) \rightarrow H_{YA}$
$Encrypt(\{Q_A, H_{YA}\}) \rightarrow P_A$
$Encrypt(\{Concat(X_A, P_A, T_1), K_{(A\text{-}TS)}\}) \rightarrow C_A$
$Hash(h(.); Concat\ (X_A, P_A, N_1)) \rightarrow ID_{A\sim T}$
$Send(\{ID_{A\sim T}, C_A\})$ to TS and Update $(ID_{A\sim T})$
$Receive(TS, (CP_A))$
$Decrypt(\{ID_{TS}, CP_A\}\ H_{Y'A})$ and Split to get $[X_B, ID_A, ID_B, Y'_A, N_1]$
$Hash(h(.); Concat\ (dX_B, ID_B, ID_A)) \rightarrow S_{kA}$

Table 3. Local Set at Trusted Server (TS).

$POSS(T_S) = \{ID_{TS}, d, K_{(TS-A)]}, K_{(TS-B)}\}$
$BEL(T_S) = \{\#(ID_{TS}), \#(K_{(TS-A)]}, \#K_{(TS-B)}\}$
$BL(T_S) =$
$Receive(A, \{C_A\})$
$Decrypt(\{ID_{A\sim T}, C_A\}K_{TS-A})$ and Split to get $[X_A, P_A, T_1]$
$check(T'_1 - T_1) \geq \Delta T$ then abort
$Hash(h(.); Mul(d, X_A)) \rightarrow H_{Y'A}$
$Decrypt(\{P_A\}H_{Y'A})$ and Split to get $[ID_A, M_A, N_1, MAC(M_A), ID_B]$
$Hash(h(.); Concat(PW_p, ID_A, ID_B)) \rightarrow M'_A$
if $MAC(M'_A)$ equals $MAC(M_A)$ else discard
if M'_A NOT equals M_A then discard

$Hash(h(.); Concat(ID_{TS}, ID_B, R_{TS})) \rightarrow Z_{TS}$
$Hash(h(.); Concat(ID_A, ID_B, N_2)) \rightarrow Q_{TS}$
$XOR\ (Z_{TS}, Q_{TS}) \rightarrow ID_{B\sim T}$
$Encrypt(\{Concat(ID_A, Z_{TS}, T_2, N_2, ID_{B\sim T}), K_{(TS-B)}\}) \rightarrow C_{TS}$
$Send(\{ID_{TS}, C_{TS}\})$ to B and Update $(ID_{B\text{-}T})$

$Receive(B, \{C_B\})$
$Decrypt(\{ID_{B\sim T}, C_B\}K_{TS-B})$ and Split to get $[X_B, P_B, T_3]$
$check(T'_3 - T_3) \geq \Delta T$ then abort
$Hash(h(.); Mul\ (d, X_B)) \rightarrow H_{Y'B}$
$Decrypt(\{P_B\}H_{Y'B})$ and Split to get $[ID_B, M_B, N_3, MAC(M_B), ID_{TS}]$
$Hash(h(.); Concat(PW_B, ID_{TS}, ID_B)) \rightarrow M'_B$
if $MAC(M'_B)$ equals $MAC(M_B)$ else discard
if M'_B NOT equals M_B then discard

$Encrypt(\{Concat(X_B, ID_A, ID_B, Y'_A, N_1), H_{Y'A}\}) \rightarrow CP_A$
$Send(\{ID_{A\sim T}, CP_A\})$ to A
$Encrypt(\{Concat(X_A, ID_A, ID_B, Y'_B, N_2), H_{Y'B}\}) \rightarrow CP_B$
$Send(\{ID_{B\sim T}, CP_B\})$ to B

Table 4. Local set at Patient/Doctor (B).

POSS(B) = {ID_B, P, R_B, K_{B-TS}, F, PW_B}
BEL(A) = {#(ID_B), #(P), #(R_B), #($K_{(B-TS)}$), #(F), #(PW_B)}
BL(A) =
Receive(TS, {C_{TS}})
Decrypt({$ID_{B\sim T}$, C_{TS}}K_{B-TS}) and Split to get [ID_A, Z_{TS}, T_2, N_2]
Hash(h(.); Concat(ID_A, ID_B, N_2)) → Q'_{TS}
check(XOR(Z_{TS}, Q'_{TS}) ! equals $ID_{B\sim T}$) then abort
Mul (R_B, P) → X_B, Mul (R_B, F) → Y_B
Hash(h(.); Concat(PW_B, ID_{TS}, ID_B)) → M_B
Concat(ID_B, M_B, N_3, MAC(M_B), ID_{TS}) → Q_B
Hash(h(.); Y_B) → H_{YB}
Encrypt({Q_B, H_{YB}}) → P_B
Encrypt({Concat(X_B, P_B,T_3),$K_{(B-TS)}$}) → C_B
Send({$ID_{B\sim T}$, C_B}) to TS and Update($ID_{B\sim T}$)

Receive(TS, (CP_B))
Decrypt({ID_{TS}, CP_B} $H_{Y'B}$) and Split to get [X_A, ID_A, ID_B, Y'_B, N_2]
Hash(h(.); Concat(dX_A, ID_B, ID_A)) → S_{kB}

5.1. SAPS Analysis and Verification

In this section, SAPS is analyzed for secure session key establishment for the patient to access their physicians anonymously for medical prescription, as discussed in section IV. In this scenario, the establishment request is initiated by the patient (A) by transmitting secret credentials generated using secure methodology established through the TS. After the sending operation, an update operation performed by the sender to refresh the security credentials for future sessions is as shown below.

- Concat(IDA, MA, N1, MAC(MA), IDB) → QA
- Encrypt({QA,H_{YA}}) → P_A
- Encrypt({Concat(X_A, P_A, T_1), $K_{(A-TS)}$}) → C_A
- Send({$ID_{A\sim T}$, C_A}) to TS and Update($ID_{A\sim T}$)
- Update()

To observe, a list of associated factors, messages, nonce numbers, actual key, ciphers, pseudo-dynamic, finite field, and one-way hash values, are kept in a possession set at the sender node, i.e., with the patient (A). In this case, during the authentication for key establishment phase, the following steps are performed.

- POSS(A) = {ID_A, P, R_p, K_{A-TS}, F, PW_p}
- BEL(A) = {#(ID_A), #(P), #(R_p), #($K_{(A-TS)}$), #(F), #(PW_p)}
- BL(A) = Mul(R_p, P) → XA, Mul(R_p, F) → YA

After sending messages to the other party and the authentication request is sent to the trusted authority, the TS decrypts the received message to get the secret credentials necessary for verification and to explore the request message. The freshness of the message is checked by comparing the timestamp threshold value, nonce number, and masked IDs value with set values. If we fulfill the threshold parameter and verify the answer, then further process calculations are processed. Otherwise, the message is discarded. MAC is calculated for message integrity and compared to hash values to ensure integrity. The participant verification and message integrity steps performed at the TS are as follows.

- Receive(A, {C_A})
- Decrypt({$ID_{A\sim T}$, C_A}K_{TS-A}) and Split to get [X_A, P_A, T_1]
- check(T$'_1$–T_1) ≥ ΔT then abort
- Hash(h(.); Mul(d, X_A)) → $H_{Y'A}$

- Decrypt($\{P_A\}H_{Y'A}$) and Split to get [ID_A, M_A, N_1, MAC(M_A), ID_B]
- Hash(h(.); Concat(PW_p, ID_A, ID_B)) → M'_A
- if MAC(M'_A) equals MAC(M_A) else discard
- if M'_A NOT equals M_A then discard

After Patient (A) verification, the TS calculates some parameters and generates a message for the other party that can provide medical services to the patient (A) as follows.

- Hash(h(.); Concat(IDTS, IDB, RTS)) → ZTS
- Hash(h(.); Concat(IDA, IDB, N2)) → QTS
- XOR(ZTS, QTS) → IDB~ T
- Encrypt($\{$Concat (IDA, ZTS, T2, N2, IDB~T), K(TS-B)$\}$) → CTS
- Send($\{$IDTS, CTS$\}$) to B and Update (IDB~ T)

Upon receiving the secret credentials sent by the TS, Doctor (B) verifies the message integrity and the TS as follows:

- Decrypt($\{ID_{B\sim T}$, $C_{TS}\}K_{B\text{-}TS}$) and Split to get [ID_A, Z_{TS}, T_2, N_2]
- Hash(h(.); Concat (ID_A, ID_B, N_2)) → Q'_{TS}
- check(XOR(Z_{TS},Q'_{TS}) ! equals $ID_{B\sim T}$) then abort

Following the authentication and verification of Party (B) by the TS, party (B) also computes some secret credentials and provides a reply message for the TS. The secret credentials are used by both parties to generate a secret key, and the transmission is secured using the shared key, as well as by calculating the hash, adding a nonce, and MAC. The steps performed at the physician's side for session key establishing are as follows:

- Mul(R_B, P) → X_B, Mul(R_B, F) → Y_B
- Hash(h(.); Concat (P_{WB}, IDTS, ID_B)) → M_B
- Concat(ID_B,M_B, N_3, MAC(M_B), IDTS) → Q_B
- Hash(h(.);Y_B) → H_{YB}
- Encrypt($\{$QB, $H_{YB}\}$) → P_B
- Encrypt($\{$Concat(X_B, P_B,T3), K(B-TS)$\}$) → C_B
- Send($\{ID_B\sim T$, $C_B\}$) to TS and Update (IDB~ T)

For verification and checking of message integrity of party (B), the TS performs the same steps as Party (A). The TS securely generates secret credentials based on the information gathered from both ends, and distributes a common key which is partially completed. Secure parameter distribution steps are shown as below, which are transmitted securely to the participants.

- Encrypt($\{$Concat (X_B, ID_A,ID_B,Y'_A, N_1), $H_{Y'A}\}$) → CP_A
- Send($\{ID_{A\sim T}$, $CP_A\}$) to A
- Encrypt($\{$Concat (X_A, ID_A,ID_B, Y'_B, N_2), $H_{Y'B}\}$) → CP_B
- Send($\{ID_{B\sim T}$, $CP_B\}$) to B

Although data/credentials transmission is performed using strong encryption techniques by the TS to increase security and un-traceability of participants, the proposed scheme has a novel approach in its partial session key mechanism. After successful authentication and session key establishment, a "Forget Operation" performed at each participating entity will result in removing temporary values like nonce value, time stamp, temporary encryption key H*, and MAC calculating parameters. These operations ensure security against forwarding secrecy and user traceability issues.

5.2. User Anonymity

The user's identity, ID, cannot be stored in plaintext at the user level, nor at the TS, and it can be transmitted via the login request. In our scheme, user identity is masked in both M_A and P_A, after the original identity registration, session request, and end-user joining request is sent to the TS in the encrypted form. The secret parameters are generated by party (A) and party (B) by choosing secret number d_A, d_B, respectively, from E with large order n as shown in steps I–III. It is not feasible for any third party to get these secret parameters and it is almost impossible to recover messages M_A, M_B to get identities without knowing the one-way hash function. It is not viable for an adversary to compute the original identities of the participant. The TS has private and public key pairs and the participants use their MAC for message integrity, masked-IDs, nonce number, and time stamp (T) for message freshness. At the trusted sever, a randomized symmetric encryption technique is used to conceal the random number $\{R_{TS}\}$ generated by the TS instead of using the XOR. Before communicating the session request of party(A) to party(B), the TS first verifies the original identity of the requested party and the message freshness by computing the inverse functions as shown in Protocols II and III. It generates a temporary public ID of each participant instead of using their original identities. The public identity, say IDV, can run the protocol. Therefore, on the basis of the above analysis, it is impossible for the adversary to get the user's identity from the proposed protocol during authentication, forwarding, the joining request, or the session key computing procedure. Therefore, we know that the proposed protocol is able to provide user anonymity.

5.3. User Un-Traceability

In our scheme, each session-based communication contains parameters $\{X_A,\ P_A,\ T_1\}$ based on X_A and P_A that are dynamic for each authentication/verification session of all participants and are different for each transmission. Moreover, a timestamp is appended to every session. The value of $(X_A,\ P_A)$, Z_{TS} and X_B, P_B, as shown in the proposed protocols to fulfill the requirements for common session key establishment, are executed in a distributed manner. Consequently, the adversary is unable to figure out that two procedures have the same users involved. It ensures that our proposal accomplishes user un-traceability. According to the pattern of the projected protocol, the participant generates a new random number $r \in Z^*_q$ to compute X_A, Z_{TS} and X_B in each session. Due to the randomness of the secret parameters, the adversary cannot find and link among messages sent by the end parties or the trusted server, and therefore is unable to follow their actions. Therefore, the proposed protocol is able to provide un-traceability during authentication, session key management, and the following data transmission procedures.

5.4. Offline Password Guessing Attacks

In offline password guessing, the adversary tries to capture the entire communication between party (A) and the TS or between the TS and party (B), but is unable to get the password. The next adversary attack may be possible.

i. $\{X_A,\ P_A,\ T_1\} \rightarrow \{TS\}$ from party(A) to TS, $\{ID_{TS},\ Z_{TS}\}$ are TS parameters, $(\{X_B,\ P_B\}, T_3)$ Party(B) to TS and $\{CP_A,\ CP_B\}$ are the communications between A, B, and the TS known by the adversary. To commence the offline secret password estimating attack, the adversary tries to regenerate PW'_p, an inverse password of party (A) and computes M_A'. Still, if the adversary gets the IDs of both participants, it is not possible for the adversary to compute $E_{H(YA)}$ and they are unable to verify the P_A as used in the protocols which contains the message and the identities of the participants.

ii. Appropriate to the un-traceability of the Computational Diffie-Hellman assumption (CDH) a difficult adversary does not get $\{Y_A = R_pF := R_pdP \rightarrow Y_A = dX_A\ F\}$ and it is impossible for the adversary to get the password.

iii.   If an adversary gets party B's password to compute the random R_{Ts} number generated by the TS, as shown in protocol-III, to compute the parameters after the received connection establishing request from party (A), it is not possible for the adversary to compute B's password without knowing YB because $Y_B = \{d_B F\}$ and has ECDLP, as shown in step-3 of protocol-III.

As a result, the proposed protocol can oppose offline password guessing attacks. To deal with online password guessing attack, the TS detects the encounter during the message validation process and the freshness procedure at the beginning of the communication.

5.5. Perfect Forward Secrecy

In our scheme, the un-traceability of CDH plays a vital role in resisting guessing previous session keys by the adversary. The session key is generated using $H(d_A, d_B P, ID_B, ID_A)$, where d_A, d_B are nonce numbers chosen by both participants specially for the specific session and are different from the nonce numbers used during the authentication process, such as N_1, N_2, N_3. In the proposed protocol, the end parties compute the session key, SK, as $H(dX_B, ID_B, ID_A)$ and $H(dX_A, ID_B, ID_A)$, where dX_A and dX_B are computed by randomly chosen numbers by both parties at their end with the help of the trusted server. Knowing the secret key of the server and the password does not help the adversary to compute a previously established session key, because the secret credentials used to compute the secure key are not based on the password and server's public key. If the adversary wants to know an old session key he/she must compute dX_A, dX_B. However, since the adversary does not know the R_p due to the hardness of ECDLP, the adversary cannot compute the secret credentials. Therefore, the proposed scheme provides perfect forward secrecy.

5.6. Replay Attack

Replay attacks can be launched while an attacker replays the original message parameters at some other time to impersonate any legal participant. In the proposed scheme, messages between the ID_A, TS, and ID_B are transmitted on the public channel. An attacker might try to use these conversations to launch a replay attack. However, in our protocol, replay attacks can be easily thwarted because an adversary cannot produce an updated timestamp. Both end parties and the TS verify message freshness with a threshold for timestamp and nonce number. If the difference exceeds this threshold, it will abort the session. It is not easy for an adversary to impersonate participants' reply messages because the nonce numbers N_1, N_2, N_3 during the authentication process, d_A, d_B for key session key generation and R_{Ts} used by the TS are newly chosen for every session. For this scenario, an adversary cannot compute the $\{X_A, P_A, T_1\}$, $S_K = H(d_A X'_B, ID_B, ID_A)$, and $(\{X_B, P_B\}, T_3)$ communication patterns of the entire network.

5.7. Forgery Attacks and Impersonation

In our scheme, TS has a pair of public-private secret keys $(d, F = dP)$, and if an adversary attempts to impersonate the participants or the TS and sends a message to the TS acting as the participants or tries to establish a connection with any party, they will remain unable to verify themself. For the verification process, it is necessary for an adversary to know the password or private key of the TS, d.

5.8. Man in the Middle Attack

An adversary may intercept the messages sent between the parties and the TS and replace them with their own messages. These forged messages need to be verified by the TS before getting the session key. However, it is not feasible as the adversary does not know the TS secret key and secret passwords of the parties. So, our scheme resists a man in middle attack.

6. Results and Analysis

We have simulated the SAPS protocol by deploying nodes for the patient, doctor/nurse, and the trusted server using TCL script in NS 2.35.The simulation parameter and system setting defined in Table 5. We have separately configured the patient and doctor/nurse for low power devices. The server is configured for high residual and transmission power. In the TCL file, communication messages are initiated and traffic sources are also configured along with packet sizes. Moreover, C/C++ files are developed for providing device-level functionalities, including send, receive, hash, encrypt, and decrypt functions. Results are extracted from the trace file by executing the AWK scripts. We have used a 160-bit key along with $f(x) = x^{167} + x^9 + x^7 + x^5 + x^3 + 1$ where the tuple $T = (m, f, (x)a, b, G, n, h)$. The performance of SAPS is evaluated regarding storage, computation, and communication costs for the base scheme TPKE [15], A-TMIS [16], EAKA [40], and AAS [41]. A list of simulation parameters is shown in Table 4.

Table 5. Simulation Parameters.

Parameters	Values
Network Field	1300×1300 m
Initial Energy at Smart Device	1000 Joules
Tx Power at Smart Device	0.819 Joules
Receiving Power	0.049 Joules
Queue Type	Queue/DropTail/PriQue
Max Packet in Queue	55 Packets
Agent Trace	ON
Router Trace	ON
Number of Nodes	500 Nodes

6.1. Storage Overhead

In the proposed protocol, we outlined the storage overhead and memory requirement, including the public/private key of the TS and the communication parties, IDs, random number, timestamp, and resultant length of the session key, as shown in Figure 4. In the view of the used parameters between the patient (A), TS, and Doctor (B), we have analyzed and compared the storage cost of TPKE [15], the smart card keeps $\{ID, B, p\}$ and thus the storage overhead is $(160 + 1022 \times 2) = 2208$ bits. A-TMIS [16] stores $(1600 + 1024 \times 3) = 3232$ bits and an efficient authentication and key agreement EAKA protocol [40] requires $(160 \times 5) = 800$ bits in the smart card for basics parameters. The AAS [41] scheme improves the protocol for TMIS and consumes 960-bits storage to process authentication and authorization which contains $\{P, u, B, R, p, q\}$.

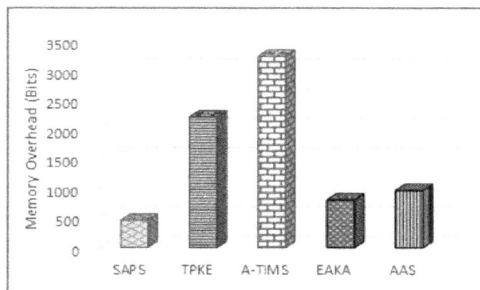

Figure 4. Storage cost for Secure Authentication and Prescription Safety (SAPS).

In our SAPS protocol, the end parties need to keep $\{P_W, ID, X_A, N_i, T_i, E_{K_{A-TS}}\}$ for identification, authentication, and session key establishment. From an evaluation point of view, it has been supposed that secret identity, one-way hash operation, and timestamps are 160-bits in size, whereas the ECC recommended size by NIST for a key is 160-bits and 64-bit for the secret key for encrypting passwords generated using the TS's shared credentials. So, the total storage overheads of proposed scheme are $(160 + 160 \times 2) = 480$ bits, which is stored at both ends and the TS has more computation and storage capabilities. In our scenario, more parameters such as ID masking, public/private key and pseudorandom generation processes are accomplished at the TS.

6.2. Communication Overhead

To appraise the message exchanging overhead of the presented protocol, the data that is transmitted between the participating parties and the TS during the identification and session key generation phase need to be considered. It is identified that the secret key of size 160-bit using ECC can yield equal security to a 1024-bit RSA secret key. For the evaluation phase, we believe that the resultant one-way hash function, participant's identities, timestamp, and nonce number are 160 bits in length. The end party sends three parameters which are $\{XA, PA, T1\}$ to the TS for authentication, and their lengths are $(160 \times 3) = 480$ bits. On the other side, in the party verification phase, the TS sends an encrypted packet CP_A using a 160-bit ECC key to the end party for session key establishment and its length is $(160 \times 2) = 320$ bits. On the basis of these computations in the proposed SAPS protocol, Patient (A) and Doctor (B) have the same communication cost during their end user confirmation and secure key generation processes. On the other hand, existing ECC- and RSA-based schemes have greater communication overheads, as depicted in Figure 5.

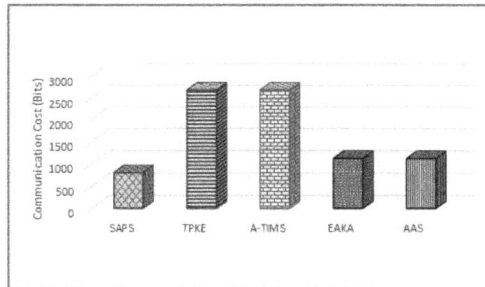

Figure 5. Communication overheads during authentication.

TPKE [15] is based on RSA which requires 1344 bits for the authentication method and 1344 bits for server to end party communication. Similarly, A-TMIS [16] consumes the same communication cost as TPKE for the whole procedure. In the login phase of Xu et al.'s protocol for EAKA [40], the server requires 640 bits of communication cost, and the server to the user requires 480-bits. AAS [41] requires 640 bits and 480 bits communication from the user to server and the server to user, respectively. By the above analysis, the proposed scheme has less communication cost by ensuring user anonymity.

6.3. Computation Complexity

Based on the simulation results and defined parameters, a 5 MHz frequency is required to compute the 160-bit elliptic curve, where 5 MHz is for one small data module in which multiple modules are included in the calculation of the elliptic curve and related mathematical operations. To elaborate in detail, we have defined some notations to describe the function of protocol like, T_E, T_{EPM}, T_{EDs}, T_H, T_X which are the time for performing an exponential operation, time for performing an elliptic curve point multiplication operation, time for computing EC point multiplication function, symmetric encryption/decryption operation time, the one way hash function computation time, and XOR operation, respectively.

According to [42,43], the computation time for an exponential operation is 0.522 ms, EC point multiplication process consumes 0.063075 ms, one-way hash operation implementation time is 0.0005 ms, and the encryption/decryption operation time is 0.0087 ms. On the user's side, the proposed scheme has lower computational overheads, as shown in Figures 6 and 7. Our SAPS protocol is more suitable for a mobile scenario when compared to existing schemes, because it has fewer rounds needed for authentication. Computing complexity for the adversary is high, whereas fewer communication rounds make it more efficient and secure.

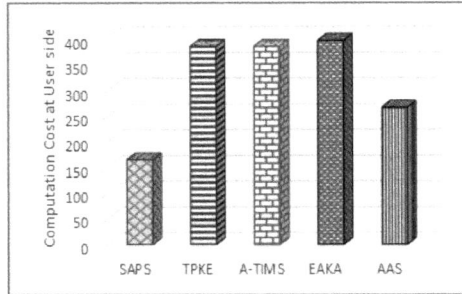

Figure 6. Computation cost at user side.

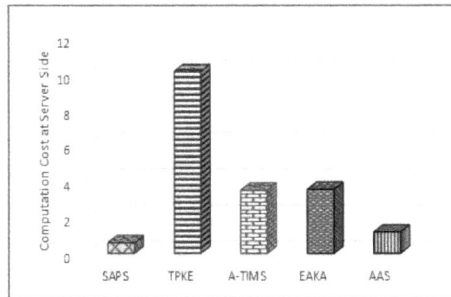

Figure 7. Computation cost at server side.

6.4. Resilience

During secure communication between the patient and doctor, devices from different regions communicate using intermediate devices. The chance of compromised devices in the path exists. The probability Pr_β that an intermediate node is compromised is given in Equation (1), where N is the number of devices in the network and β is number of devices compromised by adversary. The term $N-2$ represents that sender and receiver are considered uncompromised, whereas $N-3$ means to exclude one more intermediate device which is a direct neighbor of the sender.

$$Pr_\beta = 1 - \binom{N-3}{\beta} / \binom{N-2}{\beta} = \frac{\beta}{N-2} \tag{1}$$

Figure 8 elucidates the scenario for measuring the impact of compromising intermediate devices by calculating the probability Pr_β when the number of devices in the network varies from 100 to 500. In the case of 300 devices, the probability is 0.0167, 0.033, 0.050, and 0.067 for $\beta = 5$, 10, 15, and 20 compromised devices, respectively. If an intermediate device is compromised, then data and security credentials stored in that device are exposed. Moreover, the probability Pr_ω that a particular session key and its related credentials are compromised is given in Equation (2), where ω credentials are compromised out of a total of M devices in the network.

$$Pr_\omega = 1 - \left(\begin{array}{c} M-1 \\ \omega-1 \end{array} \right) / \left(\begin{array}{c} M \\ \omega \end{array} \right) = \frac{\omega}{M} \tag{2}$$

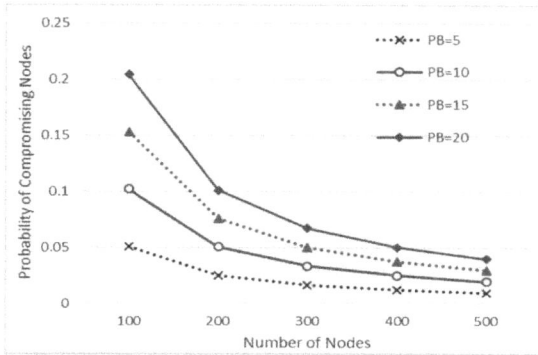

Figure 8. Probability of compromised intermediate device.

Figure 9 shows that different security credentials stored in devices can be revealed to intruders when the devices are compromised. We have considered the scenario where the number of devices is varied from 100 to 500, and the number of compromised nodes is varied from 5 to 25, respectively. In the case of 400 devices in the network where 20 of them are compromised, the number of compromised bytes are 15.62 KB, 18.75 KB, 43.12 KB, and 63.12 KB for EAKA, AAS, TPKE, and A-TIMS respectively. Our proposed SAPS method dominates and achieves better resilience against node capture attack by revealing only 8.98 KB.

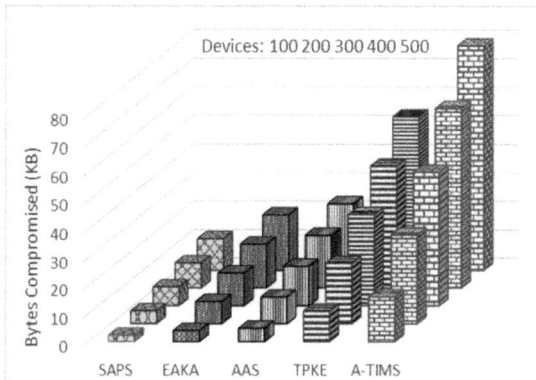

Figure 9. Bytes revealed upon device compromise.

7. Conclusions

A secure three-party key establishment technique for TMIS is presented to secure patients' medical prescriptions. It uses ECC for end-user anonymity, using the secure authentication and prescription safety (SAPS) protocol that can establish a secure connection between patients and a doctor/nurse without revealing their secret identities. The proposed scheme achieves anonymity and un-traceability of the participants. The SAPS protocol has been analyzed by applying Rubin Logic to verify security, user anonymity, and un-traceability of participants during session key generation for secure information sharing between the doctor and the patient in TMIS. Public attacks and their countermeasures are analyzed at each level. For validation of SAPS, we have performed simulation using NS-2.35 to compare the performance of SAPS for storage, communication, and computation overheads, as compared to other methods to prove its suitability for the ubiquitous TMIS network. The storage cost reduction of the proposed scheme at the user side and at the server side is approximately 38% and 41%, respectively, as compared with the mean of the four latest existing techniques. The average computation overhead reductions at both the user side and the server side are 37% and 49%, respectively, as compared with the mean average of existing four schemes. Our future work will aim to analyze the impact of chaotic map-based keying for multi-party authentication between doctors and patients to get a medical prescription for common diseases without revealing either identities on an open network.

Acknowledgments: This work was funded by the National Natural Science Foundation of China (61471035), and Fundamental Research Funds for the Central Universities (06105031, 06500010). In particular, it was supported by Cybermatics and Cyberspace International Science and Technology Cooperation Base.

Author Contributions: Zahid Mahmood and Ata Ullah conceived and designed the experiments; Zahid Mahmood performed the experiments; Huansheng Ning analyzed the data and overall proposed protocols, models, structure and flow of entire paper; Xuanxia Yao and Ata Ullah performed the formal modeling and verification of proposed scheme. Zahid Mahmood contributed reagents/materials/analysis tools and also wrote the paper along with literature.

Conflicts of Interest: The authors declare that there is no conflict of interest in this research.

References

1. Wu, Z.-Y.; Tseng, Y.-J.; Chung, Y.; Chen, Y.-C.; Lai, F. A reliable user authentication and key agreement scheme for web-based hospital-acquired infection surveillance information system. *J. Med. Syst.* **2012**, *36*, 2547–2555. [CrossRef] [PubMed]
2. Giri, D.; Maitra, T.; Amin, R.; Srivastava, P. An efficient and robust rsa-based remote user authentication for telecare medical information systems. *J. Med. Syst.* **2015**, *39*, 145. [CrossRef] [PubMed]
3. Xie, Q.; Zhang, J.; Dong, N. Robust anonymous authentication scheme for telecare medical information systems. *J. Med. Syst.* **2013**, *37*, 9911. [CrossRef] [PubMed]
4. Abdalla, M.; Fouque, P.-A.; Pointcheval, D. Password-based authenticated key exchange in the three-party setting. *IEEE Proc. Inf. Secur.* **2006**, *153*, 27–39. [CrossRef]
5. Chung, H.-R.; Ku, W.-C. Three weaknesses in a simple three-party key exchange protocol. *Inf. Sci.* **2008**, *178*, 220–229. [CrossRef]
6. Guo, H.; Li, Z.; Mu, Y.; Zhang, X. Cryptanalysis of simple three-party key exchange protocol. *Comput. Secur.* **2008**, *27*, 16–21. [CrossRef]
7. Lu, R.; Cao, Z. Simple three-party key exchange protocol. *Comput. Secur.* **2007**, *26*, 94–97. [CrossRef]
8. Huang, H.F. A simple three-party password-based key exchange protocol. *Int. J. Commun. Syst.* **2009**, *22*, 857–862. [CrossRef]
9. Nam, J.; Paik, J.; Kang, H.-K.; Kim, U.M.; Won, D. An off-line dictionary attack on a simple three-party key exchange protocol. *IEEE Commun. Lett.* **2009**, *13*, 205–207.
10. Phan, R.C.-W.; Yau, W.-C.; Goi, B.-M. Cryptanalysis of simple three-party key exchange protocol (S-3PAKE). *Inf. Sci.* **2008**, *178*, 2849–2856. [CrossRef]
11. Chen, H.-M.; Lo, J.-W.; Yeh, C.-K. An efficient and secure dynamic id-based authentication scheme for telecare medical information systems. *J. Med. Syst.* **2012**, *36*, 3907–3915. [CrossRef] [PubMed]

12. Xie, Q.; Dong, N.; Tan, X.; Wong, D.S.; Wang, G. Improvement of a three-party password-based key exchange protocol with formal verification. *Inf. Technol. Control* **2013**, *42*, 231–237. [CrossRef]

13. Wu, S.; Chen, K.; Pu, Q.; Zhu, Y. Cryptanalysis and enhancements of efficient three-party password-based key exchange scheme. *Int. J. Commun. Syst.* **2013**, *26*, 674–686. [CrossRef]

14. Wu, Z.-Y.; Lee, Y.-C.; Lai, F.; Lee, H.-C.; Chung, Y. A secure authentication scheme for telecare medicine information systems. *J. Med. Syst.* **2012**, *36*, 1529–1535. [CrossRef] [PubMed]

15. Debiao, H.; Jianhua, C.; Rui, Z. A more secure authentication scheme for telecare medicine information systems. *J. Med. Syst.* **2012**, *36*, 1989–1995. [CrossRef] [PubMed]

16. Wei, J.; Hu, X.; Liu, W. An improved authentication scheme for telecare medicine information systems. *J. Med. Syst.* **2012**, *36*, 3597–3604. [CrossRef] [PubMed]

17. Zhu, Z. An efficient authentication scheme for telecare medicine information systems. *J. Med. Syst.* **2012**, *36*, 3833–3838. [CrossRef] [PubMed]

18. Pu, Q.; Wang, J.; Zhao, R. Strong authentication scheme for telecare medicine information systems. *J. Med. Syst.* **2012**, *36*, 2609–2619. [CrossRef] [PubMed]

19. Khan, M.K.; Kim, S.-K.; Alghathbar, K. Cryptanalysis and security enhancement of a 'more efficient & secure dynamic ID-based remote user authentication scheme'. *Comput. Commun.* **2011**, *34*, 305–309.

20. Kumar, P.; Lee, S.-G.; Lee, H.-J. E-SAP: Efficient-strong authentication protocol for healthcare applications using wireless medical sensor networks. *Sensors* **2012**, *12*, 1625–1647. [CrossRef] [PubMed]

21. He, D.; Kumar, N.; Chen, J.; Lee, C.-C.; Chilamkurti, N.; Yeo, S.-S. Robust anonymous authentication protocol for health-care applications using wireless medical sensor networks. *Multimed. Syst.* **2015**, *21*, 49–60. [CrossRef]

22. Nam, J.; Choo, K.-K.R.; Han, S.; Kim, M.; Paik, J.; Won, D. Efficient and anonymous two-factor user authentication in wireless sensor networks: Achieving user anonymity with lightweight sensor computation. *PLoS ONE* **2015**, *10*, e0116709. [CrossRef] [PubMed]

23. Xue, K.; Ma, C.; Hong, P.; Ding, R. A temporal-credential-based mutual authentication and key agreement scheme for wireless sensor networks. *J. Netw. Comput. Appl.* **2013**, *36*, 316–323. [CrossRef]

24. Li, C.-T.; Weng, C.-Y.; Lee, C.-C. An advanced temporal credential-based security scheme with mutual authentication and key agreement for wireless sensor networks. *Sensors* **2013**, *13*, 9589–9603. [CrossRef] [PubMed]

25. Turkanović, M.; Brumen, B.; Hölbl, M. A novel user authentication and key agreement scheme for heterogeneous ad hoc wireless sensor networks, based on the Internet of Things notion. *Ad Hoc Netw.* **2014**, *20*, 96–112. [CrossRef]

26. Amin, R.; Islam, S.H.; Biswas, G.; Khan, M.K.; Li, X. Cryptanalysis and enhancement of anonymity preserving remote user mutual authentication and session key agreement scheme for e-health care systems. *J. Med. Syst.* **2015**, *39*, 140. [CrossRef] [PubMed]

27. Whitmore, A.; Agarwal, A.; Da Xu, L. The Internet of Things—A survey of topics and trends. *Inf. Syst. Front.* **2015**, *17*, 261–274. [CrossRef]

28. Dinh, H.T.; Lee, C.; Niyato, D.; Wang, P. A survey of mobile cloud computing: Architecture, applications, and approaches. *Wirel. Commun. Mob. Comput.* **2013**, *13*, 1587–1611. [CrossRef]

29. Moosavi, S.R.; Gia, T.N.; Nigussie, E.; Rahmani, A.-M.; Virtanen, S.; Tenhunen, H.; Isoaho, J. Session Resumption-Based End-to-End Security for Healthcare Internet-of-Things. In Proceedings of the 2015 IEEE International Conference on Computer and Information Technology; Ubiquitous Computing and Communications; Dependable, Autonomic and Secure Computing; Pervasive Intelligence and Computing (CIT/IUCC/DASC/PICOM), Liverpool, UK, 26–28 October 2015; pp. 581–588.

30. Moosavi, S.R.; Gia, T.N.; Rahmani, A.-M.; Nigussie, E.; Virtanen, S.; Isoaho, J.; Tenhunen, H. SEA: A secure and efficient authentication and authorization architecture for IoT-based healthcare using smart gateways. *Procedia Comput. Sci.* **2015**, *52*, 452–459. [CrossRef]

31. Rahmani, A.M.; Gia, T.N.; Negash, B.; Anzanpour, A.; Azimi, I.; Jiang, M.; Liljeberg, P. Exploiting smart e-health gateways at the edge of healthcare internet-of-things: A fog computing approach. *Futur. Gener. Comput. Syst.* **2017**, *78*, 641–658. [CrossRef]

32. Yeh, H.-L.; Chen, T.-H.; Liu, P.-C.; Kim, T.-H.; Wei, H.-W. A secured authentication protocol for wireless sensor networks using elliptic curves cryptography. *Sensors* **2011**, *11*, 4767–4779. [CrossRef] [PubMed]

33. Miller, V.S. Use of Elliptic Curves in Cryptography. In *Conference on the Theory and Application of Cryptographic Techniques*; Springer: Berlin/Heidelberg, Germany, 1985; pp. 417–426.

34. Koblitz, N. Elliptic curve cryptosystems. *Math. Comput.* **1987**, *48*, 203–209. [CrossRef]

35. Hankerson, D.; Menezes, A.J.; Vanstone, S. *Guide to Elliptic Curve Cryptography*; Springer Science & Business Media: New York, NY, USA, 2006.

36. Li, X.; Qiu, W.; Zheng, D.; Chen, K.; Li, J. Anonymity enhancement on robust and efficient password-authenticated key agreement using smart cards. *IEEE Trans. Ind. Electron.* **2010**, *57*, 793–800.

37. Ying, Z.; Chiou, S.-Y.; Liu, J. An Efficient Privacy Authentication Scheme Based on Cloud Models for Medical Environment. In Proceedings of the 2015 18th International Conference on Network-Based Information Systems (NBiS), Taipei, Taiwan, 2–4 September 2015; pp. 628–633.

38. Zhang, L.; Zhu, S.; Tang, S. Privacy protection for telecare medicine information systems using a chaotic map-based three-factor authenticated key agreement scheme. *IEEE J. Biomed. Health Inf.* **2017**, *21*, 465–475. [CrossRef] [PubMed]

39. Rubin, A.D.; Honeyman, P. Nonmonotonic Cryptographic Protocols. In Proceedings of the Computer Security Foundations Workshop VII (CSFW 7), Franconia, NH, USA, 14–16 June 1994; pp. 100–116.

40. Xu, X.; Jin, Z.P.; Zhang, H.; Zhu, P. A Dynamic ID-Based Authentication Scheme Based on ECC for Telecare Medicine Information Systems. In *Applied Mechanics and Materials*; Trans Tech Publ: Zürich, Switzerland, 2014; pp. 861–866.

41. Islam, S.H.; Khan, M.K. Cryptanalysis and improvement of authentication and key agreement protocols for telecare medicine information systems. *J. Med. Syst.* **2014**, *38*, 135. [CrossRef] [PubMed]

42. He, D.; Kumar, N.; Khan, M.; Lee, J.-H. Anonymous two-factor authentication for consumer roaming service in global mobility networks. *IEEE Trans. Consum. Electron.* **2013**, *59*, 811–817. [CrossRef]

43. Jiang, Q.; Ma, J.; Li, G.; Yang, L. An efficient ticket based authentication protocol with unlinkability for wireless access networks. *Wirel. Pers. Commun.* **2014**, *77*, 1489–1506. [CrossRef]

applied
sciences

MDPI

Article

Recognition Algorithm Based on Improved FCM and Rough Sets for Meibomian Gland Morphology

Fengmei Liang [1], Yajun Xu [1,*], Weixin Li [2], Xiaoling Ning [3], Xueou Liu [1] and Ajian Liu [1]

[1]   College of Information Engineering, Taiyuan University of Technology, Taiyuan 030024, Shanxi, China; fm_liang@163.com (F.L.); xueou_liu@163.com (X.L.); ajian_liu@yeah.net (A.L.)
[2]   Engineering Experimental Class of National Pilot School, School of Precision Instrument & Opto-Electronics Engineering, Tianjin University, Tianjin 300072, China; li_markmar@126.com
[3]   Shanxi Eye Hospital, Taiyuan 030002, Shanxi, China; xl_ning@yeah.net
*   Correspondence: xuyajun0032@link.tyut.edu.cn; Tel.: +86-186-0341-0966

Academic Editors: Wenbing Zhao, Xiong Luo and Tie Qiu
Received: 20 December 2016; Accepted: 13 February 2017; Published: 17 February 2017

Abstract: To overcome the limitation of artificial judgment of meibomian gland morphology, we proposed a solution based on an improved fuzzy c-means (FCM) algorithm and rough sets theory. The rough sets reduced the redundant attributes while ensuring classification accuracy, and greatly reduced the amount of computation to achieve information dimension compression and knowledge system simplification. However, before this reduction, data must be discretized, and this process causes some degree of information loss. Therefore, to maintain the integrity of the information, we used the improved FCM to make attributes fuzzy instead of discrete before continuing with attribute reduction, and thus, the implicit knowledge and decision rules were more accurate. Our algorithm overcame the defects of the traditional FCM algorithm, which is sensitive to outliers and easily falls into local optima. Our experimental results show that the proposed method improved recognition efficiency without degrading recognition accuracy, which was as high as 97.5%. Furthermore, the meibomian gland morphology was diagnosed efficiently, and thus this method can provide practical application values for the recognition of meibomian gland morphology.

Keywords: meibomian gland; fuzzy c-means; rough sets; attribute reduction; pattern recognition

1. Introduction

In recent years, a variety of new medical devices have been used to help doctors with clinical diagnosis while producing a large amount of image data. Manual interpretation of images relies too much on physician experience and is not very efficient. To this end, many scholars attempt to use computer-assisted processing of medical images. In the work by Xu et al. [1], the support vector machine was used to recognize brain magnetic resonance imaging (MRI) images with a recognition rate up to 95.45%. In another study, overcoming the influence of fracture diversity and individual differences, a decision tree was used to achieve automatic X-detection [2]. The method by Tang et al. [3] used fuzzy recognition to classify white blood cell images to solve the contradiction between real-time detection accuracy and speed. Chen et al. [4] developed a new method for the filtering of X-ray digital images of chests based on multi-resolution and rough set. This paper attempts to use image recognition technology to assist doctors in interpreting meibomian gland images and thus improve diagnostic accuracy and efficiency.

Meibomian gland dysfunction (MGD) is a very common eye disease [5]. In recent years, with the increase of electronic products, the incidence of MGD has increased dramatically, seriously affecting people's normal lives. Many experts have conducted numerous research studies on MGD in order to determine how to prevent the disease, offer timely diagnosis, and reduce the troubles caused by the disease. However, the current recognition of meibomian gland morphology still relies on the experience of doctors. With the development of pattern recognition technologies and continuous improvement of clinical diagnostic requirements, it is necessary to develop an intelligent diagnosis system that can replace human experience with advanced science and technology.

The rough sets theory was proposed in 1982 by Z. Pawlak [6], a Polish mathematician, whose main idea was to improve the accuracy and correctness of data analysis through attribute reduction under the premise of keeping the same classification ability. However, continuous attributes must be discretized before using rough sets theory to do attribute reduction for information system, and this process results in some degree of information loss. The fuzzy rough sets theory, presented by French scholars Dubois and Prade [7], combines the advantages of fuzzy sets and rough sets, and extends precise sets to fuzzy sets, and fuzzy equivalence classes are determined by the membership function, thus avoiding information loss to a certain extent. Rough sets theory has been developed in theoretical research and applied research for more than thirty years. Currently, many scholars apply rough sets theory to industrial control [8–10], agricultural science [11,12], aerospace, military applications, and other fields [13,14]. However, the application of fuzzy rough sets is not commonly used in medical image recognition, and available literature is relatively lacking. Moreover, compared with other image recognition technologies, fuzzy rough sets theory is more suitable for processing medical images with intense ambiguity and uncertainty [15].

In this paper, we propose a diagnostic algorithm based on a modified fuzzy c-means (FCM) algorithm and rough sets for the recognition of meibomian gland morphology. The FCM algorithm is one of the most widely used clustering algorithms due to its simple and fast convergence and its ability to handle large datasets [16]. In this paper, the defects of the traditional FCM algorithm are improved, such as the random selecting of the initial clustering center and the algorithm's sensitivity to isolated points. The improved FCM was used to cluster the data to obtain the fuzzy division of meibomian gland morphological parameters, thus avoiding information loss [17]. Subsequently, the rough sets theory was used to process the data in order to eliminate redundant samples and attributes. The compression of the information dimension and the simplification of knowledge system were also realized, and the most effective classification rule was extracted. The proposed algorithm improved recognition rate without reducing accuracy, and realized high efficiency diagnosis of meibomian gland morphology.

2. Materials and Methods

2.1. Basic Concepts of the Rough Sets Theory

Based on the classification mechanism, the rough sets theory's research object is the information system [18]. By introducing an indiscernibility relation as the theoretical basis, and defining the concepts of upper and lower approximations, the rough sets theory focuses on knowledge reduction and determining attribute importance. Through attribute reduction, the fuzziness and uncertainty knowledge can be described by the knowledge in the existing knowledge base.

2.1.1. Indiscernibility Relation

We defined the domain U as a non-empty finite set of the samples we are interested in, and any subset X which satisfies the condition $X \subseteq U$ can be called a concept or a category in U. Furthermore, any concept set of U can be called basic knowledge of U, which represents the individual classification in the domain U, referred to as U's knowledge. Let R be an equivalence relation on U, U/R denotes all equivalence classes, and $[x]_R$ represents equivalent classes of R that contain element x, which satisfies the condition $x \in U$. If $P \subseteq R$ and $P \neq \varnothing$, the intersection of all equivalence relations in P is also an equivalence relation, and this equivalence relation is called P-indiscernibility relation, denoted as $ind(P)$. In the process of classification, the individuals with little difference are classified into the same classification, and their relationship is an indiscernibility relation, which is equivalent to an equivalence relation on U.

The concept of indiscernibility relation is the cornerstone of the rough sets theory, which reveals the granular structure of domain knowledge. The concept assumes that some knowledge is in the domain, and uses attributes and attributes' values to describe the objects. If two objects have the same attributes and attributes' values, they have an indiscernibility relation. Mathematically, the indiscernibility relation of a set and the division of a set are equivalent concepts, one-to-one, and unique to each other. This concept means that objects in the domain can be described with different attributes' sets to express exactly the same facts.

2.1.2. Lower and Upper Approximations

Let X denote the subset of elements of the domain U ($X \subseteq U$ and $X \neq \emptyset$), and R denote an equivalence relation on U. The lower approximation of X in R, denoted as $\underline{R}X$, is defined as the union of all these elementary sets contained in X. More formally,

$$\underline{R}X = \cup\{Y \in U/R | Y \subseteq X\}.$$

The upper approximation of set X, denoted as $\overline{R}X$, is the union of these elementary sets, which have a non-empty intersection with X:

$$\overline{R}X = \cup\{Y \in U/R | Y \cap X \neq \emptyset\}.$$

In general, Figure 1 represents the upper approximation and lower approximation. The area in the black box is the domain U, the area in the green curve denotes X, the inner red curve denotes the upper approximation set $\overline{R}X$, and the blue curve denotes the lower approximation set $\underline{R}X$.

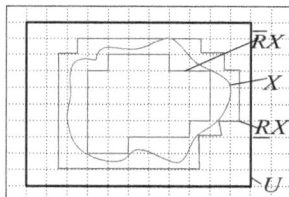

Figure 1. Schematic diagram of the upper approximation and lower approximation.

2.1.3. Core and Attribute Reduction

The concepts of core and attribute reduction are two fundamental concepts of the rough sets theory. The attribute reduction is the essential part of an information system, which can discern all dispensable objects from the original information system. The core is the basis of attribute reduction. The information system may not have only one reduction, the intersection of all reductions is called the core of the information system.

Let P be a set of equivalence relations, and $P \subseteq R$ and $P \neq \emptyset$. If $ind(R) = ind(R - P)$, then the set P can be dispensed in the set R, otherwise it cannot be dispensed. If each P in the set R is not dispensable, P is independent, otherwise it is dependent. If the set of condition attributes is independent, one may be interested in finding all possible minimal subset of attributes and the set of all indispensable attributes (core).

Given an information system $S = (U, A)$, in which U is a non-empty finite set and $A = C \cup D$ and $C \cap D \neq \emptyset$, C indicates the set of the condition attributes, and D indicates the set of decision attributes. If $B \subseteq C$ and $d \subseteq D$, $pos(d) = \cup\{\underline{B}(X) | X \in U/ind(d)\}$ is the relative positive region of the decision attribute d with respect to B.

Let P and Q be equivalence relationship sets. If $pos_{ind(P)}(ind(Q)) = pos_{ind(P-\{R\})}(ind(Q))$, then R can be reduced by P. The set of all irreducible equivalence relationships of Q in P is called the core of P, and is denoted as $core_Q(P)$. Core is the set containing the most important attributes for classification in the condition attributes, and without them, the quality of the classification will drop.

The relation between the reduction of attributes' set and the core is as follows:

$$core(P) = \cap red(P)$$

The expression $red(P)$ represents all the reductions of P. The expression $core(P)$ contains all the equivalence relations in the reduction of P, which is the important and indispensable attributes' set in P.

The concept of $core(P)$ has two meanings:

(1) the $core(P)$ is used as the basis for the calculation of attribute reduction.
(2) the $core(P)$ is a feature set that cannot be eliminated in attribute reduction.

The concept of $core(P)$ provides a powerful mathematical tool for extracting important attributes and their values from the condition attributes by attribute reduction. The attributes in the set of condition attributes are not equally important, even some of them are redundant. The processing of attribute reduction aims to reduce the unnecessary condition attributes or remove redundant attributes in the information system, and obtain the smallest set of condition attributes that can ensure correct classification. In other words, the classification quality of the reduced attributes' set is the same as that of the original attributes' set. Under the condition of guaranteeing the classification ability of the information system, attribute reduction can get a simpler and more effective decision rule. Lastly, attribute reduction is not only the approach and method of obtaining classified knowledge from an information system, but also the focus and essence of the rough sets theory research.

2.2. FCM

The FCM clustering algorithm is a fuzzy recognition unsupervised algorithm based on the division of clustering algorithm. It only provides the number of clusters, and constantly modifies the sample type, cluster centers, and membership of each sample belonging to various categories, and ultimately achieves an objective function with a best classification.

2.2.1. Traditional FCM Algorithm

Let $X = \{x_1, x_2, \cdots, x_n\}$ be a dataset containing n samples, $v_i(i = 1, 2, \cdots, c)$ is the center of each cluster, c is the number of clusters, and μ_{ik} is the membership of the sample k belonging to the class i. Dunn [19] defined the objective function as follows:

$$J(X; U, V) = \sum_{i=1}^{c} \sum_{k=1}^{n} (\mu_{ik})^m \left\| x_k - v_i \right\|_A^2$$

where U is the membership matrix, V is the matrix of cluster centers; $D_{ikA}^2 = \left\| x_k - v_i \right\|_A^2 = (x_k - v_i)^T A(x_k - v_i)$ is the Euclidean distance from samples to the cluster centers; A is a positive definite matrix; and m is a weighted index affecting the degree of fuzzy membership matrix. Generally, m is 2. The FCM clustering requires that membership meets the following condition:

$$\sum_{i=1}^{c} \mu_{ik} = 1, 1 \leq k \leq n$$

Using the Lagrange multiplier method [20,21], the condition of the objective function achieving the minimum is as follows:

$$\mu_{ik} = \frac{1}{\sum_{j=1}^{c} (D_{ikA}/D_{jkA})^{2/(m-1)}}, 1 \le i \le c, 1 \le k \le n$$

$$v_i = \frac{\sum_{k=1}^{N} \mu_{ik}^m x_k}{\sum_{k=1}^{N} \mu_{ik}^m}$$

It can be seen that the FCM clustering algorithm obtains the cluster centers through the iteration of $\mu_{.k}$ and v_i.

2.2.2. Improved FCM Algorithm

The FCM algorithm is very simple and does not need to conduct large-scale operations because the establishment of the sample category's fuzzy description can well reflect the objective world. However, when dealing with practical applications, there are still some problems [22].

First, the FCM algorithm must give the initial cluster center before clustering. Like most nonlinear optimization problems, the FCM clustering effect is directly affected by the initial value.

Second, the FCM algorithm has a good effect on data with strong regularity distribution. However, when the samples contain noise, the clustering center is shifted to the noise point, and even the noise will be selected as the cluster center, which seriously affects the clustering effect.

To solve these problems, we proposed a method for selecting the initial clustering center based on distance. Our clustering results were globally optimal. According to the Lazard's criterion [23,24], the noise point in the data is defined as follows: the deviation between the point and the mean is more than twice the standard deviation of the samples. In this paper, we located the noise points according to the sample's distance, and then dealt with them to make the algorithm insensitive to noise points.

Before introducing the improved algorithm, several related concepts are introduced as follows:

1. Distances between samples (Euclidean distance):

$$d(x_i, x_j) = \sqrt{|x_{i1} - y_{j1}|^2 + |x_{i2} - y_{j2}|^2 + \cdots + |x_{im} - y_{jm}|^2}$$

2. The mean of the distances of sample x_i to other samples:

$$m_i = \frac{1}{n} \sum_{j=1}^{n} d(x_i, x_j)$$

3. The mean of the distances of all samples:

$$d = \frac{2}{n(n+1)} \sum_{i=1}^{n} \sum_{j=1}^{i} d(x_i, x_j)$$

4. Noise point:

In the dataset X, if the sample point x_i satisfies $m_i > 2d$, we call x_i the noise point.

$X = \{x_1, x_2, \cdots, x_n\}$ is the set of classified samples, and the set of the number of clusters is c. Selecting the initial cluster center in the improved algorithm was performed as follows:

Step 1: Calculate the mean distance m_i from sample x_i to other samples, generate the sample distance vector, and take the sample point with the smallest mean distance as the first cluster center;

Step 2: Calculate the mean of the distances of all samples d, mark the sample point x_i, which satisfies $m_i > 2d$ as the noise point, and put the noise point into a separate set;

Step 3: Use the distance vector to determine the non-isolated samples whose distance from the first clustering center is larger than d, and choose the second cluster center with the smallest mean distance from the first center from among these samples.

Step 4: Repeat step 3 until c cluster centers are found.

Step 5: According to the distance, classify the noise points to the corresponding classification.

The operation flow of the improved FCM algorithm is shown in Figure 2.

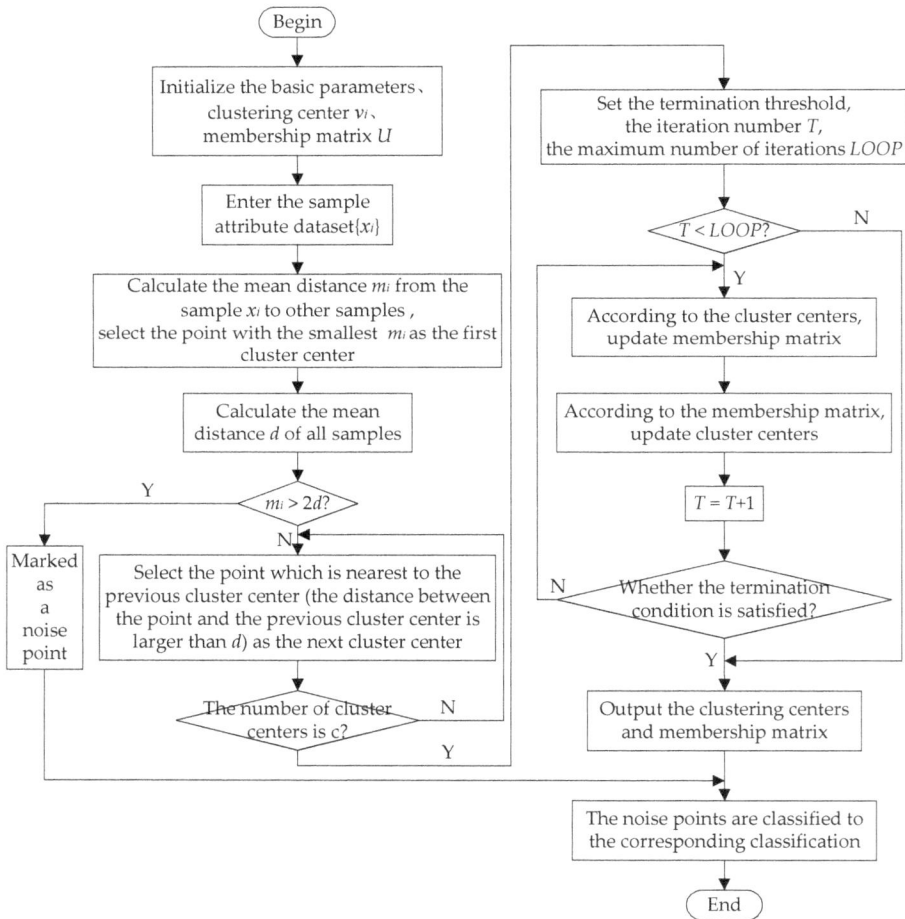

Figure 2. The workflow chart of our improved fuzzy c-means (FCM) algorithm.

2.2.3. Results Analysis of the Improved FCM Algorithm

To verify the effectiveness of the proposed algorithm, the traditional FCM algorithm and the improved version were used to cluster datasets with noise. Figure 3 shows the effect of the two kinds of clustering methods on processing the datasets, where "o", "Δ", and "+" represent different categories, and "◇" indicates the cluster center of each class. It can be seen that the clustering results were seriously affected by noise and the clustering centers were deviated using the traditional FCM algorithm. After the improved FCM was used to remove the isolated points, the clustering results became more reasonable. Table 1 shows the results of the two clustering algorithms. It can be seen that the traditional FCM was sensitive to noise and easily trapped in the local optima. Conversely, through selecting a reasonable initial clustering center and removing the influence of isolated points, the improved FCM reduced the number of iterations while clustering correctly and improving the final objective function.

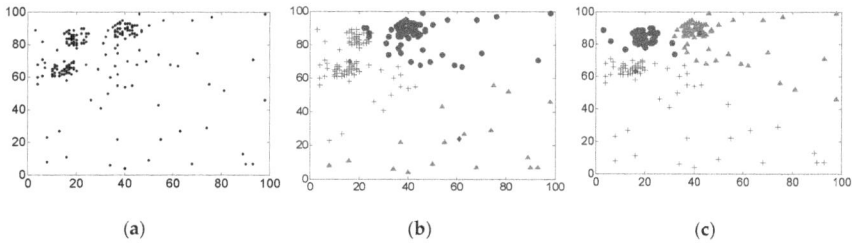

(a) (b) (c)

Figure 3. Comparison of clustering effects of two methods, they are listed as: (**a**) datasets; (**b**) clustering effect using the traditional FCM algorithm; (**c**) clustering effect using the improved FCM algorithm.

Table 1. Clustering effect comparison between the traditional FCM algorithm and the improved FCM algorithm.

Algorithm Category	Clustering Center	Number of Iterations	Objective Function
traditional FCM algorithm	(16.32,70.00), (60.96,23.88), (39.98,86.77)	31	3.49×10^4
improved FCM algorithm	(16.07,63.25), (42.24,86.78), (20.02,82.18)	16	1.95×10^4

3. MGD Identification Based on Improved FCM and Rough Sets

Different morphologies of the meibomian gland show different texture features in images. Figure 4 shows four typical kinds of meibomian glands. Figure 4a shows a normal type, the distribution of the gland ducts is uniform, and there is no expansion or deletion of the gland ducts; Figure 4b shows a shortened type, and ductal arrangement is neat, shortened, and the loss area of the gland ducts is less than one third of the total area; Figure 4c shows a deletion type, the loss of the gland ducts is obvious, and the loss area is one thirds to two thirds of the total area; Figure 4d shows a serious deletion type, the gland ducts are not obvious, and basically all of them are missing.

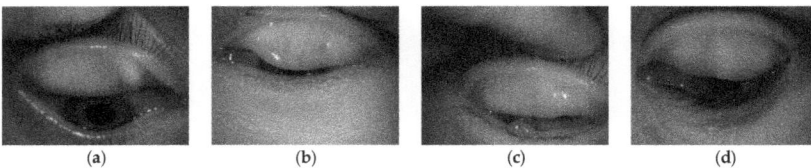

(a) (b) (c) (d)

Figure 4. Various kinds of meibomian gland images, they are listed as: (**a**) normal type; (**b**) shortened type; (**c**) deletion type; (**d**) serious deletion type.

The methods used for meibomian gland image recognition usually include image preprocessing, feature extraction, classification, and decision-making. In this paper, we applied the improved FCM and rough sets theory to meibomian gland image recognition. The workflow chart is shown in Figure 5.

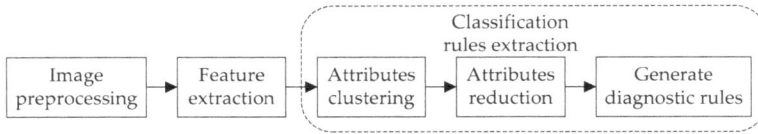

Figure 5. The workflow chart of generating the diagnosis rule table of meibomian gland dysfunction (MGD) using the proposed method.

3.1. Image Preprocessing

The purpose of image preprocessing is to improve image quality by the corresponding image processing method, making it more suitable for both observation and judgment by human eyes, and the analysis and processing by computers. Generally, image preprocessing includes image enhancement and image segmentation.

3.1.1. Image Enhancement

Images of meibomian glands are often blurred due to the limitation of equipment and man-made operation. There is no obvious gray difference in some details, so the image quality is not high, thus affecting the doctor's decision. Image enhancement improves quality and gray levels so that the enhanced details of the image are more suitable for human eyes or machine processing. In this paper, we used enhanced high-pass filter technology to eliminate ambiguity, inhibit low-frequency components, and enhance high-frequency components. These made images more clear. A Gaussian high-pass filter was used to filter the image, and the transfer function is shown as follows:

$$H(u,v) = 1 - e^{-D^2(u,v)/2\sigma^2}$$

The edge and details of the filtered image were enhanced. However, since the high-pass filter deviated from the direct-current component, the average grayscale of the image was reduced to zero. To correct this, we used high-frequency emphasis filtering. The transfer function is as follows:

$$H_f(u,v) = a + bH(u,v)$$

where $H(u,v)$ is the transfer function of the high-pass filtering, Gaussian filter used herein; a denotes the offset; and b denotes the multiplier. When offset a is less than 1 and the high-frequency multiplier b is greater than 1, the low-frequency component is suppressed, and the high frequency component is enhanced. The enhanced images are shown in Figure 6. Experiments showed that this method was convenient and effective for the enhancement of meibomian gland images, achieving greater image quality that could aid in diagnosis.

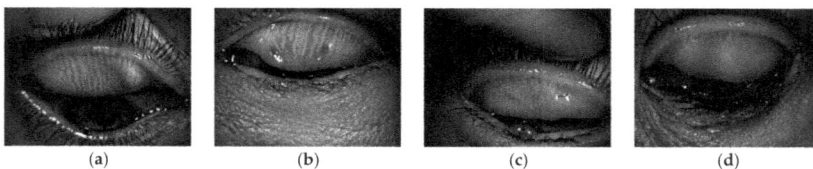

Figure 6. The enhanced meibomian gland images, they are listed as: (**a**) normal type; (**b**) shortened type; (**c**) deletion type; (**d**) serious deletion type.

3.1.2. Image Segmentation

Image segmentation segments the region of interest in the image to provide a reliable basis for subsequent analysis and processing [25]. Segmentation quality directly affects subsequent image recognition. The eyelid part is of great significance in the diagnosis of meibomian gland morphology. Using the differences of textures between the eyelid region and other regions, and combining morphological and local entropy filtering, we designed a segmentation method based on texture filtering. The local entropy is defined as an entropy operation on an area of $n \times n$ centered on the selected pixel, and the meibomian gland image was filtered using local entropy to obtain the texture image. Local entropy calculation expressions are shown as follows:

$$H = -\sum_{i=1}^{n}\sum_{j=1}^{n} p_{ij} \log p_{ij}$$

$$p_{ij} = f(i,j) / \sum_{i}^{n}\sum_{j}^{n} f(i,j)$$

where $f(i,j)$ denotes the local pixels of $n \times n$, and p_{ij} is the probability that the current pixel gray level occupies the local total gray level. The larger the local entropy is, the smaller the texture difference is in the window. Therefore, threshold segmentation can be performed according to the local entropy of the image to extract the target region. Due to the limitation of the artificially defined threshold, the segmentation result may appear over-segmentation, holes or the boundary of segmented image may not be smooth or other phenomena may result. In this paper, we used a morphological method to smooth edges, and filled the empty holes to obtain high-quality segmentation images. As shown in Figure 7, our method accurately and effectively segmented meibomian gland images while ensuring image integrity. The details of the target area were all retained, which laid the foundation for follow-up treatment.

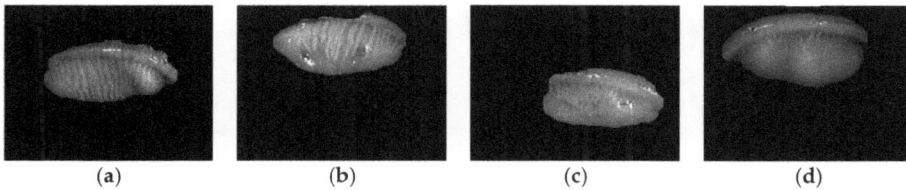

(a)   **(b)**   **(c)**   **(d)**

Figure 7. Segmented meibomian gland images. (**a**) Normal type; (**b**) shortened type; (**c**) deletion type; (**d**) serious deletion type.

3.2. Tamura Texture Feature Extraction

According to human visual perception and the basis of psychological experiments, Tamura et al. [26,27] proposed a texture feature expression, containing coarseness, contrast, directionality, line-likeness, regularity, and roughness. In this paper, we studied the characteristics of texture features of meibomian gland images.

3.2.1. Coarseness

Coarseness, the most basic texture feature, reflects particle size. Coarseness can be calculated with the following steps:

First, calculate the average intensity of the pixels in the active window of size $2^k \times 2^k$ in the image, expressed as

$$A_k(x,y) = \sum_{i=x-2^{k-1}}^{x+2^{k-1}-1} \sum_{j=y-2^{k-1}}^{y+2^{k-1}-1} g(i,j)/2^{2k}$$

where $k = 0, 1, \cdots, 5$, and $g(i,j)$ is the gray-level at (i,j).

Then, separately calculate the average intensity difference between the windows of each pixel that do not overlap in the horizontal and vertical directions, respectively. This is expressed as follows:

$$E_h(x,y) = \left| A_k(x+2^{k-1},y) - A_k(x-2^{k-1},y) \right|$$

$$E_v(x,y) = \left| A_k(x,y+2^{k-1}) - A_k(x,y-2^{k-1}) \right|$$

For each pixel, k, which maximizes the value of E, is used to set the optimum size $S_{best}(x,y) = 2^k$.

Finally, coarseness can be obtained by calculating the mean value of S_{best} in the whole image, which is expressed as follows:

$$F_{crs} = \frac{1}{mn} \sum_{i=1}^{m} \sum_{j=1}^{n} S_{best}(i,j)$$

where m and n are the effective width and height of the image, respectively.

3.2.2. Contrast

Contrast is obtained by statistical analysis of pixel intensity distribution. Generally, the contrast feature is determined by the degree of grayscale dynamic range of the image and the degree of polarization between the black and white portions of the histogram. These two factors can be defined by the kurtosis $\alpha_4 = \mu_4/\sigma^4$, where μ_4 is the fourth moment about the mean, and σ^2 which can measure the dispersion in the distribution, is the variance about the mean of the gray-levels probability distribution. Contrast can be defined as:

$$F_{con} = \frac{\sigma}{\alpha_4^{1/4}}$$

3.2.3. Directionality

The degree of direction is the global characteristics of a given texture region, and describes how textures are scattered or concentrated in some direction. First, calculate the direction of the gradient vector of each pixel. The mode and direction of the gradient vector are defined as follows:

$$|\Delta G| = (|\Delta_H| + |\Delta_V|)/2$$

$$\theta = \tan^{-1}(\Delta_V/\Delta_H) + \pi/2$$

where Δ_H and Δ_V are the amount of change in the horizontal and vertical directions of the image, respectively. When the gradient vectors of all pixels are calculated, θ can be expressed using the histogram value H_D. Finally, the overall direction of the image can be obtained by calculating the sharpness of the peaks in the histogram, which is expressed as follows:

$$F_{dir} = \sum_{P}^{n} \sum_{\Phi \in W} (\Phi - \Phi_P)^2 H_D(\Phi)$$

where P denotes the peaks in the histogram, and n is the number of peaks. For a given peak, W represents all the discrete regions contained in the peak, and Φ_P is the center of the peak.

3.2.4. Line-Likeness

Line-likeness is defined as the degree of coincidence of the co-occurrence matrix of directions of each pixel point. When calculating the co-occurrence matrix, the pixel pitch is denoted as d.

$$F_{lin} = \frac{\sum\limits_{i}^{n}\sum\limits_{j}^{n} P_{Dd}(i,j)\cos[(i-j)\frac{2\pi}{n}]}{\sum\limits_{i}^{n}\sum\limits_{j}^{n} P_{Dd}}$$

where P_{Dd} is the distance point of the co-occurrence matrix of the local area $n \times n$.

3.2.5. Regularity

Since the texture characteristics of the whole image are not regular, the variance of partitioned sub-images is calculated. Four features of the sub-image are used to measure texture regularity, which is expressed as follows:

$$F_{reg} = 1 - r(\sigma_{crs} + \sigma_{con} + \sigma_{dir} + \sigma_{lin})$$

where r is a normalizing factor and σ_{xxx} means the standard deviation of the corresponding feature F_{xxx}.

3.2.6. Roughness

According to the results of the psychological experiments on vision in the study by Yu [28], we emphasize the effects of coarseness and contrast, and approximate a measure of roughness by simply summing the coarseness and contrast measures:

$$F_{rgh} = F_{crs} + F_{con}$$

The intention lies in examining to what extent such a simple approximation corresponds to human visual perception.

3.3. Classification Rule Extraction

In this paper, the establishment of a knowledge expression system is based on Tamura features of meibomian gland image recognition. Table 2 lists the texture characteristic data of meibomian gland images obtained from the experiments. There were 96 image samples we took as the training data, and the condition attributes were coarseness, contrast, directionality, line-likeness, regularity, and roughness. The decision attributes were named I, II, III, IV, representing the normal, shortened, deletion, and serious deletion meibomian gland, respectively.

Table 2 contains the textures of the meibomian glands, and the dependencies between morphological features. However, this information is not easy to understand, and is difficult to directly be used for identification. Therefore, the data first requires further processing. The improved FCM algorithm was used to cluster six consecutive conditional variables. According to the principle of maximum membership [29], the original continuous feature space was mapped to discrete feature space using the improved FCM, as shown in Table 3.

A flow chart of attribute reduction using the rough sets algorithm is shown in Figure 8. The rough sets theory was used for attribute reduction of the data in Table 3. We then used the Johnson algorithm [29] to obtain the core of conditional attributes as {coarseness, contrast, line-likeness, regularity}. This showed that for decision attributes, these four attributes were sufficient to maintain the classification ability of the information system. By sorting the reduced decision table, the rules of precision >0.75 and coverage >0.05 were selected [30]. Finally, the typical diagnostic rule table is shown in Table 4. Using the rough sets theory effectively explored the potential laws of knowledge by simplifying unnecessary attributes, and we could extract the most concise and accurate classification rules in pattern recognition.

Table 2. Characteristic data of meibomian gland image.

Sample	Condition Attribute						Decision Attribute
	crs	con	dir	lin	reg	rgh	
1	19.018	44.011	35.55	0.22	0.943	63.028	I
2	20.416	57.585	28.821	0.248	0.9	78.001	II
3	18.599	45.586	37.261	0.178	0.949	64.185	III
4	22.711	44.708	34.895	0.205	0.905	67.418	IV
5	18.848	37.956	35.943	0.194	0.965	56.804	II
6	21.759	62.73	26.198	0.312	0.916	84.489	I
7	19.374	57.7	35.622	0.283	0.958	77.074	II
8	19.454	59.199	26.239	0.293	0.929	78.653	II
				......			
89	19.166	45.466	38.209	0.251	0.963	64.632	IV
90	20.924	58.651	38.423	0.291	0.878	79.575	III
91	21.067	41.477	29.958	0.236	0.902	62.545	III
92	21.397	60.464	32.286	0.192	0.941	81.861	IV
93	20.774	53.858	29.261	0.235	0.943	74.632	IV
94	19.844	49.788	28.553	0.216	0.94	69.632	II
95	19.443	46.836	33.736	0.266	0.938	66.279	I
96	17.613	46.098	17.812	0.282	0.901	63.711	II

crs, coarseness; con, contrast; dir, direction; lin, line-likeness; reg, regularity; rgh, roughness; I, normal; II, shortened; III, deletion; IV, serious deletion.

Table 3. Characteristic data of meibomian gland image after discretization.

Sample	Condition Attribute						Decision Attribute
	crs	con	dir	lin	reg	rgh	
1	1	2	3	2	3	2	I
2	3	4	1	3	1	4	II
3	1	2	4	1	4	2	III
4	4	2	3	1	1	3	IV
5	1	1	3	1	4	1	II
6	4	5	1	4	2	5	I
7	2	4	3	4	4	4	II
8	2	4	1	4	3	4	II
9	2	2	4	4	3	2	I
				......			
89	1	2	4	3	4	2	IV
90	3	4	4	4	1	4	III
91	3	1	1	3	1	2	III
92	4	5	2	1	3	5	IV
93	3	3	1	2	3	4	IV
94	2	3	1	2	3	3	IV
95	2	2	2	3	3	2	I
96	1	2	1	4	1	2	II

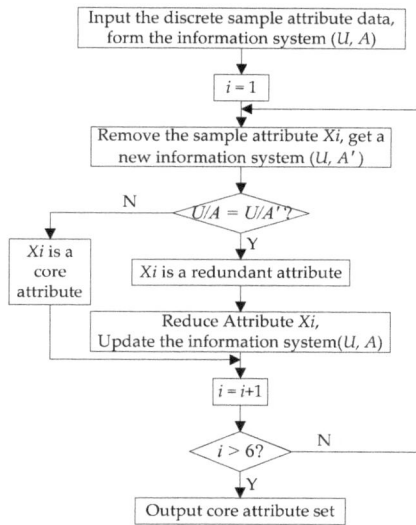

Figure 8. The flow chart of attribute reduction using rough sets algorithm.

Table 4. Typical diagnostic rule generated using the proposed method.

Diagnostic Rule
crs(1) AND con(2) AND reg(3) AND lin(2) => dec(1)
crs(3) AND con(4) AND reg(1) AND lin(3) => dec(2)
crs(1) AND con(2) AND reg(4) AND lin(1) => dec(3)
crs(4) AND con(2) AND reg(1) AND lin(1) => dec(4)
crs(1) AND con(1) AND reg(4) AND lin(1) => dec(2)
crs(4) AND con(5) AND reg(2) AND lin(4) => dec(1)
crs(2) AND con(4) AND reg(3) AND lin(4) => dec(2)
. . . . . .
crs(2) AND con(2) AND reg(3) AND lin(4) => dec(1)
crs(4) AND con(3) AND reg(2) AND lin(1) => dec(3)
crs(2) AND con(1) AND reg(4) AND lin(1) => dec(4)
crs(3) AND con(3) AND reg(3) AND lin(4) => dec(2)
crs(4) AND con(5) AND reg(1) AND lin(4) => dec(4)
crs(1) AND con(2) AND reg(4) AND lin(3) => dec(4)
crs(3) AND con(1) AND reg(1) AND lin(3) => dec(3)
crs(2) AND con(2) AND reg(3) AND lin(3) => dec(1)
crs(3) AND con(4) AND reg(1) AND lin(4) => dec(3)

4. Analysis of Experimental Results

To verify the effectiveness of the method, 40 samples were tested with our proposed method, including eight cases of the normal meibomian gland type, 14 cases of the shortened type, 10 cases of the deletion type, and eight cases of the serious deletion type. These are represented in Figure 9, in the classification labels from 1 to 4, using "o". Experimental results showed that 39 samples were classified into the correct category using the improved FCM and rough sets, while 32 cases were classified correctly using the method based on the traditional FCM and rough sets. The quantitative comparison of classification results is shown in Table 5, and comparison results are shown in Figure 9.

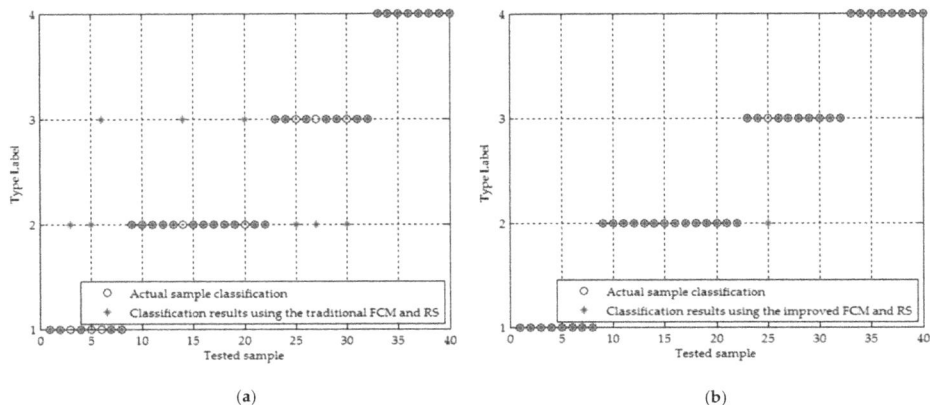

Figure 9. Comparison of classification results of the two methods, which are listed as: (**a**) classification result using the traditional FCM and rough sets (RS); (**b**) classification result using the improved FCM and rough sets (RS).

Table 5. Quantitative comparison of classification results of the two methods.

Algorithm Category	The Number of Correct Classified Samples	Accuracy
The method combining traditional FCM and rough sets	32	80%
The method combining improved FCM and rough sets	39	97.5%

From the Figure 9, it can be seen that 32 cases in the 40 samples were classified to the correct classification using the traditional FCM and rough sets, and the recognition rate was only 80% because the clustering process was affected by isolated points and the clustering centers were randomly selected. The improved FCM algorithm overcame the defects of the traditional FCM, which is sensitive to initial clustering and is susceptible to isolated points, and produced higher quality clustering results. Attribute reduction preserved more accurate classification information, and thus formed clearer and simpler classification rules. Our proposed method successfully classified 39 of 40 samples, with a recognition rate as high as 97.5%.

In order to further evaluate the proposed algorithm objectively, we used the n-fold cross validation to verify the accuracy of the algorithm. Through a large number of experiments, here we set $n = 4$, that is, the 136 data samples were divided into four copies n_1, n_2, n_3, and n_4 and each copy has 34 samples. Three of them were used as training samples and one was used as the test sample and made four simulation experiments alternately. The average accuracy of the four results with a recognition rate as high as 98.5%, was used as an estimate of the accuracy of the algorithm. The classification results are shown in Table 6.

Table 6. The classification results of the four simulations.

Simulation Time	Test Samples (34)	Training Samples (102)	The Number of Correct Classified Samples	Accuracy	The Average Accuracy
1	n_1	n_2, n_3, n_4	33	97%	
2	n_2	n_1, n_3, n_4	33	97%	98.5%
3	n_3	n_1, n_2, n_4	34	100%	
4	n_4	n_1, n_2, n_3	34	100%	

5. Conclusions

This paper mainly studied the image recognition method based on an FCM algorithm and rough sets theory, and applied it to the recognition of meibomian gland morphology. After enhancement and segmentation of the meibomian gland image, Tamura texture features were extracted and the knowledge expression system of the meibomian gland was formed. The improved FCM algorithm was used to cluster the attributes to preserve information integrity of the sample attributes. Based on the rough sets theory's advantage in attribute reduction, our method reduced the two attributes with the least influence on pattern recognition decision from the six attributes of meibomian gland morphology. The most effective data that could determine the degree of meibomian gland defect was extracted, and then the most typical diagnostic rule table was obtained. The whole process of extracting and reducing the attributes and generating the diagnostic rule table was automatic, and did not require manual specification, which improved the reliability and objectivity of its application in pattern recognition. Overall, our experimental results showed that the proposed method had higher efficiency, better classification, and practical significance for the diagnosis of meibomian gland morphology.

Acknowledgments: This work was supported by the Project of Natural Science Foundation of Shanxi Province (No. 2013011017-3).

Author Contributions: Fengmei Liang and Yajun Xu conceived and designed the experiments; Weixin Li performed the experiments; Xiaoling Ning and Xueou Liu analyzed the data; Ajian Liu contributed analysis tools; Fengmei Liang wrote the paper.

Conflicts of Interest: The authors declare no conflict of interest. The founding sponsors had no role in the design of the study; in the collection, analyses, or interpretation of data; in the writing of the manuscript, and in the decision to publish the results.

References

1. Xu, N.N.; Ge, Y.R.; Wang, J.Y. Brain MRI image recognition based on nonsubsampled contourlet transform and SVM. *Mod. Electron. Tech.* **2014**, *37*, 63–69.
2. Zhu, H.Y.; Gong, H.W. Survey on computer assisted diagnosis of bone fracture based on digital X-ray images. *China Digit. Med.* **2015**, *10*, 67–69.
3. Tang, X.M.; Lin, X.Y.; He, L. Research on automatic recognition system for leucocyte image. *J. Biomed. Eng.* **2007**, *24*, 1250–1255.
4. Chen, Z.C.; Zhang, F.; Jiang, D.Z.; Wang, H.-Y. The filtering method for x-ray digital image of chest based on multi-resolution and rough set. *Chin. J. Biomed. Eng.* **2004**, *23*, 486–489.
5. Yao, W.L.; Liang, Q.F.; Sun, X.G.; Labbe, A. Evaluation of the diagnostic value for meibomian gland dysfunction examinations. *Chin. J. Ophthalmol.* **2014**, *50*, 247–253.
6. Pawlak, Z.; Grzymala-Busse, J.; Slowinski, R.; Ziarko, W. Rough sets. *Int. J. Parallel Program.* **1982**, *11*, 341–356. [CrossRef]
7. Dubios, D.; Prade, H. Rough fuzzy sets and fuzzy rough sets. *Int. J. Gen. Syst.* **1990**, *17*, 191–209. [CrossRef]
8. Xie, K.M.; Xie, G. BGrC for superheated steam temperature system modeling in power plant. In Proceedings of the IEEE International Conference on Granular Computing, Atlanta, USA, 10–12 May 2006; pp. 708–711.
9. Valdes, J.J.; Romero, E.; Gonzalez, R. Data and knowledge visualization with virtual reality spaces, neural networks and rough sets: Application to geophysical prospecting neural networks. *Int. Jt. Conf. Neural Netw.* **2007**, *39*, 160–165.
10. Nguyen, T.T. Adaptive Classifier Construction: An Approach to Handwritten Digit Recognition. In Proceedings of the Third International Conference on Rough Sets and Current Trends in Computing, Malvern, PA, USA, 14–16 October 2002; pp. 578–585.
11. Li, W.X.; Cheng, M.; Li, B.Y. Extended dominance rough set theory's application in food safety evaluation. *Food Res. Dev.* **2008**, *29*, 152–156.
12. Du, R.Q.; Chu, X.Y.; Wang, Q.L. Application of a rough-set neural network to superfamily level in insect taxonomy. *J. China Agric. Univ.* **2007**, *12*, 33–38.
13. Hu, F.; Huang, J.G.; Chu, F.H. Grey relation evaluation model of weapon system based on rough set. *Acta Armamentarii* **2008**, *29*, 253–256.

14. Wojcik, Z.M. Detecting spots for NASA space programs using rough sets. In Proceedings of the Second International Conference on Rough Sets and Current Trends in Computing, Bnaff, AB, Canada, 16–19 October 2000; pp. 531–537.

15. Hirano, S.; Tsumoto, S. Segmentation of Medical Images Based on Approximations in Rough Set Theory. In Proceedings of the Third International Conference on Rough Sets and Current Trends in Computing, Malvern, PA, USA, 14–16 October 2002; pp. 554–563.

16. Tsai, D.M.; Lin, C.C. Fuzzy C-means based clustering for linearly and nonlinearly separable data. *Pattern Recognit.* **2011**, *44*, 1750–1760. [CrossRef]

17. Lu, W.J.; Yan, Z.Z. Improved FCM Algorithm Based on K-Means and Granular Computing. *J. Intell. Syst.* **2015**, *24*, 215–222. [CrossRef]

18. Dunn, J.C. A fuzzy relative of the isodata process and its use in detecting compact well-separated clusters. *J. Cybern.* **1973**, *3*, 32–57. [CrossRef]

19. Zhao, F.; Jiao, L.; Liu, H. Kernel generalized fuzzy c-means clustering with spatial information for image segmentation. *Digit. Signal Process.* **2013**, *23*, 184–199. [CrossRef]

20. He, J.H. A Remark on Lagrange Multiplier Method (I). *Int. J. Nonlinear Sci. Numer. Simul.* **2012**, *2*, 161–164. [CrossRef]

21. Xu, M.J.; Zhang, J.K.; Li, H. A Method for Fish Diseases Diagnosis Based on Rough Set and FCM Clustering Algorithm. In Proceedings of the 3rd International Conference on Intelligent System Design and Engineering Applications, Hong Kong, China, 16–18 January 2013; pp. 99–103.

22. Bartholdi, L.; Grigorchuk, R.I. Lie methods in growth of groups and groups of finite width. *Comput. Geom. Asp. Mod. Algebra* **2000**, *275*, 1–27.

23. Alcock, E. Flat and stably flat modules. *J. Algebra* **1999**, *220*, 612–628. [CrossRef]

24. De, A.L.; Guo, C.A. An image segmentation method based on the fusion of vector quantization and edge detection with applications to medical image processing. *Int. J. Mach. Learn. Cybern.* **2014**, *5*, 543–551. [CrossRef]

25. Wu, H.; He, L. Combining visual and textual features for medical image modality classification with ℓp-norm multiple kernel learning. *Neurocomputing* **2015**, *147*, 387–394. [CrossRef]

26. Tamura, H.; Mori, S.; Yamawaki, T. Textural features corresponding to visual perception. *IEEE Trans. Syst. Man Cybern.* **1978**, *8*, 460–473. [CrossRef]

27. Liang, Y.M.; Zhai, H.C.; Chang, S.J.; Zhang, S.-Y. Color image segmentation based on the principle of maximum degree of membership. *Acta Phys. Sin.* **2003**, *52*, 2655–2659.

28. Yu, G.J. An Algorithm for Multi-attribute Decision Making Based on Soft Rough Sets. *J. Comput. Anal. Appl.* **2016**, *20*, 1248–1258.

29. Paker, M. A decision support system to improve medical diagnosis using a combination of k-medoids clustering based attribute weighting and SVM. *J. Med. Syst.* **2016**, *40*, 1–16. [CrossRef] [PubMed]

30. Keerthika, U.; Sethukkarasi, R.; Kannan, A. A rough set based fuzzy inference system for mining temporal medical databases. *Int. J. Soft Comput.* **2012**, *3*, 41–54. [CrossRef]

![applied sciences logo] *applied sciences*

MDPI

Article

Simplified Swarm Optimization-Based Function Module Detection in Protein–Protein Interaction Networks

Xianghan Zheng [1,2], Lingting Wu [1,2], Shaozhen Ye [1,*] and Riqing Chen [3]

1 College of Mathematics and Computer Science, Fuzhou University, Fuzhou 350116, China; xianghan.zheng@fzu.edu.cn (X.Z.); mjyw_wlt@163.com (L.W.)
2 Fujian Key Laboratory of Network Computing and Intelligent Information Processing, Fuzhou 350116, China
3 College of Computer and Information, Fujian Agriculture and Forestry University, Fuzhou 350002, China; riqing.chen@fafu.edu.cn
* Correspondence: yeshzh@fzu.edu.cn; Tel.: +86-150-8002-5921

Academic Editors: Wenbing Zhao, Xiong Luo and Tie Qiu
Received: 12 February 2017; Accepted: 14 April 2017; Published: 19 April 2017

Abstract: Proteomics research has become one of the most important topics in the field of life science and natural science. At present, research on protein–protein interaction networks (PPIN) mainly focuses on detecting protein complexes or function modules. However, existing approaches are either ineffective or incomplete. In this paper, we investigate detection mechanisms of functional modules in PPIN, including open database, existing detection algorithms, and recent solutions. After that, we describe the proposed approach based on the simplified swarm optimization (SSO) algorithm and the knowledge of Gene Ontology (GO). The proposed solution implements the SSO algorithm for clustering proteins with similar function, and imports biological gene ontology knowledge for further identifying function complexes and improving detection accuracy. Furthermore, we use four different categories of species datasets for experiment: fruitfly, mouse, scere, and human. The testing and analysis result show that the proposed solution is feasible, efficient, and could achieve a higher accuracy of prediction than existing approaches.

Keywords: protein–protein interaction networks; protein function module; simplified swarm optimization

1. Introduction

Proteomics is one of the most important topics in the fields of life science and natural science [1–5]. Considering that proteins alone rarely exhibit their biological functions in individuals, the understanding of protein–protein interactions (PPI) [6] is the basis of revealing the activity of protein and promotes the study of various diseases and development of new drugs.

In the past 10 years, substantial work was conducted to promote the research in the field of PPI, such as publications in Nature [2] and Science [3], proceedings of the National Academy of Sciences [3], and nucleic acid research [7]. Available data on PPI are greatly enriched because of the fast development of high-throughput screening [7] and data mining technologies [8]. Some widely used and most complete open datasets are also released, for instance, the Biomolecular Interaction Network Database (BIND) [9], Database of Interaction Proteins (DIP) [10], IntAct [11], Human Protein Reference Database (HPRD) [12], and Molecular Interaction Database (MINT) [13,14].

However, the existing solution is incomplete or inaccurate due to the following technical challenges. On one hand, high-throughput screening technology generates a huge amount of noisy data and higher false positive rates, while the experimental method loses lots of real interactions (false negatives) [15]. On the other hand, the existing computation approaches (described in Section 2) are inefficient, computationally complex, or lack of convincing results. In this paper, we investigate protein function module detection and propose a lightweight and efficient simplified swarm optimization-based protein function module detection with the following contributions:

1. We investigate PPI datasets and existing function module detection methods and select four typical species of protein-protein interaction data from the DIP database for the experiment. A specific data crawler is developed to extract data features from these datasets.
2. The proposed PPIN function module detection is described from a few aspects: system model, feature selection, mathematical description, model optimization, etc. The proposed solution implements an SSO algorithm for clustering proteins with similar function and imports biological gene ontology knowledge for further identification.
3. Experiments are conducted to validate feasibility and efficiency of the proposed approaches. The evaluation of "degree of polymerization" and "similarity between classes" further proves the precision improvement and correctness of our proposed solution.

The paper is organized as follows. Section 2 introduces the existing research, including the graph theory-, machine learning-, and intelligent algorithm-based approaches. Section 3 describes our solution, including the system model, feature extraction, and SSO-based approach. The dataset and result evaluation are explained in Section 4. Finally, experiment conclusions are presented in Section 5.

2. Related Works

2.1. Protein–Protein Interaction Datasets

There are a few protein–protein interaction datasets described in the following:

BIND (Biomolecular Interaction Network Database) contains the known interactions among biological molecules, not only among proteins but also between proteins and DNA, RNA, small molecules, lipids, and carbohydrate substances. BIND is updated daily and has extensive coverage, including human, fruit flies, yeast, nematodes, and other species. DIP was created to establish a simple, easy-to-use, and highly credible PPI public database. It specializes in storing binary PPIs from the literature conf irmed by experiments, as well as the protein complexes from Protein Data Bank (PDB).

IntAct (Molecular Interaction Database) mainly records binary interactions and their experiment methods, experimental conditions, and interaction domain structures in people, yeast, fruit flies, escherichia coli, and other species. IntAct query is divided into basic query and advanced query (more accurate).

HPRD (Human Protein Reference Database) contains protein annotations, PPIs, posttranslational modifications, subcellular localizations, and other comprehensive information.

MINT (Molecular Interaction Database) mainly stores physical interaction of proteins, particularly PPIs of mammals. Besides, it also contains the PPIs of yeast, fruit flies, and viruses. Considering the deviation of definition and the promiscuity in different databases, Gene Ontology (GO), which is developed and maintained by the GO Consortium, should be introduced for the sharing and interoperability among bioinformatics data. Therefore, the retrieval results among different databases could be unified.

2.2. Existing Works

Existing works in the detection of protein function modules could be divided into three categories:

Graph theory-based approach. Similar to a computer network, the graph theory is introduced to improve the detection of protein functional modules, mainly based on three approaches: hierarchical algorithm, partitioning algorithm, and density algorithm [16]. The hierarchical algorithm (such as, modularity division-based method [17], etc.) is based on similarity of the connections between each node. For the partitioning algorithm, the most representative method is based on restricted neighborhood search clustering (RNSC) [18]. Although both hierarchical and partitioning algorithms are easy to understand and implement, the clustering number should be determined beforehand and the function modules cannot be overlapped.

Machine learning-based approaches. Considering the disadvantages (poor scalability and low clustering) of original Markov Clustering (MCL) algorithm, Lei et al. (2015) proposed an improved MCL clustering algorithm for PPIN [19] via importing two parameters: punishment and mutation factors. This approach improves convergence speed but leads to substantial computation complexity. In literature [20], Deddy proposed a rapid and lightweight hidden layer neural network prediction algorithm based on the Extreme Learning Machine (ELM) algorithm. It uses the speed advantage of the ELM algorithm and achieves better protein function module prediction results.

Intelligence algorithm-based approaches. Swarm intelligence algorithms are also implemented for PPIN function module detection. Examples of these algorithms include Ant Colony Optimization (ACO) [21], Particle Swarm Optimization (PSO) [22], and Artificial Bee Colony (ABC) [23]. Sallim applied ACO algorithm to the PPIN complex clustering problem, and further proposed the optimization strategies in protein interaction networks [24]. In 2012, Ji introduced a novel ACO-based functional module detection (NACO–FDM) [25] algorithm to improve the efficiency in searching for an optimal path. However, this algorithm easily falls into the local optimum. In literature, another ACO-MAE mechanism that combines ACO with the idea of multi-agent evolution (MAE) was developed to achieve better prediction accuracy.

Besides, some other works have demonstrated higher performance with a mixture of graph-based approach and machine learning-based approaches [26,27]. The algorithm is based on prior calculation of parameters on the protein residue networks and later machine learning. However, this approach still needs a lot of noted samples for training.

2.3. Clustering Evaluation

In this paper, the clustering evaluation indices include the degree of polymerization (cohesion) inside protein function module, and the deviation degree between modules (separation). Cohesion refers to the similarity degree of each data object in the same category. The higher the degree of polymerization, the higher the similarity. Separation refers to the dissimilarity between two different protein function modules. The higher degree of separation between two categories, the higher the distance between two cluster centers. From mathematics, the cohesion and separation functions are described as follows:

$$Co = \begin{cases} S + \frac{1}{D}, & D \neq 0 \\ S, & D = 0 \end{cases} \tag{1}$$

$$Se = \begin{cases} D + \frac{1}{S}, & S \neq 0 \\ D, & S = 0 \end{cases} \tag{2}$$

where S and D represent the values of protein nodes in the functional similarity matrix and distance matrix, respectively.

2.4. Discussion

However, there are still a few disadvantages in existing research. Graph-based approaches are far from being precise (with a highest precision rate of 46% [16]) because some clusters may be too thin due to the considerable weights between loosely connected nodes. Existing machine/deep learning-based approaches need huge amount of denoted sample for training, and this is difficult to implement in PPIN field. On the contrary, although intelligence algorithms (mainly ACO-related approaches) implemented have shown better precision rates and efficiency than graph-based solutions, more intelligent algorithms should be considered and implemented.

The detection of protein function modules is an NP hard problem [28]. Since the PSO-related solution is efficient and has been implemented in different kinds of NP hard problems, we propose the enhancement of PSO, Simplified Swarm Optimization (SSO) algorithms, for implementation in the detection of protein function modules. Theoretically, an SSO-based solution is capable of achieving better precision than the PSO algorithm and reduces computing complexity.

3. Simplified Swarm Optimization-Based Detection

In this section, we describe the proposed SSO-based solution in four steps: system model, feature extraction, mathematical description, and model optimization.

3.1. Interaction Model

Figure 1a–e illustrates the evolution process of protein function module detection. First, the PPI network is abstracted into the format of a protein distance matrix. The structure model is built by the measure of distance between each protein. Afterwards, the SSO algorithm is imported to search the shortest path between each node. Finally, the cutting and filtering strategies are defined and implemented to generate a clustering result.

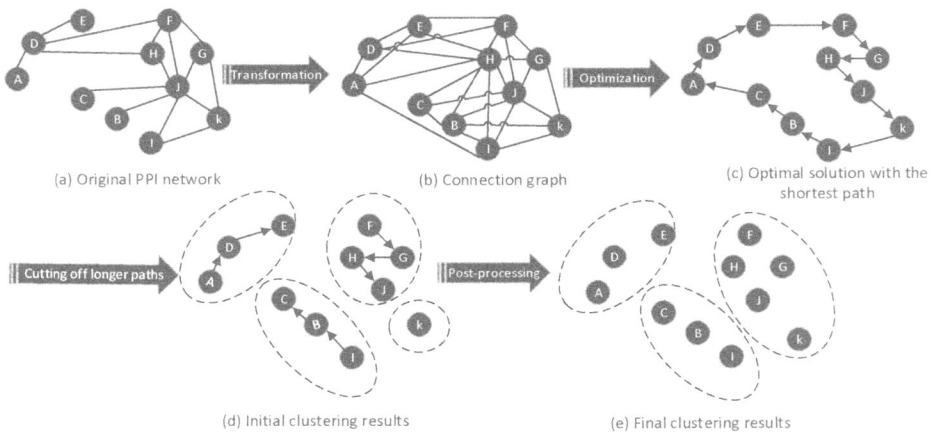

(a) Original PPI network

(b) Connection graph

(c) Optimal solution with the shortest path

(d) Initial clustering results

(e) Final clustering results

Figure 1. Interaction Model.

3.2. Feature Extraction

After acquiring a dataset from DIP and GO databases, features can be extracted in the following steps:

1. Noise Filter. Noise data refers to the existence of errors, redundant data, or abnormal data in crawled data. For example, in interaction.xml-based crawled data, the tag field "DIP-nnE" may be empty or not found. Therefore, eliminating noise and redundant data is the first step before the experiment.
2. Feature Selection. Feature selection is performed through the manual respection of protein xml data. For example, in the main part of the XML file, the tag names "interactorList" and "interactionList" indicate the interaction relationship among protein nodes. Therefore, feature data are selected through the manual inspection of protein data.
3. Feature Extraction and Reformat. After the feature selection, related data (e.g., protein id and interactor id) are extracted, reformatted, and stored in the structured database.

3.3. Mathematics Model

3.3.1. Model Establishment

Assume the initial particle swarm size n, the problem space dimensions m, the location $X_i^t = (x_{i1}^t, x_{i2}^t, \cdots, x_{im}^t)$, where $i = 1, 2, 3, \ldots n$, x_{im}^t is the value of i-th particle with respect to m-th dimension of feature space at time t; the particles in the search process reach the optimal location and are marked as p_{ij}^t; the optimal location for the group is g_{ij}^t. Therefore, the location of particle i in j dimension at time t is described in the following formulas:

$$
x_{ij}^t = \begin{cases}
X_{ij}^t, & if\ random \in [0, C_w); \\
p_{ij}^t, & if\ random \in [C_w, C_p); \\
g_{ij}^t, & if\ random \in [C_p, C_g); \\
X, & if\ random \in [C_g, 1).
\end{cases}
\tag{3}
$$

In Equation (3), X represents the new value of the particle in every dimension randomly generated; the random number is between $(0, 1)$; C_w, C_p, and C_g are the three predetermined positive constants with $C_w < C_p < C_g$.

In this study, we use the topological structure of a PPIN [29] as the basis, with the individual proteins as nodes and the interactions between proteins as lines, to construct a PPIN model (with interaction model shown in Figure 2, and adjacency matrix in Table 1). The interaction between the proteins is denoted as 1, whereas no relationship between proteins is denoted as 0.

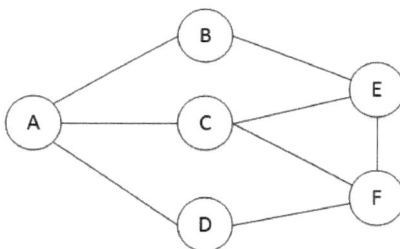

Figure 2. Protein interaction network.

Table 1. Adjacency matrix.

	A	B	C	D	E	F
A	0	1	1	1	0	0
B	1	0	0	0	1	0
C	1	0	0	0	1	1
D	1	0	0	0	0	1
E	0	1	1	0	0	1
F	0	0	1	1	1	0

Therefore, the distance between proteins d_{ij} (difference between two proteins), can be calculated according to Equation (4):

$$
d_{ij} = \frac{|Int(i) \cup Int(j)| - |Int(i) \cap Int(j)|}{|Int(i) \cup Int(j)| + |Int(i) \cap Int(j)|}
\tag{4}
$$

where i and j express the two proteins. Normally, the value of d_{ij} is greater than 0; in some special cases, when proteins i and j are in completely different function modules, d_{ij} achieves the highest value 1.

3.3.2. Parameter Setting

Parameter setting plays a key important role in detecting function modules. In SSO algorithm, the initial location of a particle swarm set to be random. In addition, C_w, C_p, and C_g are set as 0.25, 0.5, and 0.75 respectively. The values of C_w, C_p, and C_g in this paper are set as 0.1, 0.55, and 0.8 to expand the search area to a global search at the beginning of the iteration. Table 2 shows the parameter setting of the SSO and PSO algorithms used in the experiments (t expresses t-th, Max_GEN expresses maximum number of iterations).

Table 2. Parameter setting for PSO and SSO algorithm [1].

Parameter Setting	PSO	SSO
MAX_GEN	500	500
Number of Particle	100	100
Maximum Fitness	1.0	1.0
C_w, C_p, C_g	-	0.1, 0.55, 0.8
Weight	0.9–$0.4 \cdot t / \text{MAX\_GEN}$	-
c_1, c_2 [2]	2.0, $t / \text{MAX\_GEN}$	-

[1] MAX_GEN: expresses maximum number of iterations; [2] c_1, c_2 expresses learning factor.

3.4. Model Optimization

Model optimization is divided into two main parts: module planning based on function information, module planning based on topology.

3.4.1. Module Planning Based on Function Information

The objective of this step is to merge the similar protein function modules (PFMs). The basic idea is to measure the similarity of two modules. When the similarity is greater than a certain threshold, two modules can be merged, based on Equation (5):

$$S(M_S, M_T) = \frac{\sum\limits_{i \in M_S, j \in M_T} s(i, j)}{\min(|M_S|, |M_T|)} \tag{5}$$

where M_S and M_T represent the size of the two protein function modules (including the number of proteins) respectively, and $s(i, j)$ is characterized by the following Equation (6):

$$s(i, j) = \begin{cases} 1, & if\ i = j; \\ f_{ij}, & if\ i \neq j. \end{cases} \tag{6}$$

Among these paramaters, f_{ij} is the similarity function based on gene topology and is characterized by the following Equation (7) [30]:

$$f_{ij} = \frac{|g^i \cap g^j|}{|g^i \cup g^j|} \tag{7}$$

In Equation (7), g^i and g^j represent the comment values of protein i and j in the Gene Ontology respectively [31]. The greater value of f_{ij} indicates higher similarity between two proteins.

3.4.2. Module Planning Based on Topology

This step measures the density of the initial protein function module and reduces the sparse protein module through filter setting. The density is calculated according to Equation (8):

$$D_s = \frac{e}{n \cdot (n-1)/2} \tag{8}$$

where n denotes the number of current protein function module and e represents the number of interactions in the module.

4. Experiments

4.1. Dataset Description

We select four different categories of species data sets for experiment: fruitfly, mouse, scere, and human. Additionally, we use the GO (Gene Ontology) for unifying the format of four species data. Via extracting and matching, the final data statistics are illustrated in Table 3.

Table 3. Matching statistics [1].

Species	Before Matching			After Matching
	Interaction	Interactor	GO Annotation	Interactor & GO Annotation
Human	8412	4823	20,201	3394
Scere	24,668	2340	4680	2325
Mouse	2498	2259	1480	1447
Fruitfly	680	607	3299	269

[1] GO: Gene Ontology.

4.2. Evaluations

4.2.1. Complexity and Running Times

First, we compare the complexity between SSO and PSO (a typical intelligent algorithm). Assuming that the iteration number of i particles was N_i, $i = 1, 2, ..., m$, m is the maximum number of iteration, $N_1 = N_2 = \cdots = N_m = N$. Assuming that each particle in each iteration requires the computational time T_t, the total execution time of PSO algorithm for optimal operation is $N \cdot m \cdot T_t$. As for SSO, assuming that each particle in each iteration requires the computational time D_t, the total execution time in optimal operation is $N \cdot m \cdot D_t$, where $D_t = \alpha \cdot D_1 + \beta \cdot D_2 + \gamma \cdot D_3 + \lambda \cdot D_4$, $\alpha = 0.1, \beta = 0.45, \gamma = 0.25, \lambda = 0.25$. Table 4 further illustrates the experimental comparison, and shows that the SSO algorithm is more efficient than the PSO algorithm.

Table 4. The average running time comparison.

Category	SSO				PSO			
Threshold	Fruitfly	Mouse	Scere	Human	Fruitfly	Mouse	Scere	Human
0.05	4.4	71.2	171.6	731.6	5.4	148.6	205.6	710.2
0.055	4	69.4	150.4	501.4	5	167.4	217.8	650
0.06	4	75.6	181.6	451.8	5	163.2	217.8	637.8
0.065	4	73.6	150.8	407.6	5	168	203.8	683.8
0.07	4	107.4	153	418.8	5	146	204.8	629.6
0.075	4	78	150.8	375.6	5	168	204.4	758.2
0.08	4	74.6	167.2	395.2	5	166.4	206	751.2
0.085	4	76.4	158.8	402	5	167.2	205	771.2

4.2.2. Results Analysis via Threshold Setting

Besides, for four species data, eight different threshold values were selected in the experiment: 0.05, 0.055, 0.06, 0.065, 0.07, 0.075, 0.08, and 0.085, with the result illustrated in Figures 3–5. Results show that when the threshold value increases to a certain extent, the unnecessary protein filtration is greatly reduced (illustrated in Figure 3b), and the size of the protein function module (PFM) increases (illustrated in Figure 3a). However, the other four aspects of the effect including degree of polymerization in the module, the deviation degree between modules, and so on (corresponding to Figures 4 and 5) remained nearly at the same level.

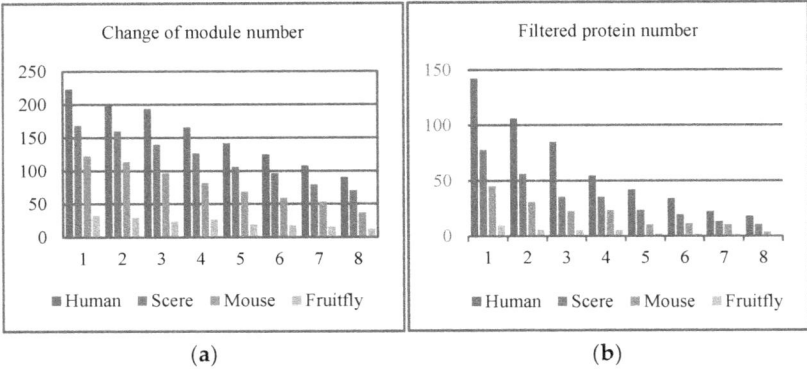

(a)

(b)

Figure 3. Four species experimental results. Threshold value changes among 1 (0.05), 2 (0.055), 3 (0.06), 4 (0.065), 5 (0.07), 6 (0.075), 7 (0.08), 8 (0.085). (**a**) Change of module number; (**b**) filtered protein number.

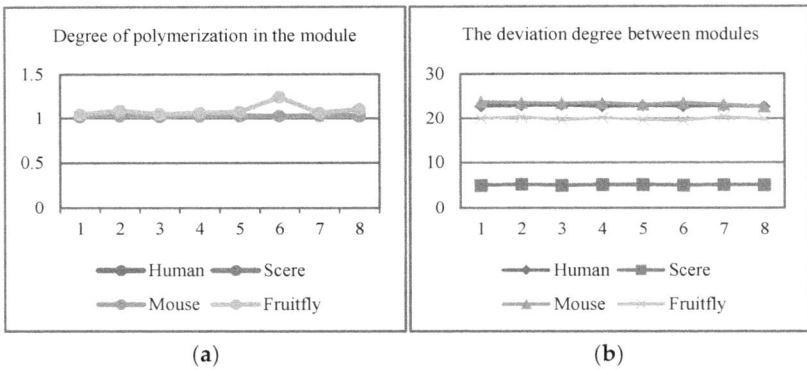

(a)

(b)

Figure 4. (**a**) Degree of polymerization in the module; (**b**) deviation degree between modules.

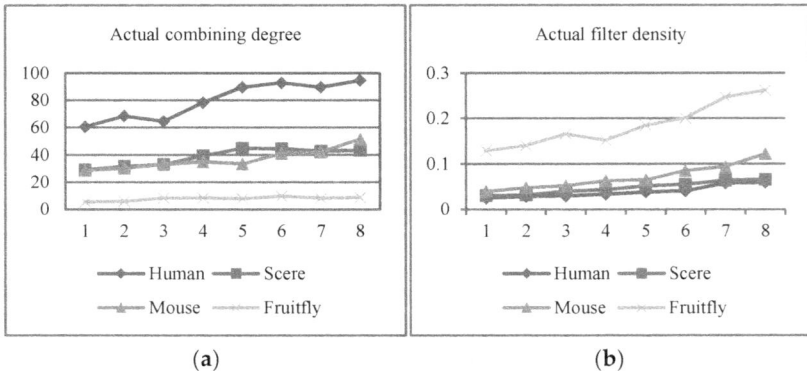

(a)

(b)

Figure 5. (**a**) Actual combining degree in each threshold; (**b**) actual filter density during the experiment.

In order to evaluate the efficiency and feasibility of SSO algorithm for protein module detection, we take the human dataset and conduct experiments for evaluation (based on cluster indices described in Section 2.3). The reason for the selection of human species is that the number of nodes is more than other experimental data and the data integrity is better, which can better reflect the characteristics of the algorithm. Figure 6 shows the results under the detection strategy of PSO and SSO.

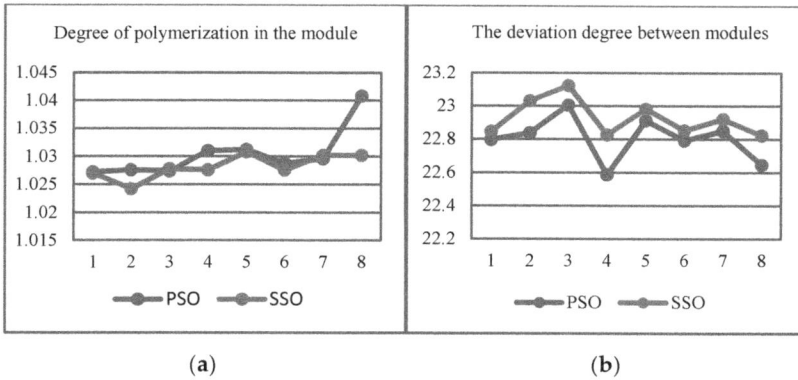

(a)   (b)

Figure 6. (a) Degree of polymerization in the module; (b) degree of deviation between modules.

In the Figure 6, we find that the curves of PSO and SSO strategies are more or less intertwined. The difference between PSO and SSO is not obvious in the index of "cohesion", however, the curve of SSO is more stable than PSO algorithm. This indicates that the SSO-based solution outperforms the PSO-based approach in "Separation".

Meanwhile, Table 5 indicates that the number of function module generated by SSO algorithm is a bit lower than PSO in fruitfly species. This may be because of the small number of protein nodes in fruitfly species. Table 6 shows the filtered protein number for PSO and SSO algorithms, which indicates that SSO is significantly better than those of PSO, especially when the number of protein increases. Table 7 shows the degree of polymerization in the module for both PSO and SSO algorithms. A higher value indicates higher similarity in the module. The result also reveals that the two algorithms are relatively close, however, the SSO algorithm has better stability.

Table 5. Change of module number for PSO and SSO algorithms.

Category	SSO				PSO			
Threshold	Fruitfly	Mouse	Scere	Human	Fruitfly	Mouse	Scere	Human
0.05	33	122.4	168.6	223	25.8	94.8	174.2	223.4
0.055	30	114	160	198.8	27	92.2	163.8	202.8
0.06	23.6	96.6	139.8	193.6	22.6	82.6	139.8	187.4
0.065	26.8	82.2	127	165.4	18	72.4	129.6	161.2
0.07	19.8	68.8	106.6	142	16.2	66	110.8	147
0.075	18.4	59	96.8	125	14.4	60.8	101.8	126
0.08	15.6	53.2	79.4	108	15.4	46.4	79.2	109
0.085	13.2	36.8	70.2	90.4	11.6	41.8	74.6	96.8

Table 6. Filtered protein number for PSO and SSO algorithm.

Category	SSO				PSO			
Threshold	Fruitfly	Mouse	Scere	Human	Fruitfly	Mouse	Scere	Human
0.05	9.8	45	77.8	142.4	10	280.2	342.4	706
0.055	5.6	30.4	56.2	106	9	172.6	205.2	432.8
0.06	5.2	22.4	35.4	84.8	6	95	102	270
0.065	5.2	23.2	35.4	54.6	4.4	56	64	234.4
0.07	2	10.4	23.2	42	3.4	45.6	35.8	157
0.075	1.6	11	19.4	33.8	4.4	17.8	33.8	100.8
0.08	1.4	10.4	13.2	22.2	1.4	12	18	70.2
0.085	0.8	3.6	10.4	17.8	1.4	6.4	13.8	48.2

Table 7. Degree of polymerization in the module for PSO and SSO algorithm.

Category	SSO				PSO			
Threshold	Fruitfly	Mouse	Scere	Human	Fruitfly	Mouse	Scere	Human
0.05	1.0448	1.028	1.016	1.027	1.0842	1.0288	1.0178	1.0272
0.055	1.0906	1.0298	1.0256	1.0242	1.0688	1.0278	1.0172	1.0276
0.06	1.0516	1.0296	1.0182	1.0278	1.0666	1.0334	1.0248	1.0274
0.065	1.0634	1.0326	1.0236	1.0276	1.071	1.031	1.025	1.031
0.07	1.0778	1.0306	1.0246	1.0308	1.0852	1.0356	1.0238	1.0312
0.075	1.2486	1.0274	1.025	1.0276	1.093	1.0296	1.0254	1.0288
0.08	1.0658	1.03	1.029	1.0302	1.098	1.0334	1.0244	1.0296
0.085	1.1094	1.0342	1.022	1.0302	1.105	1.0362	1.0282	1.0408

5. Conclusions

In this study, we introduce relevant research on protein interaction networks conducted in recent years, including the commonly used protein databases and existing detection methods. We then describe our proposed SSO algorithm for the detection problem of protein function module (PFM) in PPIN. Simultaneously, biological gene ontology knowledge is combined to improve the prediction accuracy. The performance of SSO is compared with existing work (typically PSO algorithm) through the analysis of the experimental results. Results show the feasibility and efficiency of our proposed SSO algorithm. All the datasets and code related with this paper are available from https://github.com/wulingting/PPIN-SSO-and-PSO-algorithms.

Acknowledgments: This work is supported by the National Natural Science Foundation of China under Grant No. 61502106; Fujian Major Project of Regional Industry 2014H4015.

Author Contributions: Xianghan Zheng and Lingting Wu conceived and designed the experiments; Lingting Wu performed the experiments; Xianghan Zheng and Shaozhen Ye analyzed the data; Riqing Chen contributed reagents, materials, and analysis tools; Lingting Wu wrote the paper; Xianghan Zheng participated in paper revision and made many suggestions. All authors read and approved the final manuscript.

Conflicts of Interest: The authors declare no conflict of interest.

References

1. Xu, B.; Guan, J. From function to interaction: A new paradigm for accurately predicting protein complexes based on protein-to-protein interaction networks. *IEEE/ACM Trans. Comput. Biol. Bioinform.* **2014**, *11*, 616–627. [PubMed]
2. Islam, M.F.; Hoque, M.M.; Banik, R.S.; Roy, S.; Sumi, S.S.; Hassan, F.M.N.; Tomal, M.T.S.; Ullah, A.; Rahman, K.M.T. Comparative analysis of differential network modularity in tissue specific normal and cancer protein interaction networks. *J. Clin. Bioinform.* **2013**, *3*, 19. [CrossRef] [PubMed]
3. Ahn, Y.Y.; Bagrow, J.P.; Lehmann, S. Link communities reveal multiscale complexity in networks. *Nature* **2010**, *435*, 761–764. [CrossRef] [PubMed]

4. Kachroo, A.H.; Laurent, J.M.; Yellman, C.M.; Meyer, A.G.; Wilke, C.O.; Marcotte, E.M. Systematic humanization of yeast genes reveals conserved functions and genetic modularity. *Science* **2015**, *348*, 921–925. [CrossRef] [PubMed]

5. Tanay, A.; Sharan, R.; Kupiec, M.; Shamir, R. Revealing modularity and organization in the yeast molecular network by integrated analysis of highly heterogeneous genomewide data. *Proc. Natl. Acad. Sci. USA* **2004**, *101*, 2981–2986. [CrossRef] [PubMed]

6. Szklarczyk, D.; Franceschini, A.; Wyder, S.; Forslund, K.; Heller, D.; Huerta-Cepas, J.; Simonovic, M.; Roth, A.; Santos, A.; Tsafou, K.P.; et al. Protein–protein interaction networks, integrated over the tree of life. *Nucleic Acids Res.* **2015**, *39*, D561–D568.

7. Ding, Y.; Tang, J.; Guo, F. Identification of Protein–Protein Interactions via a Novel Matrix-Based Sequence Representation Model with Amino Acid Contact Information. *Int. J. Mol. Sci.* **2016**, *17*, 1623. [CrossRef] [PubMed]

8. Szklarczyk, D.; Franceschini, A.; Kuhn, M.; Simonovic, M.; Roth, A.; Minguez, P.; Doerks, T.; Stark, M.; Muller, J.; Bork, P.; et al. The STRING database in 2011: Functional interaction networks of proteins, globally integrated and scored. *Nucleic Acids Res.* **2011**, *1093*, D561–D568. [CrossRef] [PubMed]

9. Xu, H.; Li, X.; Zhang, Z.; Song, J. Identifying Coevolution between Amino Acid Residues in Protein Families: Advances in the Improvement and Evaluation of Correlated Mutation Algorithms. *Curr. Bioinform.* **2013**, *8*, 148–160. [CrossRef]

10. Li, H.; Chang, Y.; Yang, L.; Bahar, I. The Gaussian network model database for biomolecular structural dynamics. *Nucleic Acids Res.* **2016**, *44*, D415–D422. [CrossRef] [PubMed]

11. Blohm, P.; Frishman, G.; Smialowski, P. A database of non-interacting proteins derived by literature mining, manual annotation and protein structure analysis. *Nucleic Acids Res.* **2014**, *42*, D396–D400. [CrossRef] [PubMed]

12. Orchard, S.; Ammari, M.; Aranda, B.; Breuza, L.; Briganti, L.; Broackes-Carter, F.; Nancy, H.; Campbell, G.C.; Chen, C.; del-Toro, N. The MIntAct project—IntAct as a common curation platform for 11 molecular interaction databases. *Nucleic Acids Res.* **2014**, *1093*, D358–D363. [CrossRef] [PubMed]

13. Motono, C.; Nakata, J.; Koike, R. A comprehensive database of predicted structures of all human proteins. *Nucleic Acids Res.* **2011**, *39*, D487–D493. [CrossRef] [PubMed]

14. Licata, L.; Briganti, L.; Peluso, D. MINT, the molecular interaction database: 2012 update. *Nucleic Acids Res.* **2012**, *40*, D857–D861. [CrossRef] [PubMed]

15. Ji, J.Z.; Jiao, L.; Yang, C.C.; Lv, J.W.; Zhang, A.D. MAE-FMD: Multi-agent evolutionary method for functional module detection in protein-protein interaction networks. *BMC Bioinform.* **2014**, *15*, 325. [CrossRef] [PubMed]

16. Ester, B.M.; Kriegel, H.P.; Sander, J.; Xu, X. A Density Based algorithm for discovering clusters in large spatial databases with Noise. In Proceedings of the International Conference on Knowledge Discovery and Data Mining, Chicago, IL, USA, 11–14 August 2013.

17. Newman, M.E. Fast algorithm for detecting community structure in networks. *Phys. Rev. E* **2004**, *69*, 066133. [CrossRef] [PubMed]

18. Hartuv, E.; Shamir, R. A clustering algorithm based on graph connectivity. *Inf. Proc. Lett.* **2000**, *76*, 175–181. [CrossRef]

19. Rujirapipat, S.; Mcgarry, K.; Nelson, D. Bioinformatic Analysis Using Complex Networks and Clustering Proteins Linked with Alzheimer's Disease. In *Advances in Computational Intelligence Systems*; Springer: Cham, Germany, 2017; pp. 219–230.

20. Ruan, P.; Hayashida, M.; Maruyama, O.; Akutsu, T. Prediction of heterotrimeric protein complexes by two-phase learning using neighboring kernels. *BMC Bioinform.* **2014**, *15*, S6. [CrossRef] [PubMed]

21. Lei, X.J. The Information Flow Clustering Model and Algorithm Based on the Artificial Bee Colony Mechanism of PPI Network. *Chin. J. Comput.* **2012**, *35*, 134–145. [CrossRef]

22. Dorigo, M. *Ant Colony Optimization*; MIT Press/Bradford Books: Cambridge, MA, USA, 2004.

23. Kennedy, J.; Eberhart, R. Particle swarm optimization. In Proceedings of the IEEE International Conference on Neural Networks, Perth, Australia, 27 November–1 December 1995; pp. 1942–1948.

24. Karaboga, D.; Basturk, B. On the performance of artificial bee colony (ABC) algorithm. *Appl. Soft Comput.* **2008**, *8*, 687–697. [CrossRef]

25. Ji, J.Z.; Liu, Z.J. Ant colony optimization with multi-agent evolution for detecting functional modules in protein-protein interaction networks. In Proceedings of the 3rd International Conference on Information Computing and Applications, Chengdu, China, 14–16 September 2012; pp. 445–453.

26. Rodriguez-Soca, Y.; Munteanu, C.R.; Dorado, J.; Pazos, A.; Prado-Prado, F.J.; González-Díaz, H. A web server for prediction of unique targets in trypanosome proteome by using electrostatic parameters of protein-protein interactions. *J. Proteome Res.* **2010**, *9*, 1182–1190. [CrossRef] [PubMed]

27. Rodriguez-Soca, Y.; Munteanu, C.R.; Dorado, J.; Rabuñal, J.; Pazos, A.; González-Díaz, H. A web-server predicting complex biopolymer targets in plasmodium with entropy measures of protein–protein interactions. *Polymer* **2010**, *51*, 264–273. [CrossRef]

28. Ji, J.; Liu, Z.; Zhang, A.; Jiao, L.; Liu, C. Improve ant colony optimization for detecting functional modules in protein-protein interaction networks. In Proceedings of the 3rd International Conference on Information Computing and Applications, Chengdu, China, 14–16 September 2012; pp. 404–413.

29. Debby, D.W.; Ran, W.; Hong, Y. Fast prediction of protein-protein interaction sites based on Extreme Learning Machines. *Neurocomputing* **2014**, *128*, 258–266.

30. Schlicker, A.; Albrecht, M. FunSimMat: A comprehensive functional similarity database. *Nucleic Acids Res.* **2008**, *36*, D434–D439. [CrossRef] [PubMed]

31. Ashburner, M.; Ball, C.A.; Blake, J.A.; Botstein, D.; Butler, H.; Cherry, J.M.; Davis, A.P.; Dolinski, K.; Dwight, S.S.; Eppig, J.T.; et al. Gene ontology: Tool for the unification of biology. The Gene Ontology Consortium. *Nat. Genet.* **2000**, *25*, 25–29. [CrossRef] [PubMed]

![applied sciences logo]

applied sciences

MDPI

Article

Discrimination of Aortic and Pulmonary Components from the Second Heart Sound Using Respiratory Modulation and Measurement of Respiratory Split

Hong Tang [1,*], Huaming Chen [1] and Ting Li [2]

[1] Department of Biomedical Engineering, Dalian University of Technology, No. 2, Linggong Road, Ganjingzi District, Dalian 116024, China; koreyoshi_chm@163.com

[2] College of Information and Communication Engineering, Dalian Minzu University, No. 18, Liaohe West Road, Jinzhou New District, Dalian 116600, China; liting@dlnu.edu.cn

* Correspondence: tanghong@dlut.edu.cn; Tel.: +86-411-8470-6009 (ext. 3013)

Received: 15 June 2017; Accepted: 3 July 2017; Published: 4 July 2017

Featured Application: This work proposes a method to measure the respiratory split in a quantitative way. Based on the assumption model, the aortic component can be extracted by average and the pulmonary component can be estimated by subtracting. The calculation of the split is performed by timing difference of the two components. The method can track the respiratory split and has applications in monitoring heart response to respiration.

Abstract: The second heart sound consists of aortic and pulmonary components. Analysis on the changes of the second heart sound waveform in respiration shows that the aortic component has little variation and the delay of the pulmonary component is modulated by respiration. This paper proposes a novel model to discriminate the aortic and pulmonary components using respiratory modulation. It is found that the aortic component could be simply extracted by averaging the second heart sounds over respiratory phase, and the pulmonary component could be extracted by subtraction. Hence, the split is measured by the timing difference of the two components. To validate the measurement, the method is applied to simulated second heart sounds with known varying splits. The simulation results show that the aortic and pulmonary components can be successfully extracted and the measured splits are close to the predefined splits. The method is further evaluated by data collected from 12 healthy subjects. Experimental results show that the respiratory split can be accurately measured. The minimum split generally occurs at the end of expiration and the split value is about 20 ms. Meanwhile, the maximum split is about 50 ms at the end of inspiration. Both the trend of split varying with respect to respiratory phase and the numerical range of split varying are comparable to the results disclosed by previous physiologists. The proposed method is compared to the two previous well known methods. The most attractive advantage of the proposed method is much less complexity. This method has potential applications in monitoring heart hemodynamic response to respiration.

Keywords: second heart sound; respiratory split; aortic component; pulmonary component; respiratory modulation

1. Introduction

Heart sounds are a series of mechanical vibrations produced by the interplay between heart chambers, valves, great vessels, and blood flow therein. Normal heart sounds in a cardiac cycle, in general, consist of the first heart sounds (S1) and the second heart sounds (S2). Previous studies [1,2] disclosed that the components of S1 followed the onset of the left ventricular pressure rise and closure of the mitral, tricuspid valve. Hence, S1 is considered as the sum of two components called mitral and tricuspid component. Meanwhile, S2 is considered as the sum of two components, called aortic and pulmonary component, which coincide with the closure of the aortic and pulmonary valve. Asynchronous closure of the aortic and pulmonary valves yields splitting of S2. The splitting has become widely recognized as a physiologic finding in both adults and children.

Studies about how to distinguish the aortic, pulmonary components and how to detect the splitting of S2 have progressed in recent years. The chirp model was introduced to represent the aortic and pulmonary component and to separate them [3]. The time-frequency representation (TFR) method was used to analyze S2 to get the split [4]. It can be implemented by Short Time Fourier Transform (STFT). Hence, it is referred as the STFT method in this paper. Considering S2 is a nonstationary signal, a Wigner-Ville distribution (WVD) was adopted to analyze heart sounds [5]. To solve the interference terms of the WVD, the smoothed pseudo-Wigner Ville distribution (SPWVD) was used to obtain a better time-frequency resolution [5]. The SPWVD was improved by a reassignment method which can rearrange the coefficients of the SPWVD around new zero to yield a high resolution of TFR [6]. Combining Hilbert vibration decomposition (HVD) and SPWVD, Barma et al. obtained quantitative measurement of the split [7–10]. It is referred to as the HVD method in the following. In the HVD method, an S2 signal is decomposed into several phase-fixed components and SPWVD operation is performed to each component to extract timing information.

The authors propose a novel method to measure respiratory split using ensemble information embedded in S2 collection. The aortic component could be simply extracted by averaging and the pulmonary component could be extracted by subtracting. The findings show that the respiratory split can be accurately monitored and the split variations reflect the physiological relation between respiration and heart hemodynamic response.

2. Materials and Methods

2.1. Physiology of Respiratory Split in S2

The usual explanation attributes the varying splitting to the changes of heart hemodynamics induced by respiration [11]. In inspiration, the extension of the pleura and thorax increases the volume of the thoracic cavity and lowers the pressure inside. Hence, the pressure gradient from the extra-thoracic regions to the right atrium increases, as illustrated in Figure 1. This increased gradient leads to increased blood filling of the right ventricle (RV). The increased RV end-diastolic volume (EDV) leads to an increased RV stroke volume (SV) via the Frank-Starling mechanism. The dilated RV causes the left ventricle (LV) to become less compliant by physical compression. The interventricular septum thus moves leftward, which results in reduced LV filling. Simultaneously, the distending lungs and their circulatory volume tend to reduce the pressure gradient and flow from the pulmonary veins to the LV, and the transmural diastolic aortic pressure, which is called the LV afterload, increases. These additive effects induced by respiration result in decreased LV-SV. Due to the effect of hemodynamic changes in inspiration, the aortic valve closes early and the pulmonary valve closes delay. Therefore, the splitting between the two components increases. The opposing process occurs during expiration in which RV-EDV and RV-SV decrease, while LV-EDV and LV-SV increase. So, the two components are closer, or even fused in expiration. With the opposite changes of heart hemodynamics in inspiration and expiration, the characteristics of respiratory variation in splitting is illustrated in Figure 2a. The morphology changes of heart sounds due to respiration have been investigated in recent years [12–15]. One real example of these variations of a healthy subject is shown in Figure 2b, where the S2s are sorted by respiratory phase. The aortic components are aligned in time domain to facilitate observation of the split. The respiratory variation is clearly observed.

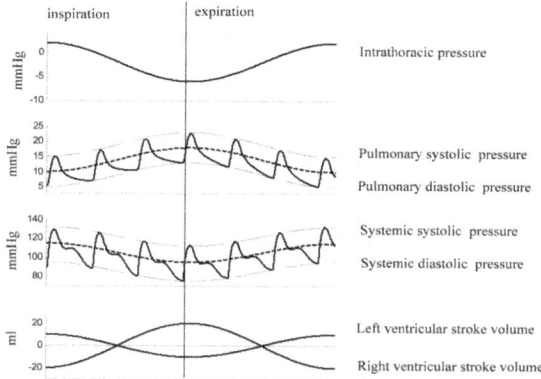

Figure 1. Diagrammatic sketch of the influence of respiration on pulmonary arterial pressure and systemic aortic pressure. (This figure is drawn by the authors. These curves are not based on clinical data of any human being or animal. They are only used to show qualitative relations).

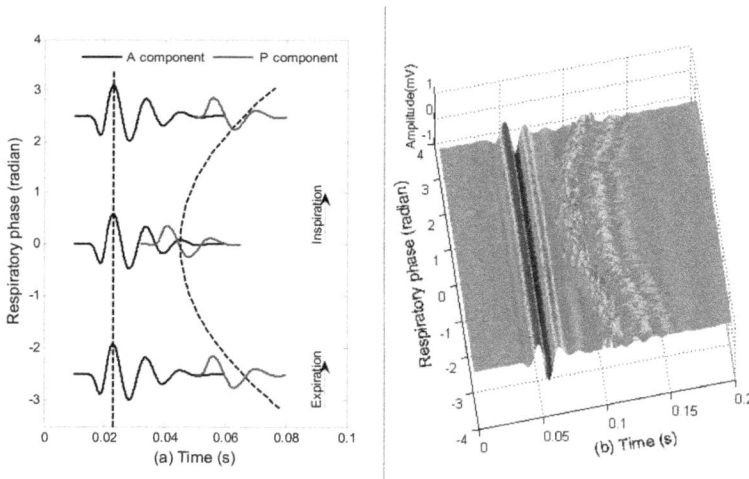

Figure 2. Illustration of the respiratory variation in spitting of the second heart sound. (**a**) Diagram of the variations. The dash lines are used as a time reference. (**b**) A real example to show the respiratory variations based on data collected from a healthy subject.

In view point of physiology, the split in S2 reflects the effect of respiration to heart hemodynamics. So, it is important to measure the split quantitatively for monitoring hemodynamic response to respiration. This paper proposes a method to measure the respiratory split of S2. The findings show that the respiratory split variations can be accurately monitored and the variations of the split reflect the physiological relation between respiration and heart hemodynamic response.

2.2. Data Collection

Twelve young male subjects aged 24 ± 1.8 years participated in the experiments. All subjects provided their consents to participate in the experiments. They were asked to remain at rest for 10 min before data collection. Each subject was asked to lie on his back in a bed during data collection.

Heart sounds, ECG lead II, and respiratory signals were simultaneously recorded at a sampling frequency of 2 kHz (PowerLab 8/35, ADinstrument, New South Wales, Australia). A heart sound microphone sensor (MLT201, ADinstrument, Australia) was placed at the left third intercostal space. The breathing transducer (MLT1132, ADinstrument, New South Wales, Australia) was a belt sensor positioned at the boundary of the thorax and abdomen to record respiratory movement. The time length of each data recording is 150–180 s. The number of cardiac cycles involved in this work of each subject is illustrated in Table 1. One portion of a recording is shown in Figure 3.

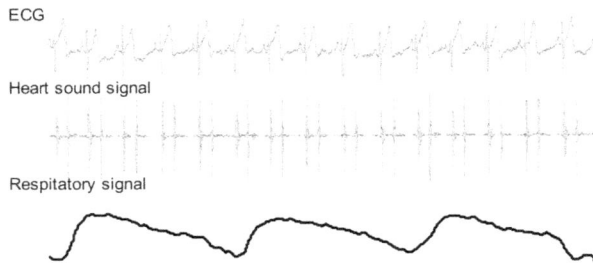

Figure 3. A portion of synchronous signals. They are scaled in amplitude for visual inspection.

Table 1. Summary of cardiac cycles involved in this work for each subject.

Subject No.	1	2	3	4	5	6
Num. of Cardiac cycles	344	331	360	367	290	311
Subject No.	7	8	9	10	11	12
Num. of Cardiac cycles	299	281	312	285	286	301

2.3. System Overview

The overview of the system workflow is illustrated in Figure 4. First, the heart sound signal and synchronous respiratory signal are bandpass filtered with zero-phase delay in the frequency band 5–200 Hz and 0.05–1 Hz, respectively. Second, all S2s from the heart sound signal were segmented and re-ordered in joint time and respiratory phase domain. Third, aortic and pulmonary components were discriminated. Fourth, the splits were measured by weighted timing.

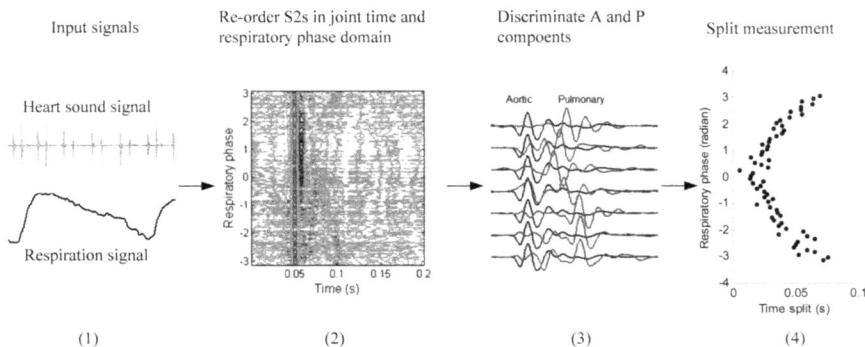

Figure 4. Overview of the workflow.

2.4. Respiratory Phase

The respiratory phase signal is extracted from the respiratory signal, i.e., the respiratory signal is mapped to respiratory phase from $-\pi$ to π. Expiration begins at $-\pi$ and ends at zero, meanwhile inspiration begins at zero and ends at π. To achieve this, the respiratory signal and its Hilbert transform form (the real part and imaginary part of an analytic signal) were used. The respiratory phase is then obtained by the phase of the analytic signal. It is assumed that $r(t)$ is a respiratory signal and $rH(t)$ is its Hilbert transform. The respiratory phase signal $\theta(t)$ is presented as

$$\theta(t) = \arctan2\left(\frac{rH(t)}{r(t)}\right)$$

where arctan2() is the operator of the four quadrant arctangent. An example of calculating respiratory phase is illustrated in Figure 5.

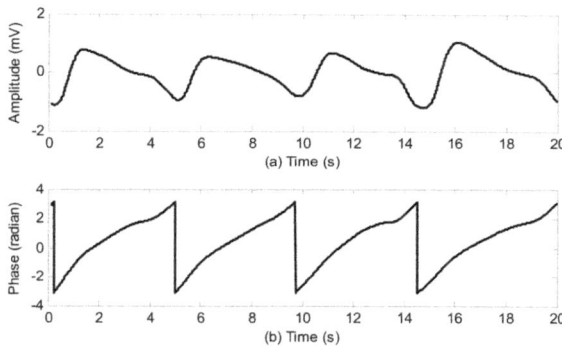

Figure 5. Illustration of respiratory phase calculation. (**a**) Respiratory signal collected from a belt sensor. (**b**) Respiratory phase. Inspiration corresponds to the phase from zero to π and expiration corresponds to the phase from $-\pi$ to zero.

2.5. Investigation on S2 Waveform Changing Modulated by Respiration

To observe the changing visually, S2s are firstly segmented from the heart sound signal using the envelope method proposed by Liang et al. [16]. The respiratory phases associated to the S2s are looked up from the respiratory phase signal with the reference of the S2s' timing. The S2s are re-ordered according to respiratory phase in ascending order. Then, the S2s are aligned in time domain and formed into a two dimensional matrix. The horizontal direction is in the time domain and the vertical direction is in the respiratory phase domain. These matrixes enable the changing to be observed clearly. This preprocessing is repeated for the twelve subjects and the contour plots of these matrixes are shown in Figure 6. A common phenomenon can be seen in that the S2s of each subject have two parts. The first parts are aligned in time domain, whose waveforms have almost no change; however the timing of the second parts varied with respect to respiratory phase. That is to say, the splits between the two parts are modulated by the respiratory phase. The split decreases in expiration where the phase is from $-\pi$ to zero and the split increases in inspiration where the phase is from zero to π. The authors believe that the first parts are the aortic components and the second parts are the pulmonary components.

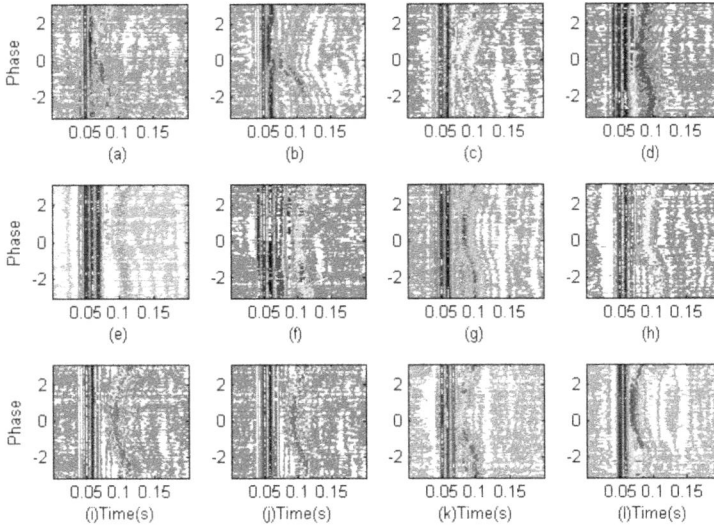

Figure 6. The second heart sounds from twelve subjects are demonstrated in joint time and respiratory phase domain. (**a–l**) subjects from No. 1 to No. 12.

2.6. Discrimination of Aortic and Pulmonary Component

Model Assumption: It is assumed that the S2 is the sum of aortic and pulmonary components with the following model

$$S_2(t,\theta) = a(t) + p(t - u(\theta)) + v(t,\theta) \tag{1}$$

where $a(t)$ is the aortic component, and $p(t - u(\theta))$ is the pulmonary component at the respiratory phase θ. $u(\theta)$ is the time delay modulated by respiration. $v(t,\theta)$ is random noise at the respiratory phase θ to contaminate the second heart sound. The purpose of this article is to measure the respiratory split, $u(\theta)$. In detail, we have further assumptions based on the mentioned observation above.

(1) $a(t)$ is assumed to have a fixed waveform over the respiratory phase, as can been seen in Figure 6.
(2) $p(t - u(\theta))$ is the time shifted version of $p(t)$. It is a delayed pulmonary component caused by respiration.
(3) $v(t,\theta)$ is assumed to be zero mean both over time and over respiratory phase, i.e., $\int v(t,\theta)dt = 0$ and $\int v(t,\theta)d\theta = 0$. It may be colored, non-Gaussian and non-stationary.

An average operation over respiratory phase is implemented on Equation (1)

$$\frac{\sum\limits_{k=1}^{K} S_2(t,\theta_k)}{K} = \frac{\sum\limits_{k=1}^{K} [a(t) + p(t - u(\theta_k)) + v(t,\theta_k)]}{K} \tag{2}$$

where K is the number of S2s involved in operation. Based on the assumption that $v(t,\theta)$ is zero mean, the average below produces a zero vector.

$$\frac{\sum\limits_{k=1}^{K} [v(t,\theta_k)]}{K} = \mathbf{0}(t) \tag{3}$$

Therefore, Equation (2) becomes

$$\frac{\sum\limits_{k=1}^{K} S_2(t,\theta_k)}{K} = a(t) + \frac{\sum\limits_{k=1}^{K} [p(t - u(\theta_k))]}{K} \qquad (4)$$

The average operation to the time shifted pulmonary components smooths the peaks and valleys. So, the average yields a small signal. To show the average operation clearly, an example is given in Figure 7. The S2 signals (blue lines) are over plotted. The solid bold red line is the averaged signal. It can be seen that the average of the time shifted pulmonary components produces so small a signal that it can be neglected considering the objective of this paper. Therefore, the second part in the right side of Equation (4) becomes

$$\frac{\sum\limits_{k=1}^{K} [p(t - u(\theta_k))]}{K} \approx \mathbf{0}(t) \qquad (5)$$

The estimated aortic component could be obtained by

$$\hat{a}(t) = \frac{\sum\limits_{k=1}^{K} S_2(t,\theta_k)}{K} \qquad (6)$$

It means that the aortic component is discriminated by the ensemble average of S2s over respiratory phase. Furthermore, considering Equation (1), the pulmonary component could be discriminated by subtracting the aortic component from the S2s,

$$\hat{p}(t - u(\theta)) = S_2(t,\theta) - \hat{a}(t) \qquad (7)$$

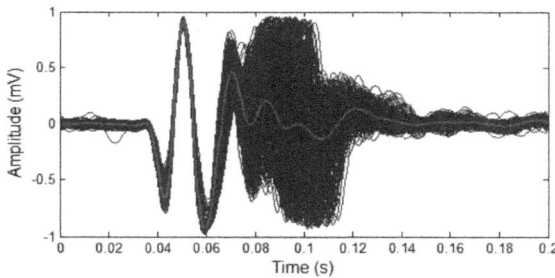

Figure 7. Average operation on S2s over respiratory phase. Blue lines are the S2s and the solid red line is the average. It can be seen that the aortic component remains. Meanwhile, the average of pulmonary components produces a very small signal.

For example, the separated components for the S2s of subject No. 4 are shown in Figure 8. It is clearly observed that the aortic components have no change, see Figure 8b. However, the estimated pulmonary components in Figure 8c have varying delay over respiratory phase. The varying delay will be estimated in the next subsection.

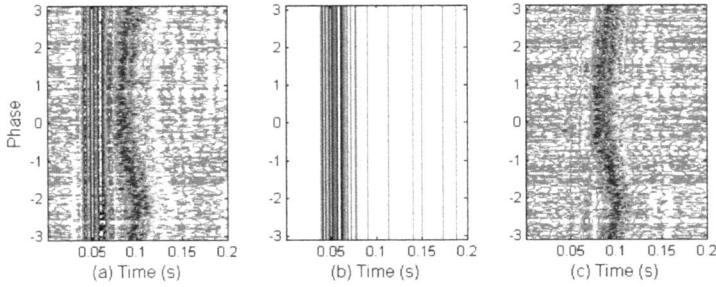

Figure 8. Example of discrimination aortic and pulmonary components for subject No. 4. (**a**) the collection of S2s shown in joint domains, (**b**) separated aortic components, (**c**) separated pulmonary components.

2.7. Estimation of Time Indices

The timings of the estimated aortic and pulmonary component are extracted from the envelope peak position. It is operated in the following. Firstly, get the upper envelope of the absolute aortic component using the local maxima with the help of cubic spline interpolation. The way to calculate the upper envelope is like extracting the upper envelope in empirical mode decomposition (EMD) [17].

$$en_a(t) = \text{upper\_envelope}(|\hat{a}(t)|) \tag{8}$$

Then, the local peaks' amplitude and associated peaks' location of the powered envelope are searched

$$[A^a, T^a] = \text{findpeaks}([en_a(t)]^k) \tag{9}$$

where k is empirically set as 8. The function of this power operation is to make the dominant peaks protruding. $A^a = [A_1^a, A_2^a, \cdots, A_M^a]$ is a vector consisting of peak amplitude, $T^a = [T_1^a, T_2^a, \cdots, T_M^a]$ is a vector consisting of peak position, and M is the number of peaks. So, the timing of the aortic component, t_a, is defined as weighted peak position

$$t_a = \frac{\sum\limits_{m=1}^{M} W_m^a T_m^a}{M} \tag{10}$$

where the weight coefficient is determined by

$$W_m^a = \frac{A_m^a}{\sum\limits_{m=1}^{M} A_m^a}$$

Similarly, get the upper envelope of the absolute pulmonary component using the local maxima with the help of cubic spline interpolation

$$en_p(t) = \text{upper\_envelope}(|\hat{p}(t)|) \tag{11}$$

The peaks of the estimated pulmonary component can be determined by

$$[A^p, T^p] = \text{findpeaks}([en_p(t)]^k) \tag{12}$$

where k is empirically set as 8. $A^p = [A^p_1, A^p_2, \cdots, A^p_N]$ is a vector consisting of peak amplitude, $T^p = [T^p_1, T^p_2, \cdots, T^p_N]$ is a vector consisting of peak position, and N is the number of peaks. So, the timing of the pulmonary component, t_p is defined as weighted peak positon

$$t_p = \frac{\sum\limits_{n=1}^{N} W^p_n T^p_n}{N} \tag{13}$$

where the weight coefficient is calculated by

$$W^p_n = \frac{A^a_n}{\sum\limits_{n=1}^{N} A^p_n}$$

The split between the aortic and pulmonary component is then estimated by the timing difference

$$\hat{u}(\theta) = |t_a - t_p| \tag{14}$$

Here is an example in Figure 9. An S2 signal is shown in Figure 9a. In Figure 9b, the blue line is the estimated aortic component and the red line is the estimated pulmonary component. The powered envelopes of the two components are given in Figure 9c. The peaks are indicated by blue stars and red squares. The associated weighted timings are shown by a black bold star and a black bold square. Hence, the split is measured by the timing difference. This processing is repeated for each S2 signal. Then, the varying split modulated by respiratory phase is obtained.

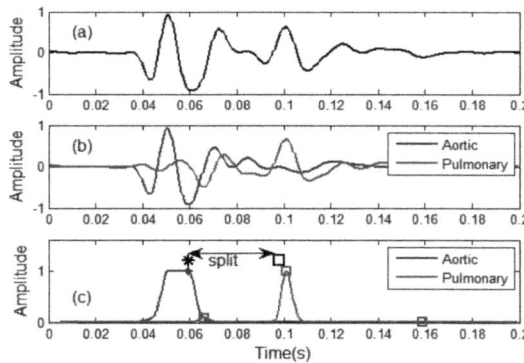

Figure 9. Estimation of timing indices for aortic and pulmonary components. (a) An S2 signal, (b) Estimated aortic and pulmonary components, (c) Timing indices estimated from weighted peak positions. The split is estimated by the timing difference between the black star and the black square.

2.8. Steps to Implement the Method

(1) Heart sound signal, respiratory signal and lead-II ECG signal are synchronously collected from a subject.
(2) Extracted respiratory phase from the respiratory signal as given in Section 2.4.
(3) Segmented all S2s from the heart sound signal and looked up the associated respiratory phase for each S2.
(4) The S2s are re-ordered with respiratory phase in ascending order in joint time and respiratory phase domain.
(5) The S2s are re-aligned in time domain.

(6) Estimated the aortic component by average operation as shown in Section 2.6.
(7) Estimated the pulmonary components by subtracting.
(8) Estimated the split by weighted peak positions as given in Section 2.7.

3. Experiments and Discussions

3.1. Computer Simulation

To validate the proposed method, we use simulated second heart sound signals with well-defined split. According to the model proposed by Xu et al. [3], the aortic component and pulmonary component are modeled as narrow-band chirp signals, i.e.,

$$A_2(t) = A_{m_A}(t)\sin(\varphi_A(t)) \tag{15}$$

$$P_2(t) = P_{m_P}(t)\sin(\varphi_P(t)) \tag{16}$$

where $A_{m_A}(t)$ and $P_{m_P}(t)$ are the amplitudes of A_2 and P_2, $\varphi_A(t)$ and $\varphi_P(t)$ are the phases. An S2 signal is simulated as

$$S_2(t) = A_2(t) + P_2(t - t_s) \tag{17}$$

where t_s is the split. To simulate varying split, it assumes that there are six hundred S2s and the splits of the S2s change in adjacent cardiac cycles from 25 ms to 80 ms like a sine wave. Then, the proposed method, the HVD method [7] and the STFT method [4] are used to detect the split variations. The simulated S2s are shown in Figure 10a. The extracted aortic and pulmonary components are shown in Figure 10b,c. The measured varying splits are illustrated in Figure 10d. A visual check shows that all the measured splits by the three methods are close to the true splits. However, in quantity, the root mean square errors of the proposed, HVD, STFT are 0.98 ms, 0.84 ms, and 1.1 ms, respectively. This computer simulation proves that the proposed method works as the authors expected.

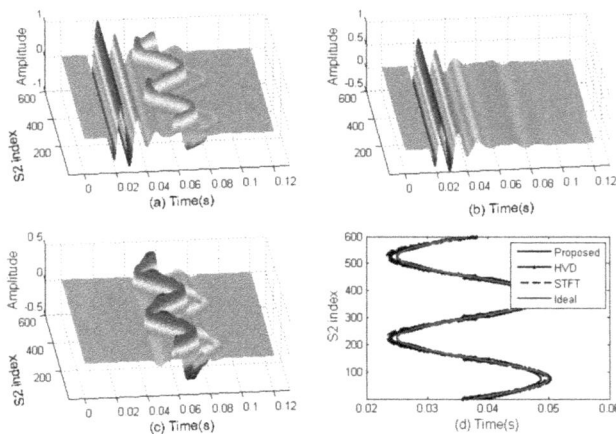

Figure 10. Validation by computer simulation. (**a**) Simulated S2 signals with varying split, (**b**) Extracted aortic components, (**c**) Extracted pulmonary components, (**d**) Comparison between the true splits and measured splits.

3.2. Measure Respiratory Variations for Human Subjects by the Proposed Method

The authors have collected data from 12 subjects and their respiratory splits are shown in Figure 11. Each recording has 3 min to 5 min consisting of several hundred cardiac cycles. A pair of respiratory phase and split can be obtained from each cardiac cycle based on the proposed method, which can be represented by a red star in the joined domain. Hence, the respiratory variations in splitting of the second heart sound can be clearly illustrated by the stars, where the measured splits are re-sorted in respiratory phase in ascending order, seen in Figure 11. We can see that the split gradually increases with the phase increasing from 0 to π (inspiration) or decreases with the phase from $-\pi$ to 0 (expiration). The minimum split generally occurs at phase zero and the split value is about 20 ms. Meanwhile, the maximum split is about 50 ms at phase π or $-\pi$. These values are comparable to the physiological results [11]. The experimental results imply that the proposed method is reasonable to monitor the respiratory variations in the split of the second heart sound. The authors wish to declare that each step of the proposed method can run automatically without any human intervention.

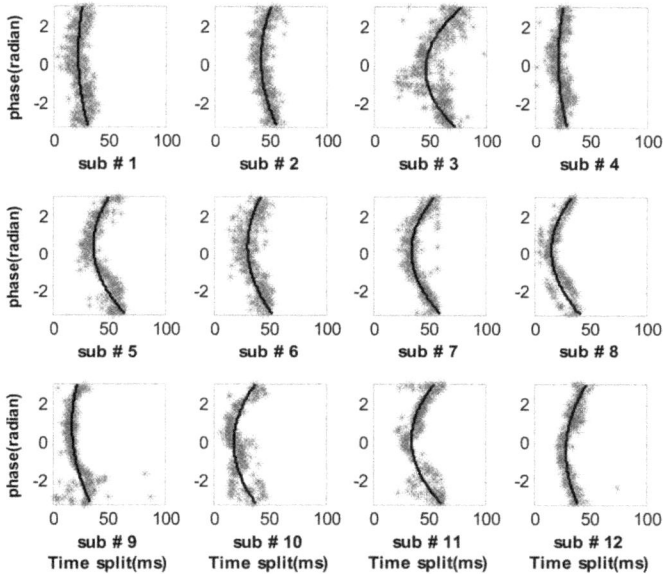

Figure 11. Measured respiratory splits of the 12 subjects by the proposed method.

3.3. Measure Respiratory Variations for Human Subjects by the Previous Methods

The respiratory splits estimated by the HVD method and the STFT method are shown in Figures 12 and 13, respectively. It can be found that the respiratory splits of all subjects estimated by the HVD method can reflect respiratory modulation. However, the respiratory splits of subject 2, 5 and 10 by the STFT method are somewhat widely disperse, as seen in Figure 13. It concludes that the STFT method is less robust than the HVD method. To evaluate the performance of the proposed method and the two previous methods quantitatively, the scatters are fitted by a second-order polynomial, as seen the black solid lines in Figures 11–13.

Hence, the difference between the scatters and the fitted values can be used to evaluate the performance. In this paper, the performance is evaluated in two ways. In the first way, the root mean square (RMS) of the difference is considered for this purpose, see Figure 14. It can be found that the proposed method has the lowest RMS for each subject. Meanwhile, the HVD has a greater RMS for subject No. 3, No. 5 and No. 10; the STFT method has a greater RMS for subject No. 2, No. 5, No. 10 and No. 12. In the second way, the authors investigate the difference distribution for all subjects. Hypothesis testing shows that the difference is like a Gaussian distribution. The confidence interval for the mean and standard deviation of the difference can be estimated by statistical theory where the confidence level is set as 0.95. Table 2 gives the confidence intervals of the two indicators. It can be seen that the intervals of both mean and standard deviation of the proposed method are narrowest in the three methods. That is to say, the proposed method has much higher consistency and much higher accuracy than the two previous methods.

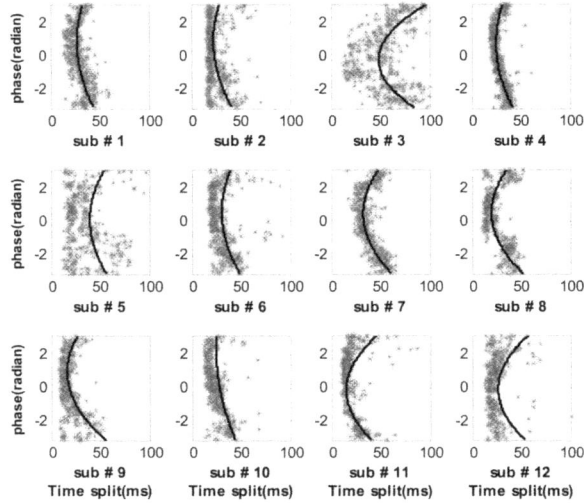

Figure 12. Measured respiratory splits of the 12 subjects by the HVD method.

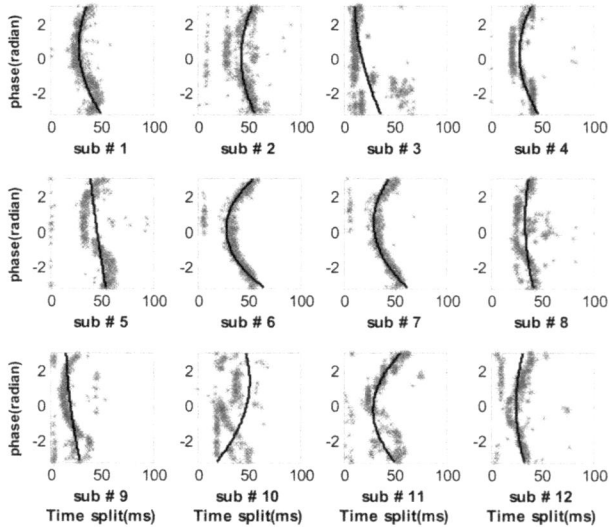

Figure 13. Measured respiratory splits of the 12 subjects by the STFT method.

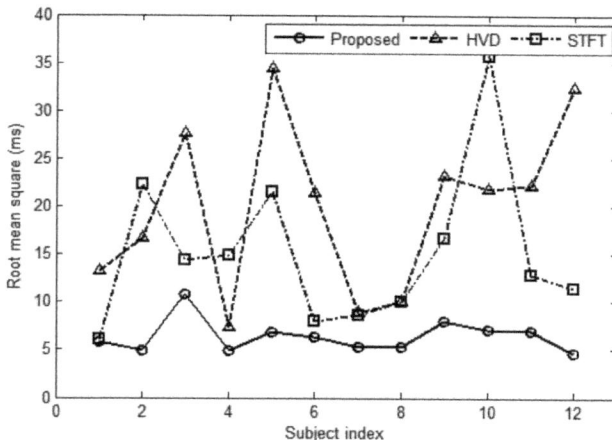

Figure 14. Performance comparison among the three methods in term of RMS.

Table 2. The confidence intervals of mean and standard deviation in 95% confidence level.

Subject Index	Indicator	HVD Method [7] (ms)	STFT Method [4] (ms)	Proposed Method (ms)
1	mean	(−1.40, 1.40)	(−0.64, 0.64)	(−0.61, 0.61)
	std	(12.30, 14.29)	(5.60, 6.50)	(5.36, 6.23)
2	mean	(−1.80, 1.80)	(−2.40, 2.40)	(−0.52, 0.52)
	std	(15.48, 18.04)	(20.66, 24.08)	(4.50, 5.25)
3	mean	(−2.85, 2.85)	(−1.48, 1.48)	(−1.11, 1.11)
	std	(25.70, 29.76)	(13.38, 15.49)	(10.05, 11.64)
4	mean	(−0.75, 0.75)	(−1.52, 1.52)	(−0.50, 0.50)
	std	(6.78, 7.83)	(13.80, 15.95)	(4.52, 5.23)
5	mean	(−3.97, 3.97)	(−2.48, 2.48)	(−0.78, 0.78)
	std	(31.78, 37.42)	(19.84, 23.37)	(6.25, 7.35)
6	mean	(−2.37, 2.37)	(−0.88, 0.88)	(−0.70, 0.70)
	std	(19.76, 23.13)	(7.33, 8.58)	(5.85, 6.85)
7	mean	(−1.01, 1.01)	(−0.97, 0.97)	(−0.60, 0.60)
	std	(8.20, 9.66)	(7.93, 9.31)	(4.93, 5.80)
8	mean	(−1.18, 1.18)	(−1.17, 1.17)	(−0.62, 0.62)
	std	(9.25, 10.93)	(9.18, 10.85)	(4.88, 5.76)
9	mean	(−2.58, 2.58)	(−1.86, 1.86)	(−0.88, 0.88)
	std	(21.47, 25.13)	(15.45, 18.09)	(7.34, 8.59)
10	mean	(−2.52, 2.52)	(−4.14, 4.14)	(−0.83, 0.83)
	std	(20.01, 23.60)	(32.84, 38.73)	(6.57, 7.75)
11	mean	(−2.57, 2.57)	(−1.49, 1.49)	(−0.81, 0.81)
	std	(20.41, 23.60)	(11.86, 13.98)	(6.46, 7.61)
12	mean	(−3.67, 3.67)	(−1.28, 1.29)	(−0.53, 0.53)
	std	(29.94, 35.15)	(10.55, 12.39)	(4.33, 5.09)

3.4. Effect of the Number of S2s

In the proposed method, the aortic component can be extracted by the average, because the average operation can smooth the pulmonary component and noise. However, the performance of average operation depends on the number of S2s involved in. It is reasonable that the greater the number of S2s involved in the average operation are, the greater possibility the assumption becomes true (i.e., the Equations (3) and (5) become true). So, the proposed method runs in block by block. A large collection of S2s is needed before it can run. The embedded ensemble information of respiration modulation are taken advantage to yield the excellent performance. The proposed method will absolutely degrade if the number of S2s is too small. The experiment experience suggests that a very good performance can be obtained if the number of S2s in a recording is greater than 200. That is, the recording time should be greater than 3 min for a normal subject. However, the HVD method and the STFT method do not run in a manner of block. They can work with a single S2 input. There is no limit on the number of cardiac cycles for the HVD method and the STFT method.

3.5. Comparisons in Computation Complexity

The main steps of the HVD method include decomposing each S2 into components by Hilbert vibration decomposition and SPWVD operation for each component to extract timing information for aortic and pulmonary components. The main step of the STFT method is performing a Short Time Fourier Transform to each S2 and extracting timing information from the time-frequency representation. Meanwhile, the main steps of the proposed method are averaging and subtracting. So, the HVD method has the greatest complexity, the STFT method is medium and the proposed method has the least complexity. The CPU time to calculate the respiratory split and the RMS error of the difference between the scatters and the fitted values for the 12 subjects are listed in Table 3 for complexity comparison and accuracy comparison. A personal computer is used to run the three methods where the CPU (Intel Core 2 Quad CPU Q8300, Intel, Kuala Lumpur, Malaysia) has two cores and the frequency is 2.5 GHz. It is found from Table 3 that the proposed method has much less complexity than those of the HVD method and the STFT method. The CPU time of the HVD method is hundreds of times longer than that of the proposed method, and that of the STFT method is over ten times longer than that the proposed method. So, the proposed method has a great attractive advantage in computation complexity. The RMS error of the proposed method is the lowest for each subject compared with the other two methods.

Table 3. Comparison of CPU time and RMS error among the three methods.

Subject Index	Number of S2s	HVD Method [7]		STFT Method [4]		Proposed Method	
		CPUtime (s)	RMSerror (ms)	CPUtime (s)	RMSerror (ms)	CPUtime (s)	RMSerror (ms)
1	344	942.1	13.2	11.5	6.0	1.3	5.8
2	331	948.1	16.7	11.4	22.3	1.2	4.9
3	360	971.4	27.7	11.6	14.3	1.2	10.8
4	367	981.1	7.3	13.1	14.8	1.1	4.9
5	290	830.1	34.5	10.1	21.5	0.9	6.8
6	311	843.3	21.4	10.6	7.9	1.0	6.3
7	299	799.3	8.9	10.2	8.6	0.9	5.4
8	281	773.5	10.1	9.5	10.0	0.9	5.3
9	312	847.3	23.2	10.4	16.7	0.9	7.9
10	285	776.7	21.7	9.7	35.7	0.9	7.1
11	286	765.3	22.2	10.4	12.9	0.9	7.0
12	301	804.2	32.4	10.2	11.4	1.0	4.7

3.6. Limitations of the Proposed Method

The proposed method has an advantage in computation complexity and accuracy. However, it has limitations too. (1) The proposed method runs in block by block. So, it is impossible to run the method in real time. The delay from inputting heart sound signal to outputting the split for a normal subject is three minutes or more. (2) A preprocessing is needed for the collection of S2s in which the S2s are aligned in time domain to facilitate average operation. If the alignment is missed or not well done, the estimated aortic and pulmonary components will be inaccurate, and consequently the performance of split estimation will degrade.

4. Conclusions

The second heart sound consists of aortic and pulmonary components. Previous physiological studies disclosed that the time delay between the two components is modulated by respiration. A novel method is proposed to quantitatively measure the delay using the respiratory modulation. A model is set up to assume that the second heart sound is the sum of aortic component and delayed pulmonary component. The aortic component could be estimated by the average of the second heart sounds over respiratory phase. Subsequently, the pulmonary component could be estimated by subtracting. The timing of the two components is further determined by the weighted powered envelope peak position. The proposed method is evaluated by both simulated data and practical data collected from healthy subjects. The experimental results clearly show that the detected splits of the second heart sound vary with respiratory phase. The values of the split and the trend of the splits coincide with previous results very well. The method is compared to the two well-known previous methods. It has advantages in computation complexity and accuracy. The results suggest the proposed method could be useful in non-invasively monitoring the hemodynamic response to respiration.

Acknowledgments: This work was supported in part by the National Natural Science Foundation of China under Grant No. 61471081, No. 61601081, and Fundamental Research Funds for the Central Universities under Grant No. DUT15QY60, DUT16QY13, DC201501056, and DCPY2016008.

Author Contributions: H.T. conceived, designed the experiments and wrote the manuscript; H.C. performed the experiments; H.C. and T.L. analyzed the data.

Conflicts of Interest: The authors declare that there is no conflict of interest.

References

1. Luisada, A.A.; Liu, C.K.; Aravanis, C.; Testelli, M.; Morris, J.; Chicago, B.A. On the mechanism of production of the heart sounds. *Am. Heart J.* **1958**, *55*, 383–399. [CrossRef]
2. Piemme, T.E.; Barnett, G.O.; Dexter, L. Relationship of heart sounds to acceleration of blood flow. *Circ. Res.* **1966**, *18*, 303–315. [CrossRef] [PubMed]
3. Xu, J.; Durand, L.-G.; Pibarot, P. Extraction of the aortic and pulmonary components of the second heart sound using a nonlinear transient chirp signal model. *IEEE Trans. Biomed. Eng.* **2001**, *48*, 277–283. [PubMed]
4. Leung, T.S.; White, P.R.; Cook, J.; Collis, W.B.; Brown, E.; Salmon, A.P. Analysis of the second heart sound for diagnosis of pediatric heart disease. *IEE Proc.-Sci. Meas. Technol.* **1998**, *145*, 285–290. [CrossRef]
5. Djebbari, A.; Reguig, F. Smoothed pseudo wigner-ville distribution of normal and aortic stenosis heart sounds. *J. Mech. Med. Biol.* **2005**, *5*, 415–428. [CrossRef]
6. Djebbari, A.; Bereksi-Reguig, F. Detection of the valvar split within the second heart sound using the reassigned smoothed pseudo Wigner-Ville distribution. *Biomed. Eng. Online* **2013**, *12*, 37–57. [CrossRef] [PubMed]
7. Barma, S.; Chen, B.; Man, K.L.; Wang, J. Quantitative measurement of split of the second heart sound. *IEEE Trans. Comput. Biol. Bioinform.* **2015**, *12*, 851–860. [CrossRef] [PubMed]
8. Feldman, M. *Hilbert Transform Application in Mechanical Vibration*; John Wiley Sons, Ltd.: West Sussex, UK, 2011; pp. 23–28.
9. Augen, F.; Flandrin, P.; Lin, Y.; Mclaughlin, S.; Meignen, S.; Oberlin, T.; Wu, H. Time-frequency reassignment and synchrosqueezing. *IEEE Signal Process. Mag.* **2013**, *30*, 32–41.
10. Auger, F.; Flandrin, P. Improving the readability of time-frequency and time-scale representations by the reassignment method. *IEEE Trans. Signal Process.* **1995**, *43*, 1068–1089. [CrossRef]
11. Castle, P.F.; Jones, K. The mechanism of respiratory variation in splitting of the second heart sound. *Circulation* **1961**, *24*, 180–184. [CrossRef] [PubMed]
12. Ishikawa, K.; Tamura, T. Study of respiratory influence on the intensity of heart sound in normal subjects. *Argiology* **1979**, *30*, 750–755. [CrossRef] [PubMed]
13. Amit, G.; Gavriely, N.; Intrator, N. Cluster analysis and classification of heart sounds. *Biomed. Signal Process. Control* **2009**, *4*, 26–36. [CrossRef]

14. Amit, G.; Shukha, K.; Gavriely, N.; Intrator, N. Respiratory modulation of heart sound morphology. *Am. J. Physiol. Heart Circ. Physiol.* **2009**, *296*, H796–H805. [CrossRef] [PubMed]

15. Tang, H.; Gao, J.; Ruan, C.; Qiu, T.; Park, Y. Modeling of heart sound morphology and analysis of the morphological variations induced by respiration. *Comput. Boil. Med.* **2013**, *43*, 1637–1644.

16. Liang, H.; Lukkarimen, S.; Hartimo, I. Heart sound segmentation algorithm based on heart sound envelogram. *Comput. Cardiol.* **1997**, *24*, 105–108.

17. Huang, N.E.; Shen, Z.; Long, S.R.; Wu, M.C.; Shih, H.H.; Zheng, Q.; Yen, N.C.; Tung, C.C.; Liu, H.H. The empirical mode decomposition and the Hilbert spectrum for nonlinear and non-stationary time series analysis. *Proc. R. Soc. A Math. Phys. Eng. Sci.* **1971**, *454*, 903–995. [CrossRef]

applied sciences

MDPI

Article

Feature Selection and Classification of Ulcerated Lesions Using Statistical Analysis for WCE Images

Shipra Suman [1,*], Fawnizu Azmadi Hussin [1], Aamir Saeed Malik [1], Shiaw Hooi Ho [2], Ida Hilmi [2], Alex Hwong-Ruey Leow [2] and Khean-Lee Goh [2]

[1] Center for Intelligent Signal & Imaging Research, Universiti Teknologi PETRONAS, Seri Iskandar 32610, Malaysia; fawnizu@utp.edu.my (F.A.H.); aamir_saeed@utp.edu.my (A.S.M.)

[2] Department of Medicine, University of Malaya Medical Center, Kuala Lumpur 50603, Malaysia; shooiho@yahoo.com (S.H.H.); i_hilmi@um.edu.my (I.H.); alexleow@gmail.com (A.H.-R.L.); klgoh56@gmail.com (K.-L.G.)

* Correspondence: suman.shipra@ieee.org; Tel.: +60-165-445-748

Received: 29 July 2017; Accepted: 18 September 2017; Published: 24 October 2017

Abstract: Wireless capsule endoscopy (WCE) is a technology developed to inspect the whole gastrointestinal tract (especially the small bowel area that is unreachable using the traditional endoscopy procedure) for various abnormalities in a non-invasive manner. However, visualization of a massive number of images is a very time-consuming and tedious task for physicians (prone to human error). Thus, an automatic scheme for lesion detection in WCE videos is a potential solution to alleviate this problem. In this work, a novel statistical approach was chosen for differentiating ulcer and non-ulcer pixels using various color spaces (or more specifically using relevant color bands). The chosen feature vector was used to compute the performance metrics using SVM with grid search method for maximum efficiency. The experimental results and analysis showed that the proposed algorithm was robust in detecting ulcers. The performance in terms of accuracy, sensitivity, and specificity are 97.89%, 96.22%, and 95.09%, respectively, which is promising.

Keywords: wireless capsule endoscopy; feature selection; color space selection; statistical analysis; support vector machine; grid search; overlapping area; classification

1. Introduction

Gastrointestinal tract (GIT) diseases, such as ulcer, bleeding, Crohn's disease, cancer or chronic diarrhea are common nowadays. Bleeding and ulcer are some common lesions which affect the small and large bowel. In the United States, approximately 1.6 million Americans currently are currently suffering from inflammatory bowel disease (IBD), representing an increase of about 200,000 since 2011.There are approximately 70,000 new cases of IBD diagnosed each year, and there may be as many as 80,000 children who are suffering from Crohn's disease (CD) or ulcerative colitis (UC) currently. Additionally, as illustrated reported in the first paper of this issue [1], the incidence number of occurrences of IBD is increasing worldwide [2]. The growth of IBD cases in newly-industrialized countries has paralleled its growth on par with that of the Western world 30 to 40 years ago. Genetic and environmental studies performed in these countries may provide new clues to the pathogenesis of IBD. However, it adds another layer of complexity since risk factors and gene-environment interactions may vary by continents and ethnicities [3]. Traditional endoscopy has been adopted for many years in order to diagnose abnormalities of GIT, whereby a physician controls a flexible endoscope to examine the lower and upper parts of GIT. This technique is limited to inspecting bowel of average length 7–8 m. It imposes high level of discomfort on the patient as well.

Wireless capsule endoscopy (WCE) [4,5] is a recent technology introduced by Given Imaging Ltd. (Yokne'am Illit, Israel) to visualize the entire GIT painlessly. It offers an efficient and comfortable way for visualizing the complete GIT. It has eight skin antennas mounted to the abdomen wall. While moving through the complete GIT, the capsule captures numerous images at approximately 2–4 frames per second (fps), and transfers them wirelessly to the data logger (DL) or recorder unit. This DL is hooked up to the patient waist and the videos/images are stored. Once the examination is complete (i.e., the WCE exits patient's body after 8 h), the images can be downloaded to a dedicated computer from DL and inspected by clinical experts through specific software. This procedure produces more than 60,000 images per examination and experts spend about 4–5 h to inspect the whole video footage very carefully. In some mild cases, clinicians have to go through each frame manually, leading to visual fatigue. This tedious and time-consuming process is the main drawback of WCE. Various image processing techniques for automatic disease detection (based on size, shape, and depth, including performance matrices) have been developed. Automatic lesion detection, on the other hand, is more efficient for chronic cases.

In this particular work, we have extracted color features for various color spaces. We have analyzed each band in order to separate the ulcer and non-ulcer pixels. Furthermore, it was combined with cross-correlation measure in order to add similarity between two images or matrices. Classification task was performed using support vector machine with and without grid search method in order to quantify the result. The main contribution of this work is the implementation of a novel computer-aided diagnostic method which is used to discriminate ulcer pixels from non-ulcerated ones with high performance in terms of sensitivity, specificity, and accuracy.

This paper is organized in the following manner: Section 2 describes the research background and the related works. Section 3 demonstrates the methodology, and Section 4 describes experimental setup, results, and discussions. Section 5 concludes the current work.

2. Background and Literature

Researchers have ventured into the technology of using automated computer-aided design (CAD) tools, such as WCE for ulcer screening. Precious clinical information in some important lesion areas can be displayed on an image [6–9]. Deeba [6] has used Retinex theory and the salient region detection method for various pathologies, such as stenosis, chylous cysts, lymphangiectasis, polypoid, bleeding, angioectasia, and ulcers. They have used a color enhancement method to improve the diagnostic yield of the CAD system. A significant improvement in detection performance using the Retinex-based color enhancement method has been achieved. An unsupervised method [10] has been used to localize the region-of-interest in order to detect angioectasia. The utility of IHb index for angioectasia detection has been pioneered to detect other abnormalities.

Yuan [8] has used a saliency detection method based on multi-level super pixel representation in order to outline the ulcer candidates. They have evaluated the corresponding saliency in accordance with the texture and the color feature of each level in the super pixel region. The images have been categorized by using saliency max-pooling with locality-constrained linear coding (LLC).

Iakovidis [9] has presented a method to detect various abnormalities in GIT by considering color as a discriminative feature. This method has been tested on a WCE model. Here, the single image (instead of the complete WCE video footage) has been analyzed. The author [11] has reviewed some current CAD methods employed in enhanced video capsule endoscopy. Various hardware and software problems have been highlighted in a review article [12] for detecting lesions in the small bowel.

Peptic ulcers are usually found in the duodenum (duodenal ulcer) and in the stomach (gastric ulcer). They can be found in small and large bowel areas of the GIT as well. They may cause severe gastrointestinal perforation or gastrointestinal bleeding [13]. Usually, it appears as a white spot in WCE images. In severe cases, these ulcers are accompanied by bleeding and other abnormalities. Ulcer lesions and normal tissue can be differentiated by using color and texture features (see Figure 1).

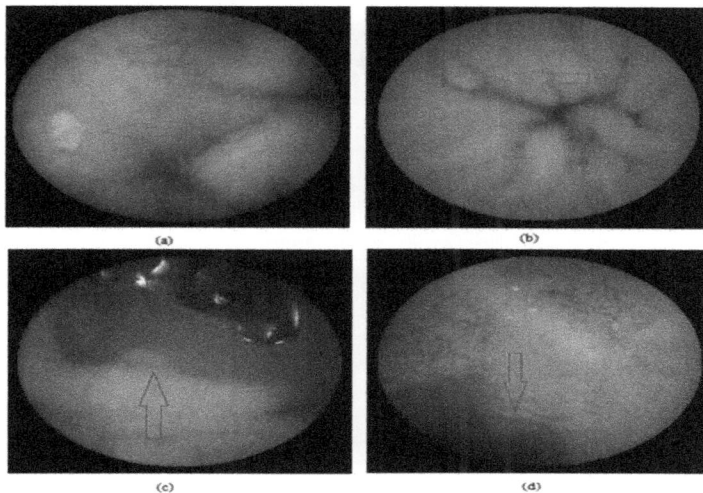

Figure 1. WCE images with bleeding and ulcer. (**a**,**b**) Ulcer image; and (**c**,**d**) bleeding images.

Feature selection [14] as practiced in machine learning is beneficial for supporting the WCE findings [15–17]. In general, feature extraction involves creating many new features mixed with the current ones. Due to the fact that the characterization of complete data variance is not possible after dimensional reduction, a highly-discriminative selecting feature [10] is undoubtedly necessary.

In order to classify the area of interest for capsule endoscopic images, first-order-histogram-based features extracted from various color spaces are very important. Relevant information can be extracted using various color spaces in order to describe the pattern of assured class. In case of bleeding detection, different color spaces [18] such as RGB (Red, Green, Blue), CMYK (Cyan, Magenta, yellow and Key [Black]), YIQ (Luma, chrominance information), CIE Lab, and HSI have been extensively investigated.

Yeh [13] used an improved CH algorithm (chosen name for the color coherence vector, CCV) to extract the color feature. The grey level co-occurrence matrix (GLCM) has been used to extract texture information. In our previous work [19], RGB and Lab color spaces have been chosen for statistical analyses of ulcer and non-ulcerated pixels. This paper extends the work of [19] by incorporating various color bands for statistical analysis.

Figueiredo et al. [20] has proposed a geometry-based automatic colorectal polyp detection method that has motivated the current work. The authors [21] have proposed a new computer-assisted bleeding detector for differentiating between bleeding and non-bleeding regions. The utilized second component from the CIE Lab color space with enhancement and segmentation techniques involves anisotropic diffusion.

3. Methodology

While analyzing the features, it is necessary to perform a few prior steps which are related to image processing. This section shows the complete flow of work. The proposed work focuses on reducing the analysis time while processing huge number of images. RGB color space is the most popular color scheme in visual system [22]; however, it has a few major disadvantages for natural images where high correlation between components can be observed [23]. Figure 2 depicts the flow of methodology for feature classification and extraction.

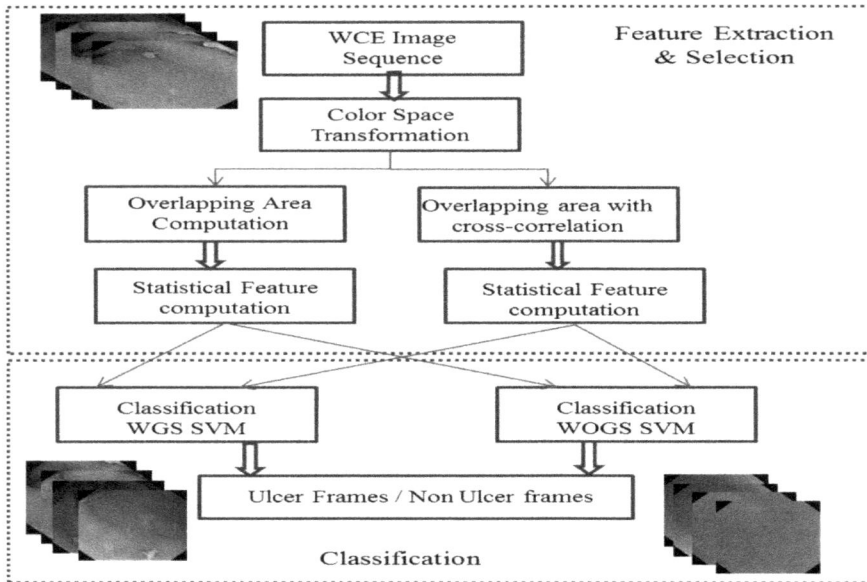

Figure 2. Methodology of proposed feature selection and classification.

3.1. Image Processing and Enhancement

The video generated after WCE examination is usually saved in a raw format and it cannot be processed directly by any programming platform. Endocapsule software (MAJ-2039) (EC 10, Olympus, Seri Iskandar, Perak, Malaysia, 2014) was used to import raw video in Audio Video Interleave (AVI) format. Subsequently, MATLAB was used to extract all images from the entire video footage in tagged image file format (TIFF) format. We have chosen the TIFF format to represent the WCE color image because it has greatest strength to support the full range of image size, color depth, and resolution. It also supports various compression techniques, where lossless compression allows this format to maintain image resolution without loss of any detail related to image [24]. Image enhancement is essential before applying any techniques in image processing. It is a technique that is able to eliminate non-essential information from an image [25]. In this particular work, we have used wavelet de-noising [26] with three levels of decomposition. Additionally, the db2 wavelet with soft thresholding method was applied to eliminate redundant noise.

3.2. Feature Extraction and Feature Selection

In this section, we have generated various normalized color spaces for feature analysis. RGB, HSV, YCbCr, CIE Lab, YUV, XYZ, and CMYK color spaces have been chosen for feature extraction and feature selection. By using these secen color spaces, we have analyzed 22 separate color bands individually. These bands contain various information of lesion and it is essential to identify the best band for the classification step.

We have used two methods to identify the best suitable band by separating foreground (non-ulcerated) and ulcer pixels. These methods involve statistical analysis of foreground and ulcer pixels in each band. We have implemented the first method (or Method 1) named as the overlapping area (OA) to measure the overlapping area between ulcer and foreground pixels. The normal distribution curve for foreground and ulcer pixels is analyzed from each pixel set. Here, we are able to highlight the index of separation for each band which shows overlapping area between foreground and ulcer pixels. Of course, lesser overlapping area signifies better separation in a particular band. The second method (or Method 2) uses overlapping area with cross-correlation (OACCorr) value in each band. Cross-correlation [27] is a standard measure for determining similarity between two images or matrices. It is more accurate and computationally more efficient. Additionally, it depends on the calculation of covariance between two bands.

The method of fast normalized cross-correlation is fast, independent, and accurate (in terms of pixel contrast and brightness values) in computing image similarity. This technique involves the estimation of correlation between all bands in the data cube of band i. Equation (1) was used to estimate the correlation values of other bands in j data cube:

$$NCC_{i,j} = \frac{\sum_{xy}\left[(D_i(x,y) - \overline{D_i}) \times (D_j(x,y) - \overline{D_j})\right]}{\sqrt{\sum_{xy}(D_i(x,y) - \overline{D_i})^2} \times \sqrt{\sum_{xy}(D_j(x,y) - \overline{D_j})^2}} \tag{1}$$

where $NCC_{i,j}$ is the normalized cross-correlation between band i and j, $D_i(x,y)$. is the intensity of pixel, (x, y) are the pixel indices within one band, and $\overline{D_i}$ is the mean of pixel intensity values of band i.

Table 1 shows the OA and OACCorr values for 22 color bands used in extracting the color features. We have used seven color spaces in the following order: RGB, HSV, YCbCr, CIE Lab, YUV, XYZ, and CMYK. The first color space is RGB with rgbR, rgbG, and rgbB color bands with allotted band numbers of 1, 2 and 3, respectively. The second color space is HSV with hsvH, hsvS, and hsvV color bands. Their allotted band numbers are 4, 5 and 6, respectively. The third color space is YCbCr with ycbcrY, ycbcrCB, and ycbcrCR color bands. Their allotted band numbers are 7, 8 and 9, respectively. The fourth color space is CIE Lab with CIE LabL, CIE LabA, and CIE LabB color bands. Their allotted band numbers are 10, 11 and 12, respectively. The fifth color space is YUV with yvuY, yvuU, and yuvV color bands of allotted band numbers 13, 14 and 15, respectively. The sixth color space is XYZ with xyzX, xyzY, and xyzZ color bands of allotted band numbers 16, 17 and 18, respectively. Finally, the seventh color space is CMYK with four bands, i.e., cmykC, cmykM, cmykY, and cmykK. Their allotted band numbers are 19, 20, 21 and 22, respectively. These entire bands are used as feature vector for further classification.

From Table 1 (columns 2 and 3), the overlapping areas of the respective band number and band name obtained using Method 1 are displayed in an incremental manner. For Method 2 (see columns 4 and 5 in Table 1), the overlapping areas added with standard measure of degree of similarity between two images are displayed in an incremental manner as well. For example, if the serial number 1 for feature extraction is analyzed using Method 1, it shows a chromium component (ycbcrCR) of YCbCr with band number 9 that has a lesser overlapping area between ulcer and foreground pixels. If the result of Method 2 is analyzed, the same band (ycbcrCR) is selected as well.

Table 1. Comparison of overlapping area with overlapping area and cross-correlation method.

Serial No.	OA		OACCorr	
	Band No.	Band Name	Band No.	Band Name
1	9	ycbcrCR	9	ycbcrCR
2	11	CIE LabA	21	cmykY
3	4	hsvH	11	CIE LabA
4	17	yuvU	4	hsvH
5	21	cmykY	3	rgbB
6	3	rgbB	17	yuvU
7	15	xyzZ	5	hsvS
8	5	hsvS	15	xyzZ
9	20	cmykM	8	ycbcrCB
10	16	yuvY	20	cmykM
11	8	ycbcrCB	16	yuvY
12	12	CIE LabB	12	CIE LabB

Table 1. *Cont.*

Serial No.	OA		OACCorr	
	Band No.	Band Name	Band No.	Band Name
13	19	cmykC	19	cmykC
14	22	cmykK	22	cmykK
15	1	rgbR	1	rgbR
16	6	hsvV	6	hsvV
17	13	xyzX	13	xyzX
18	2	rgbG	2	rgbG
19	7	ycbcrY	7	ycbcrY
20	14	xyzY	14	xyzY
21	18	yuvV	18	yuvV
22	10	CIE LabL	10	CIE LabL

3.3. Machine Learning

SVMs are accurate as they contain appropriate kernels that work well even if the data is not linearly separable in the base future space. By using the kernel functions of SVM [28], one can perform a non-linear classification more accurately by mapping its input to high-dimensional feature spaces [29]. There are various hyperplanes that separate the classes; however, it is important to select the best one which has the largest distance to the nearest data point of two classes. Grid search [30] is the conventional method of performing the optimization of hyper parameter utilizing parameter sweep or grid search through a manually specified subset of the hyper parameter of a learning algorithm. This algorithm must be guided by some performance metric, normally measured by evaluation on a held-out validation set or by cross-validation of the training dataset. For this work, we are using an SVM classifier with an RBF kernel having at least two parameters (regularization constant C and kernel hyper parameter γ) that need to be tuned to achieve high performance on the testing data. The mathematical descriptor is shown below for a binary classification problem: $\{(x_1, y_1), (x_2, y_2), \ldots, (x_k, y_k)\}$, where $x_i \in R_n$ represents the n-dimensional feature vectors, and $y_i \in \{1, -1\}$ is the corresponding class label. The SVM requires the solution of the following optimizing problem:

$$\min(\tfrac{1}{2}\omega^T\omega \; + \; C \sum_{i=1}^{k} \varepsilon_i)$$
$$\text{Subjected to } y_i \left(\omega^T \varphi(x_i) + b\right) \geq 1 - \varepsilon_i, \; \varepsilon_i \geq 0, \; i = 1, \ldots, k \tag{2}$$

Here, ε_i is the slack variable for misclassified examples, and C is the penalty parameter of error term. In addition, $K(x_i, x_j) = \varphi(x_i)^T \varphi(x_j)$ is the kernel function. Basically, there are four kernel functions used for pattern recognition and classification: linear kernel, polynomial kernel, radial basis function (RBF), and sigmoid kernel. We have adopted the RBF [28] kernel in this paper:

$$K(x_i, x_j) = \exp\left(-\gamma \parallel x_i - x_j \parallel^2\right), \; \gamma > 0 \tag{3}$$

Here, γ is the parameter which must be carefully selected in the experiment. The optimum values for parameter C and $\log_2 \gamma$ were selected from the range: $(-8, 7, 6, \ldots, 6, 7, 8)$. The grid method [29] was adopted as the searching procedure (a 0.8 step was used). Each γ and C value pair was used in the training data with ten-fold cross-validation in order to evaluate the model performance. Once the optimal values of γ and C were found, they were adopted to train a new SVM model.

4. Experimental Results and Discussions

This work was assisted by the expertise from the endoscopy unit in University of Malaya Medical Centre (UMMC), Kuala Lumpur, Malaysia for medical/clinical advises. The UTP team, on the other hand, was responsible in providing the engineering solutions. We accumulated 30 videos of various abnormalities. Moreover, the experts provided us the ground truth for these videos with labelled ulcerated lesions. This dataset serves as the reference data set for our subsequent analysis. The WCE pill used for generating the dataset was Endocapsule developed by Olympus. The resolution of the dataset provided was 288 × 288. The processor used for this work was Intel (R) Core(TM) i7-2600 CPU @3.20 GHz (Dell Optiplex 990, Seri Iskandar, Malaysia) with 8 GB memory. The chosen programming platform was MATLAB R2017a (Matlab 9.2, MathWorks, Malaysia, 2017).

4.1. Dataset Selection

Our dataset consisted of 48,000 WCE images. These images (16,000 of them) were divided into three groups. In each group, we used 8000 images to create our training set (5000 images were ulcer samples and 3000 images were normal samples) and 8000 images in testing set (5000 images were ulcer samples and 3000 images were normal samples). These images were accumulated from 30 patients and manually-labelled by gastroenterologists.

4.2. Results of Statistical Analysis

The results are presented in Table 1.

From Table 1, it is apparent that the overlapping area method (Method 1) can better reveal the ulcer information with the following bands (arranged in the descending performance): ycbcrCR, cmykY, CIE LabA, hsvH, rgbB, yuvU, and CIE LabL. Similarly, by using overlapping area with cross-correlation (Method 2), bands such as ycbcrCr, cmykY, rgbB, and hsvS contains more information for ulcer lesion. In Figure 3, we have extracted the feature vector for each band using Method 1 and Method 2. By choosing 50% of overlapping area and cross-correlation, it gives us six color bands such as ycbcrCR, cmykY, CIE LabA, hsvH, rgbB, and yuvU (i.e., the first six output rows of Table 1) using Method 1 and four color bands such as ycbcrCr, cmykY, rgbB and hsvS (i.e., the first four rows in Table 1) using Method 2. We found that the performance classifiers such as sensitivity, specificity, and accuracy are similar when more than 50% of overlapping area and cross-correlation are chosen. Otherwise, the performance is degraded and we might not be able to extract sufficient features.

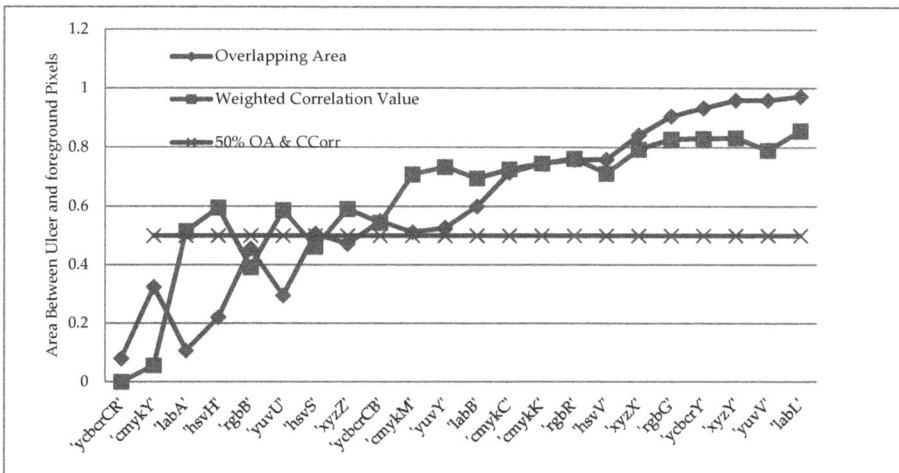

Figure 3. Comparison of overlapping area and Weighted correlation value.

The *x*-axis in Figure 3 shows the color bands for Method 2 (i.e., similar to column 5 in Table 1). A total of 50% of overlapping area (six feature vectors) and cross-correlation (four feature vectors) is taken as feature vector for Method 1 and Method 2. For Method 1 (OA), data on blue line containing ycbcrCR, cmykY, CIE LabA, hsvH, rgbB, and yuvU are chosen as feature vector as they have less overlapping area between ulcer and foreground pixels. For Method 2 (OACCorr), data on red line containing ycbcrCR, cmykC, rgbB, and hsvS are chosen as feature vector the overlapping areas added with standard measure of degree of similarity between two images are displayed in an incremental manner. The selected feature vectors were further fed into the classifier in order to analyze the algorithm performance in terms of sensitivity, specificity, and accuracy.

These bands provide the best result in terms of separating the ulcerated and non-ulcerated pixels. To enhance the result of classification, we fed the selected band to the SVM classifier. In this classifier, we used radial basis function (RBF) as kernel for the SVM. The result of classification for performance matrices is shown in Table 2.

Table 2. Sensitivity, specificity, and accuracy using SVM classifier.

Methods		Color Bands					
		Cr, Y, A, H, B, U		*Cr, Y, A, H, B*		*Cr, Y, A, H*	
Method 1	SVM (OA)	Sen	Spe	Sen	Spe	Sen	Spe
		90.32	90.55	91.98	91.56	91.58	91.23
		Cr, Y, B, S		*Cr, Y, B*		*Cr, Y*	
Method 2	SVM (OACCorr)	Sen	Spe	Sen	Spe	Sen	Spe
		92.58	91.84	93.76	92.91	93.08	91.36

4.3. Performance Metrics

Performance metrics such as accuracy (Acc), sensitivity (Sen), and specificity (Spe) were computed to evaluate the effectiveness of the proposed method. For the experimentation on GIT image data set, the positive sample represents lesion images and the negative sample represents normal images. The equations for sensitivity and specificity can be expressed as:

$$\text{Accuracy (Acc)} = TP + TN / (TP + TN + FP + FN) \tag{4}$$

$$\text{Sensitivity (Sen)} = TP / (TP + FN) \tag{5}$$

$$\text{Specificity (Spe)} = TN / (FP + TN) \tag{6}$$

where TP represents the number of true positives, TN represents the number of true negatives, FP represents the incorrect positive image samples identified and FN represents the incorrect negative image samples identified. From the clinical experts, sensitivity defines the probability of a positive analysis and specificity is the probability of a negative analysis.

In Table 2, SVM (OA) is depicted as Support vector machine for overlapping area. It is computed for seven bands, six bands, and five bands and the results are shown in Table 2. Similarly, SVM (OACCorr) is a support vector machine for overlapping area with cross-correlation value and it is computed for four bands, three bands, and two bands. Here, *Cr, Y, A, H* and *B* give better results for Method 1 (OA). On the other hand, *Cr, Y* and *B* give the best result with Method 2 (OACCorr). Specifically, Method 2 is more promising than Method 1. The above results shows that combining various color bands can provide more meaningful results.

Figure 4 shows the analyses of SVM (OACCorr) by using grid search method (WGS) and without grid search method (WOGS). The accuracies of 3 datasets have been compared. From the results taken from *Cr, Y, B* color bands, the extracted feature is more obvious using grid search method. For this method, the average accuracy, sensitivity, and specificity are 97.89%, 96.22% and 95.09%, respectively.

Additionally, we have compared our results of classification with others as presented in Table 3. It is important to note the dataset provided by other authors might be extracted from different capsule. Therefore, for comparison purpose, the dataset employed in the current work has been used for all methods, including those reported by other researchers (Table 3 shows the dataset used by other authors). The authors in [31] combined the merits of both Contourlet transform and Log Gabor filter in HSV color space; however, their dataset was very small. Author from [13] utilized RGB and HSV color space and classification was performed using MLP neural network. By using color coherence vector (CCV), a promising result was attained. As reported in [32], color wavelet covariance feature was used on various color spaces, and Texton boost was applied to classify normal and abnormal tissues. It is interesting to note that the proposed method shows higher sensitivity and higher specificity even for a very large dataset.

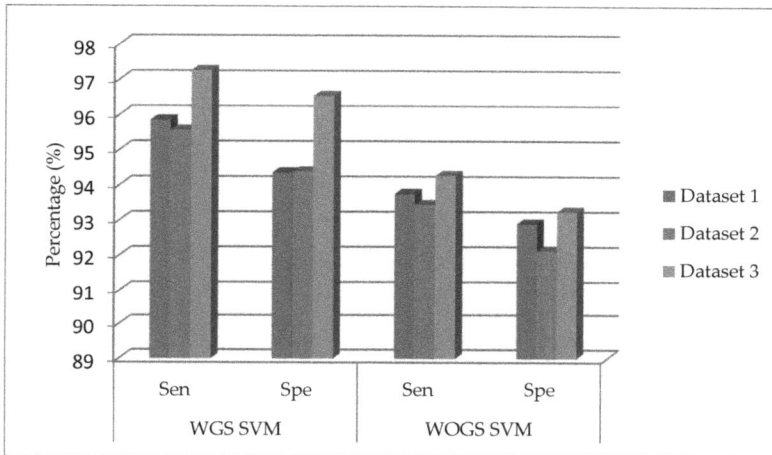

Figure 4. Performance of the proposed method.

Table 3. Comparison of performance with other author work.

Author	Color Space/Bands	Classifier	Dataset	Acc (%)	Sen (%)	Spe (%)
[31]	HSV	SVM	137 images	94.83	91.89	97.16
[13]	RGB, HSV, CCV	MLP	448 images	86.93	89.03	85.56
[32]	Various color space	Joint boost	100 images	NA	91.67	84.73
Proposed	Cr, Y, B	WGS SVM (OACCorr)	48,000 images	97.89	96.22	95.09

5. Conclusions

This paper has outlined a new method for detecting ulcer in an entire GIT. This method utilizes the divide-and-conquers technique to extract ulcer frame from a complete video footage. Statistical analysis has been performed to achieve higher separation between ulcer and non-ulcerated pixels. This technique has sub-parts for computing feature vectors in order to reveal highly-relevant information for ulcer and non-ulcer pixel discrimination which includes image enhancement, transformation of various color space, statistic feature computation, and classification. Statistical analysis has been performed to achieve higher separation between ulcer and non-ulcerated pixels by using this technique. The pixels have been classified using seven color spaces. Instead of using any single color space, it is more important to extract band information using various color spaces in order to achieve more accurate results. In this proposed method, Cr, Y, and B bands have been selected from YCbCr, CMYK, and RGB color spaces, respectively. Additionally, overlapping area with correlation using grid search method has increased the performance in separating the ulcerated pixels from normal pixels. Grid method has been adopted as the searching procedure (0.8 step was used). Each γ and C value pair has been used in the training data with ten-fold cross-validation in order to evaluate the model performance. A large dataset has been used to create training and testing dataset in order to obtain meaningful result. In this work, the sensitivity and the specificity of ulcer classification using the grid search method in SVM are 96.22% and 95.09%, respectively, which are substantially higher than those of classification without grid search method (93.76% and 92.91%, respectively). The main contribution of this work is the implementation of a novel computer aided diagnostic method which can be used to discriminate ulcer pixel from non-ulcerated pixel. The method exhibits promising performance in terms of sensitivity, specificity, and accuracy. The current work has paved the way to providing a reliable computer-aided WCE diagnosis system.

Acknowledgments: This research work is supported by the Centre for Intelligent Signal and Imaging Research (CISIR) and the Graduate Assistantship (GA) scheme, Universiti Teknologi PETRONAS, Perak, Malaysia.

Author Contributions: Shipra Suman finished the draft of this paper. Fawnizu Azmadi Hussin contributed in the design of the experimental work. Aamir Saeed malik contributed in feature extraction and feature selection algorithm for better discrimination between ulcer and foreground pixel. Shiaw Hooi Ho and Ida Hilmi contributed in the labelling of Ulcer dataset used in the experiment. Alex Hwong-Ruey Leow and Khean-Lee Goh have contribution towards disease specification and other challenges found throughout the writing and other reviewing procedure. All authors reviewed and approved the contents of this paper.

Conflicts of Interest: The authors declare no conflict of interest.

Abbreviations

AVI	Audio Video Interleaved
CAD	Computer Aided Design
CCV	Color Coherence Vector
DL	Data Logger
GIT	Gastrointestinal Tract
GLCM	Grey Level Co-Occurrence Matrix
LLC	Locality-constrained Linear Coding
OA	Overlapping Area
OACCorr	Overlapping area with Cross-correlation
RBF	Radial Basis Function
SVM	Support Vector Machine
WCE	Wireless Capsule Endoscopy
WGS	With Grid Search
WOGS	Without Grid Search

References

1. Kaplan, G.G.; Ng, S.C. Understanding and preventing the global increase of inflammatory bowel disease. *Gastroenterology* **2017**, *152*, 313–321. [CrossRef] [PubMed]
2. Kaplan, G.G.; Jess, T. The changing landscape of inflammatory bowel disease: East meets West. *Gastroenterology* **2016**, *150*, 24–26. [CrossRef] [PubMed]
3. Colombel, J.-F.; Mahadevan, U. Inflammatory Bowel Disease 2017: Innovations and Changing Paradigms. *Gastroenterology* **2017**, *152*, 309–312. [CrossRef] [PubMed]
4. Iddan, G.; Meron, G.; Glukhovsky, A.; Swain, P. Wireless capsule endoscopy. *Nature* **2000**, *405*, 417. [CrossRef] [PubMed]
5. Ghoshal, U.C. Capsule Endoscopy: A New Era of Gastrointestinal Endoscopy. In *Endoscopy of GI Tract*; InTech: Rijeka, Crotia, 2013.
6. Deeba, F.; Mohammed, S.K.; Bui, F.M.; Wahid, K.A. Unsupervised Abnormality Detection Using Saliency and Retinex Based Color Enhancement. In Proceedings of the 2016 IEEE 38th Annual International Conference of the Engineering in Medicine and Biology Society (EMBC), Orlando, FL, USA, 16–20 August 2016; pp. 3871–3874.
7. Deeba, F.; Mohammed, S.K.; Bui, F.M.; Wahid, K.A. A Saliency-Based Unsupervised Method for Angioectasia Detection in Capsule Endoscopic Images. *CMBES Proc.* **2016**, *39*, 1–11.

8. Yuan, Y.; Wang, J.; Li, B.; Meng, M.Q.-H. Saliency based ulcer detection for wireless capsule endoscopy diagnosis. *IEEE Trans. Med. Imaging* **2015**, *34*, 2046–2057. [CrossRef] [PubMed]
9. Iakovidis, D.K.; Koulaouzidis, A. Automatic lesion detection in capsule endoscopy based on color saliency: Closer to an essential adjunct for reviewing software. *Gastrointest. Endosc.* **2014**, *80*, 877–883. [CrossRef] [PubMed]
10. Charisis, V.S.; Katsimerou, C.; Hadjileontiadis, L.J.; Liatsos, C.N.; Sergiadis, G.D. Computer-Aided Capsule Endoscopy Images Evaluation Based on Color Rotation and Texture Features: An Educational Tool to Physicians. In Proceedings of the 2013 IEEE 26th International Symposium on Computer-Based Medical Systems (CBMS), Porto, Portugal, 20–22 June 2013; pp. 203–208.
11. Iakovidis, D.K.; Koulaouzidis, A. Software for enhanced video capsule endoscopy: Challenges for essential progress. *Nat. Rev. Gastroenterol. Hepatol.* **2015**, *12*, 172–186. [CrossRef] [PubMed]
12. Koulaouzidis, A.; Iakovidis, D.K.; Karargyris, A.; Plevris, J.N. Optimizing lesion detection in small-bowel capsule endoscopy: From present problems to future solutions. *Exp. Rev. Gastroenterol. Hepatol.* **2015**, *9*, 217–235. [CrossRef] [PubMed]
13. Yeh, J.-Y.; Wu, T.-H.; Tsai, W.-J. Bleeding and ulcer detection using wireless capsule endoscopy images. *J. Softw. Eng. Appl.* **2014**, *7*, 422. [CrossRef]
14. Mohammed, S.K.; Deeba, F.; Bui, F.M.; Wahid, K.A. Feature Selection Using Modified Ant Colony Optimization for Wireless Capsule Endoscopy. In Proceedings of the IEEE Annual Ubiquitous Computing, Electronics & Mobile Communication Conference (UEMCON), New York, NY, USA, 20–22 October 2016; pp. 1–4.
15. Suman, S.; Hussin, F.A.B.; Walter, N.; Malik, A.S.; Ho, S.H.; Goh, K.L. Detection and Classification of Bleeding Using Statistical Color Features for Wireless Capsule Endoscopy Images. In Proceedings of the International Conference on Signal and Information Processing (IConSIP), Vishnupuri, India, 6–8 October 2016; pp. 1–5.
16. Suman, S.; Hussin, F.A.; Walter, N.; Malik, A.S.; Hilmi, I. Automatic Detection and Removal of Bubble Frames from Wireless Capsule Endoscopy Video Sequences. In Proceedings of the 2016 6th International Conference on Intelligent and Advanced Systems (ICIAS), Kuala Lumpur, Malaysia, 15–17 August 2016; pp. 1–5.
17. Suman, S.; Hussin, F.A.; Nicolas, W.; Malik, A.S. Ulcer Detection and Classification of Wireless Capsule Endoscopy Images Using RGB Masking. *Adv. Sci. Lett.* **2016**, *22*, 2764–2768. [CrossRef]
18. Ibraheem, N.A.; Hasan, M.M.; Khan, R.Z.; Mishra, P.K. Understanding color models: A review. *ARPN J. Sci. Technol.* **2012**, *2*, 265–275.
19. Suman, S.; Walter, N.; Hussin, F.A.; Malik, A.S.; Ho, S.H.; Goh, K.L.; Hilmi, I. Optimum colour space selection for ulcerated regions using statistical analysis and classification of ulcerated frames from wce video footage. In *Neural Information Processing, Part I, Proceedings of the 22nd International Conference, ICONIP 2015, Istanbul, Turkey, 9–12 November 2015*; Arik, S., Huang, T., Lai, W.K., Liu, Q., Eds.; Springer: Cham, Switzerland, 2015; pp. 373–381.
20. Figueiredo, P.N.; Figueiredo, I.N.; Prasath, S.; Tsai, R. Automatic polyp detection in pillcam colon 2 capsule images and videos: Preliminary feasibility report. *Diagn. Ther. Endosc.* **2011**, *2011*. [CrossRef] [PubMed]
21. Figueiredo, I.N.; Kumar, S.; Leal, C.; Figueiredo, P.N. Computer-assisted bleeding detection in wireless capsule endoscopy images. *Comput. Methods Biomech. Biomed. Eng.* **2013**, *1*, 198–210. [CrossRef]
22. Colantoni, P. Color Space Transformations. Available online: http://faculty.kfupm.edu.sa/ics/lahouari/Teaching/colorspacetransform-1.0.pdf (accessed on 8 June 2017).
23. Pascale, D. A review of rgb color spaces . . . from xyy to r′g′b′. *Babel Color* **2003**, *18*, 136–152.
24. Wiggins, R.H.; Davidson, H.C.; Harnsberger, H.R.; Lauman, J.R.; Goede, P.A. Image file formats: Past, present, and future. *Radiographics* **2001**, *21*, 789–798. [CrossRef] [PubMed]
25. Suman, S.; Hussin, F.A.; Malik, A.S.; Walter, N.; Goh, K.L.; Hilmi, I.; Ho, S.h. Image Enhancement Using Geometric Mean Filter and Gamma Correction for WCE Images. In Proceedings of the 21st International Conference on Neural Information Processing, Kuching, Malaysia, 3–6 November 2014; pp. 276–283.
26. Sævarsson, B.B.; Sveinsson, J.R.; Benediktsson, J.A. Combined Curvelet and Wavelet Denoising. In Proceedings of the 7th Nordic Signal Processing Symposium, NORSIG 2006, Rejkjavik, Iceland, 7–9 June 2006; pp. 318–321.
27. Ahmed, A.; Sharkawy, M.E.; Ramly, S.E. Analysis of Inter-band Spectral Cross-Correlation Structure of Hyperspectral Data. In Proceedings of the WSEAS International Conference Recent Advances in Computer Engineering Series, Istanbul, Turkey, 21–23 August 2012.

28. Chang, C.-C.; Lin, C.-J. LIBSVM: A library for support vector machines. *ACM Trans. Intell. Syst. Technol. (TIST)* **2011**, *2*, 27. [CrossRef]

29. Hsu, C.-W.; Chang, C.-C.; Lin, C.-J. *A Practical Guide to Support Vector Classification*; National Taiwan University: Taipei City, Taiwan, 2003.

30. Bengio, Y. Practical recommendations for gradient-based training of deep architectures. In *Neural Networks: Tricks of the Trade*; Springer: Berlin/Heidelberg, Germany, 2012; pp. 437–478.

31. Koshy, N.E.; Gopi, V.P. A New Method for Ulcer Detection in Endoscopic Images. In Proceedings of the 2015 2nd International Conference on Electronics and Communication Systems (ICECS), Coimbatore, India, 26–27 Febuary 2015; pp. 1725–1729.

32. Liu, X.; Gu, J.; Xie, Y.; Xiong, J.; Qin, W. A New Approach to Detecting Ulcer and Bleeding in Wireless Capsule Endoscopy Images. In Proceedings of the 2012 IEEE-EMBS International Conference on Biomedical and Health Informatics (BHI), Hong Kong, China, 5–7 January 2012; pp. 737–740.

MDPI AG
St. Alban-Anlage 66
4052 Basel, Switzerland
Tel. +41 61 683 77 34
Fax +41 61 302 89 18
http://www.mdpi.com

Applied Sciences Editorial Office
E-mail: applsci@mdpi.com
http://www.mdpi.com/journal/applsci

www.ingramcontent.com/pod-product-compliance
Lightning Source LLC
Chambersburg PA
CBHW051710210326
41597CB00032B/5434